The Authority of EU Law

Wolfgang Heusel • Jean-Philippe Rageade
Editors

The Authority of EU Law

Do We Still Believe in It?

Springer

Editors
Wolfgang Heusel
Academy of European Law
Trier, Germany

Jean-Philippe Rageade
Academy of European Law
Trier, Germany

ISBN 978-3-662-58840-6 ISBN 978-3-662-58841-3 (eBook)
https://doi.org/10.1007/978-3-662-58841-3

This Springer imprint is published by the registered company Springer-Verlag GmbH, DE, part of Springer Nature.
The registered company address is: Heidelberger Platz 3, 14197 Berlin, Germany

Foreword by Pavel Telička*

Let me offer my warmest congratulations for this special anniversary. The Academy of European Law has been doing an invaluable job for 25 years, and it is a privilege for me, as Vice-President of the European Parliament responsible for ERA, to say that we highly honour its work. Personally, I am witnessing that work every day and I hope that we will be able to intensify this cooperation interaction.

On this special anniversary, I would like to spread some optimism. Two years ago we could read, listen and even debate the gloomiest scenarios for the EU and the European integration. It is not that long ago that, while facing national elections in some of the Member States, we were concerned that the EU could be gradually falling apart, or face what I call a "crawling disintegration". And of course we still face tremendous challenges. Take, for example, the discussion on the rule of law. We all know that the rule of law is the bedrock of our European democracies and that in some of our Member States that very principle is under threat. Let me just say that I believe the EU needs to take a particularly firm stance on this. We cannot allow to back away from the very principles we stand for. And it is also one of the areas where the expertise of ERA can be of real value added for policymakers across Europe.

But let's turn the page to today. Despite all those gloomy predictions, the EU is still around. The elections in a number of Member States give us reason for optimism. In France, the Netherlands or Germany, pro-European forces won the 2017 elections, while the extremes did not perform as well as many would have expected. We no longer use the word "crisis" in every second or third sentence. The worst scenarios have not materialised. Instead, we see an ambitious agenda on reforming the EU. We see progress on issues such as migration, the Digital Single Market or defence policies. Things are moving forward; they are evolving. And we finally have politicians who have the courage to come up with concrete ideas on where and how the EU should move forward. It will not be easy. We need to have political will. We will see national interests at stake and protectionism. But I believe that we will manage, and I think that we will see progress in advancing the regulatory environment. We have no other option than to deliver on some of the challenges where the

* Parliament's representative on ERA's Governing Board. This Foreword is based on Pavel Telička's opening speech at ERA's jubilee congress in Trier, 19 October 2017.

public does expect delivery. And that is where new legislation will come into play. We need to regulate better than we have done so far. We need to know in advance what implications legislation will have. We need to make sure that it really is better regulation. And of course we need to make sure that legislation is applied consistently across Europe. This is another important field where ERA will be of great significance.

Last year, ERA turned 25. We all know that when you are 25, life is far from over. It is the time when you are dynamic, when you have strength, you already have knowledge, you are gaining more experience and you also have the drive. And this is what I would like to wish ERA going into the next 25 years. I am looking forward to our mutual interaction but also further developing personal relationships.

Vice President
European Parliament
Strasbourg/Brussels

Pavel Telička

Preface*

On 22 June 1992, three Members of the European Parliament—Horst Langes, Willi Rothley and James Janssen van Raay—the Minister of Justice of Rhineland-Palatinate Peter Caesar, the Lord Mayor of the City of Trier Helmut Schröer and the First Councillor of the Luxembourg Ministry of Justice Charles Elsen signed the document establishing the Foundation *Academy of European Law* (ERA) in Trier. They thus laid the foundation stone for a project which the European Parliament had repeatedly called to be implemented since the late 1980s. With the entry into force of the Single European Act on 1 July 1987 and the extensive legislative programme operated by the Delors Commission to complete the Internal Market by the end of 1992, the importance of European law for practitioners in the legal profession or the judiciary and in business and administration had become ever more obvious.

It was therefore not surprising that the European Court of Justice, led by its late President Ole Due, was one of the first and most enduring supporters of the ERA project. In this sense, Ole Due was no less a founding father of ERA than Jacques Santer, then Prime Minister of the Grand Duchy of Luxembourg, whose country was the first and for a long time only EU Member State to participate in the establishment of ERA, and Peter Schmidhuber, then Member of the European Commission.

Three of these founding fathers took part in the Jubilee Congress of 19–20 October 2017 celebrating the 25th anniversary of ERA, the updated contributions to which are collected in this volume. Our heartfelt thanks go out to them—Jacques Santer, the President of our Board of Trustees; his then collaborator and later Director General of the Council of the EU Charles Elsen; and Horst Langes, Member of the European Parliament from Trier. Peter Caesar and Ole Due passed away a long time ago, but their successors Herbert Mertin and Koen Lenaerts, as well as Trier's Lord Mayor Wolfram Leibe, testified to the continuing solidarity of their institutions with ERA through their presence at the congress and with their ongoing support.

In the meantime, the Academy has grown in every respect, not least as a foundation—from one Member State in 1992 to twenty-seven in October 2017, and since,

*The text largely corresponds to the welcome speech addressed by Wolfgang Heusel to the participants of the Jubilee Congress on 19 October 2017.

to our great delight, Belgium joined last, the last missing country was Estonia, which has meanwhile also announced its accession. Represented on ERA's Governing Board, these Member States determine ERA's development and position. A key role was played by the German state of Rhineland-Palatinate, which provided generous and sustainable support whenever this was needed. We would like to express our profound thanks to all of them, the old founders and the present patrons, for whatever they have contributed to the development of our Academy.

It cannot be denied that there were no women among the founding fathers; a reason may have been an underdeveloped consideration for gender policy at that time. Very soon, however, there were great women who had significant impact on the positive development of ERA. We would like to pay tribute to three of them: first Ana Palacio, former chairwoman of the European Parliament's Legal Affairs Committee, chairwoman of the ERA Executive Board and later Spanish Foreign Minister; Diana Wallis, former Vice-President of the European Parliament, Member of ERA's Governing Board and until recently President of the European Law Institute; and Pauliine Koskelo, long-serving President of the Finnish Supreme Court, now judge of the European Court of Human Rights and chairwoman of our Board of Trustees. Diana Wallis and Pauliine Koskelo are among the authors of this commemorative publication.

When ERA was founded 25 years ago, the transformation of the European Communities into the European Union was just about to begin—the Maastricht Treaty only came into force on 1 November 1993. There were twelve Member States and little more than a Common Market policy. The fall of the Iron Curtain had occurred only a few years ago. Nevertheless, or precisely because of this, Europe was steeped in a great sense of optimism. And when we look back at the enormous progress the European Union has made since 1992, the staccato of reform treaties—Maastricht, Amsterdam, Nice, Lisbon as a replacement for the failed Constitutional Treaty; four enlargements from 12 to 28 Member States; the communitisation of judicial cooperation in civil and later even criminal matters; the common asylum policy; the introduction of the single currency; the Charter of Fundamental Rights; the institutional development with Parliament as a proper legislator, albeit with the Commission's continuing monopoly on initiatives, the increasing importance of the comitology procedure and a large number of agencies; and in addition, existential crises in the Schengen area and the Monetary Union with subsequent EU law and intergovernmental measures—it is difficult to keep track of all these breathtaking developments almost all of which have been reflected in EU law and kept ERA busy.

It is hardly surprising that the abundance of these developments has had an impact on compliance, on enforcement and hence on the authority of Union law. It is true that Walter Hallstein's early dictum of the EC as a "community of law" ("*Rechtsgemeinschaft*") continues to be present throughout the legal discourse, and primary law mentions the rule of law as one of the central values on which the Union is founded. Nevertheless, it is by no means certain that we have the same concept of the rule of law in all Member States, against which ever more frequently the principle of democracy is led into battle. And if lastly the perception has been gaining ground that the Commission, as the "guardian" of Union law, is basing its enforcement policy increasingly on political criteria, of which the effectiveness of the law seems to be just one among many, then at least this perception does not strengthen the authority of Union law.

We have therefore decided to place this challenged authority at the heart of our Jubilee Congress and approached it from various angles. We started with horizontal questions: Professor Joseph Weiler discussed the concept, while President Koen Lenaerts dealt with the Court of Justice's responsibility for the authority of EU law. A panel discussion followed on how the emergence, transparency and quality of legislation affect the authority of the Union law thus created.

The authority of Union law is also occasionally challenged by national supreme or constitutional courts when they at least in principle avail themselves of the right to no longer apply Union law on their territory if according to them the law at stake is not covered by the sovereign rights transferred to the Union. This potential for conflict, which is the consequence of a logically non-solvable tension within a supranational Union of sovereign States, is not only discussed in academic circles but also influences supreme court practice and was the subject of the second panel discussion of the Congress. In this volume, the perspectives of the Danish *Højesteret*, the French *Conseil d'Etat*, the German *Bundesverfassungsgericht*, the highest UK judiciary and the European Court of Justice are presented.

On the second day, three parallel working sessions discussed the specific challenges to the authority of EU law in three special areas—Internal Market law in the context of the economic crisis, the law of Monetary Union in the context of the Euro crisis and the respect for the rule of law in times of attacks on judicial independence in and outside the EU. In the Internal Market, the reliability and enforcement of Union law is certainly a necessity for citizens and businesses, but also for the authority of the law itself. Monetary Union, on the other hand, is a prime example of an incomplete Union in which the shortcomings of the Union's regulatory approach exacerbate the crisis, hamper the enforcement of inadequate Union law and undermine its authority, and this alongside the similarly insufficient Schengen acquis, which is lacking a consistent migration and refugee law concept and hence another example of an incomplete Union. Finally, attacks on the rule of law put at risk a cornerstone of Union law itself.

The congress programme culminated in a panel discussion which asked about the connection between the legitimacy crisis of the European project and the authority of European Union law, and which examined the possible effect of different models for the Union's further development on this legitimacy: was Brexit, for example, just a special British problem or rather the expression of a general malaise caused by a too far-pushed integration ignoring the opinions and reservations of citizens? Is the "ever closer union" still the right model to follow or do different objectives need to be set?

The congress programme was developed with the support of a twelve-member preparatory committee of the ERA Board of Trustees, most of whom delivered their own contributions to the congress programme. In addition, ERA offered participants a unique exhibition of contemporary art with works of artists from 31 European countries, an initiative of our long-serving board member Catherine Kessedjian. We would like to thank all participants, speakers, panellists and chairmen and all contributors to this publication once again for their selfless willingness to participate.

Director of the Academy
of European Law Trier, Germany
Wolfgang Heusel

Deputy Director and Programme
Director of the Academy
of European Law
Trier, Germany
Jean-Philippe Rageade

Contents

Contributors

Gerolf Annemans Committee on Economic and Monetary Affairs of the European Parliament, Brussels, Belgium

Karen Banks Legal Service of the European Commission, Brussels, Belgium

Katarina Barley Federal Ministry of Justice and Consumer Protection, Berlin, Germany

Ilya G. J. Bruggeman EuroCommerce aisbl, The European Federation for Retail and Wholesale, Brussels, Belgium

Pierre-Henri Conac Professor of Financial Markets Law, University of Luxembourg, Luxembourg, Luxembourg

ERA Board of Trustees, Trier, Germany

Emmanuel Crabit European Commission, Brussels, Belgium

Paul Craig Professor of English Law, St John's College, Oxford, UK

Wiebe de Vries Immediate Past President, International Association of Young Lawyers (AIJA), Brussels, Belgium

Hans-Jürgen Hellwig Hengeler Mueller, Frankfurt am Main, Germany

ERA Board of Trustees, Trier, Germany

Wolfgang Heusel Academy of European Law (ERA), Trier, Germany

Lars Hjortnæs Justice, Supreme Court, Copenhagen, Denmark

Bernd Kaltenhäuser Regional Office of the Deutsche Bundesbank in Rhineland-Palatinate and the Saarland, Mainz, Germany

Nadja König Chief Economist, Federal Ministry of Finance, Berlin, Germany

Pauliine Koskelo European Court of Human Rights, Strasbourg, France

ERA Board of Trustees, Trier, Germany

Francis Lamy Council of State, Paris, France

Christine Langenfeld Georg-August-Universität, Göttingen, Germany

Judge, Bundesverfassungsgericht, Karlsruhe, Germany

Koen Lenaerts Court of Justice of the European Union, Luxembourg, Luxembourg

ERA Governing Board, Trier, Germany

Giorgio Maganza Former Director, Legal Service of the Council of the European Union, Brussels, Belgium

Peter-Christian Müller-Graff Ruprecht-Karls-Universität, Heidelberg, Germany

ERA Board of Trustees, Trier, Germany

Lord Thomas of Cwmgiedd Essex Court Chambers, London, UK

Luis Ortiz Blanco EU and Competition Law Department at the Law Firm Garrigues, Madrid, Spain and Brussels, Belgium

Inger Österdahl Uppsala University, Uppsala, Sweden

Jean-Philippe Rageade Academy of European Law (ERA), Trier, Germany

Maria José Rangel de Mesquita Faculty of Law, University of Lisbon, Lisbon, Portugal

ERA Board of Trustees, Trier, Germany

Jean-Luc Sauron Vice President, Council of State, Paris, France

Jean-Marc Sauvé Council of State, Paris, France

Ludger Schuknecht Chief Economist, Federal Ministry of Finance, Berlin, Germany

Pedro Silva Pereira Member of the European Parliament, Vice-Chair of the Committee on Constitutional Affairs, Brussels, Belgium

Maciej Szpunar University of Silesia, Katowice, Poland

Court of Justice of the European Union, Luxembourg, Luxembourg

ERA Board of Trustees, Trier, Germany

Pavel Telička Vice President, European Parliament, Strasbourg, France

ERA Governing Board, Trier, Germany

Marc van der Woude General Court of the European Union, Luxembourg, Luxembourg

ERA Board of Trustees, Trier, Germany

Christian Verschueren EuroCommerce aisbl, The European Federation for Retail and Wholesale, Brussels, Belgium

Diana Wallis Senior Lecturer in Law, University of Hull, Hull, UK

Former Vice President of the European Parliament, Brussels, Belgium

Former President of the European Law Institute, Vienna, Austria

ERA Board of Trustees, Trier, Germany

Joseph H. H. Weiler European Union Jean Monnet Chair at New York University School of Law, New York, NY, USA

Part I
The authority of European law

The authority of European law: Do we still believe in it?

Joseph H. H. Weiler

1 The concept of "authority"

It is to the credit of the prestigious Academy of European Law in Trier that it did not use the occasion of its 25th Anniversary to serve up the usual bland meal typical of these occasions, extoling yet again the wonders of European law, but instead provocatively called into question the Authority of European Law and invited a sober reflection of such. It would not have done so had there not been a pervasive feeling that indeed this authority is under stress.

The term "authority" in this context is hopelessly underspecified. There are, thus, no respectable social science metrics to gauge such and one is reduced to impressions, intuitions and sporadic markers. "Compliance Pull" by principal stakeholders is one such marker, and the most crucial stakeholder, the lynch pin of the EU legal order, would be domestic courts. The simple fact is that national governments of democratic States find it much easier to defy decisions of international tribunals such as the ICJ (think Iran hostages or Nicaragua) or the WTO Appellate Body (think Beef Hormones, Bananas, Internet Gambling) than it is to defy rulings of their very own courts. Faithful application by domestic courts of ECJ rulings is the best guarantee for their authority within the EU. Take that away and that authority is called into question with a cascading and contagious effect on other branches of government. Non-faithful compliance by domestic courts also has a potentially deleterious effect on the European Court itself, where the fear that its decisions might not be followed could introduce a 'jurist's prudence' affecting its very own decision making.

J. H. H. Weiler (✉)
European Union Jean Monnet Chair at New York University School of Law, New York, NY, USA
e-mail: weilersoffice@mercury.law.nyu.edu

W. Heusel, J.-P. Rageade (eds.), *The Authority of EU Law*,
https://doi.org/10.1007/978-3-662-58841-3_1

The recent slew of defiant national courts, among them some of the most prestigious in the Union, is thus extremely worrying and probably more than any other indicator set the alarm bells ringing. It can be the *Panzer* style action of the German Constitutional Court in refusing to honor an arrest warrant from another Member State in defiance of the clear jurisprudence of the ECJ, or the much more elegant action of the Italian Constitutional Court in the *Taricco* case[1] though even there the iron fist was barely hidden within the velvet glove, to give but two recent examples. One does not need a full-scale and widespread rebellion to cause significant damage.

But compliance pull, important and crucial as it may be, sharp as it may be in the Schmittian sense, is not the only indicator of a shift, albeit subtle, in the perception of the authority of European Law. There is also an inchoate, ineffable hard to pin down dimension for which the marker might be "respect" rather than "compliance". The interesting stakeholders here are not just national courts but the broader interpretative community and even the public at large. The Law of Gravity of the law is the social and political gravitas which attach to its rule and role in society. When the statement "It's the Law!" no longer engenders the reverence and respect commensurate with its majesty as the bulwark of our civilization, then the rule of the law is undermined at its most foundational level. In the deepest sense the authority of the law depends on such.

In this respect too there are no hard social science indicators for such respect. But when the law maker itself shirks its rule by extra-Treaty devices because the Treaty itself would not allow such (as happened in the financial crisis) or when in the heroic attempts to avoid Brexit concessions were made (on free movement of workers) which no respectable lawyer would argue were consistent with the Treaty—we have markers for such expedient erosion in the gravitas of "The Law". The same has been true in the reactions of this Member State or that to the Migration saga or in the stretching of fiscal disciplines to give but two well-known examples.

And when one turns to public opinion notably as manifest in social media, these are no longer drips from a breached dyke but more like a torrent. It is of no help to brand that as manifestations of "populism". The problem with populism is that it is very popular. And when a phenomenon—disrespect of and towards EU law becomes popular, is no longer a phenomenon of the lunatic fringe but affects what have become mainstream parties in some cases in government, in other cases realistic contenders, see Austria, Italy, Poland, Hungary in the first group, and France, the Netherlands, Finland, Denmark in the second, one can both understand and justify the provocative choice of the Academy of European Law in Trier on its anniversary.

Last but not least is our own little puddle called academia. For decades and decades the academic literature on EU law in general and the European Court(s) more specifically was largely adulatory, the *Amen* Corner of Luxembourg in the Church of European Integration displaying both (well earned) respect and loyalty.

---

[1] Cases C-105/14 *Taricco and Others*, ECLI:EU:C:2015:555, and C-42/17, *M.A.S and MB (Taricco II)*, ECLI:EU:C:2017:936.

Where critique existed it was mostly of a technical nature and normative critique, when it existed, often took the form, endearingly, of critiquing the ECJ when it strayed from its own orthodoxies. And there are some spectacular examples of reactions to more robust critique which treated such as heresy. Why Hjalte Rasmussen was not invited back to teach at the College of Europe in Bruges remains a matter of controversy.

This is certainly no longer the case and has not been such for at least a decade or more. Even a cursory visit to the blogosphere attests to a different culture of commentary, yes, a whole lot less deferential and somewhat less respectful, where most decisions of note by the ECJ are subject to searching critical analysis and the dice are left to fall wherever they do.

2 Reasons for the current stress on the authority of EU law

What explains this stress, and I would not put it at more than this, on the authority of European Law? There is one principal reason and then a second ancillary one.

The principal reason is the dramatic decline in the enthusiasm for and at times commitment to, the European Union. Brexit, I am fairly sure, will remain an aberrational exception. Even the most Eurosceptic polities *de jour* Hungary, Poland, Italy, Austria and others have no appetite for leaving. They are too smart for that. But the degree to which there is a moral and social commitment to what the EU historically stood for, an engine of prosperity and civility and above all a community of shared values has taken a major hit in a large number of Member States. Make no light of this. Savigny himself quite early on alerted to the inextricable link between the cultural and moral identity of a polity and the integrity of its law.

The second explanation, ancillary, rests with the operation of the law itself, independent of the polity within which it is situated. In Europe, the central legal axis is the relationship between the European Court—principally through the ingenious mechanism of the Preliminary References and Rulings—and national jurisdictions. When this axis, this communicative channel comes under stress, there is, too, a risk to the authority of European Law.

3 Material welfare and the authority of EU law

Let me turn first, then, to an explanation to the declining sorts of the European Union in the eyes of its principal stakeholders, its very citizens, as the primary explanation in the decline in the authority of European Law.

The most common explanation endlessly given for the turn in the fortune of European integration in the eyes of its citizenry is material, indeed materialistic.

The economic crisis, the growing cleavage in prosperity between North and South and within Member States between rich and poor, all called into question (even if unjustly…) the ability of the Union, of the Single Market, of the Euro, to guarantee stability, growth and economic justice promised from the very inception of the process of European Integration.

From the Treaty of Rome:

ARTICLE 1

By this Treaty, the HIGH CONTRACTING PARTIES establish among themselves a EUROPEAN ECONOMIC COMMUNITY.

ARTICLE 2

The Community shall have as its task, by establishing a common market and progressively approximating the economic policies of Member States, to promote throughout the Community a harmonious development of economic activities, *a continuous and balanced expansion, an increase in stability, an accelerated raising of the standard of living and closer relations between the States belonging to it.* (Emphasis added).

This was the original primordial promise, interestingly, materialist, indeed, in passing, you will not find a word on democracy and human rights, let alone more transcendent human values.

Little have we learnt from history that material promise is a fickle basis on which to achieve a transformation of the soul, a loyalty to a vision greater than the difficulty of the moment.

Here is Moses offering his Article 2 to the Children of Israel after their travails in bondage, subjugation and horror (all males to be thrown into the Nile) not unlike the bondage suffered by Europe in the decades preceding the noble promise of Monnet and his associates:

> He swore to your fathers to give you, a land flowing with milk and honey … EX. XIII:5

And yet when material hardship strikes, the results are similar to contemporary reactions when GDP dips and unemployment rises:

> Then the whole congregation of the children of Israel complained against Moses and Aaron in the wilderness.[3] And the children of Israel said to them, "Oh, that we had died by the hand of the Lord in the land of Egypt, when we sat by the pots of meat *and* when we ate bread to the full! For you have brought us out into this wilderness to kill this whole assembly with hunger. (Ex. XVI:3).

Loyalty and solidarity built on material promise alone are precarious and contingent on fulfillment of that promise failure of which saw both the collapse of loyalty evident in the rapid growth of Euroscepticism and of solidarity evident in notorious statements such as that by the Dutch Chair of the Eurogroup referring to the European South and commenting

> [You] can't spend [your] money on liquor and women and then ask for help

or Merkel

> It is also about not being able to retire earlier in countries such as Greece, Spain, Portugal than in Germany, instead everyone should try a little bit to make the same efforts – that is

> important ... We can't have a common currency where some get lots of vacation time and others very little... we cannot simply show solidarity and say these countries should simply continue as before... Yes Germany will help but Germany will only help when the others try. And that must be clear...

Not surprisingly the suggestion that southern Europeans are having a nice time on the beach while the Germans are working hard for their bailouts did not go down too well:

> "This is the purest colonialism," Portuguese trade union chief Manuel Carvalho da Silva said. He blasted Merkel for showing "no solidarity" and supporting a system where "the rich continue to live at the expense of the poorest countries in a disastrous system of exploitation".[2]

So much for material-based solidarity.

Be that as it may, when the European Construct has historically placed so much emphasis on Land of Milk and Honey promises, and has placed at the center the law of the market as the instrument to guarantee such prosperity, it should not surprise us that with the (temporary) collapse of prosperity, the authority of the law which was put in place to guarantee such should also take a knock.

4 Values and the authority of EU law

But Europe has not only been a Union of markets. It has also had a robust discourse of values. And it is usually the non-material, the spiritual, which help people see their way through material hardship without losing faith in the Promised Land and without betraying their values such as solidarity with others. And yet even beyond the widespread 'populist' surge in so many countries (I prefer to refer to such as the Revolt of the Masses, giving it the dignity of the association with Ortega y Gasset even if dissociating myself from the atavistic, xenophobic and illiberal manifestations) there has been a widespread souring with the European Construct.

Why has the 'value asset' of Europe turned out to be so fragile? Unable to counteract the stem which the materialist collapse brought about?

---

[2] Statistics published by the Organisation for Economic Co-operation and Development (OECD)—a club of the richest 34 states looking at employment and economics figures—show that, in reality, Germans retire earlier than their southern European counterparts. The average "effective retirement age" shows that in 2009, German men retired when they were 61.8 years old, the same as Spaniards and slightly earlier than Greeks (61.9), but Portuguese stayed on until they were 67. Greek women, meanwhile, retire a few months earlier than their German counterparts: at 59.6 years compared to 60.5 years. But Spanish and Portuguese women still work longer, for another 3 years on average. Southerners also have a similar amount of holidays to those in Germany. According to German law, workers can have at least 20 holidays a year, but these vary from state to state and can go up to 30 days. Greek workers are also entitled to 20 days of vacation and once they have worked for more than 10 years, they get another 5 days on top. Portuguese workers go on holiday for 22 days and Spaniards for 21.

5 Two ostensibly conflicting sets of values

Let me start with Poland. When coming to Poland one sometimes gets the impression of visiting a State with two nations. The societal cleavage is painfully deep even to the outside observer such as myself. I have only witnessed similar emotional charge when in situations such as Catalonia, or Scotland, or Belgium. But in Poland we are not dealing with Catalans and Castilians, with Walloons and Flemings, with Scots and English. Yet here we are dealing with Poles and Poles. What divides the two Polish "nations" are values and emotions. What it means, or should mean to be Polish, what kind of country, as reflected in the values it privileges, should Poland be.

But now comes the crux. This is not an instance of Polish exceptionalism. It is a pan-European phenomenon, manifesting itself with different levels of intensity. Think of Brexit. The British, a proud nation, which (alongside Poland!) was the one European State which 'never surrendered' in WW II, and yet now finds itself split down the middle with a cleavage far deeper than the normal politics of Left and Right. The British, too, are divided by values and emotions regarding what it means, or should mean to be British. Make no mistake, what drove Brexit was not primarily an economic calculous but an identitarian one.

And then take a look at the fault lines that have ruptured in other European countries in a major way: Italy, and Austria, and Germany, and France to name but some of the most clamorous and visible instances. There are always local conditions, the day to day weather changes, but the overall climatic charts are very similar: an emotionally charged split about values and identity. The value crisis is European, not Polish, or British or Italian.

What are the European Values and where is the split?

The thesis I invite you to consider is simple enough. There are in fact two sets of values which underlie the crisis. One set, a very important one, an indispensable set, is the habitual often reiterated "holy trinity" of Democratic Governance, Human Rights and the Rule of Law. These values are reiterated again and again, as defining the common European value asset. They do, make no mistake.

But there is, I argue, a second set of values which are dear to the heart of Europeans, except that they have been not only depressed and repressed, but in some deep way, wrongly in my view, come to be seen as illegitimate, the unspeakable "unholy trinity". The second set consists of the following: Patriotism, the bedrock, as I shall argue, of healthy republican democracy; the celebration of uniqueness both individual and collective, which I shall argue below is but an expression of the fundamental value of human dignity; and the value of duty and responsibility, individual and collective, as the other side of our commitment to rights and entitlements. There are large segments of our European populations, which, while committed to democracy, human rights and the rule of law, hearken for a vindication of the second Trinity as well. And Europe has not merely disregarded these, but in a fatal historical misstep regarded them as contrary to the values of the Union.

The value crisis manifests itself, thus, in two interconnected ways: First the feeling of a 'value disenfranchisement' for those segments of our population which hold the second set dear, a disenfranchisement, they resent. In part we are witnessing, as mentioned above, a latter day, 'Revolt of the Masses' of which Ortega y Gasset wrote about a century ago. The second manifestation is far worse and destructive. It is the erroneous belief, increasingly widespread, that the two value trinities are oppositional, that they force a choice. The high tempers and ferocious emotions now splitting Poles is an expression of this oppositional concept of the two sets of values. And this is at the heart, the tragic feature, of the overall pan-European value crisis.

6 Democracy, human rights and the rule of law: An inextricable triad

Though we list Democratic Governance, Human Rights and the Rule of Law as three distinct values, I have used the metaphor of the Trinity advisedly. They are three but at the same time one. You cannot have one without the other and it is their unity which defines our post fascist and post Communist polities. Hitler was brought to power through democratic elections and until his death was hugely popular giving expression to the will of the vast majority of Germans. And I assure you that in the murder of six million Poles, Jewish Poles and Christian Poles in equal measure, the rule of law was scrupulously observed. The murderers were not acting on a whim, or in defiance of legal order, but executing such. And yet it was the most horrendous violation and disregard of human rights, in the modern annals of history. I could add heaps of other examples. We have come to reject a notion of democracy which simply gives expression to the will of the majority if that is not tempered with respect for fundamental rights of the minority and enforced by a judiciary constituted in accordance with the rule of law. A judiciary which is at the whim of either legislature or executive branch destroys not only its independence and hence credibility but also the principle of separation of powers fundamental for democratic governance. We reject a notion of Rule of Law, if that rule is not on the one hand an expression of democratic governance and at the same time able to oppose the majoritarian principle in protecting inviolable fundamental rights. If one compromises the rule of law in order better to give expression to majoritarian impulses, one is compromising democracy itself. To accept such should not be something imposed by Europe, something accepted as a price for membership in the Union.

I believe there is widespread commitment, in Europe and among Europeans to this Tritinity of values, the common value asset of the European Union.

7 Active citizenship, clientelism and the sense of rights and duties

What then of the other set of values? We need here to focus on Western Europe (the "Old" Europe) not because they are intrinsically more important, but because the value asset of the European Union were shaped by their experience.

To understand the story of the second set of values we have to go back in history and to three processes which begin after WW II and are reactions to such, processes which have progressed over the last six decades and which are now producing their sour grapes and are at the root of the value clash and value crisis in which Europe finds itself now.

The First Process. For reasons that are quite understandable, the very word "patriotism" became "unprintable" after the War notably in Western Europe. Fascist regimes (among others), by abusing the word and the concept, had "burned" it from collective consciousness. And in many ways this has been a positive thing. But we also pay a high price for having banished this word—and the sentiment it expresses—from our psycho-political vocabulary. Since patriotism also has a noble side: the discipline of love, the duty to take care of one's homeland and people, of accepting our civic responsibility toward the collective. In reality, true patriotism is the opposite of Fascism: "We do not belong to the State, it's the State that belongs to us." This kind of patriotism is an integral part, indeed an essential part of the republican form of democracy. And importantly, people yearn for it and feel abused and disenfranchised when any expression of patriotism is branded as illegitimate and in conflict with shared European values.

Today, we may call ourselves the Italian or French "Republic," but our democracies are no longer truly republican. There's the State, there's the government, and then there's "us".

We are like shareholders of an enterprise. If the directorate of the enterprise called "the Republic" does not produce political and material dividends, we change managers with a vote during a meeting of shareholders called "elections." If there is anything that does not work in our society, we go to the "directors"—as we do, for example, when our internet connection isn't working: "We paid (our taxes), and look at the terrible service they're giving us…" The State is always the one responsible. Never us. It's a clientelistic democracy that not only takes away our responsibility toward our society, toward our country, but also removes responsibility from our very human condition. There is nothing "Non European" in a healthy sense of patriotism; to acknowledge such is not only politically prudent because it has become self-evident that there is this wide spread yearning for such, but because of its inherent value and importance to healthy republican democracy. And yet the only time it is allowed is during international soccer competitions.

The second process which helps to explain what happened to Europe comes, once again, as a reaction to the War, and is paradoxical. We've accepted, as noted above, both at the national and international levels, a serious and irreversible obligation rooted in our Constitutions to protect the fundamental rights of individuals, even against the political tyranny of the majority. At a more general level, our political-juridical vocabulary has become a discussion of rights. The rights of, say, an Italian citizen are protected by Italian courts, and, above all, by the Italian Constitutional Court. But also by the Court of Justice of the EU in Luxembourg, and—again—by the European Court of Human Rights in Strasbourg. It's enough to make your head spin. And this is true, blessedly so, throughout the Union. Just think about how common it has become, in the political discourse of today, to speak more and more about "rights." It's enormously important. One would and should never want to live in a country in which fundamental rights are not effectively defended and that cannot be done without a truly independent judiciary. For typically rights are posited against the whims of those who govern. But here too—as with the banishment of patriotism—we pay a dear price for our rights discourse excesses. Actually, we pay two prices.

First and foremost, the noble culture of rights does indeed put the individual at the center, but little by little, almost without realizing it, it turns him or her into a self-centered individual. Atomized and at times anti-social. It is never "what can I do for society, for the State, for the Union (!) but what are my entitlements from them". No where is this clearer in the original definition of European Citizenship:

1. Citizenship of the Union is hereby established.
   Every person holding the nationality of a Member State shall be a citizen of the Union.
2. Citizens of the Union shall enjoy the rights conferred by this Treaty *and shall be subject to the duties imposed thereby*. (Emphasis added)

Take out your magnifying glass and seek for those duties. It is the blueprint, inadvertent of course, to non-republican democracy, to democracy of rights with no duties and responsibilities—apart I suppose from not breaking the law or paying taxes.

And the second effect of this "culture of rights"—which is a framework all Europeans have in common—is a kind of flattening of political and cultural specificity, of one's own unique national identity. The much vaunted Constitutional Patriotism underlies our commonality as Europeans. It flattens our uniqueness as Italians and French, as Latvians and Poles. Yet Europe is defined as United in Diversity.

The notion of human dignity—the fact that we have all been created in the image of God—contains, at one and the same time, two facets. On the one hand, it means that we are all equal in our fundamental human dignity and worth: rich and poor, Italians and Germans, men and woman, citizens and foreigners. My essential dignity is compromised and violated when I am considered less worthy than someone else.

On the other hand, recognizing human dignity means accepting that each of us is an entire universe, distinct and different from any other person. Think of yourself: In the entire history of human existence there was never anyone who lived who was quite the same as you are. We are not birds in flock. Our essential dignity is equally compromised and violated when I am treated as fungible with anyone else even if both are of equal worth. If human dignity, our essential humanity, is the bedrock value, it has to be lived through a respect for both its facets: Fundamental Equality living side by side with fundamental uniqueness. Here, too, I would argue the very human condition yearns for dignity, in both its facets. And the same duality is true for our collective and social existence as national societies. France is not intrinsically more worthy than Spain, or Germany is not intrinsically more worthy than Poland. But France is not Spain and Germany is not Poland. We yearn, too, for dignity in our collective existence. We reject the Orwellian notion that all are equal just some a bit more than others. But we also reject a notion that denies our uniqueness within the common value asset. When the legitimacy of this yearning for an acknowledgement of our unique collective national identity is derided and dismissed and disrespected, we feel again an assault on our dignity, a value disenfranchisement and we rebel.

The third long-term process is secularization. Let me be clear: this observation is not an evangelical rebuke. I do not judge a person based on his or her faith or lack thereof. And even though, for me, it's impossible to imagine the world without the Lord—The Holy Blessed Be He—I also know many religious people who are odious and many atheists of the highest moral character. This process of secularization also began with World War II. Who among us, after having seen the mountains of shoes from millions of assassinated children at Auschwitz, didn't ask the question: God, where were you?

The result of secularism lies in the fact that a voice which was at one time universal and ubiquitous, a voice in which the emphasis was on duty and not only rights, on personal responsibility in the face of what happens to us, our neighbors, our society and not the instinctive appeal to public institutions, has all but disappeared from social praxis in Western Europe and beyond. When you go to Church you do not here the priest talking to you about your rights, but about your duties and responsibilities. It is not the rights of migrants—it is our duty towards them. And here, too, there is as part of the human condition a deep yearning for duty and responsibility—for it is only through duty and responsibility that one is truly sovereign as a human being, and not the passive receiver of entitlements dependent on the good will, or benevolence of others.

It has taken decades for these three processes to mature and produce now their "sour grapes" (Is. 5:2). We see the impact everywhere, not least in matters regarding the European Union.

8 Diversity as European strength

These three values—which I ironically characterized as the "unholy Trinity"—are as European and as essential as are the Holy Trinity of Democratic Governance, Human Rights and the Rule of Law. The European clash of values, manifest in so many European societies is a result of the misperception that the first set of values are necessarily in contradiction with the second set. From the erroneous culture and praxis which subtly and not so subtly excoriated and demonized the human yearning for the love discipline of patriotism, the pride in a unique identity, and the desire to serve beyond one's immediate direct interest. And into the breech jumped politicians and parties which in good faith and bad were able to exploit such and turn frustration into a profound culture war in which Brexit is but the most extreme victim, but the poison of which has become pervasive. The sad thing is that these totally human (non atavistic and xenophobic) yearnings continue to be dismissed, degraded and unacknowledged. You will note that the entire European vision for the future is materialistic, again, whether it is from the school of Macron or Merkel or others. Euro, and Banking Union, and Minister of Economy, and a Euro Budget.

And against this climate, if European Law is associated with the Holy Trinity and is seen as negating the so called "Unholy Trinity" it is not surprising that European law instead of being seen as a law for all, as a common asset, is perceived partisan in a veritable cultural civil war, as a potent arm of one side in this "lawfare". Make no mistake: This is not to offer succor to the voices of illiberal democracy—a contradiction in terms, but to explain their mobilizing successes.

9 No *demos*, no democratic accountability, no democratic representation: the democratic deficit

There is, I fear, more. And it concerns the sad old story of the European Democracy deficit. If the law is to enjoy authority in democratic polities it must be a law the promulgation of which follows the habits and practices of democratic legitimation. Now to many this is a story which has already come to closure. Does the European Parliament not enjoy full powers as a veritable co-legislator alongside the Council of Ministers? Where, then, is the deficit?

Sadly, there is the persistent, chronic, troubling Democracy Deficit, which cannot be talked away. Although the "No-Demos" thesis seems to have receded in recent discourse, its relevance is suddenly more acute than ever. The difficulties, as will be seen, of constructing all manner of "fiscal union" type solutions for the Euro crisis are in no small measure the result of—yes, "no demos"—a lack of transcendent responsibility for the lot of one's fellow citizens and nationals. Germans and Dutch and Finns are not saying: "A Bailout is the wrong policy." They are saying: "Why should we, Germans, or Dutch, or Finns, help those lazy Italians or Portuguese or Greeks." A very visible manifestation of the No-Demos thesis of Europe's democracy crisis.

Second, there are failures of democracy which simply make it difficult to speak of governance by and of the people. The manifestations of the so-called democracy deficit are persistent and no endless repetition of the powers of the European Parliament will remove them. In essence it is the inability of the Union to develop structures and processes which adequately replicate, or 'translate,' at the Union level even the imperfect habits of governmental control, parliamentary accountability and administrative responsibility that are practiced with different modalities in the various Member States. Make no mistake: It is perfectly understood that the Union is not a State. But it is in the business of governance and has taken over extensive areas previously in the hands of the Member States. In some critical areas, such as the interface of the Union with the international trading system, the competences of the Union are exclusive. In others they are dominant. Democracy is not about States. Democracy is about the exercise of public power—and the Union exercises a huge amount of public power. We live by the credo that any exercise of public power has to be legitimated democratically and it is exactly here that process legitimacy fails.

In essence, the two primordial features of any functioning democracy are missing—the grand principles of accountability and representation.

As regards accountability, even the basic condition of representative democracy that at election time the citizens "…can throw the scoundrels out"—that is replace the Government—does not operate in Europe, the *Spitzenkandidaten* exercise notwithstanding. The form of European governance, governance without Government, is, and will remain for considerable time, perhaps forever such that there is no "Government" to throw out. Dismissing the Commission by Parliament (or approving the appointment of the Commission President) is not quite the same, not even remotely so.

Startlingly, but not surprisingly, political accountability of Europe is remarkably weak. There have been some spectacular political failures of European governance. The embarrassing Copenhagen climate fiasco; the weak (at best) realization of the much touted Lisbon Agenda (also known as Lisbon Strategy or Lisbon Process), the very story of the defunct "Constitution" to mention but three. It is hard to point in these instances to any measure of political accountability, of someone paying a political price as would be the case in national politics. In fact it is difficult to point to a single instance of accountability for political failure as distinct from personal accountability for misconduct in the annals of European integration. This is not, decidedly not, a story of corruption or malfeasance. My argument is that this failure is rooted in the very structure of European governance. It is not designed for political accountability. In similar vein, it is impossible to link in any meaningful way the results of elections to the European Parliament to the performance of the Political Groups within the preceding parliamentary session, in the way that is part of the mainstay of political accountability within the Member States. Structurally, dissatisfaction with "Europe" when it exists has no channel to affect, at the European level, the agents of European governance.

Likewise, at the most primitive level of democracy, there is simply no moment in the civic calendar of Europe where the citizen can influence directly the outcome of any policy choice facing the Community and Union in the way that citizens can when choosing between parties which offer sharply distinct programs at the national level. The political color of the European Parliament only very weakly gets translated into the legislative and administrative output of the Union.

The Political Deficit, to use the felicitous phrase of Renaud Dehousse, is at the core of the Democracy Deficit. The Commission, by its self-understanding linked to its very ontology, cannot be 'partisan' in a right-left sense, neither can the Council, by virtue of the haphazard political nature of its composition. Democracy normally must have some meaningful mechanism for expression of voter preference predicated on choice among options, typically informed by stronger or weaker ideological orientation. That is an indispensable component of politics. Democracy without Politics is an oxymoron. And yet that is not only Europe, but it is a feature of Europe—the "non-partisan" nature of the Commission—which is celebrated. The stock phrase found in endless student text books and the like, that the Supranational Commission vindicates the European Interest, whereas the intergovernmental Council is a clearing house for Member State interest, is, at best, naïve. Does the "European Interest" not necessarily involve political and ideological choices? At times explicit, but always implicit?

Thus the two most primordial norms of democracy, the principle of accountability and the principle of representation are compromised in the very structure and process of the Union.

The second manifestation of the current European circumstance is evident in a continued slide in the legitimacy and mobilizing force of the European Construct and its institutions. I pass over some of the uglier manifestations of European 'solidarity' both at governmental and popular level as regards the Euro-crisis or the near abandonment of Italy to deal with the influx of migrants from North Africa as if this was an Italian problem and not a problem for Europe as a whole. I look instead at two deeper and longer-term trends. The first is the extraordinary decline in voter participation in elections for the European Parliament. In Europe as a whole the rate of participation is below 45%, with several countries, notably in the East, with a rate below 30%. The correct comparison is, of course, with political elections to national parliaments where the numbers are considerably higher. What is striking about these figures is that the decline coincides with a continuous shift in powers to the European Parliament, which today is a veritable co-legislator with the Council. The more powers the European Parliament, supposedly the *Vox Populi*, has gained, the greater popular indifference to it seems to have developed. It is sobering but not surprising to note the absence of the European Parliament as a major player in the current crisis. But the institutional crisis runs deeper. The Commission has excelled as a creative secretariat and implementer and monitor, but neither as the sources of ideas or veritable political leadership. It has been faithful and effective as His Master's Voice. But most striking has been the disappearing act of the Council. No longer the proud leader of Europe according to the Giscardian design, but an elaborate rubber-stamp to the Union's two Presidents—Merkel and Macron. A double failure of institutional legitimacy, of Parliament and Council. Of Supranationalism and Intergovernmentalism. The resort to an extra-Union Treaty as a centerpiece of the reconstruction is but the poignant legal manifestation of this political reality.

The critique of the democracy deficit of the Union has itself been subjected to two types of critique itself. The first has simply contested the reality of the democracy deficit by essentially claiming that wrong criteria have been applied to the Union. The lines of debate are well known. For what it is worth, I have staked my position above. But I am more interested in the second type of critique which implicitly is an invocation of Result or output legitimacy. Since the Union, not being a State, cannot replicate or adequately translate the habits and practices of Statal democratic governance, its legitimacy may be found elsewhere.

In analyzing the legitimacy (and mobilizing force) of the European Union, in particular against the background of its persistent democracy deficit, political and social science has indeed long used the distinction between *process legitimacy* and *outcome legitimacy* (also known as input/output, process/result etc). The legitimacy of the Union more generally and the Commission more specifically, even if suffering from deficiencies in the state democratic sense, are said to rest on the results achieved—in the economic, social and, ultimately, political realms. The idea hearkens back to the most classic functionalist and neo-functionalist theories.

I do not want to take issue with the implied normativity of this position—a latter day *Panem et circenses* approach to democracy, which at some level at least could be considered quite troubling. It is with its empirical reality that I want to take some issue. I do not think that outcome legitimacy explains all or perhaps even most of the mobilizing force of the European Construct. But whatever role it played it is dependent on the *Panem*. Rightly or wrongly, the economic woes of Europe, which are manifest in the Euro crisis, are attributed to the European Construct. So when there suddenly is no Bread, and certainly no cake, we are treated to a different kind of circus whereby the citizens' growing indifference is turning to hostility and the ability of Europe to act as a political mobilizing force seems not only spent, but even reversed. The worst way to legitimate a war is to lose it, and Europe is suddenly seen not as an icon of success but as an emblem of austerity, thus in terms of its promise of prosperity, failure. If success breeds legitimacy, failure, even if wrongly allocated, leads to the opposite.

Thus, not surprisingly there is a seemingly contagious spread of 'Anti-Europeanism' in national politics. What was once in the province of fringe parties on the far right and left has inched its way to more central political forces. The "Question of Europe" as a central issue in political discourse was for long regarded as an 'English disease.' There is a growing contagion in Member States in North and South, East and West, where political capital is to be made among non-fringe parties by anti-European advocacy. The spill-over effect of this phenomenon is the shift of mainstream parties in this direction as a way of countering the gains at their flanks. If we are surprised by this it is only because we seem to have airbrushed out of our historical consciousness the rejection of the so-called European Constitution, an understandable amnesia since it represented a defeat of the collective political class in Europe by the *vox populi*, albeit not speaking through, but instead giving a slap in the face to, the European Institutions.

In conclusion, with a persistent and troubling deficit in the manner in which European law is made, and the evident turn away of the electorate from the law making process through elections to the European Parliament, why would we even be surprised that there would be a decline in the authority of the law so made?

10 The role of the court

At a much lower level and far less dramatic, the erosion in the authority of European Law is being chipped away by certain practices of European law itself, and not least by the most celebrated institution of European law, the Court of Justice of the European Union. It is important not to demonize the Court. It has made a singular and singularly important contribution to the noble experiment entitled European integration. But there is nothing that is so good that cannot be better, and I want to mention most briefly, since I have dealt with this elsewhere more extensively, a handful of areas where I think the Court may benefit from some thinking regarding its structure and *modus operandi*.

10.1 The selection of judges

The European Commission launched an infringement procedure against Poland over measures affecting the judiciary a day after the publication in the Polish Official Journal of the Law on the Ordinary Courts Organization on July 28, 2017. Though the infringement procedure is formally distinct from the ongoing 'Rule of Law Dialogue' and the recommendations issued just a few days before commencement of such procedure, it comes under the latter's penumbra; both form part and parcel of the Commission Press Release (IP-17-2205). If the concern was 'The Rule of Law,' at least in some respects there is more bang than buck. The President of Poland blocked the most controversial parts of the new judicial regime in Poland, so that the infringement procedure was left with just two violations.

The first concerns a different retirement age for male and female judges. It is not clear if this distinction in the Polish law is by design or inertia but the infringement seems clear: What is sauce for Sabena (RIP) cabin attendant geese, should be sauce for judicial ganders. But important as any form of gender discrimination is, this item in the Polish legislation does not directly concern the more troublesome aspects of political control over the judiciary and its independence. It seems as if Poland has corrected this anomaly.

The second item in the infringement procedure is far more serious. In the Letter of Formal Notice (the first stage in infringement procedures) the Commission raises concerns "…that by giving the Minister of Justice the discretionary power to prolong the mandate of judges who have reached retirement age, as well as dismiss and appoint Court Presidents, the independence of the Polish Courts will be undermined" (*id.*) allegedly contravening a combination of Articles 19(1) of the TEU and 47 of the EU Charter of Fundamental Rights—a legal basis which is creative but not specious.

If indeed the prolongation of the mandate of a judge reaching retirement age rests in the hands of a Minister, the government of which he or she are part and acts and/or legislation issuing from which might be subject to judicial scrutiny by said judge, it may well consciously or otherwise impact, for example, his or her conduct prior to retirement or, no less importantly, give the appearance of lack of independence. I think this is indeed a serious matter impinging on the independence and appearance of independence of the judiciary. It is one thing to have scrutiny and approval of judges by democratic bodies at the moment of appointment. But once appointed, the independence of the judge from political actors must be as absolute as possible, and this dependency described in the letter of intent clearly compromises such.

But there is an irony in this complaint. At least on two occasions proposals were put to various Intergovernmental Conferences to amend the Treaties so that appointment of Judges to the Court of Justice of the European Union should be for a fixed period of time—say 9 years—as is undoubtedly the Best Practice in Europe among higher courts where appointments are not until age of retirement. Ominously in my view, the proposals were rejected. So that now we live under a regime where the prolongation of Members of the Court(s) (Judges and the 'permanent' Advocates General) rests in the hands of national politicians whose decision and legislation may come before such judges.

I am sure one can draw all kind of Pharisaic distinction between the Polish law and the European practice. I take cold comfort from the collegial and confidential nature of proceedings as a shield guaranteeing independence and appearance of independence.

There is clearly no such shield in the case of Advocates General. The old hands among you will remember from years past at least one much commented upon Opinion of an AG which gave the appearance of being compromised by this political dependence. AGs do not give Opinions in cases where 'their' MS is a defendant in a direct action, but frequently do in Preliminary References implicating directly or indirectly same. Far be it for me to impugn the integrity of any AG, present or past. But in this area appearances are as important as actual practice.

As regards judges, the shield, too, is far from a perfect answer to the appearance of independence. (This is often given as a reason why the European Court cannot entertain the idea of dissenting opinions lest judges be exposed to undue pressure or appear to be.) Leaks apart, in most cases the Court follows the outcome proposed by the *Juge Rapporteur* (though often with modified reasoning) which given the concerns which are the subject of the infringement procedure may result in a delicate situation especially in chambers of three.

Also, recent practice (of 20 years or so) has seen Presidents serving for long terms. By not resubmitting their own national serving as President, a Member State can effectively terminate the mandate of the President of the Court.

Thus, in the case of AGs egregiously and the Court as a whole and its President more obliquely, the situation is at its core cut from the same soiled cloth as is the situation in Poland about which the Commission rightly has taken action. It does not add to the authority of European Law if its judges are subject to the same kind of political control which, rightly, was the source of the Commission's complaint against Poland.

10.2 The style of decisions

The failure to limit the term of office of judges of the Court and the resulting political control over their reappointment produces a further inimical result. Decisions of the Court of Justice are often woefully short and frequently apodictic in their style, where assertion replaces serious judicial reasoning. I do not feel it necessary to give examples. They are rife. The explanation is more interesting.

Koen Lenaerts in his remarkable essay 'The Court's Outer and Inner Selves' (to be found in *Judging Europe's Judges*, edited by Adams *et al.)* offers one possible explanation for this:

> [T]he ECJ operates under the principle of collegiality. In light of the latter principle, reaching an outcome based on consensus is of paramount importance for the daily inner-workings of the ECJ. Accordingly, for the sake of consensus, in hard cases the discourse of the ECJ cannot be as profuse as it would be if dissenting opinions were allowed. As consensus-building requires to bring on board as many opinions as possible, the argumentative discourse of the ECJ is limited to the very essential. In order to preserve consensus, the ECJ does not take 'long jumps' when expounding the rationale underpinning the solution given to novel questions of constitutional importance.

This simply underscores the argument for limiting the tenure of CJEU judges to one fixed term (following Best Practice in Europe), thus opening the door, sparingly perhaps, for dissenting opinions and allowing the Court in critical cases, even where there is no consensus, to articulate its decisions more fully and not be reduced to the lowest common denominator of consensual collegiality. And given that ECJ decisions on occasion, like similar decisions of Member State highest courts, have a meaning and significance and impact beyond the restricted ambiance of European law practitioners and beyond the national court who requested the ruling, it is sometimes essential to go beyond the 'very essential'. Sometimes, how a court explains, frames and articulates is no less important than the actual decision itself. It is important for the polity and it is important for the legitimacy of the Court itself. Mauro Cappelletti used to teach that the single most important element in legitimating judicial decisions is the quality of the reasoning. One does not expect the Court to decide issues not before it. But one expects it to decide issues before it with the quality of reasoning that a landmark decision such as *Achbita* merits, as is the practice of most European constitutional courts in similar circumstances.

10.3 The composition of the court

There is a procedure in place, and it works reasonably well, which examines the professional suitability of judges proposed for appointment to the ECJ. What there is not is any planning so that the College of Judges will have the necessary spread of expertise which its wide subject-matter docket requires. When it comes to the workings of the Single Market the Court is second to none. But what about, say, human rights? Here is the voice of one of the most authoritative commentators on the ECJ just recently published[3]:

> We are not a human rights court.' This phrase has been repeated over and again by judges and advocates general of the Court of Justice of the EU for many years. To the question of why does the Court not rely more on Strasbourg case law on human rights in the field of, say, competition, the reply was a classic: 'we are not a human rights court'. If the Court was accused of ignoring international human rights instruments in cases with a strong tie with international law, the response sounded familiar: 'we are not a human rights court'. If human rights were put aside or restricted in the name of free movement rules, the explanation was always ready to go: 'we are not a human rights court'.
>
> Indeed, the Court of Justice was not designed in its early days to be a human rights court, but its current role as the lead player of the European judicial landscape has put it in an unprecedented situation. There is no area of policy that escapes the scrutiny of the Court of Justice: the digital world has found in the Court an uncompromising upholder of private life that will not tolerate intrusions in the sphere of individuals' privacy; the effectiveness of asylum policy depends on the Court's readiness to interpret asylum rules as procedural or substantial guarantees in light of human rights; consumers throughout the continent rely on the Court's judgments to rule on how banks, digital titans or retailers treat their clients; criminal procedures have come under the umbrella of EU harmonization instruments, putting the Court in a privileged position to set standards and guarantees of criminal procedure in all Member States.

The Court will only be able to discharge this expanded jurisdiction if its composition includes with sufficient numbers experts in the various fields in which it is required to render decisions. There is plenty of evidence, and not only from the field of human rights that the Court often lacks that kind of expertise, a lack which may lead to a certain erosion in the authority and respect which its judgments deserve.

10.4 The docket

It seems that nothing to date will persuade the Court that it ought to relinquish its monopoly over Preliminary References even after more than 65 years. The damage, in my view, is palpable. It is not simply or primarily the length of time one has to wait for a Ruling. Much improvement has been seen in this regard. It is instead the dilution of the specific gravity of its decision coming down at a rate close to one a day but most importantly it is the lack of ponderation which the judgments receive all too often manifest in the less than optimal quality of the reasoning.

Reference

Sarmiento D (2018) A Court that dare not speak its name: human rights at the Court of Justice, Blog of the European Journal of International Law, published on 7 May 2018

[3] Sarmiento (2018).

The Court of Justice of the European Union as the guardian of the authority of EU law: A networking exercise

Koen Lenaerts

1 Introduction

The EU legal order is autonomous *vis-a-vis* both the national and international legal orders. It has its own constitutional framework, its own founding principles and institutional structure, as well as a full set of legal rules to ensure its operation.[1] In this legal order, the EU and its Member States—but also the Member States among themselves—are linked together in "an ever closer Union". This close relationship involves a dialogue not only between the courts of the Member States and the Court of Justice of the European Union ('Court of Justice') but also among national courts themselves. Both of those dialogues are equally vital to uphold the rule of law within the EU. This article addresses both aspects of that judicial network.

2 The dialogue between the Court of Justice and the national courts of the Member States

Article 267 TFEU provides the foundation for the judicial dialogue—which has been described as an "integrated judiciary"[2]—that exists between the Court of

This article is based on a lecture given on the occasion of the congress marking the 25th anniversary of the Academy of European Law in Trier on 19 October 2017. All opinions expressed herein are strictly personal to the author.

[1] Opinion 2/13, EU:C:2014:2454, para. 158.

[2] Halberstam (2008), p. 142.

K. Lenaerts (✉)
Court of Justice of the European Union, Luxembourg, Luxembourg

ERA Governing Board, Trier, Germany
e-mail: Ignace.maselis@curia.europa.eu

W. Heusel, J.-P. Rageade (eds.), *The Authority of EU Law*,
https://doi.org/10.1007/978-3-662-58841-3_2

Justice and the Member States' courts. As early as 1978, in *Simmenthal*, the Court held that all judges in the Member States are EU judges.[3] The power to enforce EU law is thus shared between the Court of Justice and national courts: they both ensure that in the interpretation and application of the Treaties the law is observed.[4] On the basis of the principles of primacy and direct effect, in combination with the preliminary reference procedure, national courts play an essential role in ensuring the full application of EU law and in securing judicial protection of individual rights under EU law. Together with the Court of Justice, they are the guardians of the EU legal order.[5]

Although the relationship between the Court of Justice and national courts is one of dialogue and direct cooperation,[6] the proper operation of the preliminary reference procedure—as laid down in Article 267 TFEU—is based on a division of powers between the Court of Justice and national courts. The EU courts alone have the jurisdiction to declare secondary EU law invalid.[7] As regards interpretation, the Court of Justice can only interpret EU law but not national law. It leaves to the national courts the application of EU law to the case at hand, as well as the concrete assessment of the validity of national law in the light of EU law.[8]

The fact that each judge in every Member State of the Union is an EU judge has profound implications. National courts must apply EU law in its entirety in all cases that come before them and must protect the rights which that law confers on individuals. This means that every national court must set aside provisions of national law that conflict with EU law.

The dialogue between the Court of Justice and national courts is only open to courts that are independent. This is because political considerations cannot take part in a dialogue that is based on the law, and on nothing but the law. In addition, judicial independence and effective judicial protection of EU rights go hand in hand, as only independent courts may provide effective remedies. Logically, the question arises whether EU law protects national courts that see their independence threatened by the other branches of government. In the seminal judgment in *Associação Sindical dos Juízes Portugueses*,[9] the Court of Justice held that the second subparagraph of Article 19(1) TEU may be relied upon in order to set aside national measures that call into question the independence of the national judiciary. The Court of Justice explained the relationship between the rule of law, Article 19 TEU, the principle of effective judicial protection and national courts. It held that the EU is founded on the values set out in Article 2 TEU, such as respect for the rule of law. Article 19 TEU gives concrete expression to that founding value by entrusting 'the responsibility for ensuring judicial review in the EU legal order not only to the

[3] Case 106/77, *Simmenthal*, EU:C:1978:49, para. 21.

[4] Opinion 1/09, EU:C:2011:123, para. 69.

[5] Opinion 1/09, EU:C:2011:123, para. 66-69; Lenaerts (2013), p. 40.

[6] Opinion 1/09, EU:C:2011:123, para. 84.

[7] Case 314/85, *Foto-Frost*, EU:C:1987:452.

[8] Case C-54/07, *Feryn*, EU:C:2008:397, para. 19; Lenaerts (2013), p. 41.

[9] Case C-64/16, *Associação Sindical dos Juízes Portugueses*, EU:C:2018:117.

[Court of Justice] but also to national courts and tribunals'.[10] Accordingly, the Member States are under the obligation 'to establish a system of legal remedies and procedures ensuring effective judicial protection in [the fields covered by EU law]'.[11] In that regard, the Court of Justice found that there is an unbreakable link between compliance with the rule of law and the principle of effective judicial protection: one cannot exist without the other. The bodies entrusted with responsibility for upholding the rule of law within the EU—i.e. 'courts or tribunals'—, must meet the requirements of effective judicial protection. This means, in essence, that such protection must be provided for by a body that falls within the notion of 'court or tribunal' as defined by EU law. In particular, referring to its case law on Article 267 TFEU and on Article 47 of the Charter of Fundamental Rights of the European Union (the 'Charter'), the Court of Justice held that that notion requires courts to be independent.[12]

Furthermore, national law cannot require that only certain judges may rule on a potential conflict between national and European law.[13] Indeed, under the preliminary reference procedure, any Member State court is free to engage in a dialogue with the Court of Justice and must therefore be able to draw any relevant consequences from the result of that dialogue.[14]

It follows that every national court has broad discretion in deciding whether to refer a matter to the Court of Justice, should it consider that a case pending before it raises questions on the interpretation or validity of Union law. This also applies to lower courts and even to differently constituted benches from the same court.[15]

That point was at issue in the *PFE* case.[16] The case concerned a particular procedure that exists in the Sicilian judicial system. The Sicilian Council of Administrative Justice had to make a ruling in litigation concerning public service contracts. On the basis of national procedural rules, the Sicilian Council acted as a chamber of the Italian Council of State with regard to the exercise, within that region, of the functions assigned to the Council of State. As such, the Sicilian Council of Administrative Justice was acting as a court against whose decision there was no judicial remedy under national law, which meant that it had a duty to refer questions to the Court of Justice on the basis of Article 267 TFEU.

---

[10] *Ibid.*, para 32.

[11] *Ibid.*, para. 34.

[12] *Ibid.*, paras 42, 43 and 44. Regarding Article 47 of the Charter—which contains the notion of 'independent and impartial tribunal', the Court of Justice referred to Case C-685/15, *Online Games and Others*, EU:C:2017:452, para. 60; and Case C-403/16, *El Hassani*, EU:C:2017:960, para. 40. As to the notion of 'court or tribunal' set out in Article 267 TFEU, it referred to Case C-506/04, *Wilson*, EU:C:2006:587, para. 49, and Case C-503/15, *Margarit Panicello*, EU:C:2017:126, para. 37.

[13] Case 106/77, *Simmenthal*, EU:C:1978:49, para. 21-23.

[14] Case 106/77, *Simmenthal*, EU:C:1978:49, para. 19-20; Case C-689/13, *PFE*, EU:C:2016:199, para. 38-41.

[15] Case C-378/08, *ERG*, EU:C:2010:126, para. 32.

[16] Case C-689/13, *PFE*, EU:C:2016:199.

However, a national procedural rule required the Sicilian Council of Administrative Justice, when acting as a chamber of the Italian Council of State, to apply the case law established by the plenary session of the latter Court itself, including in respect of questions concerning the interpretation and application of EU law. If the Sicilian Council of Administrative Justice did not agree with a principle of law previously stated by the plenary session of the Council of State, it was required to refer the decision to that plenary session for a ruling. In the case at hand, there seemed to be a conflict between a judgment given by the Italian Council of State and a judgment of the Court of Justice in the *Fastweb* case,[17] which, on the basis of that internal procedural rule, required the Sicilian Council of Administrative Justice to refer the case to the Council of State. In this case, the Court of Justice emphasised that national law cannot prevent a national court from complying with its obligation to refer questions to the Court of Justice. The discretion and the obligation to refer questions are an inherent part of the system of cooperation between the national courts and the Court of Justice and of the role of the courts generally in ensuring the uniform application of EU law. National rules cannot therefore interfere with the discretion or the obligation of national courts to refer questions to the Court of Justice.[18]

Another particular aspect of the preliminary reference procedure was at issue in the *Ognyanov* case, namely the requirement that the factual and legal context underlying the questions referred to the Court of Justice should be explained in the order for reference.[19] In *Ognyanov*, the Sofia City Court had referred a request for a preliminary ruling to the Court of Justice. After the reference had been made, the Sofia City Prosecutor demanded that the judges in the case should recuse themselves, on the ground that by setting out in the request for a preliminary ruling the factual and legal background to the case, that court was expressing a provisional opinion on questions of fact and law before the deliberations had begun which was contrary to a rule of national law. The referring court questioned the legality of that national rule in light of EU law. The Court of Justice held that in order for it to be able to provide an interpretation which would be of use for the national court, the latter must define the factual and legal context of the question or, at the very least, explain the assumptions of fact on which the questions were based. This is also necessary in order to afford the governments of other Member States and other interested parties a proper opportunity to submit observations.[20] The practical effect of the national rule at issue was that a national court might refrain from referring questions, which would be detrimental both to the prerogatives granted to national courts and to the dialogue between those national courts and the Court of Justice.[21]

The Court of Justice recently further emphasised the importance of the preliminary reference procedure in safeguarding the rule of law and the judicial protection

---

[17] Case C-100/12, *Fastweb*, EU:C:2013:448.

[18] Case C-689/13, *PFE*, EU:C:2016:199, para. 32-35.

[19] Case C-614/14, *Ognyanov*, EU:C:2016:514.

[20] Case C-614/14, *Ognyanov*, EU:C:2016:514, para. 22-23.

[21] Case C-614/14, *Ognyanov*, EU:C:2016:514, para. 25.

of individuals' rights. In *Rosneft*, a case concerning the imposition of restrictive measures on individuals, the Court held that it has the power—under the preliminary reference procedure—to review the legality of Common Foreign and Security Policy measures that provide for restrictive measures against natural or legal persons.[22] Article 24 TEU and Article 275 TFEU stipulate that the Court of Justice lacks jurisdiction in the CFSP, *except* to monitor compliance with Article 40 TEU and to review the legality of restrictive measures imposed on individuals. On the basis of those Treaty articles it was, however, unclear whether the Court could review the legality of restrictive measures only within the framework of a direct action for annulment or also in the context of a reference for a preliminary ruling. While recognising its limited role in the area of the Common Foreign and Security Policy, the Court of Justice nevertheless ruled that in this area of Union law, as in other fields, the judicial protection of individuals, the rule of law and the complete system of judicial protection in the EU require that the Court must have the power to review the legality of restrictive measures through the preliminary reference procedure.[23]

3 The dialogue between the national courts of the Member States

However, the EU's judicial network covers not only the judicial dialogue between the Court of Justice and the courts of the Member States. An important aspect of that judicial dialogue is the dialogue that takes place between the national courts of different Member States.

The EU's legal order is based on the fundamental premise that each Member State shares with all the other Member States a set of common values on which the EU is founded. That premise implies—and justifies—the existence of mutual trust between the Member States that those values will be recognised and, therefore, that the law of the EU that implements them will be respected. Protection of human rights is central in that respect. The rights recognised by the Charter, which has the same legal value as the Treaties, lie at the heart of the EU's legal order. Respect for those rights is a condition of the lawfulness of EU acts[24] and underpins the autonomy enjoyed by EU law in relation to the laws of the Member States, as well as in relation to international law.[25]

---

[22] Case C-72/15, *Rosneft*, EU:C:2017:236, para. 58-81.

[23] See also: Case C-455/14P, *H v Council*, EU:C:2016:569, para. 41.

[24] Case C-260/89, *ERT*, EU:C:1991:254, para. 41; Case C-299/95, *Kremzow*, EU:C:1997:254, para. 14; Case C-112/00, *Schmidberger*, EU:C:2003:333, para. 73; and Joined Cases C-402/05 P and C-415/05 P, *Kadi and Al Barakaat International Foundation* v *Council and Commission*, EU:C:2008:461, paras. 283 and 284.

[25] Case C-11/70, *Internationale Handelsgesellschaft*, EU:C:1970:114, para. 4, and Joined Cases C-402/05 P and C-415/05 P *Kadi and Al Barakaat International Foundation* v *Council and Commission*, EU:C:2008:461, para. 281-285; Opinion 2/13, EU:C:2014:2454, para. 166-170.

It must be emphasised that not only are the institutions, bodies, offices and agencies of the EU required to respect the Charter but so too are the Member States when they are implementing EU law.[26] The Member States must ensure, in their respective territories, the application of and respect for EU law, including respect for fundamental rights. That is the basis of the mutual trust that exists between the Member States. The fact that the Treaties regard all Member States as equal and that all Member States equally respect and protect the same values creates the trust that they are all equally committed to protecting the rule of law and fundamental rights.[27]

This mutual trust is thus of essential importance in the Area of Freedom, Security and Justice, as it allows for the mutual recognition of judicial decisions in civil and criminal matters. This creates an Area of Freedom, Security and Justice in which citizens and judgments can move freely. Mutual recognition implies that a court in a Member State can trust that the court in another Member State that adopted the decision provided effective judicial protection to the persons affected by the decision, including the protection of their fundamental rights. The successful operation of the system of mutual recognition is based on trust: it is because Member States trust each other in their respect for the rule of law and fundamental rights that judicial cooperation in civil and criminal matters is possible.[28]

The involvement of an independent and impartial judiciary is essential in ensuring mutual trust in the dialogue between the Member States. This is illustrated by the *Poltorak* case concerning the European Arrest Warrant. The Swedish police issued a European arrest warrant against Mr. Poltorak after he was sentenced by the District Court of Gothenburg. However, the Court of Justice determined that a European arrest warrant constitutes a judicial decision that can only be issued by a judicial authority. The term 'judiciary' cannot be extended to cover national police services.[29] Mutual trust requires that the entire surrender procedure between Member States is carried out under judicial supervision and that all decisions are taken by the judiciary. The issue of an arrest warrant by a non-judicial authority, such as a police service[30] or in the *Kovalkovas* case a Ministry,[31] cannot justify the high level of trust between the Member States upon which the European arrest warrant is predicated.[32] The trust between the judicial authorities of different Member States is therefore based on the premise that a judicial authority has intervened prior to the execution of the arrest warrant.[33]

[26] Case C-617/10, *Åkerberg Fransson*, EU:C:2013:105, para. 17-21.

[27] Lenaerts (2017), pp. 808–812.

[28] Lenaerts (2017), pp. 808–812.

[29] Case C-452/16 PPU, *Poltorak*, EU:C:2016:858, para. 28-35.

[30] See also: Case C-453/16 PPU, *Özçelik*, EU:C:2016:860.

[31] Case C-477/16 PPU, *Kovalkovas*, EU:C:2016:861.

[32] Case C-452/16 PPU, *Poltorak*, EU:C:2016:858, para. 39-45.

[33] Case C-452/16 PPU, *Poltorak*, EU:C:2016:858, para. 44.

The principle of mutual trust occupies a central role in the *raison d'être* of the EU and the creation of the Area of Freedom, Security and Justice in particular. However, it needs to be emphasised that mutual trust does not imply blind trust: mutual trust should not operate to the detriment of fundamental rights. On the other hand, the application of national (constitutional) requirements may not lead to an undermining of mutual trust.

The Court of Justice has balanced these different principles in a series of cases concerning the Area of Freedom Security and Justice. It held that 'mutual trust requires, particularly with regard to the Area of Freedom, Security and Justice, each of the Member States, save in exceptional circumstances, to consider all the other Member States to be complying with EU law and particularly with the fundamental rights recognised by EU law'. Therefore, the Member States are required, when implementing EU law, to presume that fundamental rights have been observed by the other Member States. In *Opinion 2/13* the Court clarified that this imposes two negative obligations on the Member States. Firstly, they may not require a higher level of national protection of fundamental rights from another Member State than that provided for by EU law. Secondly, save in exceptional circumstances, Member States are prevented from checking whether another Member State has actually observed the fundamental rights guaranteed by the EU in a specific case.[34] Therefore, in exceptional circumstances, the protection of fundamental rights may be invoked—temporarily—to limit the application of mutual trust and the mutual recognition of decisions. A number of cases illustrate this point.

The *N.S.* case concerned the transfer of asylum seekers under the Dublin II Regulation from the UK and Ireland to Greece. The asylum seekers challenged their transfer on the basis that in Greece they would face a real risk of being subjected to inhuman or degrading treatment because of deficiencies in the Greek asylum procedure and in the conditions for receiving them. The Court of Justice held that the presumption that all Member States comply with fundamental rights is by no means irrebuttable. The Member States cannot therefore transfer an asylum seeker to the Member State which is responsible under the Dublin II Regulation where 'they cannot be unaware that systemic deficiencies in the asylum procedure and in the reception conditions of asylum seekers in that Member State amount to substantial grounds for believing that the asylum seeker would face a real risk of being subjected to inhuman or degrading treatment within the meaning of Article 4 of the Charter'.[35] In *C.K.*, the Court of Justice clarified that this principle may also apply in certain exceptional circumstances even in the absence of systemic deficiencies and that, on the basis of particular circumstances such as serious health problems of the person concerned, the proposed transfer of an individual might need to be examined in the light of Article 4 of the Charter.[36]

In *Aranyosi and Căldăraru*, the Court of Justice came to a similar conclusion as regards the conditions under which a European arrest warrant may be executed. It

[34] Opinion 2/13, EU:C:2014:2454, para. 192.

[35] Joined Cases C-411 and 493/10, *N.S. and M.E.*, EU:C:2011:865, para. 94.

[36] Case C-578/16 PPU, *C.K.*, EU:C:2017:127, para. 91-93.

held that the operation of the principle of mutual trust may be limited in exceptional circumstances, i.e. where the execution of a European arrest warrant is liable to give rise to breaches of the prohibition of torture and inhuman or degrading treatment or punishment as laid down in Article 4 of the Charter that flow from systemic or generalised deficiencies in the prison system of the issuing Member State. In order to determine whether that is actually the case, the executing judicial authority must follow a two-step assessment.

First, it must, on the basis of objective, reliable, specific and updated information, determine whether there is a real risk of inhuman or degrading treatment for individuals who are being imprisoned in the issuing Member State.[37]

Second, when such risk is found to exist, the executing judicial authority must carry out a concrete and precise assessment of the circumstances in the particular case at hand. As such, it must verify whether there are substantial grounds for believing that the execution of the European arrest warrant at issue would entail a real risk that the prohibition laid down in Article 4 of the Charter might *actually* be breached in practice in respect of the *individual* concerned. In order to assess this, the executing judicial authority must engage in a dialogue as provided for in the Framework Decision on the arrest warrant with the issuing Member State and must give the issuing Member State the opportunity to prove that the person concerned will be detained in conditions which do not subject him or her to inhuman or degrading treatment.[38] If the judicial authority of the executing Member State believes that there is a real risk of a violation of Article 4 of the Charter, that judicial authority must postpone but not abandon the execution of the European arrest warrant. Postponing such execution gives the issuing Member State the opportunity to regain the trust of the executing judicial authority. This is important in order to avoid that a permanent state of mistrust between two Member States' judicial authorities is created. Limitations on mutual trust should therefore operate in such a way as to restore mutual trust.[39]

More recently, the two-step assessment put forward in *Aranyosi and Căldăraru* was further developed in the seminal judgment of the Court of Justice in *Minister for Justice and Equality v LM (Deficiencies in the system of justice)*.[40] The facts of the case concerned the execution of three European arrest warrants issued against LM, a Polish national, by Polish courts for the purposes of prosecuting him for drug trafficking. After being arrested in Ireland, LM did not consent to his surrender to the Polish judicial authorities, on the ground that, on account of the reforms of the Polish system of justice, he would run a real risk of not receiving a fair trial in Poland. After having cited different sources according to which the changes brought about by the Polish Government to the national system of justice might put at risk the independence of the judiciary, the High Court of Ireland made a reference to the

[37] Joined Cases C-404 and 659/15 PPU, *Aranyosi and Căldăraru*, EU:C:2016:198, para. 85-89.

[38] Joined Cases C-404 and 659/15 PPU, *Aranyosi and Căldăraru*, EU:C:2016:198, para. 93-95.

[39] Lenaerts (2017), pp. 836, 840.

[40] Case C-216/18 PPU, *Minister for Justice and Equality v LM (Deficiencies in the system of justice)*, EU:C:2018:586.

Court of Justice, asking, in essence, whether the two-step assessment put forward in *Aranyosi and Căldăraru* applied to the case at hand, or whether it was sufficient for the executing judicial authority to find that there are systemic or generalised deficiencies in the Polish system of justice, without having to assess whether the individual concerned is actually exposed to them.

At the outset, the Court of Justice pointed out that, just like Article 4 of the Charter, compliance with judicial independence, as part of the essence of the fundamental right to a fair trial enshrined in Article 47 of the Charter, is essential to the operation of the principle of mutual trust. This is because judicial independence is of cardinal importance as it guarantees the effective judicial protection of rights that EU law confers on individuals. That independence is also essential for the proper functioning of the preliminary ruling mechanism and for the free movement of European Arrest Warrants.

Next, the Court of Justice found that the executing judicial authority must follow the two-step assessment put forward in *Aranyosi and Căldăraru*. That authority must, as a first step, determine, on the basis of material that is objective, reliable, specific and properly updated, whether there is a real risk, connected with a lack of independence of the courts of the issuing Member State on account of systemic or generalised deficiencies there, of the fundamental right to a fair trial being breached. A reasoned proposal addressed by the Commission to the Council on the basis of Article 7(1) TEU might be particularly relevant for that assessment.

As a second step, the executing authority must examine whether the systemic or generalised deficiencies found are liable to have an impact at the level of the courts with jurisdiction over the proceedings to which the requested person will be subject. If that is so, the executing judicial authority must next proceed to assess whether, having regard to his personal situation, as well as to the nature of the offence and the factual context that form the basis of the European arrest warrant, there is a real risk of breach of the requested person's fundamental right to an independent tribunal and, therefore, of the essence of his fundamental right to a fair trial. A positive assessment would thus allow the executing judicial authority to refrain from giving effect to the European arrest warrant in question.

Most importantly, the Court of Justice noted that limiting the assessment to the first step (thereby foregoing the second step) would amount to suspending the implementation of the entire European Arrest Warrant mechanism in respect of the issuing Member State. However, that general suspension can only take place where the European Council decides, pursuant to Article 7 TEU, that the issuing Member State has seriously and persistently breached the principles set out in Article 2 TEU.[41] Stated differently, the second step is necessary in order not to encroach upon the political prerogatives of that EU institution.

[41] See, in this regard, recital 10 of Council Framework Decision 2002/584/JHA of 13 June 2002 on the European arrest warrant and the surrender procedures between Member States, [2002] OJ L 190/1, as amended by Council Framework Decision 2009/299/JHA of 26 February 2009, [2009] OJ 2009 L 81/24.

4 Conclusion

One can conclude that the national courts of the Member States and the Court of Justice are the joint guardians of the rule of law in the European Union. That guardianship is a networking exercise based on mutual trust. The authority of the Court of Justice rests on its capacity to encourage national courts to continue to engage in a healthy dialogue with it and to foster trust between independent and impartial national judiciaries.

References

Halberstam D (2008) Comparative federalism and the role of the judiciary. In: Whittington K, Kelmen D, Caldeira G (eds) The Oxford Handbook of Law and Politics. Oxford University Press, Oxford, p 142

Lenaerts K (2013) The Court's outer and inner selves: exploring the external and internal legitimacy of the European Court of Justice. In: Adams M, de Waele H, Meeusen J, Straetmans G (eds) Judging Europe's judges: the legitimacy of the case law of the European Court of Justice. Hart Publishing, Oxford, p 40

Lenaerts K (2017) La vie après l'avis: exploring the principle of mutual (yet not blind) trust. Common Mark Law Rev 54(3):805 ff

Part II
The impact of legislation on the authority of EU law

A view from the European Commission

Karen Banks

1 Lobbyists, delegated and implementing acts, and subsidiarity

The title of the topic for this panel discussion, as well as the bullet points proposed for development, suggest the existence of a thoroughly negative situation as regards the authority of European law, and of the processes by which it comes into being. I have to say that I do not perceive the situation as being nearly as bad as is implied. EU laws—whether primary law or delegated or implementing acts—are adopted according to the procedures laid down in the Treaties, by those authorised to do so. What are the criticisms? That *lobbyists* have too much influence? In reality, if well used by decision-makers, lobbyists can contribute to a well-informed and balanced legislative process. It is true that there are legitimate concerns about transparency in relation to the degree of influence a particular lobbyist may have. For its part, the Commission has adopted strict rules concerning the access of lobbyists to Commissioners, cabinets and Directors General, and as regards public access to information concerning meetings with such lobbyists. It is trying to persuade the other institutions to have similar rules, and discussions are on-going on that topic.

Another suggested bone of contention is *comitology* and the adoption of acts under *delegated powers*. There seems to be a suspicion of secret deals being done

---

Deputy Director-General in charge of "Quality of Legislation, Infringements and Information", Legal Service of the European Commission. Contribution to the first panel discussion for which the organisers had proposed to discuss the following bullet points: *the alleged democratic deficit, a lack of transparency in the making of the law/the role of lobbyists/comitology, a lack of legitimacy in the making of the law, ineffectiveness of the subsidiarity principle, poor quality of legislation, (…).*
Any views expressed are strictly personal to the author.

K. Banks (✉)
Legal Service of the European Commission, Brussels, Belgium
e-mail: Karen.banks@ec.europa.eu

W. Heusel, J.-P. Rageade (eds.), *The Authority of EU Law*,
https://doi.org/10.1007/978-3-662-58841-3_3

behind closed doors, an idea of a lack of democracy. But it is entirely normal in any legislative system for the legislator to adopt the essential elements of legislation and to leave the technical details to be worked out at a lower level. Not only is such a system specifically provided for in Articles 290 and 291 of the Treaty; it is in fact entirely necessary. Having lived through the extreme complexity of a reform of European agricultural legislation, I can only say that gridlock would be the inevitable result of attempting to get any more than the basic rules agreed by the co-legislators. And it should be borne in mind that each of those co-legislators has the right—which both of them have exercised when they thought it appropriate—to prevent the entry into force of a delegated act. Thus they retain ultimate control. As for implementing acts, the Member States can prevent their adoption by voting against them in the Comitology system.

Moreover the Treaty lays down strict rules as to when quasi-legislative powers may be delegated to the Commission, and the Court has shown itself vigilant in policing the respect of those rules. The first rule is that only non-essential elements may be dealt with by way of delegated act. In case C-355/10, *Parliament v Council*, which of course concerned the precursors of delegated acts, the so-called "PRAC" acts (*Procédure de Réglementation avec Contrôle*), to which the same principles applied, the Court gave a clear explanation of what are essential elements, i.e. provisions requiring political choices falling within the responsibility of the Union legislature, and did not hesitate to strike down a measure which went beyond what could be delegated to the Commission. In case C-44/16P, *Dyson v Commission*, the Court of Justice overturned a judgment of the General Court because it had not taken care to ensure that a delegated act conformed to the essential elements determined by the basic act. Even more recently, in case C-696/15P, *Czech Republic v Commission*, the Court has insisted on the requirement of Article 290 that the objectives, content, scope and duration of the delegation of power must be explicitly defined in the delegating act. As the Court put it, "a delegation of power within the meaning of Article 290 must be delimited by bounds fixed in the basic act".

As for *implementing acts*, the procedures for their adoption are laid down very explicitly in the Comitology Regulation, and the Court has underlined very recently in the *Tilly-Sabco* case (C-183/16P) that it will not countenance departures from the procedures laid down. The Court made it clear that it would insist on respect for rules which are designed to enable the representatives of the Member States to participate effectively in the decision-making process.

It is true that President Juncker has shown concern that sometimes via Comitology, the Commission is obliged to shoulder a political responsibility which should belong to the Member States. These concerns have emerged notably in the context of debates on the authorisation of GMO's, where the tendency has been for no qualified majority to emerge in the relevant committee, either for or against the authorisation in question. In such circumstances the Commission may adopt the decision, under its own responsibility. In order to seek a more political approach to these cases, the Commission has proposed to amend the Comitology Regulation as regards the Appeal Committee stage. It has notably proposed that the voting rules be changed so as only to count the votes of Member States which are present and which vote either in favour of, or against a proposal. It has also proposed that the voting positions of Member States should be made public. It remains to be seen what progress will be made with these ideas.

As for transparency concerns, I would guess that there are few Member States where so much has been done to address them as has been accomplished at EU level. Many implementing and delegated acts are available on-line for public comment for 4 weeks before their adoption; there is a public register of implementing acts which allows all stages of adoption of an act to be followed, voting results are made public, summaries of debates are published, and so on. A similar register is in preparation for delegated acts.

Turning now to the alleged ineffectiveness of the *subsidiarity* principle, I have to say (once again) that I am not convinced of the existence of a real problem. The truth is that one person's subsidiarity is another person's failure to act. I recall my own perplexity at being challenged by members of my family who wanted to know why the European Union had allowed each Member State to choose the design for one side of the euro coins. For them, the euro was a European project, and it made no sense to have coins with different images circulating around Europe having the same status and representing the same value, while of course for the authors of the project it seemed entirely appropriate to leave some share in the design of the coins to the national level. This is just one illustration of the fact that people can have very different views about the appropriate level at which a given action should be undertaken. Indeed, very often, arguments about subsidiarity are in reality more about the appropriateness of a certain action being undertaken at all, or about the intensity of that action, rather than being really focused on the appropriate level for the action.

In any event, as regards the effectiveness of the subsidiarity principle, its respect by the European legislator is safeguarded by two mechanisms, one judicial and one political, each of which has been deployed a number of times. And the control by the Court is no mere enquiry as to whether the legislator has exceeded its margin of discretion: on every occasion on which breach of the subsidiarity principle has been alleged before it, whether in the context of an action challenging the directive on the patentability of biotechnological inventions or in that of a case about cigarette packaging, the Court has conducted an autonomous examination as to whether the objective being pursued by the EU legislation could be achieved by action taken by the Member States alone or whether, because of the scale and effects of the proposed action, the objective in question could be better achieved by the Union. It is true that the outcome has always been in favour of the respect of the subsidiarity principle, but as a matter of fact that is hardly surprising given the level of political sensitivity to subsidiarity questions which exists in the Member States, so that it could only be in a highly exceptional case that a qualified majority of Member States would have voted for a measure which did not need to be adopted at European level, but could very well have been replaced by action at national level.

In order to make this eventuality even less likely, we have Protocol 2 of the TFEU which provides for control by national parliaments of legislative proposals before they become law. Even if the Commission has only been led to drop one proposal after deployment of this mechanism—and indeed has never actually admitted breach of the subsidiarity principle—the existence of the mechanism serves as a reminder of the importance of the respect of that principle, and of the possibility of political reaction if it is not respected.

In reality however, there is little risk that the Commission would overlook such a fundamental issue. The impact assessment which is carried out before any significant piece of legislation is put forward always has to examine rigorously the need for the proposed measure and possible alternatives, including that of no action at European level. If the subsidiarity issue is not fully developed in a first version of the impact assessment, one may be very sure that the Regulatory Scrutiny Board will insist on a deeper analysis of that aspect. The Juncker Commission motto "Big on big things, small on small things" makes it rather unlikely that a proposal would be let go forward if it was not quite clear that it had added value and that it needed to be advanced at the level of the EU.

Nowadays, such matters are taken very seriously in the Commission, also at the political level. Quite recently, there were lengthy discussions concerning an eco-design proposal aiming to make certain electrical products both energy efficient and recyclable. The idea of harmonising rules on hairdryers and kettles was too much for certain Commissioners. It was only after pretty intensive discussions that a reduced list of products was allowed to go forward for further study.

2 Quality of legislation

On this topic again I have to say that the angle proposed by the organisers seems to me to be overly negative. We should rather begin by recognising the many excellent pieces of legislation which have been produced by the European legislator. I myself have worked with clear, effective texts in the areas of equal opportunities, intellectual property, recognition of professional qualifications and fisheries law, to name but a few. This of course is not to say that the manner of interpreting or applying a given provision is always perfectly clear in every situation of fact—if that were so, there would be no work for lawyers, and no need for the Article 267 reference mechanism—but those difficulties of interpretation arise not because of any real fault in the legislative text but because it is impossible for the legislator to imagine in advance every factual situation which may arise in which the text in question will have to be applied. The need for litigation and judicial interpretation of legal acts is a normal part of the process of daily application of the law, and its adaptation to unforeseen or marginal circumstances.

That having been said, it is of course true that certain texts emerge from the legislative process with some of their provisions in a pretty poor state. The effects of political negotiation and compromise are not always beneficial as regards the clarity of a text. This however is part and parcel of democracy in action. We cannot complain at the same time of a lack of democratic procedures at European level and of the outcome of those very processes! I'm afraid that, in this context, there is no other remedy than relying on the Court of Justice to clarify what the legislator has left obscure, and it should be said that, in this respect, the Court does a magnificent job. It uses a purposive approach, taking account of the context and the aims of the measure in question, and generally comes up with an interpretation which is fair and just.

Where the obscurity is the result of a compromise between competing legal traditions or political views in the Member States, the advantage of the ultimate solution by the Court is that it is filtered through the legal process where political arguments necessarily become more decorous; some time is allowed to elapse; there is interaction between the Court and the national judiciary; and the final decision thus becomes more acceptable to those whose position is not (or not entirely) vindicated. Via the principle of the rule of law, and the separation of powers, the political level is brought to accept the conclusions reached by the judicial process and in this way the circle is completed and the law applied in the same way to everyone.

There is another dimension of the quality of legal texts where the Commission may have a greater role to play, and that is the quality of legal drafting. Even if it is true that the final version of a piece of legislation depends on negotiations between the co-legislators where the Commission's role is secondary, as the initiator of most legislation it nevertheless has a particular responsibility for the quality of the initial proposal. In this respect, huge challenges are faced by the Commission's legal revisers. Very often the texts prepared by the operational departments of the Commission have been written by people with no training in legal drafting, and they frequently need to be completely restructured on the basis of a thorough discussion of the intended effects of a proposed measure. In general, Trojan work is done in this regard, and the texts which emerge from legal revision are always much more understandable and better written than the initial drafts.

Two problems sometimes get in the way of optimal results; time pressure and language. As regards the former, the deadlines within which sometimes very complex pieces of legislation have to be prepared do not always allow the time for proper reflection and careful redrafting. As regards the latter, it needs to be considered that virtually all the legislative proposals put forward by the Commission are prepared in English. Now, English is not the mother tongue of most of those involved in the work, whether in the DGs or in the group of legal revisers in the Legal Service. We are obliged to maintain a multilingual group of revisers in order to be able to carry out multilingual revision of texts when necessary, but this of course means that most of the legal revisers who work on improving the drafting of legislative proposals are not English native speakers, and however good their English may be—and indeed is—their drafting in that language can never have the complete naturalness and mastery of a native speaker.

We are therefore obliged to accept a level of drafting which is good without being perfect. I am afraid that that is an inevitable consequence of the multi-cultural environment in which we work. A challenge for the future, after BREXIT, will be to maintain even today's imperfect quality when the pool of English speakers in the Commission will have diminished dramatically. This is a subject which has received little attention so far, but will certainly be a topic for considerable reflection in the future.

Can the authority of EU law be taken for granted? A tale of principles and realities

Giorgio Maganza

1 Introduction

"Do we still believe in the authority of EU law?" asks the title of the ERA Jubilee Congress. My personal, and qualified answer is yes, I still do. It is a qualified answer because, while being based on convictions about the legal principles that underlie the European construction, it has to be checked against the realities which prevail in Europe today.

The authority of European law (hereinafter "EU law") has been in-built in the system of the Treaties since their inception, 60 years ago. The respect for that authority is a natural consequence of the interplay between the Union Institutions, and between them and the Member States; it belongs in the end to the European Court of Justice (hereinafter "ECJ") to "(...) ensure that in the interpretation and application of the Treaties the law is observed".[1] Furthermore, the *rule of law* principle is amongst the values on which the Union is founded.[2]

Generally speaking, it seems fair to assume that *EU law*, as referred to what usually is "prescribed" through the institutional system set out in the EU Treaties, continues to be regarded as authoritative. We currently watch TV news on what "Brussels is expecting" this or that Member State to do in order to comply with

The views expressed are the author's alone. This text is a written development of the presentation that he made at the ERA Jubilee Congress, held in Trier on 19 and 20 October 2017, during the Panel discussion on *The Impact of Legislation on the Authority of EU Law*. It was completed on 6 February 2018.

[1] Article 19(1) of the Treaty on European Union (TEU); Article 260(1) of the Treaty on the Functioning of the European Union (TFEU) lays down the obligation for the Member States to take the necessary measures to comply with the judgments of the Court.

[2] Article 2 TEU.

G. Maganza (✉)
Former Director, Legal Service of the Council of the European Union, Brussels, Belgium

W. Heusel, J.-P. Rageade (eds.), *The Authority of EU Law*,
https://doi.org/10.1007/978-3-662-58841-3_4

European standards and rules. The "Brussels expects us to do it" way of illustrating this may look an over-simplification. But the very acceptance of the need to do what is required by the European level—even in cases when the expected action is unpopular and criticised—is a sign of the authority of EU law.

There are however reasons for being concerned. No doubt, an affirmative answer to the Congress question above would need to be confronted with recent cases where some Member States have openly challenged EU law, namely the so called second Relocation Decision,[3] and have criticised the recent ECJ judgment which dismissed the following action for annulment brought by Slovakia and Hungary against that Decision[4]; not to mention the threats to European values and possible violations of the rule of law, presently under review.[5]

It is therefore not inconceivable to wonder whether—and, if so, under which circumstances—the authority of EU law, which has been a given for decades, could become an issue or, in other words, could be open for challenge. The straightforward answer would actually be that asking that question equals questioning the very essence of the European project. A more thorough analysis can be done nevertheless of the possible conditions which would make that happen. It has for instance been suggested that European legislation might have a negative impact on the authority of EU law due to a presumed lack of legitimacy or transparency of the decision-making system; or even because of a supposedly poor quality of the law produced by that system.

As a matter of fact, that assumption is very much inspired by assessment criteria which may be valid keys to read a national constitutional order, but which are far less valid to interpret the EU system. Take the principle of parliamentary democracy: the rules governing democratic representation are not the same in the EU and in the Member States, as stressed by the *Bundesverfassungsgericht* in 2009,[6] and it would not be fair to assess democratic legitimacy under the same standards.

This paper will examine, first, whether and to what extent the authority of EU law can be affected by the way legislation is made: Does the EU decision-making system lack legitimacy? Is that system not transparent enough? Does subsidiarity make EU legislation worse? Do lobbying or comitology prevent good legislation?

---

[3] Council Decision (EU) 2015/1601 of 22 September 2015 establishing provisional measures in the area of international protection for the benefit of Italy and Greece, OJ L 248, 24.9.2015, p. 80.

[4] ECJ (Grand Chamber) Judgment of 6 September 2017 in cases C-643/15 and C-647/15.

[5] On 20 December 2017, the Commission triggered the Article 7 TEU procedure to defend judicial independence in Poland, as it concluded that "there is a clear risk of a serious breach by a Member State of the values referred to in Article 2", namely the rule of law, in that country. Earlier in 2017, the Commission had decided to follow up on the infringement procedure initiated in December 2015 against Hungary concerning its asylum law. Both Poland and Hungary "illiberal democracies"—neither of which would probably qualify for joining the European Union, as of now—have been under scrutiny by the Commission for a few years.

[6] In its Judgment of 30 June 2009 (*Bundesverfassungsgericht*, BVerfG, 2 BvE 2/08), the German Federal Constitutional Court found the Lisbon Treaty to be compatible with the Basic Law, thus opening the way for the German approval of that Treaty. It addressed however a certain amount of criticism to the EU institutional system insofar as it supposedly lacked the legitimacy which could only derive from the *one citizen-one vote* democratic principle.

And are those factors overall liable for a supposedly poor quality of the EU legislation, hence for making that legislation less authoritative? This paper will then wonder which, if any other factor may be likely to affect the authority of EU law in the near future; and what are the conditions under which the authority of EU law and more generally the European project could continue to be preserved.

2 Can the law-making affect the authority of EU law?

2.1 Democratic legitimacy

As the European Union is neither a State nor a classical international organisation, but a union of States and a union of peoples at the same time, its dual nature is reflected in the institutional system set out in the Treaties: while citizens are directly represented, at the level of the Union, in the European Parliament, Member States are represented in the European Council by the Heads of State or Government and in the Council by their respective governments, "themselves democratically accountable either to their national Parliaments, or to their citizens".[7] The dual nature of the Union is now also reflected in the double legitimacy of the Council voting system, which entered into force in November 2014 and provides that the majority of States, coupled with the majority of population, wins.[8]

The political debate on the democratic legitimacy of the European decision-making process has diminished over the years—although it may still be trendy in the media—as the powers of the European Parliament (budgetary ones in the seventies and legislative ones in the eighties and nineties) kept growing, Treaty after Treaty. Curiously enough, that did not help the Parliament to play the role which the Maastricht Treaty in particular had intended for it and to meet the expectations it had given rise to. The European citizens, whom the Parliament is supposed to directly represent, are less and less concerned by the Parliament's elections[9]; and leading politicians are not often seen running for Strasbourg.

If the democratic legitimacy of the EU institutions is hardly questioned as a whole anymore, a new criticism appeared, in particular upon the ratification of the Lisbon Treaty, specifically pointing to the unequal representation of citizens in the European Parliament, as well as to the fact that the composition of institutions generally tends to favour smaller Member States to the disadvantage of larger ones.[10] While the latter issue may be deemed to be partially addressed by the new "double majority", which builds the population element into the Council voting system, the

[7] Article 10(2)TEU. Furthermore, Article 12 TEU illustrates the way in which national parliaments may contribute to the good functioning of the Union.

[8] Article 16(4)TEU.

[9] The turnout for the European Parliament's elections has kept falling ever since the first direct elections in June 1979.

[10] See in particular the German Federal Constitutional Court decision of 2009, cited at note 6.

former will need consideration in the framework of the discussions to come on reforming Europe.

All in all, however, it would not be correct to assume that the EU decision-making system lacks democratic legitimacy. Nor do lack legitimacy, also thanks to a stronger involvement of national parliaments, the decision-making processes recently set out in the framework of European agreements concluded amongst Member States in order to tackle the financial crisis[11]—which are currently referred to as "intergovernmental method", but which it would be more appropriate to define as "Union method".

Last but not least, one could wonder about the legitimacy of the newest comitology system instead. While the former comitology gave national administrations the final say, whenever implementing measures needed to be adopted at European level—thus providing the necessary legitimacy to implementing measures that need to fit within the respective national systems, as in the end the daily implementation of Union acts belongs to Member States[12]—the new comitology shifts the balance towards the institutions, and the Commission in particular. But that is another story.

2.2 *Transparency*

The process through which legislation is made is not less transparent in the European Union than in the Member States. Most of the legislative debates are public,[13] as are the voting records in the European Parliament and in the Council. Yet, transparency in the European Union remains synonymous of a missed opportunity, more than 25 years after the debate began. What happened?

The fact is that the debate on transparency was biased from the very beginning. All of a sudden, in the early nineties, the conventional wisdom appeared that the system operated at European level was not transparent; actually, that was largely driven by the desperate wish to exorcise the panic created in the aftermath of the June 1992 failed Danish referendum on Maastricht, mixed with a genuine feeling that the public information on Europe needed improvement. Despite the fact that the Birmingham European Council, in October 1992, had clearly set citizens' information as a priority, the focus was rapidly shifted on the lack of transparency of the European Treaties—a criticism that would be recurrent in the following years—and legislation, which were both held responsible for detaching citizens from the European project. And that is how a genuinely felt need for a better information of EU citizens was turned into the easy remedy of making the European Institutions'

[11] The European Stability Mechanism (ESM) and the Treaty on Stability, Coordination and Governance (TSCG), better known as the Fiscal Compact, in 2012, as well as the Agreement on the transfer of contributions to the Single Resolution Fund in 2014.

[12] See Article 291, first paragraph of the TFEU. In the same vein, it belongs to courts and tribunals in the Member States to ensure the day to day adjudication of EU law.

[13] Article 15(2) TFEU.

deliberations public and providing for public access to documents, which the average citizen could obviously not care less about but which resulted in increased bureaucracy and costly paper work for the exclusive benefit of a few Brussels based NGOs.

No lesson was learnt though,[14] while making European citizens feel more connected to what happens and how it happens at European level remained an urgent task for all the Member States to take on.

Twenty-five years, four Treaty revisions and several referendums later, European citizens are still lacking information on the relevance of the European project for their lives. It may certainly be simpler to carry on criticising the European institutions for not being transparent enough; but it would be unfair to make that responsible for a possible lessening of the authority of EU law.

2.3 *Subsidiarity*

The principle of subsidiarity[15]—a landmark of the Maastricht Treaty—was never meant to impact the quality of EU law, but rather its quantity. It was basically a reaction to a decade of European over-legislation and intended to provide a "value-added test" for any (except in the areas of exclusive powers) EU proposed action to successfully pass before it can be voted upon. Building upon Maastricht, subsidiarity also offered a bridge, in subsequent Treaty revisions, to progressively strengthen the role of national Parliaments in the EU law-making process in order to promote closer links with the Member States' legislatures.[16]

It took some time for that principle to be properly implemented by the institutions, though it is fair to note that the legislative output of the European Union has slowed down over the past years. In the end, if the Union has finally departed from the excess of legislation, it may be also due to a new culture of subsidiarity.

2.4 *Comitology, lobbying and the quality of legislation*

"Comitology" is the "Eurospeak" term coined, a few decades ago, to describe the universe and intricacies of the committees which are in charge of assisting the Commission whenever implementing measures need to be adopted at European

[14] The same mistakes were made, as the same opportunity to improve citizens' information was missed, when public opinions were confronted with the issue of the approval of the 2004 Constitutional Treaty, which was finally rejected in the French and Dutch referenda of 2005.

[15] Article 5(3) TEU and Protocol No 2 on the application of the principles of subsidiarity and proportionality.

[16] See now Article 12 TEU on the National Parliaments' contribution to the good functioning of the Union, notably subparagraph (b).

level. As the implementation of European law is, and has always been a task for the Member States' competent authorities to carry out,[17] it was always deemed appropriate to make sure—through the involvement of the comitology committees, chaired by a representative of the Commission and composed of representatives of the Member States[18]—that European implementing measures would fit with the respective national systems, which is where the bulk of the implementation of European law is normally carried out.

It seems difficult to argue—as the European Parliament did for a long time, seeking to be granted a role in it—that comitology lowers the legitimacy of the European decision-making process or that it represents an obstacle to good legislation, which actually unfolds upstream. Quite on the contrary, it has proved for 30 years to work effectively to allow the control by Member States of the Commission's exercise of its implementing powers in order to make "European-made" implementing measures compatible with the Member States national systems. Time will tell whether it can continue to do so, under the new rules which provide for a lesser role of the Member States' representatives.

Lobbies have always existed in Brussels, like in all places where economic interests and strategic issues are debated: that is true for Member States' legislatures as for the Federal Congress in Washington. The members of the Council themselves lobby when they negotiate. Lobbying is only current at the Commission, when proposals are elaborated, or in the European Parliament when they are up for debate and voting. Preserving a proper functioning of the decision-making process rather goes through an effective regulation of the lobbying activities.

Last but not least, can one assume that the quality of legislation enacted through the EU institutional system is poor? Under which standards would such an assumption be made? Would they be national legislations' quality standards? The least one can say is that the level of quality may vary… Actually, it is easy to forget that EU legislation is the product of a complex mechanism, where elements converge from both domestic law and international law. It can be a hard task to ensure and preserve the quality of law in the making, throughout a lengthy legislative procedure. It may turn out to be a matter of quality versus the acceptability of a given text: often indeed, EU legislation embodies hard-fought compromises without which no law could be enacted at all, but which do not result in a better quality of law, when a deal is finally agreed upon. But that is the price to pay, and it does not only apply to cases where unanimity in the Council is still the rule.[19]

---

[17] See note 12 above.

[18] The first Comitology Decision dates back to 1987; it was taken by the Council in the aftermath of the Single European Act. Comitology is currently governed by Regulation (EU) No 182/2011 of the European Parliament and of the Council laying down the general rules and principles concerning mechanisms for control by Member States of the Commission's exercise of implementing powers, OJ L 55, 28.2.2011, p. 13.

[19] The difficulty of legislating when unanimity in the Council is required should not be overrated: it may be as (if not more) difficult to do so in the ordinary legislative procedure, when the Council normally acts by a qualified majority.

Overall then, it would not be fair to conclude that the authority of EU law can be affected by the way legislation is made, which is the way the Member States set out to that effect in the Treaties. The authority of EU law is not diminished, neither by a supposed lack of legitimacy or transparency in the process of making that law nor by its quality, which is not poor—though admittedly, it may not always reach the highest possible standards. It should also be added that the authority of EU law may operate irrespectively of the direct or indirect effect of the law: once it is recognised as authoritative, it works whatever way EU law is meant to apply, whether directly or through a transposition into national law.

As for European citizens, they are far less concerned by the details of the institutional mechanism which produces EU law than by the concrete, tangible results that Europe is able to bring about in their everyday life. They are not interested whether a "Community method" is used to deliver what they expect from their countries' membership of the European Union. They are not worried that EU law be drafted and adopted in the full respect of the principles of subsidiarity or transparency; and they will hardly care about the quality of that legislation, which most of them will have never even read a single piece of. What European citizens do expect from EU legislation—in fact, from the European Union—is economic growth and employment, prosperity and a decent living. That is the standard against which EU action is assessed and which may, in the end, ensure that the authority of EU law is preserved. It follows that the authority of EU law cannot—as if it were an *a priori*—be taken for granted.

3 What is most likely to affect the authority of EU law?

Over the past 3 years, Europe has been going through one of the most difficult periods ever. The euro crisis, followed by the migrant crisis, not to mention the security problems linked to the terrorist attacks, have highlighted diverging attitudes amongst Member States. Public trust in the European project has been diving to its lowest; public opinions kept distancing themselves from Europe and turned to populist movements instead, although, for the time being, their growth has been partly contained. While the economy now seems to improve again, prompting signs of renewed optimism, euro-surveys show that the economic situation is only the third cause of people's concern in Europe, far behind terrorism and immigration. And this was set against the background of a persistent weakness of the institutions, which in the same period had also to face Brexit and the risk of serious breaches of the Union's fundamental values by some Member States, in a more and more fragmented European Union.

3.1 Searching for the authority of EU law

The authority of EU law can be diminished; hence, it should not be taken for granted. But it has lesser chances to be affected by the quality of the European legislative output than by the degree to which the European project itself will continue to be accepted.

What is most likely to affect the authority of EU law is a growing distrust in the European integration project by the European Union Member States and by their citizens. What can affect the authority of EU law is an incremental divergence of views on the future and on the purpose itself of European integration, to the point where, hypothetically, even the existence of a majority in favour of a draft piece of legislation would not be sufficient either to call it a shared decision or to have it judicially enforced against any possible recalcitrant. Indeed, as already stressed above, evoking a possible challenge to the authority of EU law equals questioning the very essence of the European project.

Where then does the authority of EU law rest? It is hard to see the authority of EU law resting on its very nature or stemming from external elements such as a Crown or even a Constitution. We surely have a "Constitution" in the European meaning of that term,[20] but that is still International Law: the basic Treaties are the EU "international" Constitution that Member States can amend and withdraw from.

We all know what a strange—and beautiful—creature the European Union is. It is not a classical international organisation, even if some may have joined it truly believing that it was (and they just start realising that it isn't). And it is not a State, of course, even if some keep pretending that it acts as if it were one. The European Union has this peculiar and hybrid nature of being a union of peoples, while remaining basically a union of States; this is reflected in its institutions and, since Lisbon, also in the dual legitimacy of the Council voting system. While the first feature—a union of peoples—makes one look at the Union as a "State", with its citizens, government and parliament, the second feature is a reminder of the fact that it is still based on international law, a feature which is to remain that way for some time, probably longer than one could have thought 30 years ago, at the time of the Single European Act and the first comitology Decision.

Against this background, the Member States are those who need in the first place to remain convinced that the European integration project is still worth pursuing, because they will always be better off inside than outside it, and so will their citizens; and hopefully also because they may, after all, share a vision for the future of Europe. The continued acceptance of the European project by its authors: that is where the authority of EU law is to be found to rest.

Therefore, for the authority of EU law to remain safe and unchallenged there is a need, not only for the European citizens but also for the Member States—the signatories to the "Constitution" which EU law is based upon—to continue to support

[20] The ECJ called the Treaty "the basic constitutional charter" in 1986 (*Parti écologiste Les Verts v. European Parliament*, Case 294/83, 1986 E.C.R. I-1365, 23).

and to adhere to the European project, which needs in turn to be complied with and to be seen delivering tangible benefits in term of employment, growth and security.

3.2 *Need of support for the European project*

Member States—even more than European Institutions—bear the main responsibility for making sure that the European project itself does stay on track; and of course for keeping the quality of EU legislation high. Good, well focussed (subsidiarity!) legislation will definitely contribute to a better understanding of the European project, namely if it is better explained to European citizens by the owners of that project. Unfortunately, communication has long been Europe's "Achilles's heel".

European leaders and politicians never really undertook, with some notable exception, to explain in their constituencies what European integration was about and "who did what and why" in the European institutions. What is hardly ever highlighted in national debates is that generations of Europeans saw their quality of life improved as a result of the existence of the EU, which it would be wrong to regard as an acquis. As extraordinary as it may seem, the EU is still lacking reconnaissance and visibility amongst its citizens and only makes the headlines whenever the press and social media need a scapegoat. It is short-sighted, though common practice in politics, to keep success-stories for oneself and blame all the rest on Europe: moreover, in the long run, it might prove to be counterproductive.

That is why the role—and the responsibility—of Member States could hardly be overstated. At a time of fake news and rising populism, it is essential that European citizens are not misled on Europe. That implies that they are better informed on what is done at European level; and it goes without saying that such a task cannot be left to the European institutions, which are miles away from the ground and which were never equipped to that effect; this is a task which can only be handled at the ground level of each Member State, as part and parcel of a long-time-due general approach, starting naturally with education.

European citizens in turn need to keep their support to the European project. They need to be shown what added value the European project can bring. But in the end they also need to perceive tangible results and solidarity in order to be convinced. Anti-European narratives are easier to tell, and more difficult to counter, at a time of economic difficulties and youth unemployment. Younger European citizens are the hope of the European project, as some figures keep reminding us.[21]

[21] A poll published last year in Italy—one of the Member States presently concerned by the populist rise—on the occasion of the 60th anniversary of the Rome Treaties showed that the Italians' attitude towards the European Union was more positive than one could imagine: 76.4% of the respondents in the poll was in favour of the EU (the same poll in 1950 had only shown a favourable response of 71%); however, the share of positive responses amidst respondents between 18 and 34 years was up to 87% in favour (Doxa poll, quoted by *Il Corriere della sera* of 22 March 2017).

They deserve to be trusted to make a European choice as soon as they understand the stakes of the challenges to come.

3.3 *Need of compliance with the European project*

Member States need to show compliance and consistency vis-à-vis the European project, if this project is to have a chance to thrive. At the end of the day, that might even prove to be only a number of Member States, provided that it is a significant and consistent number of them.

The latest enlargement has highlighted a growing discrepancy of attitudes within the European Union. A number of Member States now appear to be satisfied with a lesser level of ambition, which makes it more difficult for the others to promote a common project. In such a peculiar and rather unprecedented context, the question to be answered is for how long those who are still willing to move forward—consistently with the objectives that some of them set in the founding Treaties—can and will be precluded from doing so by a lack of common agreement between all the Member States. Consistency with the European project cannot allow the long advocated reform of the euro area to be endlessly delayed, nor can it allow concrete action in the fields of Schengen and immigration to be taken by those who are ready and willing to bring that project forward. That is why recent calls to use differentiation models might have a better chance now than a few years ago; some Member States might even be tempted, this time round, to sign a separate deal among themselves in order to make, on a smaller membership basis, further steps in a few areas of integration.[22]

Standing still would be damaging for Europeans, for all Member States which care about the European project, and for the project itself, as it would affect its credibility, hence the authority of EU law.

Last but not least, Member States need to show compliance with their own project, which presupposes that they refuse to compromise when the basic values upon which that project is founded are at stake. Violations of the rule of law cannot be left unchallenged if the authority of EU law is to be upheld. In the long run, the members of the European Union, as collective owners of the project which a few of them launched 60 years ago, cannot afford to be seen letting some of them disregard the principles underlying that project.

The future of the European integration project does not only rest on the progress that will be achieved as regards the migrants issue or the reform of the euro area, or even Brexit. It will also be defined by the way in which the European Union will be able to stand up to any Member State in breach of its founding principles.

[22] See Maganza (2017), p. 479.

4 Conclusion

This chapter discusses whether the authority of EU law can be affected by different aspects of the law-making process, including the application of general principles such as subsidiarity and transparency. It finds it not to be the case, as that is not where the authority of EU law rests.

For the authority of EU law to continue to be recognised, there is a need for the Member States and for the European citizens to continue to support the European project and for that project to continue to be seen as delivering tangible progress in the Union. That requires in turn the continuing capacity and commitment of political leaders to promote that project and tell their constituencies why they do it.

At the end of the day, the authority of EU law will only be preserved as long as the European project thrives.

Reference

Maganza G (2017) Making a new start on a smaller European basis: an alternative to differentiation. In: Giegerich T, Schmitt DC, Zeitzmann S (eds) Flexibility in the EU and beyond - how much differentiation can European Integration Bear? Hart/Nomos, Oxford, p 479

A view from Parliament

Diana Wallis

1 Introductory remarks

I would wish to start by expressing my thanks to the European Law Academy. The Academy accompanied and assisted me on my journey as a European Union legislator from 2000 when I first visited the Academy as a new MEP and became aware of its huge potential in enhancing European legal education. Its importance lies as much in the high quality of its courses and conferences as in the networking role it provides as an important meeting and connecting point for European legal professionals. It is in my former capacity as both a European legislator and parliamentarian that I wish to address the challenge of the authority of European law as perceived in the work of the legislator: legislation.

Throughout my parliamentary career it was always clear to me that we needed to create a greater connection and understanding with those we represented in terms of our legislative work in order that in turn the law, which we were making should have both authority and importantly command their respect. I have often told the story of an incident, which occurred when I was canvassing or 'door-knocking' in local elections in North Yorkshire. I knocked on one door and an elderly gentleman came out to speak to me, I explained that I was there on behalf of a local candidate in Council elections but also took the chance to introduce myself as his local Member of the

---

Member of the European Parliament 1999–2012; Vice President of the European Parliament 2007–2012; President of the European Law Institute 2013–2017; member of ERA's Board of Trustees.

D. Wallis (✉)
Senior Lecturer in Law, University of Hull, Hull, UK

Former Vice President of the European Parliament, Brussels, Belgium

Former President of the European Law Institute, Vienna, Austria

ERA Board of Trustees, Trier, Germany
e-mail: d.wallis@hull.ac.uk

W. Heusel, J.-P. Rageade (eds.), *The Authority of EU Law*,
https://doi.org/10.1007/978-3-662-58841-3_5

European Parliament. He looked at me rather strangely, remaining silent for a while, he then said, 'I am really sorry but my wife and I do not travel any more.' I had little idea how to answer this rather unusual conversation stopper. It is however symptomatic of a feeling that the European Union is somewhere else and somebody else's concern and only if you move towards it or choose to interact with it will it actually concern you.

2 The politician as legislator

These worries about the lack of connection with the European legislative process nagged at me during my political life. Perhaps it is also something to do with the political process itself, particularly when perceived from the background of a lawyer. In contrast to the law in books, the actual politics of the legislative process are often messy and frustrating. Sometimes I reflected that perhaps it was just the politics that I did not like, however that is not a sufficient answer to a very serious European problem. In a sense legislation is the main product of the European Union and if Europeans cannot feel, understand or appreciate that product and the connection with their elected representatives in a positive way we have a serious problem.

The politician as a legislator and in this sense a Member of the European Parliament performs a very important task and I believe this is a task, which continues to be undervalued. This lack of value attached to the politician as legislator of course extends beyond the European context and into our national politics. Indeed it is interesting to observe that partly because of the Brexit process the British Parliament at Westminster is suddenly waking up to the fact that it does indeed have a very important job as a legislature and that these powers of law-making are critical to its role vis a vis the executive. The whole of the Article 50 litigation was angled at making sure Parliament did its job as a legislator, not just following the executive whims of the government. Conversely in a relatively young parliament, like the European Parliament I believe there was always a very much greater awareness of its powers, or indeed before recent Treaty changes, its lack of powers as a full legislator. Every piece of legislation has to be debated and checked for compliance with the appropriate Treaty provisions. This could often be contentious, but this gives a Parliament and parliamentarians a more acute sense of the value and importance of the legislative process. I have always been very struck by the writing of Jeremy Waldron on the 'dignity' of legislation.[1] I believe this is the crux; we underestimate the importance and the dignity of the act of law-making.

Within the legal world and indeed outside there is a general tendency to value much more highly the law-shaping input of courts and judges over and above the law-making work of legislators and politicians. The former are seen as calm and considered using an informed 'rights' based review of the law and critically being independent and neutral. Whereas the legislators or politicians are all too often characterised as self-serving and seeking cynical compromises. The comparison is stark

[1] Waldron (1999).

and the legislator sadly comes out of it the worse in the general estimation of the public.[2]

Sometimes I think we should remind ourselves of what legislators are trying to achieve out of what some would class as an assembly or 'rabble' of elected representatives, they are trying to consider and arrive at laws which are needed or required for the public good and reflect and resonate with public sentiment. This exercise, however messy, as long it is as robust and transparent should give legislation some dignity and authority.

3 Democracy and transparency

Against these considerations it has always been argued by some that the problem faced by the European Parliament continues to be a problem of democratic deficit, of a limit on the directly elected Parliament's law-making powers. Following the implementation of the Lisbon Treaty I would actually take the view that the European Parliament is now quite powerful enough as a directly elected body indeed in some instances having almost too much power which can out-trump its national counterparts. One only has to compare the position of European parliamentarians in the Brexit process to see that their possibilities in respect of the negotiating and conclusion of international agreements go far beyond those of their national counterparts. Some would argue to the extent of jeopardising the executive's role to make such agreements. Others would say this is an elected Parliament and legislature doing its job; carrying out the people's work. Again some commentators will also argue that the European Parliament is a lesser or flawed institution because it has no right of legislative initiative. Technically this may strictly be the case, but in practical terms one only has to observe the continued dialogue and evolution of each annual Commission Work Programme and the own initiative reports generated in Parliamentary Committees, which ultimately produce Commission legislative proposals, to see the reality is otherwise. The lack of authority attributed to European Union legislation is not a problem to be solved by giving more powers to the directly elected Parliament but rather perhaps more transparency or visibility to the legislative work, which it already does.

In terms of transparency recent years have seen huge advances in the transparency of the European legislative process especially as between Commission and Parliament as a result of the Transparency Initiative. On-line tracking of the legislative process is relatively straightforward and accessible certainly in comparison to the labyrinthine and archaic working methods of some national legislatures. The transparency requirements on public interest representatives have likewise been tightened. The main disappointment remains in the activities of the Member States in Council and more importantly the secrecy of the Trialogue process. The Parliament has the power and the possibility to insist on three legislative readings,

[2] For more on this comparison in the UK Parliament context see also Howarth (2013).

nowadays it seldom does, but arguing in favour a speedier legislative result disappears into private three way meetings with the other institutions. This activity whatever the gains in speed is not good for transparency of the legislative process and in turn visibility and trust in the process. If the process is robust and public friendly then it needs to be seen to be such.

The manner in which legislation is considered, debated and crafted by the three European institutions was in my experience normally a painstaking and credible process with much to recommend as against some of the polarised political processes seen elsewhere: making the whole of that process visible should not be problematic. It may be boring to watch but then that may go more to the dignity of the legislative process! The idea put forward during our congress that a binary democratic choice between two large European political parties following the American model would solve all our problems looks like an unhappy template for the future given the current state of American politics and hardly an end to be desired. The idea that merely allowing Europe's public the possibility 'to throw the rascals' out at each set of European parliamentary elections will solve all our problems seems to me simplistic and belonging to another age.

4 The parliamentary legislative process

I think it is helpful in this context rather to reflect on how the work of members of the European Parliament is actually organised. On the plus side members spend most of their parliamentary time working in their main legislative committees. In very general terms 2 weeks out of the normal parliamentary cycle of 4 weeks are devoted to committees and again it will be the same set of parliamentary colleagues who will together attend at and speak in individual plenary debates during the plenary session week. This distribution of working time leads to a position where a member's main friendships and loyalties often tend to revolve around those they work with closely in committee rather than ironically with their political groups, with whom in some ways they spend less time. However this working method can also lead to a form of tunnel vision. As a member is appointed as a rapporteur for a legislative file they become almost like a junior minister leading legislation in 28 countries; it is an amazing job and an amazing experience. However apart from the shadow reporters appointed by other political groups it is arguable how far other individual parliamentarians follow the work in progress in any particular detail, certainly outside of their own committee interests. Of course there are cross-cutting issues that are maybe particularly politically exciting or perhaps contain that magic word 'rights'. It was never clear to me that the majority of members know very much about what is happening on each and every particular legislative file however important. They will tend to take the lead from the rapporteur or shadow reporter within the discussions in the political group. I remember dealing with the Rome II Regulation, which to lawyers was hugely exciting, but I suspect many members thought it was probably to do with an additional Rome airport or something of that nature! Given that the rapporteur and the various shadow rapporteurs will have worked very closely together in committee to arrive at compromises there is unlikely to be any great disagreement at what should be the most visible political stage of plenary debate and therefore to the public at large it may appear the process lacks the robust political discussion that should actually take place on any new law or legislation.

In order to try to improve the connection and comprehension of the EU law-making process at national level, post the Lisbon Treaty we now have greater involvement of national parliaments in the process. However it is debatable whether the so called 'yellow-card' system, allowing a group of national parliaments being of similar mind to pause a Commission legislative proposal, has done much to reach out to the European public. Whilst done for very understandable reasons to try to increase democratic engagement down at the nation state level, the reality is that most national parliamentarians have their own main day job to be accomplishing, rather than to pay any great attention to a process that is purely negative in construct. It is therefore unrealistic save in very exceptional circumstances to expect them to follow closely any European legislative process again unless it happens to be a particular file which for some reason attracts public or political attention. Then such news that does filter out is purely negative, the intent to stop legislation rather than craft it. The result being that the majority of the good positive EU legislative work that is being done fails to engage with either parliamentarians or public at a national level.

5 Contrasting example of the European Parliament legislative process

An additional problematic faced by the European legislator is the frequent technicality of the matters under consider or conversely the simplicity of some public interventions through lobbying or other means in relation to these issues. I wish to mention two particular examples with which I was deeply involved, then finally to make at least some positive, albeit small suggestions.

5.1 European contract law

The first relates to the whole history of the attempts to deal with European contract law, the Draft Common Frame of Reference, or the European Sales law, which has now further morphed into instruments dealing with 'digital' sales. There have been years of discussing round and round this whole area in order so the argument goes to release the full benefits of the Internal Market by having a more coherent contract law across the European space, this should of course make even more sense in an age of e-commerce. It was interesting that when the European legislator was faced with a blank sheet of paper in relation to the original E-commerce Directive, and was therefore able to legislate before nation states, progress was fast and furious. However when there is an existing body of 28 national laws, especially something as deeply cultural and even constitutional, as basic contract or civil law, the situation is far more politically charged and complex. It is interesting to note that as the French recently updated their Civil Code they took the clear choice to take the technical legal arguments and keep them away from parliamentarians.[3] Europe does not do that but gets no plaudits for doing so. It might make faster progress if it did so, but would it be acceptable to deliver apparent technicalities, that often mask political choices, in to the hands of the so-called 'eurocrats'? Imagine the outcry, so there is the evidence the EU is in many ways more democratic than we think but we simply and sadly do not see it.

5.2 *The regulation on the trade in seal products*

At the opposite end of the spectrum the example I would take would be one which involved animal rights. The Regulation on the Trade in Seal Products, as Rapporteur during the process I came to note that seals are animals that have extraordinary PR. The commercial seal hunt in Canada has over many decades attracted adverse publicity and huge attention from animal rights activists, the most active organisation being the US-based Humane Society International. Here at the outset we should pause to note the main problem is centred in Canada and the main lobbying organisation in the US. However, the EU legislature became consumed by this issue in 2008/2009, in the run-up to the 2009 elections to the European Parliament. Europe of course has its own seal population, and indigenous populations that rely on it, particularly the Greenland Inuit. Whilst Greenland may now be outside the EU the issue remains sensitive for its deeply related neighbour Denmark. In addition for years the European Parliament had been issuing carefully crafted resolutions supporting these same indigenous peoples and their rights especially their traditional lifestyle, which of course includes seal hunting. Likewise for years the EU institutions had been persistently pursuing membership of the Arctic Council, the body which successfully brings together Europe's Nordic nations and neighbours plus Canada, the US and Russia. An extremely important body in relation to a fragile area of the globe deeply connected with climate change.

However whatever the importance of climate change issues, or geopolitics in the Arctic, or the rights of indigenous peoples all these were overcome by a sophisticated and professional lobbying campaign on behalf of some very attractive wild seal mammals. A campaign that took off across all of the Member States of the Union and generated huge volumes of e-mail and traditional letters from animal lovers far and wide to whom it was impossible to explain any other issues at stake.

[3] Fauvarque-Cosson (2017), pp. 337–354.

Including the fact that the beautiful white seal pups much used in the lobbying had in fact been protected by EU legislation for some years. So the EU got its ban on seal products, a ban I would have much preferred as a labelling regime that just might have had less impact on indigenous peoples, but in the slip stream the EU was refused even observer status in the Arctic Council whilst this was granted to China! Whilst these maybe deserving seals as unthreatened wild animals now arguably have greater protection than some farmed animals within the EU. If that is what the EU consumer wants then indeed the EU legislature has delivered through a very political process, however what it did not do successfully was to juxtapose the human rights of the indigenous peoples who also attempted to lobby the legislature but without the same effect. In many ways it seemed a strange outcome for a legislature that is otherwise well known for the way in which it espoused and protects human rights around the world.[4]

In both these instances some many will feel comfortable with the results, however to give the law real authority it is not the result we must view or question but the process that has led to it. Both have involved much writing and much debate, one probably did not engage the public, the other very much so. I tried my best with contract law to find an animals lovers angle and indeed had some minor success around the story of a local business promoting the sale of bespoke cat-scratching posts! However note the headline despite the endearing picture of cats.[5]

6 End thoughts

So how can the European legislator do better at engaging the public in its painstaking, technical detailed work outside of election time? I have two small practical suggestions. Firstly the Commission Annual Work Programme should form the subject of a joint debate in every national parliament, in the main chamber, just once a year when a senior member of the Commission should be given the floor along with government Ministers and MEPs should be allowed to debate together with their national colleagues under the scrutiny of their national media. This might just enhance visibility of legislation coming down the tracks.

Secondly, it is worth noting that presently every committee of the European Parliament makes visits twice a year to the capital of the incoming Council presidency. I would rather see each committee hold one public committee meeting in a city of a Member State outside of the capital just once a year. I base the effectiveness of this on two points, the huge appreciation and publicity given to local visits of the Parliament's Petitions Committee in its investigative role. In addition, the pleasure of visitors groups in actually seeing the Parliament at work. So I return to my North Yorkshire pensioner, if he will not come to 'Europe' we have to find a way of

[4] For more on this issue and analysis of the legislative process see Sellheim (2013), pp. 417–450; also Sellheim (2015), pp. 274–289.

[5] Aldridge (2011), accessed January 2018.

bringing Europe to him and making it real. Only in circumstances like this of real visibility and engagement with the EU legislators will EU legislation begin to command the respect of our citizens and have the necessary authority.

References

Aldridge A, How a European Single Contract Law could Erode English Hegemony, Guardian October 2011, Accessed Jan 2018

Fauvarque-Cosson B (2017) The French contract law reform and the political process. Eur Rev Contract Law 13:337–354

Howarth D (2013) Law as engineering; thinking about what lawyers do. Edward Elgar, Cheltenham

Sellheim N (2013) The neglected tradition? – The genesis of the EU seal products ban and commercial sealing. Yearb Polar Law 5:417–450

Sellheim N (2015) The goals of the EU seal products trade regulation – from effectiveness to consequence. Polar Record 51(3):274–289

Waldron J (1999) The dignity of legislation. Cambridge University Press, Cambridge

Part III
The authority of EU law: A view from Constitutional and Supreme Courts

L'autorité du droit de l'Union européenne – Le point de vue d'un juge français

Jean-Marc Sauvé

A ses débuts, mais encore aujourd'hui, l'approche finaliste de la Cour de justice de l'Union européenne a pu dérouter certains Etats membres et les cours constitutionnelles nationales peu accoutumés à se voir ainsi imposer un droit « extérieur ». Les tensions constatées dans les années 1960 entre les cours constitutionnelles allemande et italienne et la Cour de justice des Communautés européennes au sujet du respect des droits fondamentaux par les institutions européennes n'ont été que les premières illustrations des débats animés qui ont encore cours aujourd'hui dans certains pays d'Europe continentale sur la réception de la jurisprudence européenne en droit interne et sur l'articulation des ordres constitutionnels nationaux et européen. Les risques de confrontation entre le droit de l'Union et les droits nationaux ne sont en effet pas théoriques, comme en témoignent de récentes décisions des cours suprêmes nationales : l'arrêt de la Cour constitutionnelle tchèque du 31 janvier 2012 dans l'affaire « *des pensions slovaques* »[1], la saga *Gauweiler*[2] devant la Cour constitutionnelle fédérale allemande et la décision *Ajos* de la Cour suprême du Danemark du 6 décembre 2016[3].

C'est, par conséquent, sur un sujet d'une grande actualité que je souhaiterais livrer quelques éléments de l'appréciation d'un juge français sur ces questions.

Vice-président du Conseil d'Etat de France. Ce texte a été écrit en collaboration avec Sarah Houllier, magistrat administratif, chargée de mission auprès du vice-président du Conseil d'Etat.

[1] Cour constitutionnelle tchèque, 31 janvier 2012, Pl. US 5/12, qui fait suite à l'arrêt de la CJUE du 22 juin 2011, *Landtova*, aff. C-399/09.

[2] Cour constitutionnelle fédérale allemande, 21 juin 2016, 2 BvR 2728/13, qui fait suite à l'arrêt de la CJUE du 16 juin 2015, *Gauweiler*, aff. C-62/14.

[3] Cour suprême du Danemark, 6 décembre 2016, *Ajos*, 15/2014, qui fait suite à l'arrêt de la CJUE du 19 avril 2016, *DI*, aff. C-441/14.

J.-M. Sauvé (✉)
Council of State, Paris, France
e-mail: sarah.houllier@conseil-etat.fr; secretariat.vicepresident@conseil-etat.fr

W. Heusel, J.-P. Rageade (eds.), *The Authority of EU Law*,
https://doi.org/10.1007/978-3-662-58841-3_6

1 Les juges français ont élaboré des mécanismes d'articulation qui limitent les risques de conflit entre le droit européen et le droit national

1.1 En prenant appui sur la notion d'identité constitutionnelle, les juges français parviennent à concilier la primauté du droit de l'Union et le respect des normes constitutionnelles

En France, l'article 54 de la Constitution instaure la primauté des normes constitutionnelles, y compris sur les normes de droit international[4]. L'articulation de cette règle avec le principe de primauté du droit de l'Union européenne[5] ne pouvait qu'être périlleuse. Pour surmonter cette tension, le Conseil d'Etat s'est inspiré des décisions *Loi pour l'économie numérique* de 2004[6] et *Loi relative au droit d'auteur* de 2006[7] par lesquelles le Conseil constitutionnel, après avoir rappelé l'obligation de transposition des directives qui résulte de l'article 88-1 de notre Constitution, a jugé qu'il ne lui appartenait pas de contrôler la conformité des lois de transposition à la Constitution sauf en présence de dispositions incompatibles avec un principe inhérent à l'identité constitutionnelle de la France. Le Conseil d'Etat a adopté une logique similaire dans son arrêt *Arcelor* du 8 février 2007 en jugeant que pour examiner si un acte de transposition des dispositions précises et inconditionnelles d'une directive méconnaît un principe de valeur constitutionnelle, il doit d'abord rechercher si un principe similaire existe et se trouve effectivement protégé en droit de l'Union, auquel cas il lui revient de contrôler la conformité de la directive à ce principe, le cas échéant en posant une question préjudicielle à la Cour de justice de l'Union[8]. Si, en revanche, le principe constitutionnel invoqué ne fait pas l'objet d'une protection effective en droit de l'Union, le juge administratif accepte de contrôler directement la conformité à la Constitution de l'acte contesté.

Le Conseil d'Etat s'est ainsi attaché à mieux coordonner les différentes « primautés ». Mais il n'a jamais fait céder la primauté de la norme constitutionnelle française, en particulier en ce qu'elle définit les règles procédurales d'adoption de la loi. Le contrôle de conventionnalité de la loi ne concerne en effet que les règles de fond et il ne vaut pas pour les règles procédurales définies par la Constitution qui, à ce titre, continuent de primer en droit interne[9], sauf dans les cas où c'est le droit de l'Union européenne qui ajoute des règles de procédure, lesquelles doivent dès

[4] Confirmé par CE Ass., 30 octobre 1998, *Sarran et Levacher*, Rec. 368, n° 200286 et 200287.

[5] CJCE, 9 mars 1978, *Simmenthal*, aff. 106/77; CJCE, 17 décembre 1970, *Internationale Handelsgesellschaft*, aff. 11/70; CJCE, 8 septembre 2010, *Winner Wetten*, aff. C-409/06.

[6] CC, 10 juin 2004, *Loi pour la confiance dans l'économie numérique*, n° 2004-496 DC.

[7] CC, 27 juillet 2006, *Loi relative au droit d'auteur et aux droits voisins dans la société d'information*, n° 2006-540 DC.

[8] CE Ass., 8 février 2007, *Société Arcelor Atlantique et Lorraine*, n° 287110.

[9] CE, 27 octobre 2015, *M. Allenbach et autres*, n° 393026 confirmé par CE, 20 mai 2016, *Commune d'Aix-en-Provence et Commune de Pertuis*, n° 394016 et 394218.

lors être suivies au risque d'entacher d'un vice de procédure les dispositions législatives en cause[10].

L'articulation du droit de l'Union européenne et du droit constitutionnel repose principalement sur la réserve de l'identité constitutionnelle nationale qui s'avère un outil très utile en ce qu'il permet aux juges nationaux de se conformer à leurs obligations au regard de l'engagement européen de la France, tout en préservant la primauté de la norme constitutionnelle dans l'ordre interne. A ce jour, cette réserve n'a jamais été activée par l'une ou l'autre des juridictions françaises. S'il n'est pas exclu qu'elle puisse un jour l'être, la clause de l'identité constitutionnelle doit cependant être précisément définie et délimitée afin de ne pas être maniée de manière unilatérale ou imprévisible. Dès lors qu'il s'agit d'une notion permettant de déroger au principe d'uniformité du droit de l'Union européenne, son usage ne pourrait qu'être exceptionnel.

La reconnaissance de l'autorité du droit de l'Union européenne se traduit également dans l'articulation du renvoi préjudiciel et de la question prioritaire de constitutionnalité. Dès 2010, le Conseil constitutionnel a jugé qu'au cours de l'examen d'une question prioritaire de constitutionnalité, il appartient aux juges administratifs et judiciaires de prendre toutes les mesures nécessaires pour empêcher qu'une disposition législative nationale incompatible avec le droit de l'Union européenne ne produise des effets. Il a ajouté que les dispositions relatives à la question prioritaire de constitutionnalité ne privent aucunement le juge français de son pouvoir de poser une question préjudicielle à la Cour de justice, y compris lorsqu'il transmet une question préjudicielle de constitutionnalité, que le législateur a pourtant qualifiée de prioritaire[11]. Au même moment, le Conseil d'Etat a jugé la même chose[12]. Plus récemment, il a encore précisé les modalités d'articulation de ces deux procédures préjudicielles[13] dans une affaire dans laquelle le requérant se prévalait de la méconnaissance, par les dispositions de la loi nationale, telles qu'interprétées par le Conseil d'Etat, des objectifs d'une directive européenne. Il soutenait, aussi, par le biais d'une question prioritaire de constitutionnalité, qu'en cas d'incompatibilité entre l'interprétation faite par le juge administratif de la loi française et les dispositions de la directive européenne que cette loi transpose, il découlerait de la loi nationale une discrimination à rebours contraire au principe constitutionnel d'égalité devant les charges publiques. Confronté à une difficulté sérieuse d'interprétation, le Conseil d'Etat a décidé de renvoyer une question préjudicielle à la Cour de justice et il a jugé que si, en l'état, il n'y avait pas lieu de transmettre une question prioritaire de constitutionnalité au Conseil constitutionnel, le requérant pourrait, si la réponse de la Cour de justice le justifiait, solliciter à nouveau la transmission de cette question au Conseil constitutionnel.

---

[10] CE, 9 mars 2016, *Société Uber France et autres*, n° 388213, 388343 et 388357.

[11] CC, 12 mai 2010, *Loi relative à l'ouverture à la concurrence et à la régulation du secteur des jeux d'argent et de hasard en ligne*, n° 2010-605 DC, pts. 10 à 21.

[12] CE, 14 mai 2010, *M. Rujovic*, n° 312305.

[13] CE Ass., 31 mai 2016, *M. Jacob*, n° 393881.

Cette articulation des règles de fond et de procédure traduit bien la volonté de coordination exprimée par la jurisprudence du Conseil d'Etat.

1.2 *Des techniques jurisprudentielles pragmatiques sont venues renforcer ce dispositif de conciliation*

Pendant de la primauté du droit de l'Union européenne consacré par la Cour de justice, le principe de coopération loyale[14] impose aux Etats membres de prendre toutes les mesures nécessaires à la mise en œuvre de leurs obligations. Les administrations, comme les juges nationaux, sont ainsi tenues d'écarter l'application d'une disposition de droit interne incompatible avec le droit de l'Union européenne[15] et elles doivent tirer toutes les conséquences de l'incompatibilité d'une loi avec les objectifs d'une directive européenne[16] en s'interdisant d'en prendre les décrets d'application[17] ou, plus radicalement, d'en faire application[18] lorsqu'il n'est pas possible de donner à la loi une interprétation conforme à une directive européenne[19]. Par la technique de l'interprétation conforme, le juge administratif s'assure en effet que les règles internes sont interprétées conformément aux règles et aux principes du droit de l'Union. Ainsi, le Conseil d'Etat[20], en cohérence avec le Conseil constitutionnel[21], a interprété les dispositions nationales relatives à la question prioritaire de constitutionnalité conformément au droit de l'Union, comme l'a ensuite confirmé la Cour de justice dans son arrêt *Melki*[22]. La Cour de justice a en effet jugé que le juge national, juge de droit commun du droit de l'Union européenne, ne remplirait pas son office si, en transmettant une question prioritaire de constitutionnalité, il paralysait par là l'effet utile de dispositions du droit de l'Union. Le contrôle national de constitutionnalité des lois doit, par conséquent, se conjuguer

---

[14] Article 4 du Traité sur l'Union européenne.

[15] CJCE, 6 mars 2007, *Procédures pénales c. Massimiliano Placanica*, aff. C-338/04, C-359/04 et C-360/04.

[16] CE Sect., 3 décembre 1999, *Association ornithologique et mammalogique de Saône-et-Loire et Rassemblement des opposants à la chasse*, n° 164789 et 165122.

[17] CE, 24 février 1999, *Association de patients de la médecine d'orientation anthroposophique*, n° 195354.

[18] CE, 30 juillet 2003, *Association « L'Avenir de la langue française »*, n° 245076. Jurisprudence également applicable aux les traités internationaux « classiques » (CE, 16 juillet 2008, *M. Masson*, n° 300458).

[19] CE, 30 juillet 2003, *Association « L'Avenir de la langue française »*, n° 24507.

[20] CE, 14 mai 2010, *Rujovic*, n° 312305.

[21] CC, 12 mai 2010, *Loi relative à l'ouverture à la concurrence et à la régulation du secteur des jeux d'argent et de hasard en ligne*, n° 2010-605 DC. La procédure de QPC a été jugée conforme au droit de l'Union européenne par la Cour de justice de l'Union européenne (CJUE, 22 juin 2010, *Melki et Abdeli*, aff. C-188/10 et C-189/10).

[22] CJUE, 22 juin 2010, *Melki et Abdeli*, aff. C-188/10 et C-189/10.

avec la pleine et entière application du droit de l'Union. C'est sous réserve de cette interprétation qu'il est compatible avec lui.

La technique de « l'équivalence de protection » contribue, pour sa part, à prévenir les contradictions éventuelles entre les garanties nationales et européennes des droits, en faisant primer sur une logique de hiérarchie des ordres juridiques celle de la nécessaire protection des droits fondamentaux[23]. La reconnaissance d'une équivalence dans la protection des droits fondamentaux entre l'Allemagne et l'Union européenne a notamment fondé la décision *Arcelor* du Conseil d'Etat[24], inspirée de la jurisprudence *Solange* de la Cour constitutionnelle allemande[25].

La théorie de l'acte clair, qui résulte d'une jurisprudence du Conseil d'Etat[26], ensuite admise par la Cour de justice de l'Union européenne[27], permet quant à elle un recours raisonné à la technique des renvois préjudiciels. Le juge national n'est, par conséquent, tenu de procéder à un renvoi que lorsque c'est nécessaire, permettant ainsi de préserver l'autonomie des juridictions nationales, sans méconnaître l'autorité du droit de l'Union européenne, ni le principe de coopération loyale[28]. La décision du Conseil d'Etat de France *Conseil national des Barreaux* est un exemple de cette coopération[29]. Le Conseil d'Etat, s'estimant déjà suffisamment éclairé par une réponse de la Cour de justice à une question posée par la Cour constitutionnelle de Belgique, s'est abstenu de procéder à un nouveau renvoi préjudiciel et il s'est directement prononcé sur la conformité des dispositions de la deuxième directive relative à la prévention du blanchiment des capitaux aux stipulations non seulement de l'article 6, mais aussi de l'article 8 de la Convention européenne des droits de l'Homme. Par ailleurs, l'Etat peut désormais voir sa responsabilité engagée en cas de méconnaissance du droit de l'Union par une décision juridictionnelle[30].

L'articulation des ordres juridiques interne et européen repose ainsi au premier chef sur les juges nationaux, juges de droit commun du droit de l'Union européenne, qui par leur jurisprudence et l'attitude qu'ils adoptent à l'égard des renvois préjudiciels définissent le cadre dans lequel s'exerce la mission de la Cour de justice de l'Union européenne.

---

[23] Millet (2012), n° 2, p. 307.

[24] CE Ass., 8 février 2007, *Société Arcelor Atlantique et Lorraine*, n° 287110.

[25] Cour constitutionnelle allemande, 29 mai 1974, *Solange I* ; 22 octobre 1986, *Solange II*; 7 juin 2000, *Solange III*.

[26] CE Ass., 19 juin 1964, *Société des pétroles Shell-Berre*, Rec. 344.

[27] CJCE, 6 octobre 1982, *CILFIT*, aff. 283/81.

[28] Article 4 § 3 du Traité sur l'Union européenne.

[29] CE Sect., 10 avril 2008, *Conseil national des barreaux*, n° 296845.

[30] CE, 18 juin 2008, *Gestas*, n° 295831 reprenant les principes édictés dans CJCE, 2003, *Köbler*, aff. C-224/01.

2 Cette œuvre prétorienne ne suffit toutefois pas à aplanir toutes les difficultés

2.1 *La Cour de justice continue de rendre des décisions qui divergent parfois de l'appréciation des autorités nationales.*

Dans certains cas, la Cour de justice de l'Union européenne a adopté une interprétation du droit de l'Union à laquelle les autorités nationales, administratives ou judiciaires, ne souscrivaient pas. C'est le cas de l'arrêt *Melloni* par lequel, à rebours de ce qu'avait jugé le Tribunal constitutionnel espagnol, la Cour de justice a refusé de lire dans l'article 53 de la Charte des droits fondamentaux de l'Union la possibilité pour les Etats membres de se prévaloir des garanties offertes par leur Constitution pour déroger au droit de l'Union européenne, même lorsque ces garanties sont plus protectrices[31]. C'est aussi le cas avec l'arrêt, plus récent, *Tele2 Sverige* du 21 décembre 2016[32] qui a précisé, dans un sens restrictif, la jurisprudence résultant de l'arrêt *Digital Rights Ireland* de 2014 invalidant la directive de 2006 sur la conservation des données au motif que la possibilité donnée aux Etats membres d'imposer aux opérateurs de communications de conserver l'ensemble des données de connexion des utilisateurs pour une durée maximale comprise entre six mois et deux ans méconnaissait le droit au respect de la vie privée des personnes et le droit à la protection des données personnelles[33]. Cette décision pouvait faire l'objet de deux interprétations : une interprétation souple selon laquelle la collecte et la conservation indifférenciées de données sont possibles à condition d'être justifiées par des objectifs sérieux et d'être assorties de garanties suffisantes ; une interprétation stricte conduisant à écarter toute forme de collecte et de conservation indifférenciée des données, y compris pour des motifs d'intérêt général. Dans son étude annuelle 2014[34], puis en formation juridictionnelle[35], le Conseil d'Etat avait pris position en faveur de la première interprétation. Par son arrêt *Tele2 Sverige*, la Cour de justice n'a pas retenu cette analyse et elle a considérablement réduit la marge d'appréciation des Etats en ce qui concerne la possibilité d'ordonner la conservation des données de connexion, y compris dans le cadre de la lutte contre le terrorisme ou la criminalité organisée.

Il est aussi arrivé que le Conseil d'Etat se reconnaisse une autonomie lui permettant de s'écarter de l'appréciation de la Cour de justice. Ce fut le cas dans l'arrêt *Quintanel* du 27 mars 2015 relatif à un avantage réservé aux femmes en matière de pensions : la bonification de pension pour enfants[36]. Peu de temps auparavant, la

[31] CJUE, 26 février 2013, *Stefano Melloni c. Ministerio fiscal*, C-399/11.

[32] CJUE, 21 décembre 2016, *Tele2 Sverige* et *Secretary of State for the Home Department*, aff. C-203/15 et C-698/15.

[33] CJUE, 8 avril 2014, *Digital Rights Ireland* et *K. Landesregierung*, aff. C-293/12 et C-594/12.

[34] Etude annuelle 2014 du Conseil d'Etat, *Le numérique et les droits fondamentaux*, La documentation française.

[35] CE, 12 février 2016, *Association French Data Network et autres*, n° 388134 et n° 388255.

[36] CE Ass., 27 mars 2015, *M. Quintanel*, n° 372426.

Cour de justice avait estimé que cette inégalité de traitement ne semblait pas justifiée par des critères objectifs étrangers à toute discrimination fondée sur le sexe, mais que si sa jurisprudence fournissait « des indications (…) de nature à permettre à la juridiction nationale de statuer », seul le juge national pouvait interpréter la législation de son pays et qu'il dispose pour ce faire d'une certaine marge d'appréciation[37]. Reprenant cette formulation, le Conseil d'Etat a fait usage de cette latitude et il a jugé qu'une telle loi était justifiée par un objectif légitime de politique sociale : celui de compenser les désavantages objectivement constatés et subis par les femmes dans le déroulement de leur carrière en raison des interruptions liées à la naissance ou l'éducation d'un enfant. Une loi prévoyant que la bonification des droits à pension pour les personnes ayant élevé trois enfants ou plus est subordonnée à une interruption d'activité d'une durée continue au moins égale à deux mois n'est, par conséquent, pas contraire au droit de l'Union européenne[38].

2.2 *Des divergences d'appréciation entre les juridictions nationales suprêmes et la Cour de justice de l'Union seraient susceptibles de porter atteinte à la légitimité et l'autorité du droit de l'Union*

De réelles tensions peuvent naître entre juridictions nationales et juridictions européennes. La mise en œuvre des dispositions relatives au mandat d'arrêt européen a, par exemple, donné lieu à un dialogue juridictionnel actif, certaines juridictions nationales ayant exprimé la crainte d'un nivellement par le bas compte tenu de la disparité des protections et des procédures dans les différents Etats-membres[39]. La Cour constitutionnelle fédérale d'Allemagne[40] a ainsi estimé qu'en cas de méconnaissance d'un principe inhérent à l'identité constitutionnelle allemande, il était possible de ne pas appliquer le droit de l'Union. En l'occurrence, elle a jugé que si la décision-cadre relative au mandat d'arrêt européen prévoit des garanties suffisantes pour les personnes jugées en leur absence, il existait dans l'affaire en litige un doute sur l'effectivité de leur mise en œuvre en Italie, ce pays ne prévoyant pas la possibilité d'un nouveau jugement lorsque la personne a été jugée par contumace. La Cour de justice de l'Union a, en retour, infléchi sa jurisprudence par ses arrêts *Aranyosi* et *Căldăraru* du 15 avril 2016 en prenant appui sur la Charte des droits fondamentaux de l'Union européenne[41]. Saisie d'une question préjudicielle sur la possibilité de remettre un suspect à un pays dans lequel il risquerait de subir des traitements inhumains ou dégradants, la Cour de justice de l'Union s'est en effet

[37] CJUE, 17 juillet 2014, *M. et Mme Leone*, aff. C-173/13.

[38] CE Ass., 27 mars 2015, *M. Quintanel*, n° 372426.

[39] Gaillet (2016), p. 1112.

[40] Cour constitutionnelle fédérale allemande, 15 décembre 2015, 2BvR 2735/14.

[41] CJUE, 15 avril 2016, *Pál Aranyosi et Robert Căldăraru*, aff. C-404/15 et C-695/15 PPU.

prononcée en faveur de la garantie la plus élevée des droits fondamentaux. Si, sur la base d'éléments concrets et étayés, les juridictions nationales jugent qu'il existe un risque réel de traitement inhumain ou dégradant pour les personnes recherchées, elles doivent suspendre l'exécution du mandat d'arrêt européen ou y mettre un terme, le cas échéant. En plaçant le juge national au cœur de la conciliation entre la primauté du droit de l'Union et la protection des droits fondamentaux tels que protégés, notamment, par la Charte des droits fondamentaux, la Cour de justice de l'Union a, dans cette affaire, permis d'éviter un conflit potentiellement dévastateur entre la Constitution allemande et la mise en œuvre du mandat d'arrêt européen[42]. Plus récemment, l'application de la jurisprudence *Mangold*[43] de la Cour de justice a provoqué de vives tensions avec la Cour suprême du Danemark. La décision *Mangold* avait déjà été vivement critiquée en 2005, au motif que la Cour de justice avait adopté une lecture trop extensive des dispositions de la directive en consacrant un principe de non-discrimination en fonction de l'âge, lui reconnaissant ainsi un effet horizontal, alors qu'une directive ne produit en principe qu'un effet vertical[44]. Après avoir saisi la Cour de justice d'une question préjudicielle, la Cour suprême du Danemark a estimé, contrairement à l'interprétation des juges européens, que le principe de primauté du droit de l'Union ne pouvait lui imposer d'interpréter le droit danois *contra legem* et que le principe de non-discrimination en raison de l'âge devait être tempéré par celui de sécurité juridique et de confiance légitime[45].

Bien que ces tensions soient faiblement ressenties au-delà de la communauté juridique, elles sont génératrices de risques dont il ne faut pas sous-estimer la gravité ou les conséquences. Il est, par conséquent, nécessaire que les juridictions nationales et européennes poursuivent le dialogue engagé depuis plusieurs années pour aplanir les difficultés futures qui pourraient émerger. Ainsi, le Conseil d'Etat et la Cour de justice de l'Union pratiquent, ces dernières années, un dialogue des juges « décomplexé », selon le mot de certains commentateurs[46]. Alors que le Conseil d'Etat n'avait transmis à la Cour de justice que 18 questions préjudicielles en vingt ans, de 1970 à 1999, il en a déjà transmis 108 depuis 2000, dont 13 au titre de la seule année 2017. Par exemple, dans quatre affaires récentes, relatives aux conséquences à tirer de l'arrêt *Google Spain* du 13 mai 2014 de la Cour de justice de l'Union[47], le Conseil d'Etat a renvoyé plusieurs questions préjudicielles relatives aux modalités de mise

[42] Gazin (2016), n°6, p. 192.

[43] CJCE, 22 novembre 2005, *Werner Mangold*, aff. C-144/04.

[44] Cette approche a toutefois été confirmée à plusieurs reprises par la Cour de justice de l'Union européenne (CJUE, 19 octobre 2010, *Kücükdeveci*, aff. C-555/07.

[45] Cour suprême du Danemark, 6 décembre 2016, *Ajos*, 15/2014, qui fait suite à l'arrêt de la CJUE du 19 avril 2016, *DI*, aff. C-441/14. – Voir la contribution du juge Lars Hjortnæs, membre de la Cour suprême du Danemark, expliquant le raisonnement de la Cour, dans ce livre (p. …).

[46] G. Odinet et S. Roussel (2017), p. 740 au sujet de l'affaire *Chupin* (CE Ass., 24 février 2017, n° 391000).

[47] CJUE, gr.ch., 13 mai 2014, *Google Spain SL, Google Inc. c. Agencia Española de protección de datos (AEPD), M. Costeja Gonzalez*, aff. C-131/12.

en œuvre du droit à l'oubli[48] et ce, alors même qu'aucun requérant ne l'avait demandé et qu'il ressortait des conclusions du rapporteur public que certaines questions au moins pouvaient directement être tranchées par le juge national, conformément à la jurisprudence selon laquelle il lui appartient de qualifier les faits et de tirer les conséquences de l'interprétation de la Cour[49]. Sur la portée géographique du droit au déréférencement cette fois, le Conseil d'Etat a transmis trois nouvelles questions préjudicielles à la Cour de justice par une décision du 19 juillet 2017[50]. Le Conseil d'Etat a aussi essayé, par ces renvois préjudiciels, d'infléchir la jurisprudence de la Cour de justice conformément à l'analyse qui était la sienne. Ce fut le cas, avec succès, par sa décision *France Nature Environnement* du 26 juin 2015[51] au sujet de la modulation dans le temps des effets des déclarations d'illégalité d'une disposition nationale contraire au droit de l'Union[52]. Il faut en outre relever que le juge constitutionnel français joue désormais également le jeu du dialogue européen et qu'il a, en 2013, transmis à la Cour de justice de l'Union européenne sa première question préjudicielle au sujet de l'interprétation de la décision-cadre relative au mandat d'arrêt européen[53].

La vigueur des débats et l'acuité des tensions qui ont vu le jour ou peuvent exister entre les juridictions nationales suprêmes et la Cour de justice de l'Union européenne ne doivent pas faire oublier que cette dernière a su faire preuve de mesure et d'esprit de conciliation dans de nombreux cas. Les décisions *Melki*[54], *Aranyosi*[55], ou même *Gauweiler*[56], témoignent de la volonté de la Cour de s'inscrire dans un véritable dialogue avec les plus hautes juridictions nationales[57]. L'une des solutions

---

[48] CE Ass., 24 février 2017, *Mme Chupin et autres*, n° 391000.

[49] CE Ass., 11 décembre 2006, *Société De Groot En Slot Allium*, n° 234560.

[50] CE, 19 juillet 2017, *Google Inc.*, n° 399922.

[51] CE, 26 juin 2015, *France Nature Environnement*, n° 360212.

[52] La CJUE a estimé qu'une juridiction nationale pouvait, lorsque le droit interne le permettait, limiter dans le temps les effets d'une déclaration d'illégalité d'une disposition nationale adoptée en méconnaissance du droit de l'Union à condition que cette limitation soit exceptionnelle et qu'elle s'impose par une considération impérieuse et compte tenu des circonstances spécifiques de l'affaire dont elle est saisie (CJUE, 28 juillet 2016, *Association France Nature Environnement*, aff. C-379/15, dont le Conseil d'Etat a tiré les conséquences dans CE, 3 novembre 2016, *France Nature Environnement*, n° 360212).

[53] CC, 4 avril 2013, n° 2013-314P QPC; CJUE, 30 mai 2013; CC, 14 juin 2013, *M. Jeremy F.*, n° 2013-314 QPC.

[54] CJUE, 22 juin 2010, *Melki et Abdeli*, aff. C-188/10 et C-189/10.

[55] CJUE, 15 avril 2016, *Pál Aranyosi et Robert Căldăraru*, aff. C-404/15 et C-695/15 PPU.

[56] CJUE, 16 juin 2015, *Gauweiler*, aff. C-62/14.

[57] C'est précisément cet esprit de dialogue et, plus encore, de responsabilité partagée et de confiance dans les juridictions suprêmes nationales qui a gravement fait défaut dans l'arrêt de la Cour de justice rendu le 4 octobre 2018 dans l'affaire C-416/17. Alors même que le Conseil d'Etat de France avait dans cette affaire tiré les conséquences d'un premier arrêt rendu à sa demande, à titre préjudiciel, par la Cour de justice et avait pris en compte une autre décision récente de cette juridiction, la Cour, par un simple arrêt de chambre, a cru pouvoir balayer son argumentation rigoureuse pour, de surcroît, déduire mécaniquement de l'analyse, selon elle erronée du Conseil d'Etat, un manquement à l'obligation de renvoi préjudiciel résultant de l'article 267, alinéa 3, TFUE. Elle a

aux conflits susceptibles de surgir réside, comme la décision *Aranyosi* l'a montré, dans l'élévation des standards européens de contrôle – en l'occurrence, des mandats d'arrêt européens –, de telle sorte que puisse être évité un écart entre la garantie nationale des droits fondamentaux – qui serait plus élevée – et la garantie européenne – qui serait plus lâche. Seul un dialogue régulier et approfondi des juridictions nationales suprêmes et des juridictions européennes peut permettre une articulation des ordres juridiques qui ne se fasse au détriment ni de l'autorité du droit de l'Union, ni de celle des normes suprêmes de droit national.

Ce dialogue peut être rugueux et sans complaisance. Il doit cependant se conclure dans la convergence et la concorde. Parce que nous sommes des juges, il nous appartient de respecter la hiérarchie des normes qui s'impose à nous, le mandat qui nous est donné par les textes fondateurs qui nous instituent et la légitimité démocratique dès lors que nous appliquons des lois qui sont l'expression de la souveraineté populaire. Parce que nous sommes des juges, nous sommes aussi des sages ou nous devons nous efforcer de l'être. Par conséquent, il ne peut être envisagé de se résoudre à des chocs frontaux et il convient de tout mettre en œuvre pour préserver les acquis de la construction européenne à laquelle les juges ont apporté une éminente contribution. Ce que nous avons entrepris ensemble depuis 60 ans, à tous les niveaux des pouvoirs publics, y compris au niveau juridictionnel, est plus important que ce qui peut séparer les juges nationaux et européens. Il nous faut par conséquent maintenir et faire progresser cette construction. Les techniques de conciliation et d'articulation entre les ordres et les principes juridiques doivent nous permettre de surmonter les difficultés conjoncturelles auxquelles nous pouvons être confrontés. Il y a toujours d'autres solutions à trouver que le refuge ou le repli dans l'absolutisation des principes et des jurisprudences nationales ou le glissement dans l'activisme judiciaire au niveau européen : l'élévation de la garantie des droits fondamentaux pour assurer des protections équivalentes aux plans européen et national en fait clairement partie. C'est ainsi que nous respecterons la primauté, l'unité et l'effectivité du droit de l'Union et que nous sauvegarderons les légitimes identités constitutionnelles nationales. Les premières et les secondes sont appelées à coexister durablement et pacifiquement et à se conjuguer dans une dynamique qui permettra de

---

ainsi fait prévaloir une lecture extrêmement rigide et même tatillonne de sa jurisprudence *CILFIT*, sans aucune évaluation de la gravité et de la portée dans le dossier de l'erreur de droit invoquée, ni référence aux circonstances particulières de cette affaire, ni, au plan formel, analyse étayée au regard des critères de l'arrêt *CILFIT*, dont nul n'avait jamais compris, bien au contraire, qu'il imposait, en matière de renvoi préjudiciel, une pareille contrainte aux juridictions nationales suprêmes. Outre que le constat d'un tel manquement devrait engendrer une multiplication des questions préjudicielles de nature à submerger la Cour de justice, ce n'est pas de cette manière que se construira dans la durée un dialogue des juges efficace, mûr et serein en Europe et que se renforcera l'autorité du droit de l'Union. Ce dialogue exige bien sûr que les juridictions nationales suprêmes respectent la Cour de justice de l'Union européenne. Il exige en retour que la Cour de justice de l'Union respecte les juridictions nationales suprêmes et, par conséquent, sache leur faire raisonnablement confiance et ne s'inscrive pas de manière automatique dans des rapports disciplinaires. Le présent article ayant été écrit en octobre 2017 n'a pu tenir compte, sauf dans cette note tardive, de ce regrettable épisode jurisprudentiel.

combler les angles morts de la mise en cohérence de nos systèmes de droit et de surmonter et régler les points de désaccord qui pourraient encore surgir.

References

Gaillet A (2016) Confiance et méfiance autour du mandat d'arrêt européen. AJDA, p 1112

Gazin F (2016) Droits fondamentaux. Mandat d'arrêt européen. Europe 6:192

Millet F-X (2012) Réflexions sur la notion de protection équivalente des droits fondamentaux. RFDA 2:307

Odinet G et Roussel S (2017) Renvoi préjudiciel: le dialogue des juges décomplexé. AJDA, p 740

A view from the Danish Supreme Court in light of the *Ajos* Judgment

Lars Hjortnæs

The *Ajos* judgment of the Danish Supreme Court of December 2016 has to many seemed to raise questions about the authority of EU Law because of the non-compliant result. I will try to briefly explain the Supreme Court's reasoning behind the judgment and the rather unheard-of non-compliance with a preliminary ruling from the CJEU. In this ruling the CJEU obliged the Supreme Court to give an EU principle prohibiting discrimination on grounds of age precedence over clear and contravening Danish law in a dispute between an employee and a private employer called Ajos. The dispute was about the entitlement of the employee to a special severance allowance. The CJEU told the Danish Supreme Court to rule *contra legem* and thus against the employer Ajos, as it would go against the said principle not to give the employee a severance allowance.

1 Brief introduction to the *Ajos* judgment and background of the case

I do not think that I will offend anyone by saying that this case was not a major one, at least not considering the size of the severance allowance at issue. However, as the saying goes, little strokes fell great oaks.

Ajos A/S is basically a quite ordinary private Danish business. In May 2009, it terminated the contract with an employee who had been with the company for more than 25 years. He was 60 years old at the time. Before he turned 50, he had joined a scheme that entitled him to old-age pension from Ajos, his employer, from the age of 60. He could have chosen to activate this pension when his contract was

L. Hjortnæs (✉)
Justice, Supreme Court, Copenhagen, Denmark
e-mail: LarsHjortnaes@Hoejesteret.dk

W. Heusel, J.-P. Rageade (eds.), *The Authority of EU Law*,
https://doi.org/10.1007/978-3-662-58841-3_7

terminated, but he did not. Instead, he transferred the pension scheme to a new employer later that year, thereby postponing his retirement.

As a general rule under the Danish Salaried Employees Act, an employee whose contract terminated after that many years of employment is entitled to a special severance allowance. However, in 2009, the Act contained an exception in cases where salaried employees "receive an old-age pension from the employer", and the employee has joined the pension scheme in question before attaining the age of 50. Since the early 1970s, this derogating provision had been interpreted by the courts, including the Supreme Court in several rulings, to the effect that this applied regardless of whether the employee actually activated the pension or not. What mattered was whether the employee was entitled to a pension.

Citing this provision, Ajos did not pay severance allowance to the terminated employee. And that was fully acceptable under the provisions of the Salaried Employees Act.

But, then the EU Court of Justice delivered the *Ole Andersen* judgment in 2010,[1] ruling that such derogating provision, which applied notwithstanding that the employee did not exercise his right to retire but chose to continue in another job, was in contravention of the prohibition of discrimination on grounds of age in the Employment Directive. The CJEU held that this amounted to disproportionate discrimination of older workers relative to young workers who had been employed for the same period of time by the same employer and also continued working. Unlike the older workers, they were entitled to receive severance allowance, because they had not yet reached retirement age.

On the face of it, this judgment was not relevant to Ajos, because Ajos is a private business and it is clear from the CJEU's case-law that directives do not have a direct effect on individuals. And the Salaried Employees Act had not been amended with retroactive effect.

But the terminated employee still chose to make another claim for payment of the severance allowance. Briefly put, his reasoning was as follows: The derogating rule in the Salaried Employees Act now also had to be viewed in the light of the fact that the CJEU in some judgments had held the prohibition of discrimination on grounds of age in the Employment Directive to be only a concrete expression of a general principle of EU law on the prohibition of discrimination on grounds of age, and that this principle may be directly applied in the relationships between private persons. And since the CJEU had now determined that the Danish Salaried Employees Act was contrary to the Directive, the rule also had to be inconsistent with the general principle of EU law. This meant that, if required, he could claim his severance allowance directly under this EU law principle. It was this disagreement between the terminated employee and Ajos A/S that ended up being brought before the Supreme Court, and is now known as the *Ajos* case.

To begin with, the Supreme Court stayed the appeal and referred two questions to the CJEU for a preliminary ruling. To provide the background to the case, the

[1] C-499/08 Ingeniørforeningen i Danmark, acting on behalf of *Ole Andersen*, v Region Syddanmark, 12.10.2010, ECLI:EU:C:2010:600.

Supreme Court explained that the state of the law according to the Danish Salaried Employees Act had been interpreted in the case-law, and that it would be *contra legem* to interpret the derogating provision in the Act such that it was brought in line with the Employment Directive as interpreted by the CJEU in the *Ole Andersen* case. Both questions sought to clarify the precise nature of the general principle under EU law prohibiting discrimination on grounds of age.

The Supreme Court's first question to the CJEU was whether the general principle has the same content and scope as the Employment Directive, including whether the derogating provision in the Salaried Employees Act was also contrary to the EU law principle, considering that it was contrary to the Employment Directive according to the CJEU's judgment in the *Ole Andersen* case. The gist of the CJEU's reply to this question was that the scope of the protection against discrimination on grounds of age conferred by the Employment Directive does not go beyond that afforded by that principle, meaning that the derogating provision in the Salaried Employees Act was also contrary to the principle.

The Supreme Court's second question was whether, if the CJEU responded to the first question as it actually did, it would be consistent with EU law to weigh the principle of EU law against the principle of legal certainty, which is another principle held by the CJEU to apply, and to conclude on that basis that the principle of legal certainty must take precedence over the principle prohibiting discrimination on grounds of age, such that Ajos in this case could rely on the national rule in the Salaried Employees Act applicable at that time. The CJEU's reply to that question was as follows: No, according to EU law, such balancing of different principles cannot lead to a citizen losing his or her protection under the EU law principle of the prohibition of discrimination. If the Danish Salaried Employees Act could not be interpreted in conformity with EU law, the Supreme Court would be obliged to disapply the provision in the Act that did not comply with this principle.

On this basis, the Supreme Court went on to make its final decision in the case. And it ruled in favour of Ajos, confirming that it was entitled to adhere to the then applicable Danish rule in the Salaried Employees Act and was not required to follow the principle of prohibition against discrimination on grounds of age.

So the Supreme Court did not do what the CJEU had told us to do. This is not something that happens every day, and it is no wonder that it has resounded in Denmark and created some stir in Europe. But *why* or perhaps rather *how* did the Supreme Court reach this conclusion?

In the Supreme Court's grounds, the principal issues in the case have been divided into two distinct subsections: (1) Could the company left by Ajos' now deceased employee be successful in its appeal pursuant to *Danish* law, that is, based on an interpretation of the Salaried Employees Act that is in conformity with EU law? And (2) If such interpretation was not possible, could the company then succeed based on directly applicable *EU law*, namely a principle under EU law prohibiting discrimination on the grounds of age with direct effect on the relationship between private persons? Of course, dividing the case into these two questions was obvious, if not necessary, due to the dissenting opinion in the case, which only concerned question (2); however, this is also an expression of the fundamentally dualistic approach applied in the judgment.

2 Interpreting Danish law in conformity with EU law

The first main point in the grounds was the issue of interpretation of Danish law in conformity with EU law.

It is probably quite easy to tell from the Supreme Court's reference order in the case that we had no idea that the question of interpretation of the Salaried Employees Act in conformity with EU law would become a key issue in this case. As mentioned earlier, the questions that the Supreme Court referred to the CJEU did not concern the obligation to interpret national law in conformity with EU law, but rather the scope and legal effect of the principle of prohibition of discrimination on grounds of age in EU law. However, in its reply, the CJEU to a certain extent called into question the Supreme Court's assumption in its questions for a preliminary ruling that a "*contra legem* situation" existed, meaning that the derogating provision in the Salaried Employees Act could not be interpreted in such a way that it was consistent with the EU principle. For this reason—and, of course, based on the company's and Ajos' final arguments in the case—the Supreme Court went into detail about the issue of interpretation in conformity with EU law and "*contra legem*" in the grounds for the final judgment.

As we know, according to the C JEU case law, the national courts must, as far as possible, in applying national law, interpret EU directives in the light of their wording and purpose in order to achieve the result sought by the directive. This has been established in several judgments, including the *Domínguez* judgment from 2012.[2] According to the CJEU,[3] the national courts' obligation to refer to the content of a directive when interpreting and applying the relevant rules of domestic law is limited by general principles of law (including the principle of legal certainty), and it cannot serve as the basis for an interpretation of national law *contra legem*. In paragraph 27 of the *Domínguez* judgment, the CJEU explained that national courts are required to do whatever lies within their jurisdiction to interpret national law in conformity with directives, taking the whole body of domestic law into consideration and applying the interpretative methods recognised by domestic law. It is therefore clear that the obligation to interpret national law in conformity with EU law cannot lead to an outcome that is "*contra legem*".

In the *Ajos* case, the CJEU reiterated these guidelines in paragraphs 30–32, which are also referenced in the Supreme Court's grounds. Danish courts would probably also essentially have come to this conclusion in accordance with the rules of international law, had the CJEU not said it.

[2] C-282/10 Maribel *Domínguez* v Centre informatique du Centre Ouest Atlantique, Préfet de la région Centre, 24.1.2012, ECLI:EU:C:2012:33 (paragraph 24).

[3] Cf. e.g. paragraph 25 of the *Domínguez* judgment.

In hindsight, the Supreme Court should probably have elaborated a bit more on this issue in its reference order in the *Ajos* case. We only wrote that "In Danish case-law, Section 2a(3) of the Salaried Employees Act (that is the derogating provision) has been consistently interpreted as meaning that…" etc. And then we wrote that "Against that background it would be *contra legem* to interpret Section 2a(3) in such a manner as to bring the provision into line with the Employment Directive as interpreted by the EU Court of Justice in the *Ole Andersen* case". We had thus only described *how* the derogating provision in Section 2a(3) of the Salaried Employees Act had been interpreted in practice, but we had not explained *why*, just as we had failed to mention that the Danish Parliament had based its subsequent amendments of the Act on this interpretation. This was probably why the CJEU in its judgment on the reference for a preliminary ruling felt called upon to explain in paragraphs 33 and 34 that the requirement to interpret national law in conformity with EU law entails the obligation for national courts to change its established case-law where necessary, if it is based on an interpretation of national law that is incompatible with the objectives of a directive, and that the Supreme Court could "not validly claim in the main proceedings that it is impossible for it to interpret the national provision at issue in a manner that is consistent with EU law by mere reason of the fact that it has consistently interpreted that provision in a manner that is incompatible with EU law".

Despite the use of the words "by mere reason of", this wording might well raise the question of whether the CJEU was actually trying to interfere more with the Supreme Court's concrete interpretation of the Danish legal provision.

In paragraphs 68–69 of Advocate General Bot's opinion, he stated that *contra legem* is an interpretation that contradicts the very *wording* of the national provision—and *only* that—and that this is not the situation in the case of the derogating provision in Section 2a(3) of the Salaried Employees Act. In the Advocate General's opinion, the Supreme Court would not be making any incursion into the sphere of competence of the national legislature by interpreting the Act in conformity with the Directive. If the European Court of Justice had come to the same conclusion, it cannot be ruled out that this could have given rise to questioning, among other things, the interaction with Article 267 of the Treaty on the Functioning of the European Union (TFEU) on the division of responsibilities between the CJEU and the national courts in connection with references for a preliminary ruling.

But, the CJEU did *not* come to the same conclusion—and one could indeed argue that only considering the wording in a possible *contra legem* situation and leaving everything else left out of the equation would have been a little difficult to reconcile with the Court's own general guideline, according to which all recognised interpretation methods must be applied in the interpretation of national legislation.

To this should, of course, be added that in paragraph 37 of the preliminary ruling, the CJEU said that, if the Supreme Court considers that it is impossible for it to interpret the national provision at issue in a manner that is consistent with EU law, it must disapply that provision. We could only take this to mean that the question of whether a *contra legem* situation existed was left open and up to the Supreme Court to decide.

We thus interpreted the CJEU's wording in paragraphs 33 and 34 of the preliminary ruling as the Court merely trying to convey something like "if you don't have a better argument than 'case-law', well, that just won't cut it". This meant that it would probably be uncontroversial if the Supreme Court with more elaborate grounds than in the reference order reached the same conclusion, namely that re-interpreting the derogating provision in the Salaried Employees Act in conformity with EU law would be *contra legem*.

In the Supreme Court's judgment, two things in particular were therefore added to the grounds:

- Firstly, that the Supreme Court's decision to maintain its interpretation of the rule in the Salaried Employees Act was—well, of course—not taken out of thin air, but was rather justified by the wording and the legislative material. This is a standard purposive interpretation, which is indisputably a recognised interpretation method under Danish law. Actually, purposive interpretation was applied in the very first Supreme Court judgment.[4]
- Secondly, it was added that the Danish Parliament when amending the Salaried Employees Act back in 1996, had taken account of a Supreme Court judgment of 1991, which confirmed the case-law that a person did not have a claim for severance allowance if he or she only had the right to, and thus the possibility of receiving, pension, and that the Parliament had decided not to change this state of play.

The Supreme Court also considered whether Section 1 of the Danish Act on Prohibition against Discrimination on the Labour Market, which prohibits indirect discrimination on grounds of age, among other things, could take precedence over the then current derogating provision in the Salaried Employees Act, so as to achieve an interpretation of the Salaried Employees Act that is consistent with the Directive. As described in the Supreme Court's grounds,[5] the problem with that solution was that when the Employment Directive's rules prohibiting discrimination on grounds of age were implemented in 2004 through the amendment of the Anti-Discrimination Act, the Danish Parliament expressly stated that Section 2a of the Salaried Employees Act on severance allowance should not be amended as a result of the Directive.

With these clarifications, the Supreme Court's conclusion was the same as that in the reference order, namely that the legal position was clear and that this was a *contra legem* situation.

If you are extremely well-versed in EU case-law, you may ask yourself why paragraph 13 in the CJEU's so-called *Björnekulla* judgment from 2004[6] is not mentioned in the Supreme Court's ruling. Some authors have interpreted this paragraph as implying that the CJEU has ruled that legislative material for national legislation cannot be used as basis for not interpreting the law in conformity with EU law. But

[4] Weekly Law Reports (UfR) 1973, p. 317.

[5] P. 38 of the judgment.

[6] C-371/02*Björnekulla* Fruktindustrier AB v Procordia Food AB, 29.4.2004, ECLI:EU:C:2004:275.

the CJEU has not chosen to refer to this paragraph in subsequent judgments. Why that is, I cannot say. One might however venture the guess that the reason is that the CJEU has repeatedly—both before and after the *Björnekulla* judgment—held that when assessing whether it is possible to interpret national law in conformity with a directive, *all* recognised principles of interpretation must be applied. Another reason might be that paragraph 13 actually dictated that the obligation to interpret national law in conformity with a directive applies notwithstanding "any contrary interpretation which *may* arise" from the legislative history behind the national rule". This is not the same as completely disregarding the legislative history.

The Supreme Court's decision on interpretation in conformity with the Directive and *contra legem* is largely parallel to the decision in the so-called *Holiday Act* Case.[7]

3 The binding effect of a principle of EU law

I come now to the question of the binding effect of the EU law principle on Ajos in a *contra legem* situation. Let me start by explaining that the majority of the Supreme Court uses slightly varying terminology on this binding effect in the grounds, such as "direct effect (thereby creating obligations) and [...] precedence over conflicting Danish law in a dispute between individuals", "direct effect in a dispute between individuals" and "directly applicable". All of these mean the same, namely the former, i.e. direct horizontal effect in a dispute between individuals. The only reason that the legally more ambiguous term "directly applicable" has been used in some places is to make it less wordy and vary the language a bit.

There are various ways to explain this part of the judgment. I have chosen to select four "focal points" in the majority's grounds in the judgment that I will then delve further into. The *first* focal point may be summed up as follows:

> It is for the CJEU to determine how to interpret EU law, including whether a rule under EU law has direct effect in a dispute between individuals and is thereby allowed to take precedence over a conflicting Danish rule. But whether a rule under EU law can be given direct effect in Danish law, as required under EU law, turns on Danish law, and first and foremost on the Accession Act.

You do not have to know much about constitutional law to see that the majority—which I will from now refer to as "the Supreme Court", with all due respect to the dissenting judge—is expressing a fundamentally dualistic approach to the case. However, in this context, there was a central *Treaty* provision—which there was no need to mention—namely Article 5(2) TEU, according to which "competences not conferred upon the Union *in the Treaties* remain with the Member States".

Accordingly, when considering the principal issue in the case concerning the effect of the EU law principle in a *contra legem* situation, it should be borne in mind

[7] Weekly Law Reports (UfR) 2014, p. 914.

that the EU Court of Justice has a sovereign right to determine the substance of EU law. And Denmark then has the dualistic system, according to which it must be considered whether—in this case—an EU law principle with direct effect in a dispute between individuals and taking precedence over national law has been adopted under Danish law. This dualistic approach is also applied in the Supreme Court's grounds in a previous judgment on the Maastricht Treaty.[8]

The *second* focal point may be summed up like this:

> The CJEU's case law must be construed as meaning that the principle prohibiting discrimination on grounds of age is inferred from legal sources outside the EU Treaties and does not have any basis in a specific Treaty provision, but still applies at Treaty level.

This is, of course, a pivotal point in the judgment. In the grounds, the Supreme Court quotes the central paragraph 22 in the CJEU's judgment on the reference for a preliminary ruling. This makes it clear that the CJEU does not link the principle prohibiting discrimination on grounds of age to the Treaties. The Court infers the principle from various international instruments and the constitutional traditions common to the Member States, but it does not refer to any EU Treaty. So this is an activity creating a legal effect that is completely detached from the Treaty. The Court mentions that the principle is now enshrined in Article 21 of the Charter, but this is to emphasise that a principle that prohibits discrimination on grounds of age actually *applies*—this principle is *not laid down* in Article 21. Also, there is no reference to the Lisbon Treaty in Article 6(3). On top of this, it should of course also be noted that the facts of the *Ajos* case took place before the Charter entered into force.

I have heard it described by some that the CJEU has, in effect, drafted an addendum to the Treaty with horizontal direct effect, and this description does indeed give you food for thought.

As mentioned earlier, the Supreme Court's reference order sought clarification of the EU law principle, and in its order, the Supreme Court referred to some opinions of Advocates General who had expressed reservations about the legal basis for the principle with direct horizontal effect which the CJEU established in, among others, the *Mangold* judgment[9] and now also in this case.

During the CJEU's hearing of the reference for a preliminary ruling, the Danish Government, among others, pointed to other ambiguities in the CJEU's previous judgments with regard to the precise nature of the principle and the basis for attributing direct horizontal effect to it. The Government strongly questioned the basis for attributing direct horizontal effect to the principle, stating that the CJEU has held that the Employment Directive gives concrete expression to the principle, while the CJEU at the same time has made it completely clear that directives are not directly applicable in the relationship between individuals. Its question was "Does this not indirectly make directives directly applicable?" It is fair to say that the CJEU now

[8] Weekly Law Review (UfR) 1998. p. 800 (in paragraph 9.5).

[9] C-144/04 *Mangold*, 22.11.2005, ECLI:EU:C:2005:709.

had an opportunity to account for the legal basis in the Treaty for the principle's horizontal effect—if there was one.

The *third* focal point is the judgment's analysis of the Danish Accession Act which may be summed up as follows:

> A situation in which a principle at Treaty level is to have direct effect in a dispute between individuals and be allowed to take precedence over conflicting Danish law, without the principle having any basis in a specific Treaty provision is not foreseen in the Accession Act. And, following a detailed analysis of the Act and its history, read in conjunction with the Treaty basis, the conclusion is that the Accession Act does not provide the legal basis to allow the unwritten principle prohibiting discrimination on grounds of age to take precedence over the then current provision in the Salaried Employees Act.

The problem becomes clear when considering that it is not foreseen in the Accession Act that a situation such as this could actually occur, where a principle at Treaty level according to EU law is to create obligations and thus be allowed to take precedence over conflicting Danish law in a dispute between individuals, without this principle being enshrined in any Treaty provision. The wording "not foreseen" is a bit unusual in this context, but the aim is to describe the fact that the legal situation that has now occurred is not something that anyone could have ever imagined.

The Supreme Court then goes on to explain this by delving into the possible arguments that could be used to show how the unwritten EU law principle with direct effect in disputes between individuals has been adopted in Danish law. Here, the Supreme Court plays it safe, you could say, and goes through some Treaty provisions which the CJEU did not even refer to as legal basis for the EU law principle with direct horizontal effect. And, of course, the reason for this approach is that the fundamental purpose of the Accession Act is to implement Treaty provisions in Danish law.

The Supreme Court starts by mentioning that the Danish legislature was aware from the outset that the provisions in the Treaties themselves can be directly applicable, and these provisions became part of Danish law through Section 3 of the Accession Act. However, this is about provisions in the Treaties, which is not the case here.

The Supreme Court then goes on to say that it is well known that the CJEU can develop and establish general principles that are to be found in the European Convention on Human Rights and similar Treaties and constitutional traditions common to the Member States. But what is important is that such general unwritten principles according to the Accession Act and its history may *not* be invoked in disputes between individuals. Here, the Supreme Court refers to the provision in Article 6(3) of the TEU, according to which the European Human Rights Convention constitutes general principles of the Union's law. As this provision was first introduced with the Maastricht Treaty, the view was taken that the provision was not among the provisions covered by Section 2 of the Accession Act on transfer of powers or Section 3 on Treaty provisions, which are directly applicable in Denmark. It was considered that the provision was a codification of the CJEU's case-law, according to which the Court, in examining a specific EU legal act, ascertains whether the act infringes rights laid down in, for example, the ECHR or in the Member States' constitutions. And in subsequent amendments to the Accession Act, it was confirmed that the provision is not covered by Section 2 or 3. In its judgment on the reference for a preliminary ruling, the CJEU uses wording similar to that in Article 6(3), but the Court does not refer to the provision, and this must be taken to mean that the CJEU also believes that Article 6(3) makes it possible to develop principles, but not to give them horizontal effect and allow them to take precedence over national law to the detriment of citizens. And, as mentioned earlier, everything in the history behind the Accession Act discussing fundamental rights etc. is about protecting citizens against the State and the EU institutions, and not about protecting citizens against each other. So, there is no mention of a horizontal direct effect, and it is fair to say that there is, what can best be described as, a quantum leap between bestowing rights on citizens and bestowing obligations on them.

The Supreme Court then goes on to look at Article 6(1) TEU, and on Article 21(1) of the Charter, which prohibit discrimination on grounds of age, among other things. According to TEU Article 6(1), the Charter does not extend in any way the competences of the Union as defined in the Treaties. And it follows from Article 51 of the Charter that the Charter is addressed to the institutions and bodies of the Union and to the Member States only when they are implementing Union law. The Charter does not establish any new power or task, or modify powers and tasks defined by the Treaties. That the Charter does not extend the EU's competences was also made clear in the report from the Danish Ministry of Foreign Affairs to the Danish Parliament in connection with the amendment of the Accession Act after the adoption of the Lisbon Treaty. And the Supreme Court also mentions that it is expressly stated in the Minister for Foreign Affairs' answer to a question from the Parliament's European Affairs Committee concerning the bill amending the Accession Act that the Charter does *not* entail legal obligations for the citizens.

It is against this background that the Supreme Court reached the conclusion that the Accession Act has not brought the EU law principle prohibiting discrimination on grounds of age into Danish law with direct horizontal effect.

There was, however, the small snag that the direct effect of the principle in disputes between individuals was established by the CJEU in the so-called *Mangold* judgment in 2005. This judgment was from the time before the most recent amendment of the Accession Act in 2008. You could maybe say that this judgment had to somehow be part of the amendment. According to the Supreme Court, on that ground alone that the amendment in 2008 was a result of the Lisbon Treaty only, and the *Mangold* judgment was not mentioned anywhere in the legislative material to the Act, the judgment cannot give rise to the Accession Act subsequently being interpreted differently in this respect. So, you could say that the Danish Parliament could not be caught out just because it had not taken the *Mangold* judgment into account. Further in support of this, the Supreme Court added that there was a plausible explanation for the judgment not being mentioned in the legislative material, namely that in the *Mangold* judgment the CJEU had not decided on or considered the issue of whether EU law permits not setting aside conflicting national law by way of balancing the principle prohibiting discrimination on grounds of age against the principle of legal certainty for the citizens. Incidentally, this point was also raised by the Danish Government in its submission to the CJEU in the *Ajos* case.

I would like to mention one further Treaty provision that one could have imagined the CJEU to refer to as legal basis, namely Article 19 TFEU on legal acts to combat discrimination on grounds of age. However, this provision grants authority to the Council, and, on top of that, it requires unanimity. Some might venture the guess that the CJEU knows that it would not likely get away with effectively transferring this power to itself. In any event, the Court has opted not to refer to this provision, just as the Supreme Court has not found it necessary to mention it in its grounds.

I would also like to add that Ajos argued before the Supreme Court that giving the unwritten EU law principle direct effect in Denmark would run counter to a Danish principle of legal certainty, which could allegedly be inferred directly from Section 3 of the Danish Constitution. However, this is not mentioned anywhere in the Supreme Court's grounds either.

In the light of the dissenting opinion in the Supreme Court's judgment, it is of course relevant to ask in which respect the majority thought that the *Ajos* case differed from the Supreme Court's judgment in the *Maastricht* case of 1998 with regard to the significance of the CJEU's activity creating a legal effect. This is only provided indirectly in the argumentation, you might say. To put it very simply, the difference is that, in the *Maastricht* judgment,[10] the Supreme Court spoke about this CJEU activity "when interpreting the *Treaty*". In connection with the adoption and subsequent amendments of the Accession Act, account was taken of the fact that the EU Court of Justice adopts a dynamic interpretation of Treaty provisions; however, this interpretation is anchored in these provisions. As mentioned earlier, in the *Ajos* case the activity creating legal effect is detached from the Treaty.

My final comments for this focal point are that I have heard the argument that the Supreme Court should have interpreted not only the Salaried Employees Act, but also the Accession Act in conformity with EU law, including for example by reading the preparatory material as being merely descriptive and not legally normative. Here, I think I can only confirm that the majority's grounds contain nothing to the effect that the Supreme Court has felt obliged to interpret the Accession Act itself in a special way that is consistent with EU law.

So, to sum up, the Supreme Court's words "is not foreseen" are really key, because they reflect that no-one in the Danish legislature (or society at large) had ever, nor could have imagined even in their wildest fantasies that the CJEU would think of making a principle not enshrined in any Treaty provision create obligations for private citizens by requiring it to take precedence over contravening national law in disputes between individuals. In other words, no-one had ever thought it possible or even given it a thought that the CJEU would in effect draft an addendum to the Treaty, as it were, despite TFEU Article 19 and not allowing for the EU principle of legal certainty to play any role when deciding whether to apply the non-discrimination principle directly and horizontally.

---

[10] UfR 1998, p. 800.

The legislative history showed this. And so, under these very unusual circumstances the Danish courts' usual method of "consistent" interpretation of Danish law in order to fulfil Denmark's international obligations was not relevant or not sufficient.

The *fourth* and last focal point is the most publicly quoted part of the judgment:

> The Supreme Court would be acting outside the scope of its powers as a judicial authority if it were to disapply the provision in the Salaried Employees Act in this situation.

You could say that, after the previous conclusion on the legal basis, this sentence is superfluous—it does not add anything that has not already been said by the Supreme Court. And this is quite true. The sentence really just says that, according to Section 3 of the Constitution, Danish courts are only the judicial authority, and also that the judges must be governed solely by the law according to Section 64. And as there was no legal basis in this case to not comply with the derogating provision in the Salaried Employees Act, well, the rest is self-explanatory.

But with the attention that this sentence has attracted, it would be fair to say that it served its purpose which is not to prescribe, but primarily to show what is at stake and which league that this case is in.

4 Perspectives

I have heard some critics "accuse" the *Ajos* judgment of effectively introducing a new Danish opt-out from the EU. To this I will just say that there is indeed a difference between something that the Danish Parliament and people have decided to opt out of, and something that the Parliament, and perhaps also the people, have still to decide to opt in to.

The *Ajos* judgment cannot be perceived as taking an anti-EU stance in any respect. The Danish Supreme Court of course has no opinion whatsoever on the optimal role and competence of the CJEU. The judgment only maintains that, if Danish courts are to refrain from basing their judgments on the applicable Danish law, this must be something that has been allowed by the Danish legislature, it cannot be decided by the CJEU alone.

The *Ajos* judgment thus reaffirms the dualistic Danish constitutional system. In this particular case this was to the effect that whereas the Danish legislator through the Accession Act has certainly allowed dynamic Treaty interpretations by the CJEU to impact on Danish law, and whereas Denmark through the Accession Act has also allowed "unwritten" principles to guide Danish authorities when implementing Community or Union law, Denmark has not yet allowed the CJEU to make its own rules in this field detached from the Treaties and give them precedence over contravening Danish law in disputes between private citizens.

The Supreme Court's grounds for non-compliance are not based on an "ultra vires" assumption. Some have claimed, though, that indirectly it is even worse because the Supreme Court in effect says that the CJEU has acted so much on its own that it is even beyond Denmark's accession—or in other words: "Ultra vires" comes into play within the scope of accession, and you are not even within that scope! This may be something to think about.

Lifting my eyes from the *Ajos* judgment, I would like to offer a few comments on the general issue of "judicial activism", "dynamic" interpretations and legitimacy. By judicial activism I mean that a court extends its own competence without the usual basis in written law or legislative history.

I think that judicial activism is less an inherent risk of any Supreme Court or international court because it is supreme or international than it has to do with the legal framework under which the court operates. The task of the CJEU is to interpret a Treaty which lays down specific aims on a constitutional level guiding the way in which the Union should develop, thus making dynamic interpretations more natural. The Danish constitution, on the contrary, is more like a blank sheet of paper in that sense—it does not in the same way lay down specific political aims guiding the way society should develop. So, basically it is understandable (or even necessary) that the CJEU interprets the Treaties and EU law dynamically. I do not think that in my country the authority of EU law is being questioned because of dynamic interpretations per se.

This is—perhaps—slightly different at times with regard to the legitimacy of certain decisions. For instance, it created some dismay when the CJEU in the *Pereda* case[11] dynamically disregarded an obvious reference to national law and national practice in the Directive in question and invented, so to speak, a new annual leave-regime which the Directive said nothing about and which went against an annual leave practice solidly established on the Danish labour market since 1938. Such dynamism might put the general trust and respect for the authority of EU law at risk, since it may seem to disregard fundamental needs both for legal certainty and for democratic influence. In other words, the dynamic interpretation can become so excessive that it may challenge the popular trust in the EU's respect for national democratic processes and balanced compromises.

[11] C-277/08 Pereda v Madrid Movilidad SA, judment of 10.9.2009, ECLI:EU:C:2009:542.

EuGH-EGMR-BVerfG: Von der Multipolarität zum Verbund der Gerichtsbarkeiten im Bereich des Grundrechtsschutzes

Christine Langenfeld

1 Vorbemerkung

Das Zusammenwirken von Bundesverfassungsgericht, dem Gerichtshof der Europäischen Union (EuGH) sowie dem Europäischen Gerichtshof für Menschenrechte (EGMR) lässt sich als eine prozesshafte Entwicklung beschreiben. Zentral für das Verhältnis dieser Höchstgerichte ist der Begriff des (Verfassungs-)Gerichtsverbundes.[1] Hierbei beschreibt der Begriff „Verbund" nicht etwa den materiellen Zustand einer einmal erreichten Einheit, sondern steht für den Dialog und die Kooperation der genannten Gerichte. Im Rahmen dieses Verbundes besteht eine Reihe prozeduraler und materieller Vorkehrungen[2], die das Verhältnis der Gerichte und der verschiedenen Rechtsschichten, d.h. des Verfassungsrechts, des Unionsrechts und des Konventionsrechts zueinander regulieren. Der Präsident des Bundesverfassungsgerichts *Andreas Voßkuhle*, hat den komplexen Tatbestand folgendermaßen zusammengefasst: Der Begriff des Verbundes

> "ermöglicht [...] den Verzicht auf räumliche, stark vereinfachende Bilder wie ‚Gleichordnung, Über- und Unterordnung'. Stattdessen eröffnet er die Möglichkeit einer differenzierten Umschreibung anhand unterschiedlicher Ordnungsgesichtspunkte wie Einheit, Differenz

Die Autorin ist Richterin des Bundesverfassungsgerichts und Direktorin der Abteilung für Staatsrecht des Instituts für Öffentliches Recht an der Georg-August-Universität Göttingen.

[1] Vgl. Voßkuhle (2010), S. 1 ff.

[2] Insofern ist auch von materieller und prozessualer bzw. prozeduraler „Kohärenzsteuerung" die Rede, siehe Voßkuhle (2010), S. 4 f.; Lenaerts and Hartmann (2017), S. 323.

C. Langenfeld (✉)
Georg-August-Universität, Göttingen, Germany

Judge, Bundesverfassungsgericht, Karlsruhe, Germany
e-mail: clangenfeld@jura.uni-goettingen.de

W. Heusel, J.-P. Rageade (eds.), *The Authority of EU Law*,
https://doi.org/10.1007/978-3-662-58841-3_8

und Vielfalt, Homogenität und Pluralität, Abgrenzung, Zusammenspiel und Verschränkung. Im Gedanken des Verbundes sind Eigenständigkeit, Rücksichtnahme und Fähigkeit zu gemeinsamem Handeln gleichermaßen angelegt."[3]

2 Der Gerichtsverbund im Bereich des Grundrechtsschutzes – Marksteine der Rechtsprechung des Bundesverfassungsgerichts

2.1 Die Herausforderung: Gewährleistung eines gemeineuropäischen Grundrechtsschutzes

Innerhalb der Europäischen Union sind drei Normschichten zu unterscheiden. In Art. 6 EUV wird dies besonders plastisch. Danach gelten zum einen die Grundrechte, wie sie in der Europäischen Menschenrechtskonvention (EMRK) verbürgt sind und wie sie sich aus den gemeinsamen Verfassungsüberlieferungen der Mitgliedstaaten ergeben, als allgemeine Rechtsgrundsätze des Unionsrechts gemäß Art. 6 Abs. 3 EUV. Hinzugetreten ist 2009 die Grundrechtecharta (GR-Charta), die gemäß Art. 6 Abs. 1 EUV denselben Rang beansprucht wie das Primärrecht und neben den hergebrachten Grundrechten eine Reihe weiterer „moderner" Grundrechte gewährleistet. Die Charta enthält in Artt. 52 und 53 Bestimmungen, die die Auslegung der EU-Grundrechte mit Blick auf die EMRK-Grundrechte und die gemeinsamen Verfassungsüberlieferungen und Grundrechtsstandards der Mitgliedstaaten regeln und hierbei ein möglichst hohes Schutzniveau garantieren möchten. Und schließlich gelten die Grundrechte, die durch die Verfassungen der EU-Mitgliedstaaten, in Deutschland durch das Grundgesetz, garantiert sind und von den nationalen Verfassungsgerichten durchgesetzt werden. Es besteht also kein Mangel an Grundrechtsgarantien. Man ist verführt, mit *Christian Kohler* von einem „embarras de richesses"[4] zu sprechen.

Der gerichtliche Schutz dieser auf mehreren Ebenen gewährleisteten Grundrechte ist komplex und mehrspurig ausgestaltet.[5] Die Herausforderung liegt darin, zur Gewährleistung eines konsistenten Grundrechtsschutzes die verschiedenen Grundrechtsschichten voneinander abzugrenzen, zugleich aber auch aufeinander zu beziehen und miteinander zu verschränken. Im europäischen Gerichtsverbund geschieht dies über Instrumente prozessualer bzw. prozeduraler und materieller „Kohärenzsteuerung"[6]. Die Einbeziehung von EuGH und EGMR durch das Bundesverfassungsgericht erfolgt in unterschiedlicher Weise: In Hinblick auf den EuGH vor allen Dingen im Wege des Vorabentscheidungsverfahrens (Art. 267 AEUV), die Rechtsprechung des EGMR wird nach dem Grundsatz der

[3] Voßkuhle (2010), S. 3.
[4] Kohler (2002), S. 375.
[5] Kohler (2002), S. 375.
[6] Siehe Voßkuhle (2010), S. 4 f.; Lenaerts and Hartmann (2017), S. 323.

Völkerrechtsfreundlichkeit durch die Einpassung in das einfache Recht und die Heranziehung als Auslegungshilfe für die Grundrechte des Grundgesetzes und seine rechtsstaatlichen Prinzipien berücksichtigt. Die Marksteine dieser Rechtsprechung sollen im Folgenden näher entfaltet werden.

2.2 Bundesverfassungsgericht und EuGH - von der Bipolarität zum Gerichtsverbund

2.2.1 Vorrang des Unionsrechts und Europarechtsfreundlichkeit des Grundgesetzes

Grundlage für die Funktionsfähigkeit des Rechtsprechungsverbundes innerhalb der EU ist die Anerkennung des Vorrangs des Unionsrechts und seiner unmittelbaren Geltung.[7] Der Vorrang gilt nach Maßgabe von Art. 23 Abs. 1 GG indes nicht grenzenlos; die Ausnahmen von diesem Prinzip sind allerdings eng. Die vom Bundesverfassungsgericht insoweit in Anspruch genommenen Kontrollbefugnisse sind entsprechend dem Grundsatz der Europarechtsfreundlichkeit, den das Gericht aus dem in Art. 23 Abs. 1 S. 1 GG verankerten Verfassungsauftrag, an der europäischen Integration mitzuwirken, abgeleitet hat[8], „zurückhaltend und europarechtsfreundlich“[9] auszuüben. Hieraus folgt, dass das Bundesverfassungsgericht vor einer Entscheidung über die Unanwendbarkeit eines Unionsrechtsaktes in Deutschland den EuGH im Wege des Vorabentscheidungsverfahrens anruft, um über die Auslegung und Gültigkeit der betreffenden Norm zu entscheiden. Bei der anschließenden Entscheidung legt das Gericht seiner Prüfung jene Auslegung zugrunde, die das Unionsrecht durch den EuGH erfahren hat.

2.2.2 Sicherung eines adäquaten Grundrechtsschutzes im Rechtsprechungsverbund – zur Rechtsprechung des Bundesverfassungsgerichts

Der Solange-Vorbehalt - die vertikale Dimension

Seit Beginn der europäischen Integration hat sich der Grundrechtsschutz als besonders bedeutsames Feld des gerichtlichen Zusammenwirkens, aber auch der wechselseitigen Selbstbehauptung dargestellt. In der berühmten *Solange-I*-Entscheidung aus dem Jahr 1974[10] hatte der Zweite Senat des

---

[7] Grundlegend EuGH, Rs. 26/62 *van Gend & Loos* – Slg. 1963, S. 1; Rs. C-6/64 *Costa/ENEL* – Slg. 1964, S. 1251; anerkennend und zugleich begrenzend BVerfGE 73, 339 (375 f.).

[8] BVerfGE 123, 267 (346 f.).

[9] BVerfGE 126, 286 (303).

[10] BVerfGE 37, 271.

Bundesverfassungsgerichts die Zulässigkeit einer fachgerichtlichen Vorlage im Rahmen eines konkreten Normenkontrollverfahrens (Art. 100 Abs. 1 S. 1 GG) und damit seine eigene Zuständigkeit mit Verweis auf die seinerzeit noch für lückenhaft befundene gemeinschaftsrechtliche Grundrechtsordnung bejaht und dabei die bekannte Formel aufgestellt:

> "Solange der Integrationsprozeß der Gemeinschaft nicht so weit fortgeschritten ist, daß das Gemeinschaftsrecht auch einen von einem Parlament beschlossenen und in Geltung stehenden formulierten Katalog von Grundrechten enthält, der dem Grundrechtskatalog des Grundgesetzes adäquat ist, ist nach Einholung der in Art. 177 des Vertrags [des EWG-Vertrags; Anm. d. Verf.] geforderten Entscheidung des Europäischen Gerichtshofs die Vorlage eines Gerichts der Bundesrepublik Deutschland an das Bundesverfassungsgericht im Normenkontrollverfahren zulässig und geboten, wenn das Gericht die für es entscheidungserhebliche Vorschrift des Gemeinschaftsrechts in der vom Europäischen Gerichtshof gegebenen Auslegung für unanwendbar hält, weil und soweit sie mit einem der Grundrechte des Grundgesetzes kollidiert."[11]

Die im Senat umstrittene Entscheidung formulierte indes vier Vorbehalte für die nationale Grundrechtskontrolle: Europäische Rechtsakte konnten nicht direkt angegriffen werden, d.h. nur europarechtlich determinierte nationale Akte konnten tauglicher Prüfungsgegenstand sein[12]; das vorlegende Fachgericht musste vorab dem Europäischen Gerichtshof vorgelegt haben[13]; das Bundesverfassungsgericht konnte bei Vorliegen einer Grundrechtsverletzung nicht die Ungültigkeit, sondern nur die Unanwendbarkeit des europäischen Rechtsakts feststellen[14] und, zuletzt, das Fachgericht im Ausgangsverfahren durfte letzteres nicht, d.h. das Bundesverfassungsgericht reklamierte das „Verwerfungsmonopol“[15] für sich. Der verfassungsgerichtliche Zugriff seitens der Senatsmehrheit[16] beruhte dabei auf der Prämisse, dass der damals maßgebliche Art. 24 GG es nicht erlaube, „die Grundstruktur der Verfassung, auf der ihre Identität beruht, [...] zu ändern.“[17] Zur Verfassungsidentität, die damit schon lange vor der Lissabon-Entscheidung als Integrationsgrenze erkannt wurde, gehörte danach „der Grundrechtsteil des Grundgesetzes“, der nur dann gegenüber gemeinschaftsrechtlichen Akten außer Anwendung gelassen werden konnte, soweit das Anwendungsvorrang beanspruchende europäische Recht – so der Senat damals – ebenfalls über einen „kodifizierten Grundrechtskatalog[s], dessen Inhalt ebenso zuverlässig und für die Zukunft unzweideutig feststeht wie der des Grundgesetzes“, verfügen würde.[18]

---

[11] BVerfGE 37, 271 (285).

[12] BVerfGE 37, 271 (284 f.).

[13] BVerfGE 37, 271 (285).

[14] BVerfGE 37, 271 (281 f.).

[15] BVerfGE 37, 271 (284).

[16] Vgl. die Sondervoten der Richter *Rupp*, *Hirsch* und *Wand*, die aus der Autonomie des Gemeinschaftsrechts die Unzulässigkeit des Normenkontrollantrags ableiteten, in BVerfGE 37, 271 (291 ff.).

[17] BVerfGE 37, 271 (279).

[18] Siehe BVerfGE 37, 271 (280).

In dem zwölf Jahre später ergangenen *Solange-II*-Beschluss[19] verlangte der Senat indes keinen kodifizierten Katalog auf europäischer Ebene mehr und ließ es genügen, dass der EuGH die Gemeinschaftsgrundrechte auf Grundlage der Verfassungsüberlieferungen der Mitgliedstaaten und der alle Mitgliedstaaten bindenden EMRK im Sinne allgemeiner Rechtsgrundsätze richterrechtlich gewährleistete.[20] Die „fallweise" erfolgende Grundrechtsentwicklung war trotz noch zu konstatierender Lücken im Ergebnis grundgesetzadäquat und zwar mit Blick auf die beim Gerichtshof durch das Bundesverfassungsgericht inzwischen beobachtete „prinzipielle Haltung [...] gegenüber der Grundrechtsgebundenheit der Gemeinschaft".[21] Mit anderen Worten: Obwohl der europarechtliche Grundrechtskanon seinerzeit noch nicht perfekt erschien, gab am Ende das institutionelle Vertrauen den Ausschlag und bildete die eigentliche Grundlage für die zweite, bis heute[22] prinzipiell gültige Formel:

> "Solange die Europäischen Gemeinschaften, insbesondere die Rechtsprechung des Gerichtshofs der Gemeinschaften einen wirksamen Schutz der Grundrechte gegenüber der Hoheitsgewalt der Gemeinschaften *generell* [Hervorh. d. Verf.] gewährleisten, der dem vom Grundgesetz als unabdingbar gebotenen Grundrechtsschutz im wesentlichen gleichzuachten ist, zumal den Wesensgehalt der Grundrechte generell verbürgt, wird das Bundesverfassungsgericht seine Gerichtsbarkeit über die Anwendbarkeit von abgeleitetem Gemeinschaftsrecht, das als Rechtsgrundlage für ein Verhalten deutscher Gerichte und Behörden im Hoheitsbereich der Bundesrepublik Deutschland in Anspruch genommen wird, nicht mehr ausüben und dieses Recht mithin nicht mehr am Maßstab der Grundrechte des Grundgesetzes überprüfen; entsprechende Vorlagen nach Art. 100 Abs. 1 GG sind somit unzulässig."[23]

Der Solange II-Vorbehalt bedeutet, dass eine vorbehaltlose Prüfung deutscher Umsetzungsakte in Hinblick auf den Vorrang des Unionsrechts am Maßstab der Grundrechte des Grundgesetzes nur insoweit erfolgen kann, als sie sich im Bereich unionsrechtlich nicht determinierter Umsetzungsspielräume bewegen. Im Urteil zur Vorratsdatenspeicherung aus dem Jahre 2010 hat das Bundesverfassungsgericht indes auch die grundrechtliche Überprüfung von Vorschriften zugelassen, die auf zwingendem Sekundärrecht beruhten, um eine Vorlage an den EuGH zu ermöglichen.[24] Würde dieser den Sekundärrechtsakt (etwa wegen Verstoßes gegen europäische Grundrechte) für nichtig erklären, wäre der Weg für eine Überprüfung des deutschen Umsetzungsgesetzes am Maßstab der deutschen Grundrechte wieder frei. Allerdings muss es sich um entscheidungserhebliches Unionsrecht handeln, d.h. es muss für den Ausgang des verfassungsgerichtlichen Verfahrens auf die Auslegung bzw. Wirksamkeit des Unionsrechts ankommen. Dies ist dann nicht der Fall, wenn die geforderte Umsetzung des Sekundärrechts ohne Grundrechtsverstoß

[19] BVerfGE 73, 339.

[20] Vgl. BVerfGE 73, 339 (378).

[21] Siehe BVerfGE 73, 339 (383).

[22] Bestätigt durch BVerfGE 102, 147.

[23] BVerfGE 73, 339 (387).

[24] BVerfGE 125, 260 (307).

möglich ist.[25] Dann liegt in der Feststellung der Grundrechtskonformität keine Beeinträchtigung der Wirksamkeit des Unionsrechts. Würde hingegen die geforderte Umsetzung mit einer Verletzung der Grundrechte einhergehen, käme es darauf an, ob der zugrunde liegende Sekundärrechtsakt gültig ist und damit am Vorrang des Unionsrechts auch gegenüber den Grundrechten des Grundgesetzes teilhat. Über die Frage der Gültigkeit kann nur der EuGH entscheiden.

Außerhalb des Anwendungsbereichs der Unionsgrundrechte bleiben die Grundrechtssphären ohnedies klar getrennt. Wie weit jener Anwendungsbereich reicht, hängt wiederum davon ab, ob der Durchführungsbegriff in Art. 51 Abs. 1 S. 1 GR-Charta, der die Anwendbarkeit der Unionsgrundrechte dem Grunde nach auslöst, eher extensiv oder restriktiv ausgelegt wird. Nach Ansicht des EuGH ist der Anwendungsbereich auch dann eröffnet, wenn es um die Beschränkung einer Grundfreiheit durch eine nationale Maßnahme geht („ERT-Konstellation"), d.h. in einem Bereich, der vom Unionsgesetzgeber ausdrücklich nicht harmonisiert worden ist, und insofern für die Mitgliedstaaten noch Raum lässt für die Geltendmachung von zwingenden Erfordernissen („Cassis-Formel") zur Einschränkung der Grundfreiheiten.[26] Gegen eine Anwendung der nationalen Grundrechte können in diesen Fällen keine Einwände bestehen, denn verstößt eine beschränkende Maßnahme gegen ein nationales Grundrecht, so dient dies gerade der Effektivität des Unionsrechts, welches beschränkende Maßnahmen gerade nicht einfordert; hier laufen Grundfreiheit und nationales Grundrecht also parallel. Liegt ein Grundrechtsverstoß indessen nicht vor, hindert dies den EuGH wiederum nicht daran, die nationale Maßnahme für unvereinbar mit dem Unionsrecht zu erklären und damit die für grundgesetzkonform gehaltene nationale Maßnahme zu beseitigen.

Anders lag die Konstellation hingegen in der *Åkerberg-Fransson*-Entscheidung, in der der EuGH einen denkbar weiten Zugriff bei der Auslegung von Art. 51 Abs. 1 S. 1 GR-Charta wählte und auf diesem Wege Umsetzungsverpflichtungen der Mitgliedstaaten begründete, die dem Regime der Grundrechtecharta unterfielen.[27] Setzte sich dieser Ansatz dauerhaft durch, hätte dies zur Folge, dass praktisch jedes mitgliedstaatliche Handeln mit Bezug zum Unionsrecht am Maßstab der Grundrechtecharta zu messen wäre. Die Kritik an dieser Rechtsprechung fiel deutlich aus[28]. Rund ein Jahr später kam der EuGH dann auch zu einer deutlich restriktiveren Interpretation von Art. 51 Abs. 1 S. 1 GR-Charta.[29] Insgesamt aber fehlt es

---

[25] BVerfGE 125, 260 (308).

[26] EuGH, Rs. C-260/89, *ERT* – Slg. 1991, I-2951 (2963). Dazu m.w.Nw. zur Kritik Franzius (2015), S. 386 f; vgl. zur sog. „Cassis-Formel" EuGH, Rs. 120/78 *Cassis de Dijon* – Slg. 1979, S. 649.

[27] Vgl. Rs. C-671/10 *Åkerberg Fransson*, EU:C:2013:105, Rdnr. 19: „in allen unionsrechtlich geregelten Fallgestaltungen" bzw. wenn die nationale „Vorschrift in den Geltungsbereich des Unionsrechts fällt".

[28] Vgl. etwa bei Britz (2015), S. 278; Voßkuhle (2016), S. 164 f.; Ludwigs and Sikora (2017), S. 385 ff.; Safferling (2014), S. 545 ff.; Mannefeld (2017), S. 158 f.

[29] Vgl. Rs. C-206/13 *Siragusa*, EU:C:2013:124, Rdnrn. 20 ff. Der Gerichtshof hält an der Definition aus der vorgenannten Entscheidung fest, erweitert diese aber, unter Rückgriff auf weitere Entscheidungen, um einschränkende Merkmale; danach ist in Hinblick auf die nationale Vorschrift ergänzend „zu prüfen, ob mit ihr eine Durchführung einer Bestimmung des Unionsrechts bezweckt

an einer einheitlichen Linie.[30] In Reaktion auf das Urteil des EuGH in *Åkerberg-Fransson* hatte das Bundesverfassungsgericht im Urteil zur Anti-Terror-Datei deutlich gemacht, dass jene Entscheidung nicht so verstanden werden könne, dass jeder sachliche Bezug einer Regelung zum abstrakten Anwendungsbereich des Unionsrechts oder rein tatsächliche Auswirkungen auf dieses für eine Bindung der Mitgliedstaaten an die Grundrechtecharta ausreiche.[31] In der Tat wäre eine uferlose Ausweitung des Anwendungsbereichs der Charta einem differenzierten und zielgenauen Grundrechtsschutz innerhalb der Europäischen Union nicht dienlich. Die notwendige Sachnähe des Grundrechtsschutzes, gerade auch in mehrpoligen Grundrechtsverhältnissen, lässt sich kaum durch eine umfassende Hochzonung von der nationalen auf die supranationale Ebene und einer Zentralisierung ebendort bewerkstelligen.

Die menschenwürdesichernde Identitätskontrolle – die (neue) horizontale Dimension

Das Vorhandensein des prinzipiellen Vertrauens in die Leistungsfähigkeit des unionsrechtlichen Grundrechtsschutzes nach Maßgabe der Solange II-Formel wurde durch die Entscheidung des Bundesverfassungsgerichts zum Europäischen Haftbefehl im Jahr 2015[32] nicht grundsätzlich in Frage gestellt, zugleich wurde allerdings markiert, dass unionsrechtlich eingefordertes gegenseitiges Vertrauen in die Rechtsstaatlichkeit anderer Mitgliedstaaten im Rahmen der Kooperation im Raum der Freiheit, der Sicherheit und des Rechts Grenzen kennen muss, sofern der grundrechtliche Realbefund eine Verletzung der Menschenwürde besorgen lässt. Es handelt sich hier um eine Konstellation, in der es um den Schutz der Unionsgrundrechte zwischen den Mitgliedstaaten geht. In der Literatur wird in diesem Zusammenhang verschiedentlich von einem horizontalen Solange-Prinzip gesprochen: Solange alle Mitgliedstaaten wesentliche Unionsgrundrechte befolgen, gilt zwischen den Mitgliedstaaten das Prinzip des gegenseitigen Vertrauens im Raum der Freiheit, der Sicherheit und des Rechts.[33]

Die Einhaltung der Grenzen dieses Vertrauens wird durch das Bundesverfassungsgericht prozessual über die Identitätskontrolle[34] abgesichert. Mit dem Instrument der Identitätskontrolle wird die grundrechtliche Überprüfbarkeit unionsrechtlich determinierter nationaler Rechtsakte, hier eines gerichtlichen

wird, welchen Charakter diese Regelung hat und ob mit ihr andere als die unter das Unionsrecht fallenden Ziele verfolgt werden, selbst wenn sie das Unionsrecht mittelbar beeinflussen kann, sowie ferner, ob es eine Regelung des Unionsrechts gibt, die für diesen Bereich spezifisch ist oder ihn beeinflussen kann", vgl. ebd., Rdnr. 25. Vgl. jetzt auch Rs. C-198/13 *Hernàndez*, EU:C:2014:2055, Rdnr. 37; in eine andere Richtung weisend aber Rs. C-390/12 *Pfleger*, EU:C:2014:281, Rdnr. 30 ff.

[30] Britz (2015), S. 275 m.Nw. zur schwankenden Rspr. des EuGH.

[31] BVerfGE 133, 277 (316 Rn. 91); vgl. dazu auch Voßkuhle (2016), S. 164.

[32] BVerfGE 140, 317.

[33] Franzius (2015), S. 407 m.w.Nw.

[34] Vgl. zu diesem Instrument BVerfGE 123, 267 (339 ff.); 142, 123 (203 ff.).

Überstellungsbeschlusses auf Grundlage eines europäischen Haftbefehls, zur Sicherung des „nach dem Grundgesetz unabdingbaren und von der Garantie der Menschenwürde nach Art. 1 Abs. 1 GG umfassten“[35] Grundrechtsstandards, hier bezüglich der basalen strafprozessualen Verteidigungsrechte im Ausstellungsstaat, im Einzelfall eröffnet und zwar ausdrücklich „ungeachtet“[36] der Solange-II-Rechtsprechung. Die im konkreten Fall vorgebrachte Grundrechtsrüge eines durch ein italienisches Strafgericht in Abwesenheit verurteilten US-Bürgers (bei nicht ausgeräumten Zweifeln über die Möglichkeit zur Durchführung einer neuen mündlichen Verhandlung in Italien) überprüfte das Bundesverfassungsgericht in Hinblick auf die „für integrationsfest erklärten Schutzgüter“[37] wie eben Art. 1 Abs. 1 GG. Die Entscheidung stellt damit klar, dass der Schutz der Verfassungsidentität auch „im Einzelfall sicherzustellen“[38] ist. Einen generellen Kontrollverzicht entsprechend dem Solange-II-Vorbehalt soll es im Fall möglicher Verletzungen der Menschenwürde nicht geben. Dabei erwies sich im konkreten Fall die zulässige Identitätsrüge zwar als begründet, dies jedoch nicht, weil dem zugrunde liegenden unionalen Rechtsakt, hier dem Rahmenbeschluss[39], grundrechtliche Mängel anhafteten. Vielmehr bedurfte es im Ergebnis

> “[e]iner unter Rückgriff auf Art. 79 Abs. 3 GG in Verbindung mit Art. 1 Abs. 1 GG begründeten Begrenzung des dem Rahmenbeschluss zukommenden Anwendungsvorrangs [...] im vorliegenden Zusammenhang jedoch nicht, weil sowohl der Rahmenbeschluss selbst [...] als auch das diesen umsetzende Gesetz über die internationale Rechtshilfe in Strafsachen [...] eine Auslegung gebieten, die den von Art. 1 Abs. 1 GG geforderten Mindestgarantien von Beschuldigtenrechten bei einer Auslieferung Rechnung trägt. Insofern genügen die einschlägigen Vorgaben des Unionsrechts den durch das Grundgesetz zur Absicherung des integrationsfesten Schuldprinzips gebotenen Mindestgarantien von Beschuldigtenrechten.”[40]

Mit anderen Worten: Die Verletzung der Menschenwürde und somit der Verfassungsidentität war hier allein dem deutschen Gericht anzulasten, welches bei hinreichender Berücksichtigung der *europäischen* Grundrechte zu einem anderen Ergebnis hätte kommen müssen, welches dann auch dem über Art. 1 Abs. 1 GG zu fordernden Standard entsprochen hätte. Damit steht die Entscheidung – jedenfalls in ihrem konkreten Ergebnis – auch mit der *Melloni*-Entscheidung des EuGH in Übereinstimmung, in der der Gerichtshof anerkannt hat, dass die Überprüfung einer Überstellungsentscheidung am Maßstab der nationalen Grundrechte in Hinblick auf Art. 53 GR-Charta, wonach das Schutzniveau nationaler Grundrechte nicht beeinträchtigt werden soll, möglich ist, „sofern durch diese Anwendung weder das Schutzniveau der Charta, wie sie vom Gerichtshof ausgelegt wird, noch der Vorrang, die Einheit und die Wirksamkeit des Unionsrechts beeinträchtigt werden.“[41] Einer

---

[35] BVerfGE 140, 317 (333).

[36] BVerfGE 140, 317 (334).

[37] BVerfGE 140, 317 (341).

[38] BVerfGE 140, 317 (334).

[39] Rahmenbeschlusses 2002/584/JI des Rates vom 13. Juni 2002 über den Europäischen Haftbefehl und die Übergabeverfahren zwischen den Mitgliedstaaten (ABl. L 190, S. 1) in der Fassung des Rahmenbeschlusses 2009/299/JI des Rates vom 26. Februar 2009 (ABl. L 81, S. 24).

[40] BVerfGE 140, 317 (355 f.).

[41] Rs. C-399/11 *Melloni*, EU:C:2013:107, Rdnr. 60.

parallelen Anwendbarkeit von unionalen und nationalen Grundrechten im Bereich eines unionsrechtlich eingeräumten Umsetzungsspielraums sind danach Grenzen gesetzt, die dann, aber auch nur dann, zum Tragen kommen, wenn Unterschiede im Grundrechtsschutz die einheitliche Anwendung und den Vorrang des Unionsrechts gefährden würden. Im Fall *Melloni* hatte der Gerichtshof eine Verletzung von Unionsgrundrechten durch die Überstellung eines in Italien in Abwesenheit Verurteilten verneint und damit einer auf die spanische Verfassung gestützten Verweigerung der Vollstreckung des Europäischen Haftbefehls die Grundlage entzogen.[42]

Die Möglichkeit eines einzelfallbezogenen verfassungsprozessualen Zugriffs im Rahmen der Identitätskontrolle wurde im Übrigen jüngst, im Dezember 2017, durch das Bundesverfassungsgericht in einer weiteren Haftbefehlssache[43] bestätigt: Die auf Art. 1 Abs. 1 GG gestützte Identitätsrüge, gerichtet gegen eine positive Auslieferungsentscheidung auf einen in Rumänien ausgestellten Europäischen Haftbefehl war zulässig; im konkreten Fall bestand die Möglichkeit einer Menschenwürdeverletzung des Beschwerdeführers infolge bestimmter als menschenrechtswidrig gerügter Haftbedingungen in Rumänien.[44] Die Begründetheit ergab sich indes bereits aus Art. 101 Abs. 1 S. 2 GG in Hinblick auf die unterlassene Vorlage des Fachgerichts an den EuGH, der die europäischen Grundrechtsstandards bezogen auf die hier problematische Mindestgröße der Hafträume noch nicht konkret ausbuchstabiert hatte.[45] Die Stattgabe der Identitätsrüge war also auch hier nicht ‚gegen' die Union und ihre Organe, namentlich den Gerichtshof, gerichtet. Vielmehr wurde letzterem die Möglichkeit gegeben, sich an der Fortentwicklung des gemeineuropäischen Grundrechtsschutzes in dieser Frage zu beteiligen. In der erstgenannten Haftbefehlsentscheidung hatte das Bundesverfassungsgericht das Vorliegen einer Vorlagepflicht für sich selbst verneint, da sich die Verletzung des Unionsrechts durch das deutsche Fachgericht als „derart offenkundig (darstellte), dass für einen vernünftigen Zweifel keinerlei Raum bleibt (‚acte clair' […]).“[46] Im Ergebnis erzielte das Gericht hier einen „ebenenübergreifenden Gleichklang der materiellen Gewährleistungsgehalte“[47] mit der Folge, dass beiden Rechtsordnungen mitsamt ihren normativen Erwartungshorizonten Genüge getan wurde. Die Identitätskontrolle führte dementsprechend dazu, eine Überprüfung des Vollzugs des Unionsrechts, hier des europäischen Haftbefehls, an dem auf das Schutzgut der Menschenwürde reduzierten Maßstab des Grundgesetzes zu eröffnen, der wegen der unionsrechtlichen Determinierung des nationalen Handelns ansonsten nicht zur Verfügung stünde. In einer solchen Konstellation, in der der europäische

---

[42] Vgl. die Folgeentscheidung des spanischen Verfassungsgerichts vom 13. Februar 2014, Nr. 26/2014, in englischer Übersetzung abgedruckt in HRLJ 2014, S. 475, in der dem Urteil des EuGH in differenzierter Weise Rechnung getragen wird.

[43] BVerfG, Beschluss vom 19. Dezember 2017, 2 BvR 424/17.

[44] Vgl. BVerfG, Beschluss vom 19. Dezember 2017, 2 BvR 424/17, Rdnr. 34.

[45] Vgl. BVerfG, Beschluss vom 19. Dezember 2017, 2 BvR 424/17, Rdnrn. 35 ff.

[46] BVerfGE 140, 317 (376).

[47] So treffend Reinbacher and Wendel (2016), S. 342.

Grundrechtsschutz dem grundgesetzlich gebotenen Mindestschutz entspricht, verhilft die Identitätskontrolle nicht nur Art. 1 GG, sondern auch den europäischen Grundrechten und damit der Identität der europäischen Grundrechtsordnung insgesamt zur Durchsetzung.

2.2.3 Materielle und formelle Verschränkungen

In der Haftbefehlsentscheidung aus dem Jahr 2015 ist das Bundesverfassungsgericht auch und gerade für den Fall der grundrechtsbezogenen Identitätskontrolle im Einzelfall von dem grundlegenden Erfordernis einer vorhergehenden Vorlage zum EuGH ausgegangen und hat, wie erwähnt, lediglich im konkreten Fall das Vorliegen der Voraussetzungen einer Vorlagepflicht aus Art. 267 AEUV verneint.[48] Die grundsätzlich vor einer möglichen Versagung der Anwendung eines europäischen Rechtsakts bestehende Vorlageverpflichtung reflektiert dabei den Umstand, dass der durch das Bundesverfassungsgericht seit der *Solange-I*-Entscheidung[49] fortlaufend eingeforderte Reservevorbehalt als Element eines gerichtlichen „kohärenzsichernden Kontrollverbundes"[50] zu verstehen ist, wonach der verfassungsgerichtliche „Ausnahmevorbehalt" gegenüber dem gewissermaßen als „Grundtatbestand" fungierenden Anwendungsvorrang des Unionsrechts[51] eine vorhergehende Befassung des EuGH notwendig erscheinen lässt. Soweit in der Literatur der Ansatz vertreten wird, dass das Loyalitätsgebot aus Art. 4 Abs. 3 EUV als Anknüpfungspunkt für eine „Wechselbezogenheit der Rechtsordnungen"[52] dienen kann und auf weitergehende Konzeptionen wie die eines „europäischen Normenverbundes" mitsamt einer „geteilten Normativität oder Verbundnormativität"[53] verwiesen wird[54], bringt dies – ungeachtet des verfassungsrechtlich determinierten Grundsatzes, wonach „Grund und Grenze für die Geltung des Rechts der Europäischen Union in der Bundesrepublik Deutschland [...] der im Zustimmungsgesetz enthaltene Rechtsanwendungsbefehl, der nur im Rahmen der geltenden Verfassungsordnung erteilt werden kann"[55], ist – treffend zum Ausdruck, dass aus Sicht des Bundesverfassungsgerichts kein ‚Gegeneinander', sondern vielmehr ein ‚Miteinander' anzustreben ist.[56]

Aus unionsrechtlicher Sicht sind Vorabentscheidungsersuchen in derartigen Konstellationen zulässig, obwohl sich das Bundesverfassungsgericht vorbehält, nach der Entscheidung des Gerichtshofs den Ausnahmevorbehalt vom Vorrang des

---

[48] Vgl. BVerfGE 140, 317 (376).

[49] Oben „Der Solange-Vorbehalt - die vertikale Dimension".

[50] Schmidt-Aßmann (2016), S. 90.

[51] So die Terminologie bei Schmidt-Aßmann (2016), S. 90.

[52] Schmidt-Aßmann (2016), S. 90.

[53] Siehe Burchardt (2015), S. 196 ff., insbes. 198 ff.

[54] Vgl. Schmidt-Aßmann (2016), S. 90.

[55] BVerfGE 123, 267 (402); vgl. auch BVerfGE 140, 317 (336). Dies sehen im Übrigen die meisten nationalen Gerichte so, vgl. Haltern (2017), S. 433 f., Rdnr. 1064.

[56] In diesem Sinne vgl. auch Lenaerts and Hartmann (2017), S. 322 f.

Unionsrechts gegebenenfalls geltend zu machen. Auch wenn nach Auffassung des Generalanwalts *Cruz Villalón* in seinen Schlussanträgen zu der auf den OMT-Vorlagebeschluss[57] des Bundesverfassungsgerichts ergangenen Vorabentscheidung „der ‚Einschub' des Vorabentscheidungsersuchens in den Verfahrensgang der abschließenden Beurteilung einer *Ultra-vires*-Handlung durch das nationale Gericht Probleme aufwirft [Hervorh. i. Orig.]"[58], so hat er doch das Ersuchen des Bundesverfassungsgerichts als „Ausdruck des zwischen beiden Gerichten bestehenden ‚Kooperationsverhältnisses'" gewürdigt.[59] Dieses komme dadurch zum Tragen, dass das Bundesverfassungsgericht sich „von einer gegenüber dem Unionsrecht offenen und aufgeschlossenen, ‚europarechtsfreundlichen' Haltung"[60] leiten lasse. Dementsprechend ging der Generalanwalt davon aus, dass „es nicht von vornherein auszuschließen und sogar darauf zu vertrauen [sei], dass das nationale Gericht in Anbetracht und unter Berücksichtigung der Antwort, die es vom Gerichtshof auf seine Vorlagefragen erhalten hat, unbeschadet der Wahrnehmung seiner eigenen Verantwortung diese Antwort als für im Ausgangsverfahren maßgeblich erachten werde."[61]

Der Gerichtshof schloss sich dem an, betonte freilich noch etwas stärker die Bindungswirkung seiner Vorabentscheidung.[62] In dem im Nachgang zur Entscheidung des EuGH ergangenen OMT-Urteil aus dem Jahr 2016 stellte das Bundesverfassungsgericht wiederum fest, dass die durch den Gerichtshof vorgenommene, unionsrechtskonforme Auslegung des Beschlusses der Europäischen Zentralbank (EZB) vom 6. September 2012, beruhend auf der Prämisse einer „primär verfahrensrechtlichen Einhegung" ebendieses EZB-Beschlusses, die für die Vermeidung eines Ultra-vires-Verstoßes notwendige „Annahme eines jedenfalls im Schwerpunkt geldpolitischen Charakters des OMT-Programms [...] als vertretbar erscheinen" ließ.[63] Deutlich wurde hier einmal mehr, dass bedeutsame formelle und materielle Verschränkungen zwischen den Gerichten und somit zwischen den Rechtsordnungen bestehen.

Bezogen auf den Grundrechtsbereich bedeutet dies zweierlei. Aus der formellen Verschränktheit der Rechtsordnungen folgt, dass vor Annahme eines Grundrechtsverstoßes durch das Bundesverfassungsgericht grundsätzlich der EuGH als gesetzlicher Richter gemäß Art. 101 Abs. 1 S. 2 GG im Wege der Vorabentscheidung einzubeziehen ist, je nach prozessualer Konstellation entweder durch das Bundesverfassungsgericht selbst oder aber durch die im Instanzenzug angerufenen Fachgerichte. Eine Verletzung des Art. 101 Abs. 1 S. 2 GG durch das Fachgericht

57 BVerfGE 134, 366.

58 GA *Cruz Villalón*, Rs. C-62/14 *Gauweiler u.a. ./. Deutscher Bundestag*, EU:C:2015:7, Rdnr. 46.

59 GA *Cruz Villalón*, Rs. C-62/14 *Gauweiler u.a. ./. Deutscher Bundestag*, EU:C:2015:7, Rdnr. 47. Vgl. zum Kooperationsverhältnis grundlegend BVerfGE 89, 155 (175), aufgegriffen in BVerfGE 102, 147 (163).

60 GA *Cruz Villalón*, Rs. C-62/14 *Gauweiler u.a. ./. Deutscher Bundestag*, EU:C:2015:7, Rdnr. 48.

61 GA *Cruz Villalón*, Rs. C-62/14 *Gauweiler u.a. ./. Deutscher Bundestag*, EU:C:2015:7, Rdnr. 67.

62 Vgl. Rs. C-61/14 *Gauweiler u.a. ./. Deutscher Bundestag*, EU:C:2015:400, Rdnr. 16.

63 Siehe BVerfGE 142, 123 (225).

kann gegebenenfalls mit der Verfassungsbeschwerde vor dem Bundesverfassungsgericht gerügt werden. Aus der materiellen Verschränktheit der Grundrechtsordnungen folgt zweitens, dass das Bundesverfassungsgericht nur eingreift, wenn auf der europäischen Ebene ein hinreichender Grundrechtsschutz generell nicht mehr gewährt wird (Solange-II-Vorbehalt) oder im Einzelfall vor allem in horizontaler Hinsicht der aus Gründen der Verfassungsidentität unabdingbare Menschenwürdeschutz bedroht erscheint (Identitätsvorbehalt).

Auf die Haftbefehlsentscheidung des Bundesverfassungsgerichts aus dem Jahr 2015[64] hat der EuGH wenige Monate später in der Entscheidung *Aranyosi und Căldăraru* dadurch reagiert, dass im Fall eines ungarischen und eines rumänischen Überstellungsersuchens an Deutschland den mitgliedstaatlichen Behörden die Möglichkeit eingeräumt wurde, bei „Vorliegen systemischer oder allgemeiner, bestimmte Personengruppen oder bestimmte Haftanstalten betreffender Mängel" in dem Staat, der einen Europäischen Haftbefehl ausgestellt hat, die Überstellung mit Rücksicht auf das Verbot der erniedrigenden und unmenschlichen Behandlung aus Art. 4 der Grundrechtecharta nötigenfalls auszusetzen beziehungsweise, bei Nichtbehebung der Mängel, zu verweigern.[65] Im Gefolge der Haftbefehlsentscheidung aus dem Jahr 2017[66], durch welche das für die Überstellungsentscheidung (nach Rumänien) zuständige Gericht durch das Bundesverfassungsgericht verpflichtet wurde, ein Vorabentscheidungsersuchen nach Art. 267 AEUV zu stellen, ist der Gerichtshof nun ebenfalls am Zug und wird in Hinblick auf die im Überstellungsverfahren gerügte Unterschreitung der grundrechtlich gebotenen Mindestgröße von Hafträumen im rumänischen Strafvollzug eine konkrete Antwort geben müssen. In einem ähnlich gelagerten Verfahren hat der EuGH jüngst, auf Vorlage eines deutschen Gerichts in Hinblick auf eine mögliche Überstellung nach Ungarn, bereits einige konkrete Aussagen zur Haftraumgröße gemacht und sich hierbei wiederum an der Rechtsprechung des EGMR orientiert; er hat allerdings auch klar gestellt, dass das Gericht des überstellenden Staates „nur die Haftbedingungen in den Haftanstalten prüfen muss, in denen die genannte Person nach den dieser Behörde vorliegenden Informationen wahrscheinlich, sei es auch nur vorübergehend oder zu Übergangszwecken, inhaftiert sein wird" und nicht in allen Haftanstalten des ersuchenden Staates.[67] Auch hier zeigt sich, welch produktive Wirkung im Sinne eines effektiven Grundrechtsschutzes das Miteinander von Karlsruhe und Luxemburg haben kann, wenn es darum geht, „[g]rundrechtliche

---

[64] Oben „Die menschenwürdesichernde Identitätskontrolle – die (neue) horizontale Dimension", Fn. 32.

[65] Rs. C-404/15 und C-659/15 PPU *Aranyosi* und *Căldăraru*, EU:C:2016:198, Rdnr. 104.

[66] Oben „Die menschenwürdesichernde Identitätskontrolle – die (neue) horizontale Dimension", Fn. 43.

[67] Siehe Rs. C-220/18 PPU *ML ./. Generalstaatsanwaltschaft Bremen*, EU:C:2018:589, Rdnrn. 92 ff., 117.

Sollbruchstellen des Anerkennungsgrundsatzes“[68] auszumachen. Insofern kann von einer „gerichtliche[n] Auslegungs- und Dialogverantwortung“[69] gesprochen werden.

2.3 *Der dritte Spieler auf dem Feld des Grundrechtsschutzes: der EGMR*

2.3.1 Zur „Architektonik des europäischen Grundrechtsraumes“

Nimmt man nun den EGMR in den Blick, so ist das Verhältnis dieses dritten Spielers auf dem Feld des Grundrechtsschutzes zum Bundesverfassungsgericht wie auch zum EuGH auszuloten. Es geht gewissermaßen um die „Architektonik des europäischen Grundrechtsraums“ in Hinblick auf die „spannungsreiche Verflechtung nationaler, supranationaler und internationaler Grundrechtsregime in Europa“.[70] Dabei ist das Verhältnis zwischen Bundesverfassungsgericht und EGMR ein anderes als dasjenige zwischen letzterem und dem EuGH. Das erste Verhältnis ist bestimmt durch die völkerrechtlich begründete und ausgestaltete Eigenschaft der Bundesrepublik als Vertragsstaat der EMRK, die sich von der ebenfalls völkerrechtlich begründeten, indes supranational ausgestalteten Mitgliedschaft Deutschlands in der Europäischen Union fundamental unterscheidet. Das Verhältnis des EuGH zum EGMR ist wiederum gänzlich anderer Natur, weil die Europäische Union weiterhin keine Vertragspartei der EMRK ist, obgleich mit dem Inkrafttreten des 14. Zusatzprotokolls und der dadurch bewirkten Einfügung des neuen Art. 59 Abs. 2 EMRK im Jahr 2010[71] ein Vertragsbeitritt seitens der Union nunmehr möglich wäre. Infolge des negativen Gutachtens des EuGH[72] zu dem bereits ausgehandelten Beitrittsabkommen ist der Beitrittsprozess zunächst unterbrochen[73], der Beitritt ist indes gem. Art. 6 Abs. 2 S. 1 EUV weiterhin Ziel der Union.[74] Damit bleibt es für die Bestimmung des Verhältnisses zwischen Straßburger und Luxemburger Gericht einstweilen bei Art. 6 Abs. 3 EUV, der die Konventionsrechte „als allgemeine Grundsätze [als] Teil des Unionsrechts“ ausweist[75], sowie bei den Regelungen aus Artt. 52 Abs. 3 und 53 GR-Charta, wonach einerseits die unionalen Grundrechte

[68] Zu diesen ausf. Schwarz (2016), S. 264 ff.

[69] So Reinbacher and Wendel (2016), S. 342.

[70] So Dederer (2006), S. 575 f.

[71] Vgl. Art. 17 Nr. 1 des Protokolls Nr. 14 vom 13. Mai 2004 zur Konvention zum Schutz der Menschenrechte und Grundfreiheiten über die Änderung des Kontrollsystems der Konvention, BGBl. 2006 II, S. 139 (144 f.), sowie die Bekanntmachung der entsprechenden Neufassung, BGBl. 2010 II, S. 1198 (1216).

[72] Gutachten 2/13 des Gerichtshofs *EMRK-Beitritt II*, EU:C:2014:2454.

[73] Zum Ablauf und zu möglichen Perspektiven statt vieler Engel (2015), S.10 ff., 331.

[74] Vgl. dazu Stellungnahme der Generalanwältin *Kokott*, Gutachtenverfahren 2/13 *EMRK-Beitritt II*, EU:C:2014:2454, Rdnr. 3.

[75] Dabei dient die EMRK in ihrer Auslegung seitens des EGMR nach h.M. als Rechtserkenntnisquelle, vgl. statt vieler Engel (2015), S. 19 ff. m.W.Nw.

möglichst konform zu den Konventionsrechten auszulegen sind[76] und andererseits unter dem Gesichtspunkt der Meistbegünstigung die nationalen Grundrechte und internationalen Menschenrechte in ihrer eigenständigen Geltung soweit wie möglich unberührt bleiben sollen.[77]

2.3.2 Setzung von Mindeststandards in einem System pluralen Grundrechtsschutzes

Die Aufgabe des EGMR besteht darin, den Grundrechtsschutz in den 47 Konventionsstaaten sicherzustellen und dabei Mindeststandards zu setzen.[78] Im Verhältnis zu den nationalen Rechtsordnungen spielt der Subsidiaritätsgrundsatz eine entscheidende Rolle. Infolge des Inkrafttretens des 15. Zusatzprotokolls[79] wurde die Präambel der EMRK um ein ausdrückliches Bekenntnis zur Wahrung ebendieses Prinzips sowie zum Beurteilungsspielraum der Vertragsstaaten – beides ist in der Rechtsprechung des Gerichtshofs seit langem anerkannt[80] – ergänzt. Durch den Verweis auf das Subsidiaritätsprinzip und auf die Doktrin vom Beurteilungsspielraum (*margin of appreciation*) sind diese beiden Rechtsfiguren somit nun auch in den Konventionstext inkorporiert. Subsidiarität bedeutet dabei, dass „in erster Linie die staatlichen Behörden, insbesondere die staatlichen Gerichte, für die Anwendung und Durchsetzung der Konvention verantwortlich" sein sollen.[81] Daraus folgt auch, dass das Bundesverfassungsgericht eine besondere Rolle bei der Gewährleistung der Konventionsrechte spielt, indem es bei der Auslegung der Grundrechte die Konvention einschließlich der Rechtsprechung des EGMR miteinbezieht.[82]

Aber allein mit dem Schlagwort Subsidiarität ist das rechte Verhältnis zwischen nationalen Rechtsordnungen und der EMRK nicht beschrieben, denn es gibt Bereiche, in denen wiederum das Unionsrecht den Grundrechtsstandard abschließend vorgibt. Handelt es sich um eine Konstellation, in der staatliches Handeln unionsrechtlich determiniert ist, nimmt der EGMR seine Kontrollkompetenz, gestützt auf die generelle Vermutung eines adäquaten

[76] Nach Jarass (2016), Art. 52, Rdnrn. 62 f. fungiert die Europäische Menschenrechtskonvention hier gewissermaßen als „Untergrenze".

[77] Jarass (2016), Art. 53, Rdnr. 2.

[78] Engel (2015), S. 32 f.

[79] Protokoll Nr. 15 vom 24. Juni 2013 zur Änderung der Konvention zum Schutze der Menschenrechte und Grundfreiheiten, BGBl. 2014 II, S. 1034. Die Änderung diente auch der Umsetzung eines der zentralen Postulate der Erklärung von Brighton, vgl. BT-Drs. 18/2847, S. 10; Baade (2017), S. 235 f.

[80] Vgl. zu beidem Meyer-Ladewig et al. (2017), Einleitung, Rdnrn. 27 f.; krit. zum Mehrwert der Textänderung daher Baade (2017), S. 235 f.

[81] Meyer-Ladewig et al. (2017), Einleitung, Rdnr. 28 [i. Orig. m. Hervorh.]. Dies ergibt sich auch aus Art. 1 EMRK und kommt in den Art. 13 und 35 EMRK zum Ausdruck, siehe ebd., Rdn. 28.

[82] Grundlegend BVerfGE 111, 307 (317).

Grundrechtsschutzes auf unionaler Ebene, zurück.[83] Gerade hier ist durch den EuGH besonders darauf Bedacht zu nehmen, dass die grundrechtlichen Vorgaben des Unionsrechts einem gemeineuropäischen Standard, also jedenfalls der EMRK, entsprechen, wie es in Art. 52 Abs. 3 und Art. 53 GR-Charta vorgegeben ist. Ein eindrucksvolles Beispiel stellt hier die bereits erwähnte[84] *Aranyosi und Căldăraru*-Entscheidung des EuGH dar, in der der Gerichtshof in Hinblick auf die als grund- bzw. menschenrechtswidrig gerügten Haftbedingungen in Rumänien und Ungarn bei der Auslegung des grundrechtlich normierten Verbots unmenschlicher und erniedrigender Behandlung aus Art. 4 GR-Charta eine konforme Auslegung zum gleichlautenden Art. 3 EMRK, unter sorgfältiger Heranziehung der einschlägigen Rechtsprechung des EGMR, vorgenommen hat.[85]

2.3.3 Verknüpfung der Grundrechte des Grundgesetzes mit der EMRK

Wenngleich aus der Perspektive des Bundesverfassungsgerichts keine direkte verfahrensmäßige Verknüpfung mit dem EGMR besteht, sind die beiden Gerichte indirekt dadurch prozedural verbunden, dass die Möglichkeit der Individualbeschwerde zum EGMR gegen deutsche Rechtsakte erst nach Erschöpfung des Rechtsweges (Art. 35 Abs. 1 EMRK) möglich ist, wozu bei entsprechender Möglichkeit auch die erfolglose Erhebung der Verfassungsbeschwerde zählt. Materiell erfolgt nach Maßgabe des *Görgülü*-Beschlusses aus dem Jahr 2004[86] und der Entscheidung zur Sicherungsverwahrung[87] grundsätzlich eine Verknüpfung des deutschen Grundrechtsschutzes mit den Konventionsgewährleistungen. Trotz des Ranges der EMRK als einfaches Gesetz (vgl. Art. 59 Abs. 2 GG) hat das Bundesverfassungsgericht ihr unter Verweis auf die besondere Bedeutung der unveräußerlichen Menschenrechte in Art. 1 Abs. 2 GG und den Grundsatz der Völkerrechtsfreundlichkeit verfassungsrechtliche Bedeutung zuerkannt. Die EMRK in der Auslegung durch den EGMR ist als Auslegungshilfe bei der Bestimmung von Inhalt und Reichweite der Grundrechte und rechtsstaatlichen Grundsätze des Grundgesetzes heranzuziehen.[88] Die mit einer Gewährleistung der EMRK befassten Fachgerichte sind darüber hinaus verpflichtet, die EMRK und die Rechtsprechung des EGMR bei der Auslegung und Anwendung des deutschen Rechts zu beachten.[89] Denn zur Bindung an Recht und Gesetz nach Art. 20 Abs. 3 GG gehört auch die Berücksichtigung der Gewährleistungen der EMRK und der Entscheidungen des

---

[83] Vgl. EGMR, Nr. 45036/98 *Bosphorus Hava Yollari Turizm ve Ticaret Anonim Sirketi ./. Ireland*; dazu näher 2.3.4.

[84] Oben 2.2.3., Fn. 65.

[85] Vgl. Rs. C-404/15 und C-659/15 PPU *Aranyosi* und *Căldăraru*, EU:C:2016:198, Rdnr. 86 ff; restriktiv noch Rs. C-399/11 *Melloni*, EU:C:2013:107.

[86] BVerfGE 111, 307 (315 ff.).

[87] BVerfGE 128, 326 (368 ff.).

[88] BVerfGE 111, 307 (317); 128, 326 (370).

[89] BVerfGE 111, 307 (317); vgl. auch 128, 326 (370 ff.).

Gerichtshofs.[90] Eine Verletzung dieser Verpflichtung kann unter Berufung auf das konkret betroffene Grundrecht in Verbindung mit dem Rechtsstaatsprinzip gerügt werden.[91] Die Verpflichtung der Berücksichtigung der EMRK gemäß der Auslegung durch den EGMR durch die Fachgerichte wie auch das Bundesverfassungsgericht gilt sowohl bei Entscheidungen des EGMR, in denen Deutschland als Prozesspartei unmittelbar betroffen ist, als auch – wegen der faktischen Orientierungs- und Leitfunktion der Rechtsprechung des Straßburger Gerichts – für andere Verfahren.[92]

Entscheidend für die Frage der Berücksichtigungsfähigkeit der EMRK und der einschlägigen Straßburger Rechtsprechung ist dabei auch, inwiefern „im Rahmen geltender methodischer Standards Auslegungs- und Abwägungsspielräume eröffnet sind“[93], denn „‚berücksichtigen' bedeutet, die Konventionsbestimmung in der Auslegung des Gerichtshofs zur Kenntnis zu nehmen und auf den Fall anzuwenden, soweit die Anwendung nicht gegen höherrangiges Recht, insbesondere das Verfassungsrecht verstößt.“[94] Das Gebot der Völkerrechtsfreundlichkeit verlangt „keine schematische Parallelisierung [...] sondern eine möglichst vollständige Übernahme der materiellen Wertungen [wie sie vom EGMR konkretisiert worden sind, Anm. d. Verf.] – soweit dies methodisch vertretbar und mit den Vorgaben des Grundgesetzes vereinbar ist“.[95] Möchte ein Gericht in Anwendung dieser Vorgaben ausnahmsweise von einem Urteil des EGMR abweichen, so muss es dies nachvollziehbar begründen. Eine weitere Grenze der konventionsfreundlichen Auslegung von Grundrechten liegt darin, dass die Beachtung der Konvention nicht zu einem geringeren Grundrechtsschutz führen darf, als er vom Grundgesetz vorgesehen ist. Dieses Problem stellt sich vor allen Dingen dann, wenn mehrpolige Grundrechtsverhältnisse[96] betroffen sind, in denen ein „Mehr“ an Freiheit für den einen ein „Weniger“ an Grundrechtsschutz für den anderen Grundrechtsträger bedeutet.[97] Und schließlich dürfen Gesetzgeber und Gerichte bis hin zum Bundesverfassungsgericht im Falle einer Normenkollision die vom EGMR vorgenommene Auslegung der Konvention ausnahmsweise unbeachtet lassen, wenn diese Auslegung gegen tragende Grundsätze des Grundgesetzes verstieße.[98]

---

[90] BVerfGE 111, 307 (315 f.).

[91] BVerfGE 111, 307 (323 f.).

[92] BVerfGE 111, 307 (319 ff.); vgl. auch BVerfGE 128, 326 (368 f.) sowie Voßkuhle (2010), S. 4 f.

[93] BVerfGE 111, 307 (329).

[94] BVerfGE 111, 307 (329).

[95] BVerfGE 141, 1 (30).

[96] Vgl. dazu in diesem Kontext Voßkuhle (2016), S. 164.

[97] Vgl. etwa zum Verhältnis von Persönlichkeitsrecht und Pressefreiheit den sog. Caroline-von-Monaco-Fall in BVerfGE 104, 361 und EGMR, Nr. 40660/08 und 60641/08 *von Hannover ./. Germany*.

[98] BVerfGE 111, 307 (319).

2.3.4 Das Verhältnis des EuGH zum EGMR – die „Bosphorus"- Vermutung und ihre Grenzen

Das Verhältnis zwischen EuGH und EGMR ist wiederum geprägt von dem seitens des Straßburger Gerichts in der bereits erwähnten *Bosphorus*-Entscheidung im Verhältnis zum Luxemburger Gericht etablierten Grundsatz der Vermutung der Äquivalenz des unionsrechtlichen Grundrechtsschutzes gegenüber den Standards der Konvention.[99] Der EGMR verzichtete hier auf die Überprüfung der Übereinstimmung einer durch den irischen Staat angeordneten Beschlagnahme eines Flugzeugs am Maßstab von Art. 1 ZP 1, nachdem der EuGH zuvor festgestellt hatte, dass das streitgegenständliche Luftfahrzeug, welches durch eine türkische Fluggesellschaft von der staatlichen Fluggesellschaft der damaligen Bundesrepublik Jugoslawien geleast worden war, unter eine die Mitgliedstaaten zur Beschlagnahme verpflichtende Bestimmung aus einer Verordnung zur Umsetzung von Embargobeschlüssen des UN-Sicherheitsrats fiel. Aus dem Umstand, dass die irischen Behörden zwingenden Verpflichtungen aus dem Unionsrecht nachgekommen waren, folgerte der Straßburger Gerichtshof die Vermutung der Konventionskonformität des behördlichen Handelns im Vertrauen auf einen grundsätzlich äquivalenten Grundrechtsschutz innerhalb der Union: „[...] State action taken in compliance with such legal obligations is justified as long as the relevant organisation is considered to protect fundamental rights [...] in a manner which can be considered at least equivalent to that for which the Convention provides [...]."[100]

Die Ähnlichkeiten zur *Solange-II*-Entscheidung des Bundesverfassungsgerichts sind unübersehbar.[101] Es bestehen indes zwei gewichtige Unterschiede. Zum einen folgt aus der Vermutungsregel nicht schon die Unzulässigkeit der Individualbeschwerde, sondern lediglich die Unbegründetheit als Folge der (vermuteten) Rechtfertigung der Beeinträchtigung des einschlägigen Konventionsrechts.[102] Zum anderen ist eine Widerlegung der Vermutungswirkung in Hinblick auf Grundrechtsdefizite im Einzelfall[103] („in the circumstances of a particular case"[104]) möglich, wohingegen für die Aktivierung des *Solange-II*-Vorbehalts „die Begründung der Vorlage oder einer Verfassungsbeschwerde im Einzelnen darlegen [muss], dass der jeweils als unabdingbar gebotene Grundrechtsschutz [auf

---

[99] EGMR, Nr. 45036/98 *Bosphorus Hava Yollari Turizm ve Ticaret Anonim Sirketi ./. Ireland*, Rdnr. 165.

[100] EGMR, Nr. 45036/98 *Bosphorus Hava Yollari Turizm ve Ticaret Anonim Sirketi ./. Ireland*, Rdnr. 155.

[101] Vgl. ausf. *Haratsch* (2006), S. 928 f., 932 ff.

[102] Haratsch (2006), S. 932 f. Theoretisch könnte wegen offensichtlicher Unbegründetheit die Beschwerde aber auch als unzulässig (Art. 35 Abs. 3 EMRK) zurückgewiesen werden, siehe ebd.

[103] Haratsch (2006), S. 943; vgl. EGMR, Nr. 45036/98 *Bosphorus Hava Yollari Turizm ve Ticaret Anonim Sirketi ./. Ireland*, Rdnrn. 149 ff.

[104] EGMR, Nr. 45036/98 *Bosphorus Hava Yollari Turizm ve Ticaret Anonim Sirketi ./. Ireland*, Rdnr. 156.

Unionsebene; Anm. d. Verf.] generell nicht gewährleistet ist."[105] Unberührt davon bleibt allerdings die Identitätskontrolle durch das Bundesverfassungsgericht, die im Einzelfall – zur Abwehr von Menschenwürdeverletzungen im Gefolge der Durchsetzung von zwingendem Unionsrecht – dem Vorrang des Unionsrechts Grenzen setzt.[106]

In Bereichen, die unionsrechtlich vom Grundsatz des gegenseitigen Vertrauens zwischen den Mitgliedstaaten beherrscht sind, bedeutet die Anwendung der Bosphorus-Formel, dass die „Reichweite der den mitgliedstaatlichen Behörden rechtlich eingeräumten Spielräume [...] hier zugleich die Reichweite der Grundrechtskontrolle durch das Bundesverfassungsgericht und der völkerrechtlichen Menschenrechtskontrolle durch den EGMR [...]" bestimmt.[107] Der auf der sogenannten *Bosphorus*-Vermutung beruhende Kontrollverzicht stößt allerdings nicht nur im Fall systemischer Grundrechtsmängel an seine Grenzen, sondern auch im Einzelfall, in dem der durch die EU gewährleistete Grundrechtsschutz offensichtlich unzureichend ist.[108] Aus Sicht des EGMR geht es hier um die rechte „Koordination des Grundrechtsschutzes in Europa" im Angesicht teilweise in den Vertragsstaaten zu beobachtender grundlegender Mängel im Grundrechtsschutz.[109] Dass systemische Mängel das unionsrechtlich eingeforderte gegenseitige Vertrauen etwa im Bereich des Vollzugs Europäischer Haftbefehle oder bei Überstellungen von Schutzsuchenden nach der Dublin-III-Verordnung[110] beeinträchtigen können, liegt auf der Hand. Die jüngere Rechtsprechung des EuGH zeigt, dass dieser trotz der grundlegenden Bedeutung, die er dem Grundsatz des gegenseitigen Vertrauens für die Funktionsfähigkeit des Gemeinsamen Raums der Freiheit, der Sicherheit und des Rechts zumisst, erkennt, dass in bestimmten Situationen, in denen durch den Vollzug des Unionsrechts schwere Grundrechtsverletzungen, etwa in Form einer unmenschlichen Behandlung zu besorgen sind, dieses Vertrauen an seine Grenzen stoßen muss. Kontrafaktischem und „blindem" Systemvertrauen wird damit eine Absage erteilt. Aufgabe von EuGH, EGMR und Bundesverfassungsgericht ist es hier, die notwendige institutionelle Sichtweise in Hinblick auf die Funktionsfähigkeit der horizontalen Kooperation zwischen den Mitgliedstaaten als Integrationsprinzip in der EU mit der Notwendigkeit der Sicherung elementarer Grundrechtsstandards zu verbinden.

---

[105] BVerfGE 102, 147, Ls. 2.

[106] Vgl. dazu näher oben „Die menschenwürdesichernde Identitätskontrolle – die (neue) horizontale Dimension".

[107] Wendel (2015), S. 738.

[108] Vgl. etwa EGMR, Nr. 17502/07 *Avotins ./. Latvia;* EGMR, Nr. 29217/12 *Tarakhel ./. Switzerland.*

[109] So mit Bezug auf das damals noch anhängige *Avotins*-Verfahren Keller and Kühne (2016), S. 307.

[110] Verordnung (EU) Nr.604/2013 des Europäischen Parlaments und des Rates vom 26. Juni 2013 zur Festlegung der Kriterien und Verfahren zur Bestimmung des Mitgliedstaats, der für die Prüfung eines von einem Drittstaatsangehörigen oder Staatenlosen in einem Mitgliedstaat gestellten Antrags auf internationalen Schutz zuständig ist (ABl. L 180/31).

Klärungsbedarf besteht freilich noch in Hinblick auf die Höhe der Schwelle, bei deren Überschreiten der Vertrauensgrundsatz zurücksteht. Für einen kohärenten Grundrechtsschutz in der EU ist es notwendig, die unionsrechtliche Vermutung der nationalen Grundrechtskonformität und die *Bosphorus*-Vermutung des äquivalenten Grundrechtsschutzes innerhalb der Union aufeinander abzustimmen und nicht so zu verstehen, dass über eine Aneinanderreihung von Vermutungen eine Verkürzung des Grundrechtsschutzes eintritt. Denn ein solches Ergebnis wäre, wie der EGMR im *Avotins*-Urteil betont, tatsächlich paradox.[111] Andererseits sind die Standards nicht zu hoch zu setzen. Es müssen in den Worten des EuGH „objektive, zuverlässige, genaue und gebührend aktualisierte Angaben [...], die das Vorliegen systemischer oder allgemeiner [...] Mängel [...] belegen", vorhanden sein, um in einem zweiten Schritt überprüfen zu können, „ob es ernsthafte und durch Tatsachen bestätigte Gründe für die Annahme gibt", dass jemand der „echten Gefahr" einer Grundrechtsverletzung ausgesetzt ist.[112]

In der *Tarakhel*-Entscheidung aus dem Jahr 2014[113] ist der EGMR über eine sehr weitgehende Interpretation der Selbsteintrittsklausel in (damals noch) Art. 3 Abs. 2 Dublin-II-Verordnung[114] in den durch das Prinzip des gegenseitigen Vertrauens geschützten Bereich des Unionsrechts eingebrochen.[115] Die einzelfallbezogene Sichtweise des EGMR, die sich von der das Asyl- oder Strafrechtssystem eines Mitgliedstaates insgesamt in den Blick nehmenden Perspektive des EuGH abhebt, ist aus Sicht eines Menschenrechtsgerichtshofes folgerichtig, auch wenn man sich im Fall *Tarakhel* mit dem Sondervotum[116] die Frage stellen muss, ob hier tatsächlich der Schutzbereich von Art. 3 EMRK eröffnet war. Bereits seit dem Fall *Soering*[117], in dem es allerdings um eine Auslieferung an einen Drittstaat, die USA ging, wird

---

[111] Vgl. EGMR, Nr. 17502/07 *Avotins ./. Latvia*, Rdnr. 115: „The Court emphasises that this results, paradoxically, in a twofold limitation of the domestic court's review of the observance of fundamental rights, due to the combined effect of the presumption on which mutual recognition is founded and the *Bosphorus* presumption of equivalent protection."

[112] Rs. C-404/15 und C-659/15 PPU *Aranyosi* und *Caldararu*, EU:C:2016:198, Rdnr. 104. Vgl. in diesem Sinne auch das jüngst ergangene Urteil in der Rs. C-216/18 PPU *Minister for Justice and Equality v LM (Celmer)*, ECLI:EU:C:2018:586, insbes. Rdnr. 68 (Vollstreckung in Polen erlassener Europäischer Haftbefehle bei Geltendmachung systemischer Mängel der Rechtsstaatlichkeit in Polen).

[113] EGMR, Nr. 29217/12 *Tarakhel ./. Switzerland*, Rdnrn. 88 ff.

[114] Verordnung (EG) Nr. 343/2003 des Rates vom 18. Februar 2003 zur Festlegung der Kriterien und Verfahren zur Bestimmung des Mitgliedstaats, der für die Prüfung eines von einem Drittstaatsangehörigen in einem Mitgliedstaat gestellten Asylantrags zuständig ist (ABl. L 50, S. 1).

[115] Der Zugriff wurde dadurch ermöglicht, dass die *Bosphorus*-Formel nach der Ansicht des Gerichtshofs nicht eingriff, da die Inanspruchnahme der Selbsteintrittsklausel im Ermessen der Mitgliedstaaten gelegen und insoweit keine Determination durch Unionsrecht vorgelegen habe; dazu krit. Wendel (2015), S. 739.

[116] Krit. zur Vorverlagerung des Menschenrechtsschutzes die dissentierenden Richterinnen und Richter *Casadevall*, *Berro-Lefèvre* und *Jäderblom*, vgl. EGMR, Nr. 29217/12 *Tarakhel ./. Switzerland.*

[117] EGMR, Nr.1/1989/161/217 *Soering ./. United Kingdom.*

die Kontrolle von Art. 3 EMRK auch präventiv gegenüber anderen Staaten ausgeübt, d.h. die Konventionsgarantie verpflichtet die Mitgliedstaaten, vorbeugend schwerwiegenden Grundrechtsverletzungen entgegenzutreten. In gewisser Weise steht dies quer zu einem Gemeinsamen Raum der Freiheit, der Sicherheit und des Rechts, dessen Funktionsfähigkeit im Bereich der Justiz- und Verwaltungskooperation von einer sorgfältig austarierten Balance zwischen dem unionsrechtlichen Grundsatz des gegenseitigen Vertrauens und der präventiven Vorverlagerung des Menschenrechtsschutzes durch die Fachgerichte des kooperierenden EU-Staates abhängt. Eine vorbeugende Grundrechtskontrolle im Einzelfall sollte außerhalb des Vorliegens systemischer Mängel daher auf Härtefälle beschränkt bleiben, in denen auch der Verweis auf Rechtsschutz im Zielstaat, der seinerseits an die EMRK gebunden ist, nicht weiterhilft.

Die Beschränkung auf Härtefälle führt allerdings dann nicht weiter, wenn die Vollstreckung eines Europäischen Haftbefehls in Rede steht und sich Fragen stellen in Hinblick auf die Erfüllung rechtsstaatlicher Mindestanforderungen des Strafverfahrens im Ausstellungsstaat. Hier geht es trotz verbliebener nationaler Zuständigkeit für das Strafverfahren um die unionsgrundrechtliche Sicherung rechtsstaatlicher Mindestanforderungen des Strafverfahrens, die über den Grundsatz der gegenseitigen Anerkennung im Europäischen Haftbefehlssystem nicht unterlaufen werden dürfen. Dies ist auch das zentrale Anliegen der vom Bundesverfassungsgericht ausgeübten Identitätskontrolle. Deren Notwendigkeit entfällt, je nachhaltiger der EuGH seine Aufgabe als Grundrechtsgericht im Zusammenwirken mit den nationalen Fachgerichten wahrnimmt.

3 Herausforderungen und Zielsetzungen des Gerichtsverbunds im Bereich des Grundrechtsschutzes

Als Zielsetzungen des Verbunds und der in ihm stattfindenden Kooperation lassen sich die Sicherung eines hohen Grundrechtsschutzes, hoher rechtsstaatlicher Standards und einer hohen Qualität der Reflexion[118] bei der notwendigen Abwägung möglicherweise gegenläufiger Rechtsgüter ausmachen. Dabei sollte gesehen werden, dass eine „Zentralisierung des Grundrechtsschutzes bei einem Gericht […] dem Konzept einer föderal angelegten Rechtsgemeinschaft mit geteilten Verantwortungen zuwider [liefe].“[119] Es darf nicht – ohne dass dies zur Sicherung der Effektivität des Unionsrechts zwingend geboten wäre – zu einer Verengung „politische[r] Spielräume“ und zur Überlagerung des vorhandenen „ausdifferenzierten, historisch gewachsenen Grundrechtsschutz[es] in den Mitgliedstaaten“ kommen.[120]

[118] Zum „Ringen um die ‚beste Lösung'“ Voßkuhle (2010), S. 8.

[119] Voßkuhle (2016), S. 164.

[120] So Voßkuhle (2016), S. 164.

Welche problematischen Wirkungen eine solche Entwicklung haben kann, zeigt das Beispiel der Rechtsprechung von Luxemburg und Karlsruhe zur Vorratsdatenspeicherung. Das Bundesverfassungsgericht hatte im Jahr 2010 einzelne Regelungen der Strafprozessordnung zu anlassunabhängigen Speicherungen von Telekommunikationsverkehrsdaten – sog. Vorratsdatenspeicherung (VDS) – für grundrechtswidrig befunden.[121] Da die VDS-Richtlinie[122] im Wesentlichen die Speicherungspflicht an sich regelte, konnte die Ausgestaltung in Hinblick auf Fragen des Behördenzugriffs oder der Datensicherheit am Maßstab des Grundgesetzes geprüft werden.[123] Nachdem die unionsrechtliche Pflicht zur mindestens sechsmonatigen Datenspeicherung infolge der Ungültigerklärung dieser Richtlinie durch den EuGH wegen Verstoßes gegen Unionsgrundrechte im Jahr 2014[124] entfallen war, war allgemein davon ausgegangen worden, dass die Entscheidung über die Zulässigkeit der Vorratsdatenspeicherung mangels unionsrechtlicher Vorgabe nunmehr wieder allein am Maßstab der nationalen Grundrechte zu messen sei. In einer Entscheidung aus dem Jahr 2016[125] unterwarf der Gerichtshof die nationalen Regelungen zur Vorratsdatenspeicherung gleichwohl der Kontrolle durch die Unionsgrundrechte. Als unionsrechtlichen Maßstab für die Regulierung der Vorratsdatenspeicherung auf mitgliedstaatlicher Ebene griff der EuGH nunmehr auf die Datenschutzrichtlinie für die digitale Kommunikation (sog. ePrivacy-RL)[126] zurück, welche in Art. 15 festlegt, dass die Mitgliedstaaten

> "Rechtsvorschriften erlassen [können], die die Rechte und Pflichten gemäß Artikel [...] beschränken, sofern eine solche Beschränkung [...] für die nationale Sicherheit (d. h. die Sicherheit des Staates), die Landesverteidigung, die öffentliche Sicherheit sowie die Verhütung, Ermittlung, Feststellung und Verfolgung von Straftaten oder des unzulässigen Gebrauchs von elektronischen Kommunikationssystemen in einer demokratischen Gesellschaft notwendig, angemessen und verhältnismäßig ist. Zu diesem Zweck können die Mitgliedstaaten unter anderem durch Rechtsvorschriften vorsehen, dass Daten aus den in diesem Absatz aufgeführten Gründen während einer begrenzten Zeit aufbewahrt werden."

Der Gerichtshof legte diese Bestimmung als „sekundärrechtliche Grundlage für eine normative Regelung über die Vorratsdatenspeicherung auf mitgliedstaatlicher

---

[121] BVerfGE 125, 260.

[122] Richtlinie 2006/24/EG des Europäischen Parlaments und des Rates vom 15. März 2006 über die Vorratsspeicherung von Daten, die bei der Bereitstellung öffentlich zugänglicher elektronischer Kommunikationsdienste oder öffentlicher Kommunikationsnetze erzeugt oder verarbeitet werden, und zur Änderung der Richtlinie 2002/58/EG (ABl. L 105/54).

[123] BVerfGE 125, 260 (308 f.).

[124] Rs. C-293/12 u. C-594/12 *Digital Rights Ireland Ltd*, EU:C:2014:238, Rdnrn 64 f.

[125] Rs. C-203/15 u. C-698/15 *Tele2 Sverige AB*, EU:C:2016:970, Rdnrn. 81 ff.

[126] Richtlinie 2002/58/EG des Europäischen Parlaments und des Rates vom 12.Juli 2002 über die Verarbeitung personenbezogener Daten und den Schutz der Privatsphäre in der elektronischen Kommunikation (Datenschutzrichtlinie für elektronische Kommunikation), ABl. L 201/37, in der durch die Richtlinie 2009/136/EG des Europäischen Parlaments und des Rates vom 25. November 2009 (ABl. L 337/11) geänderten Fassung.

Ebene“[127] aus und brachte damit die Unionsgrundrechte als Maßstab erneut ins Spiel. In der Literatur ist der EuGH für dieses weit ausgreifende Verständnis mit dem nachvollziehbaren Argument kritisiert worden, Art. 15 ePrivacy-RL stelle lediglich eine „die Kompetenzgrenzen markierende Öffnungsklausel“[128] dar, die den Anwendungsbereich der Unionsgrundrechte gerade nicht eröffne. Verwiesen wurde zudem[129] auf Art. 1 Abs. 3 der Richtlinie, wonach diese „nicht für Tätigkeiten [gilt], die nicht in den Anwendungsbereich des Vertrags zur Gründung der Europäischen Gemeinschaft fallen [...], und auf keinen Fall für Tätigkeiten betreffend die öffentliche Sicherheit, die Landesverteidigung, die Sicherheit des Staates [...] und die Tätigkeiten des Staates im strafrechtlichen Bereich.“

Die beschriebene Problemkonstellation offenbart die außerordentliche Diffizilität der Abgrenzung der Grundrechtssphären bei Vorliegen verschachtelter Normenkomplexe. Zutreffend wurde in der Literatur angemerkt, dass die Datenspeicherungspflicht zu den „unionsrechtlich nur schwach determinierten Bereichen“[130] zählt, so dass hier besondere Sensibilität für die jeweils andere Grundrechtsordnung angezeigt erscheint, zumal wenn, wie im Fall der Vorratsdatenspeicherung geschehen, bereits eine detaillierte und überaus differenzierte Grundrechtsprüfung[131] erfolgt ist. Die seinerzeit vom Bundesverfassungsgericht zur Beurteilung der Grundrechtskonformität der Regelungen zur Vorratsdatenspeicherung vorgenommene Differenzierung zwischen dem grundsätzlichen „Ob“ und dem konkreten „Wie“ einer „Ausgestaltung, die dem besonderen Gewicht des hierin liegenden Eingriffs hinreichend Rechnung trägt“[132], führte dazu, die Speicherpflicht als solche nicht bereits als von vornherein grundrechtswidrig einzustufen. Der weite Zugriff des EuGH richtet sich nun aber gegen jede nationale Regelung, „die für Zwecke der Bekämpfung von Straftaten eine allgemeine und unterschiedslose Vorratsspeicherung sämtlicher Verkehrs- und Standortdaten aller Teilnehmer und registrierten Nutzer in Bezug auf alle elektronischen Kommunikationsmittel vorsieht“.[133] Dies hat zur Folge, dass sogar die in Hinblick auf die Vorgaben[134] des Bundesverfassungsgerichts neu und deutlich restriktiver gefassten Regelungen zur Speicherung von Verkehrsdaten[135], die zudem eine massive Absenkung der Speicherungsdauer vorsehen[136], in der deutschen

[127] Schiedermair and Mrozek (2016), S. 92.

[128] Sandhu (2017), S. 458.

[129] Vgl. Derksen (2017), S. 1005.

[130] Wollenschläger and Krönke (2016), S. 909.

[131] Vgl. BVerfGE 125, 260 (316 ff.).

[132] BVerfGE 125, 260 (316).

[133] Rs. C-203/15 u. C-698/15 *Tele2 Sverige AB*, EU:C:2016:970; Rdnr. 112.

[134] Vgl. BT-Drs. 18/5088, S. 2.

[135] Insbes. § 100g StPO und § 113a-g des Telekommunikationsgesetzes (TKG), neugefasst bzw. eingeführt durch Artt. 1 und 2 des Gesetzes zur Einführung einer Speicherpflicht und einer Höchstspeicherfrist für Verkehrsdaten vom 10. Dezember 2015, BGBl. I, S. 2218.

[136] Während § 113a TKG a.F. für alle genannten Verkehrsdaten eine Speicherdauer von sechs Monaten vorsah, differenziert § 113b TKG nun zwischen Verbindungs- und Standortdaten und

Rechtsprechung nun als „objektiv-rechtlich mit Unionsrecht unvereinbar" gelten.[137] Die Bundesnetzagentur hat in Hinblick darauf entschieden, einstweilen „von Anordnungen und sonstigen Maßnahmen zur Durchsetzung der in § 113b TKG geregelten Speicherverpflichtungen gegenüber allen verpflichteten Unternehmen" abzusehen.[138] Das in dieser Konstellation zu Tage tretende Spannungsverhältnis wird noch im Einzelnen ausbuchstabiert werden müssen, denn ein Grundsatz, wonach im Grundrechteverbund stets das höhere Grundrechtsschutzniveau vorzuziehen sei, besteht nicht. Es sollte vielmehr im Grundrechteverbund keinen gegenseitigen Überbietungswettbewerb in Richtung eines „Immer Mehr" an Grundrechtsschutz geben. Dies gilt umso mehr in Hinblick auf mehrpolige Grundrechtskonstellationen, in denen etwa – und so verhält es sich bei der Vorratsdatenspeicherung – wegen bestehender grundrechtlicher Schutzpflichten das „Mehr" auf der einen mit einem „Weniger" auf der anderen Seite einhergeht und in denen auch legitime und gewichtige Gemeinwohlbelange wie etwa die Effektivierung von Strafverfolgung und Gefahrenabwehr zur Rechtfertigung von Eingriffen in Grundrechte geltend gemacht werden.

Zentral für die Funktionsfähigkeit und auch die Legitimität und Akzeptanz des europäischen Grundrechteverbunds wäre demgegenüber, dass dieser Raum für eine „Interaktion der Rechtsebenen lässt", um eine „inhaltliche Gleichschaltung unter der Ägide des überstaatlichen Rechts" zu vermeiden.[139] Vielmehr besteht von vornherein die Notwendigkeit, „dass auf überstaatlicher Ebene normative Rückversicherungen vor einer ausgreifenden Unitarisierung bestehen und strukturelle Erwägungen sicherstellen, dass derartige vielfaltswahrende Regeln und Prinzipien den Mitgliedstaaten in der Praxis einen Freiraum zur partikularen Identitätskonstruktion belassen."[140] In den Worten von *Andreas Voßkuhle*: Eine „Zentralisierung des Grundrechtsschutzes" auf der Unionsebene „würde potentiell zu einer von der Kompetenzverteilung zwischen Union und Mitgliedstaaten nicht getragenen Vereinheitlichung verschiedenster Rechtsmaterien vom Datenschutzrecht über das Versicherungsrecht bis hin zum Strafrecht führen, […] die nicht mehr vom Willen der Mitgliedstaaten getragen wäre."[141]

Die in jüngerer Zeit ebenfalls zu beobachtenden Tendenzen des EuGH zur stärkeren Freilassung nationaler Grundrechtsspielräume sind daher umso ausdrücklicher zu begrüßen. Zuletzt hat der EuGH im Rahmen eines Vorabentscheidungsverfahrens auf Vorlage des italienischen Verfassungsgerichtshofs (*Corte Costituzionale*) die italienische Praxis, Verjährungsvorschriften als

---

sieht für erstere einen Zeitraum von zehn Wochen, für letztere von vier Wochen vor. Dies soll dem „Gebot einer möglichst grundrechtsschonenden Regelung" genügen, so BT-Drs. 18/5088, S. 37.

[137] Vgl. den Beschluss des OVG Münster vom 22. Juni 2017, Az.: 13 B 238/17, insbes. Rdnr. 136.

[138] Vgl. die Mitteilung der Bundesnetzagentur vom 28. Juni 2017, abrufbar unter: https://www.bundesnetzagentur.de/DE/Sachgebiete/Telekommunikation/Unternehmen_Institutionen/Anbieterpflichten/OeffentlicheSicherheit/Umsetzung110TKG/VDS_113aTKG/VDS.html [letzter Abruf am 4. März 2019].

[139] Siehe Thym (2015), S. 58.

[140] Thym (2015), S. 58.

[141] Voßkuhle (2016), S. 164.

Bestandteil des materiellen Strafrechts zu erfassen und somit dem Grundsatz der Gesetzmäßigkeit der Strafe zu unterstellen, trotz in einer früheren Entscheidung bereits festgestellter[142] und in bestimmten Konstellationen bestehender Kollisionen mit dem Gebot effektiver Mehrwertsteuerbetrugsbekämpfung aus Art. 325 AEUV, gebilligt und klargestellt, dass die (insbesondere rückwirkende) Unanwendbarkeit von unionsrechtswidrigen Verjährungsvorschriften nicht verlangt sei, wenn dies nach italienischem Verfassungsverständnis zu einem Verstoß gegen den Gesetzmäßigkeitsgrundsatz führt.[143] Dies ist auch im grundrechtlichen Kontext bedeutsam, bezieht der EuGH doch die bei der Bekämpfung des Mehrwertsteuerbetrugs unionsrechtlich geforderte Grundrechtsbeachtungspflicht ausdrücklich auf die Möglichkeit, „nationale Schutzstandards für die Grundrechte anzuwenden".[144] Auch in diesem Fall hat der EuGH bewusst Raum für eigene grund- und verfassungsrechtliche Wertungen der nationalen Verfassungsgerichte gelassen und dies unter Hervorhebung des Umstandes, dass im Rahmen des Vorabentscheidungsverfahrens „zwischen dem Gerichtshof und den Gerichten der Mitgliedstaaten ein[en] Dialog von Gericht zu Gericht"[145] möglich ist.

4 Schlussbemerkung

Was kann der skizzierte Verbund für die Akzeptanz des Unionsrechts und des nationalen Europaverfassungsrechts leisten? Wenn er in der beschriebenen Weise, d.h. behutsam und unter Wahrung gegenseitigen Respekts gestaltet wird, dann wird er – bei aller Kritik an einzelnen Entscheidungen und Dialogbausteinen – der Akzeptanz des Unionsrechts dienen und damit auch seiner Durchsetzung. Zentral ist hier, dass jedes für seine Sphäre zuständige Gericht besondere Rücksicht gegenüber den jeweils anderen Sphären walten lässt, d.h. vor allen Dingen um eine konstruktive Abgrenzung (und gegebenenfalls Verzahnung im Sinne einer komplementären Geltung) der jeweils anwendbaren Grundrechtsordnungen in Hinblick auf die Notwendigkeiten der Effektivität des Unionsrechts bemüht ist. Der Mehrwert grundrechtlicher Pluralität wird sich nur einstellen, wenn die Gerichte nach einem „solidarischen Kooperationsprinzip[s]" agieren.[146] Der oftmals beklagte Verlust der ausschließlichen Zuständigkeit des Bundesverfassungsgerichts zur Überprüfung des in Deutschland anwendbaren Rechts wird dabei durch ein anderes Element kompensiert: die Mitwirkung an einer verbindlichen gemeineuropäischen Verfassungsordnung mit europaweiten Grundrechtsstandards. Wie fruchtbar dies

---

[142] EuGH, Rs. C-105/14 *Ivo Taricco u.a.*, ECLI:EU:C:2015:555.

[143] EuGH, Rs. C-42/17 *M.A.S. und M.B.* („Taricco II"), ECLI:EU:C:2017:936, Rdnrn. 29 ff.

[144] Vgl. EuGH, Rs. C- 42/17 *M.A.S. und M.B.* („Taricco II"), ECLI:EU:C:2017:936, Rdnrn. 46 f.

[145] EuGH, Rs. C-42/17 *M.A.S. und M.B.* („Taricco II"), ECLI:EU:C:2017:936, Rdnr. 22; vgl. zur Dialogfunktion auch Voßkuhle (2016), S. 5.

[146] So Lenaerts and Hartmann (2017), S. 322 f.

sein kann, zeigen nicht zuletzt die referierten Entscheidungen zum Europäischen Haftbefehl.

Literaturverzeichnis

Baade B (2017) Der Europäische Gerichtshof für Menschenrechte als Diskurswächter. Springer, Berlin-Heidelberg

Britz G (2015) Grundrechtsschutz durch das Bundesverfassungsgericht und den Europäischen Gerichtshof. EuGRZ:274–281

Burchardt D (2015) Die Rangfrage im europäischen Normenverbund. Mohr Siebeck, Tübingen

Dederer H-G (2006) Die Architektonik des europäischen Grundrechtsraums. ZaöRV 66:575–624

Derksen R (2017) Unionsrechtskonforme Spielräume für anlasslose Speicherung von Verkehrsdaten. NVwZ:1005–1009

Engel D (2015) Der Beitritt der Europäischen Union zur EMRK. Mohr Siebeck, Tübingen

Franzius C (2015) Grundrechtsschutz in Europa. Zwischen Selbstbehauptungen und Selbstbeschränkungen der Rechtsordnungen und ihrer Gerichte. ZaöRV 75:383–412

Haltern U (2017) Europarecht. Dogmatik im Kontext. Band II: Rule of Law – Verbunddogmatik – Grundrechte, 3. Auflage. Mohr Siebeck, Tübingen

Haratsch A (2006) Die *Solange*-Rechtsprechung des Europäischen Gerichtshofs für Menschenrechte. ZaöRV 66:927–947

Jarass HD (2016) Charta der Grundrechte der Europäischen Union, 3. Auflage. C.H.Beck, München

Keller H, Kühne D (2016) Zur Verfassungsgerichtsbarkeit des Europäischen Gerichtshofs für Menschenrechte. ZaöRV 76:245–306

Kohler Ch (2002) Vom EuGVÜ zur EuGVVO: Grenzen und Konsequenzen der Vergemeinschaftung. In: Schütze RA (Hrsg.) Einheit und Vielfalt des Rechts. Festschrift für Reinhold Geimer zum 65. Geburtstag. C.H. Beck, München

Lenaerts K, Hartmann M (2017) Der europäische Rechtsprechungsverbund in der Wirtschafts- und Währungsunion. JZ:321–332

Ludwigs P, Sikora M (2017) Grundrechtsschutz im Spannungsfeld von Grundgesetz, EMRK und Grundrechtecharta. JuS:385–393

Mannefeld L-K (2017) Verfassungsrechtliche Vorgaben für die europäische Integration. Mohr Siebeck, Tübingen

Meyer-Ladewig J, Nettesheim M, Von Raumer S (2017) EMRK, 4. Auflage. Nomos, Baden-Baden

Reinbacher T, Wendel M (2016) Menschenwürde und Europäischer Haftbefehl – Zum ebenenübergreifenden Schutz grundrechtlicher Elementargarantien im europäischen Auslieferungsverfahren. EuGRZ:333–343

Safferling C (2014) Der EuGH, die Grundrechtecharta und nationales Recht: Die Fälle Akerberg Fransson und Melloni. NStZ:545–551

Sandhu A (2017) Die Tele2-Entscheidung des EuGH zur Vorratsdatenspeicherung in den Mitgliedstaaten und ihre Auswirkungen auf die Rechtslage in Deutschland und in der Europäischen Union. EuR:453–470

Schiedermair S, Mrozek A (2016) Die Vorratsdatenspeicherung im Zahnräderwerk des europäischen Mehrebenensystems. DÖV:89–97

Schmidt-Aßmann E (2016) Einheit und Kohärenz der europäischen Mehrebenenrechtsordnung. EuGRZ:85–92

Schwarz M (2016) Grundlinien der Anerkennung im Raum der Freiheit, der Sicherheit und des Rechts. Mohr Siebeck, Tübingen

Thym D (2015) Vereinigt die Grundrechte! JZ:53–63

Voßkuhle A (2010) Der europäische Verfassungsverbund. NVwZ:1–8

Voßkuhle A (2016) Integration durch Recht – Der Beitrag des Bundesverfassungsgerichts. JZ:161–168
Wendel M (2015) Menschenrechtliche Überstellungsverbote: Völkerrechtliche Grundlagen und verwaltungsrechtliche Konkretisierung. DVBl:731–741
Wollenschläger F, Krönke L (2016) Telekommunikationsüberwachung und Verkehrsdatenspeicherung - eine Frage des EU-Grundrechtsschutzes? NJW:906–910

The authority of EU law as viewed from a National Court: The United Kingdom

Lord Thomas of Cwmgiedd

1 Introduction

At first sight, the authority of the law of the European Union (EU law) would appear to depend on the power and logic of the reasoning of the decisions of the court that ultimately decides what EU law is—the Court of Justice of the European Union (CJEU).

However, I do not think that this approach is necessarily the best way of approaching the issues that have been raised about the authority of EU law. These need to be looked at in the more general context of the role of courts and their relationship to the legislative and executive powers of the state and in the specific context of the relationship of the CJEU to the national courts and other EU institutions.

2 The role of courts

Although the UK has had a long tradition going back to the seventeenth century of courts playing a central role on the development of constitutional law and in the mid-twentieth century in the development of judicial review, the role of the courts has in recent years come in for substantial critical examination. Elsewhere the role of judges and courts has also been the subject of critical examination and sometimes abuse. The CJEU is not exempt from this. Indeed the role of the CJEU has been an important factor in the decision of the UK to give notice under Article 50 TEU of its

Until October 2017, Chief Justice of England and Wales.

Lord Thomas of Cwmgiedd (✉)
Essex Court Chambers, London, UK
e-mail: LordThomas@essexcourt.com

W. Heusel, J.-P. Rageade (eds.), *The Authority of EU Law*,
https://doi.org/10.1007/978-3-662-58841-3_9

intention to leave the EU and in the subsequent and ongoing negotiations and discussions as to the future relationship between the EU and the UK.

As far as I am aware there has been no real research into the reasons why in general the role of judges has come in for such critical examination, but I would venture to suggest seven particular causes for the generally critical examination of the role of judges. I have spoken elsewhere of this at greater length, but the points can be briefly summarised.

First, there is the universal acknowledgement of the fundamental importance of the rule of law as underpinning the way in which our respective states operate and society is maintained. Although the rule of law can be seen to have different meanings, the application of the rule of law, in whichever way the rule of law is defined, depends upon the judiciary. The position of judges has therefore moved to a more central position.

Second, arising out of the application of the rule of law, has been the growth of judicial review of administrative action taken by the executive power (or branch) of the state. The judiciary has thus been seen to provide an important element of enforcing the rule of law over the executive power, insisting on a proper and impartial analysis of the issues which arise, examining the lawfulness of what the executive power proposes to do and telling the executive power that it is wrong when it does not act in accordance with the rule of law. In some states the judiciary has been a far more effective fetter on the executive power than the legislature.

However, even in Europe, this is not everywhere the case. In contrast, again arising out of the application of the rule of law, the judiciary, by buttressing those who wish to resist change, can be seen as the institution that supports the executive power rather than fettering it. This is possibly a reversion in some state to what was long perceived to be the role of judges—supporting the status quo and in punishing those who try to change it, even by peaceful means. However such states are the exception in Europe. By and large, judges have come in most democratic states to be seen as the institution of the state which will uphold the rule of law as it is usually now understood; the judges have established in this way huge capital by way of credit within their own state.

Third, even though the position of judges in enforcing procedural compliance with the law has become well established, politicians have nonetheless been prepared in legislation and treaties to give judges powers to decide issues that traditionally had not been for judges to decide. The EU Treaties, the European Convention on Human Rights and the Charter of Fundamental Rights and Freedoms give judges significant new scope for making decisions in relation to issues that were formerly regarded as issues for the legislature. Judges have for some time exercised these powers when requested to do so at the suit of litigants; such litigants have come to see the judiciary in most democratic states as the institution of the state that is prepared to bring about change in a way that had not hitherto happened. Indeed, the development of the jurisprudence under such instruments is an example of how significant change can be made by judges to the way in which society works and lives in harmony.

Fourth, this growing influence of the judiciary and the changes judges can make to society has therefore led to a much more critical examination of the role of the judiciary and its decisions. That such criticism is sometimes robust is hardly surprising given the fact that we live in an era characterised by the decline of deference to institutions. Given the role judges have assumed, such criticism is an essential part of a democracy; judges should not only accept this, but welcome the fact that what they do is challenged in a critical manner. In some states, the judiciary have reacted positively to criticism by becoming more conscious of the need to explain its role and its decisions, a subject to which I will return.

Fifth, within this expanded role, judges have sometimes made decisions which politicians in the legislature or executive do not like. Though it was the politicians in the legislature who had given judges a considerably expanded scope for deciding issues, politicians have castigated judges as "activist" when, in exercising their powers as expanded in scope by such politicians, they make decisions the politicians do not like, particularly if the decisions protect a minority against the views of the majority or expand the powers of an institution that politicians did not want expanded.

Sixth, the perception of judicial activism has blended with the perception of the judiciary who insist on proper compliance with the rule of law to provide the opportunity to castigate judges; they are characterised as the "unelected" and the "unaccountable" who develop or change the law without democratic legislative action and hence legitimacy. In other words such attacks have begun to erode the capital judges had built up over the years.

Seventh with the rebirth of populism such attacks have increased, as the judiciary is seen by populists as the most significant institution that can insist on compliance with constitutional conventions and procedures and the rule of law. In their perception, the judiciary therefore forms a barrier to reliance on the populists' mantra—"the will of the people" and on occasions to abuse the judiciary, such as castigating judges as "enemies of the people".[1]

In my view, the issues relating to the authority of EU law must be seen first in this much wider context. In addition to these seven general matters which are applicable to national courts and the CJEU, there are at least four further specific matters which are relevant to the position of the authority of EU law and the CJEU.

First, the lose textured drafting of much Community legislation gives judges yet more scope in which to give decisions that make or develop the law. In general the UK Parliament is reluctant to draft legislation in this way. Sometimes when EU legislators cannot agree, they leave the text open so that the CJEU can decide what is best (I have been present when this has happened). This exposes the judiciary to the criticism that they are making law under the guise of interpretation, even though it is the legislative powers that have put the court in this position.

Second, the application and interpretation of the Charter of Fundamental Rights and Freedoms confers rights that are wider in scope than the European Convention

[1]After the decision of the Divisional Court in *R (Miller) v Secretary of State for Exiting the European Union* [2017] 2 WLR 583, some of the UK press attacked the judges in these terms.

on Human Rights. Again this gives rise to the considerations which I have already outlined.

Third the CJEU is perceived (and I emphasise this is a perception that may be without foundation) as having a preconceived broad purposive direction of travel when interpreting EU legislation. This direction of travel is often seen as support for ever closer union rather than pursuing a conventional interpretation based on the text under consideration.

Fourth, the CJEU has to deal with the relationship with national Courts at their highest level. Such courts have traditionally been supreme in their respective spheres of competence within the state and regarded themselves as the ultimate guardian of the rule of law in their states. In some states the courts at the highest level have developed sophisticated jurisprudence over the centuries. Perhaps not unsurprisingly a perception (which again may be without foundation) has arisen that the CJEU has not taken sufficient account of their position and not been prepared sufficiently to acknowledge the contribution that they have made and continue to make to the development of both national and EU law.

I have set out these matters as I think it is difficult to examine the authority of EU law without paying close attention to the position of the national courts and the CJEU at the current time, as well as having regard to perceptions, whether they be unfounded or not and whether they are fair or not. Perceptions have to be addressed and efforts made to correct them, even if they are ill founded or unfair.

3 The perceived position of the CJEU in relation to UK political and public opinion

A first example of the manifestation of these concerns can be found in the way in which the CJEU has been treated in the period leading up to and during the campaigns for a referendum on Brexit, as the role played by the CJEU became an important issue. Since the referendum its role has also become one of the "redlines" adopted by the UK government, particularly against the background of the view some UK politicians and some of the public had taken of the European Court of Human Rights in the immediately preceding period.

Again it is not clear precisely why this has happened. If an attempt is made to isolate decisions where politicians have criticised specific decisions of the CJEU (in contradistinction to the European Court of Human Rights), they are few and far between. For example one Minister criticised the judgments on data protection as hobbling the growth of internet companies[2]; another criticised the *SiMAP*[3] and

[2] Vote Leave, 20 February 2016.

[3] (2000) C-303/98.

Jaeger[4] decisions on the Working Time Directive as they affected work in hospitals.[5]

However, it appears that the real criticism is based on the perception of the CJEU as making decisions on issues regarded as political in nature from which there is no appeal and which it is difficult to change, in contrast to decisions of UK national courts that can be reversed by the legislature. Three examples of this may help explain the reasons for this perception. The first is the interpretation of the UK opt-out in respect of the Charter of Fundamental Rights and Freedoms; there was a popular perception amongst politicians that the opt-out was very far-reaching, but the decisions of the court in their eyes unduly restricted the scope of the opt-out. The second is the perception of the use of the Charter by the CJEU in developing rights rather than allowing the jurisprudence of the European Court of Human Rights to have primacy; this has a particular importance to the UK for two reasons. First, as the UK courts do not have to accept the decisions of the European Court of Human Rights, but merely take account of them; second neither the European Court of Human Rights nor the UK courts can invalidate UK legislation that contravenes the European Convention on Human Rights; it is left to Parliament to decide what to do. The third example is the perception that the CJEU in its decisions has shown it does not understand the ways in which the UK Parliament has balanced protection against the threat of terrorism, the powers of the Security Services and the secrecy of information with the need for liberty and open justice.

It is not my purpose to examine whether there is any basis whatsoever in these perceptions. What matters is that the perceptions have arisen in the general context I have endeavoured to explain; of particular importance is the view amongst some that the CJEU has made decisions that should not be taken by judges, but left to the legislature; and, even if taken by judges, such decisions do not have to be followed by the legislature or can be reversed by the legislature.

These perceptions have given rise to much more populist disparagement, manifesting itself in matters such as the claim that the UK loses more than 60% of its cases before the CJEU, that the CJEU enjoys doing down the UK, that the CJEU is always shifting the goal posts and that the CJEU is eroding laws enacted to protect the public against terrorism. Although each of these populist claims is unfounded in fact, it is a matter of real concern that such unfounded populist disparagement can gain sway amongst a significant part of the public.

4 The case law in relation to age discrimination

It is in this context that I approach the second example of the manifestation of the concerns I have expressed—the rejection by the Danish Supreme Court of the decisions of the CJEU in cases that form the focus of the panel discussion held at the

[4] (2003) C-151/02.

[5] House of Commons Hansard, 26 April 2012.

ERA jubilee congress—*Mangold v Helm* (2005),[6] *Pereda v Madrid Movilidad* (2009),[7] *Kücükdevici v Swedex* (2010)[8] and *Ajos v Rasmussen* (April 2016).[9] Each is a decision about the compatibility of national law enacted by national legislatures in relation to the general principle of EU law developed by the court prohibiting age discrimination. As the decisions make clear this principle was developed by the court from Directive 2000/78, various international instruments and the constitutional traditions common to the Member States and said by the court to be enshrined in Article 21 of the Charter; the effect was to prohibit national legislatures from enacting legislation that breached this general principle.

In the context of the matters to which I have referred, I do not think it was unsurprising that the Danish Supreme Court in its December 2016 decision *Ajos* refused to apply the CJEU decision in *Ajos*, holding that the Danish accession law did not provide a legal basis to permit the principle set out in these cases to take precedence over specific Danish legislation.

There is much literature on the development of the general principle originating from *Mangold* (some of it critical) and some commentaries questioning the approach of the Danish Supreme Court. However, I do not think it is necessary to analyse the comparative merits of the legal issues raised, as I think it unwise to see these questions as purely legal questions. Each court has used the tools of the law at its disposal to achieve the result it thinks right. What is more important are the much deeper questions as to the role of judges, their underlying approach to their functions and the issues of the relationships between courts and the legislature and the national courts and the CJEU. Any failure to address these questions is a failure to address serious issues currently facing the authority of law and the judiciary in our democracies.

5 The need to reconsider the approach of courts

The part the role of the CJEU has played in relation to the Brexit referendum and subsequent events in the UK and the decision of the Danish Supreme Court in *Ajos* are in my view very different examples of perceptions and concerns that have arisen as to the way in which EU law is developed and hence its authority.

Courts, of course, have a role in developing the law; the developments of commercial law in England by Lord Mansfield and his nineteenth century successors and the development of judicial review in the twentieth century are striking historical examples of the benefits of judge-made law. There are therefore plainly benefits from the substantial development of EU law by the CJEU, but they are not without substantial dangers which may not readily be appreciated.

---

[6] C-144/04.

[7] C-277/08.

[8] C-555/07.

[9] C-441/14.

It therefore may be wise in considering the development by judges of the law to reflect on the more general issues that relate to the position of courts and in particular the relationships with the other branches of the state. There have been of late some calls for self-restraint by the courts or, as it may be better put, role recognition.[10] It is, in my view, unwise of judges in any jurisdiction to fail to heed the limits of judicial power and the potential of the damage judges can do by such a failure. Unthinking activism can be very damaging the credit that the judiciary has built up.

I have also expressed the view that it is important for the judiciary of a democratic state to understand the principles of both independence and interdependence. The former is well known and a relatively easy call for judges; they must be independent of all interested in the outcome, protected from improper influences and decide cases without fear of making others unhappy and angry. Indeed one of the most important duties of a judge is to utilise that independence to protect an unpopular minority whose liberty or position might be threatened by the majority.

Interdependence[11] is a much more difficult call for judges as it takes them into an unfamiliar area. I have described it as comprising[12]:

- A clear understanding by each of the three powers (or branches) of the state of the constitutional functions and responsibilities of the other powers of the state;
- Mutual support by each of the powers of the other powers when carrying out the functions and responsibilities which the constitution has assigned to the other powers;
- Non-interference in the proper working of the functions and responsibilities which the constitution has assigned to another power by showing a proper and mutual respect for the role of the other powers.

On a national level, interdependence entails national courts engaging in dialogue with the other powers of the state on the basis of mutual respect and understanding of each other's functions, particularly with regard to the role of each in the development of the law. One consideration in that mutual understanding is the ease or difficulty in changing or amending the law as made; for example judges have to be more cautious in a given area, if it is difficult to change or amend the law as determined by judges.

---

[10] A term used by Lord Hodge of the UK Supreme Court in his lecture at Stellenbosch University *Judicial Law-making in a changing constitution* [2105] 26 Stellenbosch Law Review 471.

[11] A term used by Jackson J in the US Supreme Court in *Youngtown Co v Sawyer* 343 US 579 (1952) at 635:

> While the Constitution diffuses power the better to secure liberty, it also contemplates that practice will integrate the dispersed powers into a workable government. It enjoins upon its branches separateness but interdependence, autonomy but reciprocity.

[12] I examine this at much greater length in The Ryle Memorial Lecture given in June 2017 at the Palace of Westminster. *The judiciary within the State—the relationship between the three branches of the State.* https://www.judiciary.gov.uk/wp-content/uploads/2017/06/lcj-michael-ryle-memorial-lecture-20170616.pdf.

It seems to me that the principle of interdependence recognised within in a state can be adapted and applied at a supranational level. There is a direct parallel in the relationships with the other institutions of the supranational structure. By parity of reasoning, the principles of interdependence can also apply to the relationship between a supranational court such as the CJEU and the national courts. At the core of interdependence in such a relationship should be a more clearly defined relationship between the supranational court and the national courts. For example, the relationship should reflect the fact that national courts have a closer understanding not only of national law (even though research can be carried out by advocates and the staff of the supranational court), but also of the way in which particular issues are perceived in their state—not just law, but a wider understanding of the operation of the whole of the government of a state, as the judicial power is one part of the state. The definition of the relationship would involve the development of a more clear delineation of the nature of the dialogue between national courts and the CJEU. Such dialogues should be based not on deference, but on mutual respect for and acknowledgement of each other's functions and contributions to the development of the law. It is, in my view, important that the position of national courts at the highest level is respected not only as the supreme judicial body within their own state, but also as an essential part of the EU legal order. Although ultimately there has, of course, to be a court whose decisions are final, such a court can only achieve respect for its decisions by dialogue and an acknowledgement of the importance of the views of national courts. The relationship with respect to EU law might best be expressed on the basis of primus inter pares and not on the basis it is a superior court. The discussion and development of such a relationship based on the principles of interdependence would, in my view, considerably strengthen the authority of EU law and address some of the background factors I have outlined.

There are two other matters which may also assist given the context in which the judiciary now operates—proper communication and accountability. National judges have in recent years learnt that it is not enough to explain their decisions in language that can be understood only by lawyers and other judges; nor is it wise simply to blame newspapers or social media as biased and uninformed, for that is to ignore their influence. It is necessary for judges to find a means of communicating their decisions directly in their own words in terms that are readily understandable by all interested in the decision. Pithy summaries written by judges themselves in everyday language rather than a press office or a judicial assistant are, it has been found, the best way of doing this. This is a valuable lesson no court, whether national or supranational, should fail to observe, for much of the court's legitimacy is dependent on its ability to communicate directly and to explain its decision in the context of the factors I have outlined. For if a court is not prepared to engage directly in the explanation of its role and its decisions, particularly where judges make law, there are many others prepared to do it for them, in terms that they may not like and with consequences that may not only wipe out the credit balance the judiciary has achieved but also begin to undermine the authority of the law.

The accountability of the judiciary is a subject that is seldom sufficiently addressed in this context. Ordinarily accountability is provided by open hearings and clearly expressed reasoning. I question, however, whether more cannot be done to demonstrate judicial accountability. At any level this can be done by providing regular information about the way a court deals with the business before it—speed, workload, cost are obvious indicators. But should judges go further?

6 The development of a separate UK EU jurisprudence

There is one final matter to raise by way of a footnote. At present, the CJEU is the only court which finally determines issues of EU law; that will remain the case after Brexit, but the Supreme Court of the UK may provide an alternative view on some legal issues which the CJEU cannot overrule, but simply disapprove.

At present it is intended that the UK will incorporate the acquis as it exists at the date of Brexit, with very limited exceptions (such as the omission of the Charter of Fundamental Rights and Freedoms and the law as to damages as established by the decision in *Francovich*[13]). After that date there will be no new references to the CJEU. It is also intended that the UK courts will be free to develop their own jurisprudence in relation to the acquis; the Supreme Court will be given power to overrule or otherwise depart from decisions of the CJEU given at any time whilst the UK was a Member State.

For the future, it may be of interest to see how the UK Supreme Court develops its jurisprudence on the acquis. It must be recalled that the common law has been enriched by the developments in the courts of the United States for over two centuries and much more recently in states such as Australia, Singapore, New Zealand and Canada, where the Supreme Courts have from time to time arrived at different strands of law which have subsequently influenced English law. Is it possible the same may happen to some strands of the acquis after Brexit? If so, may be it will enrich the acquis and hence the authority of EU law. If so, it will be an unintended consequence of Brexit.

[13] Case C-6/90 and C-9/90; [1991] ECR I-5357.

The authority of EU law: The case of horizontal application of fundamental rights

Maciej Szpunar

1 Introductory remarks

The relationship between the Court of Justice and national supreme courts has been discussed and analysed from different angles for many years. While some of the controversies constitute evergreens in doctrinal analysis, others have been revealed in the case-law of national supreme courts. In some—admittedly rare—decisions of national supreme courts, the authority of the Court of Justice—as the supreme jurisdiction for the interpretation of EU law—has been challenged.

In the times we live in it is very often not only EU law but the law in general whose authority is challenged. In a similar vein, it is not only the authority of the Court of Justice which is challenged, but often the authority of courts at large.

When we speak about the authority of EU law, it appears to me a bit awkward that the debate is concentrated almost exclusively on the question whether the Court of Justice has, in some instances, acted *ultra vires*, that is to say outside its own jurisdiction or outside the jurisdiction of the Union. Indeed, the debate is often presented as a dispute between the Court of Justice and supreme courts of the Member States.

This is unfortunate. It goes without saying that the Court of Justice retains the supreme role in the interpretation of EU law. But at the same time it is national courts that apply EU law in the first place. And, just as the Court of Justice, they do so, all across Europe, on a daily basis. In fact, it is only a tiny minority of disputes

All views expressed in this article are strictly personal.

M. Szpunar (✉)
University of Silesia, Katowice, Poland

Court of Justice of the European Union, Luxembourg, Luxembourg

ERA Board of Trustees, Trier, Germany
e-mail: maciej.szpunar@curia.europa.eu

W. Heusel, J.-P. Rageade (eds.), *The Authority of EU Law*,
https://doi.org/10.1007/978-3-662-58841-3_10

involving EU law where the Court of Justice has a chance to interpret EU law within the framework of the preliminary ruling procedure. For this reason I would dare to assert that national courts, and especially supreme jurisdictions, contribute to the authority of EU law almost to the same extent as the Court of Justice. Before turning to the merits of the analysis, I should like to recall some basic principles of EU law that I deem useful in the light of further considerations.

First, the legal order within the European Union is 'multicentric'[1] in nature. The law applicable in the Member States is not created by a single legislature. In addition to the respective laws of the Member States, there is the legal order of the Union, and, not to forget, the legal order based on the European Convention for the Protection of Human Rights and Fundamental Freedoms. It is clear that the relationship between the legal order of the Union and the respective legal orders of the Member States is the most important one. However, when referring to the European legal space, one cannot ignore the Convention—even if it is not supranational in nature.

Secondly, the difference between these legal orders is not solely the result of the existence of numerous centres of legislative power: it is above all the result of the existence of numerous centres of judicial power. The judicial power within the European legal space is not based on a hierarchical system. In other words, constitutional and supreme courts in the Member States are not subordinate to the Court of Justice; likewise, the Court of Justice is not subordinate to the judicial authorities of the Member States. Each of these courts retains its own jurisdiction: the Court of Justice as regards the interpretation of EU law and the assessment of the validity of EU secondary law; and the courts of the Member States as regards the interpretation of national law and the determination of the disputes pending before them. In the context of the preliminary reference procedure, the Court of Justice does not settle the dispute: it merely interprets EU law.

Thirdly, the legal order of the Union is not a "closed" system. With the exception, perhaps, of the law governing the institutions, EU law cannot function independently of the legal orders of the Member States. This has both a procedural aspect, insofar as EU law is applied primarily by the judicial authorities of the Member States, and a substantive aspect, in that the rights stemming from EU law are often implemented with the help of national law, in the context of what is commonly termed as the procedural autonomy of the Member States. In this context, it should also be borne in mind that, for instance, the judicial decisions based on EU law are, as a rule, enforced on the basis of the enforcement provisions specific to the Member States.

[1] I use the term "multicentric" following publications of the renowned Polish scholar Łętowska (2002), p. 1127.

2 Interpretation of fundamental rights and general principles of law as a challenge to the authority of EU law

On the basis of these introductory remarks, I will address the main problem of the present analysis, which is the authority of EU law.

The case law of both the Court of Justice and national supreme jurisdictions as well as problems analysed in the legal writings show that potential conflicts arise first and foremost in the area of fundamental rights and general principles of EU law, often in connection with EU secondary law. Indeed, the *Solange* saga started off with fundamental rights in the 1970s.[2] Moreover, fundamental rights, being part of primary law, constitute a domain of EU law where the judge-made law may—potentially—prevail over legislation. It is here where the danger of switching power from the legislator to the judiciary may occur.

The general reproach made to the Court of Justice is that of '*ultra vires* acts'. Given that I am a member of that institution, it will not be surprising that I do not entirely share such reproaches.

3 Autonomy of EU law

It is not the autonomy of EU law in general that sometimes comes under fire from constitutional and supreme courts. Indeed, this principle which is well established and which has surfaced mainly in three Opinions of the Court (1/91, EEA Agreement[3]; 1/09, Patent Court[4]; and 2/13, Accession to the ECHR[5]) and in the recent decision in *Achmea*[6] does not seem to me to be questioned in general. What seems to provoke the debate about the Court of Justice acting allegedly *ultra vires* is the horizontal application of fundamental rights and general principles of EU law. I will, therefore, devote my analysis to this particular problem, bearing in mind that there are also other domains in which the case law of the Court of Justice may provoke controversies.

[2] Federal Constitutional Court of Germany, judgment of 29 May 1974, *Solange I* (BVerfGE 37, 271); Federal Constitutional Court of Germany, judgment of 22 October 1986, *Solange II* (BVerfGE 73, 339).

[3] Opinion of 14 December 1991, EU:C:1991:490.

[4] Opinion of 8 March 2011, EU:C:2011:123.

[5] Opinion of 18 December 2014, EU:C:2014:2454.

[6] Judgment of 6 March 2018, *Achmea*, C-284/16, EU:C:2018:158.

4 General principles in horizontal situations

What tends to irk national courts is when the Court—as they perceive it—pulls concepts out of the hat which they did not reckon with. This occurs first and foremost in the area of horizontal application of general principles of EU law.

As I will demonstrate, there is an issue when it comes to the relationship between fundamental rights and general principles of EU law and their horizontal application.

As is well known, EU fundamental rights which were first developed by the Court of Justice as (unwritten, as in 'not written into the Treaties') principles of EU law have been—to a large extent—codified in the Charter of Fundamental Rights and this for good reason: a right enshrined in a text of a constitutional nature has more clout and visibility than one to be searched in the European Court Reports.

Following classical liberal doctrine, fundamental rights, in general, should not be invoked against individuals in that otherwise individual liberty would be curtailed too much.[7] A right of one person is always the obligation of another person. This should always be borne in mind in horizontal situations which are, as a rule, governed by the principle of private autonomy and the ensuing freedom between parties. This freedom is in the first place exemplified by the freedom of contract.

5 What does "horizontal application" mean?

The horizontal application of a particular legal norm is very often confused with the problem whether, in litigation involving a private party, this party should bear the negative consequences of the application of that legal norm. By horizontal application of a legal norm one should understand that a private individual is a direct addressee of this norm. In other words, this norm is capable of regulating directly the behaviour of private individuals. This is for example the case of Art. 101 TFEU which is addressed to all undertakings, be they public or private, and stipulates how undertakings should (not) behave on the market.[8]

It does not mean that a legal norm that is deprived of horizontal application cannot affect the outcome of proceedings involving private parties. If one takes the example of Art. 34 TFEU prohibiting quantitative restrictions on imports and all measures having equivalent effect, it is clear in the case law of the Court of Justice that this provision has no horizontal direct effect since it is not addressed to private individuals. It means that the behaviour of a private individual cannot be assessed solely in the light of this provision. Nevertheless, it is not excluded that this provision

[7] See e.g. Safjan and Miklaszewicz (2010), p. 479. These authors correctly point out that "According to the dominant opinion formulated in the constitutional doctrine, the nature of the fundamental rights and freedoms is strongly differentiated. Certain fundamental rights cannot, by virtue of their very nature, produce horizontal effects at least in a narrower meaning limited to the direct effect."

[8] See Prechal and de Vries (2009), p. 12 et seq.

can be invoked in proceedings between individuals. This is the case when a national court is called upon to assess the compatibility of national law or EU secondary legislation under Art. 34 TFEU.[9] It follows that, even though Art. 34 TFEU has no horizontal direct effect and is not addressed to individuals, its application may have negative consequences for private parties. A typical example would be that of a private individual relying on a national legislation that turns out to be incompatible with Art. 34 TFEU and is for this reason inapplicable.

We are dealing with a similar situation in the case of the application of fundamental rights which, in principle, are not applicable horizontally. One could easily imagine a situation in which an individual invokes against another individual a fundamental right in order to plead that, either, an act of EU law has to be interpreted in conformity with this fundamental right, or, an act of EU law is contrary to this right. Here, we are not dealing with the horizontal application of fundamental rights. In these kinds of disputes an individual is not invoking a fundamental right in order to impose obligations on another individual. The fundamental right in question serves only as an instrument in the light of which an act of EU law—that constitutes a legal base on which the dispute has to be resolved—is to be assessed. It is clear that EU acts of secondary law cannot be contrary to the fundamental rights including those stemming from the Charter.[10]

6 The effect of Art. 51 of the Charter

In accordance with its Art. 51, the fundamental rights of the Charter are addressed to public authorities[11]: those of the EU and those of the Member States when they are implementing EU law, which means when they act within the scope of application of EU law.[12] As a consequence, fundamental rights of the Charter cannot be addressed to individuals and for this reason are not capable of imposing on them direct obligations.[13]

---

[9] Judgments of 10 November 1982, *Rau Lebensmittelwerke*, 261/81, EU:C:1982:382, and of 4 November 1997, *Parfums Christian Dior*, C-337/95, EU:C:1997:517.

[10] The notion of direct effect in its classical meaning cannot be confused with the doctrinal proposal of distinguishing between the so called 'invocability of exclusion' (fr. 'invocabilité d'exclusion') and 'invocability of substitution' (fr. invocabilité de substitution'). This distinction was initially proposed by AG Léger in his opinion in the case *Linster* (C-287/98, paras 57 et seq.) and, then developed further in legal writings. In his analysis, AG Léger relied, in particular, on the publication of Galmot and Bonichot (1988), p. 10 et seq. In my view this distinction, even though attractive from the doctrinal point of view, should not have any influence on the application of EU law in practice.

[11] It is debated in legal writings to what extent this provision of the Charter can be understood as having the same consequences as the Treaty provision (Art. 288(3) TFEU) excluding the horizontal direct effect of directives—see: Leczykiewicz (2013), pp. 485–486.

[12] Judgment of 26 February 2013, *Åkerberg Fransson*, C-617/10, EU:C:2013:105.

[13] This is also very well explained by Advocate General Trstenjak in her Opinion in *Domínguez*, C-282/10, EU:C:2011:559, paras 80–83; see also Trstenjak and Beysen (2013), p. (293) 308. It has

The Court's case-law to date bears testimony to this. Thus, for instance, in *AMS*,[14] it was held that Article 27 of the Charter (by itself or in conjunction with the provisions of Directive 2002/14 establishing a general framework for informing and consulting employees) cannot impose obligations on individuals.

7 Do the general principles of EU law matter after the Charter became a binding instrument?

The fact that the Charter became a binding instrument and many of the existing general principles of EU law have been incorporated into the Charter does not mean that the former are obsolete. There is nothing in the wording of the Charter that could suggest that the fundamental rights of the Charter affect the existence of the general principles of law in the EU legal order. First of all, the general principles of the EU constitute an open catalogue of fundamental rights and principles that—by definition—cannot be exhaustively listed in a legal document. Secondly, as I will demonstrate below, some of the restrictions on the application of the Charter may not necessarily affect the application of the general principles of EU law. Thirdly, the Court itself ruled that some provisions of the Charter must be understood as a confirmation of already existing general principles of law which have their source in various instruments of international law and in constitutional traditions common to the Member States.[15]

8 May the general principles of EU law apply in horizontal situations?

It has to be asserted that, as a rule, the general principles of EU law apply in vertical situations only, the rationale being analogous to that of fundamental rights. However, this principle is subject to some exceptions. For example, the principles of non-discrimination with respect to pay, enshrined in Article 157 TFEU, and of free movement of workers under Article 45 TFEU were held, by the Court, to apply in

---

to be emphasised, however, that the recent judgment of the Court in the case *Egenberger*, C-414/16, did not refer to Article 51 of the Charter while discussing the horizontal direct effect of Articles 21 and 47 of the Charter. Nevertheless one must bear in mind that at the same time the Court considered that the prohibition of discrimination based on religion or belief constitutes a general principle of EU law (para 76 of this judgment).

[14] Judgment of 15 January 2014, *Association de médiation sociale*, C-176/12, EU:C:2014:2.

[15] Para 75 of the *Egenberger* decision.

both vertical and horizontal situations in the cases *Defrenne*[16] and *Angonese*[17] respectively.

In addition to this, since *Mangold,*[18] the Court also holds the principle of non-discrimination on grounds of age has to apply in horizontal situations. The Court has confirmed this in decisions such as *Kücükdeveci*[19] and *DI*,[20] also known as *Ajos*. Moreover, in *Egenberger* the Court held that the prohibition of discrimination based on religion or belief may also apply horizontally.[21] And it is here that there is a source of conflict.

I do not need to go in detail into the *Ajos* saga, for this has already been discussed extensively in legal writings.[22] But I would like to stress that the point of contention for the Danish Supreme Court was that the principle of non-discrimination on grounds of age was judge-made, as opposed to written in a Treaty and therefore apparently of secondary quality.

The legal argument in defence of the Court of Justice is straightforward. Whether written into Treaties or derived out of the context and objectives of the Treaties, a general principle of EU law, in the form it is shaped by the Court of Justice, constitutes a part of primary law[23] which is, moreover, supreme over national law in case of conflict. This amounts to saying that whatever the interpretation of the Court is, it has to be followed by the courts of the Member States. The Court is not precluded from finding that some general principles of EU law may be horizontally applicable and may be addressed to acts of private individuals.

While this is certainly true, the real question appears to me, however, to be the following: what is the precise delimitation between fundamental rights and general principles of EU law when it comes to horizontal application?[24] It has to be recalled that by virtue of its Art. 51, the Charter is addressed to public bodies only and for this reason it cannot impose obligations on individuals. Does this, therefore, mean that the possibility to apply general principles of EU law horizontally may, in some way or another, amount to a circumvention of Art. 51 of the Charter?

---

[16] Judgment of 25 May 1971, *Defrenne*, 80/70, EU:C:1971:55.

[17] Judgment of 6 June 2000, *Angonese*, C-281/98, EU:C:2000:296.

[18] Judgment of 22 November 2005, *Mangold*, C-144/04, EU:C:2005:709.

[19] Judgment of 19 January 2010, *Kücükdeveci*, C-555/07, EU:C:2010:21.

[20] Judgment of 19 April 2016, *DI*, C-441/14, EU:C:2016:278.

[21] Judgment of 17 April 2018, *Egenberger*, C-414/16, para 77.

[22] See, e.g.; Reuter (2015), pp. 279–282; Picod (2016), p. 871; Kainer (2016), pp. 262–270; Dubout (2016), pp. 287–297; Holdgaard et al. (2018), pp. 17–54.

[23] '(…) *general principles of EU law enjoy a "constitutional status*"', see Lenaerts and Gutiérrez-Fons (2010), p. 1629, at 1647 et seq.; Lenaerts (2013), p. 470.

[24] I am not speaking here about 'principles' enshrined into the Charter itself. The distinction between rights and principles of the Charter is another story. In the latter context see Safjan and Miklaszewicz (2010), p. 480 who claim that: "[t]he Charter distinguishes between rights and principles. In particular, principles should be 'judicially cognizable only in the interpretation' of EU acts and national acts implementing European Union law and 'in the ruling on their legality' (Article 52(5) of the Charter). This provision seems, at first glance, to exclude any direct effect of the principles enshrined in the Charter".

This problem is in particular illustrated by the decisions in *Mangold* and *Kücükdeveci*, in which the Court of Justice, by reference to general principles of EU law, *de facto* allowed for the horizontal application of directive provisions, which is normally excluded by virtue of EU law. The Court of Justice ruled that certain provisions of a directive constituted a concretisation of the general principle of non-discrimination on grounds of age. Since this general principle of EU law could be applied horizontally, it was also possible to apply horizontally provisions of a directive that were simply confirming the existence and the scope of this principle.

If in legal doctrine the Court is criticised for not following the reasoning of *Kücükdeveci* in *AMS*, I would retort: for good reason, given that *AMS* is the rule and *Kücükdeveci* should be seen as the exception.[25]

Indeed, if we were to assimilate fundamental rights of the Charter to general principles of EU law, we would end up circumventing the limitation of the personal scope of the application of the Charter resulting from its Art. 51.[26] To illustrate this point: if the Court had followed this reasoning in *AMS*, there would have been no obstacle to apply horizontally all directives on consumer protection. After all, a high level of consumer protection is proclaimed in Art. 38 of the Charter.

In this context it is worth mentioning the reasoning of the Court in *Egenberger*. As has already been stated above, the prohibition of discrimination based on religion or belief constitutes a general principle of EU law which has its source in various instruments of international law and in the constitutional traditions common to the Member States.[27] For the Court, this prohibition is sufficient in itself to confer on individuals a right that can be invoked against another individual.[28] In that sense, the nature of this prohibition—which is laid down in Article 21 of the Charter—is similar to certain Treaty provisions on the internal market.[29]

We must therefore accept that the relation between fundamental rights of the Charter and general principles of EU law—that may exceptionally be applicable horizontally—is delicate and more complex than one might imagine at first sight. I personally and consciously defend the view that the mere inclusion of a particular right into the Charter does not mean that this right is automatically recognised as a general principle of EU law which could be invoked in a horizontal situation.

Furthermore, I am convinced that, as a rule, general principles of EU law should not be applied horizontally, for the very reason that, as I outlined already, horizontal application amounts to curtailing private autonomy.[30] As a consequence, we should perhaps envisage allowing for a horizontal application only in exceptional cases such as in the case of the principle of non-discrimination.[31]

---

[25] Opinion of Advocate General Mengozzi in *Fenoll*, C-316/13, EU:C:2014:1753, paras 59–60.

[26] See: Fornasier (2015), p. 41 with the cited literature: Pech (2012), p. (1841) 1869.

[27] Para 75.

[28] Para 76.

[29] This can be inferred from para 77 of the judgment.

[30] Basedow (2016), pp. 345–346.

[31] This cautious view is shared e.g. by Basedow (2016), p. 349; Leczykiewicz (2013), p. 486; Muir (2011), p. 47—"*Either the Court opts for the unitary approach, thus supporting a very ambitious*

9 Consistent interpretation of national law: limits resulting from non *contra legem*

Another problem that stems from the *Ajos* decision concerns the limits of so-called consistent interpretation.

To me it is clear that it is for national law to determine what constitutes an interpretation *contra legem*. We are here in a situation of, as you would say in French: *obligation de moyens et non pas de résultat*. The Court of Justice cannot impose on national courts to interpret national law in such a way as to reach a concrete result. Even the following passage from *Ajos* does not alter this principle:

> The national court [the Danish Supreme Court] cannot validly claim that it is impossible for it to interpret the national provision at issue in a manner that is consistent with EU law by mere reason of the fact that it has consistently interpreted that provision in a manner that is incompatible with EU law.[32]

What the Court of Justice is saying is simply that if the only reason why a national rule cannot be interpreted in conformity with EU law is that, until now, this rule has been interpreted differently, this amounts to a breach of the *obligation de moyens*.[33] If there are, however, other reasons stemming from national rules on interpretation—which of course fall outside the scope of EU law—the result could be different.

10 Legal certainty for individuals

Also Advocate General Trstenjak, in her opinion in the *Domínguez*[34] case, had reservations regarding the legal certainty for private individuals and the risk of mixing sources of law with regard to directives as secondary law and general principles as primary EU law. About the absence of legal certainty[35] for private individuals she emphasised:

> The principle of legal certainty requires that rules involving negative consequences for individuals should be clear and precise and their application predictable for those subject to them. However, as it will never be possible for a private individual to be certain when an unwritten general principle given specific expression by a directive will gain acceptance

understanding of the process of European integration, or it opts for the more humble dual approach and consequently ought to justify giving direct effect to provisions of EU law on a case-by case basis".

32 Para 34.

33 See also para 73 of the judgment in *Egenberger*.

34 Opinion of Advocate General Trstenjak in *Domínguez*, C-282/10, EU:C:2011:559.

35 Timmermans (2016), p. 676 "*Direct intervention of EU law in private law relationships* ***raises*** *delicate questions of legal certainty. It also raises questions of legitimacy in cases where Treaty law does not explicitly allow EU law directly to grant rights to and impose obligations on private parties*".

over written national law there would, from his point of view, be uncertainty as to the application of national law similar to that experienced where a directive is directly applied in a relationship between private individuals.[36]

In this context it seems appropriate to emphasise that the principle according to which general principles of EU law cannot be applied horizontally is not strict. The argument that no obligations may be imposed on a private party through the applications of the general principles of EU law cannot be considered as a rule without any exceptions.

Let us analyse for example the consequences of consistent interpretation. In this respect I would like to refer to the obligation to interpret EU secondary law as well as national law in the light of the Charter and general principles of EU law. In every dispute between two private individuals, the obligation to interpret national law in conformity with EU law would be favourable to one party only and disadvantageous to the other party. It is equally true as far as the obligation to interpret EU secondary law in the light of the Charter and general principles of EU law is concerned. Private parties must sometimes also bear the negative consequences of consistent interpretation. It is clear that in many situations the outcome of particular proceedings is different whether a particular provision of EU secondary law or national law is or is not interpreted in conformity with superior legal norms.

It has to be underlined that the limitations concerning the negative consequences of consistent interpretation in the field of criminal liability do not apply in the context of horizontal situations. It follows from the decision in *Pupino*,[37] in which the Court of Justice introduced this kind of limitation that the consistent interpretation may not lead to establishing or enhancing the criminal liability of an individual. In any event this decision cannot be understood as introducing any limitations on negative consequences of the consistent interpretation for a private party in disputes involving claims of private law.

This means that the argument stemming from the absence of legal certainty for private individuals, if we accept—to some limited extent—the horizontal effect of fundamental rights, cannot be understood strictly. Indeed, can we really say that the obligation to respect the principle of non-discrimination of workers violates the legitimate expectations of the employer? Even if a particular means of discrimination (in this case "discrimination based on age") is not expressly prohibited or prohibited only by a directive that was not implemented into national law?

Let me finish by presenting another observation. I have the impression that the importance of distinction between private/public entities is slightly exaggerated. This distinction is of course the result of the fact that the constitutional charter of EU law is based on international treaties. Therefore, the concept of a state and its emanations plays a pivotal role. We all see, however, that this distinction reflects neither economic nor social reality. There is no doubt that there are entities which even though cannot be considered as emanations of Member States, but which

---

[36] See Opinion of Advocate General Trstenjak in Domínguez, C-282/10, EU:C:2011:559, para 164.

[37] Judgment of 16 June 2005, *Pupino*, C-105/03, EU:C:2005:386.

nevertheless exercise substantive influence on economic and social life. For this reason it is perfectly justified that the Court ruled that certain Treaty provisions concerning the internal market like Art. 45, Art. 49 and Art. 56 TFEU are also addressed to individuals which cannot be considered as "emanations of the state". To what extent this reasoning could also apply to the personal scope of certain general principles of EU law is a different story.

In this context one has to draw attention to two interesting cases that have recently been decided by the Court of Justice, *Max Planck Gesellschaft e.V.* (C-684/16) as well as *Bauer and Willmeroth* (C-569/16 and C-570/16). These proceedings concern the possibility of relying on Art. 31 paragraph 2 of the Charter in order to justify the horizontal direct effect of some provisions of Directive 2003/88 concerning certain aspects of the organisation of working time.

While in the first case the Court solely relied on the Charter, in the second it relied on the combined application of the Directive and the Charter. These cases perfectly illustrate current challenges. There will certainly be further challenges in the years to come. The Court of Justice will thus continue to need to position itself in relation to this phenomenon. But it cannot do it properly without the help of national courts, especially supreme jurisdictions.

11 Conclusions

By way of conclusion it should be reminded that we are living at a time when the idea of European integration and, on that basis, the functioning of the European legal space are being put to a test. From that aspect, the proper functioning of European justice, and the fact of ensuring the legitimacy of our decisions and reacting in an opportune fashion to the challenges of our era, assume particular importance.

To my mind, it is essential—in the present era, in particular—for the Court of Justice and the constitutional and supreme courts of the Member States to be in a relationship of mutual trust.

The authority and the legitimacy of all European jurisdictions are very closely linked. The rule of law must impose itself in the same way, within both the Member States and the European Union.

References

Basedow J (2016) General principles of European private law and interest analysis some reflections in the light of Mangold and Audiolux. Eur Rev Private Law (3 & 4):345

Dubout E (2016) Grandeur et décadence de l'obligation d'interprétation conforme aux directives dans les litiges horizontaux. Revue des affaires européennes:287

Fornasier M (2015) The impact of EU fundamental rights on private relationships: direct or indirect effect? Eur Rev Private Law 23(1):41

Galmot Y, Bonichot J-C (1988) La Cour de justice des Communautés européennes et la transposition des directives en droit national. Revue française de droit administratif 4(1):10
Holdgaard R, Elkan D, Schaldemose GK (2018) From cooperation to collision: the ECJ's *Ajos* ruling and the Danish Supreme Court's refusal to comply. Common Mark Law Rev 55(1):17
Kainer F (2016) Zu den Grenzen richtlinienkonformer Auslegung und horizontalen Richtlinienwirkungen. Zeitschrift für Gemeinschaftsprivatrecht:262
Leczykiewicz D (2013) Horizontal application of the charter of fundamental rights. Eur Law Rev 38(4)
Lenaerts K (2013) The principle of equal treatment and the European Court of Justice. Il Diritto dell'Unione Europea Anno XVIII (3):470
Lenaerts K, Gutiérrez-Fons JA (2010) The constitutional allocation of powers and general principles of EU law. Common Mark Law Rev 47(6):1629
Łętowska E (2002) Multicentryczność współczesnego system prawa i wykładnia jej przyjazna. In: Ogiegło L, Popiołek W, Szpunar M (eds) Rozprawy prawnicze. Księga pamiątkowa Profesora Maksymiliana Pazdana. Zakamycze, Kraków, p 1127
Muir E (2011) Of ages in-and edges of-EU law. Common Mark Law Rev 48:39
Pech L (2012) Between judicial minimalism and avoidance: the Court of Justice's sidestepping of fundamental constitutional issues in *Römer and Dominguez*. Common Mark Law Rev 49:1841
Picod F (2016) Non-discrimination en fonction de l'âge dans un litige entre particuliers, La Semaine Juridique - édition générale, n° 17 p 871
Prechal S, de Vries D (2009) Seamless web of judicial protection in the internal market? Eur Law Rev 34(1):5
Reuter M (2015) Zeitschrift für europäisches Sozial- und Arbeitsrecht. pp 279–282
Safjan M, Miklaszewicz P (2010) Horizontal effect of the general principles of EU law in the sphere of private law. Eur Rev Private Law 18(3):479
Timmermans C (2016) Horizontal direct/indirect effect or direct/indirect horizontal effect: what's in a name? Eur Rev Private Law 24(3-4):676
Trstenjak V, Beysen E (2013) The growing overlap of fundamental freedoms and fundamental rights in the case law of the CJEU. Eur Law Rev 38:293

Part IV
Remaining and new obstacles to the single market rules: Does the economic crisis justify a weakening of the authority of EU law?

The authority of the law: Some personal reflections on the internal market and European integration

Marc van der Woude

1 Introduction

Before joining the General Court in 2010, I had the pleasure of working in the Brussels office of a well-reputed Belgo-Dutch law firm. As any international firm combining people of various origins, generations and social background, it had its internal tensions. As one could expect, the relations between the Dutch and the Belgians were not always perfect. Neither were the relations between the Dutch speakers and the French speaking colleagues always harmonious. Even so, it was (and still is) an enjoyable and successful firm. With hindsight, I see two important factors that contributed to overcoming internal frictions. The first factor was explained to me by the then office manager of the firm.[1] In his view, and now also mine, human conflicts often arise because of perceptions, which do not necessarily coincide with objective facts and true intentions. The stronger emotions are, the wider this gap tends to become. Lifting the veil of perceptions, therefore, helps to avoid and solve conflicts. The second factor that contributed to the firm's success was a sense of common purpose. There were no fundamental doubts about the objectives pursued by the partnership: offering a good service and being paid accordingly. Readers may wonder what these personal recollections have to do with the internal market project and European integration. Now, the answers to this question relate to the two factors mentioned above: the contrast between perceptions and reality and the absence of uncertainties as to the objectives pursued.

[1]The manager in question, Marc Janssen passed away in 2014. He was an exceptional individual: a humanist and intellectual with a great sense of humour.

M. van der Woude (✉)
General Court of the European Union, Luxembourg, Luxembourg

ERA Board of Trustees, Trier, Germany
e-mail: marc.Van_der_woude@curia.europa.eu

W. Heusel, J.-P. Rageade (eds.), *The Authority of EU Law*,
https://doi.org/10.1007/978-3-662-58841-3_11

Let me start with the gap between perceptions and reality. Whereas the common and, later, the internal market used to be a clear and relatively well understood objective in the first decades of European integration, it is no longer perceived as such. European citizens take it for granted as if it had always existed and had not taken any effort to be achieved or maintained. As the Brexit discussions about the internal market show, it is only when one threatens to lose the benefits of this wealth-creating project that one starts to understand its real value. Or, to put it differently, money becomes an issue again when realism overtakes emotions. It is not only the general public that lost the internal market project out of sight but also the community of European integration experts. Internal market law or the rules of free movement, which used to be at the forefront of any academic study programme on European law, are now one of the numerous disciplines taught to young European lawyers. Obviously, European law is much broader now than it was 30 years ago, but these other disciplines would most probably not have existed in the absence of an internal market. As I will try to explain below, the internal market project, which still is the basis of the EU prosperity and attractiveness, has lost its relative importance in the public's perception. Other policy objectives ranging from monetary policy to immigration issues seem to attract more attention. Rows over these other policy objectives not only affect the policies concerned, but undermine the entire EU integration project, including its internal market.

The second factor concerning the clarity of the objectives pursued leads me to the issue of the authority of the law, which was the overarching theme of ERA's 25th birthday symposium. I do not have any pretentions to elaborate on this lofty issue. The only thing which I would like to mention here is my modest understanding that uncertainties regarding the objectives of the common venture and the methods used to achieve them undermine the authority of the law. This concept and the related concept of the rule of law rely on mutual trust and confidence in the institutions that are supposed to make and enforce the law. Both concepts are essential for the proper functioning of democracies. They not only allow citizens to embark on future projects without having to fear that the rules of today no longer apply tomorrow, but also to protect one generation against the whims of another. Since the European integration is an abstract project without armed law enforcement forces, its success entirely relies on the authority of its rules and the willingness of Member States to enforce them. For example, the functioning of the internal market is based on that premise. Exporters of goods and services as well as workers and investors must be confident that they will be treated fairly in the receiving Member State and that they will enjoy adequate judicial protection to enforce their rights. Here again, the authority of the rules is threatened by doubts which the European citizens increasingly have as regards the objectives pursues by the integration project as well as with respect to the values they are supposed to share.

Against this backdrop, I would like to focus on a, not very original, question which many Europeans ask themselves and which was discussed during one of the panels organised during ERA's 25th anniversary symposium: what are the possible causes of the relative loss of confidence in the European project, as expressed in the Brexit vote and the relatively good performance of Eurosceptic parties in most

Member States? In the first part of my essay I will try to identify the moment in time when this lack of trust may have occurred. I submit that this moment probably coincides with the completion date of the Internal Market, i.e. on 1 January 1993. The second part of my contribution will focus on some of the numerous uncertainties that currently affect the European integration project and that may explain the, real or perceived, absence of popular support. I submit that some uncertainties ultimately relate to the lack of certitude about the objectives pursued by this project. There is no clarity, neither at governmental level, nor in the public opinion, as to the destiny of the common venture. The third and last part of my essay is even less structured than the two previous ones. It contains some loose ideas which could help to overcome the uncertainties identified in the second part and restore the confidence in the integration project and, hence, in the rules that go with it.

2 When did it go wrong?

The European integration process is not a smooth one. It jumps from one crisis to another. During the first decades, the difficulties primarily stemmed from the relations between the governments of the Member States. None of them has ever been eager to pay into the budget and all of them have always been very keen to receive from it. The European public learned about negotiation marathons on issues such as monetary compensatory amounts, intervention prices and budget rebates. It probably looked at these discussions with some cynical amusement, but never expressed doubts as to the integration project as such. On the contrary, governments were criticised for their obstructive attitude. In his book, 'The Passage to Europe', Luc van Middelaar refers to a mass demonstration that took place in 1985 during a European Council meeting in Milan. As improbable as it may sound today, protesters were denouncing the lack of progress made by governments.[2]

Ultimately, progress was made under the Commission led by Jacques Delors. Under his leadership and with strong support from the European industry (the European round table of industrialists) the European Economic Community and the Member States embarked on the Internal Market project which would become an area in which workers, goods, services and service providers, investors and capital could circulate freely. The rules underlying this project were laid down in the European Single Act, which was signed in 1986. The ratification process was delayed because of constitutional issues in Ireland. These difficulties were solved by a referendum that took place in 1987 and which expressed wide support for the Single Market project: it was approved with 70% in favour and 30% against. Here again, such results are probably hard to reproduce today, but they did not surprise at the time.

In parallel with the adoption of the European Single Act and the implementation of the 300 measures proposed in Lord Cockfield's White Paper, the European Court

[2] van Middelaar (2011), p. 149.

of Justice actively contributed to the opening of national markets by its interpretation of the free market rules in sectors such as air transport, banking, insurance and telecommunications. Services that were beyond reach for the normal European citizen became suddenly affordable.[3] Moreover, five Member States linked the Internal Market process to a free travel zone for all their citizens by concluding the Schengen agreement in 1985 and reinforcing it in 1990.

It is true that it is hard to fall in love with a market, as Jacques Delors is supposed to have said. In addition, product harmonisation rules can lead to strange results. We all heard stories about square eggs and straight bananas. Even so, at the time, the opening of the Internal Market provided concrete benefits to European citizens. As a young Commission official serving under the Delors Commission, I vividly remember how popular the project was at the time. My colleagues and I were invited throughout Europe to promote the Internal Market project. It was a relatively easy sell, since it offered European citizens the perspective of free travel (and shopping) throughout the Community. There was a large electronic display on the Berlaymont building counting down the number of days that were still left until 1 January 1993. When going to work, I looked at this display with confidence.

Boosted by the success of the internal market process, the Commission and the Member States explored new areas for European integration, especially in the fields of economic and monetary integration (EMU), justice and home affairs (JHA) and common foreign and security policy (CFSP), which are areas closely connected to traditional regal powers. These initiatives led to the signature of the Maastricht Treaty in 1992. The ratification process turned out to be more difficult than the ratification of the European Single Act. In the United Kingdom, where the Internal Market project had enjoyed support, the ratification process nearly led to the fall of the Major government, despite the opt-outs concerning the EMU. The ratification process in France also turned out to be a bumpy road. The outcome of the referendum was a close call with 50.8% in favour. But it was Denmark that created the most important hurdle. The Danish population turned down the Treaty in a referendum with 50.7% of negative votes. Subsequently, the Member States agreed in Edinburgh that Denmark was not obliged to participate in the EMU, JHA and CFSP. In addition, European citizenship rules would not apply to Danish citizens. With these opt-outs the Danish population voted in a second referendum with 56.7% in favour of the revised Maastricht Treaty.

The difficulties in the process of ratifying the Maastricht Treaty showed that the engineers of the European integration project started to lose public understanding and support. One may speculate about the reasons of this disconnect. In my perception, there are at least three major reasons.

The first concerns precipitation. After the fall of the Berlin wall, the geopolitical landscape changed. Reunited Germany had to reinvent and imbed itself in the

[3] I would like to refer especially to *Ministère public v. Asjes*, C-209/84 of 30 April 1986. I discussed the case with Professor Valentine Korah on the day on which it was delivered on a roof terrace of UCL in London, where I had arrived on the same day by aeroplane from Brussels. With the price of that 45 min trip, Europeans can now fly to New York and beyond.

European project so as to reassure its traditional partners. Nor was the European project a purely western affair any longer. A common home had to be built for all Europeans, including for those who had suffered under communist rule and who aspired to freedom and prosperity. It was felt that the European house should be refurbished first before greeting its new coproprietors. Finding the right balance between the enlargement process and the deepening of the integration project proved to be a difficult and delicate exercise. Even so, European leaders frenetically started redrafting the founding treaties: whilst the ink of one Treaty revision was still drying, EU leaders were already engaged in negotiating the next one, in Amsterdam, Nice or Lisbon. One may wonder whether the outcome of this process was entirely satisfactory. In many respects, the integration project is still an uncompleted and fragile edifice. The financial crisis of 2008 showed the risks of having an EMU without common economic governance. Similarly, the migration crisis of 2015 revealed the weakness of having a large open free movement area without an external border policy. Even from a purely legal point of view, the current Treaties basically consist of lists of various policy areas. Their structure lacks the intellectual rigour that characterised the structure of the 1957 Treaties.

This leads me to the second reason that may explain the disconnect between the ambitions of Europe's leaders and its populations. It concerns the degree of abstractness of the integration project. Whereas an internal market is relatively easy to understand and explain, the new policy areas introduced by the Maastricht Treaty require considerably more efforts both in terms of understanding and explanation, especially where these policies touch upon issues such as citizenship, currency and police, which are directly associated with the exercise of regal powers. It is not surprising that the divide between integrationists (the "maastrichards") and sovereignists (the "anti-maastrichards") particularly marked the political debate on the ratification of the Maastricht Treaty in France and continued to do so ever since. In addition, this debate has become more difficult to hold with the rise of so called populism. The complex narrative that is often needed to present and to defend the integration project contrasts sharply with the one-liners that denounce a loss of national powers, or more accurately, rely on a nostalgic perception of what these powers once were.

The third and last reason directly follows from the second and has to do with hubris. Those involved in pushing the European project ahead did probably not realise immediately that they were losing contact with the European people. For many of them, the lack of public adherence to the project resulted from a mere misunderstanding. They sincerely thought that explaining the project and its good intentions would suffice to get the people onboard. I belonged to this group. I remember having said during a debate on the draft Constitutional Treaty in 2005 that I could not see any intellectually valid reason to vote against it. Obviously, this type of arrogance does not help. People may have perfectly valid reasons to be against a political project. Even so, European leaders pushed the integration project ahead, believing that amending draft treaties would suffice to obtain approval for the new treaties. Indeed, changes to the Maastricht Treaty secured a positive vote at the 1993 referendum in Denmark. A similar approach was followed in 2001 and

2002 to obtain public support for the Nice Treaty in Ireland. And, last but not least, after the rejection of the draft Constitutional Treaty in France and the Netherlands, the texts were recast into a more traditional and classic form that led to the Lisbon Treaty, which was ratified without referenda in all Member States, with the exception of Ireland. In that country, the population ultimately voted in favour of the Treaty after having obtained some assurances on Irish neutrality, abortion rules and Irish representation in the institutions.

Whatever one may think of the Lisbon Treaty itself, the change and approve tactics probably led to resentment amongst the voters who objected to the draft Constitutional Treaty in the first place. They may, rightly or wrongly, feel that their votes simply did not matter and that the integration project would be pursued with or without their support. The impression or perception of loss of control over the course of events has been reinforced ever since by the process of globalisation and the relative decline of Europe's importance. For some, European integration and globalisation go hand in hand. The circumstances in which the Lisbon Treaty was ultimately ratified affected not only the perception which European citizens have of the integration project as a kind of runaway train, but also that of its leaders. The latter seem paralysed and averse to any Treaty change or referenda.[4] But the tide seems to be turning. After the Brexit vote in 2016 and the election of Mr Macron in 2017 as president of the French republic, institutional reform is on the agenda again. In addition, the current international climate and the instability of old alliances compel the EU to reconsider its functioning.

Now, if this process were to lead to Treaty changes, it is essential that the errors made in the past are avoided. New rules and institutional structures must provide clear answers to problems that Europe's citizens understand to be of common concern. Spelling out the problem must precede the proposed solution. The Internal Market project leading to the Single European Act may be seen as an example to follow. Jacques Delors and his team first identified the shortcomings of the then existing Common Market, then mobilised the societal forces and political will to address these problems and, subsequently, proposed the corresponding solutions. Of course, the Internal Market project was a child of its time and there is no guarantee that this formula should or could be replicated today. Even so, I believe that any integration project is bound to fail, if it is not problem driven. This leads me to the many uncertainties that prevent Europeans to see the problems that they have in common, and to identify those that they would like to be resolved by common solutions.

[4] With the exception of specific monetary treaties and the agreement on the Unified Patent Court between some but not all Member States, no new treaties were signed.

3 Some uncertainties

Uncertainty is a very relative concept. For some, it reflects the simple fact that one cannot predict the future. For others, uncertainty is associated with fear of the unknown. Moreover, some have strong convictions of what the future should be whereas others are more inclined to wait and see what future brings. Uncertainties that are unbearable for some are not necessarily perceived as problematic by others. Now, as submitted above, it does not have much sense to offer common solutions to those who do not see the existence of a common problem. To avoid misunderstandings and disappointments, it may be useful to start making an inventory of the uncertainties or deficiencies that undermine the integration project as it exists today. I do not pretend to make an exhaustive list. I will just list the issues which jumped to my mind during the panel debates that took place in Trier on 20 October 2017.

First, it seems to me that the European institutions are in a state of flux. The institutional machinery as we know it today finds its origin in the founding Treaties of the fifties. These Treaties, and especially the ECSC Treaty envisaged a supranational structure in which political management and the right of initiative were entrusted to a collective administrative body, initially the High Authority and subsequently the Commission. The case law of the Court of Justice and the evolution of the powers of the Parliament also underlined the supranational character of the European integration project. This supranational character was mitigated from the very beginning, since the supranational bodies set up by the founding Treaties are composed of national representatives: each State insisting on having its own Commissioner, Judge or Auditor. This also holds true for the Parliament, whose members are elected on a national basis and are not free to meet where they want. In addition, the centre of gravity has gradually shifted over time from the supranational institutions towards the Member States whose leaders regularly meet in the context of the European Council. Moreover, national administrations, integrated in Council working groups, management committees or common services, seem to have overtaken, at least partially, the Commission's executive role. It is nowadays hard to say where the national administration stops, and where the Union executive starts[5]

In this complex machinery, that is often referred to as "Brussels", powers and, hence responsibilities are diffuse and dispersed. Decision making in this multifaceted system is not an easy affair and is sometimes better served by the discretion of traditional diplomacy than by transparency and public debate.[6] The ensuing lack of clarity and accountability facilitates double speak by European leaders whose positions within the decision-making bodies do not necessarily coincide with the statements they make before their national voters. These complexity and opacity may affect the authority of the rules that the institutional machinery produces. Indeed,

---

[5] See for example, Brito Bastos (2018), pp. 101–134.

[6] See for a very outspoken position, inaugural lecture by Prof. Deirdre Curtin at the University of Amsterdam, "*Top Secret Europe*", 20 October 2011.

citizens may find it difficult to identify the author of the rule and even the very reason why it was adopted.

Second, European integration may have gone too fast or too far for its citizens. The process that culminated in the Lisbon Treaty affects numerous aspects of their daily life. They may find out, often to their surprise, that national or even local authorities are not free to take the decisions they would like to see adopted. Environmental or State aid rules may indeed have a very local impact. Despite the efforts made by the European and national institutions to render European rules and documentation accessible,[7] the problem remains that the EU is still perceived as complex and distant. Even the national judiciary may have sometimes, rightly or wrongly, the impression of being confronted with rules to which the State did not sign up for.[8] In short, the scope of European rules and powers remains unclear to many. One could argue that the same holds true for local, regional or national rules and that the absence of clarity of these rules does not necessarily undermine their authority. The answer to that argument is that the European rules find their legitimacy and hence their authority in the principle of conferral, as defined by Articles 4 and 5 TEU. The EU is competent only when powers are conferred to it, whereas competence at national level most often simply pre-exists.

I already referred to the third uncertainty in the introduction to this essay. It concerns the finality of the European integration project. Creating an internal market is a clear objective, albeit more open-ended than one imagines at first sight. A process towards an ever-closer Union between the peoples of Europe as mentioned in Article 1 TEU is less clear. Whereas this lofty objective may have appealed to the generations marked by the Second World War, its power of attraction is less certain today. It could be perceived by some as a *carte blanche* for the transfer of new powers to what they see as a kind of super-state. Whatever one may think of Article 1 TEU, it does not define a final destination. Unlike my old law firm, the integration project does not have a clearly defined common purpose. The discomfort to which this uncertainty may give rise, is likely to be exacerbated by the undefined geographical scope of the integration project, as Europe does not have clear borders. The concerns about what some perceive as a borderless Europe became particularly acute with the migration crisis that unfolded in 2015 and may compromise future enlargements. If the members of the family are unknown, one should not expect familyhood.

The fourth uncertainty which could possibly erode the authority of the law in the Union is even more delicate than the third. It relates to the belief in democratic values and the rule of law. Recent elections in Central Europe have led to regimes that have different perceptions or a different understanding of these concepts than regimes in other European States. That is not a problem as such, but it starts to

[7] For example, I would like to congratulate the European Commission and DG COMP especially for its clear websites. Similarly, the website of the Dutch association of municipalities (VNG) provides clear and detailed explanations about European rules and subsidies: https://vng.nl/onderwerpenindex/europa.

[8] See Holdgard et al. (2018), pp. 17–53.

become one if these differences erode the trust upon which the European project relies.[9] If judges in one Member State start having doubts about the impartiality of their colleagues in other Member States, they may be less inclined to extradite suspected criminals to those latter states, to return asylum seekers to them or recognise the authority of their judgments. I do not think, however, that the rule of law issue is a binary one: whether the rule is respected or not will most often depend on the specific circumstances of the case. Impartiality concerns are not necessarily systematic in nature, they may also relate to one specific judge, court, area of the law or political issue. Moreover, whereas doubts about due process are a real cause of concern in matters falling within the ambit of Article 6 ECHR, they may be less so in purely technical, commercial or regulatory matters.

It would not take much of an effort to add other uncertainties to the above list. Making such a list is not a very original exercise. Nor is it very useful to lament about, a perceived or real, erosion of the authority of the law. A consensus starts to emerge that the current integration project is at the end of a cycle and that it needs revision. As mentioned above, Mr Macron has already expressed his views on future Treaty revisions at various occasions.[10] Moreover, the German coalition agreement of 7 February 2018 bears the ambitious title ‘A new start for Europe’. Some of the ideas expressed by French and German leaders correspond to the scenarios described in the Commission’s White Paper of 1 March 2017.[11] I do not pretend to take part in this debate. Nor am I in a position to do so. What I can do, however, is explore some avenues that could deal with the uncertainties listed above.

4 Dealing with uncertainty

Let me start with the Internal Market, since that was the central theme of our panel discussion. When the Brits voted for Brexit in June 2016, they voted against the EU as they perceived it. They may have voted against the project as a whole, but not necessarily against all its constituent parts. What the vote really meant is still uncertain today. For example, I do not think any Brit was against the Erasmus project or against cheap air travel to Mediterranean holiday destinations. Nor were they asked to vote on the question as to whether they wanted to stay in a customs union, a common market or an internal market. What would have been the outcome of the referendum if the Brits had been offered, for example in a subsequent referendum, a choice between the EU, EEA membership, a customs union or comparable types of arrangements or no integration model at all? If this question had been asked upfront,

[9] Opinion 2/13 (Accession of the European Union to the ECHR) of 18 December 2014, EU:C:2014:2454.

[10] See in particular speech at the Sorbonne on 26 September 2017. See for another approach, speech by Mr. Rutte at Bertelsmann Stiftung, Berlin 2 March 2018.

[11] White Paper on the Future of Europe—Reflections and scenarios for the EU27 by 2025, COM(2017)2025 of 1 March 2017.

British politics would probably have had less difficulties in interpreting the outcome of the referendum and in defining what type of (trade) relations they would like to have with their fellow Europeans in general and with the Irish neighbours in particular. By now, the formula 'Brexit means Brexit' seems over-simplistic, as one-liners often are.

When seeking public support for future integration projects, European leaders may draw an important lesson from the Brexit referendum: confronting voters with binary yes/no type questions does not provide useful guidance as to what voters really want. Instead, they could be offered choices between various options or consulted in various subsequent rounds to distil the preferred option. Obviously, offering a choice for public approval purposes presupposes that choices can be made. Until now the European Treaties have been conceived in a holistic manner; one adopts or rejects the plan, while intermediate solutions were not envisaged from the outset. But such solutions do exist in practice. Modifications, attenuations, opt-outs and guarantees have been agreed upon ex post to secure support for the signing or ratification process after initial resistance, as illustrated above. Even so, they are corrections to a scheme rather than part of it.[12] This flexibility could also be foreseen as an integral part of the design of any new reform. This idea is not new. It has been referred to as Europe with a variable geometry (*l'Europe à géométrie variable*) or *l'Europe à la carte*.

Under the existing Treaty structure, this pragmatic *à la carte* approach stands at odds with the current objectives of the EU Treaties which qualify the integration process as an ongoing one towards an ever closer union between the peoples of Europe or to put it in matrimonial terms, a union for better and for worse and not an occasional relationship. Abandoning this objective is not inconceivable: for some Member States the present degree of integration possibly suffices or could even be rolled back, whereas others might prefer to go ahead. But all should have a clear idea of what they signed up to. Obviously, managing various degrees of integration would cause serious difficulties in terms of financing and institutions. Here again, some solutions already exist. Agency and network structures dealing with specific policy areas could be a means to provide institutional flexibility. Such agency or network models already operate in a wide range of sector-specific policy areas, such as telecommunications, energy, food safety, chemicals, medicines, as well as educational and scientific research programmes.[13] States could participate in these systems without necessarily having to participate in the wider scheme consisting of the Internal Market, the traditional environmental and cohesion policies, the EMU, JHA and the CFSP.[14] They could even join, albeit to a lesser extent, the networks

[12] With the possible exception of Article 20 TEU allowing for reinforced cooperation among groups of Member States.

[13] For example, Israel already participates in various EU research programmes.

[14] For example, third States that are connected to the EU's energy networks could participate in the EU's regulatory energy network scheme, without participating in its Internal Market for other goods and services. This is already the case for some Balkan States that cooperate within the European Energy Community. Conversely, States that are in the Internal Market must obviously participate in that scheme.

that exist in more regal policy areas such as air transport control, data protection, prudential supervision, competition policy, police, procurement of military equipment. Moreover, as shown by Switzerland and Norway, third States can even join the Schengen zone.

Of course, there are limits to a pick and choose model. First, the Member States that participate in the core of the scheme, which still is, at least in my perception, the Internal Market, should participate in those policy areas that are indispensable for its proper functioning, such as standardisation, social protection, trade defence, competition and, increasingly, environmental policies, as well as its cohesion policies, such as agriculture and structural development funds. This economic foundation can be distinguished and detached from more politically sensitive policy areas, such as the EMU, JHA, CFSP and defence, which could function on an opt-in basis.

Second, participation in one or more of the various packages has consequences. Those who sign up must be aware of membership conditions. A State that wants to participate in a free travel zone must realise that this choice has an impact on its powers to regulate borders, asylum and extraditions. Similarly, the tighter the integration, the higher the requirements in terms of adequate judicial protection. All this to say, that integration has a price: States and their citizens should be made conscious of the pros and cons of their choices. If they are not prepared to pay that price, they should not join the policy area concerned and perhaps opt for a lighter option or no option at all.

Third, strong institutions will be needed, not only to manage the inner circle of the integration project, but also to ensure the coordination of the various cooperation schemes. The continuation of intergovernmental cooperation forms is hard to reconcile with these tasks. The executive power should preferably be efficiency-driven and accountable to representative bodies, which, since we were in Trier on the 20th October 2017, could find their inspiration in the German model of a Bundesrat with national representatives and a Bundestag with directly elected European delegates.

Fourth, one could object to these ideas as they might lead to a complex patchwork of various integration forms. That is most probably true. I submit however that the current system is even more complex and difficult to understand, both for the ordinary citizen and the average legal expert. The new scheme could essentially consist of three groups of members: those who participate in the Internal Market, which would still be at the core of the new edifice, those who would like to go further in terms of economic, monetary, security and foreign policies—and finally those who opt for looser forms of cooperation by joining agency and network models dealing with specific policy issues, gravitating around the Internal Market.

The image thus created is one of a living and diverse institutional organism that can adapt itself to internal challenges and external dangers. Diversity and flexibility have been Europe's strengths throughout the ages and will hopefully remain so for the era to come.[15]

---

[15] See, Diamond (1999), pp. 393–395.

References

Brito Bastos F (2018) Derivative illegality in European composite administrative procedures. Common Mark Law Rev, pp 101–134

Diamond J (1999) Guns, germs and steel. Norton & Company, New York, Epilogue, pp 393–395

Holdgard R, Elkan D, Schaldemose GK (2018) From cooperation to collision. The ECJ's Ajos ruling and the Danish Supreme Court's refusal to comply. Common Mark Law Rev, pp 17–53

van Middelaar L (2011) De Passage naar Europa

The authority of EU law: What does it require and why is it fading?

Hans-Jürgen Hellwig

1 Introduction

I would like to begin with some personal remarks. My presentation will be rather critical of the present state of affairs of EU law. It is the critical position of a convinced European. My father and I myself were born in Saarbrücken, the capital of the Saar region which throughout history has been the focus of conflicts between France and Germany: Each side wanted to have an integrated coal and steel industry that would be based on the coal mines of the Saar region and the ore mines of neighbouring Lorraine. All of you know what these and similar conflicts have led to in 1870/71, in 1914–1919 and in 1939–1945.

That is why the European idea was one of my parents' most important messages to me.

That is why my father served the European idea, in the 1950s as member of the German *Bundestag* and from 1959 to 1970 as member of the High Authority of the European Coal and Steel Community and thereafter as Vice-President of the European Commission.

And that is why I myself devoted a large part of my work to the European idea, in the German Bar Association as a Member of the Board and as a Vice-President for European Affairs and in the Council of Bars and Law Societies of Europe (CCBE) as Head of the German Delegation, Vice-President and President.

I repeatedly discussed my concerns with my father before he died in July 2017, a few weeks before his 105th birthday, and I find comfort in the fact that my father who was present at the creation of the European Communities, fully shared my concerns.

H.-J. Hellwig (✉)
Hengeler Mueller, Frankfurt am Main, Germany

ERA Board of Trustees, Trier, Germany
e-mail: Hans-Juergen.Hellwig@hengeler.com

W. Heusel, J.-P. Rageade (eds.), *The Authority of EU Law*,
https://doi.org/10.1007/978-3-662-58841-3_12

Anyone who enters the Supreme Court of Poland passes by a pillar which in golden letters carries the phrase "*Quid est enim civitas nisi iuris societas civium*?"—What is a state other than the community of law of its citizens? The phrase on the column is a citation from Cicero's "*De re publica*" (I, 49). Cicero in this phrase not only defines a state but also describes the function of the law in a state: It is the law that holds the people and the state together.

Neither morals nor ethics nor religions can do so. They rather have the tendency of dividing people as history shows. People in Europe learned that lesson once and forever from the devastating effects of the Thirty Years' War between Catholics and Protestants in the seventeenth century, and as a result of that lesson they agreed in the era of enlightenment that it should be the law as overarching common denominator that holds people and state together.

The authority of EU law—as lawyers we associate with this topic a large number of legal concepts such as priority of EU law over national law, the obligation of national courts of last instance to refer questions of interpretation of EU law to the CJEU, non-implementation or inadequate implementation of EU directives, infringement actions in case of violation of EU law, etc. I shall not deal with such issues of detail. I shall rather take a more basic approach to the topic, and in doing so I shall also address what the people, and not merely what we lawyers think about EU law.

The conclusion of my presentation is in a nutshell: The greatest danger for the authority of EU law comes from EU law itself.

2 Constitutive elements of the authority of the law

The law can have the authority to unite the people only when it has been properly made, when its content is basically accepted as a law, when it is respected, and when it is properly enforced in case of violations.

Proper making of the law requires a process that is transparent and democratically legitimised.

Transparency: Even lawyers have difficulties with the EU law making process. It is much more complex and thus less transparent than the processes at national Member States level that more or less all people in a given state are familiar with.

Democratic legitimacy: The EU institutional structure, as we all know, is government-heavy. Thus the law-making process is to a large part legitimised only indirectly from the elections at Member State level. That was acceptable in the early days of the European Economic Community (EEC) which was a mere economic community. But: The broader the scope of competencies, the greater the need for democratic legitimisation. Communitisation and unionisation by now have progressed to such an extent that they cover basically all aspects of daily life of individuals and businesses. The role of the European Parliament (EP) has been strengthened, however not up to the competencies of national parliaments. Democratic legitimisation therefore continues to lag behind the scope of EU competencies. Commission and Council continue to be the decisive EU institutions, and both enjoy only indirect democratic legitimisation. I am aware of the argument why this cannot be different, given the fact that the EU is not a full state in its own right. However, that argument does not change the finding that there is a lack of democratic legitimisation which is bad for the authority of EU law and which prompts the counter-question whether the EU and EU law have reached the limits of what can be achieved under the present institutional structure of the EU without triggering effects of self-destruction.

Most people in the street do not understand these details of democratic legitimacy, however the many so-called civil society organisations that today exist at Member State level do understand, and they criticise the existing imbalance between competencies and democratic legitimacy. It was in my mind a mistake not to discuss this issue at all when the EU competencies were expanded and expanded again. One conclusion is clear: Proclamations of self-legitimisation as we keep hearing them from EU Commission and European Council are not sufficient. They are rather counter-productive for the perception of the people.

Perception of the people: Philosophers tell us reality does not exist in an absolute sense. Reality is subjective. What matters in the context of the authority of EU law is not what we lawyers think is the reality but what the people at large perceive as reality—perception is reality. After all it is the people at large that must accept and respect the law—acceptance and respect by the lawyers is not sufficient.

General acceptance of and respect for the law also requires that in terms of content, leaving aside details, people think that the law should indeed deal with the subject matter in question. This at first sight seems to be the issue of subsidiarity, but in fact it goes deeper. At stake is not so much the division of competencies between EU and Member States, at stake is rather whether the issue in question should be dealt with by the law in the first place. People still today ridicule the attempt by the Commission to regulate the bending of cucumbers. Nothing undermines someone's authority more than making jokes about him. That holds true not only for individual politicians but also for political institutions. Making jokes about a political institution undermines the authority of the institution and all of its activities.

3 Realism as a precondition for respecting the authority of the law

Regarding the subject matter of the law, its authority also suffers from overambitious, unrealistic goals. In the following I shall list some examples in EU law.

The Treaty of Maastricht of 1992 imposed certain ceilings upon Member States debts. These so-called Maastricht criteria were unrealistic right from the beginning and were so perceived by most of the people. A study of 2017 published by Swiss bank Vontobel has shown that from 1999 to 2015, the deficit ceiling of 3% of Gross Domestic Product (GDP) of a Member State was violated in a total of 114 cases where the conditions for exceptions from the ceiling were not met. Leading perpetrators were France with eleven and Greece, Poland and Portugal each with ten breaches. Only Luxembourg, Estonia and Sweden were able to always meet the 3% ceiling. The most prominent perpetrators rather early on were France and Germany, and they got away with it without any consequences. The French and German violations thus became an open invitation for other Member States to also knowingly disregard the Maastricht criteria. This eventually led to an outright state debt crisis in Greece, Italy, Portugal and Spain which then triggered the Euro crisis. What a mess of totally unrealistic but legally binding law! The peak of absurdity in the authority of EU law was reached when the Commission took no measure whatsoever vis-à-vis a recent new violation of the Maastricht criteria by France and explained that passivity with the simple words: "*C'est la France*"—It is France![1]

After the breakdown of the Soviet Union and the fall of the Iron Curtain there was an intensive discussion whether the Union should be enlarged (by accession of former Eastern Block States) or rather focus on further deepening of the existing Union. As a compromise, the Nice summit of 2000 agreed that both goals should be pursued in parallel. How in the world can one deepen a Community when a significant number of members, namely the new Accession States, are missing almost 50 years of joint EC experience? Each society has a deep normative structure formed by history. The Nice summit compromise simply disregarded the differences in sociological and psychological structures between the existing EU Member States and the new Accession States as if these differences did not exist. The deepening of the Union has totally overstrained the Accession States and their people which, as required for accession, had implemented the *acquis communautaire* on paper but not yet in mental reality.

As CCBE President in 2004 I welcomed the organisations of the legal professions from the Accession States, and I have been in close touch with them before and after accession. In spite of all their efforts they just felt lost. I urged the Commission to finance education in EU law for lawyers, judges and civil servants in all Accession States in an effort to turn the *acquis communautaire* from law on paper into law in the minds. The Commission acknowledged the problem, but they had funds only for EU law training in States outside the EU—the export of EU law into bordering states was more important than the training in EU law in the new Member States.

As a result, the Accession States and their people where overstrained by the demands coming from existing EU law and even more so by the demands coming from the legislative process for new EU law. This overstrain is a major explanation for the revitalisation of the Visegrád Group of 1991 which comprises Hungary, Poland, Czech Republic and Slovakia—a group of former communist block states within the EU which is occasionally joined by Bulgaria and Romania. The Iron

[1] "The European Commission has given France leeway on fiscal rules "because it is France," the president of the EU executive Jean-Claude Juncker said on Tuesday", according to Reuters, 31.5.2016 (https://uk.reuters.com/article/uk-eu-deficit-france/eu-gives-budget-leeway-to-france-because-it-is-france-juncker-idUKKCN0YM1N0).

Curtain as a physical divide of Europe has disappeared but has there been a true growing together of the minds? I am afraid the mental divide that was created by the Iron Curtain over more two generations—free democratic societies with their market economies in an ongoing dynamic communitisation process on the one hand and static societies under communist dictatorship with state-planned economies on the other hand—has not yet disappeared in the minds of many people in the Accession States. A major reason in my mind is the unfortunate Nice compromise which was cast into binding EU law, the Treaty of Nice. From the outset This law was unrealistic and in my view counter-productive for the authority of EU law at large.

4 The Monetary Union

I now turn to the Euro currency union, another overambitious goal. The French politician, economist, lawyer and ECJ Judge (1952–1962) Jacques Rueff once said: "*L'Europe se fera par la monnaie ou se ne fera pas*"—Europe will come via the currency, or it will not come at all. This sentence is right with respect to the psychology of the people, but it is silent on the preconditions for a European currency. History tells us that all currency unions that were not accompanied by a however structured fiscal union, sooner or later failed. There is a striking example in more recent European history. Europe from 1865 onwards knew the so-called Latin Mint Union where the exchange ratios between the gold and silver coins of the participating states and their metal content were fixed by treaty. Problems arose when some States financed their budget deficits not only by State debt but also by inflation—they printed paper money or reduced the metal content of their coins which damaged the other States' currencies. Main violators of the Mint Union were Greece and Italy. Greece became insolvent in 1893, was forced to leave the Union in 1908, agreed with its creditors on a debt cut, and re-joined the Union again in 1910. As one of the consequences of the First World War, the Union came to an end in 1919.

I do not mean to say that the introduction of the Euro currency union without fiscal union was legally incorrect. I only question the economic and political wisdom of that decision. It was meant to create unity but in fact it led to bitter conflicts on legal issues such as the no-bail out clause of Art. 125 TFEU. Lawyer Christine Lagarde, today Director of the International Monetary Fund, exclaimed in the days of the Euro and sovereign debt crisis when she was French Economic and Finance Minister: "Forget about the Treaties!" What a blow to the authority of EU law! Even worse is the fact that the Euro and sovereign debt crisis caused outright animosities between—in simplified terms—northern and southern Member States of the Euro union. There were other negative structural effects that I will discuss below. Summing up, the Euro crisis with its dividing consequences is dormant for now, but it can come back again at any time as a result of a new sovereign debt or banking crisis.

5 Migration

Another example of overambitious law-making is the free movement union. The Schengen regime deals with the free movement of persons within Europe, and the Dublin regime with travel and immigration from the outside world into Europe. From the outset both regimes could work out only as long as the Member States situated at the external borders of the EU could effectively control these borders. This failed to be the case in Italy and Greece. In spite of their efforts and lacking support from the other EU Member States, due to the absence of a general EU programme, they were unable to control their borders when they were flooded by immigrants. Under Dublin rules these high numbers of immigrants were immigrants into Greece and Italy. A high percentage of these immigrants moved on "flooding" other Member States, in particular after they felt invited into Germany by Angela Merkel. In reaction thereto, the adjacent states closed the Balkan route. Even Germany and some Nordic States, too, introduced border controls for all travellers. Many people across Europe felt the same way when Angela Merkel said: "Dublin is obsolete". So far, all efforts for a fair burden sharing with regard to the immigrants into Italy and Greece have failed, and Hungary has announced that it will defy the CJEU decision of 6 September 2017 which confirmed the Council Decision on the allocation of immigrants.[2] Legally the Dublin rules may still be in force, as the Court says, for the psychology of people they have failed and are dead. In addition, when Germany in the urgency of the situation opened its borders to the flood of immigrants by unilateral measure, without prior consultation with the other EU Member States, and later, like Greece and Italy had done, asked for a fair reallocation of these immigrants within the entire EU, the reaction from other Member States was understandably bitter and critical. So the overambitious Dublin goals based on the assumption of an effective control of the EU's external borders have not only led to a flood of immigrants but also to a rift between the EU Member States. It is not just a rift between governments, it is also and in particular a rift between the people in the Member States.

6 A Europe of variable geographic composition and various speeds

Setting aside the overambitious goals of EU law, the question is what do we mean by EU law in the first place? There is no one uniform EU law any longer. We have several different Europes each with its own laws à la carte. We have the Treaties (TEU and TFEU) as the general framework, however there are many exceptions, the most notorious for the time being the budget rebate for the UK—greetings from Margaret Thatcher's "I want my money back". Then we have the Euro currency

[2] Case C-643/15, ECLI:EU:C:2017:631.

union consisting of some, not all EU Member States, and the Schengen/Dublin union as another sectorial union, consisting also of only some EU Member States. All these sectorial unions are in a geographical sense partial unions within the EU, they cover only parts of the EU territory, and they are not even identical in composition. There are many more such sectorial partial unions. This development will continue: Every "Enhanced Cooperation" under Art. 326 ss TFEU will create its own little union within the larger EU. One cannot but say: The more partial unionisation we have among some Member States, the greater the fragmentation. We lawyers have difficulties to cope with this maze of patchwork unions, the people at large are at a loss. How then, under these circumstances, can the people in all Member States develop a common feeling of all-encompassing identification with the EU at large?

Why did the EU get into this state of its own internal legal setup? Because it was unable to find among all Member States the necessary consent for dealing with old issues and new ones as they came up. Enlargement was achieved with the simple act of accession, the much more difficult process of deepening the entire EU for all Member States turned out to be largely impossible. So the EU settled for more partial unionisation at the price of fragmentation.

7 Intergovernmental versus community solutions

To this fragmentation within the EU legal structure must be added the trend to intergovernmental cooperation which takes place completely outside the framework of EU law. The most prominent example is the European Stability Mechanism (ESM) of 2012. The EU was unable to deal with the Euro crisis caused by the sovereign debt levels of several members of the Euro union. So the other Euro States jumped in and set up the ESM as rescue tool. Another example of intergovernmental cooperation is the European Fiscal Compact (Treaty on Stability, Coordination and Governance in the Economic and Monetary Union) of 2012 for greater budget discipline of EMU Member States that introduced i.a. the possibility for financial sanctions in case the Maastricht criteria are violated—possible sanctions of which no use was made when recently France violated the criteria—*C'est la France*! Also the financing of the Single Resolution Mechanism (SRM) for banks of 2014[3] by the banking industry is based on an intergovernmental cooperation. This entire development shows: In the area of sovereign debt and financial services the EU is at the limits of its ability to act.

The ESM has led to regular meetings of the Finance Ministers of all Euro States. These meetings have become a de-facto institution without a basis in the law. They are today the real power centre, outside the EU framework but with a most significant

[3] Regulation (EU) No 806/2014 of the European Parliament and of the Council of 15 July 2014 establishing uniform rules and a uniform procedure for the resolution of credit institutions and certain investment firms in the framework of a Single Resolution Mechanism and a Single Resolution Fund and amending Regulation (EU) No 1093/2010, OJ L225, 30.7.2014.

influence on all of the inside of the EU. Thus partial unionisation in the Euro currency union has led to de-unionisation. No wonder President Juncker wants to turn the ESM into an EU institution. In their first reactions, the Euro Finance Ministers have refused to go ahead with this, arguing that unionisation of the ESM would require a modification of the Treaties by unanimity among all Member States, including referenda required in some Member States under national law. Would the Finance Ministers in the first place be prepared to waive special rules and rights that have been agreed upon intergovernmentally? Would Germany, given the case law of the German Constitutional Court, even be permitted to give up its present right of veto in the ESM?

In particular, the ESM as an instrument of intergovernmental co-operation must be seen in a wider historic context. One of the goals pursued by the Treaty of the European Coal and Steel Community of 1951 has been to provide a structural framework that would also serve as containment for excessive national influence of individual Member States. This is why the independent High Authority of said Community was given far-reaching executive powers in the coal and steel sector, it truly was an independent supranational Authority. Then came the European Economic Community (EEC) created by the Treaty of Rome of 1957 for all sectors of economy outside coal and steel. However, in comparison with the High Authority, the Commission of the new Community was given reduced competences only, and corresponding thereto the Council of Ministers of the Economic Community, consisting of the relevant department ministers from the Member States, was more powerful than the Council of Ministers of the Coal and Steel Community. Then French President de Gaulle, through his "empty chair" policy in 1964/65 practically ruled out majority decisions of the Council, thus introducing a factual veto right of a given Member State. The resulting impasse was resolved in 1969 through the introduction of regular summit meetings of the Heads of State and Governments which would work mostly by consensus. In 1979, UK Prime Minister Margaret Thatcher used this consensus principle for threatening to block all future integration measures unless the UK net budget contribution to the Community were significantly reduced. That blackmail was successful.

The regular summit meetings of Heads of State and Government were regulated by law for the first time only in 1986 in the Single European Act (SEA). At that time the European Council still remained outside the institutional structure of the EU. It was only the Treaty of Maastricht of 1992 which made the European Council of Heads of State and Government an official EU institution. This European Council which assembles the highest representatives of the nations that as Member States form the EU, is not included in the EU legislative process, yet it is today undoubtedly the most powerful institution in the EU. The Treaty of Maastricht also brought foreign policy, security policy and justice as well as home affairs into the competencies of the EU, with the proviso, however, that use of these new competencies should to the greatest extent be made by means of intergovernmental cooperation. These two elements—the intergovernmental cooperation and the European Council as the assembly of Heads of State and Governments of the Member States—are proof of the fact that the supranational nature of the Union has decreased while the powers and influence of the Member States have increased. The price for an increase in communitisation has thus been a decrease of supranationality of the EU and a greater vulnerability vis-à-vis political decisions in a given single Member State.

Intergovernmental cooperation by means of treaties under international public law such as the ESM does not have any built-in structural containment of national power politics. So it is only realistic to acknowledge the fact that the ultimate effect is a revitalisation of the old nation states. The manner in which the sovereign debt crisis of Greece, Italy, Spain, Portugal and Ireland was dealt with is characterised by the fact that the interests of the rescuing Member States, with Germany, but also France in the front whose banks were particularly affected, in many respects prevailed over the interests of the crisis States. When Germany and France had violated the Maastricht criteria they were pardoned by unanimous consent of all Member States in the European Council because all of them had a common interest, namely to loosen the binding effects of the Maastricht criteria. Who in all these cases spoke for the interests of the Union? Is such a state of affairs what the founding fathers of the Communities intended to achieve? Is there not reason for reflection following from the fact that when Greece was rescued by the ESM and the International Monetary Fund (IMF), the neutral IMF repeatedly, in particular regarding the question of a general cut of parts of the Greek State debt, took openly position for Greece and against the main financers Germany and France?

There is another important systemic aspect in connection with the creation of the ESM. History tells us that every crisis is the hour of governments at the expense of parliaments. Ever since the Euro sovereign debt crisis and the post-Lehman shutdown banking crisis, financial Europe has been in crisis mode—remember the extremely difficult recurring negotiations with Greece. Once again, the prerogative of government in times of crisis comes at the expense of parliament. This upsets the normal separation of powers as we have learned from Montesquieu. In the preceding financial crises, the German *Bundestag* had a few hours only to read, and to vote on, bills coming from the government with several hundreds of pages! Is that what we understand by control and last decision of parliament as the democratic representative of the people?

8 Enforcement

For the law, to have authority requires not only a transparent and democratic process of adoption and basic acceptance of the subject matter to be dealt with, but also enforcement in case of violations. That is why Art. 17 para. 1 TEU says that the Commission shall oversee the application of Union law under the control of the Court of Justice of the Union—the Commission is the guardian of EU law. According to the Court's jurisprudence the Commission has a certain degree of discretion when deciding whether to initiate infringement proceedings against a Member State under Art. 258 TFEU. One would think that the decisive criterion in that respect is the seriousness of the violation of the law. However, in a Communication of

21 December 2016 the Commission announced for the future that: ".... the Commission will examine the impact of an infringement on the attainment of important EU policy objectives .... It will distinguish between cases according to the added value which can be achieved by an infringement procedure and will close cases when it considers this to be appropriate from a policy point of view." Thus, EU law is to be enforced only when the enforcement leads to an added value with respect to "economic important EU policy objectives". The Communication is silent on what it means by "important EU policy objectives" and by "from a policy point of view". It does not say that in a given case of violation the respective policy is the one defined by EU law. It does not say either that the importance of an EU policy objective will—at least *inter alia*—depend on the impact of the infringement. According to the wording of the Communication, an important EU policy objective can be any policy as determined by the Commission, including a policy that disregards objectives of existing EU law—policy decisions by the EU Commission then have priority. It is by now an almost open secret in Brussels that an earlier draft of the Communication had defined important EU policies by reference to the ten policy areas that Jean-Claude Juncker, then newly elected President of the Commission, in July 2014 presented to the European Parliament as his agenda for the future. This reference, it seems, was deleted from the draft after having met criticism from EU Commission staff. However, what does that deletion change when there is no definition at all of "important EU policy objectives"? The guardian decides when he wishes to guard the law and when not. The Commission as a result is no longer the guardian of EU law but of its own policies. I seriously wonder whether that Communication is in conformity with Art. 17 para. 1 TEU. Commission Vice-President Frans Timmermanns once said that, the EU being based on treaties and rules, these have to be respected, otherwise that would make the law the plaything of politics.[4] He said so in connection with the reforms of the Supreme Court in Poland with which the Commission takes exception, and not in connection with the Commission's own Communication of 21 December 2016.

From a systemic aspect, the Commission's Communication is even more serious in view of the fact that the TEU architecture on EU law infringements in reality has gone out of balance due to the renaissance of national political power plays—intergovernmental agreements do not provide for a containment as said before. To put it in one question: Can anyone imagine that Greece will dare in whichever part of EU law to bring an infringement action against Germany whose financial support it needs for the ongoing financing of its state budget? And can one be so naive to think that this political power play will not take place, too, within the architecture of the Treaties, e.g. in cases referred to the CJEU? Taking the example of the *Erzberger v. TUI* case, the question at stake in that reference to the CJEU was whether the exclusion of employees working abroad from the right of election, and of standing for election, to the supervisory board of a German parent corporation as provided in the German co-determination rules is in conformity with EU law. In its written submission to the Court made before the Communication of December 2016 the

[4] Frankfurter Allgemeine Zeitung, 20.7.2017.

Commission said that there is a violation of EU law. In the subsequent hearing before the Court which took place after the Communication was published the Commission said that there is no violation. Apparently the first position of the Commission had not met the added value test. Honny soit qui mal y pense ….

To sum up: Under the Treaties the Commission has an almost total monopoly for EU law initiatives. The decline in real relevance of infringement actions by Member States described above makes infringement actions by the Commission even more important for the authority of EU law. And now the Commission says that it will exercise that guardianship function depending on its "policy point of view"….

9 Public support

Let us now turn to the question how people have reacted and continue to react to all these developments. This is an extremely important question—after all EU law and politics are made by politicians, but they are made for the people and not for the politicians. At the beginning of the European Communities, the sentiments of the people were extremely positive and optimistic. There was unlimited confidence in the European institutions. People saw that confidence was justified—Europe went through an unprecedented long period of continuing economic growth and peace, notwithstanding the difficulties and outright wars in other parts of the world. People did not care about the ever growing legal complexity of the EU. What mattered to them were the positive results of Community politics.

Over time, the pro-European sentiments became weaker and weaker. Over time, the invaluable positive aspects of the Union—peace, economic success, fundamental freedoms etc.—were taken for granted. For the new generations in "old" EU Member States these benefits came without saying. German poet Johann Wolfgang von Goethe once said: "*Was Du ererbt von Deinen Vätern hast, erwirb es, um es zu besitzen*"—You must yourself acquire for your own possession what your ancestors bequeath on you. This process of permanent identification with the European idea, generation by generation, did not take place, at least not to the necessary extent. So people started to feel unsecure. They did not understand how the European institutions work, how EU law is made etc. They did see however that matters where different from what they were used to at the national level. They became confused when national politicians criticised EU laws at home after they had voted for them in Brussels and Strasbourg. 2004 and 2007 saw the accession of new Member States two of which, as even the Commission stated, had serious rule of law deficits, and people in these countries had a quite different socio-biography. People in "old Europe" were not given sufficient explanation why this accession was necessary. They did however realise one thing: Enlargement and deepening of the Union in parallel did not fit their own practical life experiences.

The introduction of the Euro was welcomed with enthusiasm by the people in all Euro-states. The subsequent sovereign debt crisis in some Euro States however caused a lot of frustration and even anger—people in the non-crisis States where frustrated and angry over the bailouts of the crisis States, and people in the crisis States where frustrated and angry over the tight bail-out conditions imposed upon them. The Euro now is not only at the core of currency union but also a cause of contention between Member States and nations. Matters are similar with the free movement of persons union. Schengen was welcomed with enthusiasm, but the flood of immigrants resulting from the failure of the Dublin system caused the biggest political earthquake ever in the history of European integration.

In summary, the sentiment of many people in the Member States vis-a-vis the EU has by now turned from enthusiasm, trust and confidence into scepticism, distrust and even suspicion. This development is not only a matter of psychology but also of law. Over a time, this development will destroy the basis for the mutual recognition principle on which much of EU law is based.

Where and how do the people react? They react in elections. And since the European institutions and their policy-making processes are far away and difficult to understand they express their dissatisfaction in national elections—national politicians and parties get the blame. I do not mean to say that these EU-sourced problems are the sole factor. There are also other very basic problems on the mind of people, e.g. globalisation, digitalisation, over-aging societies, the ever growing splits in societies, etc. Many people, however, have the impression that the EU has so far not been able to provide satisfactory answers and, even worse, see the EU as part of the problem. So people more and more seek answers and solutions at Member State level—a renaissance of the old nation-state thinking now on the part of the people. And, depending on the degree of dissatisfaction with national politicians, that trend can then produce a strong push for outright nationalistic parties in the Member States. That does not mean to say that the sentiment of the people is bound to be totally anti-European. The 2017 election of President Macron in France rather shows that right-wing nationalistic trends can be successfully countered by a revitalisation of the European idea.

There is another possible reaction at Member State level that one should not forget. In difficult times people develop a desire for strong leadership. The most prominent example at present is Hungary and maybe also Poland.

10 The reaction of EU institutions

What is the reaction of the European institutions to all these developments of the Union and of Union law? The referenda on the European Constitution in France and the Netherlands, the political tensions between Member States and the animosities between their people caused in particular by the Euro currency union/sovereign debt crisis and also by the immigration crisis, the move of Member States politics back to putting national interests first, the Brexit referendum, the trend in Member States elections to right wing parties and—all of that should have been a strong signal to Brussels to pause and reflect. Instead, the Commission, it seems, continues to be happy with what it has achieved so far, happy with its inventions that bear funny names such as Two-Pack and Six-Pack and European Semester by which people in the street rather understand packs of bottles of beer and a university studies term respectively. The Commission did neither get the message by EP President Martin Schulz that Europe is close to implosion. The Commission does not seem to care about the question why today many people are sceptical, distrustful and even suspicious about many aspects of the EU; about the question whether the reasons for Brexit may possibly be on the EU side, too; and about the question why a Member State like Poland light-handedly puts into jeopardy some basic rule of law principles of the EU. The Commission simply goes on with all its regulatory activities and apparently does not even realise the danger of counterproductive overregulation.

Walter Hallstein once said the European Community is a community of the law. Unlike a nation state that has as basis its people, its territory and its laws, the sole basis of the EU is the law. This makes the EU so vulnerable—its entire existence depends on the law, and its credibility depends on the authority of that law. This ought to be reason enough to pay the greatest attention possible not to undermine the authority of EU law.

The White Paper published by the Commission some time after the June 2016 Brexit referendum listed several possibilities for action, and in the meantime the Commission has announced that it has decided for future deepening of the EU, for pressing to turn the ESM into an EU institution. However, what is necessary in the first place is not hasty action but rather a thorough analysis of the reasons for the present state of the EU and of EU law. The Commission seems to be convinced that the EU institutions are the solution to the problems without asking the question whether in reality they are not part of the problems.

The Commission seems convinced that lawyers will eventually find solutions to the present problems. But will these solutions last? Will they not further erode the European idea and the authority of EU law in the eyes of the people?

What is my suggestion to give matters a positive turn?

I definitely think that more attention must be given to the psycho-logic than to the law-logic of the present problems. The analysis of the reasons for these problems should definitely reach out beyond politicians and should include representatives from civil society organisations at Member State level.

Years ago we had a Convention to prepare a draft for a European Constitution. Why not have a similar body do the necessary diagnosis of the European patient and to develop possible therapies? A body that would try to find out which kind of Europe people have in mind for a positive European idea—an all-encompassing supranational Europe, a Europe without any supranationality or a Europe that is partly supranational (in which areas?) and in other respects characterised by nation states, or which other kind of structure? A body that would do so in a transparent process to be in line with peoples' expectations for transparency in today's information age. A body that would get into the process in a structured manner also the social media which today probably have the greatest influence of all media on public opinion. In my opinion, it will be impossible to revitalise the European idea with the people unless the social media are included in the process. What matters most in this context is the process as such and not so much the result. People must be given the feeling of being involved. Europe must again become a bottom-up idea like in the 1950s. A European idea top-down in the long-term has no chance.

The Commission is taking that top-down approach. It continues its politics of "*la fuite en avant*"—shut your eyes, grind your teeth and go forward! This way the Union and the law on which alone it is based, resemble a train. Some passenger cars are in flames. The engine driver instead of bringing the train to a halt accelerates more and more, in the hope that the force of the speed wind will extinguish the fire. In fact the wind will do the opposite—it will nourish the flames to grow more and more.

Let me conclude with some thoughts expressed by Joachim Gauck, who as President of the Federal Republic of Germany in a speech of February 2013 stressed the need for the European project to take the people along. He quoted Massimo D'Azeglio who said in 1861, the year of Italian unification: "We have created Italy. Now we must create the Italians." The parallel to our topic goes without saying. President Gauck added to that quote the following sentence: "Speed and depth of European integration are determined by the citizens of Europe." Let us do everything possible to replace the Union scepticism of today that exists with many if not most people, by the Union optimism that existed at the founding days of the European Communities. And let us bequeath on our children and grandchildren that the integration of Europe is not something that can be and is achieved once and for all times, it must rather be fought for and realised anew again and again all the time.

Hans-Jürgen Hellwig *Rechtsanwalt*, former President of the CCBE, honorary professor at the University of Heidelberg; partner at Hengeler Mueller, Frankfurt am Main. – A German version of this paper has been published in EuZW 2018, 222–228 (*Die Autorität des Unionsrechts – Glauben wir noch daran?*).

"Questions identitaires" as challenges to the single market

Luis Ortiz Blanco

First of all, I would like to thank the Academy of European Law for inviting me to its 25th Anniversary—congratulations—and for accepting that I address the "questions of identity" in Member States as a threat to the proper functioning of the Internal Market (in French "*questions identitaires*"). This is not a completely novel obstacle for the Internal Market, but its recent intensity is definitely novel.

The existence of numerous regions of Member States with their own culture, their differentiated "identities" and—for our purposes more relevant—their legislative and executive powers has been a "classic" obstacle to the Internal Market. In some Member States regional identities and aspirations of self-government have been dealt with by attributing great powers to regional entities; a *quid pro quo* between diversity and solidarity that has served well national and EU interests. Unfortunately, the balance risks to be broken because there are new threats lurking on the horizon.

Let me first deal with "classic" obstacles stemming from this reality (diversity) with a brief overview of selected cases; I will deal with more recent threats later.

It is well known that in some Member States regions enjoy wide competences to legislate and enforce rules on education, health, environmental protection, taxation, commerce regulation and consumer protection, to name but a few. These rules are liable to create obstacles to the Internal Market.

The case law of the Court of Justice of the European Union has clearly established that, to be considered contrary to the principle of free movement, national rules only need to apply to a part, and often a very small part, of the national territory. In this sense, not only national but regional and even municipal measures have been considered as contrary to the Treaty. For example, rules on labelling in regional languages.

L. Ortiz Blanco (✉)
EU and Competition Law Department at the Law Firm Garrigues, Madrid, Spain

EU and Competition Law Department at the Law Firm Garrigues, Brussels, Belgium
e-mail: Luis.Ortiz.Blanco@garrigues.com

W. Heusel, J.-P. Rageade (eds.), *The Authority of EU Law*,
https://doi.org/10.1007/978-3-662-58841-3_13

Linguistic issues have been dealt with by the European Court of Justice in regard to official languages, for example in cases *Piageme*[1] and *Geffroy*,[2] and in regard to regional and non-official languages, for example in cases *Colim*[3] and *Schwarzkopf*.[4]

In all of them the Court is sympathetic to linguistic requirements. In essence, it makes clear that the obligation to use a given language at stages prior to sale to the final consumer cannot be justified on consumer protection grounds, since this type of requirement is not necessary. However sales to the final consumer are a different matter: the Court accepts linguistic requirements provided they are justifiable and proportionate. The Member States may adopt national measures requiring that certain particulars of domestic or imported products be given in a language that is easily understood by the consumer, but this national measure must not exclude the possible use of other means of informing consumers, such as designs, symbols and pictograms, and in all circumstances, a measure of that kind must be restricted to the information made mandatory by the Member State concerned and for which the use of means other than translation would not be suitable for providing consumers with the appropriate information.

So, proportionality is the key, and proportionality requires a case-by-case approach. In the case *New Valmar*,[5] for example, the Court was tougher on regional linguistic requirements on the basis that it was disproportionate that legislation of a federal entity of a Member State requires every undertaking that has its place of establishment within the territory of that entity to draw up all the details on invoices relating to cross-border transactions exclusively in the official language of that entity, failing which those invoices are to be declared null and void by the national courts of their own motion. Such legislation can be justified neither by the objective of promoting and encouraging the use of one of the official languages of a Member State nor by the need to protect the effectiveness of fiscal supervision, since it goes beyond what is necessary to attain those objectives and thus cannot be regarded as proportionate.

However, there is much more than linguistic requirements.

For example, health concerns are very present in case *Aragonesa de Publicidad Exterior*,[6] which has a certain flavour of *Cassis* (*de Dijon*, of course). It refers to a law enacted by the Parliament of Catalonia prohibiting the advertising of alcoholic beverages over 23 degrees in the media, on streets and highways (except to indicate centres of production and sale), in cinemas and on public transport. The companies concerned were fined for not complying with such rule and argued in their appeal that the law on which those fines were based was contrary to Article 30 EEC (Article

[1] Judgment of 12 October 1995, *Piageme v Peeters*, C-85/94, EU:C:1995:312.

[2] Judgment of 12 September 2000, *Geffroy*, C-366/98, EU:C:2000:430.

[3] Judgment of 3 June 1999, *Colim*, C-33/97, EU:C:1999:274.

[4] Judgment of 13 September 2001, *Schwarzkopf*, C-169/99, EU:C:2001:439.

[5] Judgment of 21 June 2016, *New Valmar*, C-15/15, EU:C:2016:464.

[6] Judgment of 25 July 1991, *Aragonesa de Publicidad Exterior and Publivia v Departamento de Sanidad y Seguridad Social de Cataluña*, C-1/90, EU:C:1991:327.

34 TFEU), as by virtue of the advertising restrictions it affected marketing opportunities for beverages originating in other Member States.

While according to its case law legislation which restricts or prohibits certain forms of advertising and certain means of sales promotion can be considered as measures having equivalent effect within the meaning of Article 30 EEC (now 34 TFEU), the Court considered that in this case such a measure protected public health, as "*advertising acts as an encouragement to consumption and the existence of rules restricting the advertising of alcoholic beverages in order to combat alcoholism reflects public health concerns*", and was proportionate to the objective to be attained, as it restricted advertising of those products only to a limited extent. In the same vein, the Court considered that this measure did not represent a disguised restriction on trade between Member States.

Indeed, even if it is not necessary for a measure to have the effect of favouring national products as a whole or placing only imported products at a disadvantage to be considered protective or discriminatory, and although Catalonia produced more beverages having an alcoholic strength of less than 23 degrees than beverages with a higher alcohol content, the Court considered that the legislation did not distinguish between products according to their origin and did not restrict imports.

Environmental protection by regional authorities has also been subject to the scrutiny of the European Court of Justice. The *Walloon Waste* Case[7] concerns a regional Belgian measure adopted by the Walloon Regional Executive power, whereby it prohibited the storage, tipping or dumping in Wallonia of waste originating in another Member State or in a region of Belgium other than Wallonia. Such a measure was considered contrary to an existing Directive in the area concerned. However, it was not deemed contrary to Articles 30 and 36 EEC (Articles 34 and 36 TFEU). The Court clearly stated that waste must be considered as "goods" under the free movement provisions, but it determined that the Walloon measure was justified by imperative requirements of environmental protection, as it could not be considered discriminatory, on the basis of the self-sufficiency and proximity principles contained in the Basel Convention (1989) and on the principle that environmental damage should as a matter of priority be remedied at source.

The *Ligur Carni* case[8] concerned an Italian Royal Decree providing that "*the bringing into a municipality of fresh meat for the purpose of marketing, after slaughter elsewhere, is authorised on condition, in particular, that the meat 'undergoes a further inspection by the veterinarian at the municipality of destination', in addition to the one which has taken place in the municipality of origin*". On this basis, the Liguria region in Italy adopted a Regional Law providing for the payment of charges by individuals using such veterinary services. Moreover, in a determined municipality, La Sapienza, for the marketing of meat an importer had to use the services of CO.GE.SE.MA., a cooperative company to which the municipal authority had granted an exclusive concession for the handling of goods in the municipal

[7] Judgment of 9 July 1992, *Commission v Belgium*, C-2/90, EU:C:1992:310.

[8] Judgment of 15 December 1993, *Ligur Carni and Others v Unità Sanitaria Locale n° XV di Genova and Others*, Joined cases C-277/91, C-318/91 and C-319/91, EU:C:1993:927.

slaughterhouse as well as their carriage to the places of final destination. The trader could have the goods distributed by its own means, but CO.GE.SE.MA. had to be paid anyway. The Court found, firstly, that the Regional measure was contrary to EU law on the basis of its non-compliance with the relevant Directives; secondly, that the levying of such charges on importers was also considered to constitute an obstacle to free movement; and finally, that the municipal measures on the exclusive concession on handling were also considered as contrary to Article 30 EEC (Article 34 TFEU).

Moving now to taxation, the *Carbonati Apuani* case[9] concerns a measure by which a tax was established in favor of a municipality, Comune di Carrara, on marble leaving its territory. The application and collection of the tax, as well as the determination of the tax rate, had to be carried out by the local authorities and on the basis of municipal rules. The Court reminds the distinction to be made between internal taxation and measures which have to be considered as charges having equivalent effect to customs duties. However, it did not consider that such a tax could be deemed to relate to a system of internal taxation, as the chargeable event consisted on the crossing of the boundaries of the region at issue, and not on objective criteria. Instead, the Court made reference to its case law,[10] according to which "*a charge imposed when goods cross a territorial boundary within a Member State constitutes a charge having effect equivalent to a customs duty*". The size of the territorial administrative authority levying the tax is immaterial to classify a tax as a charge having effect equivalent to a customs duty, so the Court concluded that such a tax was contrary to free movement of goods provisions.

Also on taxation and more recently, the *ANGED* cases[11] relate to several requests for a preliminary ruling from the Spanish Supreme Court lodged by the National Association of Large Distribution Companies (ANGED) against the Generalitat de Catalunya, the Principado de Asturias and the Diputación General de Aragón. The case concerns several regional taxes imposed on the use of individual large retail spaces with sales areas of various sizes—in the Catalan case, 2500 m^2 or more—due to their potential effect on planning, the environment and urban retailing patterns in the region. As a matter of law, the tax applies irrespective of whether or not such retail establishments are actually situated in a consolidated urban area, and in practice it usually affects undertakings from other Member States. ANGED has challenged this tax on the basis of Articles 49 TFEU and 54 TFEU; but also on the basis of Article 107(1) TFEU because—allegedly—this regional legislation provides for full and partial tax exemptions in certain cases that constitute State aid.

[9] Judgment of 9 September 2004, *Carbonati Apuani*, C-72/03, EU:C:2004:506.

[10] Judgment of 16 July 1992, *Administration des douanes and droits indirects v Legros and Others*, C-163/90, EU:C:1992:326; Judgment of 9 August 1994, *Lancry and Others v Direction générale des douanes and Others*, joined cases C-363/93, C-407/93, C-408/93, C-409/93, C-410/93 and C-411/93, EU:C:1994:315; and Judgment of 14 September 1995, *Simitzi v Dimos Kos*, Joined cases C-485/93 and C-486/93., EU:C:1995:281.

[11] Judgments of 26 April 2018, *ANGED*, joined cases C-233/16, C-234/16, C-235/16, C-236/16 and C-237/16, EU:C:2018:280; EU:C:2018:281; EU:C:2018:291.

Even more recently, a group of organisations representing farmers, food processors, distributors, hotels and catering companies have opposed the autonomic tax on sugar drinks approved in Catalonia (IBAE) on 30 May 2017, on the basis that it goes against the free movement of goods, the unity of the Spanish market and the principle of equality and non-discrimination. These organisations have asked the Spanish Government to challenge this tax before the Spanish Constitutional Court.

To sum up, when regional legislation is liable to restrict trade within Member States’ national markets *and* other EU national markets, EU law and the Court of Justice can help integrate EU Member States’ national markets. However, when that regional legislation creates “purely internal solutions”, EU law would not apply. In such a case a Member State can only rely on its own Constitution to solve the problem, possibly legislating like Spain did with Law 20/2013, of 9 December, on the safeguard of the unity of the market—which has itself been challenged by some regional Governments before the Spanish Constitutional Court.

Turning to the most novel and most serious threat not only to the Internal Market, but to the very existence of the European Union and to peace in Europe, let me touch on the Catalan crisis.

Spain is a full democracy and a most reliable and enthusiastic partner of the European Union. For some European media, the Catalan events may have cast a different light on Spain—perhaps a gloomier, older light. But we are still the same people, the same reliable partner.

The Spanish Government has perhaps made some mistakes, but it has made them trying to defend the rule of law in Spain and to oppose a unilateral declaration of independence of a substantial part of its territory. Spain is an advanced democracy by all standards, and should be given credit and backing from the EU institutions and Member States in defending the rule of law.

The EU and particularly Spain have gone through a major economic crisis which is dying hard and has made many people lose faith in politics and made Spain the prey of populist miracle sellers. Other European countries are experiencing the same problem.

Nationalism—the very opposite of the idea of an ever closer union among the people of Europe—is trying to divide European countries further, creating new borders in smaller regions with the aim of reducing solidarity within the territories of Member States. At the end—at least in Europe—a State is a territory in which its constituent regions help each other to promote common goals; in sum, an area of solidarity.

Spain is undergoing an attack from powerful nationalist and populist forces; many other countries could suffer the same fate if the EU institutions and Member States did not differentiate between the defenders and the attackers of solidarity and of the rule of law. Luckily they do.

Nationalism and populism are not only the enemies of Spain; they are the enemies of the EU and of peace in Europe. No matter how right President Juncker may be in stating that it would be impossible to handle a European Union of 98 States, former French Prime Minister Manuel Valls is even righter: it could be war in Europe, again. Let’s not forget about our history.

Protectionism in Central and Eastern Europe and the EU Internal Market: the case of retail

Ilya G. J. Bruggeman and Christian Verschueren

1 Introduction

Populism and protectionism are not only phenomena in the media, in which trust has diminished,[1] but they are also affecting our daily lives and the EU Internal Market. Businesses operating cross-border suffer from new national rules and practices that restrict their freedom to conduct their business. A survey among EuroCommerce members showed that, for the coming years, the main challenges, apart from the digital transformation of the economy, are protectionism and trade barriers.[2] The economic evidence in literature demonstrating how protectionism hampers economic growth and jobs is overwhelming. Nevertheless, policy-makers undermine competition in the market. This reduces consumer's choice, purchasing power, and confidence on the one hand, and legal certainty for businesses on the other. It also prevents the Internal Market from reaching its full potential to provide jobs and growth. Ultimately, it is the citizen, whether as a consumer or a jobseeker, who suffers the consequences of these policies.

By working with retailers in EuroCommerce,[3] the European umbrella organisation for retail and wholesale businesses, we have built up significant experience of dealing with these protectionist measures and trade restrictions in a number of countries, in particular in Central and Eastern Europe: how to identify and deal with

[1] Edelman (2018): In the yearly global Trust Barometer of Edelman, correspondents have been asked about their trust in four institutions: NGOs, business, government and media. This year correspondents have identified media as the least trusted institution.

[2] The EuroCommerce online membership survey was carried out in December 2017 and January 2018. The e-survey was sent to all member contacts of EuroCommerce and received 140 replies which represents a 15% response rate.

[3] www.eurocommerce.eu.

I. G. J. Bruggeman (✉) · C. Verschueren
EuroCommerce aisbl, The European Federation for Retail and Wholesale, Brussels, Belgium
e-mail: bruggeman@eurocommerce.eu; guedes@eurocommerce.eu

W. Heusel, J.-P. Rageade (eds.), *The Authority of EU Law*,
https://doi.org/10.1007/978-3-662-58841-3_14

them, but also how this impacts the Internal Market. We have seen over many years a diminution of respect for the rule of law and its institutions, and increasing fragmentation of the Internal Market.

After 60 years of European construction, we still do not have one Internal Market in Europe, free from unnecessary, unjustified and disproportionate restrictions. Yet everyone recognises that achieving this will bring benefits to society: increasing wealth, jobs, growth and choice for consumers. We believe that this increased welfare will give citizens more opportunities to live their lives the way they want, and that all of Europe's nations will be so economically and culturally intertwined that the costs of protectionism are unimaginably high, and that war becomes an archaic concept. The Single Market has already provided those enterprises with countless opportunities to expand their businesses and trade with other businesses and consumers all over Europe. The digital transformation is facilitating this further; with a few mouse clicks, customers have access to products and services anywhere. For years now, the growth rates of e-commerce sales (even during the financial crisis) have been in double digits.[4] We want to find a way to preserve our current EU achievements, and use and develop further the governance of the Internal Market to contain the wave of protectionist and populist policies in a more effective way.

In this paper, we discuss protectionist trends in the EU, our experience with dealing with protectionist and populist policies, the weaknesses in current Single Market governance, and possible ways of improving governance further.

2 The rise of protectionism and populism

Protectionism and populism have become growing global trends over the past decade. Obviously, protectionism and populism are not the same thing, but they often go hand in hand. In the EU (the focus of this paper), we see that almost all populists display protectionist tendencies. Protectionism often involves conscious government policies and practices aimed at giving a direct or indirect advantage to local businesses vis-à-vis foreign businesses. Populism is harder to define, however, and literature offers many definitions and ideas. Cas Mudde and Cristóbal Rovira Kaltwasser[5] offer an 'ideational approach' of populism, which combines different definitions found in the literature. They define populism as "a thin-centred ideology that considers society to be ultimately separated into two homogeneous and antagonistic camps: the pure people versus the corrupt elite. They argue that politics should be an expression of the general will of the people. Most notably, political actors have combined populism with a variety of other thin- and thick-centred ideologies, including agrarianism, nationalism, neoliberalism, and socialism."[6]

[4] Eurostat (2017).

[5] Mudde and Rovira Kaltwasser (2017).

[6] Mudde and Rovira Kaltwasser (2017).

A recent study published by the Tony Blair Institute[7] shows that more and more people in Europe are voting for populist parties. In 2000, on average 8.5% of the votes went to populist parties. Today, that number almost tripled at 24.1%. While populist parties in Eastern Europe took an average of 9.2% of the national vote in 2000, their vote share has since then even more than tripled, reaching 31.6% in 2017.

Examples of growing populism among voters and in political leadership abound in Europe. For example, in Poland, the ruling PiS party continues to enjoy wide acceptance[8]; in Hungary, Prime Minister Orban's Fidesz party has secured its dominant position institutionally and electorally[9,10]; since last year Austria has a new coalition government including the far-right FPÖ[11]; in the Netherlands, the populist Geert Wilders gained more votes than ever in last year's parliamentary elections[12]; in France, Marine Le Pen won more votes than ever in the presidential elections, even though she ultimately lost out to Emmanuel Macron[13]; in Germany, the AfD's major gains in the last election made building a coalition of the centre unusually difficult[14]; in Italy, the Five Star Movement and Lega won together more than 50% of the votes in the 2018 elections.

According to an analysis by the Economist[15] more and more populist parties are being brought into coalitions,[16] co-opted and their policies copied. Even if populism is still not the dominant force in national politics, it is widespread. However, voters in general are not necessarily anti-EU. Last year has shown a steep increase of people throughout Europe having favourable views of the EU. But, while few citizens on the European continent are eager to see their own country depart the EU, many have expressed the wish to have their voice heard through their own referendum on EU membership.[17]

The above seems to imply that populism is far from dead, and it might even grow further if the trend revealed in the Tony Blair Institute study would continue.

Where does this populism come from and why are populist parties gaining so much ground? In a study, the World Bank sought to look into the socio-economic

---

[7] Tony Blair Institute (2017).

[8] Reuters (2017).

[9] New York Times (2018).

[10] Financial Times (2018).

[11] Guardian (2017).

[12] NRC (2017).

[13] Le Monde (2017), 10.6 million votes were cast for Marie Le Pen in the second round of the presidential elections in 2017, in the second round of 2015 Front National received in the regional elections 6.8 million votes.

[14] Spiegel (2017).

[15] Economist (2018).

[16] For example, FPÖ in Austrian government since 2017 and from 2000 to 2007, PVV supporting minority government in the Netherlands from 2010 to 2012, PS in Finland from 2015 to 2017 and its splinter Finns Party in the government coalition until today.

[17] Pew Research Center (2017).

aspects that drive populism. They concluded that perhaps one root case is the structural challenges and resulting social and political tensions in many countries. Mistrust in established institutions is increasing, and concern about job security is growing. Even though common economic indicators show that peoples' economic conditions have improved, they do not necessarily perceive it that way. This may reflect decreased optimism about the future, more jobs have become flexible or part-time, and a shift in demand for skills due to digital technology has made jobs not requiring those skills rarer or more precarious. More academic research is needed to investigate this further, the World Bank concluded.[18]

In The Toronto Globe and Mail, Darrel Bricker and John Ibbitson argue that populism is not mainly driven by economic insecurities but by fear of immigrants. They call this nativism "a fear of foreigners coming into your community and undermining your culture and way of life." They claim that for example that resentment towards immigrants caused people to vote for Brexit. "Today's populist rebellions are nothing more than the exploitation of gullible voters by politicians who are willing to stoke nativist resentment that other elites ignore and who couldn't care less about how badly they damage their societies in the process." Interestingly, they say that politicians and the media should "play down the grand theories about the advantages of immigration, globalization and economic diversification. It'll all be labelled fake news."[19]

Their views become more interesting if we take a look at an article on global demographic developments until 2050 from Jean-Michel Boussemart and Michel Godet, which was published by the Fondation Robert Schuman. While the population of Europe remains stable at about 500 million, in Africa the population is expected to more than double from 1186 million in 2015 to 2478 million in 2050. An increase of 1292 million people, of which a 130 million will be born in North Africa. "In other words, the migratory pressure on Europe will be greater than ever! (…) Yet nobody in Europe is talking about it, let alone preparing for it."[20] One could therefore conclude that, if fear of immigrants is one of the drivers of populism, it will certainly not disappear in the following decades. This makes it even more important to have a real debate about populism and protectionism, and about the role of our institutions to guard against those.

[18] World Bank Group (2016).

[19] The Globe and Mail (2018).

[20] Fondation Robert Schuman (2018).

3 Protectionism against Western retailers in Central and Eastern Europe

While the digital revolution is fundamentally changing the shape of retail, we still need brick & mortar stores, products still need to be produced somewhere and will still have to cross borders. In 2017 intra-EU trade was valued at EUR 3347 billion.[21] While many barriers to e-commerce are created by outdated rules or new rules designed for a non-digital economy, over the past ten years, international retailers from Western Europe have seen a strong rise in protectionism everywhere in Europe, and particularly in member states in Central and Eastern Europe.[22] The Czech Republic, Hungary, Poland and Slovakia have united in the Visegrad Group,[23] which has become more and more influential, often strengthening and reinforcing each other's position.[24] Business sectors that are considered strategic and where foreign players, mostly from Western Europe, dominate, like banking, telecom, media, energy, and food retail have been targeted. Control of the media is of particular interest to populist regimes, as we see in the Czech Republic,[25] Hungary or Poland.

In retail, we mainly see protectionist laws restricting Western food retailers. They face significant barriers to establish stores in another Member State and to operate their businesses in an open and fair way. They are often bluntly discriminated against in favour of local players and local product assortment.

Sometimes protectionism is indirect and difficult to detect, because one needs a thorough understanding of market mechanisms involved. However, often, it can also be very obvious, as in countries like in Poland[26] and Hungary[27] where the Rule of Law is clearly under threat. This undermines legal certainty for businesses and undermines trust for foreign investors. If we look in particular to the food retail sector, there are a number of ways in which regimes in Central and Eastern Europe usually try to regulate the sector:

1. **competition and (unfair) trading laws** that prohibit or restrict certain B2B trading practices, redefine concepts as 'dominant market position' or 'significant market power', oblige large foreign-owned players to publish market sensitive data, or impose disproportionate fines;
2. **food laws** that introduce new labelling and reporting obligations, disproportionate fines, sourcing obligations, or disproportionate inspection fees;

[21] Eurostat, http://ec.europa.eu/eurostat/statistics-explained/index.php/International_trade_in_goods, last visited 21 May 2018.

[22] Central and Eastern Europe covering in this paper Bulgaria, Croatia, Czech Republic, Hungary, Poland, Romania, Slovakia and Slovenia.

[23] http://www.visegradgroup.eu/.

[24] Visegrad Group (2018).

[25] The two leading newspapers *Lidové noviny* and *Mladá fronta DNES* are owned by the current Prime Minister Andrej Babiš.

[26] European Commission (2017a).

[27] European Parliament (2017a).

3. **tax laws** that introduce discriminatory and disproportionate retail taxes or 'fees';
4. **product laws** that make foreign products less attractive vis-à-vis local products;
5. **establishment laws** that restrict the market-entry or expansion of new or foreign-based players.

These mechanisms are used by governments to limit international food retailers' ability to compete in the market, which limits choice for consumers, raises costs and curbs investment and innovation. In Table 1, we present some examples of these laws. A more extensive but non-exhaustive overview of specific laws is available on the website of EuroCommerce.[28]

Many of these laws target the business model of Western European retailers. This usually differs substantially from local players or national chains: (1) they are usually centrally organised and have integrated businesses, while local players often operate under franchise or in a network of independent retailers; (2) international retailers have complex global supply chains and multifaceted agreements with a great number of local and large multinational suppliers, whilst local players have often less complex supply chains; (3) international retailers often operate with large stores, while local players often focus on smaller stores; (4) international retailers need to achieve economies of scale in a new market to make their investment profitable. Because of these differences between international and local players, it is often easy for policy-makers to design laws in such a way to undermine the business model of international retailers or benefit the business model of local players.

We also see a pattern emerging of Member States mimicking each other's laws: examples include the introduction or consideration of a staggered retail tax (Poland, Hungary, Romania, Slovakia), a reporting obligation on the origin of foods (Czech Republic and Slovakia), the prohibition of certain listing fees (Croatia, Czech Republic, Romania, Slovakia), and the redefinition of market power (Czech Republic and Hungary). This makes it more important to have a Single Market in which the rules are clear and well enforced. If one Member State gets away with a specific measure, others are likely to follow.

In addition to business-unfriendly legislation, EuroCommerce members also suffer discrimination in enforcement. Very intense and more frequent inspections (e.g. food, taxation, compliance) are used to find minor violations and punish retailers. With every successive violation, fines may increase exponentially. It also happens that, under the threat of fines, local authorities make illegal suggestions on how these fines can be avoided, e.g. by selling more (of a specific) local product(s). These discriminatory or disproportionate practices by public authorities are difficult to document, and the retailer cannot reveal the practice without revealing its own identity and risk retaliation. In some Member States, we see that public opinion is very hostile towards foreign-owned retailers.[29] The media regularly reports on

---

[28] www.eurocommerce.eu, search for 'Single Market Barriers Overview' under the tab resources. The overview is regularly updated.

[29] Budapest Business Journal (2016).

Table 1 Examples of protectionist laws

Czech Significant Market Power Act (Act No. 395/2009 on Significant Market Power in the sale of agricultural and food products and the abuse thereof) Among others, retailers that have a turnover higher than CZK 5 billion (≅€200 million) are deemed to have significant market power. No additional assessment of economical dependencies between retailers and suppliers is necessary, or the actual impact on competitiveness. Businesses can be fined up to 10% of turnover. Suppliers' payments are limited to 3% of the value of the delivered food products. There is a list of prohibited activities such as commonly used listing fees. Retailers have to publish their payment conditions. Publication of payment terms undermines competition. Many of the practices that are prohibited are common commercial practices which are legitimate in other EU Member States. The prohibitions undermine the business model of modern retail.
Slovak Food Act (152/1995 Coll) The law foresees a very steep fine system for violations of the law, including minor violations that have limited or no risks for consumer health e.g. expiry of the best before date, spots on fruit and vegetables. The first fine is between €1000 and €500,000, the second fine is double the first fine i.e. €2000 and €1,000,000, the third fine is €1,000,000 to €5,000,000. These high fines create high legal uncertainty for all retail businesses, especially when stores already have two fines. They are also disproportionate to the violation, as these are usually minor. There is no indication that food sold in Slovak supermarkets is less safe or safer than elsewhere in the EU. So far, mainly foreign-owned retailers have been fined and only those have received €1 million fines.
Romanian Food Act (Act 150/2016 of 18 July 2015 on Food Trade) Among others, the law requires large retailers to source 51% of merchandise volumes in core product categories via the (still undefined) short supply. There is an obligation to display and promote Romanian products in stores. There is a total prohibition of listing fees. These are fees charged by retailers to suppliers for services provided e.g. logistics, promotion campaigns, etc.
Polish Act on the Retail Sales Tax of 6 July 2016 (Published in the Polish Official Gazette on 1 August 2016) The tax would only have applied to retailers. Franchisees and online sales were exempt. The tax would have been charged based on a: • monthly turnover of less than 17M Zloty would be exempt from the tax • monthly turnover of 17M to 170M Zloty would be subject to a 0.8% tax • monthly turnover exceeding 170M Zloty would be subject to a 1.4% tax The largest portion of the tax would have been paid by foreign-owned retailers. In average, many of them have a higher turnover than local players, not least because they operate less frequently via a franchise system.
Hungarian Food Supply Chain Fee (2014 amendment to the Food Chain Act) The law would have introduced a tax based on the total turnover of retail businesses. Franchise chains (only local) would have been taxed based on the turnover of individual franchisees. The staggered rate was as follows: • the first 500 million HUF turnover exempt • between 500 million HUF and 50 billion HUF 0.1% • between 50 billion and 100 billion HUF 1% • between 100 billion and 150 billion HUF 2% • between 150 billion and 200 billion HUF 3% • between 200 billion and 250 billion HUF 4% • between 250 billion and 300 billion HUF 5% • above 300 billion HUF 6% The tax was justified by the need to finance food controls. The revenue was estimated at €100 million, almost all to be paid by foreign-owned retailers.

(continued)

Table 1 (continued)

Czech Reporting Obligation (Act 110/1997 on foodstuff and tobacco products and on amendments to certain related acts—Amendment 139/2014) Retailers with a turnover greater than CZK 5 billion were obliged to disclose a list of the five countries of which the highest percentage of food products is sold in the Czech Republic, including the percentage, at the entrance of the store, and report to the government. The intention of the law was to influence consumer behaviour, in the hope they would shop at stores that reported high percentages of local (Czech) products.
Ban World Heritage Sites (Act CXII of 2014 on Modification of Act CLXIV of 2005 on Trade in connection with operation of undertakings in the interest of fair market practice) The ban entered into force on 1 January 2015, and prohibits to establish or operate discounters, large supermarkets or hypermarkets in urban living areas of World Heritage Sites and their buffer zones, i.e. an area of 967 hectares in the inner districts of Budapest. After a three year's transition period from 1 January 2018, it is prohibited to establish and operate discount stores (400 m^2 and above), supermarkets (2500–5000 m^2) or hypermarkets (5000 m^2 and above) on places belonging to the World Heritage defined by a separate law. The only existing stores covered by the law were of foreign-owned retailers.

allegations by producers, farmers and politicians against foreign-owned retailers of bad behaviour, often demanding government intervention and regulation. In this environment, retailers operate under constant threat of arbitrary action. In some countries, foreign-owned retailers are refused access to key policy-makers, or policy-makers fear that being seen to support retailers may damage their reputation. Speaking up in public or going to court where a retailer believes it is mistreated or subjected to protectionist measures may have consequences in future dealing with national authorities and make them cautious about doing so.

4 Economic impact of protectionism

How can we assess if the Single Market is functioning, or if there is a Single Market at all?[30] Could we measure this by the level of harmonisation within the EU? Or the number of national rules deviating from the four freedoms based on overriding reasons of public interest? Is it possible to measure the additional economic growth since the Single Market project has started or how much we still have to gain, or the welfare loss due to non-integration? This goes beyond the scope of this paper. In this chapter, we will instead try to identify some key issues relating to how protectionist policies undermine the functioning of the Single Market.

The European Parliamentary Research Services has published several studies on the "Cost of Non-Europe".[31] The fourth edition estimates an annual cost (in terms of

[30] Erixon and Georgieva (2016) is an interesting read, as it discusses if the Single Market delivered anything at all and if current harmonisation policies are creating barriers instead of removing them.

[31] European Parliament (2017b).

lost opportunities) of some €1751 billion, 12% of EU-28 GDP (2016). €615 billion could be gained by completing the Single Market for consumers and citizens, and €415 billion by completing the digital Single Market. The €615 billion cover completion of the Single Market for goods, which would gain €183 billion, and completion of the Single Market for services, worth an extra €338 billion. Both are key for retail and wholesale businesses. Especially for services the potential is high. It is widely recognised that the Services Directive has not brought the benefits people expected from it. In 2016 the European Court of Auditors (ECA) published its assessment of the implementation of the Services Directive,[32] in which it concludes that among others the Commission has not applied the announced zero-tolerance policy against Member States infringing the Services Directive, the number of infringement cases is extremely low, the Commission has not created a systematic strategy to strengthen the Single Market in services, overall the Commission has only been partially effective in ensuring the implementation of the Directive. The ECA makes one interesting recommendation (number 5), namely strengthening the notification procedure with a standstill period. This procedure is a preventive tool that may be an effective way of tackling protectionism, as we will explain in chapter 6. To conclude, the ECA report seems to indicate the Commission seriously underperformed here. But it seems unfair to put all the blame on the Commission, it were in the end the Member States that did not implement the Services Directive properly and continued to protect local interests instead.

The Organisation for Economic Co-operation and Development (OECD) took another angle to look at the performance of the Single Market. It compared the EU with the United States in a 2016 report on completing the Single Market.[33] In the EU intra-EU trade in manufactured goods was in 2012 21% of GPD, in comparison with 35% of GDP with interstate trade in the United States. A staggering gap that seems to indicate that cross-border trade in the EU could easily double when barriers are removed.

While these are impressive figures, it is unclear how far they stem from protectionist policies connected with populist regimes. However, we can say something more concrete about the impact of restricting retail operations on the overall competitiveness of the market. A very recent communication by the Commission concludes that the retail is a heavily regulated sector, and that overregulation may lead to less competition in the local retail markets. "[T]he productivity of the EU retail sector has been lagging behind other sectors and is less dynamic than in other comparable economies." Main points of attention are barriers to retail establishment, operational restrictions and compliance costs.[34] One of the conclusions of an underpinning study of the communication on retail establishment that was commissioned by the Commission on the legal framework for retail establishment in the 28 Member States was that "the regulatory framework in the Member States regarding the establishment of retail outlets tends to be (very) complex... [P]rocedure(s) to be

[32] European Court of Auditors (2016).

[33] OECD (2016).

[34] European Commission (2018a).

followed (are) usually quite burdensome." In the accompanying economic analysis the researchers found that the level of restrictiveness was negatively correlated with the opening or expansion of stores. It also concluded that the most concentrated markets have the lowest level of opening new stores. This might be indirectly linked with the level of regulation.[35]

A study published in 2014 commissioned by DG COMP tried to measure the impact of modern retail on choice and innovation in the EU food sector.[36] This and other studies found evidence that new shop openings led to more competition, and that there is a link between the level of restrictive regulation of retail and innovation, and competition in the retail market. Although scientific evidence is still limited, one could conclude that protectionist policies that undermine competition in the retail market undermine the free movement of goods and services, and thereby the working of the Single Market. In more general terms, the OECD Services Trade Restrictiveness Index (STRI) shows that consumers and firms pay the cost of trade restrictions: entry barriers allow incumbent firms to gain market power, limit competition, and delay innovation. The costs of a policy environment that reduces competition from new entrants, whether domestic or foreign, is ultimately borne by consumers and downstream business customers, who pay higher prices and enjoy less choice than they would in more competitive markets. The resulting price increases for domestic users of services can be quantified as a sales tax equivalent on their purchases, imposing substantial additional costs on manufacturing enterprises and eventually on final customers.[37]

To give a better idea of the practical implications we have listed in Table 2 the known impact of some protectionist laws or the possible impact these would have had.

While these effects might look limited in themselves, over time the missed potential accumulates and consumers will experience less choice, higher prices and less jobs.

5 Filing cases for infringements against EU law

In this challenging context, EuroCommerce has supported its members in addressing various sometimes blatant infringements against the freedoms laid down in the EU Treaties.

If a national protectionist measure breaches EU law, there are two main forms of remedies one may consider: invoking the breach of EU law in proceedings before the national courts or lodging a complaint with the European Commission for

[35] HVG (2016).

[36] European Commission (2014a).

[37] OECD (2018).

Table 2 Economic impact of some protectionist laws in retail

Hungarian crisis tax for the retail sector	A total amount of €300 million paid over 2010, 2011 and 2012. (Estimated amount mainly paid by foreign-owned retailers based on public sources)
Hungarian Supplier Act[a]	Between 2013 and 2014, the quantity of imported UHT milk in Hungary decreased from about 75% to 50% in favour of locally produced milk.
Polish Act on the Retail Sales Tax	€350 million annually (Estimated amount that should have been paid by foreign-owned retailers out of total tax revenue of €450 million annually based on public resources)
Hungarian Food Supply Chain Fee	€100 million annually (Estimated amount that should have been paid by foreign-owned retailers based on public sources)

[a]The law prescribes that the profit margin on local and foreign agricultural products should be the same. In practice it is mainly applied to imported UHT milk, which has led to a steep decline of imported UHT milk. Showing it clearly affects the free movement of goods within the EU

infringement of EU law. We discuss both approaches and our experience in dealing with both approaches below.

5.1 *National procedures*

Businesses should pursue national appeal procedures and an EU complaint at the same time. A national procedure is not always opportune, as stated earlier, as it may lead to retaliation and attacks in the media. However, if the national procedure raises questions of EU Law, the national court could decide to refer the case to the Court of Justice of the European Union for guidance. In the absence of an infringement procedure by the European Commission, such a referral may resolve the case but only if the right questions are referred to the ECJ. It is also possible to run a national case and an EU infringement procedure in parallel. From experience, we know that this may delay a decision by the Commission on an infringement procedure. However, such a referral order to the ECJ could take quite some time before being concluded. During an infringement procedure, the European Commission usually enters into a dialogue with the accused Member State to change its policies and bring them in line with EU law before the case is referred to the ECJ by the Commission. In certain cases, this can be a faster and more permanent solution than a preliminary ruling of the Court.

Having a national case next to lodging a complaint against a Member States with the European Commission is relevant for a number of other reasons. The European Commission might decide not to pursue the case at all. In 2016, the European Commission handled 3458 complaints; of those, 3026 were closed for different reasons: no EU laws were breached (2253), no power to act (86), the correspondence did not qualify as a complaint (667), and 20 cases were withdrawn.[38] This means that only 1 out of 8 complaints led to a real case against a Member State that year.

In some cases, the decision by the European Commission for not pursuing a complaint further may be driven by a reluctance to enter into action it may not win, or as a result of lack of resources. For example there is little case law about disproportionate fines, and EU law gives the Member States a lot of room for manoeuvre.

Another reason that plays a role is the Commission's ambition to be 'bigger and more ambitious on big things, and smaller and more modest on small things'.[39] Basically, meaning the European Commission is no longer the guardian of the Treaties if it is an infringement with a limited impact. We have had several complaints that were not pursued due to their limited impact.

In addition, the European Parliament and Member States are looking for opportunities that serve their interest. The Commission may not want to pursue an infringement case that may work against gaining the Member State's political support in, for example, a new piece of legislation. For instance, the opening of infringement cases is frequently delayed during the months before national elections. Although this delay might be understandable, in the meantime businesses have to abide the infringing national law and change the way they operate.

Simply waiting for the Commission to take immediate action is an uncertain strategy, and even when the Commission opens a case this may not lead to swift solutions. Therefore, it is worthwhile for businesses to pursue a national solution, next to lodging a complaint with the Commission.

5.2 Lodging complaints for infringements against EU law

Below we discuss some lessons learned from lodging complaints and infringement cases. In principle, lodging a complaint should be a last resort. It means all other options at national and EU level have failed and the only way to resolve the matter is by lodging a complaint against a Member State with the Commission.

The Commission has tried to act fast and took our complaints seriously. In most cases, the complaint led to the opening of an EU pilot[40] or a formal infringement procedure. However, we see a number of issues that prevent or delay the opening of a procedure, or slow down its progress. All these make this Single Market governance tool less effective in fighting Member States breaching EU law in general, and protectionism in particular.

---

[38] European Commission (2017b).

[39] European Commission (2017c).

[40] The so-called "EU pilot" procedure used to be a procedure preceding the formal infringement investigation.

In general, the most effective policy tool the Commission has is in Competition Law. The Directorate General for Competition can open an in-depth investigation about possible unlawful State aid and issue a suspension injunction on the implementation of the alleged unlawful State aid. Even in cases where the implementation of the state aid is not suspended, if the Commission concludes, at the end of the State aid investigation, that the State aid is unlawful, the Member State has to recover the State aid. A suspension provides businesses with immediate redress, while an infringement procedure against legislation will only conclude that a law breaches EU law and has to be adjusted accordingly. It is up to businesses and citizens to seek redress in a national court. However, in our experience, only a limited number of cases qualify for the State aid case criteria. Yet, the Commission has strong powers when unlawful State aid is given, but this contrasts with cases where Internal Market law is breached.

If we look at how the Commission handles infringement cases, a number of things stand out. Even if one has a strong case, this does not mean the Commission will immediately act. Complaints are not only assessed from a legal perspective, but also from a 'political urgency' perspective. Getting support further up the Commission's hierarchy accelerates the handling of a complaint, but it can be difficult to pinpoint why a decision is sometimes delayed by many months or even years.

When an infringement procedure is finally opened, a cat-and-mouse game may begin between the Commission and Member State. Although on paper the Commission and Member States are bound by deadlines to reply to each other's correspondence, there are no penalties for taking more time. What we have experienced in certain cases is that Member States reply just before or after the deadline to maximise the duration of a procedure. Member States provide the Commission with insufficient or even false information, they propose superficial solutions, or even push the national parliament to initiate a never-ending and confusing discussion of amending the contested law. This creates the impression that the contested law might be amended for the better soon, but no clarity over how the amended law will look. We also see that in some cases, the wording of the law is changed, but the impact remains the same. All these tactics are difficult for the Commission to handle. It feels forced to play by the rules, even though it knows it is being played with.

Another effective delaying tactic is a Member State announcing that it will change the law in line with the Commission's instructions, and then only doing so with considerable delay. Even though, legally speaking, a business is no longer obliged to apply the law, in practice a business will do so, because it may lead to repercussions by local authorities e.g. more inspections, fines and create legal uncertainty.

To conclude, we see that Single Market governance in theory is very clear. The Commission is the guardian of the Treaties, and it can initiate infringement procedures against Member States. Business can exercise their Single Market rights and go to court or file a complaint with the Commission. In reality, we see that the Commission can be held back by various factors from policing the Single Market, businesses may fear retaliation when complaining in public, and certain Member

States may be very inventive in preventing or delaying infringement procedures. In a time where populism and protectionism seem to go hand in hand and can act to undermine the EU and the Single Market, this is of major concern. We would like to see more resources and proactive policing of the Single Market, effective governance and institutions able to protect the rights of citizens and business. In Sects. 6.1 and 6.2 below, we look at ways of aiding the process by allowing early action before national measure are adopted.

5.3 *Respect for the rule of law*

The threat to the functioning of our institutions is not imaginary: the European Commission felt it necessary to adopt 'A new EU Framework to strengthen the Rule of Law' in 2014.[41] The Communication starts by saying: 'The rule of law is the backbone of any modern constitutional democracy. (…) respect for the rule of law is a precondition for EU membership'. This is a strong and clear statement aimed at Member States. The Communication sets out a procedure for a dialogue between the Commission and a Member State adopting questionable practices, before activating the mechanism in Article 7 TEU, under which the European Council could ultimately suspend the voting powers of, and the financial support to the accused Member State. This would require unanimity by the Council, of course with the exception of the Member State involved. This new EU framework is currently being put to the test with regard to Poland and Hungary. The European Commission asked the Council by the end of 2017 to activate Article 7(1) against Poland[42] and in September 2018 the European Parliament adopted a resolution regarding Hungary[43]; at the time of writing the Council had not yet decided to support the Commission's Decision or Parliament's Resolution. On 1 March 2018, the European Parliament backed the Commission's decision on Poland.[44] Whether Poland or Hungary will ever suffer the ultimate sanction foreseen in Article 7 is questionable. Hungary and Poland both expressed their intentions to vote against imposing sanctions under the Article 7 procedure against each other. In Hungary, this was confirmed by a vote in the Hungarian Parliament calling upon the Hungarian government to support Poland in its fight against the European Commission.[45] The Commission proposal for the 2021-27 Multi-annual Financial Framework suggests using "reverse qualified majority" voting to break this logjam.[46]

The European Commission and European Parliament do not stand alone in this debate. The Venice Commission of the Council of Europe has raised its concerns

[41] European Commission (2014b).

[42] European Commission (2017d).

[43] European Parliament (2018a).

[44] European Parliament (2018b).

[45] Politico (2018).

[46] European Commission (2018b).

multiple times. In its last opinion on several Polish draft laws amending the judicial system it concludes "that the Act and the Draft Acts, especially taken together and seen in the context of the 2016 Act on the Public Prosecutor's Office, enable the legislative and executive powers to interfere in a severe and extensive manner in the administration of justice, and thereby pose a grave threat to the judicial independence as a key element of the rule of law."[47]

To conclude, we see a strong political trend in Europe of populist forces that seem unlikely to change direction in the years to come. It is likely that the populist footprint will grow stronger. At the same time, we see that in countries like Hungary and Poland populist governments reform their institutions, which undermine the Rule of Law, infringe EU law and disrespect EU values. This undermines legal certainty for businesses, especially foreign businesses. This makes it clear that Single Market governance is becoming more and more important to protect the four freedoms and the rule of law. In the next chapter, we will suggest some ideas to improve Single Market governance.

6 Prevention is better than cure

We believe that the focus of the EU institutions should shift more to the prevention of infringements. Prevention of infringements is attractive from several points of view:

- no harm has occurred yet;
- it is politically and procedurally easier to adjust draft measures than measures already adopted by the national or local legislative bodies;
- infringement cases may drag on for years, and the result is uncertain. In the meantime, citizens and businesses are forced to change their behaviour and may suffer damages;
- stronger prevention could lead to better quality legislation that ensures better compliance with EU law and reduces the number of infringements;
- EU institutions would have more resources available to focus on other relevant EU files (e.g. in 2016, 3783 complaints were filed with the Commission. The number of new complaints in 2016 is the highest since 2011, at the end of 2016, 1657 infringement cases were open).[48]

Mechanisms should be set in place or better utilised to detect possible infringements at an early stage and solutions should be put forward before a national measure is adopted or enters into force. Some of these mechanisms are already there or are in the pipeline. Below we will discuss some of them.

[47] Council of Europe (2017).

[48] European Commission (2017b).

6.1 Single Market Transparency Directive (EU) 2015/1535

There is a notification procedure for national technical product legislation and information society services, which is set out in the Single Market Transparency Directive (EU) 2015/1535 (SMTD). This procedure is best known as 'TRIS': the Technical Regulation Information System.[49] Member States must notify draft measures at least three months before adoption (the so-called standstill period). The notifications are translated by the Commission in all official EU languages, are submitted to a public database,[50] are accessible to all stakeholders and one can easily submit a contribution via the website. Member States and the European Commission may submit an observation or a detailed opinion. In case of the latter, an additional three months standstill is introduced preventing the notifying Member State to adopt the measure after the initial standstill period expired. In principle, the notifying Member State has to respond to the observations and detailed opinion and take them into account in the final draft put to vote in the national parliament. If the notifying Member State would ignore the Commission's detailed opinion or not amend the draft measure sufficiently, the Commission may open an infringement procedure (the burden of proof is on the Commission). According to case law,[51] when a Member State has not notified a measure, it renders it null and void. This procedure provides a strong incentive for Member States to fulfil their obligations under the SMTD.

The notification helps stakeholders to be aware at an early stage of national technical product legislation. Member States do notify most of the relevant measures (about 700 notifications per year) and the procedure enables a dialogue with the notifying Member States. Regularly, the initial standstill period is extended, and other Member States and the Commission submit observations or a detailed opinion. It leads to debate and changes in the final measures[52] and sometimes Member States even abstain from its adoption.[53]

Most stakeholders and the EU institutions agree this procedure works quite well. However, transparency could be increased by making the observations and detailed opinions public. It is unclear whether the Commission's detailed opinion takes account of all arguments put forward by stakeholders. The Commission's opinion could also be relevant in the national debate. Now governments cannot be held accountable for the accurate application of the Commission's opinion. It might also be worthwhile to extend the notifications to general product rules. For example, generic provisions that apply to all products do not fall within the scope of the notification procedure, but in some cases one would appreciate a review of such a measure to assess the compatibly with EU law.

[49] http://ec.europa.eu/growth/tools-databases/tris/en/.

[50] http://ec.europa.eu/growth/tools-databases/tris/en/search/.

[51] Beca Engineering, Case C-285/15, EU:C:2016:295, paragraph 37, Ince, Case C-336/14, EU:C:2016:72, paragraphs 67–68.

[52] For example TRIS notification 2016/318/BG.

[53] For example TRIS notification 2017/199/HU.

6.2 *More effective notification procedure for services*

The Services Directive[54] also has a notification procedure for legislative changes affecting the freedom of establishment in Article 15(7). Draft national measures or newly adopted measures falling within the scope of the Services Directive should be notified. The Commission theoretically has the opportunity to take a decision within three months of notification, and to request the notifying Member State to either withdraw the draft measure or abolish the adopted measure if it infringes the Services Directive. Unfortunately, this legislation is at present ignored by most Member States. Between 2009 and 2015, the Commission received 1639 notifications, five Member States never notified anything and the majority of notifications was from only seven Member States.[55] Some reasons brought forward by Member States for not fulfilling their obligations were a lack of awareness of the obligations, absence of standard practice, and a lack of any clear consequences in case of non-notification. EuroCommerce advocated a review of the procedure in 2015.[56] The Commission issued a proposal on 10 January 2017 for a new Directive further clarifying and strengthening the procedure.[57] The proposal would strengthen the obligation for Member States to notify a draft measure three months prior to adoption; the notification would be published on a public website; the Commission, other Member States and stakeholders would have the possibility to provide comments; in case of concerns, the Commission could issue an alert which would require the notifying Member State to refrain from adoption another three months. Not fulfilling obligations as a Member State would constitute a procedural defect of a serious nature. In such a case, the Court of Justice of the European Union could be expected to rule that a not notified measure is null and void. The proposal aims at a structured and transparent procedure for dialogue between the notifying Member States, the Commission and other Member States, with the aim of preventing infringing laws of being adopted. The Council has now agreed a general approach[58] and the Internal Market and Consumer Protection Committee of the European Parliament adopted its report on the proposal.[59] Both have tried to water down the Commission proposal, but kept intact the obligation on all Member States to notify draft measures three months prior to adoption and the ability of the Commission to issue a decision (burden of proof on Member State) or recommendation (burden of proof on Commission) requesting (instead of requiring) a Member State to refrain from adopting or abolishing the measure. At the moment of writing, the EU institutions are in trilogue to find an agreement.

---

[54] Directive 2006/123/EC of the European Parliament and of the Council of 12 December 2006 on services in the Internal Market.

[55] European Commission (2017e).

[56] EuroCommerce (2015).

[57] European Commission (2017f).

[58] Council of the European Union (2017).

[59] European Parliament (2017c).

We are convinced that a strong procedure that enables the Commission to assess draft laws on their proportionality and compatibility with EU law is an effective way to prevent infringements. Giving stakeholders the opportunity to provide timely comments will be of great value as well. In the case of EuroCommerce, members regularly report on regulatory developments in their countries. Members have an in-depth understanding of their own regulatory decision-making process and how new regulation may impact the market. Because of this, they can provide the Commission with important information that enables it to make a better assessment of draft measures.

Obviously, such a notification system needs to be proportionate and should not prevent Member States from regulating their markets appropriately.

6.3 Extend the power of suspensive injunction to Internal Market law

Article 13(1) of Council Regulation (EU) 2015/1589 on State aid gives the European Commission the power to "adopt a decision requiring the Member State to suspend any unlawful aid until the Commission has taken a decision on the compatibility of the aid with the Internal Market": the so-called *suspension injunction*. This is a powerful tool for a number of reasons. First, the Commission may issue such a suspension injunction before any harm has occurred. It also sends a strong signal to Member States that the Commission has the power to act immediately in case it considers a measure constituting unlawful State aid. This contrasts with the standard infringement procedure where the process of opening a procedure may take many months and the procedure itself years. If ultimately no resolution is found, the Commission has to resort to the Court of Justice to establish that the Member State is infringing EU law. During the infringement procedure, businesses and citizens may suffer damage, may be deprived of their rights under EU Law, and be subject to sanctions. If the Court does rule that a Member State has infringed EU law, no compensation is provided for businesses and citizens. They have to go to court separately to seek redress.

It is remarkable that, today, in case of a clear breach of Internal Market law the Commission first has to open an infringement procedure with the possibility that a Member State will use all the tricks in the book to delay the procedure. We see a great added value in introducing the right of a suspension injunction under Internal Market law if there is a clear breach. This should always be followed by an in-depth investigation, similar to State aid law. We believe this would lead to better quality law-making by Member States, would solve the problem of short-term infringements that last shorter than completing an infringement procedure and improve compliance by Member States.

6.4 *Link EU funding with upholding the rule of law*

In the recent discussion at EU level, the idea has been raised to establish a stronger link between EU funding and upholding the Rule of Law by Member States. This has now been taken up in the recent Commission proposal for a multiannual financial framework 2021–2027.[60] Even though crude, such a mechanism could work. As mentioned earlier, it is now difficult for the Commission to penalise a Member State via the earlier mentioned Article 7 procedure. A number of Member States are heavily dependent on the EU structural and cohesion funds. For CEE Member States, the money flowing in from the EU represents literally percentages of their GDP.[61] Cutting off all or some of the funding would lead to immediate economic problems. The question remains of course if one would ever want to bring a Member State's government on its knees like this, it would be mostly a deterrent instrument and when used it could backfire in the sense that the 'EU'[62] is imposing its dictates on the Member States. Nevertheless, it makes sense to cut off Member States from EU funding if they do not uphold the Rule of Law and EU values anymore. In this case, it should be best used as a preventive tool, to withhold Member States to infringe EU law in a very grave manner.

6.5 *Make infringement procedures more automatic and transparent*

We described earlier that the European Commission may have a number of reasons to abstain from or delay an infringement procedure. Our impression is that this is not likely to change in the near future. At a certain moment, Member States may start expecting the Commission to take into account local sensitivities by default. If the Commission would then ignore those and go ahead with enforcement actions, Member States may object, leading the Commission to be even more hesitant next time.

At the same time, the Commission and the Member States are not always transparent about infringement procedures. Almost all correspondence and argumentation during most of the enforcement steps is kept confidential, with even complainants only having very limited access to information.

The lack of transparency and the lack of a more automatic infringement procedure undermine legal certainty. Member States can get away with infringements for

[60] European Commission (2018b).

[61] http://ec.europa.eu/budget/figures/interactive/index_en.cfm, webpage visited on 21 May 2018.

[62] Even though people often refer to the EU or 'Brussels' as acting entities, both are nothing of the sort. It is among others the institutional dynamic between the Council, Commission and European Parliament that leads to EU actions. In that sense, all policies seen as adverse by the Member States are approved by at least a qualified majority or by unanimity by those same Member States in one way or the other.

a long time and different Member States may end up receiving different treatments.

Therefore, we believe infringement procedures should be made more automatic, by setting clear criteria taking a next step, and decisions based on these conditions should not be influenced by external factors. This would make infringement procedures more predictable and diminish the impact of extraneous political considerations. The Commission could also set out in more detail why it is pursuing or closing an infringement procedure. Providing greater clarity of the Commission's considerations in specific cases could act as a deterrent to Member States infringing EU law, and reduce the scope to exert political pressure on Commission decisions. With much more predictable and automatic infringement procedures, Member States would have a strong incentive to assess the compatibility of new laws with EU law ahead of taking a decision to propose them, thus avoiding public reprimand.

7 Conclusion: The Single Market more important than before?

At the beginning of this paper we asked ourselves if Single Market governance could play a role in containing protectionist and populist policies and maintain our Single Market achievements. First, we looked at populism and protectionism as trends in Europe and concluded that they have become more dominant over the past decade and were likely to even increase further. Then we looked at our experience in dealing with protectionism and infringement procedures. We saw that State aid law as an instrument was fairly effective, but could only be used in a limited number of cases. The use of infringement procedures as a single market governance instrument has its limits. We see that in a number of cases it helped to abolish the infringement, but the Commission is sometimes held back from opening an infringement and taking fast and decisive next steps. Additionally, Member States can be very resourceful in preventing or delaying infringement procedures.

This leads to a situation where the ultimate tool of the European Commission to enforce Single Market rules has become less effective over time. We see that certain Member States are behaving in a more and more protectionist way to protect local interests. We also showed that the cost of this protectionism and the gaps in the Single Market are significant, involving hundreds of billions of euros in opportunity costs. We also saw that the cost impact of individual laws can easily be hundreds of millions of Euros. If we believe that increased welfare is beneficial for Europe's citizens, all European stakeholders and decision-makers have an interest to defend the integrity of the Single Market and fight protectionism.

The question remains of what the most successful strategy would be to contain or fight protectionist policies via Single Market governance. We believe that in the current timeframe, we should focus on prevention, rather than demand stronger enforcement by the European Commission. Over the years, demands for stronger enforcement have not been very effective and it is questionable if Member States would allow it. This is why we put forward a number of concrete ideas that we believe could prevent infringements from happening by assessing more and better draft laws affecting the free movement of goods and services, introducing a deterrent power of suspension injunction in case of clear breaches of Internal Market law, linking EU funding with upholding the Rule of Law, making infringement procedures more automatic and less political, and improve transparency of notifications of draft laws and infringement procedures for all stakeholders.

We believe this will help preserve Europe's competitiveness and provide economic welfare gains for future generations. Populism may grow stronger, but a well-functioning Single Market will create economic benefits for all regardless their political preferences, and just possibly by stimulating growth and jobs, reduce some of the underlying reasons for illiberal political tendencies which threaten the very fabric of the European project.

References

Budapest Business Journal (2016) Lázár: Multinational food retailers should leave Hungary, 16 June 2016, https://bbj.hu/politics/lazar-multinational-food-retailers-should-leave-hungary_117833

Council of Europe (2017) Poland - Opinion on the Draft Act amending the Act on the National Council of the Judiciary; on the Draft Act amending the Act on the Supreme Court, proposed by the President of Poland, and on the Act on the Organisation of Ordinary Courts, CDL-AD(2017)031-e, 8-9 December 2017

Council of the European Union (2017) Proposal for a DIRECTIVE OF THE EUROPEAN PARLIAMENT AND OF THE COUNCIL on the enforcement of the Directive 2006/123/EC on services in the Internal Market, laying down a notification procedure for authorisation schemes and requirements related to services, and amending Directive 2006/123/EC and Regulation (EU) No 1024/2012 on administrative cooperation through the Internal Market Information System - General approach, 9507/17, 22 May 2017

Economist (2018) Dancing with danger, Europe's populist are waltzing into the mainstream, 3 February 2018

Edelman (2018) 2018 Edelman Trust Barometer, Global Report, 2018, https://www.edelman.com/trust-barometer

Erixon F, Georgieva R (2016) What is wrong with the Single Market, Five Freedoms Project at European Centre for International Political Economy, Working Paper No 1/2016, 2016

EuroCommerce (2015) Contribution to the forthcoming Commission Single Market strategy 2015, position paper, 3 July 2015, https://www.eurocommerce.eu/resource-centre.aspx#PositionPaper/9555

European Commission (2014a) The economic impact of modern retail on choice and innovation in the EU food sector, September 2014

European Commission (2014b) A new EU Framework to strengthen the Rule of Law, Communication from the Commission to the European Parliament and the Council, COM(2014) 158 final, 11 March 2014

European Commission (2017a) European Commission acts to preserve the rule of law in Poland, press release, 26 July 2017

European Commission (2017b) Report from the Commission, Monitoring the application of European Union Law, 2016 Annual Report, COM(2017) 370 final, 6 July 2017

European Commission (2017c) Communication from the Commission, EU law: Better results through better application, Official Journal of the European Union, (2017/C 18/02), 19 January 2017

European Commission (2017d) Rule of Law: European Commission acts to defend judicial independence in Poland, press release, 20 December 2017, http://europa.eu/rapid/press-release_IP-17-5367_en.htm

European Commission (2017e) Impact Assessment, Accompanying the document, Proposal for a Directive of the European Parliament and of the Council on the enforcement of the Directive 2006/123/EC on services in the Internal Market, laying down a notification procedure for authorisation schemes and requirements related to services, and amending Directive 2006/123/EC and Regulation (EU) No 1024/2012 on administrative cooperation through the Internal Market Information System, SWD(2016) 434 final, 10 January 2017

European Commission (2017f) Proposal for a Directive of the European Parliament and of the Council on the enforcement of the Directive 2006/123/EC on services in the Internal Market, laying down a notification procedure for authorisation schemes and requirements related to services, and amending Directive 2006/123/EC and Regulation (EU) No 1024/2012 on administrative cooperation through the Internal Market Information System, COM(2016) 821 final, 10 January 2017

European Commission (2018a) A European retail sector fit for the 21st century, European Commission, Communication from the Commission to the European Parliament, the Council, the European Economic and Social Committee and the Committee of the Regions, COM(2018) 219 final, 19 April 2018

European Commission (2018b) A Modern Budget for a Union that Protects, Empowers and Defends, The Multiannual Financial Framework for 2021–2027, European Commission, Communication from the Commission to the European Parliament, the Council, the European Economic and Social Committee and the Committee of the Regions, COM(2018) 321 final, 2 May 2018

European Court of Auditors (2016) Has the Commission ensured effective implementation of the Services Directive?, Special report No 5/2016, 2016

European Parliament (2017a) Fundamental rights in Hungary: MEPs call for triggering Article 7, press release, 15 May 2017

European Parliamentary Research Service (2017b) Mapping the Cost of Non-Europe 2014-2019, Fourth edition, PE 603.239, December 2017

European Parliament, Committee on the Internal Market and Consumer Protection (2017c) Report on the proposal for a directive of the European Parliament and of the Council on the enforcement of the Directive 2006/123/EC on services in the Internal Market, laying down a notification procedure for authorisation schemes and requirements related to services, and amending Directive 2006/123/EC and Regulation (EU) No 1024/2012 on administrative cooperation through the Internal Market Information System, A8-0396/2017, 8 December 2017

European Parliament (2018a) Rule of law in Hungary: Parliament calls on the EU to act, press release, 12 September 2018, http://www.europarl.europa.eu/news/en/press-room/20180906IPR12104/rule-of-law-in-hungary-parliament-calls-on-the-eu-to-act

European Parliament (2018b) Rule of law in Poland: Parliament supports EU action, press release, 1 March 2018, http://www.europarl.europa.eu/news/en/press-room/20180226IPR98615/rule-of-law-in-poland-parliament-supports-eu-action

Eurostat (2017) File:V1 E-sales and turnover from e-sales, 2008 to 2016, EU28 (% enterprises, % total turnover).png, webpage was modified on 5 December 2017, http://ec.europa.eu/eurostat/statistics-explained/index.php/File:V1_E-sales_and_turnover_from_e-sales,_2008_to_2016,_EU28_(%25_enterprises,_%25_total_turnover).png

Eurostat (2018). http://ec.europa.eu/eurostat/statistics-explained/index.php/International_trade_in_goods, webpage visited 21 May 2018

Financial Times (2018) The rise and rise of Viktor Orban, 25 January 2018

Fondation Robert Schuman (2018) Boussemart J, Godet M, Europe 2050: Demographic Suicide, European issues, n° 462, 13 February 2018

Guardian (2017) Muted protests in Vienna as far-right ministers enter Austria's government, 18 December 2017, https://www.theguardian.com/world/2017/dec/18/thousands-protest-as-far-right-ministers-enter-government-in-austria

HVG (2016) Legal study on retail establishment through the 28 Member States, Restrictions and freedom of establishment: final report. Volume I, 4 April 2016

Le Monde (2017) Le second tour de la présidentielle 2017 en 8 chiffres, 7 May 2017, http://www.lemonde.fr/les-decodeurs/article/2017/05/07/le-second-tour-de-la-presidentielle-2017-en-8-chiffres_5123931_4355770.html

Mudde C, Rovira Kaltwasser C (2017) Populism, a very short introduction. Oxford University Press

New York Times (2018) As West Fears the Rise of Autocrats, Hungary Shows What's Possible, 10 February 2018

NRC (2017) nrc.nl, Uitslagenkaart Tweede Kamerverkiezingen 2017, 15 March 2017, https://www.nrc.nl/nieuws/2017/03/15/tk2017-a1550054

Organisation for Economic Co-operation and Development (2016) Priorities for completing the European Union's Single Market, Jan Stráský, OECD Economics Department Working Papers No. 1315, 20 July 2016

Organisation for Economic Co-operation and Development (2018) Services Trade Restrictiveness Index, http://www.oecd.org/tad/services-trade/services-trade-restrictiveness-index.htm, webpage visited 20 March 2018

Pew Research Center (2017) Stokes B., Wike R. and Manevich D., Post-Brexit, Europeans More Favorable Toward EU, But many back empowering national governments on migration and trade, and they want their own vote on EU, Pew Research Center, 15 June 2017

Politico (2018) Politico.eu, Hungarian parliament votes to support Poland in fight against EU, 20 February 2018, https://www.politico.eu/article/hungarian-parliament-votes-to-support-poland-in-fight-against-eu/

Reuters (2017) Support for Polish ruling nationalists at all-time high, 13 October 2017, https://uk.reuters.com/article/uk-poland-politics-poll/support-for-polish-ruling-nationalists-at-all-time-high-idUKKBN1CI26M

Spiegel (2017) spiegel.de, Endgültiges Ergebnis, 13 October 2017, http://www.spiegel.de/politik/deutschland/bundestagswahl-2017-alle-ergebnisse-im-ueberblick-a-1167247.html

The Globe and Mail (2018) What's driving populism? It isn't the economy, stupid, 9 February 2018, https://www.theglobeandmail.com/opinion/what-is-driving-populism-it-isnt-the-economy-stupid/article37899813/

Tony Blair Institute (2017) Eiermann M., Mounk Y., Gultchin L., European Populism: Trends, Threats and Future Prospects, REPORT, 29th December 2017, https://institute.global/insight/renewing-centre/european-populism-trends-threats-and-future-prospects

Visegrad Group (2018) V4 Statement on the Future of Europe, 26 January 2018, http://www.visegradgroup.eu/v4-statement-on-the-180129

World Bank Group (2016) Polarization and Populism, Europe and Central Asia Economic Update, Office of the Chief Economist, November 2016

Part V
The Economic and Monetary Union as an illustration of "the incomplete union": The authority of EU law stuck half-way between supranational and national sovereignty

Die Wirtschafts- und Währungsunion als Herausforderung der Autorität des Unionsrechts

Peter-Christian Müller-Graff

Die Wirtschafts- und Währungsunion als Herausforderung des Unionsrechts oder als Illustration der „unvollständigen" Union ist Teilthema der Leitfrage des Jubiläumskongresses der Europäischen Rechtsakademie nach der Autorität des Unionsrechts mit der provokativen Frage „Glauben wir noch daran?" Sie versteht sich vor dem Hintergrund der Großprobleme von Staatsverschuldungsproblemen einzelner Eurostaaten, Rechtsstaatskrisen einzelner Beitrittsstaaten, Migrationsdruck auf die Europäische Union und britischem Austrittswillen. Aufgeworfen sind damit gleichermaßen die Fragen nach der Bedeutung der Autorität des Unionsrechts (1.), nach den Herausforderungen der Wirtschafts- und Währungsunion für diese Autorität (2.) und nach den möglichen Antworten auf die Herausforderungen (3.).

1 Zur Bedeutung der Frage nach der Autorität des Unionsrechts

Die Frage, ob wir noch an die Autorität des Unionsrechts glauben, ist eine elementare Frage für Bestand und Zukunft der Europäischen Union. Auch wenn das Recht allein den gemeinsamen politischen Willen des Zusammenhalts auf Dauer nicht ersetzen kann, vermag es aber doch Schwächeperioden stabilisierend zu überbrücken. Dass der *politische* Wille lebt, zeigen beispielhaft die zahlreichen Reaktionen auf das Austrittsvotum im Vereinigten Königreich auf dem Kontinent

Prof. Dr. Dr. habil. Dr. h.c. mult. Peter-Christian Müller-Graff, Ph.D.h.c., MAE, Ruprecht-Karls-Universität Heidelberg.

P.-C. Müller-Graff (✉)
Ruprecht-Karls-Universität, Heidelberg, Germany

ERA Board of Trustees, Trier, Germany

W. Heusel, J.-P. Rageade (eds.), *The Authority of EU Law*,
https://doi.org/10.1007/978-3-662-58841-3_15

wie Bürgerbewegungen wie „Pulse of Europe“,[1] die gelebte Einigkeit von 27 Mitgliedstaaten gegenüber dem Vereinigten Königreich[2] und, wie jüngst, die kraftvollen Reden des französischen Präsidenten[3] und des Präsidenten der Kommission der Europäischen Union.[4] Dass dieser Zusammenhalt aber *nicht ohne die Autorität gemeinsamen Rechts* im Sinne von Akzeptanz, Befolgung und Durchsetzung gelingt, ist allen selbstverständlich, die in der Achtung des Rechts einen Schutz gegen allfälligen politischen und oder administrativen Wankelmut und gegen Willkür sehen. Dies bedeutet innerhalb eines Staates die Achtung der Verfassung und der Gesetze und innerhalb der Union die Achtung ihres Primär- und Sekundärrechts, unbeschadet dessen Änderbarkeit und Entwicklung. Die Union beruht seit Beginn der supranationalen europäischen Integration in den Jahren 1952 mit dem Montanvertrag (EGKSV) und 1958 mit den Verträgen zur Gründung der Europäischen Wirtschaftsgemeinschaft (EWGV) und der Europäischen Atomgemeinschaft (EAGV) auf der Idee der Rechtsgemeinschaft (1.1) und zugleich der Erwartung der Integrationsentwicklung durch Recht (1.2) und gründet auf der Annahme eines gemeinsamen Verständnisses der realen Relevanz von Recht in den Mitgliedstaaten (1.3).[5]

1.1 Die Europäische Union als Rechtsgemeinschaft

Das Wort der Europäischen Gemeinschaft als Rechtsgemeinschaft wird bekanntlich dem ersten Präsidenten der Kommission der EWG und Mitverfasser der Römischen Verträge zugeschrieben: *Walter Hallstein*, einem ehemaligen Professor für Privatrecht und Wirtschaftsrecht. Aber weder war dies ein spezifisch deutsches Verständnis noch war Hallstein allein mit dieser Idee und ihrer Verwirklichung. Viele teilten sie. *Antoine Vauchez* nennt in seinem jüngstem Buch „L´Union par le Droit“[6] einen *Kreis wirkungsmächtiger Praktiker* dieses Gedankens in der Ursprungszeit, darunter, neben Hallstein, aus den anderen Gründerstaaten, u.a. *Michel Gaudet* (französischer Mitverfasser der Römischen Verträge und erster Generaldirektor des Juristischen Dienstes der Kommission seit 1958), *Andreas Donner* (niederländischer Präsident des EuGH seit 1958), *Robert Lecourt*

---

[1] Vgl. https://pulseofeurope.eu/de/ ; Haupt (2017).

[2] Beginnend mit der Erklärung der Informellen Tagung der 27 v. 29.6.2016 in Brüssel; sich fortsetzend in der Erklärung von Bratislava v. 16.9.2016.

[3] Vgl. namentlich: Emmanuel Macron fordert Neugründung der EU, in: ZEIT ONLINE v. 26.9.2017, 17:52; Macron fordert „Wiedergeburt Europas“, in: Spiegel ONLINE v. 17.4.2018, 14:17.

[4] Europäische Kommission, Rede von Jean-Claude Juncker zur Lage der Union 2017 v. 13.9.2017.

[5] Die nachfolgenden Ausführungen des Teils 1.1 beruhen auf einem Vortrag, den *Verf.* am 28.3.2017 auf der Veranstaltung des Europäischen Parlaments in Verbindung mit der Europäischen Rechtsakademie zum 60. Jahrestag der Unterzeichnung der Römischen Verträge und zum 25. Jahrestag der Unterzeichnung des Vertrages von Maastricht in Brüssel gehalten hat.

[6] Vauchez (2013).

(französischer Richter am EuGH seit 1962, später dessen Präsident); *Alberto Trabucchi* (italienischer Richter am EuGH seit 1962, später Generalanwalt), *Fernand Dehousse* (belgischer Präsident der Parlamentarischen Versammlung des Europarats seit 1956, später Abgeordneter im Europäischen Parlament). Hinzuzufügen ist aus Luxemburg *Pierre Werner* (luxemburgischer Ministerpräsident seit 1959).

Kern dieser Idee ist der Gedanke, europäische Gemeinsamkeit auf die *stablisierende Autorität von Recht* zu gründen, genauer auf vertragliche, also *freiwillig* eingegangene und demokratisch ratifizierte Verpflichtungen. Es ist die Vision, dadurch den Zusammenhalt inhaltlich und institutionell dauerhaft *gegen politische* Launenwechsel, Erschütterungen und Rückfälle in trostlose nationale Konflikte des Kontinents mit sich selbst zu immunisieren. Es ist das Konzept, damit die Gemeinsamkeit zu gründen auf *gemeinsame Ziele* wie bei einem Gesellschaftsvertrag,[7] auf wechselseitige inhaltliche Verpflichtungen der Mitglieder (ursprünglich namentlich zur Errichtung eines Gemeinsamen Marktes),[8] auf die gesicherte Ermöglichung grenzüberschreitender wirtschaftlicher Privatinitiative,[9] auf außerstaatliche gemeinsame Institutionen mit legislativen und administrativen Kompetenzen[10] und auf Rechtsschutz und Streitlösung durch ein gemeinsames Gericht.[11] Es ist die Erwartung, den Umgang der staatlichen Egoismen mittels gemeinsamen Rechts und mittels Rechtssicherheit für die Akteure eines gemeinsamen Wirtschaftsraums zu zivilisieren. Dieser Gedanke der Rechtsgemeinschaft hatte von Anfang an *zwei* Dimensionen: die *statische* Dimension des Respekts für die vertraglich festgelegte Gemeinsamkeit und die *dynamische* Dimension der fortschreitenden Schaffung neuer verbindlicher Gemeinsamkeiten, mithin der Integration durch Recht (dazu 1.2).

1.2 Integrationsentwicklung durch Recht

Die Annahme der Integrationsentwicklung durch Recht ist ein großes Thema, das integrationswissenschaftlich der Sache nach vor allem als neofunktionalistische Theorie[12] im Unterschied zur intergouvernementalen Theorie[13] behandelt wird. Die Literatur zu diesem Ansatz ist abundant. So hat dazu beispielsweise vor dreißig Jahren *Mauro Cappeletti* zusammen mit vielen anderen am Europäischen Hochschulinstitut eine Forschungsreihe im institutionellen und materiellen

---

[7] Müller-Graff (2017)., Rdnr 1.

[8] Vgl. EuGH, Rs. 26/62, ECLI:EU:C:1963:1 (*Van Gend & Loos*).

[9] Müller-Graff (1987), *S. 17, 27;* Müller-Graff (1991), *S.17.*

[10] Monnet (1976), S. 353.

[11] Ipsen (1972), S. 366.

[12] Dazu z.B. Haas (1958); Zu neo-institutionellen Erklärungen z.B. Taschowsky (2001), S. 4ff, 7ff.

[13] Dazu z.B. Hoffmann (1965); Moravcsik (1998).

Europarecht aufgelegt.[14] In jüngerer Zeit hat diesen Ansatz ein von *Daniel Augenstein* herausgegebener Sammelband neu beleuchtet.[15] Im Kern der verschiedenen Varianten geht es dabei um Recht nicht nur als ein *Objekt* politischer Gestaltung und als stabilisierendes *Instrument*, sondern als aktiv gestaltendes *Subjekt* und als *Agent* der europäischen Integration. Damit wird zum einen gesagt, dass *Recht transnationale Wirklichkeit gestaltet*. Der Gedanke beinhaltet zum anderen zugleich, dass das Integrationsrecht, einmal in die Welt gesetzt, aus seiner inneren, dem Recht eigenen *Vernunft pfadabhängig* neue Herausforderungen der Gemeinsamkeit zu bewältigen und den Bau des europäischen Gemeinwesens zu fördern vermag. Recht bewirkt neue wirtschaftliche, soziale und politische Realität und neues Recht. Integrationswissenschaftlich fügt sich diese Annahme in den neofunktionalen Erklärungsansatz.[16]

Tatsächlich blieb es nicht bei bloßen Erwartungen. Es kam zu großen Errungenschaften und zur Emanzipation des Integrationsrechts von klassischen Merkmalen des Völkervertragsrechts.[17] Schon das epochal neue Konzept einer Hohen Behörde im Jahre 1951 war notwendig mit dem Schutzsystem einer obligatorischen Gerichtsbarkeit zu verbinden. Denn die Ausübung administrativer Hoheitsrechte bedarf gerichtlicher Kontrolle. Der damit eingeschlagene Weg europäischer Hoheitsrechte wurde sukzessive fortgesetzt – über die EWG und EG bis in die heutige EU von Lissabon – und sukzessive aus der inneren Systemlogik des Marktrechts auch in benachbarte Politikbereiche verbreitert: so besonders markant in das Währungswesen mit dem Ziel der Währungsunion[18] und in die gesicherte räumliche Freizügigkeit der dazu Berechtigten mit dem Ziel des grenzkontrollfreien Binnenraums (des jetzt so genannten Raums der Freiheit, der Sicherheit und des Rechts[19]). Es erwuchs aus dem innovativ-dynamischen Konzept des Gemeinsamen Marktes dank des EuGH, dessen stabilisierende Leistung für das europäische Zusammenwirken nicht hoch genug gewürdigt werden kann, der Gedanke der unmittelbar anwendbaren subjektiven transnationalen Marktzugangsrechte[20] mit Anwendungsvorrang vor abweichendem nationalen Recht.[21] Es erwuchsen aus der Ermächtigung der Gemeinschaften zur Rechtsetzung das qualifizierte Mehrheitsprinzip im Rat[22] bis hin zum Einbau des demographischen Faktors,[23] die

[14] Cappeletti et al. (1985).

[15] Augenstein (2012).

[16] Haas (1958); Zu neo-institutionellen Erklärungen z.B. Taschowsky (2001), S. 4ff, 7ff.; grundlegend Mitrany (1943).

[17] Zu diesen Schritten im Einzelnen Müller-Graff (2007), 407ff.

[18] Art. 119, 127ff. AEUV.

[19] Art. 67ff.; dazu Müller-Graff (2017), Art. 67ff. AEUV.

[20] Grundlegend EuGH, Vgl. EuGH, Rs. 26/62, ECLI:EU:C:1963:1 (*Van Gend & Loos*).

[21] EuGH, 6/64, ECLI:EU:C:1964:6 (*Costa/ENEL*).

[22] Ein besonders markanter Schritt war die Einführung dieses Entscheidungsprinzips für die binnenmarktfördernde Rechtsangleichung durch die Einheitliche Europäische Akte, vgl. dazu Müller-Graff (1989).

[23] In Übernahme der Regelung des Verfassungsvertrags durch den Vertrag von Lissabon: jetzt: Art. 16 Abs. 4 EUV.

Direktwahl des Europäischen Parlaments[24] und das ordentliche Gesetzgebungsverfahren.[25] Es erwuchs aus der neuartigen Budgethoheit der Gemeinschaften der Gedanke des Eigenmittelsystems.[26] Es ergab sich aus dem Aufwuchs der europäischen Hoheitsbefugnisse folgerichtig das Erfordernis des Grundrechtsschutzes.[27] Es sprossen aus der Verdichtung der Gemeinsamkeit das Konzept der Unionsbürgerschaft mit vereinzelten Teilhaberechten an Hoheitsaufgaben anderer Mitgliedstaaten (Stichwort: kommunales Wahlrecht)[28] und das Ziel der Verfolgung gemeinsamer, konkret benannter Grundwerte, darunter auch der Rechtsstaatlichkeit.[29] Dies alles lässt sich durchaus als ein Siegeszug der Integration durch Recht bezeichnen.

Allerdings gibt es auch die *Kehrseite* der *Nichtbeachtung* von Integrationsrecht. Jedoch ist hierbei zu *differenzieren*: erstens zwischen der einfach-gelegentlichen und der gravierenden Nichtbeachtung; zweitens zwischen den Sachbereichen (die gravierende Nichtbeachtung betraf in jüngerer Zeit namentlich den intergouvernementalen Bereich der Wirtschaftsunion – Stichwort: nationale Haushaltspolitik unter Missachtung Art. 126 AEUV – und den gleichfalls anspruchsvollen, allerdings supranationalen Bereich des sekundären Flüchtlingsrechts – Art. 78 AEUV); und drittens zwischen den Mitgliedstaaten (dazu 1.3).

1.3 Die Autorität des Rechts in den Mitgliedstaaten

Die Frage, ob alle Mitgliedstaaten dasselbe Verständnis von Recht teilen, hat zwei Ebenen: die generelle nach Recht als Autorität im nationalen Zusammenleben und die spezielle nach Recht als Autorität im unionalen Zusammenleben.

Es scheint, als ob die *erste* innerhalb der Union rechtskulturwissenschaftlich vergleichende Ebene bislang zu wenig systematische Aufmerksamkeit gefunden hat. Diese Aufgabe kann auch im Zusammenhang mit dem hier im Vordergrund stehenden Thema nicht hinreichend behandelt, sondern nur angesprochen werden. Pointiert geht es um die Frage, ob Rechtsnormen und Gerichte in allen Mitgliedstaaten, in Nord und Süd, in Ost und West, in *gleichwertiger* Weise respektiert und ernst genommen werden. Bei der Lektüre von *Hans Magnus Enzensbergers* literarischen Ländervignetten in seinem Buch „Ach Europa!“[30] mag man mit rechtlich unterlegtem Blick historisch nachwirkende Unterschiede herauslesen:

---

[24] Zum Direktwahlakt Müller-Graff (1979); heute: Art. 14 Abs. 3 EUV.

[25] In Übernahme der Terminologie des Verfassungsvertrags durch den Vertrag von Lissabon, jetzt: Art. 289 Abs. 1, 294 AEUV.

[26] Heute: Art. 311 AEUV.

[27] Beginnend mit EuGH, Rs. 29/69, ECLI:EU:C:1969:57 (*Stauder/Ulm*); heute Art. 6 EUV und GRC.

[28] Heute: Art. 22 Abs. 1 AEUV.

[29] Heute: Art. 2 EUV; Müller-Graff (2017), Art. 3 EUV, Rdnr. 7ff.

[30] Enzensberger (1987).

stark vergröbert beispielsweise einerseits Rechtstreue als Überlebenselement in der einstigen Wildnis des schwedischen Nordens,[31] andererseits Recht als allgemeine Regel mit Ausnahmen für den souveränen Renaissance-Menschen südlich der Alpen.[32] Die Frage ist der Untersuchung wert, ob oder inwieweit Unterschiede im kollektiven Verständnis zur Rolle des Rechts im Sozialleben substantiiert verifizierbar bestehen und ob gegebenenfalls tiefenwirksame Faktoren wirken, vielleicht aus historisch unterschiedlicher konfessioneller Prägung des Normdenkens, vielleicht aus historisch unterschiedlichen Erfahrungen der Gewaltenteilung. Dies alles ist spekulativ und führt kulturwissenschaftlich, rechtssoziologisch und sozialempirisch in schwer zu strukturierende und zu verifizierende Zusammenhänge.[33] Auffällig ist aber doch, dass beispielsweise das rechtsstaatliche Zentralthema der Rolle der unabhängigen dritten Gewalt durch die erste und zweite Gewalt ausgerechnet in zwei Transformationsstaaten aktuell geworden ist und der nahezu unbegrenzte Zugang zu behördlichen Dokumenten in den protestantisch geprägten skandinavischen Staaten am stärksten ausgeprägt zu sein scheint.[34]

Dies alles könnte in der Vielfalt Europas auf sich beruhen, wäre mit der europäischen Rechtsgemeinschaft nicht die *zweitgenannte* Ebene betroffen, nämlich die Autorität des Rechts im *unionalen* Zusammenleben. Hier geht es um die *reale* Verlässlichkeit der Freiheitsgarantien des Binnenmarktes[35] und generell die Anwendung von Unionsrecht und insbesondere um die rechtlichen und faktischen Umsetzungspflichten von Richtlinien der Union,[36] um die – Vertrauen in die Gleichwertigkeit voraussetzende – gegenseitige Anerkennung zivilrechtlicher und strafrechtlicher Entscheidungen,[37] um das wechselseitige Vertrauen in Verwaltungsentscheidungen,[38] um die Wirklichkeit des Grundrechtsschutzes[39] und

---

[31] Enzensberger (1987), S. 35ff.

[32] Enzensberger (1987), S. 68ff.

[33] Zum sehr abstrakten Fragenspektrum der einzelnen mit „Recht als Tatsache" befassten Wissenschaftsrichtungen im Allgemeinen Baer (2017), S. 67f, 71ff, 74ff.

[34] Vgl. Söderman (1998), S. 313, 339.

[35] Vgl. Art. 28ff. AEUV.

[36] Vgl. dazu den instruktiven Bericht der Kommission, Kontrolle der Anwendung des EU-Rechts, Jahresbericht 2016 v. 6.7.2017, COM(2017) 370 final: mit Statistiken und Säulendiagrammen zur Richtlinienumsetzung im Vergleich der Mitgliedstaaten (S. 31ff.).

[37] Vgl. zu diesen Fragen der gegenseitigen Anerkennung Müller-Graff (2012a), S. 72-86; Zur Kategorie des „Vertrauens" „als wertende europapolitische Perspektive, als rechtswissenschaftliches Analyseraster oder gar Rechtsgrundsatz" sowie den Erkenntnissen der allgemeinen Vertrauensforschung von Bogdandy (2017), *S.* 487, 499ff., 507ff.

[38] Grundlegend EuGH, Rs. 120/78, ECLI:EU:C:1979:42 (*Cassis de Dijon*); vgl. ferner EuGH, Rs. C-340/89, ECLI:EU:C:1991:193 (*Vlassopoulou*); zu Konsequenzen für die Warenverkehrsfreiheit namentlich Mitteilung der Kommission zu Auslegungsfragen – Erleichterung des Marktzugangs für Waren in einem anderen Mitgliedstaat: praktische Anwendung des Prinzips der gegenseitigen Anerkennung, ABl. 2003 C 265/2.

[39] Namentlich auch die Anwendung der Grundrechte-Charta der Europäischen Union im Rahmen des Art. 51 GRCh.

der Rechtsstaatlichkeit in jedem Mitgliedstaat[40] und um das reibungslose Funktionieren der Verbindung zwischen nationalen Gerichten und dem EuGH in der Praxis des Unionsrechts.[41] Vor diesem Hintergrund kann das *reale Verständnis* der Relevanz von Recht und Gerichten in den Mitgliedstaaten und ihrer Bevölkerung nicht nebensächlich sein. Im Gegenteil fordert Art. 2 Satz 1 des Unionsvertrags (EUV) explizit die Rechtsstaatlichkeit der Mitgliedstaaten. Dies ist ein berechtigtes Ziel. Denn das Gelingen der Europäischen Union fordert die gelebte Achtung des Rechts und unabhängiger Gerichte in allen Mitgliedstaaten. Dieser Gedanke ist unverändert frisch: 25 Jahre nach Unterzeichnung des Vertrages von Maastricht, 60 Jahre nach Unterzeichnung der Römischen Verträge, 66 Jahre nach Unterzeichnung des Montanvertrages. Er ist ein zeitloser Anker des gemeinsamen Gedeihens in Europa.

2 Die Befolgung des Rechts der Wirtschafts- und Währungsunion als Herausforderung für die Autorität des Unionsrechts

Das Unionsrecht der Wirtschafts- und Währungsunion stellt sich angesichts der Probleme bei seiner Befolgung und Durchsetzung seit geraumer Zeit als eine Herausforderung der Autorität des Unionsrechts dar.[42] Dies gilt für die öffentliche Wahrnehmung (2.1.) und für die Ursachenidentifizierung (2.2.)

2.1 Die Wahrnehmung in der Öffentlichkeit

Das Unionsrecht der Wirtschafts- und Währungsunion ist ein Sachgegenstand, der als Ausdruck einer von manchen als „unvollständig“ verstandenen Union[43] in besonderem Maße in der von den Artt. 119 ff. AEUV begründeten Spannung zwischen supranationalen und nationalen Hoheitsrechten siedelt: zum einen das Unionsrecht der Währungsunion in supranationaler Ausprägung[44] und zum anderen das Unionsrecht der Wirtschaftsunion, also der Wirtschafts- und Haushaltspolitik in

[40] Generelle unionsrechtliche Verpflichtung der Mitgliedstaaten nach Art. 2 S. 2 EUV; s. auch Art. 7 EUV.

[41] Scil.: Vorabentscheidungsverfahren gemäß Art. 267 AEUV.

[42] Vgl. dazu z.B. Caesar (2015), S. 129ff.; s. auch schon Kösters and Caesar (2004), S. 288ff.

[43] So der Obertitel der zweiten Abteilung des Jubiläumskongresses. Für “Schritte zur Vollendung der Wirtschafts- und Währungsunion“ die gleichnamige Mitteilung der Kommission an das Europäische Parlament, den Rat und die Europäische Zentralbank, KOM(2015) 600 endg. Für eine „'more perfect' Economic and Monetary Union” Fabbrini (2016), S. 271ff.

[44] Zu den rechtlichen Grundprinzipien der Währungsunion ausführlich Selmayr (2015), § 23, Rdnr. 80ff. (S. 1461ff).

intergouvernementaler Ausformung ihrer Kernelemente[45], wenn auch krisenreaktiv seit 2010 mit verstärkter „zentralisierter" Einfassung.[46] In diesem Bereich ist die Autorität des Unionsrechts seit Ausbruch der Staatsschuldenkrisen im Euroraum namentlich in der deutschen Öffentlichkeit sehr heftig in Zweifel gezogen worden: so von nahezu jedem Beobachter die Verlässlichkeit des Gebots des Art. 126 AEUV, dass die Mitgliedstaaten übermäßige öffentliche Defizite vermeiden; so von Ökonomen und einzelnen Staatsrechtlern (mit dem Vorwurf des „Rechtsbruchs"[47]) die Einhaltung der Aussage des Art. 125 AEUV, dass ein Mitgliedstaat nicht für die Verbindlichkeiten eines anderen Mitgliedstaats haftet und nicht für derartige Verbindlichkeiten eintritt; und erst jüngst hat das Bundesverfassungsgericht erneut seine Zweifel an der Einhaltung des in Art. 123 AEUV verankerten Verbots der monetären Staatsfinanzierung durch die Europäische Zentralbank (EZB) dem EuGH vorgelegt.[48] In der deutschen Öffentlichkeit findet sich auch latent der Verdacht, dass die Politik der EZB verbotene monetäre Staatsfinanzierung mit unverständlichen Anglizismen und ökonomischen Termini verschleiert. Kundige Unionsrechtler mögen solche Beurteilung jedenfalls teilweise für überzogen halten: zwar nicht hinsichtlich der Missachtung des übermäßigen öffentlichen Verschuldungsverbots (Art. 126 Abs. 1 AEUV), wohl aber hinsichtlich des Art. 125 AEUV, das bei pauschaler Bezeichnung als „Bail-Out-Verbot" Missverständnisse auslösen kann und vielmehr differenziert zu lesen ist.[49] Aber die Existenz der verbreiteten kritischen öffentlichen Wahrnehmung der Umsetzung des Unionsrechts der Wirtschafts- und Währungsunion lässt sich nicht mit leichter Hand abtun und schon gar nicht hinsichtlich der Geldpolitik der EZB bei schwer nachvollziehbaren Begründungen wie etwa der Rechtfertigung des „Quantitative Easing" zum Zweck der Deflationsbekämpfung.[50]

[45] Zu den Grundlagen des Rechts der Europäischen Wirtschaftsunion ausführlich Hufeld (2015), Das Recht der Europäischen Wirtschaftsunion, § 22, Rdnr. 1ff. (S. 1305ff.); zu supranationalen Elementen *infra* 3.1.1.

[46] Als Analyse zur „Governance" Fabbrini (2016), S. 23ff, 60f; zur rechtlichen Entwicklung Müller-Graff (2012b), S. 2-14.

[47] Vgl. z.B. Issing (2011), S. 257, 258; Seidel (2011), S. 241; Ruffert (2011), S.1777, 1785ff; Degenhart (2012), 157ff., S. 161 m.w.N.; a.A. EuGH, Rs. C-370/12, ECLI:EU:C:2012:756, Rdnr. 125ff., 137 (*Pringle*); dazu Müller-Graff (2013), *S. 111ff*; zuvor schon *ders.*, in: F.A.Z. v. 20.5.2010, S. 8 (= in: Müller (Hrsg.) (2011), S. 52ff.; Herrmann (2010), S. 413, 415; Wieland (2011), S. 340, 342.

[48] BVerfG, Rs. 2 BvR 859/15 u.a., ECLI:DE:BVerfG:rs20170718.bvr085915; zuvor schon die Vorlage des Bundesverfassungsgerichts zum OMT-Programm der EZB, die zum Urteil des EuGH in der Rs. C-62/14, ECLI:EU:C:2015:40 (*Gauweiler*) und zu der abschließenden Entscheidung des BVerfG, Rs. BvR 2728/13 u.a., ECLI:DE:BVerfG:rs20160621.2bvr272813 führte.

[49] So auch EuGH, Rs. C-370/12, ECLI:EU:C:2012:756 (*Pringle*), Rdnr. 125ff.

[50] Dazu Plickert (2014); kritisch zur ökonomischen Begründung des EZB-Programms z.B. *Hans-Werner Sinn*, laut F.A.Z. v. 9.3.2015 (EZB-Programm – Ökonom Sinn schilt die EZB), 12:49.

2.2 *Die Ursachenidentifizierung*

Die Ursachenidentifizierung für die Herausforderungen der Autorität des Unionsrechts der Wirtschafts- und Währungsunion hat zu differenzieren. Zum einen ist zu fragen, ob oder inwieweit bereits die *normpositiven Regeln* und das zugrundeliegende *Konzept* des geltenden Unionsrechts der Wirtschafts- und Währungsunion Probleme für die hinreichende Autorität für deren Einhaltung aufwerfen (1.). Zum anderen stellt sich die Frage, ob oder inwieweit die *Handhabung* des geltenden Unionsrechts der Wirtschafts- und Währungsunion seine Autorität untergräbt (2.).

2.2.1 Autoritätsgefährdung durch den Normrahmen selbst?

Rechtsnormen können mit ihrer Sollensanordnung aus verschiedenen Gründen in die Gefahr der Selbstgefährdung ihrer Autorität geraten. Dies kann eintreten, wenn sie inhaltlich nicht überzeugen, realitätsfremd sind oder hinreichender Durchsetzungsmechanismen ermangeln. Dieser Prüfung muss auch das Unionsrecht der Wirtschafts- und Währungsunion standhalten, will es in den wechselnden wirtschaftlichen und politischen Herausforderungen dauerhaft bestehen.

a. *Inhaltlich* bemisst sich die Überzeugungskraft des Regelwerks der Artt. 119 ff. AEUV nicht allein aus deren *spezifischen* Einzelvorschriften, sondern beruht zugleich auf der Überzeugungskraft der Prämissen der *primärrechtlichen Gesamtordnung* (oder: Verfassungsvertragsordnung[51]), innerhalb derer sie sich bewegen.

aa. Diese Prämissen sind im gesellschaftsvertragsartig formulierten Zielartikel des Art. 3 EUV niedergelegt und insbesondere durch die vier operativen Hauptziele gekennzeichnet, mit denen die Union ihre hochabstrakte Leitzieltrias der Förderung des Friedens, ihrer Werte und des Wohlergehens ihrer Völker zu verwirklichen hat: erstens durch die Grundentscheidung für die Errichtung eines Binnenmarktes (Art. 3 Abs. 3 EUV) in der definierten Form der vier Grundfreiheiten des Art. 26 Abs. 2 AEUV im sozialen Ordnungsrahmen („gemäß den Bestimmungen der Verträge") mit der daraus erfolgenden Ermöglichung transnationalen Wettbewerbs der Marktteilnehmer und dem Erfordernis eines Systems, das den Wettbewerb vor Verfälschungen schützt (Protokoll Nr. 27 über den Binnenmarkt und den Wettbewerb); zweitens durch das daraus erwachsene Ziel der Errichtung einer Wirtschafts- und Währungsunion (Art. 3 Abs. 4 EUV) in der definierten Form der Artt. 119 ff. AEUV mit seinem Bekenntnis zur wettbewerblichen Marktwirtschaft („offene Marktwirtschaft mit freiem Wettbewerb"), die nach Art. 3 Abs. 3 EUV

[51] Zu diesem Wesensmerkmal des Primärrechts Müller-Graff (2002), S. 206, 209ff.; in diesem Sinne einer „europäischen Verfassung im funktionellen Sinne" BVerfG, Rs. 2 BvE 2/08 u.a., ECLI:DE:BVerfG:2009:es20090630.2bve000208 = BVerfGE 123, 267, Rn. 231.

zugleich eine soziale Marktwirtschaft sein soll;[52] drittens durch das gleichermaßen aus der Entscheidung für den Binnenmarkt entstandene Ziel der Gewährleistung eines grenzkontrollfreien Binnenraums im Sinne eines „Raums der Freiheit, der Sicherheit und Rechts" (Art. 3 Abs. 2 EUV) im definierten Sinne der Artt. 67 ff. AEUV; und viertens durch das Ziel gemeinsamen auswärtigen Handelns (Art. 3 Abs. 5 EUV) in der definierten Form der Artt. 21 ff. EUV und Artt. 205 ff. AEUV.

Diese Ziele stehen nicht verbindungslos nebeneinander. Vielmehr beruhen die drei letztgenannten operativen Hauptziele konzeptionell und faktisch im Wesentlichen auf der Marktintegration. Dies ergibt sich aus der Gegenprobe. Dächte man das Binnenmarktziel der Union weg, verlören die anderen drei operativen Hauptziele ihre integrationskonzeptionellen und faktischen Voraussetzungen. Diese Funktion lässt sich aus der bereits oben angesprochenen historischen Entwicklungslinie der vertraglich vereinbarten Integrationsagenda seit 1958 erkennen. Aus der inneren Systemlogik des transnationalen Marktrechts kam es zu jeweils neu vereinbarten und ratifizierten Zuständigkeiten für benachbarte Bereiche der Marktintegration: so namentlich für die binnenmarktfördernde transeuropäische Vernetzung der Infrastruktur (Straßen, Schienen, Brücken, Energie, Telekommunikation);[53] für die Politiken zum möglichst präventiven genuinen (also über den primär markintegrativ begründeten Schutz[54] hinausgehenden) Schutz von Verbrauchern[55] und Arbeitnehmern,[56] von Gesundheit[57] und Umwelt;[58] für die Politik des wirtschaftlichen, sozialen und territorialen Zusammenhalts zum Zweck der Dämpfung integrationsgefährdender (gegebenenfalls auch binnenmarktverstärkter) asymmetrischer regionaler Wirtschaftsentwicklungen;[59] für das Währungswesen mit dem Ziel einer Währungsunion zur Vermeidung großflächiger Wettbewerbsverzerrungen infolge schwankender Wechselkursrelationen verschiedener Währungen;[60] für die Gewährleistung eines grenzkontrollfreien Binnenraums[61] (zunächst zur Erleichterung des Wirtschaftsverkehrs[62]) mit der Konsequenz der Ermöglichung einer gemeinsamen Politik zur Sicherung der Außengrenzen,[63] des

[52] Dazu Müller-Graff (2011), S. 600ff.

[53] Vgl. heute Artt. 170ff. AEUV.

[54] So namentlich mittels der marktintegrativen Rechtsangleichung, insbesondere auf der Grundlage der Artt. 114, 115 AEUV.

[55] Vgl. Art. 169 AEUV.

[56] Vgl. Artt. 151ff. AEUV.

[57] Vgl. Art. 168 AEUV.

[58] Vgl. Artt. 191ff. AEUV.

[59] Vgl. Artt. 174ff. AEUV.

[60] Vgl. Artt. 119 Abs. 2, 127 AEUV (eingefügt durch den Vertrag von Maastricht).

[61] Vgl. Artt. 67 Abs. 2, 77 Abs. 1 Buchst. a AEUV (als „Raum der Freiheit, der Sicherheit und des Rechts" terminologisch zusammengefasstes Konzept durch den Vertrag von Amsterdam).

[62] Vgl. Art. 26 Abs. 2 AEUV: Raum ohne Binnengrenzen" (eingefügt durch die Einheitliche Europäische Akte).

[63] Vgl. Art. 77 Abs. 1 Buchst. b AEUV.

Visawesens,[64] der Flüchtlingsfragen[65] und – bislang freilich nur rudimentär – der Wirtschaftsmigration[66] sowie der justiziellen und polizeilichen Zusammenarbeit zur Prävention und Bekämpfung von Straftaten und Terrorismus[67] (mit der jüngst erfolgten Errichtung einer Europäischen Staatsanwaltschaft[68]); und für das über die Gemeinsame Handelspolitik als Außenseite des Binnenmarktes[69] hinausgehende, vom Vertrag von Maastricht in die Union eingestellte auswärtige Handeln auch in der Außen-, Sicherheits- und Verteidigungspolitik.[70]

bb. In diesem Gesamtrahmen sind für die Bewertung der inhaltlichen Überzeugungskraft des spezifischen unionsrechtlichen Normrahmens der Wirtschafts- und Währungsunion vor allem zwei vorgelagerte primärrechtliche Prämissen von Bedeutung: die Entscheidungen für den Binnenmarkt und für eine Wirtschaftsordnung der wettbewerblichen Marktwirtschaft.

Die Grundentscheidung für den *Binnenmarkt* (Art. 3 Abs. 3 EUV, Art. 26 Abs. 2 AEUV, Protokoll 27 über den Binnenmarkt und den Wettbewerb) ist, wie gezeigt, grundlegend für die Struktur der europäischen Integration und deren ausstrahlende Dynamik. Sie wurde in der Vorläuferform des „Gemeinsamen Marktes" als „relance européenne" in einer Zeit getroffen, in der sich mit dem Scheitern der Europäischen Verteidigungsgemeinschaft und der Europäischen Politischen Gemeinschaft das Bemühen um derartige föderale Schritte als undurchführbar erwiesen hatte.[71] Sie entfesselte mit ihrer innovativen, sich von traditionellen wirtschaftsvölkerrechtlichen Verträgen lösenden Vernetzungskonzeption über den Markt die diesem eigenen millionenfachen privatautonomen Initiativkräfte der freien Koordination freier Präferenzentscheidungen von Angebot und Nachfrage zum Nutzen der sozialen und politischen Integration.[72] Die Überzeugungskraft dieses Grundkonzepts für Integration und Zusammenhalt ist ungeschmälert. Nicht zuletzt die transnationale soziale Vernetzungswirkung ist in den seit dem Ergebnis des britischen Referendums von 2016 vielfach artikulierten binnenmarktbezogenen Trennungsschmerzen der seit 45 Jahren gewachsenen Zugehörigkeit des Vereinigten Königreichs zum gemeinsamen europäischen Marktraum erkennbar.[73]

Ein auf die transnationalen Marktgrundfreiheiten von Verkäufern und Käufern, Dienstleistenden und Dienstleistungsempfängern, Arbeitnehmern und Arbeitgebern, Selbständigen und Unternehmen, Kapitalgebern und Kapitalnehmern setzendes

---

[64] Vgl. Art. 77 Abs. 2 Buchst. b AEUV.

[65] Vgl. Art. 78 AEUV.

[66] Vgl. Art. 79 AEUV.

[67] Vgl. Artt. 82ff. AEUV.

[68] Verordnung (EU) 2017/1939 des Rates v. 12.10.2017, ABLEU 2017 L 283/1.

[69] Vgl. Artt. 205ff. AEUV.

[70] Vgl. heute Artt. 21ff. EUV.

[71] Vgl. dazu Clemens et al. (2008), S. 108ff, 119ff.

[72] Vgl. z.B. Müller-Graff (2016), § 2 Rdnr. 46, S. 103f.

[73] Vgl. zur innerbritischen Diskussion z.B. Gardiner (2017).

Integrationskonzept beinhaltet immanent die *Ermöglichung von Wettbewerb.*[74] Es impliziert die Grundentscheidung für das Wirtschaftsordnungsprinzip der *freien wettbewerblichen Marktwirtschaft.*[75] Seit dem Reformvertrag von Maastricht ist dieser Orientierungspunkt für die Wirtschafts- und Währungspolitik folgerichtig auch ausdrücklich vertragspositiv formuliert (heute: Art. 119 Abs. 1 und 2 AEUV). Die Überzeugungskraft dieser wirtschaftsordnungsrechtlichen Grundentscheidung für den gemeinsamen Wirtschaftsraum basiert auf der Erwartung der positiven Funktionen, die dem wirtschaftlichen Wettbewerb gesamtwirtschaftlich (Wettbewerb als „effizienter Einsatz der Ressourcen"[76]), aber auch gesellschaftspolitisch (Wettbewerb als Freiheitssicherung[77] und als „Entmachtungsinstrument"[78]) und innovationspolitisch („Wettbewerb als Entdeckungsverfahren"[79]) zugeschrieben werden.[80] Insoweit ist sie ungeschmälert, sofern die wettbewerbliche Marktwirtschaft im sozialstaatlich erforderlichen Ordnungs- und Schutzgutrahmen („soziale Marktwirtschaft"; Art. 3 Abs. 3 UAbs. 1 S. 2 EUV[81]) eingebettet ist.

b. In diesem axiomatischen Rahmen hat sich die Autorität des *spezifischen* Rechts der Wirtschafts- und Währungsunion in seinen Grundentscheidungen und ausfüllenden Einzelregelungen unter den Gesichtspunkten deren inhaltlicher Überzeugungskraft, Realitätsfähigkeit und Durchsetzungskraft zu behaupten.

aa. Die *inhaltliche* Überzeugungskraft der *Grund*entscheidungen zentriert in den normativen Eckpunkten der Koordinierung der Wirtschaftspolitik (Art. 119 Abs. 1 AEUV) und der Währungsunion (Art. 119 Abs. 2 AEUV).

Die bereits vom EWG-Vertrag getroffene Entscheidung für eine Koordinierung der Wirtschaftspolitik[82] ist, ebenso wie es deren Supranationalisierung wäre, *folgerichtig* zu den beiden Grundentscheidungen für Binnenmarkt und wettbewerbliche Marktwirtschaft. Denn zum einen kann binnenmarktweiter Wettbewerb regional asymmetrische Wirtschaftsentwicklungen hervorrufen oder verstärken. Und zum anderen können nicht koordinierte präventive oder reaktive mitgliedstaatliche

---

[74] Müller-Graff (2010), S. 329ff.; Müller-Graff (2015a), § 9 Rdnr. 5ff, S. 488ff.

[75] Vgl. dazu schon Ophüls (1962), S. 134ff; *Ernst-Joachim* Mestmäcker (1965), S. 345ff.; von Simson (1967), S. 55ff; s. auch Müller-Graff (1984). S. 280ff.; Müller-Graff (2015b), § 1 Rdnr. 24ff, S. 68ff.

[76] So die ausdrückliche in Art. 120 Abs. 1 S. 2 AEUV ausgesprochene Erwartung der Mitgliedstaaten. Diese kann sich auf gleichlautende Annahmen im Schrifttum stützen: z.B. Bork (1978), *S. 111.*

[77] z.B. Tolksdorf (1994), S. 11; Eucken (1965), S. 196ff, 240ff.

[78] Böhm (1933), Nachdruck 2010.

[79] von Hayek (1968) , S. 119ff.

[80] Vgl. gebündelte Auflistung m.w.N. Möschel (1972), S. 338f.

[81] Dazu Müller-Graff (2002), S. 206, 209ff.; in diesem Sinne einer „europäischen Verfassung im funktionellen Sinne" BVerfG, Rs. 2 BvE 2/08 u.a., ECLI:DE:BVerfG:2009:es20090630.2 bve000208 = BVerfGE 123, 267, Rn. 231.

[82] Zum historischen Kontext, zur rechtspolitischen Einordnung und zur Ausfaltung vgl. Hufeld (2015), § 22 Rdnr. 17ff., 21ff., 25ff. (S. 1311ff.).

Wirtschaftspolitiken (im Sinne aller wirtschaftsrelevanten Politiken wie insbesondere Struktur-, Regional-, Konjunktur-, Beschäftigungs-, Preis-, Investitions-, öffentliche Einnahme- und Ausgabepolitiken) und wirtschaftsrelevante Maßnahmen der Union in der wettbewerblichen Binnenmarktwirtschaft wettbewerbsverzerrend, kontraproduktiv oder fruchtlos wirken.

Unter dem Gesichtspunkt der wirtschaftsrelevanten Politiken ist auch die (terminologisch ungewöhnliche) Einbeziehung der mitgliedstaatlichen Haushaltspolitiken angesichts der (auch ohne *keynesianische* Konnotierung[83]) volkswirtschaftlichen Bedeutung öffentlicher Budgets in dieses Koordinierungsziel sinnfällig. Sie unterliegt im Vergleich zu den anderen Varianten der „Wirtschaftspolitik" insoweit einer Sonderregelung, als bereits das Primärrecht definierte Koordinierungsentscheidungen beinhaltet: so das Gebot der Vermeidung übermäßiger öffentlicher Defizite in Art. 126 Abs. 1 AEUV und dessen Flankierung durch die Verbote der notenbankpolitischen Haushaltsfinanzierung (Art. 123 AEUV) und des bevorrechtigten Zugangs öffentlicher Einrichtungen zu Finanzinstituten (Art. 124 AEUV) sowie des Haftungsausschlusses von Union und Mitgliedstaaten für die Verbindlichkeiten eines Mitgliedstaates (Art. 125 AEUV) – letztere mit dem gemeinsamen Ziel, eine Schwächung des Bemühens um Haushaltsdisziplin und um Steigerung der Wettbewerbsfähigkeit zu vermeiden.[84] Allerdings sind diese Regelungen nicht zwingend aus dem Binnenmarktziel oder dem Wirtschaftsordnungsprinzip der wettbewerblichen Binnenmarktwirtschaft geboten, sondern verstehen sich in Verbindung mit den eigenständigen Prämissen der mitgliedstaatlichen haushaltspolitischen Eigenverantwortung[85] und des Prinzips solider Haushaltsführung[86] sowie aus dem Ziel der Preisstabilität.[87]

bb. Allerdings stellt sich die Frage, ob eine Gesamtkonstruktion der wirtschafts- und haushaltspolitischen Eigenverantwortung ohne flankierende Förder- oder Beistandsmechanismen in einer wettbewerblichen Marktwirtschaft für die Verwirklichung des angestrebten Ziels der Kompatibilisierung der Wirtschaftspolitiken und der mitgliedstaatlichen Haushaltsdisziplin *hinreichend realitätsnah* ist[88] oder aber mangels Realitätsnähe die Autorität der betroffenen Normen gefährdet. Schon früh haben Ökonomen, darunter z.B. *Clemens Fuest*, das in der unionsrechtlichen Architektur inhärente Konstruktionsproblem für die Stabilität der Währungsunion aus zentraler

---

[83] Scil.: Antizyklische Haushaltspolitik zur Dämpfung von Konjunkturzyklen.

[84] Vgl. zu Art. 125 AEUV *Ruffert M (2015)*, S. 4ff.

[85] Vgl. z.B.: Herrmann (2017), Rdnr. 13; Hufeld (2015), § 22, Rdnr. 101, S. 1345.

[86] Vgl. Art. 119 Abs. 3 AEUV: Einhaltung des richtungsweisenden Grundsatzes „gesunder öffentlicher Finanzen"; zu deren elementarem staatserhaltenden Sinn markant Hufeld (2015), § 22, Rdnr. 190, S. 1383.

[87] Dies ist ein nicht nur für die Euro-Staaten primärrechtlich ausgewiesenes Ziel: vgl. Art. 3 Abs. 3 UAbs. 1 S. 2 EUV und Art. 119 Abs. 3 AEUV. Zusätzlich ist die Gewährleistung der Preisstabilität als „vorrangiges Ziel" des ESZB von Art. 127 Abs. 1 S.1 AEUV normiert.

[88] Langfristige Tragfähigkeit der aktuellen Konstruktion der Währungsunion wird jüngst etwa verneint von Tober and Theobald (2018), S. 5.

Geldpolitik und dezentralisierter Fiskalpolitik bei gleichzeitiger Kombination einer „No-Bail-Out"-Klausel mit einem schwachen Defizitverfahren benannt.[89] Diese Spannung wird im Falle auseinanderdriftender Wirtschaftsentwicklungen in den Mitgliedstaaten infolge unterschiedlicher Wirtschaftspolitiken und Wettbewerbsfähigkeiten der dort angesiedelten Unternehmen mit daraus mitangetriebenen Haushaltsschwierigkeiten verstärkt. Dies verbindet die Frage nach der Realitätsnähe der Grundkonstruktion mit derjenigen nach den vorgesehenen Durchsetzungsmechanismen (s. cc).

cc. Die Autorität des Unionsrechts hängt auch von seiner *Durchsetzbarkeit* ab. Zwar bestehen immerhin die unionsrechtlichen Verfahren der wirtschaftspolitischen Koordinierung (Art. 121 AEUV) und der Defizitaufsicht (Art. 126 AEUV). Indes kennzeichnet das Defizitverfahren eine Schwerfälligkeit,[90] die durch die so genannte „Six-Pack"/"Two-Pack"-Legislation[91] mit dem Verfahren der umgekehrten qualifizierten Mehrheit bei sekundärrechtlichen Entscheidungen[92] und durch Art. 7 des (völkerrechtlichen) Vertrages über Stabilität, Koordinierung und Steuerung in der Wirtschafts- und Währungsunion (SKS-Vertrag) mit der Unterstützungspflicht der Eurostaaten für Empfehlungen und Vorschläge der Kommission im Defizitverfahren zwar abgemildert, aber nicht gänzlich behoben wurde. Hinzu kommen das Eignungsproblem des Sanktionsregimes des Art. 126 Abs. 11 AEUV,[93] das „die Maastrichter Stabilitätshoffnungen nicht erfüllt [hat]", auch nicht „edukatorisch",[94] und das Fehlen von Sanktionen in Art. 121 AEUV. Die Autorität des Unionsrechts der Wirtschafts- und Währungsunion ist daher durch diese inneren Durchsetzungsschwächen latent gefährdet. Zu diesen Problemen gesellt sich der Ausschluss des Vertragsverletzungsverfahrens der Art. 258 und 259 AEUV vor dem EuGH bei Verstößen der Haushaltsführung gegen die Vorschriften der Art. 126 Abs. 1 bis 9 AEUV (Art. 126 Abs. 10 AEUV). Die Reparaturmechanismen des SKS-V für die Koordinierung der Wirtschaftspolitik und der ESM-V als Stabilitätseinrichtung der Euro-Staaten siedeln als völkerrechtliche Verträge[95] zur Wirtschaftspolitik der jeweils beteiligten Mitgliedstaaten außerhalb des Unionsrechts. Sie dienen allerdings dessen Verwirklichung und können, wenn sie zielgemäß durchgeführt werden, die Autorität des Unionsrechts stützen.

[89] Fuest (1993), *S.* 539ff., 545.

[90] Darstellung im Einzelnen z.B. Herrmann (2017), Rdnr. 26ff.

[91] Vgl. im Einzelnen Hamer (2015), Rdnr. 25ff, 44ff.

[92] Dazu Hamer (2015), Rdnr. 41f.

[93] Angesprochen für die primärrechtliche Geldbuße von Hamer (2015), Rdnr. 127; zweifelnd auch Häde (2016), Rdnr. 73; demgegenüber auf „edukatorische Wirkung" abstellend *Bernhard Kempen*, in: Streinz (2012), Art. 126 AEUV, Rdnr. 39.

[94] Hufeld (2015), § 22, Rdnr. 133, S. 1360.

[95] Dazu Uerpmann-Wittzack (2013), S. 49ff.

2.2.2 Autoritätsgefährdung durch Normhandhabung

Zu den aufgezeigten Gefährdungen der Autorität des Unionsrechts aus dem unionsrechtlichen Normrahmen der Wirtschafts- und Währungsunion gesellen sich in der öffentlichen Wahrnehmung Autoritätsgefährdungen aus der Handhabung der einschlägigen unionsrechtlichen Normen durch die Mitgliedstaaten, die politischen Unionsorgane und die EZB.

a. Unter diesem Gesichtspunkt dürfte es unzweifelhaft sein, dass die primäre Gefährdung von *Mitgliedstaaten* ausgeht, die das Gebot der Haushaltsdisziplin des Art. 126 Abs. 1 AEUV nicht einhalten. Zwar entspricht es infolge des kategorialen Unterschieds zwischen Sollen und Sein der Lebenswirklichkeit, dass Sollensnormen nicht durchgängig eingehalten werden. Jedoch ist der Anspruch an die Befolgung vereinbarter und ratifizierter Regeln durch Staaten als Hoheitsträger naturgemäß besonders hoch. Um so tiefenwirksamer erschüttert deren Missachtung das Vertrauen in deren Verlässlichkeit und damit auch in deren Autorität. Bereits das Haushaltsgebaren Deutschlands und Frankreichs zum Jahrhundertbeginn und die (später vom EuGH für nichtig erklärte[96]) Aussetzung des Defizitverfahrens durch den Rat im Jahre 2003 erzeugte daher Unruhe. Hinsichtlich der vereinbarten Haushaltsdisziplin machten die Budgetkrisen einzelner Euro-Staaten ab dem Jahre 2010 und deren Ursachenaufdeckung dieses Spannungsverhältnis zwischen unionsrechtlicher Anforderung und tatsächlichem Staatsverhalten[97] breitenwirksam publik.

Befeuert wurden diese Zweifel der Öffentlichkeit an der Vertragstreue der Mitgliedstaaten im Bereich der Wirtschaftsunion sodann, wie oben gezeigt, durch die gegen die freiwilligen internen „Rettungsschirme" zugunsten von Euro-Staaten, die in budgetäre Schieflage geraten und im Zugang zum Kapitalmarkt gefährdet waren,[98] von Ökonomen und einzelnen Staatsrechtlern breitenwirksam vertretene,[99] wenn auch unionsrechtlich nach dem Verständnis des EuGH nicht stichhaltige[100] Annahme der Missachtung des Haftungs- und Einstehensausschlusses von Mitgliedstaaten für die Schulden eines Mitgliedstaats (Art. 125 AEUV). Erst die – auf der Grundlage der Auslegung des EuGH an sich überflüssige, aber im Kern klarstellende – Vertragsergänzung um Art. 136 Abs. 3 AEUV hat diese Zweifel in vertraglich positivierter Weise beseitigt. Danach können die Euro-Staaten einen

---

[96] EuGH, Rs. C-27/04, ECLI:EU:C:2004:436, Rdnr. 97 (*Kommission/Rat*).

[97] *Supra* 2.1.

[98] Zunächst der Griechenland-Hilfsbeschluss v. 7.5.2010 (Erklärung der Staats- und Regierungschefs des Euro-Währungsgebiets), sodann die Schaffung der Europäischen Finanzstabilisierungsfazilität (Beschluss der im Rat der EU vereinigten Vertreter der Regierungen der dem Euro-Währungsgebiet angehörenden Mitgliedstaaten v. 10.5.2010) und schließlich die Einrichtung des Europäischen Stabilitätsmechanismus (Vertrag zur Einrichtung des Europäischen Stabilitätsmechanismus, in Kraft getreten am 27.9.2012).

[99] *Supra* B I.

[100] Vgl. EuGH, Rs. C-370/12, ECLI:EU:C:2012:756 (*Pringle*).

Stabilitätsmechanismus einrichten, der aktiviert wird, wenn dies unabdingbar ist, um die Stabilität des Euro-Währungsgebietes insgesamt zu wahren.[101]

b. Lässt sich daher bei realitätsnaher Betrachtung das normabweichende Verhalten auch eines staatlichen Normadressaten entgegen der von ihm freiwillig eingegangenen Verpflichtung nicht ausschließen, so spielt für die Autorität der verletzten Norm die Anwendung der Sanktionsvorschriften durch die mit ihrer Durchsetzung betrauten *politischen Unionsorgane* eine maßgebliche Rolle. Insoweit kam es im Hinblick auf das vom Rat für Deutschland und Frankreich im Jahre 2003 festgestellte „übermäßige Defizit"[102] zu einer ersten Erschütterung durch die Aussetzung des Defizitverfahrens durch den Rat.[103] Indes vermochte hier die nachfolgende judikative Nichtigkeitserklärung der Aussetzung durch den EuGH[104] den im Defizitverfahren einzuhaltenden Vorschriften zumindest symbolischen Respekt zu verschaffen. In der im Jahre 2010 ausbrechenden Budgetkrise einzelner Mitgliedstaaten wurde die Aktivierung des Art. 122 Abs. 2 AEUV für die Schaffung des Europäischen Finanzstabilisierungsmechanismus (EFSM)[105] in seiner Begründbarkeit aus „außergewöhnlichen Ereignissen, die sich seiner (scil.: eines Mitgliedstaates) Kontrolle entziehen" als zweifelhaft wahrgenommen.[106] Eine Gefährdung der Autorität des Art. 126 Abs. 1 AEUV besteht vor allem auch dann, wenn Äußerungen der Kommission oder von Ratsmitgliedern in der Öffentlichkeit als großzügiger Umgang mit den maßgeblichen unionsrechtlichen Vorschriften zur Haushaltsdisziplinierung verstanden werden.[107] Derartige Verlautbarungen nach Art „because it is France" widersprechen einem Verständnis, das die Regeln zur Durchsetzung der Haushaltsdisziplin als „ausnahmefeindlich"[108] begreift.

c. Eine dritte Gefährdungsquelle der Autorität des Unionsrechts in der Wirtschafts- und Währungsunion durch dessen Handhabung liegt in der Politik und in den Maßnahmen der mit geldpolitischer Unabhängigkeit ausgestatteten[109] *EZB* im Hinblick auf das Verbot der direkten Staatsfinanzierung des Art. 123 AEUV. Zweifel bestehen insoweit namentlich in der deutschen Öffentlichkeit unter dem Gesichtspunkt der Umgehung des Verbots des unmittelbaren

[101] Zur Entstehung Smulders and Keppenne (2015), Art. 136 AEUV, Rdnr. 13.

[102] Entscheidung 2003/89/EG v. 21.1.2003; Entscheidung 2003/487/EG v. 3.6.2003.

[103] Schlussfolgerungen des Rates v. 25.11.2003.

[104] EuGH, Rs. C-27/04, ECLI:EU:C:2004:436 (*Kommission/Rat*).

[105] Verordnung (EU) Nr. 407/2010 des Rates v. 11.5.2010 zur Einführung eines europäischen Finanzstabilisierungsmechanismus, ABl. 2010 L 118/1.

[106] Vgl. dazu Müller-Graff (2012b), S. 3f.

[107] Vgl. als Beispiele *Francesco Guarascio*, EU gives budget leeway to France "because it is France" (Reuters – Business News, May 31, 2016 / 3:26 PM) und die (unsägliche und zudem rechtlich wohl unzutreffende) Aussage der seinerzeitigen französischen Finanzministerin zur Rettungsaktion im Mai 2010 "we violated all the rules" (Reuters – Business News, December 18, 2010 / 2:44 PM).

[108] Ausdruck von Ruffert (2015), S. 32.

[109] Art. 130 AEUV.

Ankaufs staatlicher Anleihen insbesondere hinsichtlich des so genannten „Outright Monetary Transaction“-Beschlusses des EZB-Rates vom 6. September 2012 (OMT-Beschluss)[110] und der Politik des so genannten „Quantitative Easing“ (QE-Programm).[111] Hinzu kommen die öffentliche Problematisierung der Entwicklung der Target-Salden zwischen den Mitgliedstaaten als ein (intransparenter) Umgehungsmechanismus[112] und die gleichfalls unter Verdacht der Schwächung des unionsrechtlichen Konzepts der Haushaltsdisziplin stehenden, allerdings im Bankenrecht wurzelnden „Eigenkapitalprivilegien bei Staatsanleihen“.[113]

Der OMT-Beschluss und das QE-Programm haben bekanntlich zu Verfassungsbeschwerden vor dem Bundesverfassungsgericht und zu bislang zwei Vorlagen des Bundesverfassungsgerichts beim EuGH[114] geführt (die anhängige jüngste zur Frage der Gültigkeit des EZB-Beschlusses (EU) 2015/774 über ein Programm zum Ankauf von Wertpapieren des öffentlichen Sektors an den Sekundärmärkten[115]), die OMT-Problematik zu einem Urteil des EuGH[116] und einem Schlussurteil des Bundesverfassungsgerichts.[117] Die Nutzung der judikativen Kontrolle der Maßnahmen der EZB durch den EuGH ist unter dem Gesichtspunkt der Autorität des Unionsrechts zu begrüßen. Sie birgt, unabhängig vom Ausgang eines konkreten Verfahrens, die Chance, mittels überzeugender Begründungen des gerichtlichen Urteils der Gefährdung der Autorität des Unionsrechts durch dessen Handhabung seitens der EZB entgegenzuwirken. Allerdings erfordert die unionsrechtliche Verteilung der sachpolitischen Letztverantwortlichkeit in der Geldpolitik die Einräumung eines weiten Ermessensspielraums in der nach Art. 5 Abs. 4 EUV vorzunehmenden Verhältnismäßigkeitsprüfung einer Maßnahme unter den Gesichtspunkten deren Eignung und Erforderlichkeit. Dieses wird dem ESZB durch

[110] EZB, Press Release (2012).

[111] Schulz (2015).

[112] Sinn and Wollmershäuser (2011).

[113] Vgl. dazu z.B. Heinemann (2016).

[114] BVerfG, Rs. 2 BvR 2728/13 u.a., ECLI:DE:BVerfG:2014:rs20140114.2bvr272813 = BVerfGE 134, 366; BVerfG, Rs. 2 BvR 859/15 u.a., ECLI:DE:BVerfG:2017:rs20170718.2bvr085915.

[115] So genanntes PSPP-Programm (ABl. 2015 L 121/20). Das BVerfG führt dazu in Rdnr. 80 aus: „Das PSPP betrifft Anleihen von Staaten, staatlichen Unternehmen und anderen staatlichen Einrichtungen sowie von europäischen Institutionen. Diese Anleihen werden zwar ausschließlich auf dem Sekundärmarkt erworben. Für einen Verstoß des PSPP-Beschlusses gegen Art. 123 AEUV spricht jedoch, dass Einzelheiten der Ankäufe in einer Art und Weise angekündigt werden, die auf den Märkten die faktische Gewissheit begründen könnten, dass das Eurosystem emittierte Staatsanleihen auch erwerben wird …, dass die Einhaltung bestimmter Mindestfristen zwischen der Ausgabe eines Schuldtitels auf dem Primärmarkt und seinem Ankauf auf dem Sekundärmarkt nicht nachprüfbar ist …, erworbene Anleihen bislang durchweg bis zur Endfälligkeit gehalten werden und darüber hinaus Anleihen erworben werden, die von vornherein eine negative Rendite aufweisen.“ Vgl. dazu jetzt EuGH, Rs. C-493/17, ECLI:EU:C:2018:1000 (Weiss u.a.).

[116] EuGH, Rs. C-62/14, ECLI:EU:C:2015:40 (*Gauweiler*).

[117] BVerfG, Rs. 2 BvR 2728/13 u.a., ECLI:DE:BVerfG:2016:rs20160621.2bvr272813 = BVerfGE 142, 123.

den EuGH wegen der Notwendigkeit von „Entscheidungen technischer Natur" und von „komplexen Prognosen und Beurteilungen" im Bereich der Offenmarktgeschäfte einleuchtenderweise auch mit der Folge eingeräumt,[118] dass er sich bei der Eignungsprüfung auf „offensichtliche Beurteilungsfehler"[119] und bei der Erforderlichkeitsprüfung auf die Anwendung des Kriteriums beschränkt, ob eine Maßnahme „nicht offensichtlich über das hinausgeht, was zur Erreichung der Ziele erforderlich ist".[120] Davon unbeeinträchtigt hat indes richtigerweise die Kontrolle der Einhaltung verfahrensrechtlicher Garantien zu bleiben.[121]

3 Antworten auf die Herausforderungen

Antworten auf die aufgezeigten Herausforderungen der Autorität des Unionsrechts in der Wirtschafts- und Währungsunion lassen sich auf verschiedene Weise geben: de lege ferenda und de lege lata.

3.1 Rechtspolitische Antworten

Rechtspolitische Antworten lassen sich danach unterscheiden, ob sie primär modellgeleitet präventiv gestaltend oder primär problemreaktiv erfolgen.

3.1.1 Modellgeleitete Gestaltung des Unionsrechts der Wirtschafts- und Währungsunion

Die modellgeleitete Gestaltung des Unionsrechts der Wirtschafts- und Währungsunion ist, wenn man Überlegungen zur Einschränkung des derzeitigen Teilnehmerkreises der Währungsunion oder deren gänzlicher Verabschiedung[122] beiseite lässt, seit Beginn dessen Positivierung im Vertrag von Maastricht kontroverser Gegenstand der politischen Debatte und Kräfte zwischen dem „supranationalen" und „intergouvernementalen" Ansatz. Sie wird, wie oben aufgezeigt,[123] üblicherweise dahingehend beschrieben, dass die Währungsunion unionsrechtlich „supranational", die Wirtschaftsunion hingegen „intergouvernemental" strukturiert

---

118 EuGH, Rs. C-62/14, ECLI:EU:C:2015:40 (Gauweiler), Rdnr. 68.

119 EuGH, Rs. C-62/14, ECLI:EU:C:2015:40 (*Gauweiler*), Rdnr. 74.

120 EuGH, Rs. C-62/14, ECLI:EU:C:2015:40 (*Gauweiler*), Rdnr. 81; affirmativ Lehmann (2017), S. 112, 127.

121 EuGH, Rs. C-62/14, ECLI:EU:C:2015:40 (*Gauweiler*), Rdnr. 69.

122 Vgl. dazu z.B. Bernau (2011) mit im Übrigen unzutreffendem Verständnis des vereinfachten Vertragsänderungsverfahrens des Art. 48 Abs. 6 AEUV.

123 *Supra* 2.1.

ist. Dies ist insoweit zutreffend, als die „Währungspolitik der Mitgliedstaaten, deren Währung der Euro ist", ausdrücklich der ausschließlichen Zuständigkeit der Union zugewiesen ist (Art. 3 Abs. 1 lit. c AEUV), wohingegen das Primärrecht zur Wirtschaftsunion die Wirtschaftspolitik der Mitgliedstaaten als Gegenstand der „Koordinierung" (Art. 119 Abs. 1 AEUV) benennt und namentlich in der allgemeinen Kompetenzklassifizierung die Formulierung wählt: „die Mitgliedstaaten koordinieren ihre Wirtschaftspolitik innerhalb der Union" (Art. 5 Abs. 1 AEUV). Eine Zuständigkeitsübertragung an die Union liegt darin nicht, weil diese dann wegen der Formulierung des Art. 4 Abs. 1 AEUV („außerhalb der in den Artikeln 3 und 6 genannten Bereiche") als geteilte Zuständigkeit im Sinne des Art. 2 Abs 2 AEUV mit der damit verbundenen Möglichkeit der Ausübungssperre der mitgliedstaatlichen Zuständigkeit zu qualifizieren wäre.[124]

a. Eine kantenscharfe Ausgrenzung des kompletten unionsrechtlichen Normenbestands der Wirtschaftsunion aus der „Supranationalität" im geltenden Primärrecht scheint indes zweifelhaft, wenn der Maßstab der Einzelelemente der Supranationalität angelegt wird.

Zwar lässt sich eine *unmittelbare Anwendbarkeit* für Art. 121 Abs 1 und 126 Abs. 1 AEUV nicht erkennen, wohl aber ist dies anhand der allgemeinen Kriterien der unmittelbaren Anwendbarkeit[125] für die Verbote der Kreditfazilitäten bei der EZB oder den nationalen Zentralbanken und des unmittelbaren Erwerbs von Schuldtiteln durch die EZB oder den nationalen Zentralbanken zu bejahen.[126]

Die *Handlungsinstrumente* von Kommission und Rat in der *Koordinierung der Wirtschaftspolitik* überschreiten nicht die unverbindliche Empfehlung im Sinne des Art. 288 Abs. 5 AEUV, wozu auch die „Verwarnung" (Art. 121 Abs. 4 UAbs. 1 S. 1 AEUV) zu rechnen ist. Aber zumindest die Einzelheiten des Verfahrens der multilateralen Überwachung nach Art. 121 Abs. 3 und 4 AEUV können durch Verordnung im ordentlichen Gesetzgebungsverfahren festgelegt werden (Art. 121 Abs. 6 AEUV). Im *Haushaltsüberwachungsverfahren* dominieren zwar die Empfehlungen, doch hat der Rat im fortgeschrittenen Stadium auch definierte Beschlussmöglichkeiten und diese mit qualifizierter Mehrheit (Art. 126 Abs. 9 UAbs. 1 AEUV: Inverzugsetzung; Art. 126 Abs. 11 AEUV: Sanktionen) ebenso wie Beschlusskompetenzen (mit Einstimmigkeit) im Hinblick auf das Protokoll über das Verfahren bei einem übermäßigen Defizit (Art. 126 Abs. 14 AEUV).

Die *judikative* Kontrolle durch den EuGH ist nicht über eine Klageerhebung nach den Artikeln 258 und 259 AEUV wegen Verletzung des Art. 126 Abs. 1 bis 9 AEUV erreichbar (Art. 126 Abs. 10 AEUV), wohl aber bei Verstoß gegen Art. 126

---

[124] Ebenso Streinz (2012) , Art. 6 AEUV, Rdnr. 2.

[125] Vgl. dazu EuGH, Rs. 26/62, ECLI:EU:C:1963:1 (*Van Gend & Loos*).

[126] Tutsch (2015), Art. 123, Rdnr. 3; der Sache nach auch *Christoph Herrmann/Corinna Dornacher*, a.a.O. (Fn. 85), Art. 123 AEUV, Rdnr. 37 (Rechtsfolge eines Verstoßes: Nichtigkeit des jeweiligen Vertrages).

Abs. 11 AEUV und mittels Untätigkeitsklagen gegen die Kommission und Nichtigkeitsklagen gegen Entscheidungen des Rates.[127]

b. Vor diesem primärrechtlichen Hintergrund vollzieht sich die Diskussion um eine (weitere) Supranationalisierung der Wirtschaftsunion. Sie ist von zahlreichen, oftmals wenig präzisierten Vorschlägen und meist von einer Tendenz zur Stärkung des verbindlichen Entscheidungsradius der Union geprägt: so namentlich von Vorschlägen zur Etablierung eines europäischen Finanzministers (mit oder ohne Überwachungskompetenzen über die mitgliedstaatlichen Haushalte),[128] zur Schaffung eines spezifischen Eurostaaten-Haushaltes,[129] zur Überführung des ESM in einen Europäischen Währungsfonds auf unionsrechtlicher Grundlage,[130] zur Aktivierung eines transferorientierten Solidaritätskonzepts innerhalb der Union.[131] Hinzu kommen Vorschläge zur Ausgabe gemeinsamer Anleihen der Eurostaaten („Eurobonds“[132]) und zur Vollendung der Bankenunion mit, u.a., fiskalischer Letztsicherung des einheitlichen Abwicklungsfonds und der Einführung eines europäischen Einlagensicherungssystems (EDIS),[133] aber auch zur Abschaffung der Nullgewichtung von Staatsanleihen in der Bankenbilanz.[134]

Inwieweit diese politischen Vorschläge für das „Wohlergehen der Völker“ der Union (Art. 3 Abs. 1 EUV) und für „eine immer engere Union der Völker Europas“ (Art. 1 Abs. 2 EUV) zielführend[135] und mit verfassungsrechtlichen Vorgaben einzelner Mitgliedstaaten vereinbar[136] sind, ist für die vorliegende Frage nach der Autorität des Unionsrechts nicht zu beurteilen. Es ist aber nicht zu verkennen, dass deren eventuelle unionsrechtliche Umsetzung im Einzelnen Rückwirkungen auf die Autorität des Unionsrechts haben kann und daher den oben genannten Maßstäben der Überzeugungskraft, Realitätsfähigkeit und Durchsetzbarkeit genügen muss und den Zusammenhalt der Union nicht schwächen darf. Eine unionsrechtliche Supranationalisierung, die diese Richtpunkte nicht beachtet, gefährdet die Autorität

---

[127] Rodi (2018), Art. 126 AEUV, Rdnr. 30.

[128] Vgl. z.B. den Vorschlag von *Jean-Claude Juncker* laut ZEIT ONLINE v. 6.12.2017, 13:50 („Juncker schlägt Europäischen Währungsfonds vor“).

[129] So der Vorschlag von *Emmanuel Macron* laut Deutsche Wirtschaftsnachrichten v. 31.8.2017, 11:51 („Macron fordert gemeinsamen Haushalt aller Euro-Staaten“).

[130] Jean-Claude Juncker laut ZEIT ONLINE v. 6.12.2017, 13:50, s. auch Koalitionsvertrag CDU, CSU und SPD v. 7.2.2018, S. 9 (Zeilen 247-250).

[131] Zu dieser Diskussion z.B.: Schieritz and Tatje (2011).

[132] Delpla and von Weizsäcker (2011).

[133] European Commission, Communication to the European Parliament, the European Council, the European Central Bank, the European Economic and Social Committee and the Committee of Regions on completing the Banking Union, COM(2017) 592 final v. 11.10.2017.

[134] Heinemann (2016).

[135] Kritisch das gemeinsame Papier von acht „Nordstaaten“ der EU laut Mussler (2018).

[136] Zur Rolle des Legitimationspotenzials mitgliedstaatlicher Parlamente in diesem Kontext vgl. BVerfG, Rs. 2 BvE 4/11, ECLI:DE:BVerfG:2012:es20120619.2bve000411 = BVerfGE 131, 152, 189, Rdnr. 98.

des Unionsrechts und im schlimmsten Fall den Zusammenhalt der Union. So würde etwa die Einführung eines EDIS ohne vorhergehende glaubwürdige Sanierung der Bilanzen aller beteiligten Banken und einer verlässlich-strengen Bankenaufsicht vorhersehbar Sprengkraft entfalten. Ein Zuwachs an Supranationalität führt im Fall der Spannung zu mitgliedstaatlicher Gestaltungssouveränität nicht zwangsläufig zu höherer Autorität des Unionsrechts. Andererseits beinhaltet ein Zuwachs an ambitiösem, rechtlich aber nicht durchsetzbarem intergouvernementalem Unionsrecht die Gefahr, die Autorität des Unionsrechts zu schwächen. Orientierungspunkt für die Gestaltung des Unionsrechts der Wirtschafts- und Währungsunion ist daher, nur dasjenige in Rechtsnormen zu fassen, von dem ernsthaft erwartet werden kann, dass es von den Mitgliedstaaten grundsätzlich auch befolgt werden kann und wird.

3.1.2 Der problemreaktive Evolutivprozess der gegenstandsgerechten Rechtsfassung

Die Alternative zur modellgeleiteten Gestaltung des Unionsrechts der Wirtschafts- und Währungsunion ist der reaktive Evolutionsprozess der gegenstandsgerechten Rechtsfassung. Diese scheint derzeit in einer am Ziel der Wirtschafts- und Währungsunion ausgerichteten, zum geltenden Unionsrecht sich pfadabhängig herausbildenden rechtskategorialen Mischform zu liegen. Denn die seit 2010 entwickelten rechtlichen Neuerungen für die Wirtschaftsunion siedeln sowohl im Unionsrecht, soweit dieses Ermächtigungsgrundlagen für den Erlass sekundären Unionsrechts enthält („Six-Pack", „Two-Pack"),[137] als auch außerhalb des Unionsrechts im herkömmlichem Völkervertragsrecht zwischen den Mitgliedstaaten als „Ausweichordnung",[138] soweit es sich um „Wirtschaftspolitik" im Sinne des AEUV handelt wie beim solidarischen „Rütlischwur"[139] des ESM-Vertrages der Eurostaaten.[140] Inwieweit der Vertrag über Stabilität, Koordinierung und Steuerung in der Wirtschafts- und Währungsunion (SKS-Vertrag)[141] kompetenziell außerhalb des Unionsrechts verbleiben muss, ist gesonderter rechtspolitischer Überprüfung bedürftig.[142] Immerhin wird dessen Art. 3 wegen der Verpflichtungen zu einem ausgeglichenen gesamtstaatlichen Haushalt[143] und zur verbindlichen und dauerhaften Übernahme dieser Regelungen in das einzelstaatliche Recht „in verbindlicher und

[137] Vgl. Nachweise Hamer (2015).

[138] Uerpmann-Wittzack (2013), S. 49ff.; s. auch Hölscheidt (2013), S. 61ff.

[139] Hufeld (2015), § 22, Rdnr. 156, S. 1369.

[140] Vertrag zur Errichtung des Europäischen Stabilitätsmechanismus v. 2.2.2012; Bekanntmachung über das Inkrafttreten des ESMV v. 1.10.2012, BGBl. II, S. 978; dazu Häde (2014), § 17, S. 891ff.

[141] Vertrag über Stabilität, Koordinierung und Steuerung in der Wirtschafts- und Währungsunion v. 2.3.2012; Bekanntmachung über das Inkrafttreten des VSKS v. 14.1.2013, BGBl. II, S. 162.

[142] Der SKS-Vertrag erklärt es in seiner Präambel als Ziel, seine Bestimmungen „sobald wie möglich in die Verträge, auf denen die Europäische Union beruht, zu überführen."

[143] Art. 3 Abs. 1 SKSV.

dauerhafter Art, vorzugsweise mit Verfassungsrang“[144] als „nunmehr Zentralgestirn des WWU-Haushaltsrechts“ gedeutet.[145]

Der Autorität des Unionsrechts kann eine derart problemreaktive Evolution dienlich sein, soweit dadurch seine Befolgung gefördert wird. Dies erfordert Rechtstreue auch gegenüber dem die Wirtschafts- und Währungsunion fördernden intergouvernementalen Recht außerhalb des Unionsrechts.[146] Die problemreaktive Reaktion sollte aber nicht die Orientierung auf eine modellgeleitete unionsrechtliche Gestaltung der Wirtschafts- und Währungsunion dämpfen. Die seit 2010 eingetretene „enorme Verkomplizierung des Rechts“[147] kann kontraproduktiv zum Vertrauen in dieses wirken. Andererseits erinnert diese Evolution an das generelle rechtspolitische Postulat, diejenige rechtliche Fassung vorzunehmen, die nicht mangels inhaltlicher Überzeugungskraft, Realitätsnähe oder Durchsetzbarkeit eine Gefährdung der Autorität des Unionsrechts auslöst. Dies dient letztlich der Stabilität der Wirtschafts- und Währungsunion und damit der Europäischen Union selbst.

3.2 *Die verlässliche Einhaltung geltenden Unionsrechts*

Jenseits rechtspolitischer Entwicklungsüberlegungen ist entscheidender Faktor für die Autorität des Unionsrechts auch im Recht der Wirtschafts- und Währungsunion dessen verlässliche Einhaltung in der vereinbarten bzw. beschlossenen Fassung, solange es in Kraft ist. Dies gilt für das von den Mitgliedstaaten ratifizierte und damit nicht nur völkerrechtlich, sondern auch demokratisch legitimierte Primärrecht der Wirtschafts- und Währungsunion ebenso wie für das von den dazu kraft Primärrechts legitimierten Unionsorganen erlassenen Sekundärrecht. Ohne verlässliche Einhaltung verlässt die reale Gestalt der Wirtschafts- und Währungsunion ihre legitimatorische Basis und gerät in Konflikt mit völkerrechtlichen, demokratischen und rechtsstaatlichen Erfordernissen. Dies zu vermeiden und die Legitimation des Unionshandelns und der Union insgesamt zu gewährleisten, dient die Autorität des Unionsrechts zuallererst.

Literaturverzeichnis

Augenstein D (ed) (2012) “Integration Through Law” Revisited: The Making of the European Polity

Baer S (2017) Rechtssoziologie, 3. Auflage, S. 67f, 71ff, 74ff

---

[144] Art. 3 Abs. 2 SKSV; anschaulich als „Selbstverfassungsgebot“ bezeichnet von Hufeld (2015), § 22, Rdnr. 137, S. 1362.

[145] So Hufeld (2015), § 22, Rdnr. 136, S. 1362.

[146] Zweifelnd insoweit am Beschluss des Gouverneursrats des ESM v. 17.7.2015 nach Art. 13 Abs. 2 ESMV Ruffert (2015), S. 26f.

[147] Rodi (2018), Art. 126 AEUV, Rdnr. 34.

Bernau P (2011) Ende der Währungsunion - Der Euro-Ausstieg ist machbar, F.A.Z. v. 31.12.2011, 12:17
Böhm F (1933) Wettbewerb und Monopolkampf (Nachdruck 2010)
Bork RH (1978) The Antitrust Paradox
Caesar R (2015) Ist die EU noch eine Rechtgemeinschaft? Anmerkungen aus ökonomischer Sicht. In: Behrens P, Kotzur M, Lammers K (Hrsg.) Sechs Dekaden europäischer Integration – eine Standortbestimmung, S. 129ff
Cappeletti M, Seccombe M, Weiler JH (eds) (1985) Integration through Law
Clemens G, Reinfeldt A, Wille G (2008) Geschichte der europäischen Integration, S. 108ff, S. 119ff
Degenhart C (2012) Missachtung rechtlicher Vorgaben bei der Umsetzung der Währungsunion, Bonner Rechtsjournal 2/2012, 157ff, S. 161
Delpla J, von Weizsäcker J (2011) Eurobonds. Das Blue Bond-Konzept und seine Implikationen, Friedrich-Ebert-Stiftung, Juni 2011
Enzensberger HM (1987) Ach Europa!
Eucken W (1965) Grundlagen der Nationalökonomie, 8. Auflage, S. 196ff, 40ff
EZB, Press Release (2012) Technical features of Outright Monetary Transactions, 6. September 2012
Fabbrini F (2016) Economic Governance in Europe, S. 271ff; S. 23ff, 60f
Fuest C (1993) Stabile fiskalpolitische Institutionen für die Europäische Währungsunion, WiD 1993, 539ff, 545
Gardiner B (2017) Brexit means leaving the single market and the customs union. Here's why. The Guardian 17:55 BST
Haas EB (1958) The uniting of Europe: political, social and economic forces 1950–1957
Häde U (2014) Der Europäische Stabilitätsmechanismus. In: Hatje A, Müller-Graff P-C (Hrsg.), Europäisches Organisations- und Verfassungsrecht (Enzyklopädie Europarecht, Band 1), § 17 (S. 891 ff)
Häde U (2016) in: Calliess C, Ruffert M (Hrsg.), EUV/AEUV, 5. Auflage, Art. 126 AEUV, Rdnr. 73
Hamer J (2015) in: von der Groeben H, Schwarze J, Hatje A (Hrsg.), Europäisches Unionsrecht, 7. Auflage, Art. 126 AEUV, Rdnr. 25ff, 44ff; Art. 126 AEUV, Rdnr. 41f; Art. 126 AEUV, Rdnr. 127
Haupt F (2017) Sie gehen für Europa auf die Straße, F.A.Z. v. 8.2.2017, 12:14
Heinemann F (2016) in: ZEW-Aktuell, Wirtschaftspolitik aus erster Hand – Die Dramaturgie der Eurokrise, 5.10.2016
Herrmann C (2010) Griechische Tragödie, EuZW 2010, 413, 415
Herrmann C (2017) in: Pechstein M, Nowak C, Häde U (Hrsg.), Frankfurter Kommentar, EUV-GRC-AEUV, Art. 126 AEUV, Rdnr. 13; Art. 126 AEUV, Rdnr. 26ff
Hoffmann S (1965) The State of War: Essays on the Theory and Practice of International Politics
Hölscheidt S (2013) Intergouvernementale Zusammenarbeit in der Krise – Garant oder Gefahr für die Einheit der Union – aus der Sicht des Bundestages, in: EuR, Beiheft 2/2013
Hufeld U (2015) Das Recht der Europäischen Wirtschaftsunion, in: Müller-Graff P-C (Hrsg.), Europäisches Wirtschaftsordnungsrecht (Enzyklopädie Europarecht Band 4), § 22 Rdnr. 1ff (S. 1305ff); § 22 Rdnr. 17ff, 21ff, 25ff (S. 1311ff); §22 Rdnr. 101 (S. 1345); §22 Rdnr. 190 (S.1383); § 22 Rdnr. 133 (S. 1360); § 22 Rdnr. 156 (S. 1369); § 22 Rdnr. 136 (S. 1362)
Ipsen HP (1972) Europäisches Gemeinschaftsrecht, S. 366
Issing O (2011) Die Währungsunion im Spannungsfeld zwischen Politik und Ökonomie, EWS 2011, 257, 258
Kempen B (2012) in: Streinz R(Hrsg.), EUV/AEUV, 2.Auflage
Kösters W, Caesar R (2004) Europäische Wirtschafts- und Währungsunion: Europäische Verfassung versus Maastrichter Vertrag. Integration 27(4):288ff
Lehmann M (2017) Varying standards of judicial scrutiny over central bank actions. In: ECB Legal Conference 2017 – Shaping a new legal order: a tale of crises and opportunities, S. 112, 127

Mestmäcker E-J (1965) Offene Märkte im System unverfälschten Wettbewerbs. In: Coing H, Kronstein H, Mestmäcker E-J (Hrsg.), Wirtschaftsordnung und Rechtsordnung. Festschrift für Franz Böhm, S. 345ff

Mitrany D (1943) A Working Peace System: An Argument for the Functional Development of International Organisation

Monnet J (1976) Mémoires, S. 353

Moravcsik A (1998) The Choice for Europe. Social Purpose and State Power from Messina to Maastricht

Möschel W (1972) Das Wirtschaftsrecht der Banken, S. 338f

Müller R (Hrsg.) (2011) Staat und Recht

Müller-Graff P-C (1979) Die Direktwahl des Europäischen Parlaments, 2. Auflage

Müller-Graff P-C (1984) Unternehmensinvestitionen und Investitionssteuerung im Marktrecht, S. 280ff

Müller-Graff P-C (1987) Privatrecht und Europäisches Gemeinschaftsrecht, in: Müller-Graff P-C/ Zuleeg M (Hrsg.), Staat und Wirtschaft in der EG, S. 17, 27

Müller-Graff P-C (1989) Die Rechtsangleichung zur Verwirklichung des Binnenmarktes, EuR 1989, 107ff EEA

Müller-Graff P-C (1991) Privatrecht und Europäisches Gemeinschaftsrecht – Gemeinschaftsprivatrecht, 2. Auflage, S. 17

Müller-Graff P-C (2002) Europäische Verfassungsordnung, in: EWS 2002, 206, 209ff

Müller-Graff P-C (2007) Primärrechtliche Entwicklungsschritte der Gemeinschaftsintegration zu einem transnationalen Gemeinwesen. Integration 30 (4), S. 407ff

Müller-Graff P-C (2010) Die Marktfreiheiten als Herzstück der europäischen Wettbewerbsidee: Funktion und Wirkungen. In: Blanke H-J, Scherzberg A, Wegner G (Hrsg.), Dimensionen des Wettbewerbs, S. 329ff

Müller-Graff P-C (2011) Soziale Marktwirtschaft als neuer Primärrechtsbegriff der Europäischen Union. In: Müller-Graff P-C/Schmahl S/Skouris V (Hrsg.), Europäische Recht zwischen Bewährung und Wandel. Festschrift für Dieter H. Scheuing, S. 600ff

Müller-Graff P-C (2012a) Gegenseitige Anerkennung im Europäischen Unionsrecht. ZVglRWiss 111:72–86

Müller-Graff P-C (2012b) Die rechtliche Neujustierung der Europäischen Wirtschafts- und Währungsunion. ZHR 176:2–14

Müller-Graff P-C (2013) Das EuGH-Urteil zum Europäischen Stabilitätsmechanismus – Die itio in partes in der Europäischen Wirtschaftsunion: EU und ESM, in: RIW 2013, 111ff

Müller-Graff P-C (2015a) Grundfreiheiten und Wettbewerbsordnung. In: Hatje A, Müller-Graff P-C (Hrsg.), Europäisches Organisations- und Verfassungsrecht (Enzyklopädie Europarecht, Band 1), §9, 5ff (S. 488ff)

Müller-Graff P-C (2015b) Europäisches Wirtschaftsordnungsrecht. Das System. In: Müller-Graff P-C (Hrsg.), Europäisches Wirtschaftsordnungsrecht (Enzyklopädie Europarecht Band 4), §1 Rdnr. 24ff (S. 68ff)

Müller-Graff P-C (2016) Allgemeines Gemeinschaftsprivatrecht. In: Gebauer M, Teichmann C (Hrsg.), Europäisches Privat- und Unternehmensrecht (Enzyklopädie Europarecht, Band 6), §2, Rdnr. 46 (S. 103f)

Müller-Graff P-C (2017) in: Pechstein M/ Nowak C/ Häde U (Hrsg.) Frankfurter Kommentar EUV-GRC-AEUV, Art. 3 EUV, Rdnr. 1; Art. 3 EUV Rdnr. 7; Art. 67ff AEUV

Mussler W (2018) Nord-Allianz stellt sich gegen Euroideen, F.A.Z. v. 7.3.2018, 8:00

Ophüls CF (1962) Grundzüge europäischer Wirtschaftsverfassung, ZHR 124

Plickert P (2014) Leitzins bleibt auf Rekordtief – Draghi wagt Tabubruch, F.A.Z. v. 3.4.2014, 13:51

Rodi M (2018) in: Vedder C/Heintschel von Heinegg W (Hrsg.), Europäisches Unionsrecht, Art. 126 AEUV, Rdnr. 30; Art. 126 AEUV Rdnr. 34

Ruffert M (2011) The European debt crisis and European Union law. CMLRev 48:1777, 1785ff

Ruffert M (2015) Europäische Währungspolitik als Herausforderung des Rechts, S. 4ff; S. 31

Schieritz M, Tatje C (2011) Wieviel Solidarität braucht der Euro? in: ZEIT ONLINE v. 17.3.2011
Schulz J (2015) Der 1.140.000.000.000-Euro-Plan, in: Süddeutsche Zeitung, 22. Januar 2015, 16:56
Seidel M (2011) Die „No-Bail-Out"-Klausel des Art. 125 AEUV als Beistandsverbot, EuZW 2011
Selmayr M (2015) Das Recht der Europäischen Währungsunion. In: Müller-Graff P-C (Hrsg.), Europäisches Wirtschaftsordnungsrecht (Enzyklopädie Europarecht Band 4), § 23, Rdnr. 80ff (S. 1461ff)
Sinn H-W, Wollmershäuser T (2011) Target-Kredite, Leistungsbilanzsalden und Kapitalverkehr: Der Rettungsschirm der EZB, Ifo Working Paper No. 105 v. 24. Juni 2011
Smulders B, Keppenne J-P (2015) in: von der Groeben H/Schwarze J/Hatje A (Hrsg.), Europäisches Unionsrecht, 7. Auflage, Art. 136 AEUV, Rdnr. 13
Söderman J (1998) Rapport Général, in: XVIII Congrès FIDE, Le Citoyen, l´Administration et le Droit Européen
Streinz (Hrsg.) (2012) EUV/AEUV, 2.Auflage, Art. 6 AEUV, Rdnr. 2
Taschowsky P (2001) Neuer Institutionalismus und die europäische Sozialpolitik, ISSN 0949-9962, S. 4ff, 7ff
Tober S, Theobald T (2018) Geldpolitische Herausforderungen. Zinspolitische Wende, sichere Staatsanleihen und digitaler Euro, IMK Report Nr. 135, März 2018, S. 5
Tolksdorf M (1994) Dynamischer Wettbewerb, S. 11
Tutsch R (2015) in: von der Groeben H, Schwarze J, Hatje A (Hrsg.), Europäisches Unionsrecht, 7. Auflage
Uerpmann-Wittzack R (2013) Völkerrecht als Ausweichordnung – am Beispiel der Euro-Rettung, in: EuR, Beiheft 2/2013, S. 49ff
Vauchez A (2013) L´Union par le Droit – L´invention d´un programme institutionnel pour l`Europe, S. 49ff
von Bogdandy A (2017) Jenseits der Rechtsgemeinschaft, EuR 2017, 487, 499ff, 507ff
von Hayek FA (1968) Der Wettbewerb als Entdeckungsverfahren, in: Internationales Institut „Österreichische Schule der Nationalökonomie" (Hrsg.), Die Österreichische Schule der Nationalökonomie. Texte, Band II, S. 119ff
von Simson W (1967) Die Marktwirtschaft als Verfassungsprinzip in den europäischen Gemeinschaften, in: Rechts- und Staatswissenschaftliche Fakultät der Albert-Ludwigs-Universität Freiburg/Br. (Hrsg.), Zur Einheit der Rechts- und Staatswissenschaften, S. 55ff
Wieland J (2011) Der Rettungsschirm für Irland, NVwZ 2011

The need to complete the EMU: cui bono?

Gerolf Annemans

1 Introduction

Readers should be aware that the author of this contribution is an EU-critical MEP representing resistance against the federal EU model that is spiralling out of control and becoming the instrument that crushes our nation states. The European Union is in my view no longer about cooperation in the way that I defend her. It is about multilateral and multicultural supra-nationalism. Especially the Euro zone is an efficient 'crushing mechanism'.

Stage two of the 2015 roadmap to deepen the EMU, the so-called *"Five Presidents Report"* comprises the completion of the Economic and Monetary Union (hereafter: EMU). The completion of the EMU is based on five pillars: the establishment of an EU Finance Minister, the transformation of the European Stability Mechanism (hereafter: ESM) into a European Monetary Fund (EMF), the expansion of the Euro area and the subsequent phase-out of non-Euro EU Member States, further convergence of tax policies, and finally increased risk-sharing and risk-reduction.[1] The goal of deepening the EMU is two-fold: on the one hand risk-sharing, and on the other hand risk-reduction. I will discuss each of the five points separately and balance their advantages and disadvantages.

[1] The Five Presidents' Report: Completing Europe's Economic and Monetary Union, European Commission, 22 June 2015.

G. Annemans (✉)
Committee on Economic and Monetary Affairs of the European Parliament,
Brussels, Belgium
e-mail: gerolf.annemans@ep.europa.eu

W. Heusel, J.-P. Rageade (eds.), *The Authority of EU Law*,
https://doi.org/10.1007/978-3-662-58841-3_16

2 Establishing an EU Finance Minister

An EU Finance Minister, as currently envisioned,[2] would be a double-hatted function, in which a European Commissioner for economic affairs also acts as the chair of the Eurogroup. He or she would also represent the Euro area at global level. What seems positive at first glance, is that budgetary discipline would be easier to enforce when the Euro-policy is coordinated centrally and supra-nationally. A better policy coordination in the general interest of the EU/Euro could improve fiscal governance of the Euro and economic and political governance in the Member States. Also important is that the Finance Minister would be accountable to the European Parliament, which now is not the case for the Eurogroup president, who is often criticised for that.[3] And rightly so. Currently, national finance ministers are not accountable before the European Parliament, and the ECB's independence as a central bank prevents them from taking or defending political decisions. The proposal is also linked with the project to establish a EMF which should serve as a solidarity mechanism between Member States (see Sect. 3 below).

On the other hand, the idea of an EU Finance Minister would imply a whole range of disadvantages and dangers. I will name four:

(1) A European Minister of Finance would be inconsistent with the concept of the exclusive competences of the Member States in fiscal and monetary affairs. National ministers of finance as well as national parliaments would become very limited in their legislative and fiscal competences to an extent that would conflict with their constitutional contexts. Not only would a European Minister of Finance require a change in primary EU Treaty law, it would also have to be balanced with national constitutions.

(2) The double function of the Minister of Finance (Commissioner and president of the Eurogroup) contains a conflict of interests: by definition, the economic policy of the Eurogroup would become the economic policy of the whole EU, while countries such as Denmark[4] (and to some extent Sweden) have an agreement that they are not obliged or expected to become a member of the Euro area. This implies that there could never be a Danish or Swedish EU Minister of Finance, even though the Danish and Swedish taxpayer would be subject to the solidity and solidarity requirements implemented and controlled by the European Minister of Finance. Non-Euro Member States would be forced to adjust their economic policies to that of the Euro countries and would be politically pressed to join the Euro scheme, since they would be obliged to contribute

[2] European Commission President Jean-Claude Juncker, State of the Union Address, 13 September 2017.

[3] Thierry Chopin, "Euro zone, legitimacy and democracy: how do we solve the European democratic problem?", Fondation Robert Schuman, *European issues* n°387, 5 April 2016.

[4] Protocol on certain provisions relating to Denmark, annexed to the Treaty establishing the European Community (1992).

to the EMF, which is aimed at supporting members of the Euro area only. This would constitute in any case a form of political blackmail.

(3) A European Minister of Finance would turn the inter-institutional balance upside-down, as it would give the Commission out-of-scale competence at the expense of the Council: a European Minister of Finance, who would be both a Commissioner and head of the Eurogroup, would have substantial leverage to push an economic agenda top-down, effectively bypassing the Council and thus the Member States. This is logical, since the Minister would render the competences of the national finance ministers mostly void.

3 Turning the European Stability Mechanism (ESM) into a European Monetary Fund (EMF)

The European Stability Mechanism was established in 2012 outside of the EU framework by an intergovernmental treaty as mechanism aimed at safeguarding the financial stability of the Euro area. The EGOV paper on the ESM presents more information. The ESM provides loans to Euro Area Member States facing financial distress, conditionally to the implementation of policy measures. It borrows money on financial markets, guaranteed by around 700 billion Euros as authorised capital by the 19 participating Member States.

The European Parliament reiterated on several occasions that it is in favour of the incorporation of the ESM into the EU legal framework provided that there is appropriate democratic accountability.

In December 2017, the Commission presented a proposal for a Council Regulation on the establishment of the European Monetary Fund.[5] The proposal would make the EMF a unique body of EU law, governed by its own board of Directors and board of Governors, the latter being composed of the ministers of finance of the Euro Member States.

The EMF would serve as a fiscally neutral common backstop to the Single Resolution Fund; support can be provided also by participating non-Euro area Member States (Article 22) in the framework of the second pillar of the Banking Union. Unanimity is required for decisions with financial impact (capital calls), however a new reinforced qualified majority (85% of the votes) is proposed for decisions on stability support, disbursement and the deployment of the backstop. This would make it harder for the Member States to block solidarity pay-outs to Euro area economies in need of liquidities.

On the one hand, the EMF would function as a solidarity mechanism between the Member States. In this way, banks and strategic industries in Member States could be supported with liquidity and capital from other Member States. The current solidarity mechanism is under control of the Council and the ECB, and therefore

[5] Proposal for a Council Regulation on the establishment of the European Monetary Fund, Brussels, 6.12.2017 COM(2017) 827 final 2017/0333 (APP).

detached from the Commission which is responsible for the economic governance of the Union. In the negotiations regarding the Greek debt, we have also seen that the ESM is underequipped compared to the IMF, which have better staff, were better prepared and eventually took the lead in the negotiations and the final compromise. An EMF would increase the bargaining power of the EU in financial crises vis-à-vis international organisations such as the IMF, which operates without any form of scrutiny and democratic control.

On the other hand, the EMF would essentially be a European bail-out fund. At the moment, support measures are discussed at Council level. Individual Member States and governments would have much less influence on such support measures, especially if the qualified majority rule will be implemented. Besides, the EU institutions are currently working on the new bail-in rules in the Banking Package, the so-called Banking Resolution Directive (BRRD).[6] This makes bail-outs impossible on paper and instead opts for bail-ins, meaning resolution of banks at the expense of bond and shareholders. The EMF would effectively de facto reinstate a bail-out mechanism, which would contradict the whole exercise we are undertaking presently on the BRRD. Last but certainly not least, it is uncertain if the EMF would be deemed constitutional in all EU Member States. In 2014, the German Constitutional Court upheld the legality of the ESM since it ruled that the German parliament had sufficient powers to control national liabilities.[7] It remains to be seen whether the controlling powers of the Parliament will still be sufficient after the qualified majority rule is implemented.

4 Expansion of the Euro area

At present, all EU member states, apart from Sweden and Denmark (and the UK), are "supposed" to join the Euro area as soon as they meet the criteria of the Maastricht Treaty. Non-Euro Member States, through the European Semester, are actively encouraged to meet those criteria (low public debt, budget deficit below 3% of GDP etc.). But there are important economic incentives for non-Euro Member States not to join the Monetary Union. For example Italy: the Italian Lira was a competitive currency because of its low value compared to the German Mark. Since the introduction of the Euro, the Italian economy has lost up to 40% of its competitive power compared to Germany,[8] which was able to benefit much more from the common currency which was highly overvalued with respect to the Italian export.

[6] Directive 2014/59/EU of the European Parliament and of the Council of 15 May 2014 establishing a framework for the recovery and resolution of credit institutions and investment firms and amending Council Directive 82/891/EEC, and Directives 2001/24/EC, 2002/47/EC, 2004/25/EC, 2005/56/EC, 2007/36/EC, 2011/35/EU, 2012/30/EU and 2013/36/EU, and Regulations (EU) No 1093/2010 and (EU) No 648/2012, of the European Parliament and of the Council.

[7] BVerfG, Urteil des Zweiten Senats vom 18. März 2014, 2 BvR 1390/12 - Rn. (1-245).

[8] Paolo Manasse, The roots of the Italian stagnation, VoxEU.org, 19 June 2013.

So a country like Bulgaria which has reached the Maastricht target is still reluctant to join the Euro area. Of course, it would become easier to trade goods within the Union, but the country would lose competitive power worldwide, just like the Italians did in the last two decades. In addition to that, a cheaper currency also implies cheaper labour and more return on capital investments. For example: in order to avoid tax increases levied after the economic crisis, thousands of Greek companies have moved across the border to Bulgaria. In 2015 alone, 2000 undertakings did so. In total, over 15,000 Greek undertakings have been registered in Bulgaria since 2008, which accounts for 5 billion euros per year which has been added to the Bulgarian economy instead of the Greek economy.[9] Why? Because the taxes are lower and the currency is cheaper. Bulgaria would not win when deciding to join the Euro area now.

From an EU and ECB perspective, it makes sense to end monetary sovereignty in Eastern Europe, since their respective national banks can easier adopt interest policies to economic changes. It is therefore in the interest of the Euro area to monopolise the economic policy of the whole EU in the hands of the Euro area. This would mean that the Euro area would be able to set VAT and other tax rates in Bulgaria and regulate the registration of undertakings without the Bulgarians being able to apply for the position of EU Finance Minister. In order to weigh in on economic policy, Bulgaria, just like any other non-Euro Member State, would have to join the Euro area. In this way, non-Euro Member States will be less reluctant to join the Euro area. Such a monopolisation will also strengthen the hegemony of the Euro in the light of sensitive new legislation, such as the new enhanced Cash Controls Regulation,[10] which would lead to increased controls on money physically leaving the EU, the EU's war on cash, namely the abolishment of small coins and big notes[11] and mandatory electronic payment over certain thresholds[12] etc.

However, in his State of the European Union speech on 13 September 2017, Jean-Claude Juncker stressed explicitly that Denmark and Sweden are exempt from adopting the Euro. This would mean that both countries would de facto never be able to apply for the position of EU Minister of Finance, since that post could by definition only be held by a minister appointed by a member state from the euro area. Does this not constitute a flagrant form of institutionalised discrimination by the EU institutions?

---

[9] "Greece Losing Businesses to Bulgaria, Freelancers to Cyprus", *The National Harald*, 23 October 2017.

[10] Regulation (EC) No 1889/2005 of the European Parliament and of the Council of 26 October 2005 on controls of cash entering or leaving the Community.

[11] Regulation (EU) No 651/2012 on the issuance of euro coins (OJ L 201, 27.7.2012, p. 135).

[12] Directive (EU) 2015/2366 of the European Parliament and of the Council of 25 November 2015 on payment services in the internal market, amending Directives 2002/65/EC, 2009/110/EC and 2013/36/EU and Regulation (EU) No 1093/2010, and repealing Directive 2007/64/EC.

5 Further convergence of tax policies

Another important pillar of the EMU is further convergence of tax policies. Neutralising fiscal competition between the Member States will make it easier for the Commission to control the Member States, which can now sabotage most of the fiscal legislation at Council level. With an initiative such as the Common Consolidated Corporate Tax Base (CCCTB),[13] it will become much harder for Member States to craft their own fiscal policies and attract foreign investment. This is especially problematic for smaller Member States who have little to no key national industries, and need to compete with larger industrial nations such as Germany or France with fiscal incentives. Tax harmonisation would effectively centralise economic power with the great industrial nations, at the expense of the smaller Member States who specialise in the digital and service economy.

Furthermore, initiatives such as the Fourth Anti-Money Laundering Directive[14] and the EU blacklist of non-cooperative jurisdictions for tax purposes in 2018 would make it impossible for individual Member States to set their own bilateral economic relations with countries who happen to find themselves on the blacklist.

Finally, Jean-Claude Juncker stressed in his State of the European Union speech of 19 September 2017 that the Council should drop some veto powers in taxation measures. This would complete the objective of the European Finance Minister and the EMU, namely to effectively neutralise the powers of national finance ministers, and, mutatis mutandis, national parliaments.

6 Risk-sharing and risk-reduction

Compared to the United States of America (USA), the Euro area has only one third of the capacity to mitigate and smooth out output shocks.[15] The US has a more centralised economic policy, less fiscal competition between the states, who have themselves more limited fiscal powers, and states which are culturally and economically more homogenous. In order to make the European economy sounder to output shocks, a more centralised economic supervisory control system seems in order, where enhanced risk-sharing and risk-reduction go hand in hand. The EU has proposed a few measures to mitigate these shocks.

---

[13] COM/2016/0685 final—2016/0337 and COM/2016/0683 final—2016/0336.

[14] Directive (EU) 2015/849 of the European Parliament and of the Council of 20 May 2015 on the prevention of the use of the financial system for the purposes of money laundering or terrorist financing, amending Regulation (EU) No 648/2012 of the European Parliament and of the Council, and repealing Directive 2005/60/EC of the European Parliament and of the Council and Commission Directive 2006/70/EC.

[15] Cinzia Alcidi and Gilles Thirion, "Assessing the Euro Area's Shock-Absorption Capacity Risk sharing, consumption smoothing and fiscal policy", *CEPS, European Commission*, January 2017.

Firstly, the EU is envisioning a common EU employment insurance. This is the prime example of risk-sharing. This would de facto mean that northern European taxpayers, who adhere to healthier and more solvable social services such as unemployment schemes, would subsidise unemployment benefits of southern Europeans, who live in countries where such schemes tend to be less performant.

Another example is the common European Deposit Insurance Scheme (EDIS).[16] EDIS is the third pillar of the Banking Union. The EDIS proposal builds on the system of national deposit guarantee schemes (DGS) regulated by Directive 2014/49/EU. This system already ensures that all deposits up to €100,000 are protected through national DGS all over the EU. EDIS would provide a stronger and more uniform degree of insurance cover in the Euro area. This would reduce the vulnerability of national DGS to large local shocks, ensuring that the level of depositor confidence in a bank would not depend on the bank's location and weakening the link between banks and their national sovereigns. EDIS would apply to deposits below €100,000 of all banks in the Banking Union. When one of these banks is placed into insolvency or in resolution and it is necessary to pay out deposits or to finance their transfer to another bank, the national DGS and EDIS will intervene via the Deposit Insurance Fund up to 20% of the shortfall. This would reduce the liquidity risk for troubled banks and illiquid national guarantee schemes, but would on the other hand incentivise these banks to take on more risks, because deposit holders will be eventually saved by EDIS, i.e. deposit holders in other EU Member States. It would therefore increase risk instead of reducing it, and would require the EU to step up its efforts regarding banking supervision.

Furthermore, Andrea Enria, the Italian president of the European Banking Authority (EBA) which conducts the stress tests on European banks to increase transparency in the European financial system and identifying weaknesses in banks' capital structures, has proposed an EU-wide bad bank for non-performing loans, funded by the European taxpayers. Such a bad bank could buy up billions in non-performing loans, predominantly from southern European countries.[17] Eurogroup president Centeno said the creation of an EU-wide bad bank, known as an "Asset Management Company", would be welcome, but faced complications under the EU rules on State aid. This would mean that northern European taxpayers in countries such as Belgium, which has the lowest amount of NPLs due to a well-developed mortgage market and home-ownership cultures, would be footed the bill from Italian bankers who failed to assess the creditworthiness of their clients, and from shareholders who didn't instruct their CEO's to reduce the NPL ratio on the banks' balance sheet.

Other forms of risk-mutualisation include the EU Rainy Day Fund,[18] which is a mechanism to counter asymmetric shocks in the Euro area of around 100 to 200

[16] COM/2015/0586 final—2015/0270.

[17] Addendum to the ECB Guidance to banks on nonperforming loans: Prudential provisioning backstop for non-performing exposures, ECB 15 March 2018.

[18] European Commission Communication to the European Parliament, the European Council, the Council and the European Central Bank: New budgetary instruments for a stable Euro area within the Union framework, Brussels, 6.12.2017, COM(2017) 822.

billion Euros and which would be triggered if the economy of one Member State plummets, eurobonds[19] and sovereign bond-backed securities.[20]

The adverse effects of these risk-sharing measures, namely increased risky behaviour of banks and governments in southern European Member States, would have to be curbed by increased risk-reduction and oversight by the Commission. To this end, the Commission proposed a number of legislative initiatives, such as the enhanced Capital Requirements Regulation (CRR) and Capital Requirements Directive (CRD), which set out prudential requirements for credit institutions and investment firms and rules on governance and supervision, and the Bank Recovery and Resolution Directive (BRRD) and the Single Resolution Mechanism Regulation (SRMR) which spell out the rules on the recovery and resolution of failing institutions. It remains to be seen if enhanced levels of total loss-absorbing capacity and minimum requirements for own funds and eligible liabilities will be beneficial for healthy, yet smaller banks in Northern and Eastern Europe, as well as for highly indebted, almost insolvable institutional financial players in the southern European market. It would also put the entire financial sector of countries like Italy, Cyprus and Greece under enhanced European supervision from Brussels. A more proactive banking resolution policy from Brussels may also lead to market consolidation in Southern Europe.[21] It is highly uncertain if further market consolidation in the financial sector is beneficial for the European market in the long run.

7 Conclusions

The completion of the EMU poses a whole range of questions, uncertainties and hazards for the sustainability of the European economy. The five pillars of deepening the Economic and Monetary Union will lead to enhanced decision power for the Commission at the expense of national parliaments and the Council. A European Minister of Finance and the transition of the ESM into an EMF will effectively bully non-Euro Member States into the Euro area, which will accelerate the federalisation process and undermine any opposition from the Member States against certain files. Enhanced risk-sharing between national economies, financial institutions and taxpayers will perverse incentives for highly indebted countries to reduce risk, which will in turn trigger more supervisory power at EU level. Enhanced risk-reduction will de facto put the southern European financial sector under northern European

[19] European Commission Green Paper on the feasibility of introducing Stability Bonds, European Commission, 23 November 2011.

[20] Enabling regulatory framework for the development of sovereign bond-backed securities, European Commission, Ares(2018)400473, 23 January 2018.

[21] Regular public hearing with Danièle Nouy, Chair of the Single Supervisory Mechanism, European Parliament, Committee for Economic and Monetary Affairs, 19 June 2017; "Banco Popular acquisition - Creating shareholder value through in-market consolidation", p. 34, as published by Santander on 7 June 2017.

control, which raises concerns regarding accountability and democratic legitimation. This will lead to a situation where the EU will spend more and more resources in supervising markets and curbing the loss of value from economic sources, rather than in creating the circumstances in which new wealth can be generated. The Economic Union will inevitably lead to a Command and Control Union, which will not benefit European taxpayers, undertakings and financial institutions.

Completing v. rethinking the European Monetary Union?

Pierre-Henri Conac

I am a convinced European and I fully support the European Union (EU). However, the situation has become too serious to simply continue like before.

Professor Fabbrini, in his presentation at ERA's jubilee congress, noted that the European Economic Constitution has been changed by the 2010 Eurozone crisis. I agree with this view and I actually think it is a welcome development. Following this crisis, a new economic architecture has been adopted. These changes towards more centralisation of power and more financial support and solidarity among Member States have been endorsed by the European Court of Justice (ECJ). The ECJ has supported these developments by interpreting the EU Treaties in a very flexible way. This has been done first in the *Pringle* case of 2012 where the core provisions of the Economic and Monetary Union (Articles 121–127 of the Treaty on the Functioning of the European Union) were systematically examined for the first time. In this decision, the ECJ validated the European Stability Mechanism (ESM) which was designed to stabilise Member States facing a financial crisis.

In 2015, in the *Gauweiler* case, the ECJ held that the OMT (Outright Monetary Transactions) programme, authorising the European System of Central Banks (ESCB) to purchase on secondary markets government bonds of Member States of the Euro area, announced by the ECB in September 2012 was compatible with EU law. Essentially, the ECJ validated the *Quantitative easing* programme of the European Central Bank (ECB) which saved the Eurozone after Mario Draghi's declaration in July 2012 to do "[w]hatever it takes to save the Euro, and believe me, it will be enough". This statement saved the Euro and it would have been doubtful,

Written version of the author's panel presentation at the Jubilee congress of the Academy of European Law in Trier, 20 October 2017.

P.-H. Conac (✉)
Professor of Financial Markets Law, University of Luxembourg, Luxembourg, Luxembourg

ERA Board of Trustees, Trier, Germany
e-mail: Pierre-Henri.CONAC@uni.lu

W. Heusel, J.-P. Rageade (eds.), *The Authority of EU Law*,
https://doi.org/10.1007/978-3-662-58841-3_17

from a democratic point of view, that judges could strike down the Euro which had been decided by national Parliaments, and sometimes people by referendum, when the Maastricht Treaty was adopted and ratified. Finally, the ECJ also adopted a very supportive and flexible interpretation of the Treaties, and especially of the "Meroni doctrine", when it held in 2014 that the powers granted on the European Securities and Markets Authority (ESMA) did not imply discretion.

In all those cases, it could have been convincingly argued that the Treaties had been violated by actions taken by the EU legislator, if not their letter, at least certainly their spirit. **Those decisions reflected implicit amendments of the EU Treaties to validate actions taken, sometimes in emergency, during and after the Eurozone crisis of 2010** and the great financial crisis of 2008. Although, a Treaty change would have offered a stronger legal ground, it is traditional and acceptable to have constitutional changes decided by courts. This is the way constitutions do evolve and this allows flexibility. This is exactly what happened in the United States during the *New deal* era in the 1930s'. However, those constitutional changes lack the democratic support of a popular vote.

The changes brought by the EU legislator and validated by the ECJ in the Economic and Monetary Union (EMU) constitute a powerful move towards more centralisation and federalism. Following these developments, the "Five presidents report" on "Completing Europe's Economic and Monetary Union" of 2015 suggested to strengthen further the Eurozone. More recently and following the 2016 Brexit vote, the European Commission issued on 31st May 2017 a "Reflection paper on the deepening of the EMU". The report argues, among other measures, for creating European bonds and having a Euro area Treasury. This would essentially create a fiscal union. One striking feature of this report is that, despite its technocratic language, it lacks a strong analysis and actually fails to make a convincing case for the fiscal union apart from arguing that it is a logical and inescapable consequence of the EMU. It is another illustration of the unfortunate "There is no alternative" (TINA) approach which has already been harmful to the EU legitimacy as people consider that their opinion is not taken into account by technocrats. Implementing this report would be a huge federalist step forward.

This proposal fits very well with the idea of Professor Fabbrini to create a European tax for the EU budget. It strikes me as very strange and naïve that a European tax would make European integration more popular. Quite to the contrary, it could only increase the backlash against the EU. I cannot think of any example in history where increasing taxes has increased the popularity of a government or a ruler. These proposals also fits well with the view held by Emmanuel Macron in France that the Brexit opens a "window of opportunity" for a federalist move since the United Kingdom (UK), which was always opposed to a federalist approach, will not be able to block it.

The issue with such proposals, which call for going deeper and faster, is that the EU is facing a popular revolt and the hostility towards a federalist move is very strong. The Brexit is a disaster for the UK but also for the EU. It is also a serious red flag which shows a "successful" case of anti-Europeans being able to remove a

Member State of the European Unions despite severe negative consequences for its own population.

Moving towards more federalism and political integration, even limited to the Eurozone, is like waving a red flag in front of powerful anti-European political forces. To say it differently, waving a red flag in the face of a raging bull might not be the best idea. Hostility towards more federalism was often blamed on the UK alone but this shows a deep lack of understanding of the Member States. Scandinavian countries, for instance, are also reluctant towards more federalism and will oppose such moves. Do we want to lose Scandinavia, too? In addition, Germany might not be as federalist as France thinks or hopes.

There is a democratic issue in the EU with not taking into account popular feelings. In France and the Netherlands, the 2005 referendums on the European Constitution were unfortunately lost. The Constitution was replaced by the Lisbon Treaty of 2007, which essentially implemented the Constitution, like if there had been no opposing vote.

Also, there are many questions on whether the ECB policy of *Quantitative easing* is a success. Some argue that it inflates real estate values and distorts financial assets prices, contributing to wealth inequality while doing little, quite to the contrary, to trigger reforms in some Member States like Italy. Has QE been used for too long? Also, it makes some people believe that the ECB is replacing politicians which raises another issue of democratic accountability at the EU level.

Therefore, making a federalist step now looks like a giant gamble which could backfire. As a convinced European, it seems to me that cautiousness is warranted instead. The time now is to save the European Union, as it is a precious gift to be protected at all costs, rather than to embark on a grand scheme that might lead to stronger opposition and finally weaken or even destroy the European construction through a "populist" revolt in several Member States.

Therefore I support, at least for the time being, a more technical and cautious approach. What is needed is to improve what already exists in the banking and financial sector and which is technical. For instance, a reform of the governance of the European Supervisory Authorities (ESAs) should be introduced in order to allow supervisory convergence since it is necessary but almost impossible with the current arrangement. Also, the Meroni doctrine should be removed either through case law or through a targeted Treaty change as it prevents a larger attribution of powers to the ESAs.

It is also necessary to complete the Banking Union through two key measures. The first one is the adoption of the European Depositary Scheme (EDS) to protect deposits in the Eurozone. This will imply that Germany accepts to use its sovereign balance sheet to protect depositors and savers in southern Europe countries. This would be a significant step and not an easy one to accept in Germany, but it is necessary since otherwise the EMU could be undermined by a new banking crisis. The second step is to adopt a fiscal backstop for the Single Resolution Board (SRB) in order to make resolution work.

The real debate here should not be so much between pro and the anti-Europeans but among pro-Europeans. It is among the pro-Europeans themselves, between the

"Euro-realists" and the "Euro-happy", those who think that nothing has happened in the last 15 years and that it is "business as usual". Unfortunately, the European project is in serious trouble having already faced serious setbacks (lost referendums) and a historical loss with the Brexit. The situation reminds me of Rome during the second Punic war after the consecutive defeats of La Trebia and Lake Trasimeno to Hannibal. After some time, the cautious approach of the Roman "dictator" Fabius *cunctator* (the patient), designed to weaken Hannibal and avoid battle at all cost, was abandoned. The new young and ambitious Roman leadership, which replaced Fabius, overestimated its strength and underestimated the danger posed by Hannibal's tactical genius and army. It ended up in the field of Cannae in 216 BC with a devastating and potentially mortal blow for Rome.

The EU needs to avoid such fate. Several would-be Hannibals are operating in the Member States, including at the heart of the Eurozone. Giving them a chance to destroy the EU, by not listening to the European people and promoting a strong federalist agenda, needs to be avoided at all costs. An incremental and cautious approach promoting technical, yet key improvements, is the way forward. This popular revolt needs to be heard rather than ignored in order to protect and save Europe.

Completing v. rethinking the European Monetary Union?

Bernd Kaltenhäuser

Having been invited to add an economic viewpoint to the debate on the question of "Completing v. Rethinking the EMU", I would like to emphasise the premise that the Deutsche Bundesbank, the institution I work for, is an integral part of the Eurosystem and as such has its very own interest in the stability of our currency, the Euro, and the stability of the Monetary Union.

1 Foundations of the Monetary Union

The Economic and Monetary Union is based on two main pillars: on the one hand, a centralised monetary policy with the primary objective of price stability and the independent Governing Council of the ECB to implement the decisions that need to be made towards that goal.

On the other hand, there are 19 governments and parliaments, each of which is tasked with deciding the fiscal policy path for its country. Two mechanisms are in place to prevent countries from over-borrowing in the market: first, risk-adequate pricing and, second, the legal provisions of the EU Treaty and the Stability and Growth Pact such as the no-bail-out clause, the 3% deficit ceiling and the 60% debt level ceiling.

The primary objective of price stability is defined by the Governing Council as an increase in the harmonised consumer price index of below, but close to 2% per

Written version of the author's panel presentation at the Jubilee congress of the Academy of European Law in Trier, 20 October 2017.

B. Kaltenhäuser (✉)
Regional Office of the Deutsche Bundesbank in Rhineland-Palatinate and the Saarland, Mainz, Germany
e-mail: bernd.kaltenhaeuser@bundesbank.de

W. Heusel, J.-P. Rageade (eds.), *The Authority of EU Law*,
https://doi.org/10.1007/978-3-662-58841-3_18

year over the medium term. Since the introduction of the Euro in 1999, inflation has averaged about 1.8% per year. Hence, we can safely conclude that monetary policy has achieved its objective in the first 18 years of Economic and Monetary Union.

Unfortunately, the expectations for fiscal policy have not been met. Both mechanisms designed to keep public debt at bay have failed to deliver the desired results. In the first decade of the Euro, market participants did not differentiate enough between Member States. All Member States were able to borrow at nearly the same interest rates. Moreover, the Stability and Growth Pact could not prevent some Member States from running excessive deficits over several consecutive years, and their debt levels rose accordingly. One cardinal error was certainly that Germany and France stopped a proposal by the European Commission to escalate their respective deficit procedures in 2003. There have been a total of 109 violations of the 3% deficit criterion since 1999. In other words: in 40% of all reviews, the 3% ceiling was violated.[1] And remember, the target was a deficit below 1%, not 3% of gross domestic product. In the end, the rules of the Stability and Growth Pact were modified several times and the European Commission was given greater leeway in interpreting these rules.

2 The evolution of the EMU

The foundations of the Economic and Monetary Union, as defined in the EU Treaty, remain unchanged. But its architecture has continued to evolve. With the crises in Greece, Ireland, Portugal and Spain, the European Stability Mechanism (formerly European Financial Stability Facility) and the Fiscal Compact were added by way of inter-governmental treaties.

The European Stability Mechanism was founded to provide financial assistance to countries that were no longer able to borrow in private financial markets. Its funds prevented a harsh cut in public transfers or services, which would have been inevitable if no one had provided fresh money. Of course, rescue funds came with conditionality attached. In the end, the European Stability Mechanism opened a time window which was to be used to correct the imbalances and to enable the country in question to stand on its own feet again.

The European Stability Mechanism created a new element of risk sharing, as other Euro area countries are providing cash and guarantees out of their respective budgets. To avoid an inappropriate use of funds, Member States agreed that the mechanism must only be activated if there is a threat to the stability of the Euro area as a whole. Moreover, the European Stability Mechanism can mitigate only liquidity shortages but not solvency problems. Solvency problems would raise the question of a debt restructuring, and the no-bail-out clause would clearly prohibit the use of European Stability Mechanism funds in that case.

---

[1] Deutsche Bundesbank, Monthly Report June 2017, p. 32.

The Bundesbank assessed the European Stability Mechanism as being acceptable provided the agreed rules are heeded. The German Constitutional Court also confirmed its constitutionality.

It is important to remember that solidarity and solidity are two sides of the same coin. In order to reinforce the solidity aspect, all Eurozone countries ratified the Fiscal Compact, which requires all countries to implement a limit on debt and to maintain structural deficits of less than 0.5% of gross domestic product.

3 Future perspectives

This is the background against which the current debate evolves. I do not wish to comment on catchwords like European Monetary Fund or European Finance Minister, as they are very unclear at this point, or are defined very differently by different stakeholders. In my view, we need to focus the discussion on some guiding principles.

First and foremost, we should not separate the decision maker from the entity that bears the costs. If a decision is taken nationally, then other countries should not be liable for the consequences. One example illustrates this point perfectly: a common European unemployment insurance. As long as national governments and parliaments are responsible for setting the parameters of the labour market, such as access to vocational training or the length and conditions of unemployment benefits, it is difficult to make the case for a common budget to finance the resulting level of unemployment. However, if legal control over the key labour market parameters were transferred to the European level one could justify a common European unemployment insurance.

From time to time it is suggested that external economic shocks should be buffered by some sort of enhanced risk sharing. One has to keep in mind, however, that the European Union with its common market already provides a considerable amount of risk sharing. Also, one has to answer the question whether a higher degree of risk sharing requires more public transfers. The private sector, too, could assume a meaningful portion of shock absorption. People are already migrating within the EU, and the Capital Markets Union could also play a useful role. There are studies which show that risk sharing is better provided by capital markets, especially the market for equity. In the US, integrated capital markets are estimated to account for 40% of the absorption of regional economic shocks, while fiscal policy accounts for only 10–20%.[2]

A number of other measures could likewise improve the functioning of the Economic and Monetary Union in the future, and the Bundesbank publishes an overview of them regularly in its *Monthly Report*. They range from financial stability to fiscal and economic policy to monetary policy.

---

[2] Asdrubali et al. (1996), pp. 1081–1110.

I would like to emphasise two proposals which could greatly enhance resilience in the Euro area. First, we need to disentangle banks' balance sheets and the state of public finances, especially in their respective home countries. We have learned the hard way that government bonds are not risk-free and could drown the domestic banking system. Therefore, banks should be mandated to provide capital on a risk-weighted basis for government bonds on their balance sheets, which is currently not the case in the European Union. As with private sector debt, there should also be exposure limits for government bonds. These measures would also be necessary preconditions for further steps towards a banking union with a European deposit insurance scheme.

While the first proposal of disentangling banks and states aims at crisis prevention, the second proposal aims at crisis resolution. In 2013, Euro area Member States included collective action clauses in their bond contracts to facilitate debt restructuring by a qualified majority. It would be in keeping with Economic and Monetary Union principles if the maturity of outstanding government bonds were automatically prolonged by three years in the event that a Member State applies for European Stability Mechanism funds.

It would not only strengthen market discipline but also offer a time window to correct imbalances without a debt restructuring. Furthermore, the limited resources of the European Stability Mechanism could be protected because funds would only be needed to cover the current deficit and not to pay out private bond holders.

Finally, I wish to come back to fiscal policies in the Euro area. The currently benign economic environment and ultra-expansionary monetary policy have shrunk deficits in many countries to below the 3% ceiling. However, two countries are still subject to an excessive deficit procedure, and debt levels in many countries remain elevated. Seven out of 19 member states have debt levels of more than 90% of gross domestic product. Just to remind us, Member States agreed to reduce the amount of debt that exceeds the 60% threshold by 1/20th per year.

Therefore, monitoring public deficits and debt levels should follow simple, transparent and easily comprehensible rules. Ideally, it should be conducted by an independent agency such as the European Stability Mechanism.[3] Strengthening the link between liability and control would serve the Euro best. I don't think any of us wants to see the Austrian comedian Werner Schneyder vindicated, who said: "Europe consists of countries which don't want to follow the rules they themselves have enacted".

Reference

Asdrubali P, Sørensen B, Yosha O (1996) Channels of interstate risk sharing: US 1963–1990. Q J Econ 111(4):1081–1110

[3] Deutsche Bundesbank, Monthly Report July 2016, p. 64.

Part VI
Current Threats to the rule of law in the EU: The fundaments on which the authority of EU law rests

Article 7 TEU and the rule of law mechanism: A dissuasive weapon or a paper tiger?

Inger Österdahl

1 Introduction

This contribution deals with the ability or not of the European Union (EU) to act in situations of serious systemic violations of the rule of law in a Member State. It does this by looking at the different available mechanisms including Article 7 in the Treaty on European Union (TEU) and the new Rule of Law Framework and excluding infringement procedures before the Court of Justice of the EU. The contribution also discusses whether as a result of a serious breach of the TEU a Member State could be expelled from the organisation. The TEU contains no provision on expulsion, but the Vienna Convention on the Law of Treaties potentially does. In conclusion, the contribution finds that neither mechanism can be likened to a weapon, nor are they probably dissuasive, but they might be persuasive thanks to a persistent and protracted dialogue. The EU has no realistic choice but to be a gentle civiliser of Member States.

2 Article 7: The mother of all mechanisms?

Article 7 in the TEU concerning potential breaches by Member States of the fundamental values underpinning the organisation was introduced in 1997 through the Treaty of Amsterdam.[1] According to the Treaty of Amsterdam, the Council of the

[1] Treaty of Amsterdam amending the Treaty on European Union, the Treaties establishing the European Communities and certain related acts, Official Journal (O.J.) C 340/01, 10 November 1997.

I. Österdahl (✉)
Uppsala University, Uppsala, Sweden
e-mail: Inger.Osterdahl@jur.uu.se

W. Heusel, J.-P. Rageade (eds.), *The Authority of EU Law*,
https://doi.org/10.1007/978-3-662-58841-3_19

EU meeting in the composition of the Heads of State or Government could determine the existence of a serious and persistent breach by a Member State of the founding principles of the EU, at the time laid down in Article 6.

In 2002, through the Treaty of Nice, a preventive component was added to Article 7 of the TEU by means of which the Council, as an initial step, could determine that there was a clear risk of a serious breach by a Member State of the fundamental principles of the EU, and then address appropriate recommendations to that State.[2] The possibility for the Council meeting in the composition of the Heads of State or Government to determine the existence of a serious and persistent breach of the principles remained, and was not conditioned on the Council having previously determined the presence of a clear risk of a serious breach and having addressed appropriate recommendations to the faulting Member State.

Then in 2007 Article 7 in its current form was laid down in the Treaty of Lisbon.[3] The Council may still determine that there is a clear risk of a serious breach by a Member State of the founding values of the EU, now stated in Article 2 of the TEU, and the Council may address recommendations to the Member State in question.[4] In the more sanctioning end of the procedure under Article 7, the European Council, not the Council, may henceforth determine the existence of a serious and persistent breach by a Member State of the values contained in Article 2. The procedure under Article 7 in its current version will now be examined in some detail.[5] A lot of procedural steps will reveal themselves.

Before Article 7 is scrutinised, however, let us remind ourselves of the founding values of the EU laid down in Article 2 of the TEU: respect for human dignity, freedom, democracy, equality, the rule of law and respect for human rights, including the rights of persons belonging to minorities. And then, "[t]hese values are common to the Member States in a society in which pluralism, non-discrimination, tolerance, justice, solidarity and equality between women and men prevail".

If the Council is considering issuing a determination under Article 7 that there is a clear risk of a serious breach by a Member State of the values in Article 2, the Council must, first, hear the Member State in question and may, secondly, address recommendations to it. Then, thirdly, on a reasoned proposal by one third of the Member States, by the European Parliament (EP) or by the European Commission (Commission), the Council may by a majority of four fifths of its members after obtaining the consent of the European Parliament determine that there is a clear risk of a serious breach by the Member State of the values listed in Article 2.[6] Fourthly,

---

[2] Treaty of Nice amending the Treaty on European Union, the Treaties establishing the European Communities and certain related acts, O.J. C 80/01, 26 February 2001.

[3] Treaty of Lisbon amending the Treaty on European Union and the Treaty establishing the European Community, O.J. C 306/01, 13 December 2007.

[4] Consolidated version of the Treaty on European Union, O.J. C 202/1, p. 13, 7 June 2016.

[5] See also for instance Raulus (2016), pp. 25–37.

[6] As stated in Article 7(5) of the TEU, the voting arrangements applying to the EP, the European Council and the Council for the purposes of Article 7 are laid down in Article 354 of the Treaty on the Functioning of the European Union (TFEU) (Consolidated version of the TFEU, O.J. C 202/1

according to Article 7, the Council shall regularly verify that the grounds on which such a determination was made continue to apply.

Fifthly, if the European Council, consisting of the Heads of State or Government, would consider taking up the issue of a Member State breaching the values in Article 2, the European Council must invite the Member State in question to submit its observations. After that, sixthly, the European Council, acting by unanimity on a proposal by one third of the Member States or by the Commission and after obtaining the consent of the Parliament, may determine the existence of a serious and persistent breach by a Member State of the founding values of the EU.

Seventhly, where such a determination by the European Council has been made that a serious and persistent breach exists, which it must be added is a purely hypothetical scenario so far, the Council, acting by a qualified majority, may decide to suspend certain of the rights deriving from the application of the "Treaties" to the Member State in question. The "Treaties" according to Article 1 of the TEU (and according to Article 1 of the TFEU) refers to the TEU and the TFEU.

There is no restriction on the type of rights that may be suspended nor on the number of rights that may be suspended at any one time. The only limitation that may be inferred from the text of the provision is perhaps that not all rights deriving from the application of the Treaties to the Member State in question may be suspended at the same time; the qualification "'certain' of the rights" would seem to point in that direction. This can be compared with Article 60 of the Vienna Convention on the Law of Treaties, in particular point 2, which states that a material breach of a multilateral treaty by one of the parties entitles the other parties among other things to "suspend the operation of the treaty *in whole* or in part (emphasis added)".[7]

The Vienna Convention applies if nothing else has been agreed by the parties to the treaty and it would seem as if the parties to the TEU have agreed at least implicitly that the suspension of the operation of the Treaties as a whole would not be an option. A "material breach" in the Vienna Convention is defined in Article 60 (3) (b) as "the violation of a provision essential to the accomplishment of the object or purpose of the treaty" and regardless of the fact whether the TEU allows the suspension in whole or only in part of the EU Treaties, Article 2 of the TEU the breach of which is in focus in Article 7 would seem to qualify as a provision essential to the accomplishment of the object or purpose of the TEU and indirectly of the TFEU. Below we will come back to the issue of material breach under the VCLT and its possible consequences in the EU context.

The only explicit specification contained in Article 7 concerning the kind of rights that may be suspended in case of a serious and persistent breach by a Member State of the values referred to in Article 2, is the voting rights of the representative of the government of that Member State in the Council. Putting aside the condition

---

p. 47, 7 June 2016). The voting arrangements and their significance will not be entered into further here.

[7]Adopted on 23 May 1969, 1155 UNTS (United Nations Treaty Series), p. 331; on treaty law see generally, for instance, Aust (2013), Kolb (2016) and Tams et al. (2014).

that the determination of the existence of a serious and persistent breach of the values in Article 2 must take place through a unanimous decision by the European Council, which constitutes an obvious hurdle to overcome before a decision on the suspension of rights might potentially be taken by the Council, acting by a qualified majority, the suspension of the voting rights of a Member State in the Council might potentially constitute a fearful weapon in the hands of the rest of the Member States of the EU when trying to stop ongoing breaches of the founding values of the EU on the part of one of its members. Since it is the only type of suspension which is explicitly mentioned and judging from the way the provision is drafted generally with the possibility to suspend the voting rights mentioned last and presumably as the "jewel in the crown" of possible rights to suspend, the wording of Article 7(3) suggests that the drafters of the TEU considered the suspension of voting rights to be a serious sanction indeed. From the point of view of principle and symbolically, it certainly is. From the point of view of practice, other kinds of sanctions may be even more severe.[8]

However, eighthly, the Council is reminded in the last sentence of Article 7(3) that if contemplating to introduce a suspension of the rights deriving from the application of the Treaties to the faulting Member State, the Council must take into account the possible consequences of such a suspension on the rights and obligations of natural and legal persons. This would seem to constitute a further indirect qualification of the powers of the Council, in addition to the initial condition that the determination of the existence of a serious and persistent breach by the Member State in question of the values in Article 2 is made through a unanimous decision by the European Council. Achieving unanimity among the remaining members of the European Council would currently seem to be the most difficult condition of all to fulfil.

Considering the close relationship in many areas and on many levels between the different Member States of the EU and their inhabitants, it is likely that a suspension of rights deriving from the application of the Treaties to a Member State, for instance the right to free movement or any right to economic subsidies, will negatively affect the rights and obligations of natural and legal persons, like companies. If the rights and obligations of natural and legal persons are not negatively affected, on the other hand, it might be that the suspension would not be effective enough as a sanction. Moreover, there is the further complication that an effective sanction in principle with grave consequences for natural and legal persons both within the faulting Member State and potentially in other Member States, may turn out to be detrimental to the sympathies among the population at large especially in the Member State concerned toward the EU and the EU project as a whole, and may not work in favour either of the EU or the political opposition in the Member State in question

[8]According to the Statute of the Council of Europe a Member State may be suspended from its rights of representation (and ultimately expelled from the organisation) under Article 8 in case of serious violations of the rule of law or human rights and fundamental freedoms under Article 3, adopted 5 May 1949, ETS (European Treaty Series) No. 001.

or in favour of the retraction on the part of the government concerned of the threats to the rule of law giving rise to the suspension of rights.[9]

Thus, the suspension weapon in Article 7(3) would seem to risk being a double-edged sword should it ever be even theoretically possible to use it considering the fundamental rule of unanimity mentioned above. The lacking likelihood that the weapon will ever be used, due initially to the likely lack of unanimity among the remaining Member States, adds to the ambiguity or weakness of the weapon of suspension of rights on the whole. A Member State intent on breaching the values in Article 2 need not be very fearful of any eventual suspension of certain of its rights deriving from the Treaties. Should the Council decide to suspend certain rights (against all odds), Article 7 ends by stating that the obligations of the Member State in question under the Treaties shall in any case continue to be binding on that State.

Ninthly, under Article 7(4) the Council after having taken measures of suspension, may subsequently decide to vary or revoke the measures taken in response to changes in the situation which led to their being imposed. The Council shall make its decision by a qualified majority. Thus, the same decision-making rule applies to the imposition of a suspension of rights by the Council as to the decision to vary or revoke the measures taken. Prior to the imposition of a suspension of rights by the Council there is of course the need for a previous determination by the European Council, acting by unanimity, that a serious and persistent breach by a Member State of the values in Article 2 exists. It is slightly more difficult for the Council alone to determine that there is a clear risk of a serious breach by a Member State of the founding values of the EU. As we saw above, there is a need for a majority of four fifths of the members of the Council, among other requirements relating to other institutional actors involved, in order for the determination of risk to be made by the Council.

Should a qualified majority of the members of the Council by any chance for good or bad reasons not want to vary or revoke the measures of suspension taken despite changes in the situation that lead to the measures being imposed, then the measures presumably will remain in force. In addition, Article 7(4) merely states that the Council *may* decide to vary or revoke its measures of suspension. There is no obligation on the Council even in principle to adapt its measures according to changes in the situation. The (very) hypothetical situation could arise that a Member State subject to a suspension of rights under Article 7, but which is sincerely trying to improve its rule of law performance nevertheless continue to be subject to sanctions for reasons not directly related to its earlier breach of the values in Article 2. This situation could arise if the necessary qualified majority in the Council cannot be reached.

Perhaps this circumstance may also make the Council weary to impose a suspension of rights on a Member State under Article 7; the Council could never be sure that the suspension will be revoked once the situation in the Member State has possibly returned to an acceptable normal.

[9] For a forceful argument to the contrary, see Halmai (2018).

3 Expulsion from the EU?

Under Article 7 of the TEU it is possible for the Council, at least in principle, to suspend certain of the rights resulting from EU membership of the Member State who breaches the values referred to in Article 2. There is no provision in the TEU regulating the potential termination of the Treaties with the Member State in question by the remaining members, i.e. there is no provision in the TEU regulating the potential expulsion of a Member State due to its breach of the fundamental values of the organisation.

Before the Treaty of Lisbon of 2007, the potential withdrawal from the EU on the part of a Member State was not regulated either, in any provision in the TEU. The question is whether the expulsion of a Member State due to its serious and persistent breach of the values in Article 2 would still be possible, from the point of view of principle and law.

Under the Vienna Convention on the Law of Treaties (VCLT) which applies to all interstate treaties including, according to Article 5, treaties forming the foundation of international organisations, the termination or suspension of the operation of a treaty as a consequence of its breach is regulated in Article 60. In the case of multilateral treaties, a material breach by one of the parties entitles the other parties by unanimous agreement to suspend the operation of the treaty in whole or in part or to terminate it, either in the relations between themselves and the defaulting State, or as between all the parties. It can be noted already that the unanimous agreement is needed between the remaining parties before a termination of the treaty can potentially take place.

A termination of the treaty, further, presupposes a “material breach”. In the words of the VCLT Article 60(3), a material breach of a treaty, for the purposes of Article 60, consists in either (a) a repudiation of the treaty not sanctioned by the present Convention or (b) the violation of a provision essential to the accomplishment of the object or purpose of the treaty. It is the latter part of Article 60(3) of the VCLT which is of interest here. One question which presents itself is whether a serious and persistent breach by a Member State of the EU of the values referred to in Article 2 of the TEU would qualify as a material breach of the TEU.

It would seem as if a serious and persistent violation of Article 2 of the TEU would indeed qualify as a material breach considering that in the words of Article 2 “[t]he Union is founded” on the enumerated values. If the Union is founded on these values then the respect for these values would seem essential to the accomplishment of the object or purpose of the Treaty. Additional support for this argument could be found in Article 49 of the TEU which makes the respect for and the commitment to promote the values referred to in Article 2 a condition for membership in the organisation. If these values are so significant as to constitute a condition for membership then the values should also consequently be essential to the accomplishment of the object or purpose of the Treaty. The purpose of the TEU under its Article 1, furthermore, is that of “creating an ever closer union among the peoples of Europe” in which process the TEU marks a new step. As we will see below the argument could be made that the respect for the values in Article 2 and in particular the rule of law is a prerequisite for the process of integration in the EU. As far as the actual breach as such is concerned, a determination by the European Council of the existence of a "serious and persistent" breach by a Member State of the values in Article 2 would seem to signal that the breach is indeed serious.

Further indirect support for the interpretation suggested here, namely that a violation of Article 2 of the TEU would constitute a material breach of the Treaty in the sense of the VCLT, could arguably be found in Article 31 (3) (c) of the VCLT. Article 31 concerns the interpretation of treaties and among other things to take into account when interpreting a treaty are, under Article 31 (3) (c), any relevant rules of international law applicable in the relations between the parties.

With respect to the interpretation of Article 2 of the TEU concerning the fundamental values of the EU, the international law of human rights which binds all the EU Member States is particularly relevant, in particular the EU Charter of Fundamental Rights and the European Convention on Human Rights.[10] The latter two and a number of other international treaties on human rights illustrate the emphasis on human rights in a broad sense, including arguably the rule of law, which has characterised international law since the creation of the UN in general and the period after the end of the Cold War in particular. The great amount of international human rights law applicable between the Member States of the EU among which are two significant European instruments shall be taken into account in the interpretation of Article 2 of the TEU. The great amount of applicable international human rights law also gives emphasis to the importance of human rights generally and thus of the importance of respecting Article 2 of the TEU.

As a consequence, a serious and persistent breach by a Member State of the values in Article 2, in particular the respect for human rights and the rule of law, would constitute a material breach of the TEU in the sense of Article 60(3)(b) of the VCLT. The more important the contents of Article 2 of the TEU the more serious its breach becomes, should a breach occur. In addition, if the European Council would, potentially, determine the existence of a serious and persistent breach by a Member State of the founding values of the EU, it would be difficult to argue with respect to the VCLT that the issue is not one of a material breach of the TEU, giving rise to the entitlement on the part of the remaining Member States ultimately to expel the Member breaching the TEU from the organisation.

The condition in VCLT Article 60(2) that the termination of the treaty must be agreed on unanimously by the remaining parties may of course in practice constitute a hindrance to the, hypothetical, case of the exclusion of a member of the EU due to the still serious and persistent breach by that Member State of the values in Article 2 of the TEU. Another hindrance to the termination of the EU Treaties between the member breaching Article 2 of the TEU and the remaining members, still from the strictly legal point of view, would be if there was a provision in the

[10] Charter of Fundamental Rights of the European Union, O.J. C 202/2, p. 389, 7 June 2016; Convention for the Protection of Human Rights and Fundamental Freedoms, adopted 4 November 1950, ETS 005.

TEU prohibiting the termination of the Treaty due to a breach or a provision prohibiting the termination of the Treaty under any circumstances or for that matter a provision in the TEU drawing up conditions of its own for the suspension or termination of the Treaty in case of a breach.[11]

The TEU is silent on the issue of the expulsion of Member States from the organisation. As mentioned earlier, before the Treaty of Lisbon of 2007, there was no provision on the withdrawal of a Member State from the EU either. Under Article 60(4) of the VCLT, its provisions on the suspension or termination of a treaty due to a material breach are without prejudice to any provision in the treaty applicable in the event of a breach. The TEU in its turn, as just noted, is silent on the issue not of the "[suspension of] certain of the rights deriving from the application of the Treaties to the Member State in question" according to Article 7(3), but on the issue specifically of the termination of the Treaties. This silence would seem to point to Article 60(2) of the VCLT being potentially applicable in the case of the TEU; i.e. since the TEU is silent, the default rule in the VCLT stating that the termination of the treaty is possible due to a material breach would seem to be potentially applicable.

Another way of arguing could be to claim that the silence of the TEU on the matter of the termination of the Treaty due to a material breach implies that the termination of the Treaty by the remaining parties as a reaction to a material breach of the Treaty is not possible. It could be argued that the intent behind the TEU and the EU organisation is that it should not be possible to terminate the membership of any Member State except, after the Treaty of Lisbon, on the terminating State's own initiative. It could be argued that the termination of the TEU would go against the idea behind and the purpose of the organisation; the explicit purpose of the EU being under Article 1 of the TEU, as we saw earlier, the creation of an ever closer union among the peoples of Europe. Thus, it could be argued that the lack of provision in the TEU on the termination of the Treaty due to a material breach shows the intention of the drafters that the termination of the Treaty in such a situation should not be allowed; the silence constitutes an implicit provision prohibiting the forced termination of the TEU and the consequent expulsion of a member of the organisation. It could also be argued that the fact that Article 7(3) only mentions the suspension of different kinds of rights deriving from the EU membership of the State in question as a consequence of a "'serious' and 'persistent' breach" of the fundamental values of the organisation referred to in Article 2 of the TEU, i.e. a "material breach" for all practical purposes, would mean at least implicitly that the termination of the Treaty with the Member State by the remaining members is not possible. A "material breach" can only maximally lead to the suspension of rights under the TEU, it could be argued. The magnitude and seriousness of the breach would otherwise more naturally point in the direction of the termination of the Treaty on the part of the remaining members.

This alternative interpretation of Article 60(4) of the VCLT as applied to the TEU is not convincing in the opinion of the current author. The argument against the

[11] Cf. the Statute of the Council of Europe Articles 3 and 8 and the Charter of the United Nations Articles 5 and 6 (adopted 26 June 1945).

possibility of expulsion under the TEU would have been stronger before the introduction of the right of a Member State to withdraw from the EU in Article 50, but not even before the introduction of that Article would the alternative interpretation presented above have been entirely convincing.

Today, it may also be argued that the drive to expand the membership of the EU in quantitative terms and, perhaps, at any cost is not as important as it was earlier and that qualitative consolidation among the existing members has become more important and the entrenchment of the rule of law is part of this qualitative consolidation. In this light the potential loss of a Member State as a consequence of its expulsion due to the "serious and persistent breach" by that Member State of the rule of law might not be as antithetic to the EU project and thus as politically catastrophic as it might have appeared before.

If the interpretation of the VCLT and the TEU that the expulsion of a Member State due to a material breach of the TEU is indeed legally permitted, as argued here, it may become even more difficult for the European Council under Article 7(2) of the TEU to arrive at a determination that there "[exists] a serious and persistent breach by a Member State of the values referred to in Article 2", possibly after the Council has determined that there is a clear risk of a serious breach by the Member State of Article 2, which is grave, but not quite as grave as the determination by the European Council that such a breach actually exists.

The reason the determination might become (even) more difficult to pronounce for the European Council is that if the Member State in question does not change its behaviour not even as a result of the potential suspension of rights being subsequently introduced by the Council including the voting rights of the Member State in the Council, the European Council arguably has made it clear (implicitly) that in its opinion the conditions for the termination of the Treaty due to material breach in accordance with Article 60(2) of the VCLT are fulfilled. The remaining members of the EU would as a consequence be justified in expelling the Member State in question from the organisation. If the remaining members would not proceed to the expulsion of the Member State from the organisation in that situation despite the Member State's continuing obvious breach of the TEU, the weakness of the organisation becomes all the more evident. This is not to say that from other points of view than the strictly legal one, there might not be many and strong reasons to retain as many members as possible within the EU, i.e. not to expel. The Brexit procedure not least is frightening.

4 What's in the Rule of Law Framework?

4.1 The justifications

The EU Framework to strengthen the Rule of Law (Framework) was drafted by the EU Commission and came into existence in 2014.[12] Like Article 7 of the TEU, the Framework potentially involves a lot of different procedural steps the possible significance of whom will be discussed below. Before we come to the procedure, however, we will go through some important preliminary statements in the Framework.

The Framework is intended to address and resolve a situation where there is a "systemic threat" to the rule of law, the Commission states. The Framework seeks to resolve future threats to the rule of law in Member States, the Commission continues, before the conditions for activating the mechanisms foreseen in Article 7 of the TEU would be met. The Framework is not an alternative to but is rather intended to precede and complement Article 7. It is easy to agree with the Commission when it says that the thresholds for activating the preventive mechanism in Article 7(1) and the sanctioning mechanism in Article 7(2) respectively are very high. Also, the Commission points out, the Framework is without prejudice to the Commission's powers to address specific situations falling within the scope of EU law by means of infringement procedures under Article 258 of the TFEU.

The observation could be made that it is a bit strange that while being of fundamental importance to the entire organisation, in fact one could venture to say constituting its very raison d'être, Article 2 is still not considered to fall within the ambit of "EU law". Violations of the founding and presumably most important values of the EU contained in Article 2 therefore cannot be the subject of infringement procedures before the Court of Justice of the European Union (CJEU). Perhaps they should be. This line of thought, however, will not be further pursued here.[13] Currently, systematic rule of law issues, i.e. the most serious ones, can only be introduced indirectly in proceedings before the CJEU.[14]

---

[12] Communication from the Commission to the European Parliament and the Council: A New EU Framework to strengthen the Rule of Law, COM/2014/0158 final, Doc. 52014DC0158, 11 March 2014.

[13] See further Scheppele (2016), pp. 105–132; Closa and Kochenov (2016), pp. 182–186; Konstadinides (2017), pp. 153–159.

[14] See Crabit and Bel (2016), pp. 199–200; case C-192/18 European Commission v Republic of Poland brought before the CJEU on 15 March 2018 concerns the Law amending the Law on the Organisation of Ordinary Courts and focuses on equal opportunities and equal treatment of men and women in matters of employment and occupation; on 2 July 2018 the Commission launched another infringement procedure against Poland concerning the new Polish law on the Supreme Court and the focus is on judicial independence with reference to Article 19(1) TEU (thus not Article 2) and Article 47 of the EU Charter of Fundamental Rights [European Commission—Press release, Rule of Law: Commission launches infringement procedure to protect the independence of the Polish Supreme Court (http://europa.eu/rapid/press-release_IP-18-4341_en.htm)]; the Commission recently has three times referred Hungary to the CJEU, on the subject of Hungary's law on foreign-funded non-governmental organisations [European Commission—Press release,

Within the EU, the rule of law is of particular importance in three respects, according to the Framework: The rule of law is a prerequisite for the protection of all fundamental values listed in Article 2 of the TEU; it is also a prerequisite for upholding all rights and obligations deriving from the Treaties and from international law; and the confidence of all EU citizens and national authorities in the legal systems of all other Member States, which presupposes a functioning rule of law, is vital for the functioning of the whole EU as an area of freedom, security and justice without internal frontiers. These are also reasons why the EU has a strong interest in safeguarding and strengthening the rule of law threats across the Union, according to the Framework, and perhaps simultaneously constitute arguments on the part of the Commission why the Commission may legitimately deal with issues relating to the realisation of the rule of law within each Member State. The slight tension between the Commission competence and the Member State competence in this area is lurking throughout the Framework.

After the preliminary, and from the point of view of the Commission hopefully convincing, explanation of the background to and justification of the creation of the new EU Framework to strengthen the Rule of Law, the working of the Framework procedure for handling threats to the rule of law under the Framework is presented. The Framework will be activated, it is stated in the text of the Framework, in situations where the authorities of a Member State are taking measures or are tolerating situations which are likely to systematically and adversely affect the integrity, stability or the proper functioning of the institutions and the safeguard mechanisms established at national level to secure the rule of law.

The main purpose of the Framework, thus, is to address threats to the rule of law which are of a systemic nature. The political, institutional and/or legal order of a Member State as such, its constitutional structure, separation of powers, the independence or impartiality of the judiciary, or its system of judicial review including constitutional justice where it exists, must be threatened—for example as a result of the adoption of new measures of or widespread practices of public authorities and the lack of domestic redress.[15] The Framework will be activated, the Framework

---

Infringements—European Commission refers Hungary to the Court of Justice for its NGO law (http://europa.eu/rapid/press-release_IP-17-5003_en.htm)], Hungary's amended higher education law [European Commission—Press release, Commission refers Hungary to the European Court of Justice of the EU over the Higher Education Law (http://europa.eu/rapid/press-release_IP-17-5004_en.htm)], and its asylum and return legislation [European Commission—Press release, Migration and Asylum: Commission takes further steps in infringement procedures against Hungary (http://europa.eu/rapid/press-release_IP-18-4522_en.htm)]; see also case C-286/12 European Commission v Hungary, judgment of 6 November 2012 on equal treatment in employment and occupation; on the independence of national data protection authorities, see cases C-518/07 European Commission v Federal Republic of Germany, judgment of 9 March 2010, C-614/10 European Commission v Republic of Austria, judgment of 16 October 2012, C-288/12 Commission v Hungary, judgment of 8 April 2014.

[15] The (in)dependence of the judiciary has been the subject of two recent historical studies by the Norwegian law professor Graver (2015a), in which the author "surveys instances of judicial participation in oppression through the law in many countries in the twentieth century" (p. 8) and gives "advice on how to make more sound choices of action" (p. 10); and Graver (2015b) on the

goes on to say, when national "rule of law safeguards" do not seem capable of effectively addressing those threats.

The systemic threats listed in the Framework are threats to the central institutions and organising principles in liberal democratic states based on the rule of law. The creation of the rule of law Framework must imply that the Commission and the other institutions of the EU actually were of the opinion that the central functions of the rule of law were being threatened in one or more Member States. When considering the principles and institutions that must be threatened in order for the Framework to be triggered the seriousness of the current situation in some Member States of the EU, which triggered the drafting of the rule of law Framework, becomes obvious. Also, considering the seriousness of the rule of law functions that must be threatened for the rule of law Framework to be triggered, it becomes obvious that even though the Framework is supposed to be activated at a less acute stage than the Article 7 mechanism, the situation could be labelled rather acute or at least very serious already when the Rule of Law Framework is activated. The question arises how serious a situation would have to be in order for the mechanism in Article 7 to be activated.

The next question then arises how the EU could intervene at an even earlier stage than the one foreseen in the Framework in order to maintain and strengthen the central rule of law institutions while they are still working and not the subject of threat at all. Once the situation has turned into one in which "the political, institutional and/or legal order of a Member State as such, its constitutional structure, separation of powers, the independence or impartiality of the judiciary, or its system of judicial review including constitutional justice where it exists" are threatened the negative developments from the point of view of the rule of law have already come very far. If the purpose of the new EU Framework, as stated in the Framework, is to "prevent the emerging of a systemic threat to the rule of law in [a] Member State that could develop into a 'clear risk of a serious breach' within the meaning of Article 7 TEU", it would seem as if even under the Framework the Commission becomes involved at a rather late and perhaps too late a stage if it is supposed to prevent the "emerging of" a systemic threat to the rule of law in the Member State concerned.

Perhaps the Commission will nevertheless be able to intervene at a stage where it is still possible to prevent the development of the situation into a "clear risk of a serious breach" of the founding values of the EU within the meaning of Article 7. However, if the political, institutional and/or legal order of a Member State as such, its constitutional structure, separation of powers, the independence or impartiality of the judiciary, or its system of judicial review including constitutional justice where it exists are threatened as described in the Framework, in the view of this author there is already a clear risk of a serious breach, if a serious and persistent

actions of the Norwegian judiciary during the Second World War. For more current commentaries, see Sadurski (2018); Special Issue on the Crisis of Constitutional Democracy in Central and Eastern Europe, *Hague Journal on the Rule of Law*, Volume 10, April 2018, Issue 1, pp. 1–217; The Economist (2017a, b).

breach does not even already exist. Hopefully, the Commission will still be able to accomplish something of a preventive nature even at the relatively late stage in the development away from the rule of law in a Member State at which the Commission will become involved even under the new EU Framework. The Framework does not prevent the mechanisms set out in Article 7 of the TEU being activated directly, by the Commission or any other institution or group of Member States mentioned in the Article, should a sudden deterioration in a Member State require a stronger reaction from the EU.

4.2 The process

As under Article 7 of the TEU accounted for above, under the Framework the process for dealing with situations involving a systemic threat to the rule of law in a Member State consists of several steps. Where there are clear indications of a systemic threat to the rule of law in a Member State, the Framework states, the Commission will initiate a "structured exchange" with that Member State. The concept of exchange presupposes, however, that there is an entity at the other end willing to engage in an exchange.

If no one answers the calls of the Commission there will be no exchange in the first place and no room for influence through the channel foreseen in the Framework. If it is the government of a Member State who is pursuing a policy destructive of the rule of law it is not very likely that the same government will be willing to engage in a dialogue with the Commission on how to redirect its own chosen policy. Also, the fundamental issues of concern to the Commission, namely the political, institutional and/or legal order of a Member State as such, its constitutional structure, separation of powers, the independence or impartiality of the judiciary, or its system of judicial review including constitutional justice where it exists are very close to what states may consider to be their national identity in the sense of Article 4 of the TEU which the Union shall respect. For this reason engaging in a dialogue with the Commission on these issues may become even more sensitive. The structured exchange with the Member State should it take place will involve a delicate balancing act on the part of the Commission.

The process under the Framework is based on *four principles*: dialogue with the Member State concerned as we just saw, objective and thorough assessment of the situation, equal treatment of Member States, and indication of swift and concrete actions which could be taken by the Member State to address the systemic threat and to avoid the use of Article 7. Whereas the goal of obtaining a thorough assessment of the situation might be attainable, the goal of ensuring an objective assessment of the situation might be more difficult to reach in the probably very tense situation that reigns in the country concerned where opinions on what the situation implies differ radically among different observers.

The principle of equal treatment of Member States is mentioned several times in the Framework although one would have thought that it could be taken for granted.

By repeating the principle explicitly throughout the Framework the Commission may even, unintentionally of course, transmit the impression that Member States risk not being treated equally under the Framework after all. The suspicion may arise that, contrary to what the Commission claims, the Framework will not operate on the basis of the same benchmarks as to what is a systemic threat to the rule of law. Indicating swift and concrete actions to address the systemic threat should not be difficult in itself.

The process under the Framework evolves in three stages: a Commission assessment, a Commission recommendation and a follow-up to the recommendation. A stage may include more than one step on the part of the Commission.

The first step in the Commission's assessment is to collect and examine all the relevant information and to assess whether there are clear indications of a systemic threat to the rule of law. If the Commission finds that that there is indeed a situation of systemic threat to the rule of law, it will initiate a dialogue with the Member State concerned, by sending a "rule of law opinion" and substantiating its concerns, giving the Member State concerned the possibility to respond.[16]

According to the Framework, the Commission expects that the Member State concerned cooperates throughout the process and refrains from adopting any irreversible measure in relation to the issues of concern raised by the Commission, pending the assessment of the latter, in line with the duty of sincere cooperation in Article 4(3) of the TEU. This expectation on the part of the Commission as hinted above may be a little exaggerated in reality. With the exception of a stronger rule of law which the Member State expressly does not want in all probability, there is little for the Member State to gain from cooperating with the Commission. This is at short sight; in the longer run the Member State may risk becoming the subject of the mechanisms in Article 7 of the TEU if it continues on the course of weakening the rule of law.

Whether a Member State fails to cooperate in the Framework process, or even obstructs it, will be an element to take into consideration when assessing the seriousness of the threat, it is stated in the Framework.

At the assessment stage of the process, according to the Framework, while the launching of the Commission assessment and the sending of its opinion will be made public by the Commission, the content of the exchanges with the Member State concerned will, as a rule be kept confidential, in order to facilitate quickly reaching a solution.

The second stage in the process under the Framework, should the case arise, consists of the issuance by the Commission of a "rule of law recommendation".[17]

---

[16] The Commission has issued one rule of law opinion with respect to Poland, European Commission—Press release, Commission adopts Rule of Law Opinion on the situation in Poland, 1 June 2016, http://europa.eu/rapid/press-release_IP-16-2015_en.htm.

[17] The Commission has issued four rule of law recommendations with respect to Poland: European Commission—Press release, Rule of Law: Commission issues recommendation to Poland, 27 July 2016 (http://europa.eu/rapid/press-release_IP-16-2643_en.htm); European Commission—Press release, Rule of Law: Commission discusses latest developments and issues complementary Recommendation to Poland, 21 December 2016 (http://europa.eu/rapid/press-release_IP-16-

More precisely, the Framework states that unless the matter has already been satisfactorily resolved in the meantime, the Commission will issue a "rule of law recommendation" addressed to the Member State concerned, if it finds that there is objective evidence of a systemic threat and that the authorities of that Member State are not taking appropriate action to redress it.

In its recommendation, the Framework continues, the Commission will clearly indicate the reasons for its concerns and recommend that the Member State solves the problems identified within a fixed time limit and informs the Commission of the steps taken to that effect. The recommendation may include specific indications on ways and measures to resolve the situation, according to the Framework. Toward the end of the second stage in the process under the Framework, the Commission intensifies its efforts a little: Not only the sending of its recommendation but also its main content will be made public by the Commission. To the extent that the Member State concerned is sensitive to being potentially "named and shamed", the publication of the main content of the rule of law recommendation may add a means of pressure on the State concerned on the part of the Commission. It can be noted that at the first stage in the procedure under the Framework only the launching of the Commission assessment and the sending of its "rule of law opinion" will be made public, not the content of the opinion.

Given that the facts will probably already be generally well known and that wide "naming and shaming" will probably already have taken place in many different forms and fora including potentially in several of the EU institutions including in the CJEU, the sensitivity of the Member State concerned to the main content of the "rule of law recommendation" being made public by the Commission may be limited. The ways and measures in which to resolve the situation should not be unknown to the Member State concerned. In fact, the situation may have arisen due to the Member State having actively worked against precisely the kind of measures that the Commission would recommend the Member State to take in order to resolve the situation.

The escalation in normative terms from a "rule of law opinion" to a "rule of law recommendation" although useful in principle may not in itself be the decisive element that induces the Member State concerned to change its behaviour. A "recommendation" by the Commission is probably only marginally more awe-inspiring than an "opinion", from the point of view of the State.

The third and final stage in the process under the Framework is the follow-up to the Commission's "rule of law recommendation". Here the Commission will monitor the follow-up given by the Member State concerned to the recommendation addressed to it. This monitoring can be based on further exchanges with the Member State concerned, according to the Framework, presuming then that the Member

---

4476_en.htm); European Commission—Press release, European Commission acts to preserve the rule of law in Poland, 26 July 2017 (http://europa.eu/rapid/press-release_IP-17-2161_en.htm); European Commission—Press release, Rule of Law: European Commission acts to defend judicial independence in Poland, 20 December 2017 (http://europa.eu/rapid/press-release_IP-17-5367_en.htm).

State answers the calls of the Commission, and could, for example, focus on whether certain practices which raise concerns continue to occur, or on how the Member State implements the commitments it has made in the meantime to resolve the situation.

Then, potentially, comes the very last step under the Framework: If there is no satisfactory follow-up to the recommendation by the Member State concerned within the time limit set, the Commission will assess the possibility of activating one of the mechanisms set out in Article 7 of the TEU. While superficially the latter threat perhaps does not sound too impressive, the point is that the Commission can choose to go straight to the sanctioning parts of Article 7 in sections 2 and 3 instead of first having to pass via the preventive part in section 1. After the long process under the Framework, the preventive part of the mechanism in Article 7 would even seem a bit superfluous except for the fact that the preventive efforts would now be undertaken on a higher political level.[18] Under the sanctioning part of Article 7 the European Council may unanimously determine the existence of a serious and persistent breach by a Member State of the values in Article 2 which in its turn allows the EU Council to decide on the suspension of rights. It should be noted that the Framework only says that the Commission will "assess the possibility" of activating Article 7; there is no automatic transfer of the issue from the Framework to the mechanism in Article 7 if the efforts under the Framework would turn out unsuccessful from the point of view of the Commission and the rule of law.

If all the steps included in the mechanism under Article 7 of the TEU are added to the sum of possible steps in the Framework process we arrive at a total number of thirteen steps at least (including taking account of the possible consequences of a suspension of rights on the rights and obligations of natural and legal persons) before, as the absolutely final step, the decision is eventually taken to suspend certain of the rights of the Member State concerned under the TEU, including the voting rights in the Council.

The hope on the part of the EU must reasonably be that somewhere along this elaborate process the problem will be solved before the endpoint is eventually reached. Arguably, neither the rule of law-abiding Member States nor the Member State of concern to the Commission would wish the endpoint in the combined processes under the Framework first and then under Article 7 of the TEU ever to be attained. The purpose of all the steps in the procedure, it could be argued, is precisely to prevent the parties ever having to reach the end, by means of persistent persuasion of the Member State concerned. Which one of the two camps that would

[18] On 20 December 2017 the Commission submitted a reasoned proposal to the Council under Article 7(1) TEU inviting the Council to determine that there is a clear risk of a serious breach of the rule of law in Poland [European Commission—Press release, Rule of Law: European Commission acts to defend judicial independence in Poland (http://europa.eu/rapid/press-release_IP-17-5367_en.htm)]; Reasoned proposal in accordance with Article 7(1) of the Treaty on European Union regarding the rule of law in Poland, Proposal for a Council Decision on the determination of a clear risk of a serious breach by the Republic of Poland of the rule of law [COM(2017) 835 final, 2017/0360 (APP)].

have the most to win, or lose, from the arrival at the decision to suspend, or not, is an open question.

Even if the measures taken by the Commission under the Rule of Law Framework would eventually turn out ineffective and unsuccessful they would serve to indirectly support the political forces working in favour of the rule of law and probably against the policies of the government in the Member State concerned. The forces in favour of rule of law, democracy and human rights would hopefully be kept alive, awaiting a shift in policy, and being kept alive in this context might in very serious situations need to be interpreted literally and not only figuratively.

The support to forces opposing the government policies can also be more direct in the form of contacts, alluded to in the Framework, between the Commission and the judicial networks in the EU assembling high-level judicial professionals from the different Member States including the Member State of concern to the Commission. In the long run the indirect and direct outside support to different presumably oppositional forces in the Member State concerned can play a big role in order for the situation to change.

The necessary political change within the Member State concerned may have to be achieved by the citizens themselves through elections in due time bringing in a new government, if that is what the citizens want. If there is a change in government in favour of political forces supporting the rule of law then the new government may use the specific indications on ways and measures to resolve the situation that the Commission may have issued to the previous government of the Member State concerned. Also, the possible new government and the possibly weakened judiciary can take advantage of the know-how and support in rule of law matters provided by the Commission more generally.

5 Conclusion: A persuasive paper tiger?

Returning to the fundamental question of this contribution namely whether Article 7 of the TEU and the new EU Framework for the Rule of Law together constitute a dissuasive weapon or a paper tiger the issue arises whether harsher sanctions should be available against those Member States who clearly breach the rule of law. The issue also arises whether there are positive incentives which could be used more actively or more creatively in order to induce reluctant Member States to return to the rule of law. Then the question arises what could reasonably be achieved in particular by harsher sanctions in addition to the obvious result on the symbolic level that breaches of the rule of law are strongly condemned.

It is hard to believe that in reality any harsher sanctions in the form for instance of expulsion of the Member State concerned from the EU or in the form of stricter economic sanctions against the Member State would lead to decisive measures being taken in that Member State in order to strengthen the rule of law. It is easier almost to picture the contrary development namely a continued or even hastened erosion of the rule of law as a reaction to the harsh (although justified) external pressure on the (ex-)Member State. At some point, however, there must be a limit to what the EU can tolerate, and continue to be the EU as we know it.

As far as positive incentives are concerned, the most effective one should be the membership in the EU itself with all the undeniable advantages that flow from the membership to the Member States, not least to the Member States which today are subject to the concern of the outside world as to the condition of the rule of law in their countries. Emphasising the significance of all these advantages and implicitly or explicitly pointing out what would be lost without them (i.e. threatening with suspension or expulsion) could perhaps induce the Member States concerned to reinstall a reliable rule of law. Making the population feel and understand the advantages and what would be lost without them is perhaps even more important.

Perhaps a mechanism could be devised for organisational self-destruction in the, unlikely, case where a majority of the Member States would change to an ideology no longer respecting the rule of law and thus would establish a new "common understanding" of the rule of law, among other things, in which case the EU would develop into a potentially very powerful authoritarian organisation. In contradistinction to the UN, for instance, the EU is explicitly founded on liberal democratic values which forms part of the organisation's very essence and raison d'être. The question is how the original conception of the rule of law underlying the current EU can best be conserved. What kind of checkpoints could there reasonably be and at what point should the EU evaporate rather than be a vehicle for a membership embracing an ideology not respecting the rule of law? This is so far a hypothetical question.

A question more close to the current situation is what the new EU Rule of Law Framework contributes in comparison with the already existing mechanism under Article 7 of the TEU. One could say that the Framework provides a ground for earlier intervention by the Commission with respect to situations potentially involving systemic threats to the rule of law. In case of the mechanism in Article 7 there seemingly has to be a clear risk of a serious breach by a Member State of the rule of law, among other values, before the Council may take decisive action, although nothing would seem to prevent the Council from at least discussing the matter with the Member State concerned before this degree of seriousness in the situation has been reached. Under the Framework there only have to be clear indications of a systemic threat to the rule of law. What the difference between "clear risk of a serious breach" and "clear indications of a systemic threat" amounts to in practice may be difficult to estimate. Already when the Framework is being triggered the situation with respect to the rule of law may have become quite serious although the ambition presumably is to intervene at as early a stage as possible in a situation where a systemic threat to the rule of law is developing.

The Framework also provides the Commission with a procedure and a practical manual for the handling of systemic threats which perhaps will make it easier to handle such situations and dialogues with the Member State concerned as well as make it easier to be consistent when later similar situations arise. Having a procedure and a manual to follow will probably also facilitate the construction of a bank of knowledge and experience to make use of in future cases.

The naming and shaming involved in the procedure under the Framework, first milder and then a bit harsher may play a constructive and perhaps compelling role in order to make the Member State change its behaviour. However, the Member State may not at all be ashamed of its systemic demolition of the rule of law, quite the contrary, in which case the naming and presumed shaming of the State is not likely to affect its behaviour.

The Framework perhaps gives the Commission an opportunity to investigate the situation more closely and at an earlier stage than it could or used to do before, although as is pointed out in the Framework no new competences are taken on by the Commission through the Framework. The work done by the Commission under the Framework also lays the ground for a potential procedure under Article 7 in the TEU should the Member State in the end choose not implement the recommendations potentially issued by the Commission. If the procedure reaches the Council under Article 7 much of the preparatory work would seem to already having been done during the Framework procedure for which reason the procedure before the Council should be able to go faster than if the investigative preparatory work would have to begin with the Council.

The work done by the Commission may also provide the EU with a means of solving the problem before the political deadlock has become too entrenched. Less political prestige may perhaps be involved in the lower level dialogue under the Framework procedure than in a procedure under Article 7 in the Council which will also necessarily involve the European Parliament. At the higher political level compromises and solutions may perhaps be harder to reach.

The procedure under the Framework also shows that the Commission and the EU is keeping the situation in the Member State concerned under watch which may both work as a means of pressure on the Member State and as a means of directly or indirectly supporting oppositional movements within the State both political and professional. This may help the judiciary retain its rule of law ideals and it may also help the opposition survive and retain its force during what may in the end turn out to have been a temporary rule of law crisis. The contacts between the Commission and different professional judicial networks will also provide the Commission with valuable information about the state of the rule of law in the country concerned. The fact that the Commission keeps the situation under watch also shows that the Commission and the EU is taking the issue of the rule of law seriously and may perhaps convey the slightly delusive but for our purposes benign impression that the Commission, and the EU, has greater powers than it actually does to take action in cases of serious threats to the rule of law. There is also the implicit threat of eventually bringing the matter before the Council, to the extent this threat is felt as such by the Member State concerned.

With its multitude of different small procedural steps the procedure under the Framework may in reality be more promising than the procedure under Article 7 which would seem to include fewer openings for negotiation and persuasion along the way even under the so called preventive limb of the Article 7 mechanism.

Finally, the Framework would seem to work as a means of pressure on the Council to take the rule of law issue seriously not least if the matter would come before the Council at a later and more ominous stage in the development. It largely remains to be seen whether the Council will rise to the challenge.

References

Aust A (2013) Modern treaty law and practice. Cambridge University Press, Cambridge

Closa C, Kochenov D (2016) Reinforcement of the rule of law oversight in the European Union: key options. In: Schroeder W (ed) Strengthening the rule of law in Europe: from a common concept to mechanisms of implementation. Hart, Oxford, pp 173–196

Crabit E, Bel N (2016) The EU rule of law framework. In: Schroeder W (ed) Strengthening the rule of law in Europe: from a common concept to mechanisms of implementation. Hart, Oxford, pp 197–206

Graver HP (2015a) Judges against justice: on judges when the rule of law is under attack. Springer, Berlin

Graver HP (2015b) Dommernes krig: Den tyske okkupasjonen 1940–1945 og den norske rettsstaten (The war of judges: The German occupation 1940–1945 and Norwegian rule of law, this author's translation). Pax Forlag A/S, Oslo

Halmai G (2018) The possibility and desirability of rule of law conditionality. Hague J Rule Law (published online 11 June 2018)

Kolb R (2016) The law of treaties: an introduction. Edward Elgar, Cheltenham

Konstadinides T (2017) The rule of law in the European Union: the internal dimension. Hart, Oxford, pp 153–159

Raulus H (2016) The growing role of the Union in protection of rule of law. In: Goudappel FANJ, Hirsch Ballin EMH (eds) Democracy and the rule of law in the European Union: essays in honour of Jaap W. de Zwaan. T.M.C. Asser Press/Springer, The Hague/Berlin, pp 25–37

Sadurski W (2018) Polish constitutional tribunal under PiS: from an activist court, to a paralysed tribunal, to a governmental enabler. Hague J Rule Law (published online 13 June 2018)

Scheppele KL (2016) Enforcing the basic principles of EU law through systemic infringement actions. In: Closa C, Kochenov D (eds) Reinforcing rule of law oversight in the European Union. Cambridge University Press, Cambridge, pp 105–132

Special Issue on the Crisis of Constitutional Democracy in Central and Eastern Europe. Hague J Rule Law 10(1):1–217 (2018)

Tams CJ, Tzanakopoulos A, Zimmerman A (eds); Richford AE (ass ed) (2014) Research handbook on the law of treaties

The Economist (2017a) Trumping the law: conservative lawyers are among the president's biggest enablers. They will come to regret it. 25 November 2017, p 50

The Economist (2017b) Champions chained: a crackdown on independent lawyers is a setback for the rule of law in China. 17 June 2017, p 14

Upholding the rule of law for the future of Europe

Emmanuel Crabit

The rule of law is not a new principle in the EU legal order. During the last decades it has been firmly established in the case law of the Court of Justice of the European Union[1] and has been reaffirmed in Article 2 of the Treaty on European Union (TEU) which explicitly refers to the rule of law as one of the common values on which the EU is founded.

Despite being a deeply rooted principle, upholding the rule of law has never been so high on the EU agenda as it is today. Why has this value become so important and a key component of the broader debate about the future of Europe?

1 The rule of law cannot be taken for granted

The first reason explaining why the rule of law is so high on the EU agenda is that during the last years we have been facing in Europe a number of serious challenges relating to the rule of law. Even if it is one of the common values on which the EU is founded, the respect for the rule of law cannot be taken for granted. This is a serious issue for the EU because respect for the rule of law is a prerequisite for the protection of all the values listed in Article 2 TEU, including democracy and fundamental rights.

This article presents the personal views of the author and does not necessarily reflect the official position of the Commission. This article was finalised in October 2017 and contains only few factual updated information.

[1] In particular in the case 294/83, *Les Verts" v European Parliament*, [1986] ECR 01339, the Court of Justice stated that the EU is "*based on the rule of law inasmuch as neither its Member States nor its institutions can avoid a review of the question whether the measures adopted by them are in conformity with the basic Constitutional Charter, the Treaty*" (paragraph 23).

E. Crabit (✉)
European Commission, Brussels, Belgium
e-mail: Emmanuel.crabit@ec.europa.eu

W. Heusel, J.-P. Rageade (eds.), *The Authority of EU Law*,
https://doi.org/10.1007/978-3-662-58841-3_20

As explained in the Communication of the European Commission "*A new EU Framework to strengthen the Rule of Law*",[2] both the Court of Justice and the European Court of Human Rights confirmed that the rule of law principle is not a purely formal and procedural requirement. It is the vehicle for ensuring compliance with and respect for democracy and human rights. The rule of law is therefore a constitutional principle with both formal and substantive components. This means that respect for the rule of law is intrinsically linked to respect for democracy and for fundamental rights: there can be no democracy and respect for fundamental rights without respect for the rule of law and vice versa.

The experiences in the early 2010s have shown that the existing instruments at EU level were not always adequate for a swift and effective reaction against threats to the rule of law. In particular, it is important for the EU to have tools to address systemic threats to the rule of law in a Member State which cannot be addressed through infringement proceedings because they fall outside the scope of EU law, and which cannot be addressed by the mechanisms of Article 7 TEU either, because they remain below the high thresholds established in that Article.

For this reason, in 2014, the Commission established its Rule of Law Framework[3] in order to be better equipped to address emerging rule of law deficiencies in Member States.

The objective of the Framework is to allow the Commission to enter into a dialogue with the Member State concerned to prevent the escalation of systemic threats to the rule of law. In a situation where these threats cannot be effectively addressed by the safeguards and mechanisms which exist at national level to protect the rule of law ('the national rule of law safeguards'), there is reason for the EU to step in.

In January 2016, the Commission decided to apply the Framework for the first time due to the situation of the rule of law in Poland. In the case of Poland, the Commission adopted a Rule of Law Opinion, followed by three Rule of Law Recommendations.[4] The first two Recommendations focused on the situation of the Polish Constitutional Tribunal and the third Recommendation, adopted on 26 July 2017, in addition to the situation of the Constitutional Tribunal, also addressed other concerns raised by new justice reforms. In this third Recommendation, the Commission considered that four new laws adopted by the Polish Parliament would have a very significant negative impact on the independence of the Polish judiciary

---

[2] Communication from the Commission to the European Parliament and the Council "*A new EU Framework to strengthen the Rule of Law*" ('the Communication'), COM(2014) 158 final/2 and COM(2014) 158 final annexes 1 and 2.

[3] See previous footnote. On the establishment of the Rule of Law Framework, see: "*The EU Rule of Law Framework*", Crabit and Bel (2016).

[4] Commission Recommendation (EU) 2016/1374 of 27 July 2016 regarding the rule of law in Poland; OJ L 217, 12.8.2016, p. 53; see also Commission press release IP/16/2643; Commission Recommendation (EU) 2017/146 of 21 December 2016 regarding the rule of law in Poland complementary to Recommendation (EU) 2017/146, OJ L 22, 27.1.2017, p. 65; see also Commission press release IP/16/4476; Commission Recommendation (EU) 2017/1520 of 26 July 2017 regarding the rule of law in Poland complementary to Recommendation (EU) 2016/1374 and (EU) 2017/146; OJ L 228, 2.9.2017, p. 19; see also Commission press release IP/17/2161.

and would increase the systemic threat to the rule of law. In these three Recommendations, the Commission set out its serious concerns and recommended how these concerns should be addressed.

Unfortunately, despite these Recommendations, the concerns had not been resolved. On 20 December 2017, the Commission observed that within a period of 2 years more than 13 consecutive laws had been adopted affecting the entire structure of the justice system in Poland: the Constitutional Tribunal, the Supreme Court, the ordinary courts, the national Council for the Judiciary, the prosecution service and the National School of Judiciary. The common pattern of all these legislative changes is that the executive or legislative powers have been systematically enabled to interfere significantly with the composition, the powers, the administration and the functioning of these authorities and bodies. The legislative changes and their combined effect put at serious risk the independence of the judiciary and the separation of powers in Poland, two key components of the rule of law. The Commission also observed that such intense legislative activity had been conducted without proper consultation of all the stakeholders concerned, without a spirit of loyal cooperation required between State authorities and without consideration for the opinions from a wide range of European and international organisations.

For this reason, the Commission adopted on the same day three measures:

First, the Commission issued a fourth Rule of Law Recommendation,[5] setting out clearly a list of steps that the Polish authorities should take to remedy the current situation in the coming 3 months.

Second, the Commission decided to invoke the procedure provided for by Article 7(1) of the Treaty on European Union and to submit a Reasoned Proposal for a Decision of the Council on the determination of a clear risk of a serious breach of the rule of law by the Republic of Poland.[6] However, the Commission indicated that, should the Polish authorities implement the recommended actions in the coming 3 months, it stands ready, in consultation with the European Parliament and the Council, to reconsider its Reasoned Proposal.

Third, the Commission decided to take the next step in its infringement procedure against Poland for breaches of EU law by the Law on the Ordinary Courts Organisation, referring Poland to the Court of Justice (see below).[7]

---

[5] Commission Recommendation (EU) 2018/103 of 20 December 2017 regarding the rule of law in Poland complementary to Recommendations (EU) 2016/1374, (EU) 2017/146 and (EU) 2017/1520; OJ L 17, 23.1.2018, pp. 50–64; see also Commission press release IP/17/5367.

[6] Reasoned Proposal in accordance with Article 7(1) of the Treaty on European Union regarding the rule of law in Poland—Proposal for a Council Decision on the determination of a clear risk of a serious breach by the Republic of Poland of the rule of law; COM/2017/0835 final - 2017/0360 (NLE); see also Commission press release IP/17/5367.

[7] Commission press release IP/17/5367.

2 The rule of law is essential for the application of EU law

The second reason explaining the importance of the rule of law is the fact that the rule of law is a prerequisite for the effective application of EU law. EU law cannot be applied effectively without independent national justice systems. Debates on the rule of law that have been held in recent years do not only result from concrete developments in some Member States but also from the fact that the EU is paying more attention to the enforcement of EU law on the ground and the capacity of the justice systems in Member States to effectively do it. After having been seen for decades as a producer of norms, the EU is now developing a policy on the effective enforcement of EU law.

In December 2016, in its Communication on the application of EU law,[8] the Commission explained that it will encourage and help Member States to improve their capacity to enforce EU law and provide remedies in order to ensure that the end-users of EU law—whether private individuals or businesses—can fully enjoy their rights. The Commission in particular will also continue to help Member States to improve the effectiveness of their national justice systems through the European Semester (see below).

The Commission also underlined that it will give high priority to infringements that affect the capacity of national judicial systems to contribute to the effective enforcement of EU law. It will pursue cases in which national law prevents judicial systems from ensuring that EU law is applied effectively in accordance with the requirements of the rule of law and Article 47 of the Charter on Fundamental Rights of the EU.

In line with this strategic approach, in July 2017, the Commission decided to initiate an infringement procedure against Poland regarding the law of 12 July 2017 related to the Ordinary Courts Organisation.[9] According to the Commission, i.a. the discretionary power given to the Minister of Justice to prolong active mandates of judges who have reached the new lowered retirement age, as well as the discretionary power to dismiss and appoint court presidents, undermines the independence of Polish courts. On 20 December 2017, the Commission decided to refer the Polish Government to the European Court of Justice for breach of EU law as regards the discretionary power to prolong the mandate of judges which have reached retirement age.[10]

The basis of the Commission's reasoning is that national courts act as "EU courts" whenever they apply EU law, and therefore they must comply with the

---

[8] Communication from the Commission—EU law: Better results through better application; 13 December 2016; OJ C 18, 19.1.2017, pp. 10–20.

[9] Commission press release of 26 July 2017, IP/17/2161. Other grounds for the infringement are Article 157 TFEU and Directive 2006/54 on gender equality in employment since the law introduces a different retirement age for female judges (60 years) and male judges (65 years).

[10] Commission press release IP/17/5367.

requirement of the independence of the judiciary as a matter of EU law. Indeed, according to Article 47 of the Charter of Fundamental Rights, everyone whose rights and freedoms guaranteed by EU law are violated has the right to an effective remedy before a tribunal. Article 19(1) TEU also requires that Member States shall provide remedies sufficient to ensure effective legal protection in the fields covered by EU law.

In its *Wilson* case (C-506/04), the Court of Justice already highlighted that independence is a key criterion which must be satisfied by the body concerned in order to be considered as a "tribunal" and to ensure an effective judicial protection. Consequently, national measures affecting judicial independence to an extent that national courts can no longer be considered independent would prevent these courts from providing an effective remedy within the meaning of Article 47 of the Charter and 19(1) TEU.

This reasoning was developed by the Court of Justice in its recent judgment *Associação Sindical dos Juízes Portugueses*[11] interpreting Article 19(1) TEU which underlines that judicial independence is essential for ensuring the effective judicial protection.

The preliminary question from the Portuguese court was whether the principle of judicial independence precludes general salary-reduction measures from being applied to members of a Member State's judiciary, when such measures are linked to requirements to eliminate an excessive budget deficit and to an EU financial assistance programme.

In its ruling, the Court of Justice underlined that the very existence of an effective judicial review designed to ensure compliance with EU law is part of the essence of the rule of law. Member States must establish a system of legal remedies ensuring effective judicial review since national courts, in collaboration with the Court of Justice, fulfil the duty to jointly ensure that in the interpretation and application of the Treaties the law is observed. Every Member State must ensure that, in the fields covered by that law, 'courts or tribunals' meet the requirements of effective judicial protection. In order for that protection to be ensured, maintaining such a court or tribunal's independence is essential. The guarantee of independence, which is inherent in the task of adjudication, is required at the level of Member States as regards national courts.

The Court of Justice, referring to its *Wilson* case, underlines that the concept of independence presupposes, in particular, that the body concerned exercises its judicial functions wholly autonomously, without being subject to any hierarchical constraint or subordinated to any other body and without taking orders or instructions from any source whatsoever, and that it is thus protected against external interventions or pressure liable to impair the independent judgment of its members and to influence their decisions.

In the concrete case at stake, the Court of Justice concluded that the salary-reduction measures in question cannot be considered to impair the independence of

[11] Case C-64/16, Associação Sindical dos Juízes Portugueses v Tribunal de Contas, 27 February 2018.

the members of the *Tribunal de Contas*. Those measures were applied not only to the members of the *Tribunal de Contas*, but, more widely, to various public office holders and employees performing duties in the public sector, including the representatives of the legislature, the executive and the judiciary. They are, therefore, in the nature of general measures seeking a contribution from all members of the national public administration to the austerity effort dictated by the mandatory requirements for reducing the Portuguese State's excessive budget deficit. In addition, the measures in question were temporary in nature, since they entered into force on 1 October 2014 and were definitively repealed on 1 October 2016.

Judicial independence is not only important for the effective judicial protection but also for the application of EU instruments based on mutual recognition and, more generally, for the mutual trust between Member States. As underlined by the Court of Justice, "mutual trust between the Member States and, in particular, their courts and tribunals is based on the fundamental premiss that Member States share a set of common values on which the European Union is founded, as stated in Article 2 TEU".[12]

This explains why the EU judicial networks have taken public position on the situation in Poland. In particular, the Network of Presidents of the Supreme Courts of the EU and the European Network of the Councils for the Judiciary have clearly stated their concerns about the situation in Poland and its negative impact for the application of EU law and the mutual trust. Such importance of judicial independence for mutual trust has been recently illustrated by the request of the Irish High Court for a preliminary ruling in interpretation regarding the suspension of a European Arrest Warrant issued by a Polish judicial authority.[13]

Finally, judicial independence is a prerequisite for the smooth functioning of the preliminary reference procedures, which are the DNA of the EU legal order and on which relies the effective application of EU law. As recalled by the Court of Justice in its judgment *Associação Sindical dos Juízes Portugueses,* judicial independence is essential to the proper working of the judicial cooperation system embodied by the preliminary ruling mechanism under Article 267 TFEU since that mechanism may be activated only by independent courts.[14]

3 The rule of law is crucial for economic growth

The third reason explaining why the rule of law is so high on the EU agenda is its importance for the economy: respect for the rule of law is also crucial for building a business and investment-friendly environment in Europe. Where effective judicial systems guarantee the enforcement of rights, creditors are more likely to lend,

[12] Case C-64/16, paragraph 30.

[13] Judgment of 25 July 2018, Case C-216/18 PPU *Minister for Justice and Equality v LM* (Deficiencies in the system of justice), ECLI:EU:C:2018:586.

[14] Case C-64/16, paragraph 43.

businesses are dissuaded from opportunistic behaviour, transaction costs are reduced and innovative businesses are more likely to invest. The beneficial impact of well-functioning national justice systems for the economy is underlined in a wide range of literature and research, including from the International Monetary Fund, the European Central Bank, the OECD, the World Economic Forum and the World Bank.

For this reason, since 2013, improving the independence, quality and efficiency of national justice systems is a well-established priority of the European Semester, the EU's annual cycle of economic policy coordination. To achieve this priority, the Commission is monitoring justice reforms through two tools: the EU Justice Scoreboard and the country-specific assessments.

The EU Justice Scoreboard provides every year a comparative overview of the *independence*, *quality* and *efficiency* of national justice systems, which are the three key components of an *'effective justice system'*.[15] It aims at helping Member States to improve the effectiveness of their national justice systems by making easier to identify shortcomings and best practices and to keep track of challenges and progress. The Scoreboard uses various sources of information. As regards judicial independence, most of the information is collected through the judiciary itself, instead of the governments, in particular through the European Network of Councils for the Judiciary, the Network of the Presidents of the Supreme Courts of the EU and the Association of the Councils of State and Supreme Administrative Jurisdictions of the EU.

The country specific assessment aims at providing a deeper assessment which takes account of the context and characteristics of the legal systems of the Member States concerned. Country-specific assessments are carried out through a bilateral dialogue with the national authorities and stakeholders concerned and are presented every year in February in the European Semester country reports.[16]

The combined outcome of these two tools may lead to the Commission proposing to the Council to adopt country-specific recommendations on improving the effectiveness of national justice systems. In the 2017 European Semester, based on a proposal from the Commission, the Council addressed country-specific recommendations to five Member States relating to their justice system.[17] Also, an explicit

[15] The EU Justice Scoreboards are available at: https://ec.europa.eu/info/strategy/justice-and-fundamental-rights/effective-justice/eu-justice-scoreboard_en.

[16] Available at: https://ec.europa.eu/info/publications/2018-european-semester-country-reports_en.

[17] The five Member States were: Croatia, Italy, Cyprus, Portugal and Slovakia. See Council Recommendation of 11 July 2017 on the 2017 National Reform Programme of Croatia and delivering a Council opinion on the 2017 Convergence Programme of Croatia (2017/C 261/08); Council Recommendation of 11 July 2017 on the 2017 National Reform Programme of Italy and delivering a Council opinion on the 2017 Stability Programme of Italy, (2017/C 261/11); Council Recommendation of 11 July 2017 on the 2017 National Reform Programme of Cyprus and delivering a Council opinion on the 2017 Stability Programme of Cyprus, (2017/C 261/12); Council Recommendation of 11 July 2017 on the 2017 National Reform Programme of Portugal and delivering a Council opinion on the 2017 Stability Programme of Portugal, (2017/C 61/21); Council Recommendation of 11 July 2017 on the 2017 National Reform Programme of Slovakia and delivering a Council opinion on the 2017 Stability Programme of Slovakia, (2017/C 261/24).

reference to the rule of law was made in the recital of the country-specific recommendations concerning Poland. In addition to those Member States subject to country-specific recommendations, a further ten Member States are facing specific challenges regarding their justice system and are being monitored by the Commission through the European Semester as reflected in the country reports.[18]

4 The rule of law is a key component of the debate on the future of Europe

For all these reasons, upholding the common values of the EU, including the rule of law, has become a key component of the broader debate about the future of Europe.

The importance of the common values has been particularly highlighted in the White Paper on the future of the EU issued by the Commission in March 2017.[19] Whatever the scenarios, the future of Europe relies on our common values. As President Juncker said in his 2017 State of the Union address, "*the rule of law is not optional in the European Union. It is a must*".[20]

The importance of the common values is also underlined in several reflection papers issued to feed the debate on the future of Europe. In particular, the reflection paper on the future of EU finances[21] refers to the debate on the link between the disbursement of EU budget funds and the state of the rule of law in a Member State. It also underlines that there is a clear relationship between respect for the rule of law and an efficient implementation of private and public investments supported by the EU budget.[22]

In its contribution to the Informal Leaders' meeting on 23 February 2018,[23] the Commission underlined that respect for fundamental values, in particular the rule of

---

[18] The ten Member States were Belgium, Bulgaria, Ireland, Spain, Latvia, Hungary, Malta, Poland, Romania and Slovenia. These challenges have been reflected in the recitals of the country-specific recommendations and the country reports relating to these Member States. The most recent 2018 country reports are available at: https://ec.europa.eu/info/publications/2018-european-semester-country-reports_en.

[19] Available at: https://ec.europa.eu/commission/white-paper-future-europe-reflections-and-scenarios-eu27_en.

[20] President Jean-Claude Juncker's State of the Union Address 2017 before the European Parliament; 13 September 2017; available at: https://ec.europa.eu/commission/state-union-2017_en.

[21] COM(2017) 358 of 28 June 2017.

[22] The reflection paper on the future of the European Monetary Union (COM(2017) 291 of 31 May 2017) also mentions the importance of strengthening the European Semester to coordinate economic policy and refers in this context to the judicial systems.

[23] A new, modern Multiannual Financial Framework for a European Union that delivers efficiently on its priorities post-2020—The European Commission's contribution to the Informal Leaders' meeting on 23 February 2018; Communication from the Commission to the European Parliament, to the European Council and the Council of 14.2.2018, COM(2018) 98 final.

law, is an essential precondition for sound financial management of EU funding. There is a clear relationship between respect for the rule of law and an efficient implementation of the Union budget in accordance with the principles of sound financial management. The contribution envisages as an option the strengthening of the link between EU funding and the respect for the EU's fundamental values.

The reflection on the link between the disbursement of EU funds and respect for the rule of law in Member States led the Commission to present on 2 May 2018 a proposal for a Regulation of the European Parliament and of the Council on the protection of the Union's budget in case of generalised deficiencies as regards the rule of law in the Member States.[24] The proposed Regulation aims at strengthening the protection of the EU budget from financial risks linked to generalised deficiencies as regards the rule of law in the Member States. The proposed Regulation provides that appropriate measures shall be taken where generalised deficiencies as regards the rule of law in a Member State affect, or risk affecting, the principles of sound financial management or the protection of the financial interests of the Union. It could be invoked when a generalised deficiency as regards the rule of law in a Member State endangers, for example, the effective judicial review by independent courts, the proper functioning of investigation and public prosecution of fraud or corruption relating to the Union budget or the proper functioning of the authorities implementing the Union budget.

Finally, the importance the Commission attaches to the respect for the rule of law for the future of Europe is confirmed by the 2017 State of the Union address, in which President Juncker announced a new initiative to strengthen the enforcement of the Rule of Law in the EU.

All these developments, and the increased interest from EU institutions, Member States and stakeholders, show that upholding the rule of law is more than ever a matter of common interest for the EU. It is not only a fundamental legal requirement; it is not just a legal matter for lawyers and academics: it is also a policy driver for the future of the EU. From that perspective, it is reassuring to see all EU institutions reflecting on this topic. It is necessary to work towards a common understanding on how best to promote our common values, at national and at European level. The European Parliament has already proposed a new monitoring mechanism.[25] The Council is also holding an annual rule of law dialogue aiming at reinforcing a rule of law culture in Europe. The jubilee congress organised by ERA in October 2017 was yet another confirmation of this positive energy for developing the EU rule of law policy.

---

[24] Proposal for a Regulation of the European Parliament and of the Council on the protection of the Union's budget in case of generalised deficiencies as regards the rule of law in the Member States, COM(2018) 324 final; Commission press release IP/18/3570 and factsheet 'Sound financial management and the rule of law'.

[25] European Parliament resolution of 25 October 2016 with recommendations to the Commission on the establishment of an EU mechanism on democracy, the rule of law and fundamental rights (2015/2254(INL).

Reference

Crabit E, Bel N (2016) The EU rule of law framework. In: Schroeder W (ed) Strengthening the rule of law in Europe. Hart

Emmanuel Crabit PhD, is the Director of the Directorate "Fundamental rights and rule of law" in the Directorate-General for Justice and Consumers of the European Commission.

Développements récents du cadre juridique de l'Union européenne pour faire face aux menaces pour les valeurs démocratiques dans les États membres

Maria José Rangel de Mesquita

1 Remarques introductives

La prévision par les traités des principes et – depuis le Traité de Lisbonne – valeurs de l'Union européenne (article 2 du Traité sur l'Union européenne (ci-après « TUE »)), y compris l'État de droit – dont le respect est aussi, selon l'article 48 du TUE, condition *sine qua non* de l'adhésion de nouveaux États membres –, a été accompagnée par la prévision d'une *procédure spéciale de nature politique* visant à déclarer et sanctionner (et aussi, après le Traité de Nice, prévenir le risque de) leur violation – *la procédure en manquement qualifié des valeurs de l'Union.* Celle-ci existe à côté des deux autres procédures en manquement des États membres prévues aux articles 126 (procédure spéciale en manquement dans le domaine de l'Union économique) et 226-228 (procédure en manquement des obligations spécifiques découlant du droit de l'Union) du Traité sur le Fonctionnement de l'Union européenne (ci-après « TFUE »). Néanmoins, la procédure en manquement des valeurs de l'Union européenne n'avait jamais été initiée jusqu'à l'année 2017 – soit par absence d'objet (malgré le cas autrichien *infra* mentionné) et absence de volonté politique, soit en raison de sa complexité procédurale, notamment l'exigeante majorité ou unanimité requises dans les différentes phases de la procédure.

En effet, la question de la violation des valeurs fondamentales de l'Union qui se pose aujourd'hui n'est pas nouvelle et mérite un bref retour dans le passé. On rap-

---

Professeur Associé à la Faculté de Droit de l'Université de Lisbonne ; Juge au Tribunal Constitutionnel du Portugal. – Ce texte reprend l'essentiel de notre intervention au Congrès des 25 ans de l'ERA, les 19-20 Octobre 2017. Il prend également en considération les développements ultérieurs les plus importants qui ont eu lieu jusqu'en avril 2018.

M. J. Rangel de Mesquita (✉)
Faculty of Law, University of Lisbon, Lisbon, Portugal

ERA Board of Trustees, Trier, Germany
e-mail: mjrangeldemesquita@fd.ulisboa.pt

W. Heusel, J.-P. Rageade (eds.), *The Authority of EU Law*,
https://doi.org/10.1007/978-3-662-58841-3_21

pellera ainsi le cas autrichien (2000) dans lequel, malgré la crainte d'une violation de certaines valeurs de l'Union, la procédure de l'article 7 du TUE (dans sa version en vigueur à l'époque) n'avait pas été formellement déclenchée. La crise politique avait alors abouti – au-delà des mesures de droit international adoptées par les États membres – au *Rapport des trois sages* et à la modification du même article 7 par le Traité de Nice afin d'ajouter à la procédure en manquement en cause une phase préventive – dont le fonctionnement a été plus tard modifié par le Traité de Lisbonne en éliminant la possibilité d'intervention d'experts extérieurs à l'Union européenne. L'évolution récente en matière de manquement par les États membres à des valeurs fondamentales de l'Union ne laisse donc pas de convoquer les origines de la procédure de l'article 7 TUE aussi bien que le cas autrichien[1].

Ignorée depuis son inscription dans le droit primaire – même dans le contexte du cas autrichien susmentionné –, la procédure en manquement à des valeurs fondamentales de l'Union a connu un nouvel élan depuis 2013.

La caractéristique alors unique de cette procédure – proche d'ailleurs de procédures d'application de sanctions en cas de manquement prévues au sein des organisations internationales classiques (telles que l'ONU ou le Conseil de l'Europe[2]) – était sa nature plutôt politique, laquelle écartait en partie aussi bien la compétence de la Cour de Justice de l'Union européenne (ci-après « CJUE »), que le rôle prédominant de la Commission en tant que gardienne des traités et du Parlement européen (ci-après « PE ») en tant que représentant de la légitimité démocratique (démocratie représentative).

L'évolution de la réalité et du système politiques dans quelques États membres, où la question de la violation des valeurs de l'Union est devenue un problème européen – puisqu'il s'agit non seulement de violation des valeurs de l'Union, mais aussi des valeurs du cercle plus vaste du Conseil de l'Europe dont la *rule of law* est également une valeur fondamentale[3,4] – a provoqué une *évolution rapide du cadre juridique européen* à côté ou même au-delà des traités (et, à la rigueur, dans cette mesure, au moins dans une phase initiale, même des États membres), en ce qui concerne la garantie du respect de ces valeurs communes européennes.

Cette évolution, initiée par la Commission (2013-2014) – bien qu'elle fut à l'initiative du Conseil et du PE – et suivie peu après par le Conseil lui-même (surtout en 2014) et le Parlement européen (2014), a abouti à un *cadre juridique*

---

[1] Pour une analyse détaillée du cas autrichien et de ses rapports avec les modifications à la procédure prévue à l'article 7 TUE (phase préventive) introduites par le Traité de Nice, voir Frank SCHORKOPF, *Die Maßnahmen der XIV EU-Mitgliedstaaten gegen Österreich. Möglichkeiten und Grenzen einer "streitbaren Demokratie" auf europäischer Ebene*, Berlin, Springer, 2001.

[2] Voir article 5 (suspension de l'exercice des droits et privilèges inhérents à la qualité de Membre) et article 6 (exclusion de l'Organisation) de la Charte des Nations Unies ; article 8 du Statut du Conseil de l'Europe (suspension du droit de représentation, retrait et exclusion).

[3] Voir articles 3 et 1, a. du Statut du Conseil de l'Europe.

[4] Voir le document *Rule of Law Checklist* adopté par la Commission de Venise dans sa 106ème Session Plénière (11-12/3/2016) et, avant, le *Report on the Rule of Law* (CDL-AL(2011)003rev, adopté aussi par la Commission de Venise dans sa 86ème Session Plénière. Voir aussi la *Résolution* 2187(2017) *de l'Assemblée Parlementaire du Conseil de l'Europe*, adopté le 11 octobre 2017 (33e séance) – *Liste des critères de l'État de droit de la Commission de Venise.*

complexe composé de *textes et instruments multiples*. Ce corpus de règles, dont l'efficacité en soi est bien douteuse, et qui d'ailleurs fonctionne en amont de la procédure en manquement qualifié des valeurs de l'Union prévue à l'article 7, a eu pour effet de déplacer le centre de gravité de la question de la violation des valeurs de l'Union du niveau du droit originaire au niveau du *soft law,* avec toutes les conséquences juridiques qui en découlent.

Il convient donc se demander si, dans une certaine mesure, nous ne sommes pas face à un retour dans le passé (2000) dans lequel on éviterait – au moins au départ – d'appliquer (ou d'essayer d'appliquer) la procédure de l'article 7 en créant d'autres moyens alternatifs allant au-delà des dispositions du droit primaire et de la volonté originaire des *maîtres des traités.*

De plus, malgré les efforts pour laisser la question de la violation des valeurs de l'Union à l'abri d'un contrôle étendu par la CJUE, le récent arrêt de la Cour de Justice dans le cadre d'un renvoi préjudiciel du *Irish High Court* en matière de mandat d'arrêt européen porte directement sur la question de la violation du *rule of law* par la Pologne en tant qu'État membre de l'Union européenne et les développements du cadre juridique de l'Union à cet égard y compris la mise en œuvre de l'article 7 TUE[5].

2 Evolutions du cadre juridique de l'Union pour faire face aux menaces pour les valeurs de l'Union européenne

2.1 Les initiatives de la Commission, du Conseil et du Parlement européen

Les développements mentionnés ci-dessous du cadre juridique européen pour faire aux menaces pour les valeurs de l'Union européenne, y compris l'État de droit (*rule of law*), se caractérisent par une *multiplicité d'acteurs et d'instruments* et, désormais, par une articulation nébuleuse entre eux au détriment de la *cohérence* et même de l'efficacité.

On peut présenter ainsi ces développements en fonction des acteurs (institutionnels) de l'Union impliqués et leurs initiatives respectives.

Nombreux ont été les instruments juridiques adoptés à l'*initiative de la **Commission***, bien qu'à la suite de demandes du Conseil et du PE : (i) la *Communication de la Commission au Conseil et au PE sur l'article 7 du TUE – Respect et promotion des valeurs sur lesquelles l'Union est fondée* du 15 octobre 2003[6] et (ii) la *Communication de la Commission au PE et au Conseil – Un nouveau*

[5] *Infra,* 3.

[6] COM (2003) 606 final, du 15 octobre 2003.

cadre de l'Union pour renforcer l'État de droit, du 11 mars 2014 (ci-après « nouveau cadre »)[7].

La Commission a ensuite appliqué le nouveau cadre au cas de la Pologne, en rendant des avis et des recommandations qui y sont prévus, notamment des *recommandations concernant l'État de droit*, dont les dernières ont été adoptées le 26 juillet et le 20 décembre 2017[8]. Dans cette dernière (quatrième) recommandation complémentaire sur l'État de droit, la Commission a énuméré clairement les mesures que les autorités polonaises pouvaient prendre pour remédier à la situation actuelle et desquelles dépendrait la révision de la proposition motivée de décision du Conseil dont l'adoption avait été approuvée le même jour.

En effet, le 20 décembre 2017, en dépit des efforts déployés par la Commission pour engager un dialogue constructif avec la Pologne dans le contexte du nouveau cadre pour l'État de droit, la Commission a conclu à l'existence d'un risque clair de violation grave de l'État de droit dans cet État membre, en utilisant son pouvoir d'initiative prévu à l'article 7, paragraphe 1, du TUE et ainsi en proposant au Conseil d'adopter une décision en application de cet article.

Etant donné le comportement de l'État envisagé à la suite des recommandations successives sur l'État de droit dans le contexte du nouveau cadre, la Commission, qui avait d'abord envisagé (en juillet 2017) la possibilité de déclencher la procédure en manquement qualifié de l'article 7 à l'encontre de la Pologne, a finalement adopté la *Proposition motivée conformément à l'article 7, paragraphe 1, du TUE concernant l'État de droit en Pologne – Proposition de Décision du Conseil relative à la constatation d'un risque clair de violation grave, par la République de Pologne, de l'État de droit*[9]. Dans cette proposition, la Commission exprime ses inquiétudes concernant notamment l'absence de contrôle indépendant et légitime de la constitutionnalité des lois et l'indépendance du pouvoir judiciaire.

En outre, parallèlement à l'application du nouveau cadre précédant l'application de l'article 7, la Commission a également engagé en juillet 2017 une procédure d'infraction contre la Pologne, sur le fondement de l'article 226 du TFUE, au sujet des mesures empiétant sur le pouvoir judiciaire. Elle a ainsi adressé à cet État membre une *lettre de mise en demeure*, à la suite de la publication de la loi sur

[7] COM (2014) 158 final, du 11 mars 2014.

[8] *Recommandation (UE) 2016/1374 de la Commission du 27 juillet 2016 concernant l'État de droit en Pologne* (JOUE L 217, du 12.8.2016, p. 53, C(2017) 5320 final) ; *Recommandation (UE) 2017/146 de la Commission du 21 décembre* 2016 *concernant l'État de droit en Pologne complétant la Recommandation (UE) 2016/1374* (JOUE L 22 du 27.1.2017, p. 65) ; *Recommandation (UE) 2017/1520 de la Commission du 26 juillet 2017 concernant l'État de droit en Pologne complétant les recommandations (UE) 2016/1374 et (UE) 2017/146* (JOUE L 228 du 2.9.2017, p. 19) ; et, finalement, *Recommandation de la Commission (UE) du 20 décembre 2017 concernant l'État de droit en Pologne, complétant les Recommandations de la Commission (UE) 2016/1374, (UE) 2017/146 et (UE) 2017/1520* (C(2017) 9050 final) – sur celle-ci voir aussi le Communiqué de presse IP/17/5367 du 20 décembre 2017, 2. Recommandation sur l'État de droit et le document Action de la Commission concernant l'État de droit en Pologne ; questions & réponses, du 20 Décembre 2017 (MEMO/17/5368).

[9] COM (2017) 835 final du 20.12.2017 (2017/0360 (APP)). Voir aussi Communiqué de presse IP/17/5367 du 20 décembre 2017, 1. Proposition motivée de décision du Conseil.

l'organisation des juridictions de droit commun au Journal Officiel polonais du 28 juillet. La Commission voit dans cette loi notamment une discrimination fondée sur le sexe en raison de l'introduction d'un âge de départ à la retraite différent pour les femmes juges (60 ans) et les hommes juges (65 ans), distinction que la Commission considère contraire à l'article 157 du TFUE et à la directive 2006/54 sur l'égalité de traitement entre hommes et femmes en matière d'emploi[10] (et aussi une violation des articles 19, paragraphe 1, du TUE et 47 de la Charte). A la suite de la réponse des autorités polonaises le 31 août 2017, la Commission a décidé, le 12 septembre 2017, d'envoyer un *avis motivé* à la Pologne au sujet de la même loi[11]. En définitive, cette initiative, comprise dans les pouvoirs typiques de la Commission de gardienne des traités et de déclenchement de la procédure en manquement de droit commun, vient s'ajouter au dialogue en cours entre la Commission et la Pologne sur l'État de droit dans le contexte de l'application des étapes successives du nouveau cadre. Cette initiative contre la Pologne – utilisant ainsi la procédure toujours prévue dans le cas de manquement aux obligations concrètes découlant du droit de l'Union européenne (articles 226-228 du TFUE) – n'est pas restée sans suite en ce qui concerne la Pologne, notamment dans le cas de la forêt de Białowieza, dans lequel la CJUE a ordonné, le 27 juillet 2017, des mesures provisoires visant à mettre un terme à l'exploitation à grande échelle du bois de la forêt de Białowieza, que le gouvernement polonais n'a pas mises en œuvre, étant donné les craintes que la poursuite de l'abattage des arbres n'entraîne un « préjudice grave et irréparable » à la forêt au moment où la Cour procèderait à l'examen au fond de ladite affaire[12].

Ces initiatives parallèles de la Commission et de la CJUE démontrent ainsi la volonté d'utiliser tous les mécanismes prévus par les traités – soit le TUE soit le TFUE – et aussi leur complémentarité pour, dans les limites du champ d'application de chaque instrument, veiller et faire face aux situations de violation d'obligations spécifiques et concrètes du droit de l'union et aussi de ses valeurs fondamentales.

Des réponses ou réactions parallèles du Conseil et du PE – concernant le cadre juridique de garantie des valeurs fondamentales de l'Union – ont aussi été adoptées.

D'un côté, le **Conseil** a adopté les *Conclusions du Conseil de l'Union européenne et des États membres au sein du Conseil sur la garantie du respect de l'État* de

[10]Voir Communiqué de presse IP/17/2205 du 29 juillet 2017 et aussi Communiqué de presse IP/17/2161 du 26 juillet 2017, n° 2. Procédure d'infraction fondée sur le droit de l'Union européenne.

[11]Communiqué de presse IP/17/3186 du 12 septembre 2017.

[12]Affaire C-441/17, *Commission/Pologne* (Forêt de Białowieza), Ordonnance de la Cour (Grande chambre) du 20 novembre 2017, en particulier n° 80-84 (ECLI:EU:C:2017:877, curia.europa.eu). Les Conclusions de l'Avocat Général Yves Bot ont été présentées le 20 février 2018 (ECLI:EU:C:2018:80), où il propose à la CJUE de statuer que la Pologne a manqué aux obligations qui lui incombent en vertu de plusieurs articles de la Directive 92/43/CEE du Conseil, du 21 mai 1992 (conservation des habitats naturels ainsi que de la faune et de la flore sauvages) et de la Directive 2009/147/CE du PE et du Conseil du 30 novembre 2009 (conservation des oiseaux sauvages) – v. VI, Conclusion, 180, 1).

droit du 16 décembre 2014 – *le « dialogue structuré »*. Ce nouvel instrument, qui est une réponse politique à l'initiative de la Commission, établit un dialogue structuré entre les États membres afin de promouvoir et garantir l'État de droit dans le cadre des traités – lequel aura lieu, chaque année, au sein du Conseil, dans la formation Affaires générales et sera préparé par le COREPER (présidence), permettant au Conseil, s'il l'estime nécessaire, de promouvoir des débats sur des questions thématiques.

Un tel dialogue devra, selon le Conseil, respecter un ensemble de principes établis aux numéros 2 à 5, à savoir : la promotion du dialogue sur la base des principes d'objectivité, de non-discrimination et d'égalité de traitement entre les États membres ; la promotion du dialogue dans le respect du principe de la compétence d'attribution et du respect de l'identité nationale des États membres inhérente à leur structure politique et constitutionnelle respective, y compris au niveau du gouvernement régional et local, et à leurs fonctions essentielles concernant l'État – telles que le maintien de l'ordre public et la sauvegarde de la sécurité nationale – et selon le principe de la coopération loyale ; le développement du dialogue de façon à promouvoir la complémentarité avec d'autres institutions et organisation internationales, ceci dans le but d'éviter des duplications et de prendre en compte les instruments et connaissances spécialisées dans le domaine en cause.

La mise en œuvre du dialogue structuré ainsi établi par les Conclusions du Conseil a eu lieu, successivement, à travers le premier et le deuxième dialogues sur l'État de droit sous les présidences luxembourgeoise et néerlandaise en novembre 2015 et mai 2016 – le deuxième ayant revêtu une nature thématique, sur la liaison entre intégration des migrants et les valeurs fondamentales de l'Union[13]. L'évaluation du dialogue ainsi conçu, sur la base des contributions des États membres à partir d'un questionnaire et l'élaboration d'un résumé sur lesquels les États devaient se prononcer, était prévue en 2016 (et a eu et aura encore lieu, respectivement, en novembre de 2017 et en 2019)[14].

Ce qu'il faut essentiellement retenir de ce dialogue structuré institué par le Conseil est que cette institution ne procède à aucun mode d'articulation avec l'instrument institué par la Commission en 2014 – le nouveau cadre pour l'État de droit.

---

[13] Voir la *Note de la Présidence dirigée au Conseil – L'Etat de droit – Évaluation du mécanisme* (13980/16, de 9 de novembre de 2016 – FREMP 175, JAI 896, COHOM 138 et POLGEN 130).

[14] *Conclusions of the Council of the European Union and the member states meeting within the Council on ensuring respect for the rule of law* – General Affairs Council meeting, Bruxelles, 16 décembre 2016 (voir aussi Press Release of 16/12/2014, PRESSE 652 PR CO 74) ; Note de la présidence au Conseil – L'État de droit – Évaluation du mécanisme (13980/16, du 9 novembre 2016 – FREMP 175, JAI 896, COHOM 138 et POLGEN 130). Ces Conclusions ont pris en compte la Note de la Présidence italienne *Ensuring Respect for the Rule of Law* (16862/14 COR 1, du 16 décembre 2014 – FREMP 225, JAI 1009, COHOM 179 e POLGEN 191). Voir aussi le précédent document *Ensuring respect for the rule of law in the European Union* (15206/14, de 14 de novembre de 2014 – FREMP 198, JAI 846, COHOM 152 et POLGEN 156). L'évaluation, dans le final de 2016, de l'expérience acquise sur la base du dialogue est prévue au n° 7 des Conclusions.

D'un autre côté, le **Parlement Européen** a approuvé plusieurs résolutions à l'intention de la Commission et des État membres.

En ce qui concerne la Commission, le PE a approuvé, parmi d'autres, la *Résolution du PE du 25 octobre 2016* contenant des *recommandations à la Commission sur la création d'un mécanisme de l'Union pour la démocratie, l'État de droit et les droits fondamentaux*[15]. Cette résolution a été précédée d'un Rapport du 10 octobre 2016[16] et a invité la Commission à présenter une proposition avant septembre 2017[17].

Concernant des États membres, le PE a approuvé plusieurs résolutions concernant la situation en Hongrie et en Pologne[18].

Dans le cas de la *Hongrie*, le PE a adopté les résolutions du 10 juin 2015, 16 décembre 2015 et 17 mai 2017, dans lesquelles il a estimé que « *la situation actuelle en Hongrie représente un risque clair de violation grave des valeurs visées à l'article 2 du TUE et justifie le lancement de la procédure prévue à l'article 7, paragraphe 1, du TUE* ». Il a chargé sa Commission des libertés civiles, de la justice et des affaires intérieures d'engager la procédure et d'élaborer un rapport spécifique en vue de mettre aux voix en plénière une proposition motivée invitant le Conseil à agir conformément à l'article 7, paragraphe, 1, du TUE[19].

Concernant la situation en *Pologne*, le PE a adopté les résolutions du 13 avril 2016, du 14 septembre 2016 et aussi la résolution du 15 novembre 2017 concernant la situation de l'État de droit et de la démocratie en Pologne[20]. Dans cette dernière résolution, le PE a estimé que « *la situation actuelle en Pologne est porteuse d'un risque manifeste de violation grave des valeurs visées à l'article 2 TUE ; charge sa commission des libertés civiles, de la justice et des affaires intérieures (...) d'élaborer un rapport spécifique en vue de mettre aux voix une proposition motivée*

[15] P8_TA(2016)0409 du 25 octobre 2016 (2015/2254(INL)).

[16] *Rapport du 10 octobre 2016 contenant des recommandations à la Commission sur la création d'un mécanisme de l'Union pour la démocratie, l'État de droit et les droits fondamentaux* (2015/2254(INL)), Commission des libertés civiles, de la justice et des affaires intérieures, Rapporteure : Sophie in't Veld (A8-0283/2016).

[17] Cfr. *Résolution du 25 octobre 2016*, cit., n° 1.

[18] Le PE a aussi adopté la *Résolution du PE du 15 novembre 2015 sur l'État de droit à Malte* (2017/2935(RSP), P8_TA-PROV(2017)0438) – dans laquelle il déplore que l'évolution de la situation à Malte suscite de graves inquiétudes quant à l'État de droit, à la démocratie et aux droits fondamentaux y compris en ce qui concerne la liberté des media et l'indépendance de la police et de l'appareil judiciaire (cf. n° 5).

[19] *Résolution du Parlement européen du 10 juin 2015 sur la situation en Hongrie* (2015/2700(RSP), P8_TA(2015)0227) ; *Résolution du Parlement européen du 16 décembre 2015 sur la situation en Hongrie* (2015/2935 (RSP), P8_TA(2015)0461) ; *Résolution du Parlement européen du 17 mai 2017 sur la situation en Hongrie* (2017/2656 (RSP), P8_TA(2017)0216) – n.°s 9 et 10.

[20] *Résolution du Parlement européen du 13 avril 2016 sur la situation en Pologne* (2015/3031 (RSP), P8_TA(2016)0123) ; *Résolution du Parlement européen du 14 septembre 2016 sur les récentes évolutions en Pologne et leurs conséquences sur les droits fondamentaux inscrits dans la Charte de droits fondamentaux de l'Union européenne* (2016/2774(RSP), P8_TA(2016)0344) ; *Résolution du Parlement européen du 15 novembre 2017 sur la situation de l'État de droit et de la démocratie en Pologne* (2017/2931 (RSP), P8_TA-PROV(2017)0442).

invitant le Conseil à agir conformément à l'article 7, paragraphe 1, TUE » (comme il l'avait fait dans le cas de la Hongrie). Le PE y réaffirme la nécessité d'un suivi et d'un dialogue réguliers associant tous les États membres afin de sauvegarder les valeurs fondamentales de l'Union et préconise sa résolution du 25 octobre 2016 contenant des recommandations à la Commission sur la création d'un mécanisme de l'Union pour la démocratie, l'État de droit et les droits fondamentaux[21].

Pour finir, le PE a adopté la *résolution du 1er mars 2018 sur la décision de la Commission de déclencher l'article 7, paragraphe 1, du traité sur l'Union européenne en ce qui concerne la situation en Pologne*[22]. Dans cette résolution le PE, étant donné, notamment, sa précédente résolution du 15 novembre 2017, salue et appuie la décision de la Commission du 20 décembre 2017 de déclencher l'article 7, paragraphe 1, demande au Conseil de prendre rapidement les mesures conformément à cette disposition du TUE et invite la Commission et le Conseil à le tenir informé des progrès accomplis aussi bien que des mesures prises à chaque étape de la procédure en cause[23].

2.2 *Nouveaux instruments juridiques, nouvelles questions*

La multiplicité des instruments[24] susmentionnés adoptés – et quelques-uns déjà appliqués – par les institutions européennes soulève des questions juridiques nouvelles, davantage qu'elle n'apporte de réponses claires et efficaces. Seront abordées

[21] *Résolution du PE du 15 novembre 2017 sur la situation de l'État de droit et de la démocratie en Pologne*, cit., respectivement n° 16 et 17.

[22] P8_TA-PROV(2018)0055 – 2018/2541(RSP).

[23] P8_TA-PROV(2018)0055, cit., n.°s 1, 2 et 3, respectivement.

[24] Dans la doctrine voir le numéro thématique du *Journal of Common Market Studies*, vol. 54, Issue 5, september 2016 (JCMS Symposium 2016 : *The Great Rule of law Debate in the EU*, edited by Dimitry KOCHENOV, Amichai MAGEN et Laurent PECH), pp. 1045 et ss. ; en spécial, sur les initiatives et le rôle des institutions de l'Union, dans le numéro mentionné, Dimitry KOCHENOV et Laurent PECH, "Better Late than Never? On the European Commission's Rule of Law Framework and its First Activation", pp. 1062-1074 ; Peter OLIVER et Justine STEFANELLI, "Strengthtening the Rule of Law in the EU: The Council's Inaction", pp. 1075-1084 ; Judith SARGENTINI et Aleksej DIMITROVS, "The European Parliament's Role: Towards New Copenhagen Criteria for Existing Member States?", pp. 1085-1092 ; et encore Leonard BESSELINK, "The Bite, the Bark and the Howl. Article 7 TEU and the Rule of Law Initiatives", *Amsterdam Law School Legal Studies Research Paper* No. 2016-02, Amsterdam Centre for Research for European Law and Governance Research Paper No. 2016-01, in *https://ssrn.com/abstract=2715943*, pp. 17-22 ; Christophe HILLION, "Overseeing the Rule of law in the European Union. Legal mandate and means", in *European Policy Analysis*, January Issue 2016 (SIEPS), pp. 12-13 – don't la version finale a été publié in Carlos Closa et Dimitry Kochenov (eds.), *Reinforcing Rule of Law Oversight in the European Union*, Cambridge, University Press, 2016, pp. 59 et ss. ; Simon LABAYLE, "Respect des valeurs de l'Union européenne en Pologne: première application du nouveau cadre pour renforcer l'État de droit", in European papers, Vol. 1, 2016, N° 3, pp.1283-1288. Vide aussi András Jakab et Dimitry Kochenov (eds.), *The Enforcement of EU Law and Values. Ensuring member States' Compliance,* Oxford, University Press, 2017.

ci-dessous quelques-unes des interrogations soulevées par les principaux instruments adoptés ou proposés, à savoir le *nouveau cadre* sur l'État de droit et le *mécanisme de l'UE pour la démocratie, l'État de droit et les droits fondamentaux*, y compris la proposition de Pacte de l'Union européenne pour la démocratie l'État de droit et les droits fondamentaux (ci après « Pacte de l'UE DEF »).

2.2.1 Le nouveau cadre sur l'État de droit (Commission européenne)

On rappellera que le nouveau cadre avait été adopté pour diverses raisons, telles que la possibilité de menaces systémiques envers l'État de droit, l'inefficacité des moyens juridiques existants (notamment l'action en manquement prévue aux articles 258-260 TFUE, laquelle implique la violation d'une disposition spécifique du droit de l'UE et une situation qui rentre dans le champ d'application du droit de l'UE), ainsi que l'exigence des conditions d'application de l'article 7 requises dans les différentes phases de la procédure (notamment l'exigeante majorité d'approbation au sein du Conseil dans la phase préventive et l'unanimité du Conseil européen dans la phase déclarative). De plus, le nouveau cadre a pour but d'être complémentaire à la procédure prévue à l'article 7 et de prévenir les menaces à l'État de droit, en tant que *conditio sine qua non* des autres valeurs de l'Union.

Ce nouveau cadre pose toutefois un certain nombre de questions.

Tout d'abord, la base juridique sur laquelle le nouveau cadre a été approuvé est contestée par un avis du Service juridique du Conseil. Selon cet avis, il n'existe aucune base juridique dans les traités qui attribue compétence aux institutions pour créer un nouveau mécanisme de supervision du respect de l'État de droit par les États membres en plus de ce qui est prévu à l'article 7, ni pour modifier ou compléter la procédure qui est prévue à cet article et, ainsi, la Communication ne serait pas compatible avec le principe de compétence d'attribution qui s'applique aux institutions de l'Union. Toutefois, l'avis affirme, dans le même temps, que les États membres pourraient se mettre d'accord sur un système revu de contrôle du fonctionnement de l'État de droit dans les États membres, et sur ses possibles conséquences, sur la base d'un accord intergouvernemental[25] destiné à compléter le droit de l'Union et assurer le respect effectif des valeurs sur lesquelles les Etats membres ont fondé l'Union, sans que cela n'implique l'attribution à l'Union de compétences que les traités n'ont pas prévu – et aussi qu'un tel système revu par les États membres « *peut prévoir que certaines tâches soient attribués aux institutions de l'Union* » [26].

[25] Proposition que probablement a pris en compte l'exemple du *Traité sur stabilité, la coordination et la gouvernance au sein de l'Union économique et monétaire* du 2 mars 2012, *signé par plusieurs État membres* – lequel confère à certaines institutions de l'Union plusieurs compétences (cf. notamment articles 8, n° 1 et 2, 12 et 13).

[26] *Opinion of the Legal Service – Commission's Communication on a new EU Framework to strengthen the Rule of law: compatibility with the Treaties* (document 10296/14 du Conseil, du 27/05/2015), cfr. III. Legal Analysis, 15 et suiv., spécialement 24-27, et IV. Conclusion, 28. Voir le commentaire de Leonard BESSELINK, "The Bite, the Bark and the Howl. Article 7 TEU and the Rule of Law Initiatives", *cit.*, pp. 22-25 e 32-34.

On notera également que le nouveau cadre a été calqué sur les compétences de la Commission dans le cadre de la phase non contentieuse de l'action en manquement (commun) prévue aux articles 258-260 du TFUE, y compris la lettre de mise en demeure, le droit de réponse de l'État concerné et le dialogue entre la Commission et cet État et, enfin, l'avis motivé indiquant les mesures que l'État doit prendre et dans quel délai sous peine d'ouverture de la phase contentieuse devant la CJUE. En réalité, malgré la différence de nom et de procédure en manquement, tous ces éléments sont présents dans le nouveau cadre, structuré en trois étapes : évaluation (y compris évaluation par la Commission, dialogue structuré et avis sur l'État de droit), recommandation(s) sur l'État de droit, et suivi des recommandations par la Commission et évaluation de la possibilité de déclencher la phase préventive de la procédure de l'article 7. Mais avec une différence fondamentale : si la phase non contentieuse de l'action en manquement est prévue dans le TFUE (article 258, paragraphe 1), la compétence de la Commission préalable à l'exercice de son pouvoir d'initiative de la phase préventive de la procédure de l'article 7, telle que conçue dans le nouveau cadre, n'est pas expressément prévues dans le TUE.

Ensuite, la nature juridique – discrétionnaire ou obligatoire – de la procédure n'est pas évidente, si l'on considère que les actes approuvés par la Commission dans le contexte du nouveau cadre (avis et recommandations sur l'État de droit) ne lient pas (selon l'énoncé des actes typiques prévus à l'article 288, paragraphe 5, du TFUE) et donc ne produisent pas d'effets juridiques obligatoires. Ils sont dès lors *prima facie* hors du champ de contrôle de la CJUE.

De plus, le nouveau cadre pose sûrement un problème de *cohérence* : bien que le respect de l'État de droit puisse être comme la *conditio sine qua non* du respect des autres valeurs de l'Union, une dualité de traitement et de procédures peut être introduite par rapport au risque de violation des autres valeurs fondamentales de l'Union européenne (État de droit *vs* autres valeurs de l'Union, notamment le respect des droits de l'homme).

Une autre question qui découle du nouveau cadre porte sur la notion de « *menace systémique* » envers l'État de droit. En fait, selon le nouveau cadre, la raison de son adoption a été double : la possibilité d'une menace systémique envers l'État de droit – et, partant, au fonctionnement de l'Union en tant qu'espace de liberté, sécurité et justice – et le fait que cette menace systémique à l'État de droit dans les États membres ne puisse pas toujours, selon la Commission, être adressée de façon efficace par les instruments juridiques existants dans l'Union. En effet, on rappellera, d'une part, les limites à l'intervention de la Commission dans le cadre de la procédure et de l'action en manquement prévues aux articles 258-260 du TFUE et d'autre part, les conditions élevées (nature de la violation ou seuils de décision) d'application de la procédure en manquement des valeurs de l'Union de l'article 7 TUE – y compris dans des situations qui ne relèvent pas du champ d'application du droit de l'Union et qui ne peuvent donc être considérées comme infractions aux obligations découlant des traités, mais représentent ladite menace systémique à l'État de droit.

La notion de menace à l'État de droit de *nature systémique* est donc un élément central du fonctionnement du nouveau cadre puisque le but de celui-ci est précisément de répondre à cette menace. Si cette notion s'éloigne des concepts utilisés dans la procédure de l'article 7 du TUE (*risque clair de violation grave* et *violation grave et persistante*), elle s'inspire néanmoins de la notion « systémique » utilisée dans le cadre du Conseil de l'Europe[27]. La Commission densifie cette notion dans le sens de l'existence d'une menace à « *l'ordre politique, institutionnel et/ou juridique d'un État membre en tant que tel, sa structure constitutionnelle, la séparation des pouvoirs, l'indépendance ou l'impartialité du pouvoir judiciaire ou le système de contrôle juridictionnel, y compris la justice constitutionnelle lorsqu'elle existe* » – par exemple en raison de l'adoption de nouvelles mesures ou de l'existence de pratiques répandues dans les autorités publiques, et de l'absence de voies de recours à l'échelon national[28]. Selon la Communication de la Commission, le nouveau cadre sera activé lorsque les « mécanismes de protection de l'État de droit » nationaux ne sembleront pas en mesure de mettre fin à ces menaces.

Ainsi, la question de savoir dans quelle mesure le nouveau concept de *menace systémique* peut coïncider (ou coïncider au moins partiellement, concernant l'état de de droit) avec les notions de (risque de) *violation grave* ou de *violation grave et persistante* prévues à l'article 7 –, conditionnant ainsi l'appréciation et la vérification, en chaque cas, des conditions desquelles dépendent les décisions à prendre dans les phases préventive et déclarative de la procédure prévue à cet article – mérite d'être éclaircie.

De plus, il doit être souligné que la procédure prévue par le nouveau cadre (évaluation par la Commission et avis, recommandation(s) et suivi de celle(s)-ci) est aussi complexe que celle de l'article 7 du TUE, prolongeant ainsi surement le temps nécessaire pour atteindre d'adoption d'une décision (obligatoire) pour l'État membre concerné – que seule l'application de la procédure de l'article 7 peut garantir. Et si son efficacité se montrera assez réduite, n'évitant pas le déclenchement de la procédure de l'article 7, cela risquera d'atteindre l'autorité de cette procédure en manquement des valeurs de l'Union.

Finalement, et aussi du point de vue de son efficacité en tant que mécanisme conçu en amont de la procédure en manquement qualifié de l'article 7, les leçons de son application dans le cas de la Pologne – dans lequel un avis et quatre recommandations ont été adoptés par la Commission depuis 2016 – montrent que sa mise en œuvre n'a évité ni la décision de déclencher la procédure en manquement qualifié des valeurs de l'Union et, ainsi, ni l'intervention politique du Conseil à cet égard à travers une décision concernant la (première) phase préventive de la procédure – même si dans le sens d'une impossibilité d'atteindre la majorité requise dans cette

---

[27] Voir tout spécialement la Résolution *RES(2004) 3 sur les décisions de la Cour européenne des Droits de l'Homme (CourEDH) qui révèlent un problème structurel sous-jacent adopté par le Comité de Ministres du Conseil de l'Europe le 12 mai 2004 dans sa 114ème session – dans laquelle cette institution invite la CourEDH à identifier dans ses décisions qui déclarent une violation de la CEDH, ce qu'elle considère un « problème systémique sous-jacent » et sa source respective, notamment quand il sera probable qu'il pourra donner lieu à des plaintes nombreuses et, ainsi, aider l'état en cause à trouver une solution appropriée et aussi le Comité de Ministres dans la supervision de l'exécution des arrêts de la Cour.*

[28] Cf. Communication de la Commission COM(2014)158 final, du 11 mars 2014, cit., *4.1 Déclenchement des mécanismes prévus par le nouveau cadre.*

phase de la procédure. Ainsi, son efficacité est douteuse dans le premier cas de figure et, dans une certaine mesure, peut être considérée comme une duplication ou conduire à retarder la procédure de l'article 7 du TUE ainsi que son application (ou au moins sa tentative d'application), tout d'abord dans la phase préventive.

La question qui se pose porte donc sur sa réelle valeur ajoutée (juridique) – par rapport à la phase préventive de la procédure de l'article 7 du TUE – et sur le point de savoir si la Commission ne pouvait pas atteindre le même résultat sans créer un nouveau cadre avec toute son incertitude et sa complexité. En effet, combien de recommandations la Commission doit-elle adopter avant d'exercer son pouvoir d'initiative de la phase préventive de la procédure en manquement qualifié ? Ou bien, plus la Commission adopte de recommandations et moins l'État concerné reconnaît leur autorité ? Il faut s'interroger dans quelle mesure l'application préalable du nouveau cadre par la Commission avant que celle-ci ne prenne l'initiative d'ouvrir la procédure en manquement qualifié des valeurs de l'Union (comme elle l'a fait dans le cas de la Pologne en juillet 2017) aboutit – ou peut aboutir – à un affaiblissement de la procédure de manquement qualifié des valeurs de l'Union et du rôle du Conseil dans cette procédure, surtout dans le cas où l'État concerné ne prend en compte ni n'observe les recommandations successives adoptées par la Commission.

2.2.2 Le mécanisme de l'Union pour la démocratie, l'État de droit et les droits fondamentaux (Parlement européen)

Une des initiatives du PE concernant la garantie des valeurs fondamentales de l'Union est sa résolution du 25 octobre 2016 contenant des *recommandations à la Commission sur la création d'un mécanisme de l'Union pour la démocratie, l'État de droit et les droits fondamentaux* – qui a été précédée du rapport du 10 octobre 2016 –, y compris l'invitation correspondante faite à la Commission de présenter une proposition à cet égard avant septembre 2017[29].

Les traits principaux inhérents au mécanisme proposé par le PE dans sa résolution peuvent être regroupés en quatre volets – complexité structurelle, caractère élargi, spécialisation et (préoccupation de) cohérence.

En ce qui concerne sa structure, le mécanisme proposé est complexe. Il comprend un *Pacte de l'Union européenne pour la démocratie, l'État de droit et les droits fondamentaux* (Pacte DEF de l'UE), sous la forme d'un *projet d'accord interinstitutionnel*[30], avec des volets préventif et correctif, qui prévoit la définition, l'élaboration, la surveillance et l'application des valeurs et principes de l'Union et

[29] P8_TA(2016)0409 du 25 octobre 2016, cit. – *supra,* 2.1.

[30] P8_TA(2016)0409 du 25 octobre 2016, cit., Annexe, Recommandations détaillées en vue de l'élaboration d'un projet d'accord interinstitutionnel sur les dispositions concernant les procédures de surveillance et de suivi sur la situation de la démocratie, de l'État de droit et des droits fondamentaux dans les États membres et les institutions de l'Union – Projet d'accord interinstitutionnel – Pacte de l'Union européenne pour la démocratie, l'État de droit et les droits fondamentaux.

qui s'applique tant aux États membres qu'aux institutions de l'Union[31]. Le Pacte DEF de l'UE comprend à son tour quatre éléments : le rapport européen DEF (rapport annuel), le débat interparlementaire annuel qui s'appuie sur le rapport européen DEF, un cycle de politiques DEF au sein des institutions de l'Union (i.e. en faveur de la démocratie, de l'État de droit et les droits fondamentaux), ainsi que des modalités de traitement des risques potentiels et violations telles que prévues par les traités, et des conditions d'activation du volet préventif ou correctif de l'article 7 du TUE[32].

De plus, le mécanisme proposé, notamment le *Pacte DEF*, se présente comme un instrument dont le champ d'application est étendu et dont les acteurs sont multiples. D'un côté, le mécanisme concerne toutes les valeurs (et principes) majeures de l'Union, telles que prévues à l'article 2 du TUE (démocratie, État de droit et droits fondamentaux). D'un autre côté, il implique, en plus des États membres et des trois institutions qui adopteront le Pacte DEF sous la forme d'un accord interinstitutionnel, plusieurs intervenants (directement ou indirectement), notamment un *panel d'experts indépendants* (panel d'experts DEF)[33] – lequel effectue l'évaluation de la situation de la démocratie, de l'État de droit et des droits fondamentaux dans les États membres et élabore des projets de recommandations par pays –, ou d'autres organisations internationales et agences de l'Union, telles que le Conseil de l'Europe et la Commission de Venise ou l'Agence de droits fondamentaux[34] – révélant ainsi, à travers leur participation ou intervention, le volet spécialisé du mécanisme en cause.

En tout cas, et même si avec un format différent, la prévision de l'intervention d'un panel d'experts ne laisse pas d'être une sorte de retour au texte de l'article 7 dans sa version introduite par le Traité de Nice (et en application jusqu'à l'entrée en vigueur du Traité de Lisbonne) – dont le numéro 1, paragraphe 2, prévoyait que le Conseil, avant de procéder à la constatation qu'il existe un risque clair de violation grave par un État membre des principes énoncés (alors) à l'article 6, paragraphe 1 (TUE), pouvait demander à des personnalités indépendantes de présenter, dans un délai raisonnable, un rapport sur la situation dans l'État en question – comme cela avait été d'ailleurs le cas, même avant le Traité de Nice, dans l'épisode autrichien.

Le mécanisme proposé révèle un problème global de *cohérence* puisque le PE propose la création d'un « mécanisme global » qui inclurait « l'ensemble des acteurs pertinents » et que le Pacte DEF de l'UE devrait viser à offrir « *un cadre unique et cohérent en s'appuyant sur les instruments et mécanismes existants et en intégrant ces derniers, et être en mesure de remédier à toute lacune subsistante* », intégrant ainsi, alignant et complétant les mécanismes existants[35] – et non seulement le

[31] P8_TA(2016)0409 du 25 octobre 2016, cit., 1 et 4, et Annexe, art. 1.

[32] P8_TA(2016)0409 du 25 octobre 2016, Annexe, cit. Art. 2 et, en spéciale, arts. 4-7 (rapport européen DEF) et art. 10 (débat interparlementaire annuel).

[33] P8_TA(2016)0409 du 25 octobre 2016, Annexe, cit., arts. 8-9.

[34] P8_TA(2016)0409 du 25 octobre 2016, Annexe, cit., v.g. art. 6 ou art. 8.

[35] P8_TA(2016)0409 du 25 octobre 2016, cit., 1. et AL.

nouveau cadre, le dialogue structuré[36] et la procédure de l'article 7 du TUE, mais aussi d'autres instruments, tels que les rapports annuels sur l'application de la Charte ou du droit de l'Union.

Deux aspects du régime prévu dans le projet de Pacte DEF de l'UE méritent une mention particulière du point de vue du cadre juridique de contrôle et de garantie des valeurs de l'Union étant donné les questions qu'ils soulèvent : la prévision d'une « action pour violation systémique », au titre de l'article 2 du TUE et de l'article 258 du TFUE, « en regroupant plusieurs dossiers d'infraction », et le rapport qui y est prévu avec la procédure en manquement – soit la procédure en manquement de l'article 258, soit la procédure en manquement qualifié des valeurs de l'Union de l'article 7.

Selon l'article 10, quatrième trait, du projet d'accord interinstitutionnel – Pacte DEF de l'UE, sur la base du rapport européen DEF, rédigé par la Commission après consultation du panel d'experts indépendants –, la Commission peut décider d'intenter une action pour violation systémique au titre des articles 2 du TUE et 258 du TFUE, en regroupant plusieurs dossiers d'infraction – modifiant ainsi la pratique existante et allant au-delà du texte de l'article 258 en introduisant la (nouvelle) notion de violation systémique. En effet, selon l'article 10.2.1 et 10.3 du même projet d'accord, les décisions motivées (rendues publiques) à prendre par le PE, le Conseil et la Commission sont précédées (et probablement conditionnées) par les recommandations par pays (préparées par le panel d'experts DEF) dans le cas où elles indiquent qu'il existe un risque clair de violation grave des valeurs prévues à l'article 2 du TUE et qu'il existe suffisamment de raisons pour invoquer l'article 7, paragraphe 1, du TUE, ou qu'il existe une violation grave et persistante, à savoir en augmentation ou sans évolution pendant au moins deux ans, des valeurs prévues à l'article 2 du TUE et qu'il existe suffisamment de raisons pour invoquer l'article 7, paragraphe 2.

Ainsi, non seulement le projet d'accord consacre une nouvelle notion de violation – la violation *systémique* – qui implique une relecture de l'article 258 du TFUE et de son application par la Commission, mais fait dépendre l'application de l'article 7 du TUE par les institutions européennes de conditions qui ne sont à présent pas prévues dans le texte du droit originaire – sans que les États membre aient eu la possibilité de le modifier avant.

Finalement, deux remarques s'avèrent encore pertinentes concernant la résolution du PE sur le mécanisme de l'UE pour la démocratie, l'État de droit et les droits fondamentaux puisqu'elle contient aussi d'autres recommandations qui peuvent affecter le modèle en vigueur en matière de contrôle des violations imputables aux États membres, y compris en matière de valeurs de l'Union.

Tout d'abord, les recommandations dans le contexte des (sept) propositions de révision des traités, parmi lesquelles se trouvent les suivantes : (i) faire de l'article 2 du TUE et de la Charte une base juridique pour les mesures législatives à adopter

[36] P8_TA(2016)0409 du 25 octobre 2016, Annexe, cit, art. 3, qui prévoit expressément que le Pacte DEF est élargi en vue de regrouper au sein d'un instrument unique de l'Union le cadre pour l'État de droit de la Commission et le dialogue sur l'État de droit du Conseil.

dans le cadre de la procédure législative ordinaire ; (ii) permettre aux juridictions nationales, en vertu de l'article 2 du TUE et de la Charte d'intenter des actions devant la CJUE au sujet de la légalité des actions des États membres (légitimité procédurale) ; (iii) modifier l'article 7 du TUE pour faire sorte que les sanctions envers les États membres soient pertinentes et applicables, tout en précisant les droits (autre que le droit de vote au Conseil) qui peuvent être suspendus pour les États membres fautifs, par exemple des sanctions financières ou la suspension de financements européens ; (iv) permettre aux personnes physiques et morales touchées directement et individuellement par une action de saisir la CJUE en cas de violation alléguée de la Charte par les institutions de l'Union ou par un État membre, en modifiant les articles 258 et 259 du TFUE [37] ; (vi) procéder à la révision de la règle de l'unanimité dans les domaines qui ont trait au respect, à la protection et à la promotion des droits fondamentaux, comme en matière d'égalité et de non-discrimination[38].

Ensuite, la résolution du PE établit expressément un rapport entre le droit de l'Union européenne et les instruments de protection des droits fondamentaux dans le cadre du Conseil de l'Europe, en invitant la Commission à présenter, au plus tard en Juin 2017, un nouveau projet de traité d'adhésion, afin de satisfaire à l'obligation énoncée à l'article 6 du TUE en tenant compte de l'avis 2/13 de la CJUE et aussi invitant le Conseil de l'Europe à permettre l'ouverture de la signature de la Charte Sociale Européenne à des tiers de sorte que la Commission puisse entamer les négociations relatives à l'adhésion de l'Union (aussi à la CSE)[39].

3 Remarques (critiques) conclusives et réflexions pour l'avenir

L'évolution assez complexe du cadre juridique concernant la garantie des valeurs fondamentales communes de l'Union européenne pose certainement des questions nouvelles (*supra,* 2.2) et, surtout, suscite plusieurs doutes concernant son fonctionnement, le rapport avec les instruments précédents, en particulier ceux déjà prévus par le droit primaire, et son efficacité juridique dans le cadre d'une Union de droit.

[37] Proposition qui semble d'ailleurs proche du texte du *Traité qui institue la Cour de Justice de la Communauté Andine des Nations* (cf. article 25).

[38] Et, en plus, permettre à un tiers des députés au PE de saisir la CJUE d'un texte législatif de l'Union après son adoption définitive et avant sa mise en œuvre (*prima facie* une sorte de contrôle préventif de « constitutionalité » des actes normatifs européens) et supprimer l'article 51 de la Charte et transformer celle-ci en une Charte des droits de l'Union – cf. P8_TA(2016)0409 du 25 octobre 2016, cit., n° 20.

[39] P8_TA(2016)0409 du 25 octobre 2016, cit., n.° 11.

Les remarques ci-dessous mettent d'abord l'accent sur quelques-uns des doutes qu'il conviendra de clarifier ou surmonter (ou non) dans un avenir proche par les acteurs impliqués.

(i) Tout d'abord, il faut se demander si la procédure en manquement qualifié des valeurs de l'Union prévue à l'article 7 est vraiment insuffisante au point de justifier l'adoption de tout un cadre juridique nouveau (assez complexe), qui vise à précéder son application et aussi s'il y avait une base juridique claire pour l'adopter ou, au contraire, si l'approbation du nouveau cadre a dépassé la compétence d'attribution de certaines institutions de l'Union. Quoi qu'il en soit, l'éventuelle insuffisance de la procédure prévue à l'article 7 ne peut pas uniquement se fonder sur l'exigence des règles procédurales puisqu'elles sont le miroir de la complexité et de la sensibilité politique inhérente au contrôle de la violation de la base axiologique de l'Union

(ii) Deuxièmement, il faut noter qu'après l'adoption du (nouveau) cadre juridique de l'Union – et des propositions du PE – il semble exister un problème de cohérence horizontale (soit interinstitutionnelle, soit entre plusieurs procédures en manquement).

(iii) Ensuite, le nouveau cadre juridique – dans sa version actuelle (instruments parallèles), mais surtout dans la version (future) intégrée et inclusive telle que proposée par le PE – est évidement trop complexe et cette complexité affecte sa célérité et son efficacité, pouvant ainsi même mettre en cause ou affaiblir, dans le domaine du respect de valeurs fondamentales, l'autorité du droit de l'Union. De plus, l'appel à plusieurs acteurs de l'Union, comme l'Agence de Droits Fondamentaux[40], et externes à l'Union, comme le Conseil de l'Europe, implique un besoin accru d'articulation sous peine de duplication, voire de contradictions.

(iv) En ce qui concerne le rapport de ce nouveau et complexe cadre juridique de l'Union avec la procédure en manquement de l'article 7 du TUE, il existe des risques clairs de duplication (au moins temporels) de la phase préventive qui est prévue et la solution d'appel à des experts tiers (dans le mécanisme proposé par le PE) réintroduit sous une autre forme la solution du Traité de Nice écartée par le Traité de Lisbonne et donc par les *maîtres des traités*. De même, bien que le nouveau cadre approuvé par la Commission puisse être conçu comme un cadre de *self*-discipline de cette institution avant de déclencher la phase préventive de l'article 7 (donnant ainsi préalablement connaissance aux États membres du mode futur d'action pour chaque cas de violation potentielle des valeurs de l'Union), cette discipline et les appréciations successives de la Commission risquent certainement de conditionner la future appréciation du Conseil dans les phases préventive et déclarative, et ainsi aboutir à un changement de la nature (aujourd'hui) politique de la procédure prévue à l'article 7.

[40] Voir Gabriel N. TOGGENBURG et Jonas GRIMHEDEN, "Upholding Shared Values in the EU: What Role for the EU Agency for Fundamental Rights?", in JCMS, 54(2016)5, pp. 1093 et ss.

(v) En ce qui concerne le rapport de ce nouveau et complexe cadre et l'action en manquement des articles 258 à 260 du TFUE, et puisque il est proposé que la Commission puisse décider d'intenter une action pour *violation systémique* au titre des articles 2 du TUE et 258 du TFUE, en regroupant plusieurs dossiers d'infraction, il faut considérer quels sont les effets de ce nouveau concept (et de son interprétation par la CJUE) sur le mode de fonctionnement de l'action en manquement telle que prévue dans les traités ou s'il faut créer une nouvelle voie de recours (ou bien modifier celle qui existe déjà) pour cet effet.

(vi) Il faut également considérer les limites de la justiciabilité de la légalité de l'adoption des diverses initiatives prises par les institutions dans la mesure où ces mesures auront une projection sur (ou conditionneront) les instruments prévus par les traités sans une révision préalable de ceux-ci dans les termes qui y sont prévus. Et il faut aussi considérer les limites de la justiciabilité de chaque acte *in concreto* adopté soit par la Commission (dans le contexte du nouveau cadre), soit par les différents intervenants dans la version complexe proposé par le PE, dans la mesure où ils peuvent produire des effets juridiquement contraignants.

(vii) Enfin, le nouveau cadre juridique – et le futur cadre si la proposition du PE est accueillie – pose aussi un doute concernant la question de la violation des valeurs de l'Union en termes de *modèles de garantie* : est-elle une question surtout politique et les instruments pour y faire face sont (ou doivent être) plutôt des instruments politiques ou intergouvernementaux, ou est-elle une vraie question juridique et elle doit alors être adressée avec des instruments juridiques, *maxime* à travers l'intervention de la CJUE et de l'unicité de procédures en manquement en renforçant l'Union en tant que communauté *de droit* – et traduisant ainsi un nouvel équilibre de pouvoirs au sein de l'Union.

Pour finir, on soulèvera brièvement quelques pistes de réflexions dans le cadre d'une future révision des traités.

(i) Il faut tout d'abord réfléchir à la question de savoir si les compétences de l'UE en matière de valeurs fondamentales de l'Union européenne, y compris le respect des droits fondamentaux (article 2 du TUE), sont des compétences partagées (selon la clause générale de l'article 4, paragraphe 1, du TFUE) et ainsi soumises à la méthode 'communautaire', notamment au contrôle par la CJUE.

(ii) Se pose également la question de la pleine justiciabilité par la CJUE de la procédure de l'article 7, y compris sur la question de fond – à savoir l'existence d'un risque de violation ou d'une violation grave et persistante des valeurs de l'Union – élargissant ainsi le champ d'application de la méthode communautaire, aussi bien que des rapports entre celle-ci et la compétence de la Cour en matière de manquement systémique (en matière de valeurs de l'Union). Il faut donc réfléchir si le chemin est celui de rendre les procédures (et plusieurs procédures) de plus en plus complexes ou, bien au contraire, celui de la simplification et de l'unicité – chemin dans lequel la CJUE aura certainement un rôle primordial à jouer.

(iii) Étant donné la complémentarité entre les voies de recours dans l'ordre juridique de l'Union, la question de la violation de l'État de droit – malgré les limites du contrôle par la CJUE de l'application de l'article 7 – est récemment (et soudainement) parvenue à la CJUE à travers le renvoi préjudiciel effectué par le *Irish High Court* le 27 mars 2018 dans le cas *Minister for Justice and Equality v. A. Celmer.* Dans cette affaire, décidé par l' arrêt de la Cour du 25 juillet 2018, les questions posées par la juridiction nationale à la CJUE, dans le contexte du mandat d'arrêt européen, portent directement sur la question de la violation du *rule of law* dans le cas de la Pologne considérant notamment le nouveau cadre juridique de l'Union, y compris les recommandations de la Commission dans le cadre de la mise en œuvre de l'article 7 TUE[41,42] et donc le prononcé des institutions européennes dans le sens de l'existence d'une violation du *rule of* law par la Pologne. Le rapport avec l'application du droit secondaire de l'Union européenne n'a pas permis d'éviter le prononcé de la Cour de Justice dans un domaine compris dans les attributions de l'Union en rapport avec le respect des valeurs fondamentales de l'Union et le rôle central du juge européen et de son indépendance[43]. Ainsi une question d'abord plutôt politique est déjà rentrée dans le champ de compétences de la CJUE et, de cette façon, dans la sphère du judiciaire, soit du point de vue du contrôle de l'indépendance du juge national, soit du point de vue de cette indépendance en tant que condition de la confiance mutuelle entre États membres. La Cour de Justice – faisant appel notamment à sa jurisprudence *Aranyosi et Caldararu* et *Associação Sindical dos Juízes Portugueses* – considère, en ce qui concerne en particulier le rapport entre d'une part la procédure de remise à l'autorité judiciaire d'émission du mandat d'arrêt européen et le risque d'atteinte au contenu du droit fondamental à un procès équitable lié à un manque d'indépendance des juridictions de l'État d'émission et, d'autre part, la procédure de l'article 7 TUE, que : i) les informations figurant dans une proposition motivée adressée par la Commission au Conseil sur le fondement de l'article 7 paragraphe 1 TUE (celle du 20 décembre 2017 qui a été précédé par l'application du nouveau cadre pour l'État de droit), constituent des éléments particulièrement pertinents aux fins de

[41] *Minister for Justice and Equality, C-216/18PPU, demande de décision préjudicielle du 27/03/2018* et arrêt de la CJUE du 25 juillet 2018, *LM,* C-218/18 PPU (curia.europa.eu). Les conclusions de l'Avocat Général E. Tanchev ont été présentées le 28 juin 2018.

[42] Voir les commentaires de Sergio CARRERA et Valsamis MITSILEGAS, *Upholding the Rule of Law by Scrutinising Judicial Independence: The Irish Court's request for a preliminar ruling on the European Arrest Warrant* (11 avril 2018, https://www.ceps.eu); Mattias WENDEL, *Die Rechtsstaatlichkeitskrise vor Gericht: der Anfang vom Ende gegenseitigen Vertrauens* (2018/3/17); Tomasz T. KONCEWICS, *The Consensus Fights Back: European First principles Against the Rule of law Crisis (part 1 and part 2, 2018/4/05)* ; Petra BÁRD et Wouter van BALLEGOOIJ, *Judicial Independence as a Precondition for Mutual Trust* (2018/4/10, tous disponibles in *verfassungsblog.de*).

[43] La question de l'indépendance des juges a été adressée récemment dans l'arrêt de la CJUE du 27 février 2018, *Associação Sindical dos Juízes Portugueses c. Tribunal de Contas*, C-64/16, où la CJUE affirme que l'existence même d'un contrôle juridictionnel effectif destiné à assurer le respect du droit de l'Union est inhérent à un État de droit (cf. notamment les paragraphes 36 à 38).

l'évaluation de manière concrète et précise par l'autorité judiciaire d'exécution de l'existence d'un risque réel de violation du droit fondamental à un procès équitable lié à un manque d'indépendance des juridictions de l'État membre d'émission en raison de défaillances systémiques ou généralisées concernant le pouvoir judiciaire; ii) ce n'est qu'en présence d'une décision du Conseil européen constatant, dans les conditions prévues à l'article 7 paragraphe 2 TUE, une violation grave et persistante dans l'État membre d'émission des principes énoncés à l'article 2 TUE, tels que ceux inhérents à l'État de droit, suivie de la suspension par le Conseil de l'application de la décision-cadre 2002/584/JAI au regard de cet État membre, que l'autorité judiciaire d'exécution serait tenue de refuser *automatiquement* d'exécuter tout mandat européen émis par ledit État membre, sans devoir procéder à une quelconque appréciation concrète du risque réel couru par la personne concernée de voir affecter le contenu essentiel de son droit à un procès équitable[44]. Ainsi, la Cour s'est prononcée sur la question de la violation des valeurs de l'Union en rapport avec l'indépendance du pouvoir judiciaire et sur les effets de la procédure en manquement de l'article 7 TUE, bien qu'elle n'a pas écarté une intervention de l'autorité judiciaire d'exécution concernant la vérification de manière concrète et précise du risque réel de violation d'un droit fondamental en raison des défaillances systémiques ou généralisées concernant cette indépendance.

(iv) La question de savoir quels peuvent être les effets à rebours du mouvement « centralisateur » inhérent au nouveau cadre et à la proposition du Pacte DEF : si, d'un côté, le mouvement de centralisation (envers l'Union, à travers l'action de la Commission et du PE) peut aboutir à renforcer le partage de valeurs communes et de la confiance réciproque, il peut néanmoins, d'un autre côté, générer la méfiance des États membres objet de ce contrôle et poser ainsi des obstacles, dans un contexte de crises multiples, au projet européen.

(v) De plus, s'il y a bien une limite que l'Union ne peut pas laisser les États dépasser sous peine de fragmentation du *core* axiologique de l'intégration, il

---

[44] Cf. Arrêt du 25 juillet 2018, n.°s 33 et suivs., en particulier n.°s 61 et 72. La Cour a dit pour droit que «*L'article 1er, paragraphe 3, de la décision-cadre 2002/584/JAI du Conseil, du 13 juin 2002, relative au mandat d'arrêt européen et aux procédures de remise entre États membres, telle que modifiée par la décision-cadre 2009/299/JAI du Conseil, du 26 février 2009, doit être interprété en ce sens que, lorsque l'autorité judiciaire d'exécution appelée à décider de la remise d'une personne faisant l'objet d'un mandat d'arrêt européen émis aux fins de l'exercice de poursuites pénales dispose d'éléments, tels que ceux figurant dans une proposition motivée de la Commission européenne, adoptée en application de l'article 7, paragraphe 1, TUE, tendant à démontrer l'existence d'un risque réel de violation du droit fondamental à un procès équitable garanti par l'article 47, deuxième alinéa, de la charte des droits fondamentaux de l'Union européenne, en raison de défaillances systémiques ou généralisées en ce qui concerne l'indépendance du pouvoir judiciaire de l'État membre d'émission, ladite autorité doit vérifier, de manière concrète et précise, si, eu égard à la situation personnelle de cette personne, ainsi qu'à la nature de l'infraction pour laquelle elle est poursuivie et au contexte factuel qui sont à la base du mandat d'arrêt européen, et compte tenu des informations fournies par l'État membre d'émission en application de l'article 15, paragraphe 2, de la décision-cadre 2002/584, telle que modifiée, il existe des motifs sérieux et avérés de croire que ladite personne courra un tel risque, en cas de remise à ce dernier État.*»

n'est pas sûr que l'Union aujourd'hui ait vraiment des compétences pour contrôler l'activité de nature constitutionnelle des États membres sans un rapport concret avec l'application du droit de l'Union et sans qu'une révision des traités ait lieu. Et ce contrôle à présent exercé surtout par la Commission et le PE a pour objet, en fait (aussi), des options juridiques et politiques qui sont le résultat de l'externalisation du vote démocratique interne. Le problème de la violation des valeurs de l'Union (et communes aux États membres) ne peut pas donc être adressé au niveau de l'Union sans toucher au cœur des systèmes juridiques internes et de la démocratie représentative nationale. Il faut donc bien réfléchir sur la *frontière axiologique* de l'UE à la lumière de la version (encore) en vigueur de traités et de ses limites.

(vi) Enfin, il faut aussi réfléchir aux avantages des solutions verticales de contrôle et de garantie (du nouveau cadre juridique européen) des valeurs de l'Union par rapport à un recentrement du contrôle au niveau horizontal des États membres, c'est-à-dire, plutôt intergouvernemental, mais néanmoins moins complexe et, si les conditions de son application sont remplies, plus efficace, jusqu'à ce que soit adoptée une solution plus claire et qui implique l'institution judiciaire de l'Union, en ce qui concerne la violation du respect des valeurs de l'Union, telles que prévus à l'article 2, y compris dans le volet respect des droits fondamentaux et du *rule of law* – implication dont le cas irlandais susmentionné peut constituer un premier (malgré petit) pas.

Les attaques terroristes et l'état d'urgence en France

Francis Lamy

Le régime de l'état d'urgence est régi par une loi du 3 avril 1955.

C'est un des trois régimes de pouvoirs de crise dans le droit français avec l'article 16 de la Constitution, qui permet au Président de la République de prendre des mesures législatives, et l'état de siège, qui confie l'ordre public à l'autorité militaire.

L'état d'urgence est un régime de crise qui donne aux préfets et au ministre de l'intérieur certains pouvoirs de police administrative supplémentaires.

L'état d'urgence est resté en vigueur en France pendant deux ans[1]. Déclaré par le Gouvernement dans la nuit du 13 au 14 novembre 2015, à la suite des attentats terroristes de Paris et de Saint-Denis, il a été prorogé à six reprises par le Parlement, à la quasi unanimité des députés et des sénateurs au début, et à une très large majorité par la suite. Une telle application est sans précédent par sa durée et par le nombre de décisions prises sur son fondement.

L'état d'urgence avait déjà été appliqué à plusieurs reprises :

- à la fin de l'année 2005 lors de violences urbaines pendant un peu moins de deux mois ;
- à chaque fois pendant quelques semaines, dans des collectivités d'outre-mer : en 1985 en Nouvelle-Calédonie, en 1986 à Wallis et Futuna et en 1987 en Polynésie Française, à la suite de troubles graves à l'ordre public ;
- en 1961 dans le contexte de la guerre d'Algérie, à la suite d'une tentative de coup d'état, simultanément avec le recours à l'article 16 de la Constitution ;
- avant 1958 en Algérie.

Conseiller d'Etat, ancien préfet de région.

[1] Il a cessé le 1er novembre 2017.

F. Lamy (✉)
Council of State, Paris, France
e-mail: francis.lamy@conseil-etat.fr

W. Heusel, J.-P. Rageade (eds.), *The Authority of EU Law*,
https://doi.org/10.1007/978-3-662-58841-3_22

1 L'état d'urgence : un régime donnant temporairement certains pouvoirs renforcés de police administrative aux préfets et au ministre de l'intérieur, qu'ils utilisent, s'ils l'estiment nécessaire

Pour présenter ce régime particulier je dirai ce qu'il n'est pas – car des confusions sont souvent faites – et ce qu'il est.

1.1 Ce que n'est pas l'état d'urgence, et ce qu'il ne permet pas :

- Il n'est pas un régime de suspension des libertés publiques : la déclaration de l'état d'urgence ne suspend aucune liberté, aucune législation particulière ;
- Il n'est pas un régime de pleins pouvoirs : les décisions prises dans son cadre sont soumises à la légalité (notamment, les personnes visées par une mesure doivent représenter *une menace pour l'ordre public*) et à un contrôle approfondi (et rapide) du juge administratif (j'y reviendrai) ;
- Il n'entraîne pas de modification de la répartition des compétences entre les organes de l'Etat, à la différence de l'article 16 de la Constitution, qui permet au Président de la République de prendre des mesures législatives, et de l'état de siège qui transfère la police administrative de l'autorité civile à l'autorité militaire ; l'état d'urgence ne modifie notamment pas la répartition des compétences entre l'autorité administrative et l'autorité judiciaire, il renforce les pouvoirs de police administrative qui, constitutionnellement, relèvent de l'autorité administrative, et dont le contentieux des actes est de la compétence du juge administratif;
- Il n'est pas un régime de répression pénale particulier, avec des incriminations élargies ou nouvelles, des peines renforcées et des juridictions d'exception : la déclaration de l'état d'urgence n'emporte aucune conséquence de cette nature, seule la violation des mesures administratives de l'état d'urgence fait l'objet de peines spécifiques;
- Enfin l'état d'urgence ne permet pas d'*internements administratifs*, ce serait inconstitutionnel[2], ni[3] *de restrictions à la liberté de la presse ou des médias audiovisuels*, mais seulement la fermeture de sites internet provoquant à la commission d'actes de terrorisme ou en faisant l'apologie ; il ne crée pas non plus un régime particulier de déchéance de la nationalité (celles-ci sont régies par le droit commun, le code civil, et s'appliquent en dehors de l'état d'urgence).

[2] Avis du Conseil d'Etat du 17 décembre 2015 N° 390867 sur la constitutionnalité et la compatibilité avec les engagements internationaux de la France de certaines mesures de prévention du risque de terrorisme et, parmi de nombreuses décisions du Conseil Constitutionnel : décision QPC 2015-527 du 22 décembre 2015.

[3] Depuis la loi du 20 novembre 2015.

1.2 Ce qu'est l'état d'urgence : un régime temporaire de pouvoirs de police administratif renforcés, organisé par la loi du 3 avril 1955

Un régime temporaire : l'état d'urgence, comme tous les régimes de crise, est temporaire, il est déclaré pour 12 jours par le Gouvernement et ensuite, si nécessaire, prorogé par la loi, pour des durées limitées fixées par le Parlement.

Quelles sont ces mesures de police administrative de l'état d'urgence ?

- Certaines sont des mesures que l'on pourrait qualifier d'habituelles, classiques, de la police administrative : des restrictions à la circulation dans certains endroits et à certaines heures, des zones de protection ou de sécurité, des interdictions de manifestations sur la voie publique, de réunions, des fermetures de lieux de réunion, y compris de lieux de culte, des dissolutions d'associations, des contrôles d'identité préventifs, mais qui se font à la demande du préfet alors qu'en dehors de l'état d'urgence les contrôles d'identité se font sous le contrôle du procureur, des remises d'armes ou encore des réquisitions ;
- Trois mesures permises par la loi de 1955 sont plus particulièrement restrictives des libertés publiques individuelles : *assignation à résidence*[4], *perquisition administratives* et saisies informatiques[5], *interdictions de séjour.*

Ces mesures sont des mesures :

- de *police administrative*[6] : Il s'agit de prévenir, empêcher des atteintes très graves à l'ordre public, protéger, et non pas de punir ;
- *renforcées*,
- et qui doivent être *encadrées par la loi*[7] **:** pour les assignations – durée assignation, nombre d'heures à domicile, de présentation au commissariat – pour les perquisitions, déroulement de la procédure de perquisition, perquisition en principe de jour sauf impossibilité ou urgence, procédure de saisie des données informatiques sous le contrôle a priori du juge pour leur exploitation etc.

Les préfets et le ministre de l'intérieur ont la possibilité d'utiliser ces pouvoirs, s'ils l'estiment nécessaire. C'est pour eux une option parmi l'ensemble de leurs

---

[4] Mais, en dehors de l'état d'urgence, il y a les assignations à résidence des étrangers avant leur expulsion et les contrôles de retours de territoires contrôlés par des organisations terroristes (code de la sécurité intérieure).

[5] En dehors de l'état d'urgence un grand nombre de procédures administratives prévoient des contrôles dans des lieux professionnels, mais parfois le domicile, par l'administration après autorisation et sous le contrôle d'un juge.

[6] Comme l'a jugé le Conseil Constitutionnel à propos des assignations à résidence (DC 2015-527 du 22/12/2015) et des perquisitions administratives (DC 2016-536 du 19/2/2016) et en tiré la conséquence que leur contentieux relève du juge administratif.

[7] Quand elles sont insuffisamment encadrées le Conseil Constitutionnel les déclare contraires à la Constitution : par exemple, Conseil Constitutionnel N°2017-677 QPC du 1er décembre 2017.

pouvoirs et moyens de police. Pour employer une expression imagée, l'état d'urgence est une « boîte à outil ».

Il faut rappeler au passage que, même sans texte, en dehors de l'état d'urgence, le champ des mesures et actions de police administrative est très large. Les mesures de police administratives ne sont pas, comme les peines, prévues à l'avance par des textes, même si le législateur a tendance à en prévoir de plus en plus. Les pouvoirs de police administrative permettent aussi bien de limiter la vitesse des véhicules dans la traversées d'un village que, dans l'urgence et la nécessité, de faire beaucoup : enfermer une personne pendant quelques heures avant qu'une autorité judiciaire prenne le relais, neutraliser un preneur d'otage etc. – ces pouvoirs étant accrus en cas de circonstances exceptionnelles[8].

Mais ce que donne l'état d'urgence, et c'est important sur le plan opérationnel quand plusieurs milliers d'agents de police ou de gendarmes agissent, dans des conditions souvent difficiles et dangereuses, c'est un cadre juridique clair à cette action, comme c'est le cas des conditions précises dans lesquelles doit s'effectuer une interdiction de séjour. L'état d'urgence donne aussi davantage d'efficacité aux mesures: par exemple la fermeture d'un lieu de réunion peut être décidée pour une durée déterminée, et la méconnaissance des mesures est pénalement réprimée. L'exécution forcée des décisions de l'état d'urgence est prévue par la loi de 1955, alors qu'elle est souvent incertaine dans le droit commun. Enfin l'état d'urgence permet des mesures que le droit commun de la police administrative ne permet pas de prendre en l'absence de base législative, comme les perquisitions administratives ou les assignations à résidence, qui ont joué un rôle important ces deux dernières années.

2 Mise en œuvre de l'état d'urgence

2.1 Mesures adoptées

En 2005, lors des violences urbaines, les mesures consistèrent quasi exclusivement en des restrictions à la circulation des personnes, le soir et la nuit. Dix ans plus tard, à partir des attentats du 13 novembre 2015 le ministre de l'intérieur et les préfets ont fait, en raison de l'intensité des menaces pesant sur la vie de la population, un tout autre choix. Ils ont eu recours massivement à deux des mesures les plus restrictives des libertés : plusieurs centaines d'assignations à résidence et plusieurs milliers de perquisitions administratives. Mais les autres mesures ont été très largement mises en œuvre aussi : zones de protection (notamment pendant l'euro de football), contrôles d'identité, interdictions de circulation, fouilles des bagages, fermetures de mosquées radicales etc…

Quelle est la menace, le « péril imminent » qui a motivé l'état d'urgence ?

---

[8] Conseil d'Etat Heyriès du 28 juin 1918.

La menace d'attentats de masse (Bataclan, Nice) ou contre une ou deux personnes (père Hamel, deux policiers à leur domicile, un policier sur les Champs-Elysées, deux jeunes femmes en gare de Marseille…) dans un contexte qui est connu : l'islamisme radical, Daech, l'action de la France au Mali, en Irak et en Syrie, en France près de 12 000 individus radicalisés recensés, parmi lesquels des individus possiblement d'une grande dangerosité et qui ne sont pas tous sous le contrôle de la justice faute d'éléments suffisants, mais qui sont « suivis », notamment par les services de renseignement ; le retour d'individus en provenance de zones de combat en Syrie, profitant de filières de migration et de nombreux déplacements dans l'espace européen…

Le rythme des décisions prises par les préfets et le ministre en application de l'état d'urgence a été très variable : pour les perquisitions administratives il y a eu des pics, à près de 250 par jours, dans le mois suivant les attentats du 13 novembre 2015. Mais après le mois de décembre 2015 elles ont considérablement diminué. Ces derniers mois c'était de l'ordre de quelques perquisitions par mois.

Les assignations à résidence ont concerné au plus fort de la crise 350 personnes. Aujourd'hui elles sont encore 41 à être assignées à résidence, certaines depuis plus d'un an, et huit depuis le début de l'état d'urgence, celles considérées comme les plus dangereuses par l'autorité administrative.

2.2 *Le contrôle du juge administratif*

Le contrôle du juge administratif est, pour les personnes qui sont l'objet de mesures individuelles de l'état d'urgence, assignations à résidence par exemple, ou qui sont concernées par des mesures règlementaires, restrictions à la circulation par exemple, *la garantie essentielle* contre des abus de l'état d'urgence.

L'importance et l'effectivité de cette garantie résulte de la conjonction de trois éléments caractéristiques du contentieux devant le juge administratif :

- *la capacité du juge administratif à apporter une réponse rapide* aux demandes : ce sont les procédures d'urgence, à commencer par le référé liberté de 48 heures, avant la procédure au fond ; il faut souligner l'importance de l'audience, à laquelle participe naturellement la personne, même si elle est assignée à résidence, son caractère informel permettant à chacun de faire valoir ses arguments, le nombre significatif de retraits ou de modifications de mesures de l'état d'urgence à la suite de l'audience et avant même la décision du juge des référés; une procédure très efficace pour les assignations à résidence , mais non pour les perquisitions, car le juge intervient alors a posteriori (sauf pour autoriser l'exploitation des données informatiques) et c'est donc pour les perquisitions un contentieux principalement indemnitaire et au fond (Conseil d'Etat Assemblée du 6 juillet 2016 *Naipol* et autres) ;
- *un contrôle approfondi du juge administratif* : c'est le « triple test » du contrôle de proportionnalité – qui est appliqué dans presque tous les Etats européens – la

mesure doit être nécessaire, adaptée et proportionnée, ces exigences valant pour les décisions comme pour leur exécution, devant le juge du fond comme devant le juge de l'urgence ;

- *la possibilité de combiner la procédure de référé et la saisine du juge constitutionnel d'une question prioritaire de constitutionnalité*[9], ce qui a permis au Conseil Constitutionnel, en quelques jours ou semaines de se prononcer sur la constitutionnalité des dispositions de la loi de 1955 régissant les prérogatives des préfets et du ministre de l'intérieur (décision du 22 décembre 2015 du Conseil constitutionnel jugeant conformes à la Constitution les dispositions relatives aux assignations à résidence à la suite de sa saisine par la décision de la section du contentieux du Conseil d'Etat, D. n°395009 du 11 décembre 2015).

Au cours de l'état d'urgence le juge administratif, principalement les tribunaux administratifs et le Conseil d'Etat, ont été largement saisis et ont rendu plusieurs centaines des décisions. La part des satisfactions totales ou partielles pour les requérants à la suite de l'engagement d'une procédure contentieuse – entre 25%[10] et près de 50%[11] selon l'objet des mesure et si l'on tient compte des mesures prises par l'administration entre l'audience et la décision du juge, décisions alors de non lieu qui résultent de retraits ou d'aménagements de la décision attaquée – est élevée comparativement à d'autres contentieux.

La difficulté de la tâche des autorités de police administrative, de leur action dans l'urgence et dans des conditions incertaines et mouvantes, mais périlleuses, l'expliquent, davantage qu'une propension à faire un usage excessif, abusif, de ces pouvoirs de crise.

C'est du moins mon avis, et l'impression que j'ai retiré des audiences de juge des référés que j'ai présidées.

2.3 *Modification de la loi de 1955*

La loi de 1955 a été modifiée pour prévoir un contrôle particulier du Parlement sur la mise en œuvre de l'état d'urgence.

« *L'Assemblée nationale et le Sénat sont informés sans délai des mesures prises par le Gouvernement pendant l'état d'urgence. Les autorités administratives leur transmettent sans délai copie de tous les actes qu'elles prennent en application de la présente loi. L'Assemblée nationale et le Sénat peuvent requérir toute information complémentaire dans le cadre du contrôle et de l'évaluation de ces mesures*[12]. »

[9] Donc sans attendre la procédure au fond.

[10] Ainsi, concernant les procédures de référé devant les TA relatives à des assignations à résidence on comptait au 3 août 2017 205 rejets, 35 satisfactions totales ou partielles et 27 non lieu.

[11] Concernant les procédures au fond contre des perquisitions administratives devant les TA au 3 août 2017 on comptait 30 rejets et 29 satisfactions totales ou partielles.

[12] Article 4-1 de la loi du 3 avril 1955 issu de la loi du 21 juillet 2016.

Il n'y a pas, je crois, de précédent, en terme de contrôle parlementaire, c'est à dire d'une politique publique se traduisant par plusieurs milliers de décisions administratives, qui devaient donner lieu à transmission systématique et exhaustive en temps réel au Parlement.

Les commissions des lois du Sénat et de l'Assemblée nationale ont exercé un contrôle constant et particulièrement vigilant sur la mise en œuvre au jour le jour de l'état d'urgence. Des rapports parlementaires très rigoureux et précis ont permis d'informer de façon très complète députés et sénateurs et, parce qu'ils étaient publics, journalistes, universitaires et simples citoyens.

2.4 Le défenseur des droits

Le défenseur des droits[13] a été amené à intervenir, notamment sur les précautions à prendre vis à vis des enfants en cas de perquisition.

3 Appréciation sur l'état d'urgence

3.1 Le texte de la loi du 3 avril 1955 a profondément évolué à partir du 20 novembre 2015

Du fait des modifications apportées par les lois du 20 novembre 2015, du 21 juillet et 19 décembre 2016, ou encore du 11 juillet 2017 il n'est plus le même que le texte d'origine, encore appliqué en 2005.

Ces lois sont intervenues essentiellement pour encadrer davantage la mise en œuvre des pouvoirs de police administrative de l'état d'urgence et répondre ainsi aux exigences de la jurisprudence du juge constitutionnel en matière de mesures restrictives des libertés publiques, soit en anticipant un risque de censure (loi du 20 novembre 2015) soit en tirant les conséquences d'une censure, comme ce fut le cas de la loi du 11 juillet 2017 qui a rétabli les mesures d'interdiction individuelles du territoire[14], en les entourant des garanties exigées par le Conseil Constitutionnel.

Ce faisant on peut dire, sous réserve des recours encore pendants devant le Conseil Constitutionnel[15], que les dispositions de la loi de 1955 répondent aux

---

[13] Autorité constitutionnelle indépendante, qui en application de l'article 71-1 de la Constitution « *...veille au respect des droits et libertés par les administrations...* » et « *...peut être saisi ... par toute personne s'estimant lésée par le fonctionnement d'un service public...* ».

[14] Décision du Conseil Constitutionnel du 9 juin 2017 N°2017-635.

[15] L'article 5 2° de la loi du 3 avril 1955 sur les zones de protection (Conseil Constitutionnel N 2017-684 QPC du 11 janvier 2018) et l'article 8-1 sur les contrôles d'identité, fouilles des bagages et des véhicules (Conseil Constitutionnel N°2017-677 QPC du 1er décembre 2017) ont été déclarés contraires à la Constitution en raison de l'insuffisance de leur encadrement, mais, dans le deuxième

exigences de la Constitution, à commencer par celles de la déclaration des droits de l'homme et du citoyen de 1789, et par là, sous réserve de l'appréciation de la Cour, aux exigences de la CEDH[16], ainsi qu'aux valeurs de l'UE[17].

3.2 L'application de l'état d'urgence

Son déclanchement n'a pas été critiqué et n'était pas critiquable au regard des conditions posées par la loin de 1955, à l'évidence réunies : un « *péril imminent résultant d'atteintes graves à l'ordre public* ».

Il a donné lieu, comme les prorogations, en application de l'article 15 de la CEDH, à notification par le Gouvernement au secrétaire général du Conseil de l'Europe et, en application du pacte sur les droits civils et politiques, à notification au secrétaire général des Nations Unies. Il n'est pas douteux que la France, victime d'attentats de masse était dans une situation de *« danger public menaçant la vie de la nation »,* au sens de l'article 15 de la CEDH, qui permet à un Etat de déroger à la convention.

Sa mise en œuvre a pu être critiquée par certains, mais au regard des *exigences de l'Etat de droit* les droits des personnes sont effectivement garantis du fait notamment de l'action du juge administratif et du Conseil Constitutionnel.

D'un point de vue *démocratique* il faut souligner qu'il a été prorogé à la quasi unanimité ou à l'écrasante majorité de chacune des chambres du Parlement, et que ces prorogations avaient le soutien d'une nette majorité de Français.

Pour apprécier *l'utilité* de l'état d'urgence il importe de le considérer pour ce qu'il est, c'est à dire un moyen supplémentaire s'ajoutant à tous ceux mobilisés par ailleurs (renseignement, parquet antiterroriste, services généraux, action de la France sur les théâtres d'opération….) et permettant un emploi plus efficace des moyens, notamment humains, des services spécialisés et généraux participant à l'action de surveillance des personnes présentant une menace pour l'ordre public. Les assignations à résidence des personnes présentant un risque élevé pour la sécurité dans contexte de dangers élevés ont apporté un gain d'efficacité très important pour la mission de surveillance et ont permis une répartition optimale des moyens humains consacrés à la surveillance de personnes dangereuses pour la sécurité.

---

cas, reconnaissant l'intérêt de ces mesures, le Conseil a différé au 30 juin 2018 la date de l'abrogation des dispositions contestées.

[16] Le déclanchement et la prorogation de l'état d'urgence ont été notifiés au Conseil de l'Europe conformément à l'article 15 de la CEDH et l'avis de la commission de Venise n'a pas contesté le bien fondé du recours à l'état d'urgence.

[17] Article 7 du traité de l'UE sur la procédure de sanction à l'égard d'un Etat qui violerait de façon « *grave et persistante* » des valeurs énoncées à l'article 2 du traité (respect de la dignité humaine, liberté, démocratie, égalité, État de droit, respect des droits de l'homme notamment).

Il faut aussi souligner qu'il n'y a pas d'*efficacité* en soi de l'état d'urgence. Celle-ci dépend en réalité de la manière dont les autorités compétentes se servent des instruments qui sont à leur disposition.

D'autre part s'agissant d'une action préventive, ce qui est le propre de la police administrative, il est par définition difficile de comptabiliser les résultats : ceux-ci ne se limitent pas aux infractions découvertes dans le cadre de mesures de l'état d'urgence comme des perquisitions administratives. Ils comprennent aussi les attentats évités, ce qui peut s'identifier parfois, mais pas toujours, la dissuasion, ce qui est plus difficile encore à mesurer, comme les bénéfices de court et moyen terme que représente la collecte d'informations dans le cadre de ces mesures, qui est très précieuse.

Des individus très dangereux ont été surveillés, des perquisitions ont permis découvrir des armes, de permettre l'engagement de poursuites par le parquet antiterroriste[18], des lieux de cultes, foyers de radicalisme, ont été fermés provisoirement jusqu'à un changement de dirigeants, des équipes ou des individus isolés ont pu être gênés, intimidés etc.

Si l'on prend l'exemple des quelque 4 000 perquisitions administratives, la vague massive de perquisitions[19] au lendemain des attentats a permis de saisir des armes et des données informatiques qui ont été suivies par l'engagement de procédures pénales. Mais au-delà de ces procédures pénales des réseaux ont pu être désorganisés, des informations rassemblées, et une meilleure connaissance de la réalité de la menace assurée, ce qui est essentiel pour utiliser au mieux possible les moyens engagés.

L'état d'urgence a donc permis un renforcement des actions de police administrative et un relèvement de la sécurité intérieure, qui étaient nécessaires dans ce contexte de péril intense pesant sur la vie de la population, et qui étaient complémentaires de l'action judiciaire conduite avec beaucoup d'efficacité par le parquet antiterroriste de Paris.

La sortie de l'état d'urgence est pour tout Gouvernement, dans le contexte que nous vivons, une décision difficile à prendre. La sortie d'une crise liée à des troubles graves à l'ordre public est d'ailleurs toujours une phase difficile, critique. Dans le cas de cet état d'urgence cette difficulté est liée à la persistance d'une menace terroriste intense dont la France est la cible. L'attentat de Nice du 14 juillet 2016, avec 86 morts et des centaines de blessés, a par ailleurs conduit à prolonger un état d'urgence qui était sur le point d'être arrêté, comme l'avait annoncé quelques heures auparavant le Président de la République.

Mais comme le Conseil d'Etat l'a souligné à plusieurs reprises dans ses avis sur les projets de loi de prorogation « *…l'état d'urgence doit demeurer temporaire. Les menaces durables ou permanentes doivent être traitées, dans le cadre de l'Etat de droit, par des moyens permanents renforcés …* »[20]. Plusieurs lois ont, ces dernières

---

[18] Au 10 novembre 2016 elles représentaient 10% des saisines du parquet antiterroriste (hors apologie du terrorisme).

[19] Dans 16% des cas elles ont été suivies de procédures judiciaires.

[20] Avis du 18 juillet 2016 AG n° 391834.

années, renforcé ces moyens permanents.[21] Le Gouvernement a décidé de renforcer encore ces moyens permanents à travers un projet de loi sur la sécurité intérieure et la lutte contre le terrorisme. Ce projet comprend notamment des mesures analogues à certaines mesures de l'état d'urgence, mais avec des conditions différentes : assignations à résidence, créations de zones de sécurité, fermetures de lieux de culte et perquisitions administratives pouvant être décidées par las autorités de police administrative.

Le Gouvernement a annoncé que l'état d'urgence serait levé dès son adoption[22], ce qui a été fait la fin du mois d'octobre 2017.

4 Conclusion

L'état d'urgence n'est pas un symptôme, une illustration et encore moins la cause d'une crise de l'état de droit, c'est la protection des personnes et des biens dans des situations de crise d'une particulière gravité et la défense de l'état de droit, mais à condition :

- que les pouvoirs des autorités soient strictement encadrés par la loi pour assurer le bon équilibre entre garanties des libertés et protection de l'ordre public ;
- que le recours effectif devant le juge, avec un contrôle approfondi et dans des délais rapides soit garanti;
- et qu'il soit fait un usage approprié des mesures : sous cet angle une des garanties est que ce ne sont pas des pouvoirs laissés à la discrétion des services de police ou de gendarmerie, aussi compétents et de qualité soient-ils, mais qui appartiennent à des autorités administratives responsables, le ministre et, dans les territoires, le préfet.

---

[21] Notamment les lois n° 2015-912 du 24 juillet 2015 relative au renseignement, n° 2016-339 du 22 mars 2016 relative à la prévention et à la lutte contre les incivilités, contre les atteintes à la sécurité publique et contre les actes terroristes dans les transports collectifs de voyageurs et n° 2016-731 du 3 juin 2016 renforçant la lutte contre le crime organisé, le terrorisme.

[22] Ce projet a été adopté et est devenu la loi du 30 octobre 2017 renforçant la sécurité intérieure et la lutte contre le terrorisme. L'état d'urgence a été levé le lendemain.

Current threats to the rule of law in the EU: The foundation on which the authority of EU law rests

Pauliine Koskelo

1 Introductory remarks

The title of our working session evokes the rule of law as the foundation on which the authority of EU law rests. Moreover, however, the rule of law is a foundation for the European Union itself. This is spelled out in Article 2 TUE, according to which the Union is founded on the values of respect for human dignity, freedom, democracy, equality, the rule of law and respect for human rights, including the right of persons belonging to minorities. As the Article further spells out, those values underpin a society in which pluralism, non-discrimination, tolerance, justice, solidarity and equality between women and men prevail.

While Article 2 TEU cites the above elements, including democracy, the rule of law and respect for human rights, as the core "values" on which the Union is founded, some general remarks seem to me important to underline at the outset.

Firstly, it is essential not to lose sight of, or to detract from, the fact that by enshrining those elements in the Treaty, the Member States have elevated them from mere "values" to legal commitments which form the constitutional basis for the Union. As legal commitments, they have a binding character which cannot be allowed to become diluted if the Union is to be maintained as envisaged.

Secondly, while the listed core elements of the Union are conceptually distinct, they form a whole. Experience, including recent experience both outside and inside Europe, demonstrates that genuine democracy, rule of law and respect for human rights belong together in the sense that one does not survive without the other. Democracy depends on the fundamental rights and freedoms being respected and

Contribution to the Panel on the rule of law crisis in the EU and beyond.

P. Koskelo (✉)
European Court of Human Rights, Strasbourg, France

ERA Board of Trustees, Trier, Germany
e-mail: pauliine.koskelo@echr.coe.int

W. Heusel, J.-P. Rageade (eds.), *The Authority of EU Law*,
https://doi.org/10.1007/978-3-662-58841-3_23

protected, and it depends on the checks and balances provided for through effective adherence to the principles of rule of law. Respect for human rights and the rule of law, in turn, become endangered whenever democratic governance degrades into, or is replaced by, authoritarian rule.

Thirdly, it is important to bear in mind that ultimately, the issue is not about what the Union can impose on its Member States, or what the Member States can expect from each other; it is about how far Member States are, or should be, prepared to tolerate deviations from core principles in a Union which by its very nature is a matter of common concern. Ultimately, the question is not on which terms a given Member State wishes to belong to the Union but on which terms the other Member States are willing to share company, if the commitment to jointly agreed core requirements is crumbling.

In this regard, the EU is not just a club where the members share one or another activity but may differ on everything else. With free movement, mutual recognition and huge transfer mechanisms, we are more like a common household—a true union—where a community of core values is really a condition for the sustainability of that union. In a union, the partners cannot expect to be free to choose their own lifestyle alone, without risking their union itself.

In the EU, the questions that arise are not just soft and vague questions about values, they are hard and real questions about the core issues of the Union. How can mutual recognition be sustained if we cannot trust that the decisions to be recognised or enforced truly reflect and uphold the basic values of Article 2? How can we justify enormous amounts of financial support to Member States without being serious about whether the governance they practice or the policies they pursue are in line with those values? How can a union be maintained if its constitutional basis erodes? In the end, the toughest questions arise not for those who falter in their commitment to the core constitutional values but for those who do not wish to falter.

2 The rule of law and judicial independence as a key pillar of it

My assigned role in the panel has been to discuss the independence of the judiciary as an element of the rule of law and thus as an element of the core requirements underpinning the Union under Article 2 TEU. I have already mentioned some of the reasons why, in the context of that Article and its fundamental significance, the maintenance of the rule of law is crucial. It is one of the core requirements in the constitutional basis of the Union. The rule of law may sound like an easy phrase which no reasonable person would object to, or a concept well adapted to please Napoleon's taste for constitutional principles, as it may appear both "short and obscure" and thus amenable to being defined or redefined according to current needs or preferences. Yet the rule of law has developed into a constitutional notion which is rather well defined and established. Quite recently, the Council of Europe has formally adopted, on the basis of a recommendation by the Venice Commission, a set of rule of law criteria.[1]

These criteria include the following:

- *legality* (implying a procedure for the adoption of legal texts based on transparency, accountability and democracy);
- *legal certainty*;
- a *prohibition on arbitrary measures*;
- *access to justice* before independent and impartial courts with *jurisdictional control over administrative acts*;
- respect for *human rights*, and;
- *non-discrimination* and *equality before the law*.

Accordingly, the key elements are well set out, although it is inevitable that the criteria themselves leave room for interpretation and require further refinement and concrete elaboration. In the context of Article 2 TEU, it seems clear that these criteria cannot be regarded as "optional", or as matters of preference. Nor can notions such as "national identity" or constitutional identity be employed to undermine, or to justify deviations from, such core elements of the commitments required from each and every Member State. The rule of law criteria are constituent parts of the checks and balances which are necessary for maintaining both democracy, the primacy of law as well as equality before the law.

3 Constitutional guarantees: And the importance of a solidly rooted constitutional culture

For obvious reasons, the above elements of the rule of law must be enshrined at the level of constitutional law. That is necessary, but not sufficient. Experience demonstrates that there are numerous ways, often subtle and not necessarily very conspicuous or transparent ones, in which the principles that are essential underpinnings of the rule of law may be neglected or eroded. This can happen through a variety of measures, whether legislative, budgetary, organisational, administrative or other, which may not be "making news", nor appear as obvious enough to alert the general public, or even those with an active interest in the state of affairs in the society.

It is also important to note that even societies where the rule of law is seemingly well established are not free from such risks. Respect for the rule of law is not only a matter of the requisite constitutional guarantees being formally in place. It is ultimately also a matter of constitutional culture. A genuine and resilient respect for the rule of law must be solidly rooted not only in the formal legal structures or the

[1] See the "rule of law checklist" under http://www.venice.coe.int/webforms/documents/default.aspx?pdffile=CDL-AD(2016)007-e. The document has been formally endorsed by the Committee of Ministers of the Council of Europe in September 2016 and by the Parliamentary Assembly in October 2017.

rhetoric customs of the society, but in the actual practices of governance. The most testing moments are not those of harmony but situations where tensions arise.

Looking around, we see that the rule of law may become endangered, eroded or outright abandoned where its historic roots are too short or fragile. What we also detect, however, is that although the roots and traditions may be old and seasoned, even centuries old, this in itself does not necessarily provide any insurance against the emergence of political leadership with tendencies that are disconcerting from the point of view of the respect for the rule of law. For the latter to stay alive, constant care, cultivation and alertness are required.

4 Access to an independent judiciary as an element of EU law

Access to justice before independent and impartial courts is one of the key pillars of the rule of law. It is also a fundamental requirement under EU law.

Recently (after the ERA Congress of October 2017), this matter has been addressed by the CJEU in a Grand Chamber judgment of 27 February 2018, in the case of *Associação Sindical dos Juízes Portugueses* (C-64/16). In the present context, the judgment is notable in that the Court

(i) recalls that, as stated in Article 2 TEU, the European Union is a union based on the rule of law (§§ 30, 31);
(ii) makes, obiter dictum, the point of emphasising that mutual trust between the Member States and, in particular, their courts and tribunals is based on the fundamental premise that Member States share the common values on which the European Union is founded, as stated in Article 2 TEU (§ 30);
(iii) refers to Article 19 TEU as a norm which, by enshrining the requirement of effective judicial protection, gives concrete expression to the value of the rule of law stated in Article 2 TEU and which entrusts the responsibility for ensuring judicial review in the EU legal order not only to the Court of Justice but also to national courts and tribunals (§ 32);
(iv) stresses that the existence of effective judicial review designed to ensure compliance with EU law is of the essence of the rule of law (§ 36);
(v) points out that the principle of the effective judicial protection of individuals' rights under EU law, referred to in the second subparagraph of Article 19(1) TEU, is a general principle of EU law, stemming from the constitutional traditions common to the Member States and also enshrined in Articles 6 and 13 of the European Convention of Human Rights (§ 35);
(vi) underlines the duty of the Member States to ensure that their competent courts meet the requirements essential to effective judicial protection, which go to them being established by law, being permanent and independent, their jurisdiction being compulsory, their procedure being *inter partes* and based on the application of rules of law (§§ 37–38);

(vii) underlines that the independence of the courts and tribunals is essential, as the guarantee of independence is inherent in the task of adjudication (§§ 41–42);
(viii) holds that the concept of independence presupposes, in particular, that the body concerned exercises its judicial functions wholly autonomously, without being subject to any hierarchical constraint or subordinated to any other body and without taking orders or instructions from any source whatsoever, and that it is thus protected against external interventions or pressure liable to impair the independent judgment of its members and to influence their decisions (§ 44).

These findings are well in line with the point that I would stress, namely that the importance of an independent judiciary is not only a "core value" for a union such as the EU, but a functional necessity.

5 The concept of judicial independence

As reflected in the last point (viii) just cited from the above CJEU judgment, the concept of judicial independence boils down to the requirement of a wholly autonomous exercise of judicial functions. That in turn depends on several well-known elements.

Firstly, judicial independence requires the presence of *institutional guarantees*, both individual and structural, which must be secured at the level of constitutional norms.

In this category belong guarantees attaching to the *individual members* of the judiciary, i.e. the holders of judicial posts. These including the organisational and procedural norms governing recruitment, appointment and career development, the permanence of judicial tenure and the right to remain in office other than in the case of serious misconduct established under due procedural safeguards.

Among the institutional guarantees belong also the *structural protections* necessary for ensuring the independence of the courts and the judicial system as such. They concern matters such as the organisation, administration and funding of the courts.

The various institutional guarantees must be designed to secure a professional judiciary, to safeguard its integrity and judicial autonomy and to protect its freedom from undue external interference or influence.

Such guarantees are essential, but they are not sufficient to guarantee an independent exercise of judicial functions. The institutional guarantees constitute a protective shell, but what is essential as well is the substance inside, which consists of the professional competence and mindset of those exercising judicial functions. The independence of office alone provides no guarantee unless it is associated with an independence of mind. Judges must not only be institutionally but also intellectually independent and impartial. In other words, they must be genuinely able and willing to consider each issue before them with a non-biased and critical mind. One cannot be independent without wanting to be independent. It is a question of mindset and professional culture, and not merely a matter of formal legal guarantees.

Independence and impartiality mean that the judge's loyalty must be to the law and the values underpinning the rule of law, and that there may be no competing loyalties at work in the judiciary. This in turn is a matter of professional education, socialisation and judicial culture, and ultimately a matter of personal integrity and sense of duty in judicial office.

Thus, judicial independence must be both externally guaranteed and internalised as a professional mindset, as the ethos of judging. Recent evidence of the fundamental importance of these matters is available, for instance, in certain judgments of the European Court of Human Rights, offering concrete illustrations of what may transpire when the courts, which should serve as the ultimate protectors of the rights of individuals, are turned into the opposite, namely instruments of repression.

6 The EU context

The theme of our working session has been set in the context of current tendencies in certain parts of Europe, both outside and inside the EU, which represent a diversion from, or even an open rejection of, the principles on which the rule of law is based. What we had expected, and already seen, in terms of progress has turned into regression. Usually, these developments are associated with a warped conception of democracy, reduced to a rule by the parliamentary majority, the latter often portraying itself as "the people" in order to evoke and enhance the legitimacy of their pursuits.

We have currently within the EU political leaders for whom the "checks and balances" that are at the heart of the principles of the rule of law represent a form of "intellectual mediocrity".[2] Yet, for the EU, rule of law represents a foundation of the union, enshrined at the highest normative level—and in many countries approved by referenda (as has been the case in both Hungary and Poland).

When the "checks and balances", or the constraints on the exercise of power enshrined in the principles of the rule of law, are no longer considered attractive or worth adhering to, it is no surprise that the judiciary and the media are among the first targets, of various measures designed to curtail their independent and critical role in the mechanisms of control, review and accountability. In relation to the judiciary, the measures usually take the form of a reduction of competences or impact, followed by steps toward replacing the members. We see institutional guarantees being weakened, administrative independence being compromised, and judicial appointments being captured under the control of those holding political power.

In the EU, a lot is at stake, not only for individual Member States but for the Union as such. In a union with free movement and open borders, the justice system must be organised accordingly. Unless legal obligations and liabilities, whether civil

[2] Kirchick (2017), p. 59.

or criminal, can be fairly, reliably and effectively enforced, there is no level playing field in the internal market, and freedom of movement will have serious side effects in giving rise to injustices which citizens, for good reasons, will find hard to accept. It is therefore not difficult to understand why the principle of mutual recognition plays a key role in EU law and is qualified as a "structural principle of the Union's constitutional framework".

The President of the CJEU *Koen Lenaerts* has recently stated that all Member States are *deemed* to share the same degree of commitment to democratic values, fundamental rights and the rule of law and that one may therefore reasonably expect that they should trust each other, especially when acting in concert to achieve common EU objectives.[3]

The basis of this "deeming" is to be found in the legal commitment expressed in Article 2 TEU (and, in particular with a view to judicial independence, the obligations arising from Article 19 TEU, as indicated by the CJEU in *Associação Sindical dos Juízes Portugueses,* cited above). The constitutional premise according to which all Member States must be both able and willing to live up to those requirements of course begs the question of the consequences arising in a scenario where it turns out that this is no longer the case. I must confess that I find it worrying that the gravity of this question does not always appear to be sufficiently appreciated in all circles. The freedoms enshrined in Union law cannot function without the principle of mutual recognition. Mutual recognition in turn cannot be practiced without mutual trust, but the latter cannot just be pretended. It must actually be well-founded, anchored in the legal and factual realities prevailing in the Member States.

There are obvious sensitivities involved, as demands for respect for the principles and commitments enshrined in Article 2 TEU are sometimes made out as "interference" in a Member State's internal affairs. What gets lost in such an approach—in the particular context of a legal construction such as the EU—is that the respect for the requirements arising from Article 2 TEU cannot be regarded merely as a matter of "internal affairs" for individual Member States.

This is particularly conspicuous in the context of mutual recognition. Where the rule of law is not respected and a justice system is not genuinely independent or impartial, criminal proceedings may be instrumentalised for ulterior purposes, or the outcome of proceedings, whether civil or criminal, may be affected by undue influences or distorted by undue considerations. If the judicial authorities of another Member State are nevertheless called upon to recognise or enforce judgments or decisions that may be infected by such flaws, the requested authorities, in an exercise of mutual trust, will end up as being directly implicated in upholding such malfunctioning. They risk becoming "accomplices" in possible miscarriages of justice. In a union such as the EU, failings in the rule of law do not remain "internal affairs" or internal problems; through the application of mutual recognition, their consequences risk being spilled over across the borders. One should not lose sight of this when discussing the issues arising from a decline or erosion in the rule of law.

[3] Lenaerts (2017), p. 808.

Indeed, the new slogan seems to be that mutual trust does not amount to "blind" trust. But what, then, will be the concrete meaning of this reservation or qualification? One of the characteristics of mutual recognition is that the requested judicial authority is neither supposed to nor permitted to conduct a "revision de fond". Furthermore, the requested judicial authority will not necessarily be in a position to determine whether a judgment or decision in an individual case is flawed as a result of failings in the respect for the principles of the rule of law. While general problems or issues in the requesting State may be known, whether specific cases can be regarded as manifestations of such problems is a much more difficult matter to judge (not least given the tight timeframes which should be respected).

Under the circumstances, it is perhaps not surprising that the CJEU has recently received a request for a preliminary ruling, issued by the High Court of Ireland in the case of Minister for Justice and Equality v. LM,[4] whereby the referring court inquires as to the correct test to apply where the latter, as an executing judicial authority under the Framework Decision on the European Arrest Warrant, has concluded that the common value of the rule of law set out in Article 2 TEU has been breached in the issuing Member State. At the time of writing, the Court's proceedings were pending, but in the meantime, on 25 July 2018, the judgment has been delivered. While it is not possible at this point to enter into any detailed analysis of the Court's response, it is difficult to see that the judicial mechanism foreseen in the ruling could represent a sustainable solution to the underlying problem posed by a Member State that no longer adheres to the rule of law as we know it.

It is highly regrettable that the Union finds itself in a state where such issues pose themselves. As mentioned above, it may be feared that, ultimately, the toughest questions will arise not for those who falter in their commitment to the core constitutional values enshrined in Article 2 TEU, but for those who wish to remain committed to them.

References

Kirchick J (2017) The end of Europe – dictators, demagogues and the coming dark age. Yale University Press, p 59

Lenaerts K (2017) La vie après l'avis: exploring the principle of mutual (yet not blind) trust. Common Mark Law Rev 54(3):808

[4] Judgment of 25.7.2018, C-216/18 *PPU Minister for Justice and Equality v LM (Celmer)*, ECLI:EU:C:2018:586.

Part VII
The crisis of the European project undermining the authority of EU law: The EU in search for legitimacy

The EU, democracy and institutional structure: Past, present and future

Paul Craig

1 Introduction

It is commonplace to bemoan the EU's democratic deficiencies, as attested to by the wealth of literature discussing the issue from a variety of perspectives. This chapter is not a literature review. To the contrary, it advances my own view on the issue, albeit one that is informed by existing scholarship. The ensuing analysis is predicated on the assumption that a principal, albeit not exclusive, cause for concern about EU democracy is the mismatch, or absence of fit, between voter power and political responsibility.

EU decision-making is structured such that voters cannot determine the shape or direction of EU policy in the manner that occurs to a greater extent within Member States. It is not, therefore, possible in the EU for the electorate to remove the incumbents from office, and replace them with a different political party that has a different set of policies. It is this malaise that underlies Weiler's critique of EU decision-making, captured in aphorismic terms by his affirmation of the centrality to democracy of the voters' ability to 'throw the scoundrels out'.[1] It is the same malaise that informs Maduro's critique, to the effect that the 'real EU democratic deficit is the absence of European politics',[2] manifest in the lack of democratic political contestation about the content and direction of EU policy. Properly understood these are but two sides of the same coin.

The ensuing discussion takes the same starting point as Weiler and Maduro. The direction of travel thereafter is, however, rather different, insofar as we are concerned with explanation and understanding of the status quo. The assumption,

[1] Weiler et al. (1995), and Weiler (2012).

[2] Maduro (2012).

P. Craig (✉)
Professor of English Law, St John's College, Oxford, UK
e-mail: paul.craig@law.ox.ac.uk

W. Heusel, J.-P. Rageade (eds.), *The Authority of EU Law*,
https://doi.org/10.1007/978-3-662-58841-3_24

explicit or implicit, in much of the literature is that the fault for this malaise resides with the EU. The pattern of thought seems strikingly simple, shaped by the very cadence of language. This is most marked in the duality of meaning accorded to the phrase the 'EU's democratic deficit', which is used descriptively to capture the malaise adumbrated above, and deployed normatively to connote the fact that the fault resides with the EU, which is regarded as architect and author of present reality.

The academic line of argument pursued thereafter flows naturally from the preceding duality of meaning. Given that the democratic shortcoming resides descriptively and normatively with the EU, democracy must therefore remain in the Member States, which are said to be the principal sites for democratic legitimation. Some of the literature on 'demoicracy' is grounded, in part at least, on such assumptions. The discussion that follows takes issue with this descriptive and normative linkage, and hence with the conclusions drawn therefrom.

It will be argued that the preceding linkage does not withstand examination. Insofar as there is a democratic deficit of the kind identified above, it flows from choices made expressly and repeatedly by the Member States over time as to the institutional structure for decision-making which they are willing to accept. These choices could have been different. There is no a priori block in this respect. There is, to the contrary, no especial difficulty in devising an EU decision-making regime that would meet the democratic shortcomings outlined above. The EU itself is not blameless with respect to the mode of decision-making, and nothing in the present chapter is predicated on that assumption. Improvements could doubtless be made in the manner in which the principal EU institutions operate. This does not alter the fact that the Treaty architecture that frames their respective powers, and the way in which they inter-relate, is the result of Member State choice, made and re-made since the inception of the Community.

It will also be argued that there are, however, four constraints to a fit between the EU's institutional decision-making structure, and the precepts of democracy. The constraints are political, democratic, constitutional and substantive. The *political* constraint is predicated on the assumption that some form of parliamentary majoritarian regime would meet the democratic deficit articulated above, thereby ensuring a closer nexus between voter preferences and political responsibility. Change of the kind that would meet the democratic infirmity thus conceived is, however, very unlikely to occur, because the Member States will not accept it for the reasons explicated below. The *democratic* constraint is expressive of the fact that there is contestation as to whether such a parliamentary-type regime really is the most appropriate model for a polity such as the EU, or whether a different form of democratic ordering would be better suited. The *constitutional* constraint denotes the fact that EU decision-making is limited by the very nature of the constituent Treaties. National constitutions constrain political choice. It is inherent in their very nature. The EU is no different in this respect in principle, in the sense that the founding Treaties form the architecture to which legislation made thereunder must conform. The difference is one of degree, but it is significant nonetheless, since the EU Treaties are far more detailed than any national constitution, and hence the room for democratic policy choice is more circumscribed. The *substantive* constraint speaks to the democratic consequences of the imbalance between the economic and the social within the EU, as manifest in the original Treaties, and as a consequence of the EU's financial crisis.

2 Institutional structure and democracy: The past

The Community may only be 60 years old, but it is nonetheless easy to forget its institutional origins, and the conception of democracy that existed, or not as the case maybe, at the outset. The reality was that the original disposition of power in the Rome Treaty saw little role for direct democratic input. The Assembly was accorded limited power, and its only role in the legislative process was a right to be consulted where a particular Treaty article so specified. The principal institutional players were the Council and Commission, but in many respects the Rome Treaty placed the Commission in the driving seat in the development of Community policy. The Commission had the right of legislative initiative; it could alter a measure before the Council acted; its measures could only be amended by unanimity in the Council[3]; it devised the overall legislative agenda; and it had a plethora of other executive, administrative and judicial functions. The message was that, while the Council had to consent to proposed legislation, it was not easy for it to alter the Commission's proposal. The Commission might therefore have become something akin to a 'government' for the emerging Community.[4]

This vision accorded with, and was influenced by, Monnet's vision of Europe and by neofunctionalism. Monnet's conception of Europe was strongly influenced by the role of technocrats trained in the French *Grandes Ecoles*. It served to explain the structure of the ECSC, and the centrality of the High Authority therein, which embodied Monnet's technocratic approach. A corporatist style involving networks of interest groups was the other legacy of Monnet's experience with planning authorities in France.[5] It was institutionalised in the ECSC in the form of the Consultative Committee. Integration was based on the combination of benevolent technocrats and economic interest groups, which would build transnational coalitions for European policy.[6] Monnet's strategy was thus for what has been termed elite-led gradualism.[7] The Assembly's powers within the ECSC were very limited.

The same general institutional structure was to be carried over to the EEC: 'enlightened administration on behalf of uninformed publics, in cooperation with affected interests and subject to the approval of national governments, was therefore the compromise again struck in the Treaties of Rome'.[8] While Monnet favoured a

---

[3] Art 250(1) EC.

[4] Neunreither (1971–1972), p. 233.

[5] Featherstone (1994), pp. 154–155.

[6] Wallace (1993), p. 293, 300.

[7] Wallace and Smith (1995) p. 140.

[8] Ibid 143.

democratic Community 'he saw the emergence of loyalties to the Community institutions developing as a *consequence* of elite agreements for the functional organization of Europe, not as an essential *prerequisite* to that organization.'[9]

Neofunctionalism was to be the vehicle through which Community integration, conceived of as technocratic, elite-led gradualism, combined with corporatist style engagement of affected interests, was to be realised. Neofunctionalism fitted neatly with Monnet's perception of the Community. Monnet and neofunctionalists also shared the same sense of legitimacy and democracy. For Monnet, and like-minded followers, the legitimacy of the Community was to be secured through outcomes, peace and prosperity. The ECSC was established in part to prevent a third European war. The EEC was created in large part for the direct economic benefits of a common market. Peace and prosperity were potent benefits for the people in the 1950s. Democracy was, by way of contrast, a secondary consideration, since it was felt that the best way to secure peace and prosperity was by technocratic elite-led guidance.

3 Institutional structure and democracy: The present

Prognostication as to the future is perilous at the best of times, more especially so in relation to an institution such as the EU. Exogenous shocks external to the EU, which are unforeseen and unforeseeable, can shatter the very best reasoned predictions. Endogenous change from within the EU can, in similar vein, disrupt future visions that would otherwise be plausibly grounded, as attested to by the Catalonia problem in Spain, and electoral change in the Czech Republic, Austria and Italy. While prediction is, therefore, fraught with difficulty, a necessary condition for any such exercise is to be cognisant of the rationale for the status quo. To forget the lessons of history is to invite repetition of past mistakes, or it is to predicate views as to future institutional change on assumptions that are unsustainable when viewed in historical perspective. The significance of this will be apparent in the ensuing discussion, which is premised on the institutional disposition of power that currently prevails.

Space precludes detailed analysis of the passage from the initial institutional division of power in the Rome Treaty, to the schema embodied in the Lisbon Treaty.[10] Readers will be familiar with this, and reference will be made to it in the subsequent analysis. Suffice it to say for the present that the EP increased its power within the decision-making process. This occurred initially through the co-operation procedure, introduced by the Single European Act 1986, and then through the co-decision procedure in the Maastricht Treaty, as further strengthened by the Amsterdam Treaty. The EP attained something approximating to co-equal status in the legislative process with the Council, as later recognised by the Lisbon Treaty.[11]

[9] Holland (1993), p. 16. Italics in the original.

[10] Craig (2011), Ch 3.

[11] Arts 14(1), 16(1) TEU.

The European Council, as the ultimate repository of Member State power, also came to exercise an ever-increasing role in the decision-making process, de facto and de jure, which was affirmed and strengthened in the Lisbon Treaty.[12] The legal and political reality, as reflected in the Lisbon Treaty, was an institutional decision-making process in which State interests still predominated, and in which, notwithstanding the increase in the EP's power, the voters could not directly affect a change of policy direction in the EU by removing the incumbents and replacing them with those espousing different policies.

The Brexit discourse was conducted explicitly against the status quo, and implicitly against assumptions concerning ascription of responsibility for the existing schema. Thus the ills of the EU, whatsoever they might currently be, were conceived to be the responsibility of the EU, viewed in this respect primarily, but not solely, as the Commission, together with other 'powers' in Brussels. This is a great story, save for the fact that it bears little relation to reality. What is missing is considered discourse concerning the constitutional responsibility of the Member States for the status quo.

This is readily apparent in relation to the inter-institutional division of power within the EU. It is commonly acknowledged that the democratic deficit is a prominent feature of the EU's legitimacy problem, with the attendant implication, as noted in the introduction, that it is not just a problem that besets the EU, but is the EU's fault. It is the EU qua real and reified entity that suffers from this infirmity, the corollary being that blame is cast on it. The EU is not blameless in this respect, but nor are the Member States, viewed collectively and individually. This is not to deny the existence of problems in this regard, the disjunction between political power and electoral accountability being an important facet of the democracy deficit argument.[13]

It is to ask who bears responsibility for the status quo. This is all the more surprising given the sophisticated literature from international relations and political science concerning the relative influences of different players during periods of Treaty change, as well as in relation to the passage of EU legislation. The facts are not readily contestable, at least in relation to Treaty amendment. The stark reality is that the present disposition of EU institutional power is the result of successive Treaties in which the principal players have been the Member States. There may well be debate as to the relative degree of power wielded by Member States and the EU institutions in the shaping of EU legislation, but there is greater consensus on the fact that Member States have dominated at times of Treaty reform.[14]

Thus, insofar as the present arrangements divide EU policymaking de facto and de jure between the Commission, Council, European Parliament and European Council, this is reflective of power balances that the Member States were willing to accept. This is readily apparent when considering the initial Rome Treaty and any

---

[12] Art 15 TEU.

[13] Weiler et al. (1995), Follesdal and Hix (2006), p. 533; Nicolaïdis (2003, 2012).

[14] Marks et al. (1996), p. 341, 342; Risse-Kappen (1996), p. 53, Moravcsik (1993), p. 473; Moravcsik (1992), Moravcsik (1991), p. 19; Pollack, EUI Working Papers, RSC 2000/55.

of the five major Treaty reforms since then. It is powerfully exemplified by the debates concerning institutional reforms in the Constitutional Treaty, which were taken over into the Lisbon Treaty.[15] It was evident most notably in the battle as to whether the EU should have a single President who would be located in the Commission, or whether a reinforced European Council should also have a long-term President.[16] It was apparent in the debates as to Council configurations, and who would chair them. It was the frame within which the discourse took place concerning the number of Commissioners and the method of choosing them.

If blame is to be cast for the institutional status quo, and for its democratic shortcomings, then it should principally be laid at the door of the creators of the scheme, the Member States, who must bear, individually and collectively, constitutional responsibility for the status quo. The EU institutional disposition of power was the Member States' choice, which was made and reaffirmed over half a century. It was not foisted on them, and it was not a fait accompli in relation to which they had no input. To the contrary, the Member States were, and remain, the institutional architects of the status quo.

4 Institutional structure and democracy: The future—four constraints

The preceding backdrop is a necessary condition for making plausible suggestions concerning the future disposition of inter-institutional power in the EU. It might be argued that reforms could alleviate the existing democratic disjunction between electoral power and political responsibility, and that the change whereby the Commission President was indirectly elected by reason of being the candidate of the party that secured most seats in the European Parliament is a natural pointer in this direction. This could provide the foundation for true democratic contestation, whereby voters would be offered alternative political agendas for the EU, and their votes would truly determine the policy path for the next 5 years.

This could in theory happen. There are a range of democratic solutions available. It does not require some new master-plan of arrangements hitherto unknown to the world of democratic political architecture. A pretty-detailed schema, premised on some form of parliamentary democratic regime, could be sketched out. Thus, to take one possible way forward, it would be possible to have a regime in which the people voted directly for two constituent parts of the legislature, the European Parliament and Council, and for the President of the Commission and the President of the European Council. It would be possible in theory to have the previous package, but only a single elected President for the EU as whole. It would be possible for the entire Commission to be reflective of the majority party in the EP, and not just the

[15] Norman (2005).

[16] Craig (2010), Ch 3.

President of the Commission. It would be possible for the EP to have a right of legislative initiative in tandem with that of the Commission. It is possible to devise such a schema with conditions devised to protect against undesirable consequences of majoritarianism. The linkage between electoral power, substantive policy choice and accountability would be more visible and it would be strengthened. There are necessary qualifications to this type of model, which will be addressed in the section on democratic constraints below, but it provides a useful starting point for discussion.

4.1 Political constraints

4.1.1 Member States

The principal reason why nothing akin to the preceding model is likely to occur is that Member States are the main architects of Treaty change and they have never been willing to accept such a disposition of power. We must, as noted above, remember the past when planning the future. It is true that the choice between two Presidents and a single President for the EU was debated during the negotiations leading to the Constitutional Treaty. It is equally true that discourse concerning the election of the Commission President began in the 1980s. The broader reforms adumbrated above were not, however, on the political agenda during the extensive negotiations concerning institutional power in 2003–2004 that led to the Constitutional Treaty, nor in the subsequent discussions that culminated in the Lisbon Treaty.

The reason why nothing akin to the preceding model has ever appeared in formal discussion of Treaty reform is not hard to divine. The Member States would lose power in relative and absolute terms. They would no longer be masters of the Treaty. The preceding model, or something akin thereto, would alleviate the democratic deficit as conceived in the preceding sense, but in doing so it would endow the elected majority in the EP, and the duly elected Presidents of the Commission and European Council, with a mandate and an authority to discharge the promised electoral pledges. This would be a fortiori so if the members of the Council were also directly elected. Such a regime would inevitably significantly circumscribe Member State room for manoeuvre. It would create a substantive path dependency as to the direction of policy, and the priorities to be fulfilled.

It is, therefore, unsurprising that nothing akin to this has featured in serious political deliberations concerning the direction of institutional change within the EU. Viewed from this perspective, the democratic concession in the 2014 EP elections, known as the Spitzenkandidaten process, whereby the Commission President was imbued with greater legitimacy, because he was supported by the dominant political party, and canvassed as its candidate, could be accepted by the Member States because it did not fundamentally change the status quo ante. It did not create a path dependency towards a political agenda that committed the EU to a particular substantive set of reforms. It did not substantially undermine Member State power to set the pace and content of the EU agenda from within the European Council, and the Council. Moreover, the very fact that the other members of the Commission continued to be chosen by the Member States perforce limited the extent to which the Commission President, of whatever political persuasion, could shape the political agenda.

The preceding point is reinforced by the fact that the Member States have refused to confirm the continued application of the Spitzenkandidaten process in the 2019 elections.[17] The formal legal reality is that the European Council is only obliged to take account of the result in the European elections, when it proposes its candidate for Commission President to the European Parliament.[18] The European Parliament then votes on the candidate. The Commission and the EP, not surprisingly, pressed for the continuation of the Spitzenkandidaten process, arguing that it would increase public interest in EU affairs, and thereby augment the democratic legitimacy of the outcome. The Member States were, however, resistant to continuation of the schema, in part because the evidence indicated that only 5% of voters went to the polls to influence the choice of Commission President, with little if anything to show in terms of increased voter turnout. They were also resistant to continuation of the 2014 regime on the ground that while it would strengthen the linkage between the Commission and the EP, this could damage the democratic legitimacy of the Commission President. The argument was that the Spitzenkandidaten system robbed the Commission president of the 'dual legitimacy' that would otherwise flow from approval by the democratically-elected national leaders in the European Council, followed by that of the EP. While the European Council cannot, in formal terms, prevent the EP from operating the Spitzenkandidaten process, they can refuse to accept the candidate of the winning party as automatic incumbent of the office of Commission President. This would, moreover, accord the Member States further leverage ex ante, in the sense that they could influence who is nominated as a candidate by the EP political parties.

The assertion of national control over the EU's inter-institutional architecture is further evident in Member State rejection of suggestions from Jean-Claude Juncker that the Commission President could be double-hatted, functioning also as Chair of European Council meetings. The Member States showed no appetite for this suggestion in the deliberations leading to the Constitutional Treaty, and their position in this respect has not altered in the interim. Member State control is evident yet again in the reluctance to move towards a smaller Commission, which would mean that not every State would have a Commissioner all the time. While Commissioners do not formally represent their country, the Member States are, nonetheless, reluctant to give up their own national in the Commission decision-making process. It is paradoxical that these outcomes are occurring when the UK is set to leave the EU, since the UK would applaud the reaffirmation of Member State voice in EU decision-making.

---

[17] http://cer.eu/publications/archive/bulletin-article/2018/member-states-and-eu-taking-back-control.

[18] Article 17(7) TEU.

Member State opposition to reforms of the kind being considered here would, moreover, not be confined to the executive branch of government. The same sentiment would be voiced by some national Parliaments, which would not view with equanimity such institutional architecture, since it would be regarded as increasing the EU's legitimacy at the expense, inter alia, of national parliaments. Thus, while it suits the agenda of some political groupings in national parliaments to critique the EU's democratic credentials, they would, nonetheless, be resistant to change that alleviated such concerns, if it thereby enhanced the EU's democratic legitimacy by providing the linkage between electoral power and political responsibility, with the consequence that the authority of national parliaments was thereby diminished.

The diminution of State power that would be entailed by change of the kind mooted above would, moreover, be constitutionally challenged in some countries, on the ground that the EU was truly becoming a super-state. Thus, while the German Federal Constitutional Court has repeatedly chided the EU in relation to its democratic credentials, it would likely be one of the national constitutional courts to decide that an institutional configuration of the kind set out above, which addressed the democratic deficit as presently understood, would not be compatible with German constitutional law. This was because such a change would mean that the EU was moving closer to a federal state, with the consequence that the Member States could no longer be regarded as the Masters of the Treaty in the manner hitherto.

The political constraints on alleviating the democratic deficit have been exacerbated by the rise in populism in some Member States. This is not the place to engage in discourse concerning the meaning, and causes of, populism.[19] That would require a paper or book in itself, and it would not be possible to do justice to the complexities of the argument in the context of this chapter. Suffice it to say the following for the present. Whatsoever one's views concerning the meaning and causes of populism, the effect thereof has been to render States more suspicious of 'external' authority, and less inclined to accept choices that are not in accord with their own preferences. It is debatable whether this is an a priori consequence of populism, although it probably is. It is, however, certainly a contingent consequence, so far as concerns the effect of populism in EU Member States. Given that this is so, such Member States are less likely to accept changes to the institutional architecture of EU decision-making which would diminish their power over the direction of EU policy.

4.1.2 The EU

The EP would naturally favour change that would alleviate the democratic deficit. The increased conjunction between electoral power and political responsibility would enhance its power, more especially so if it resulted in the entire Commission bearing the political stamp of the dominant party in the EP. The setting of a truly EU

[19] See, e.g., Judis (2016), Moffitt (2016), Müller (2016); de Burca, SSRN 3105238.

electoral agenda, translated into political action by a Commission charged with the task of fulfilling the electoral mandate, would transform the EP's role as compared to the status quo. This would be further enhanced if there were EU political parties, and if the EP were to gain a right of legislative initiative in addition to that of the Commission.

The Commission's perspective would likely be more equivocal, since such change would entail gains and losses when viewed from its institutional perspective. There would be gains, insofar as the EU would have greater legitimacy, which would reinforce its authority over existing categories of competence, and facilitate transfer of further power. The legitimacy of the Commission within such a schema would be augmented, by reason of its electoral credentials. There would, at the same time, be losses for the Commission, since change of the kind under consideration would reduce its room for setting the policy agenda, and would constrain, in relative terms, the technocratic autonomy that it presently enjoys.

The European Council would likely fall at the other end of the spectrum. Its President is currently ensured presumptive support from the heads of the Member State, by reason of the fact that they choose the incumbent after lengthy deliberation. There could be no such guarantee if the President of the European Council were to be directly elected. The relative importance of the President would, moreover, be likely to diminish if the current method of appointment were retained, but the Commission President were to be directly elected on a party political platform, more especially if other Commissioners were similarly elected. The President of the European Council would henceforth be on the back-foot, as compared to a Commission President invested with the authority to carry out the electoral programme. Furthermore, the Heads of State within the European Council would be unlikely to view with equanimity an institutional regime in which the mode of intergovernmental adjustment were unduly constrained.

4.2 Democratic constraints

When articulating the preceding model for change that would alleviate the democratic deficit it was noted that the model would have to be qualified. It is now time to make good on that qualification.

The EU has always been grounded in two patterns of representation, the people being represented in the European Parliament, state interests in the Council and European Council. Reforms to alleviate the democratic deficit by increasing the connection between electoral power and political responsibility focus primarily on the first mode of representation, the connection between voter choice, the EP and the shaping of the EU policy agenda.

The reality is, however, that even if the broader package of reforms were adopted it could not ensure that the people would exercise electoral control over the direction of EU policy, since the European Council would still be populated by Heads of State, who would continue to have a marked influence over the policy agenda. The second mode of representation, via State interests, would perforce constrain the first, and this would be so even if the President of the European Council were to be elected. This is especially so, given the centrality of the European Council to agenda setting and the choice of priorities, such that nothing significant happens in the EU without its imprimatur.

It might be argued that there is nothing unusual in this respect, since it is a standard feature of national federal systems that there is duality of representation, the normal pattern being that state interests and those of the people are dealt with in different parts of the legislature. The duality does not prevent the offering of a coherent package to the electors. The two modes of representation do not, therefore, hinder the foundational democratic precept, viz that the voters choose who should represent them and the direction of policy, with the consequence that if parties fail to satisfy voter choice they pay the price at the ballot box.

The national analogy is instructive, precisely because it does not replicate at EU level. There is similarity insofar as both the EU and the federal systems are premised on two modes of representation, the people, and the states. The similarity is, however, superficial, and conceals deeper differences. The reality is that there is a hierarchy between the two modes of representation, which do not naturally co-exist on an equal footing. In federal states, the paradigm is that representation of the people has primacy, or there is parity between such representation and that of the states. This does not hold true for the EU, where state representation through the Council and European Council is more powerful than that of the people in the EP.

Thus in federal parliamentary regimes there are two component parts of the legislature, with the political agenda commonly set by the house elected by the people, with state interests, as represented in the other house, able to exert influence on the legislation. In federal Presidential systems, such as the USA, the balance of power between the elected houses may be different. It does not, however, alter the point made here, because voters have voice in relation to both houses, given that the incumbents are directly elected on party political tickets, republican or democrat; and given also that substantive policy will be set to some degree by the President, who is directly elected. A connection between voter choice and policy direction is thereby preserved.

The converse pertains as to the hierarchy between the two modes of representation in the EU. It is representation of state interests that is accorded primacy, de jure and de facto, through the Council and the European Council, with representation of the people through the EP being secondary in this respect when viewed from an historical perspective. This is readily apparent in the Treaty provisions concerning the institutions,[20] which are reinforced by their practical modus operandi.

The reasons for the difference between the nation state and the EU in this respect are not hard to divine. Representation of state interests within a federal polity and within the EU are markedly different. Commonality of interest, shared identity and solidarity is considerably greater in the former, than in the latter, and that is so notwithstanding that there may be policy differences between regions within a federal

---

[20] Arts 15–18 TEU.

state. Problems of domination of one state over another are, by way of contrast, considerably greater in the latter context than in the former, which serves to explain the attention given to voting rules and other mechanisms designed to alleviate this problem in the EU.

It is important, therefore, to view proposals to alleviate the EU's democratic deficit against the preceding backdrop. The reality is that such proposals entail a reordering of the hierarchy in the modes of representation as they pertain in the EU. Representation of the people is afforded elevated status, as manifest in the desire that voter choice be translated into political action, such that the gulf between electoral power and political responsibility is eradicated or significantly diminished. This necessarily involves reduction in the power wielded by the institutions that represent State interests.

It might be argued by way of response that this rebalancing is precisely what is intended, to which the counter is that the States are unlikely to accept the substantive path dependency and loss of power that would be attendant on this change. It might, alternatively, be argued that alleviation of the democratic deficit can be accomplished without the rebalancing adumbrated above, to which the answer is that such an argument must be fleshed out to test its institutional and substantive veracity.

Concerns of an analogous nature have been expressed by Scharpf,[21] who argues that an unqualified majoritarian system would be problematic in the EU. He points out that constitutional democracies, such as Switzerland, Belgium or Canada, in which there is societal division, combined with structural majorities and minorities, often resort to 'consociational' or 'consensus democracy' with bicameral legislatures, supermajoritarian decision rules and the like to protect the interests of minority groups. While it is contestable whether the EU is characterised by the persistent, reinforcing cleavages that prevail in such countries, there is little doubt that some qualifications to majoritarianism would be required.[22]

> Present decision rules could of course be modified in some ways, perhaps to relax the Commission's monopoly of legislative initiatives. But they could not be replaced by a regime of straightforward majority rule without provoking disruptive political conflicts and radical anti-European opposition in Member States whose national politico-economic and socioeconomic orders and values could be overridden by explicitly political decisions adopted by majorities of 'foreigners' in the European Parliament (EP) and in the Council. In other words, the explicit switch to majority rule would destroy the protection of persistent minorities that is presently ensured by the Community method. And it could politicise European legislation in ways that might transform the largely dormant 'no-demos issue' of EU legitimacy into conflicts that could destroy the Union.

[21] Scharpf (2015), p. 384, 395.

[22] Ibid, p. 395.

4.3 Constitutional constraints

4.3.1 Constitutionalisation: Vertical and horizontal dimensions

The discussion thus far has been concerned with political constraints to change that would alleviate the democratic deficit, these coming largely from Member State opposition for the reasons adumbrated above. There is, however, a further constraint as concerns reforms that would alleviate the democratic deficit, which would exist even if the Member States changed their view and were willing to embrace reform. The constraint flows from the constitutionalisation that attaches to all Treaty provisions. There is a duality to this constraint, which operates both vertically and horizontally.

The vertical dimension captures the effect of such constitutionalisation on relations between the Member States and the EU. It speaks to the limits placed on Member State action when subject matter falls within the sphere of EU law. Foundational EU constitutional doctrines such as supremacy, direct effect and pre-emption kick in to constrict Member State action. This is so in relation to the great majority of Treaty articles, and much of the legislation enacted pursuant to the Treaty. Disquiet as to the limits thereby placed on Member State action is exacerbated by what is perceived to be the imbalance between the economic and the social within the EU, with the consequence that constitutionalised EU law can place severe limits on this balance at Member State level.

The horizontal dimension of constitutionalisation addresses the confines thereby placed on political choice at EU level. This dimension is especially important in relation to changes designed to alleviate the democratic deficit by increasing the connection between electoral power and political responsibility. All constitutions restrict choices that can be made via every day politics. It is integral to the very nature of constitutions that they entail some pre-commitment, which confines choices that can be made thereafter, subject to any constitutional amendment. The limits may be procedural, or substantive. The difference with respect to the EU is one of degree, not of kind, but it is significant nonetheless, since the constitutionalised EU Treaty is far more detailed than any national constitution. It still leaves room for some policy choice as concerns the direction of EU policy. The EU Treaty, nonetheless, limits the range of such choice that rival political parties can place before the electorate. There is much in the Treaty that constitutes substantive path dependency for the direction of EU policy, thereby limiting politicisation.

Concerns as to the preceding vertical and horizontal constraints have been voiced by scholars such as Grimm, who has focused on what he terms the democratic costs of constitutionalisation.[23] His central thesis is that the EU Treaties are over-constitutionalised, with the consequence that they are thereby taken off the agenda of normal politics, notwithstanding the fact that many such issues that would be regarded as within the province of ordinary law in Member States: 'in the EU the

[23] Grimm (2015), p. 460.

crucial difference between the rules for political decisions and the decisions themselves is to a large extent levelled'.[24] It is inherent in the nature of constitutions that they function as the framework for political decisions, with the consequence that elections 'do not matter as far as constitutional law extends'.[25] There may be too little constitutionalism, but there may also be too much, with the consequence that the democratic process is fettered.[26] While there are no universally applicable principles for determining the content of a Constitution, the 'function of constitutions is to legitimise and to limit political power, not to replace it',[27] with the consequence that constitutions are a 'framework for politics, not the blueprint for all political decisions'.[28]

The EU Treaties fulfil many of the functions of national constitutions, specifying matters such as the inter-institutional distribution of power, the mode of law-making, and the respective competence of the EU and Member States. They also go significantly beyond the remit of national constitutions, with the consequence that a wide range of matters becomes constitutionalised and taken off the agenda of normal politics. The effect of this is further enhanced by the constitutional doctrines of direct effect and supremacy, which transformed the four economic freedoms from 'objective principles for legislation into subjective rights of the market participants who could claim them against the Member States before the national courts'.[29]

This in turn meant that there were two modes of EU integration. The Treaty precepts could be advanced through legislation enacted by the EU institutions, or they could be taken forward through judicial decisions, which were imbued with considerable force through direct effect and supremacy.[30] Member States had limited influence over the latter, and this was particularly important since the lack of differentiation between the constitutional law level and the ordinary law level, meant that the 'constitutionalization of the treaties immunises the Commission and particularly the ECJ against any attempt by the democratically responsible institutions of the EU to react to the Court's jurisprudence by changing the law'.[31] For Grimm, the remedy was to limit the EU Treaties to their truly constitutional elements and downgrade other Treaty provisions that were not of constitutional nature to the status of secondary law.

[24] Ibid, p. 470.
[25] Ibid, p. 463.
[26] Ibid, p. 464.
[27] Ibid, p. 465.
[28] Ibid, p. 465.
[29] Ibid, p. 467.
[30] Weiler (1981), p. 267, and Weiler (1991), pp. 2412–2431; Craig (1992), p. 453.
[31] Grimm (2015), p. 471.

4.3.2 Competence: Vertical and horizontal dimensions

Constitutionalisation is not the only constitutional constraint on political choice. It is also limited by the competence accorded to the EU. Political choices placed before the electorate in nation states are paradigmatically predicated on the State having plenary power. The assumption is that, subject to constitutional limits, the rival political parties can place before the electorate a range of options, which cover economic, social and political issues, broadly defined. This is the very lifeblood of normal politics, with contestation concerning matters such as economic redistribution, social welfare, health, crime and education, featuring prominently on the electoral agenda. There is a vertical and a horizontal dimension to such limitations on competence as they pertain to the EU.

The most obvious dimension of competence is on the vertical plane, insofar as it demarcates the respective spheres of authority of the EU and the Member States. It follows that, even assuming the Member States were willing to alleviate the democratic deficit by embracing political reordering of the kind set out above, the choices that rival political parties could place before the electorate are framed by the limits of EU competence. It is not, therefore, open to a political party to promise far-reaching change in social welfare or economic redistribution, since the EU does not have competence over such matters, nor does it have the tax base from which to effectuate such change, the EU still being principally a regulatory state in this regard. It is, moreover, not open to a political party to promise far-reaching change on matters that are of prime concern to voters in national elections, such as education, health, crime and the like, since the EU's powers are limited in such areas.

There is, however, a less obvious dimension of competence that resonates horizontally, insofar as it frames the exercise of political choice by the EU institutions when making EU policy. This is the consequence of the fact that not all heads of competence are created equal. The EU's power over different areas varies significantly, being dependent in part on whether the competence is exclusive, shared or complementary, and in part on the fact that even within each such category it is only by looking closely at the relevant Treaty provisions that one can determine the real scope of EU power. There is therefore no 'boilerplate' that determines the nature of power possessed by the EU in the diverse areas that fall within, for example, shared competence. The horizontal dimension to competence is, moreover, manifest in the fact that the Treaties specify to some significant degree the hierarchy of substantive provisions, as attested to most notably by the dominance of the four freedoms. This perforce shapes the political choices that the EU institutions are able to make.

There are, moreover, instances where there is a mismatch between the expectations of what the EU is expected to do, and the limits of the competence accorded to it, as powerfully exemplified by the rule of law crisis. This may, in the medium term, prove to be the most serious of the crises faced by the EU. There is a rich and sophisticated literature on the topic, which explores the limits of the powers currently available to the EU, and how they could be applied.[32] There is, moreover, a duality to the concept of national constitutional responsibility as it pertains to the rule of law crisis most especially in Poland and Hungary. There is the fact that the principal responsibility for the crisis resides with the States that introduced the illiberal measures threatening the rule of law. There is the secondary responsibility that lies with the Member States collectively, as reflected in the Treaty provisions, which give expression to the limits of the controls over Member State action that they are willing to accept. The terms of Article 7 TEU set the parameters for such action, and are predicated on the assumption that there will not be more than one misbehaving state at any point in time. The reality is that the EU is caught between a rock and a hard place, or if you prefer more classical illusions, between Scylla and Charybdis: it risks being damned for doing too little, criticised for being ineffectual; or criticised for trying to do too much, and thereby straying into the terrain of domestic politics where it lacks competence.

4.4 *Substantive constraints*

The fourth constraint on exercise of democratic political choice is substantive. It is related to the constitutional constraint, but distinct nonetheless, and hence warrants separate consideration. The balance between the economic and the social has been a contentious feature of the EEC since its inception, and continues to be so. It is manifest in two ways.

4.4.1 The economic and the social: Core treaty provisions

Scharpf has long argued that the EU embodies an asymmetry between the economic and the social, such that the former is prioritised at the expense of the latter.[33] He contends that the EU is premised on asymmetrical treatment of the economic and social spheres. The economic order has predominated, as evidenced by the Treaty provisions, and the primacy accorded to completion of the Single Market, with the attendant priority placed on market and competitive principles. Scharpf argued that it would have been possible, when the Rome Treaty was framed, to have made harmonisation of social protection a pre-condition for market integration, given that the welfare regimes of the original six Member States were relatively rudimentary and closer than they have since become.

If the Rome Treaty had been cast in this form, then the debates at EU level about the interplay between social protection and the market mechanism would have rep-

[32] von Bogdandy et al. (2012), p. 489; Canor (2013), p. 383; Carrera et al. (2013); von Bogdandy and Sonnevend (2015), Kochenov and Pech (2015), p. 512; Müller (2015), p. 141; Kochenov (2015), Jakab and Kochenov (2016), and Closa and Kochenov (2016).

[33] Scharpf (1997), p. 18; Scharpf (2002), p. 645; Scharpf (2003), pp. 79–104.

licated similar discourse at national level. Matters developed very differently. The Treaty focus was heavily on markets, with the consequence that there was a decoupling of economic integration and social protection. This led to constitutional asymmetry. Whereas at national level economic and social policy had the same constitutional status, it was economic policy that predominated at the EU level. The very predominance afforded to economic policy reduced the Member States' ability to influence their own economies or to 'realise self-defined socio-political goals'.[34]

The doctrines of direct effect and supremacy heightened these constraints. Scharpf argues that the Member States failed to recognise the impact of these twin doctrines, which laid the foundations for integration through law, whereby the Community courts could advance Treaty objectives if integration through legislation was not possible because of disagreement in the Council.[35] Negative integration through judicial decisions that deemed national laws to be inconsistent with the Treaty, became the dominant mode of integration, until the new mode of harmonisation was introduced post the Single European Act 1986, thereby facilitating positive integration.

There came to be increasing pressure for the EU to play a greater role in social policy, thereby alleviating the constitutional imbalance between the market-making and market-correcting functions of a polity. This goes much of the way to explain the inclusion of more heads of competence dealing with social policy, as well as development of the Structural Funds. There were, moreover, persistent efforts in the latter part of the previous millennium to recast the Single Market in more holistic terms, so as to include aspects of social and labour policy.[36]

Scharpf argued that it was not, however, possible at the turn of the millennium for the EU to adopt the stance towards social policy that it had declined to take when the Rome Treaty was signed. It was not possible to treat social welfare and protection through uniform rules applicable to all, because of the very diversity in welfare systems that existed within the Member States.[37] This was the rationale in part for the development of social policy through the Open Method of Coordination.[38]

> Political parties and unions promoting 'social Europe' are thus confronted by a dilemma: to ensure effectiveness, they need to assert the constitutional equality of social protection and economic integration functions at the European level—which could be achieved either through European social programmes or through the harmonisation of national social-protection systems. At the same time, however, the present diversity of national social-protection systems and the political salience of these differences make it practically impossible for them to agree on common European solutions. Faced by this dilemma, the Union opted for a new governing mode, the open method of coordination (OMC), in order to protect and promote social Europe.

---

[34] Scharpf (2002), p. 648.

[35] Scharpf (2015), pp. 386–387.

[36] Craig (2002), Chap 1; Craig (2003), p. 79.

[37] Scharpf (2002), pp. 649–651.

[38] Ibid, p. 652.

These arguments are important. The following points are, however, pertinent in this context. First, insofar as there is an imbalance between the economic and the social within the EU, this is the result of Member State choice, just as is the current institutional structure. It is of course true that judicial doctrines of direct effect and supremacy, as developed by the CJEU, have heightened this tension, but the fact remains that the centrality accorded to the four freedoms, and the relative weakness of the social as compared to the economic dimension, is reflective of what the Member States have been willing to accept, and the powers that it has been willing to accord, to a supranational polity. There is a paradox lurking here. The desire to preserve national sovereignty underpinned Member State reluctance to accord the EU power over social policy; yet the resulting predominance of the economic over the social within the EU impacted on Member State freedom to choose the balance between the economic and the social within the nation state.

Secondly, there is no doubt that legal doctrines of direct effect and supremacy sharpened the cutting edge of the four freedoms, thereby further enhancing the economic dimension of the Treaties, and the attendant negative integration resulting from the judicial doctrine. Scharpf's argument, to the effect that the Member States were not cognisant of the significance of the legal doctrine, should, nonetheless, be viewed with caution. Member States benefited from such judicial doctrine, insofar as it invested the Treaties, and rules made thereunder, with a peremptory force that they would otherwise have lacked. To put the same point in another way, these doctrines, as enforced by the EU courts, gave greater credibility to the commitments embodied in the Treaties.

4.4.2 The economic, the social and the political: EMU and the financial crisis

The financial crisis impacted significantly on the balance between the economic and the social, and more broadly on the political structure of decision-making in the EU. The effects were manifest at the EU level, insofar as the financial crisis meant that the EU's energies were concentrated on resolving the economic problems, with scant energy left for broader social policy. They were also manifest at Member State level, since relief for debtor States was subject to conditionality requirements, which imposed strict austerity limits, with attendant implications for national social and welfare policy. Concerns in this respect were voiced by many commentators.

For Scharpf, the imbalance between the economic and the social was heightened by the financial crisis, and the responses thereto.[39] This was, in part, because the euro regime, as it presently functions, exerts 'downward pressures on public sector functions and on wages—in the upswing to dampen the rise of external deficits and in the downswing to stimulate export-led recovery'[40]; it was in part also because of what Scharpf regards as the far-reaching discretion afforded to the Commission

[39] Scharpf (1999, 2015).

[40] Scharpf (2015), p. 391.

under the EU legislation enacted to strengthen EU oversight of national fiscal policy after the crisis.[41]

Wilkinson, drawing on the motif of authoritarian liberalism, voiced the concern that 'democratic processes have been side-lined, albeit largely with the complicity of national political and economic elites, not to assert strong statehood but for the purpose of maintaining a project of economic integration said to depend on the success of the single currency'.[42] In similar vein he deprecates the fact that 'democratic authority is replaced by a combination of executive power and market rationality, defended by the perceived necessity of acting swiftly and bypassing public debate'.[43]

In similar vein, Dawson and de Witte express disquiet at the way in which the financial crisis de facto shifted the substantive boundaries as to the intrusion of the EU into Member States, 'by increasingly making in-roads in Member State autonomy in redistributive, fiscal and budgetary matters',[44] as manifest in the conditionality criteria imposed on debtor states. They too voice worry about the increased executive dominance in decision-making, with agenda setting being done to an ever greater extent by the European Council. They acknowledge that the rationale for executive control in proposals for reform of EMU is that 'only executives and governments carry the competence, speed, credibility and legitimacy to mandate and direct significant EU intervention in core state powers such as fiscal policy'.[45] They, nonetheless, deprecate reform initiatives that further enhance executive power. Reform should, they argue, be such that the substantive direction of EU policy can be truly deliberated and contested,[46] thereby meeting a basic precept of political self-determination, that 'government is conducted not just *for* but *by* the people'.[47]

There is force in the preceding arguments. Thus, it is assuredly correct that the Commission has discretion pursuant to various regulations enacted post the financial crisis. The salient regulations were, however, approved through the ordinary legislative procedure, with significant input from the EP as well as the Council, although the room for parliamentary involvement thereafter is limited.[48] It is, moreover, important not to be asymmetrical in this respect. It is the executives of the Member States that are very much in the driving seat when it comes to setting their national budget. They commonly exercise considerable discretion in this regard, such that it is difficult to ensure parliamentary accountability. There may be reasons why the national executive is willing to tolerate significant budgetary imbalance, or feels powerless to address the issue. This can in turn have serious consequences for other Member States, through the strain thereby placed on the euro. The existence of Commission discretion should, therefore, be viewed in this light. The post-

[41] Ibid, p. 392.
[42] Wilkinson (2015), p. 313, 315.
[43] Ibid, p. 327.
[44] Dawson and de Witte (2015), p. 371, 372.
[45] Ibid, p. 374.
[46] Ibid, p. 375.
[47] Ibid, p. 382. Italics in the original.
[48] Fasone (2014), p. 2.

financial crisis legislative schema is, moreover, premised on such Commission discretion, coupled with increased provision for national budgetary targets that can be policed by national legislatures more readily than hitherto.

5 Institutional structure and democracy: The paradox

There is a paradox of cause and effect in the EU's inter-institutional configuration of power as it presently exists, and as it is likely to remain in the future. The cause captures the facts as set out hitherto. The Member States have shaped the present configuration of EU inter-institutional power, which is beset by a democratic deficit insofar as there is scant connection between electoral vote and political power or responsibility, such that it is difficult for the voters to express a view as to the direction of EU policy that will be translated into action. Member States bear the principal responsibility for the status quo, since they devised the current schema.

The effect captures the way in which we think about democratic legitimation in the EU. The infirmities in EU decision-making constitute the driver for the argument that EU legitimacy and democracy must be grounded in the Member States, not merely as one mode of representation within the EU. The argument becomes more 'visceral and foundational', in the sense that it is the Member States, and the national parliaments therein, that are regarded as the true bedrock of democracy. Their claims in this regard are grounded in the EU's democratic deficiencies, and this in turn is used to fuel the argument that such parliaments should participate in EU decision-making.

The paradox resides in the conjunction of cause and effect: Member State choice is central to the institutional architecture at EU level and the democratic infirmity that is reflected therein. The infirmity cannot, by definition, be resolved at EU level, given the nature of the choice thus made, with the consequence that the solution must be found elsewhere. The paradox is exacerbated by reason of the fact that, as argued above, most national parliaments would be in accord with their national executives in resisting change that would alleviate the democratic deficit within the EU, because of the effect that this could have on their own power. Thus, while 'a true political Union would involve not suppressing, but channelling and promoting meaningful conflict over the EU's substantive goals',[49] and while reinvigoration in this respect may be especially pertinent post the financial crisis, there is scant likelihood of this occurring.

It should be made clear that nothing in the preceding argument presumes the idea of a single demos for the entire EU; it is not predicated on the denial of plurality in the political choices made by the EU; it does not rest on assumptions of a particular kind of federal order or anything akin thereto; it presumes no particular distribution of power between the EU and the Member States; and it is perfectly consistent with a role for national parliaments.

[49] Dawson and de Witte (2015), p. 382.

The paradox is, by way of contrast, simply reflective of the politics concerning the disposition of inter-institutional power as it has unfolded since the inception of the EEC. It is reflective also of normative assumptions as to the type of Community or Union that the Member States are willing to create, and the powers that they are content to invest in it. The enduring paradox persists: Member State refusal to allow institutional change that would alleviate the democratic deficiency in EU decision-making remains a principal cause of the malaise, the consequential effect being that the problem can only be addressed at State level.

The paradox is all the more important because it comes with a 'political bite', which is doubly undermining for the EU. Member States prefer to off-load blame concerning deficiencies in EU decision-making to the EU institutions themselves, and divest themselves of responsibility. They do not readily concede their role as institutional architects of the status quo. It is, moreover, these very institutional deficiencies that serve to rob the EU of the legitimacy that it requires to tackle difficult social or economic issues. The EU is caught between a rock and a hard place, berated in equal measure for its over-attachment to the economic at the expense of the social, while castigated for lacking the democratic legitimacy to make dispositive social or redistributive decisions.

References

Canor I (2013) My brother's keeper? Horizontal *Solange*: "an ever closer *Distrust* among the peoples of Europe". Common Mark Law Rev 50:383

Carrera S, Guild E, Hernanz N (2013) The triangular relationship between fundamental rights, democracy and the rule of law in the EU, towards an EU Copenhagen mechanism. CEPS

Closa C, Kochenov D (eds) (2016) Reinforcing the rule of law oversight in the European Union. Cambridge University Press

Craig P (1992) Once upon a time in the west: direct effect and the federalization of EEC law. Oxf J Legal Stud 12:453

Craig P (2002) The evolution of the single market. In: Barnard C, Scott J (eds) The law of the single European market, unpacking the premises. Hart, Chap 1

Craig P (2003) The community political order. Indiana J Global Legal Stud 10:79

Craig P (2010) The Lisbon treaty, law, politics and treaty reform. Oxford University Press, Ch 3

Craig P (2011) Institutions, power and institutional balance. In: Craig P, de Burca G (eds) The evolution of EU law, 2nd edn. Oxford University Press, Ch 3

Dawson M, de Witte F (2015) Self-determination in the constitutional future of the EU. Eur Law J 21:371, 372

de Burca G. Is EU Supranational Governance a Challenge to Liberal Constitutionalism?. SSRN 3105238

Fasone C (2014) European economic governance and parliamentary representation: what place for the European Parliament? Eur Law J 20:2

Featherstone K (1994) Jean Monnet and the "Democratic Deficit" in the European Union. J Common Mark Stud 32:149

Follesdal A, Hix S (2006) Why there is a democratic deficit in the EU: a response to Majone and Moravcsik. J Common Mark Stud 44:533

Grimm D (2015) The democratic costs of constitutionalization: the European case. Eur Law J 21:460

Holland M (1993) European community integration. St. Martin's Press, p 16
Jakab A, Kochenov D (eds) (2016) The enforcement of EU law and values: methods against defiance. Oxford University Press
Judis J (2016) The populist explosion: how the great recession transformed American and European politics. Columbia Global Reports
Kochenov D (2015) EU law without the rule of law: is the veneration of autonomy worth it? Yearb Eur Law 34:74–96
Kochenov D, Pech L (2015) Monitoring and enforcement of the rule of law in the EU: rhetoric and reality. Eur Const Law Rev 11:512
Maduro M (2012) A new governance for the European Union and the euro: democracy and justice. RSCAS Policy Paper 2012/11, 1
Marks G, Hooghe L, Blank K (1996) European integration from the 1980s: state-centric v. Multiple-level governance. J Common Mark Stud 34:341
Moffitt B (2016) The global rise of populism: performance, political style, and representation. Stanford University Press
Moravcsik A (1991) Negotiating the single European act: national interests and conventional statecraft in the European community. Int Organ 45:19
Moravcsik A (1992) National preference formation and interstate bargaining in the European community, 1955–1986. Harvard University Press
Moravcsik A (1993) Preferences and power in the European community: a liberal intergovernmentalist approach. J Common Mark Stud 31:473
Müller J-W (2015) Should the European Union protect democracy and the rule of law in its Member States. Eur Law J 21:141
Müller J-W (2016) What is populism? University of Pennsylvania Press
Neunreither K (1971–1972) Transformation of a political role: reconsidering the case of the commission of the European communities. J Common Mark Stud 10:233
Nicolaïdis K (2003) Our European Demoi-cracy: is this constitution a third way for Europe?. In: Nicolaïdis K, Weatherill S (eds) Whose Europe? National models and the constitution of the European Union. Oxford University Press
Nicolaïdis K (2012) The idea of European Demoicracy. In: Dickson J, Eleftheriadis P (eds) Philosophical foundations of EU law. Oxford University Press
Norman P (2005) The accidental constitution, the making of Europe's constitutional treaty, 2nd edn. EuroComment
Pollack M. International relations theory and European integration. EUI Working Papers, RSC 2000/55
Risse-Kappen T (1996) Exploring the nature of the beast: international relations theory and comparative policy analysis meet the European Union. J Common Mark Stud 34:53A
Scharpf F (1997) Economic integration, democracy and the welfare state. J Eur Public Policy 4:18
Scharpf F (1999) Governing in Europe: effective and democratic? Oxford University Press
Scharpf F (2002) The European social model: coping with the challenges of diversity. J Common Mark Stud 40:645
Scharpf F (2003) Legitimate diversity: the new challenge of European integration. In: Borzel T, Cichowski R (eds) The state of the European Union, Vol. 6: law, politics and society. Oxford University Press, pp 79–104
Scharpf F (2015) After the crash: a perspective on multilevel European democracy. Eur Law J 21:384
von Bogdandy A, Sonnevend P (eds) (2015) Constitutional crisis in the European constitutional area: theory, law and politics in Hungary and Romania. Hart
von Bogdandy A, Kottmann M, Antpöhler C, Dickschen J, Hentrei S, Smrkolj M (2012) Reverse Solange–protecting the essence of fundamental rights against EU Member States. Common Mark Law Rev 49:489
Wallace H (1993) European governance in turbulent times. J Common Mark Stud 31:293, 300

Wallace W, Smith J (1995) Democracy or technocracy? European integration and the problem of popular consent. In: Hayward J (ed) The crisis of representation in Europe. Frank Cass, p 140
Weiler J (1981) The community system: the dual character of supranationalism. Yearb Eur Law 1:267
Weiler J (1991) The transformation of Europe. Yale Law J 100:2403
Weiler JHH (2012) Europe in crisis – on "political messianism", "legitimacy" and the "rule of law"'. Singap J Leg Stud, p 248
Weiler JHH, Haltern U, Mayer F (1995) European democracy and its critique. In: Hayward J (ed) The crisis of representation in Europe. Frank Cass
Wilkinson MA (2015) Authoritarian liberalism in the European constitutional imagination: second time as farce? Eur Law J 21:313

Legitimität und Finalität des europäischen Projekts

Wolfgang Heusel

"Au vingtième siècle, il y aura une nation extraordinaire. Cette nation sera grande, ce qui ne l'empêchera pas d'être libre. Elle sera illustre, riche, pensante, pacifique, cordiale au reste de l'humanité. … Une bataille entre Italiens et Allemands, entre Anglais et Russes, entre Prussiens et Français, lui apparaîtra comme nous apparaît une bataille entre Picards et Bourguignons. … Elle sera plus que nation, elle sera civilisation ; elle sera mieux que civilisation, elle sera famille. Unité de langue, unité de monnaie, unité de mètre, unité de méridien, unité de code ; …

Cette nation aura pour capitale Paris, et ne s'appellera point la France ; elle s'appellera l'Europe."

Victor Hugo, Introduction au « Paris-guide de l'exposition universelle de 1869 », Paris 1867, Chap. Ier « L'Avenir »

Seit seinen Anfängen 1952 war das europäische Integrationsprojekt immer wieder durch Krisen bedroht, und immer wieder ist es erst in Krisen gewachsen. Das überrascht wenig angesichts der radikalen Neuartigkeit und Ambition seines Konzepts. Den entscheidenden Anstoß verdankte es dem Scheitern der Europäischen Verteidigungsgemeinschaft 1954. Schwere Rückschläge brachten die Krise des leeren Stuhls in den 60er und die lähmende Eurosklerose in den 70er und frühen 80er Jahren, bis es Jacques Delors mit der Einheitlichen Europäischen Akte 1986 und dem Kunstgriff eines allgemein akzeptierten Countdowns zur Vollendung des Binnenmarktes 1992 gelang, die Integration nachhaltig zu beschleunigen. Die Zeitenwende 1989/1990 zwang die Mitgliedstaaten, Vertiefung und Erweiterung in den Vertragsrevisionen von Maastricht 1992, Amsterdam 1997 und Nizza 2001 sowie der Norderweiterung 1995 und der großen Osterweiterung 2004 zu verbinden, bis die Ablehnung des Verfassungsvertrages in Volksabstimmungen in den Gründungsmitgliedstaaten Niederlande und Frankreich 2005 die nächste große Krise auslöste. Dass der in den Niederlanden und Frankreich dann nur noch

W. Heusel (✉)
Academy of European Law (ERA), Trier, Germany
e-mail: wheusel@era.int

W. Heusel, J.-P. Rageade (eds.), *The Authority of EU Law*,
https://doi.org/10.1007/978-3-662-58841-3_25

parlamentarisch verabschiedete Lissabonner Reformvertrag die wesentlichen Bestimmungen des gescheiterten Verfassungsvertrages übernahm, beschädigte Glaubwürdigkeit und Legitimität des europäischen Projekts nicht nur in diesen Ländern. Die Banken- und Schuldenkrise seit 2008 und die Flüchtlingskrise 2015 schließlich zeigten die Anfälligkeit unvollständiger gemeinschaftlicher Regelungskomplexe, deren negative Folgen in erster Linie intergouvernemental begrenzt werden konnten, deren abschließende gemeinschaftliche Regelung aber durch manifeste Interessengegensätze der Mitgliedstaaten bisher verhindert wurde.

In vielen Mitgliedstaaten ist seit Jahren ein Erstarken EU-kritischer Parteien und Bewegungen zu beobachten, die vor einer Gefährdung nationaler Interessen und Identitäten durch die europäische Integration warnen oder gleich den Austritt ihres Landes aus der Union anstreben, wie dies im britischen Fall zur Notifizierung des Austrittsentschlusses nach Artikel 50 EUV am 29. März 2017 geführt hat. Es stellt sich daher die Frage, ob das europäische Projekt heute Gefahr läuft, an Überambition zugrunde zu gehen, und ob es erforderlich ist, die Union durch effektive Beschränkung auf diejenigen Politikbereiche, in denen die Integration echten Mehrwert gewährleistet, auf Dauer zu bewahren und fortzuentwickeln.

1 Das Legitimitätsproblem der Union: Ursachen und Wirkung

1.1 Die politischen Errungenschaften: Friede, Demokratie, Menschenrechte, Rechtsstaatlichkeit

Sechzig Jahre nach Errichtung der Europäischen Gemeinschaft für Kohle und Stahl, die just zu Beginn desselben Jahres in der EU aufgegangen war, erhielt die Europäische Union 2012 den Friedensnobelpreis „*for over six decades contributed to the advancement of peace and reconciliation, democracy and human rights in Europe*“[1].

Die Verleihung des Friedensnobelpreises war durchaus Ausdruck einer allgemeinen Wertschätzung der EU als Friedensprojekt. Tatsächlich bestreitet niemand ernsthaft den herausragenden Beitrag des europäischen Integrationsprozesses, wie er in der Europäischen Union Gestalt angenommen hat, zu Friedenssicherung und Versöhnung ehemals verfeindeter Völker in Europa. Vor dem Hintergrund von Krieg und Elend in der Welt ist diese Errungenschaft in der Tat von unvergleichlichem Wert; schon aus diesem Grund darf die Europäische Union niemals aufs Spiel gesetzt werden. Doch bietet das große Ziel der Friedenssicherung in Europa allein noch keine Antwort auf die Frage, wie weit die europäische Integration getrieben und welche Kompetenzen der europäischen Ebene zulasten der Mitgliedstaaten übertragen werden sollen. Erst recht gibt die Friedenssicherung nach innen noch

[1] The Nobel Peace Prize 2012, https://www.nobelprize.org/prizes/peace/2012/summary/.

keine Antwort auf die Frage, ob und wie die Europäische Union den Frieden auch nach außer sichern kann und soll – so wie die Pax Romana zwar den inneren Landfrieden gewährleistete, das Reich aber keineswegs von der Führung imperialer Eroberungskriege abhielt.

Etwas weniger offensichtlich als bei der Friedenssicherung nach innen ist der Beitrag der Europäischen Union[2] zur Förderung von Demokratie und Menschenrechten, den das Nobelkomitee hervorhebt. Letztere wurden vom Europäischen Gerichtshof bekanntlich erst nach vielen Jahren gemeinschaftsrechtlicher Entwicklung überhaupt als allgemeine Grundsätze des Gemeinschaftsrechts anerkannt[3] und schließlich im Maastrichter Unionsvertrag erstmals primärrechtlich sanktioniert[4], doch macht ungeachtet der eher extensiven Grundrechtejudikatur des Gerichtshofs auf der Grundlage der 2009 in Kraft gesetzten Charta dessen fortbestehender Widerwille gegen den primärrechtlich angeordneten Beitritt zur Europäischen Menschenrechtskonvention stutzig.

Auch das Demokratieprinzip war für die EU zunächst eher stillschweigend vorausgesetztes Organisationsprinzip der Mitgliedstaaten als eigenes Ziel und fand in den Gründungsverträgen keine Erwähnung. Die demokratische Rückbindung der EU-Organe selbst war bis zur Einführung der Direktwahl des Parlaments 1979 nur eine indirekte und ist ungeachtet der beeindruckenden Kompetenzzuwächse des Parlaments schon insofern unvollständig geblieben, als die Unionsbürger bis heute nicht gleichberechtigt wählen. Noch schwerer für die Legitimität politischer Willensbildung auf EU-Ebene wiegt die nicht nur von Weiler[5] seit langem beklagte Unmöglichkeit, den Kurs der europäischen Politik durch die Wahlen zum Europäischen Parlament wesentlich zu verändern: der strukturell begründeten immerwährenden Großen Koalition im Parlament stehen anders als in der Schweiz keine Volksrechte gegenüber und es überrascht wenig, dass sich allfälliger demokratischer Protest einerseits in Wahlmüdigkeit und andererseits in Stimmen für antieuropäische Parteien niederschlägt.

Das demokratische Defizit der EU klingt nach im Maastrichter Unionsvertrag, in dem sich die Union gut zwei Jahre nach dem Fall der Berliner Mauer erstmals ausdrücklich „zu den Grundsätzen der … Demokratie“ bekennt[6], im übrigen aber die demokratischen Regierungssysteme der Mitgliedstaaten als Element ihrer Identität benennt (Art. F Abs. 1) und die Stärkung der Demokratie eher als Ziel der Zusammenarbeit mit Drittstaaten definiert (Art. J Abs. 2 EUV und Art. 130u Abs. 2 EGV). Auch wenn die vom Europäischen Rat am 22. Juni 1993 festgelegten berühmten „Kopenhagener Kriterien“ unter anderem eine „demokratische und

[2] Der Begriff „Europäische Union“ umfasst im Folgenden auch die Europäischen Gemeinschaften als Vorgänger der EU.

[3] Erstmals in der Entscheidung *Stauder*, Rs. C-29/69 vom 12.11.1969.

[4] Art. F Abs. 2 EUV idF des Vertrages von Maastricht vom 7.2.1992.

[5] Weiler (in diesem Band Kapitel 1); Craig (in diesem Band Kapitel 24).

[6] Dritter Erwägungsgrund: „IN BESTÄTIGUNG ihres Bekenntnisses zu den Grundsätzen der Freiheit, der Demokratie und der Achtung der Menschenrechte und Grundfreiheiten und der Rechtsstaatlichkeit;“

rechtsstaatliche Ordnung", die „Wahrung der Menschenrechte" (und den Schutz von Minderheiten) als Bedingung für die Aufnahme in die Union formuliert hatten, beschritten die ehemals sozialistischen Staaten Mittel- und Osteuropas den Weg zur Demokratie eher aus eigenem Antrieb. Die Kopenhagener Kriterien trugen sicherlich zur Festigung demokratischer Strukturen und insbesondere zum Minderheitenschutz in den Reformstaaten bei, jedenfalls bis zu deren Beitritt; nach dem Beitritt entfalten sie keine Wirkung mehr, und der Schutz von Demokratie und Rechtsstaatlichkeit unter gleichberechtigten Mitgliedstaaten wird zum politischen Dilemma, dem mit juristischen Mitteln nur schwer beizukommen ist. Dies zeigen die mühsamen Versuche zur Aktivierung von Artikel 7 EUV gegenüber Polen und Ungarn und die Rechtsprechung des Europäischen Gerichtshofs zuletzt im Fall *LM*[7], und auch die von der Kommission für die nächste Haushaltsperiode vorgeschlagene Sanktionierung von Rechtsstaatsmängeln durch die Suspendierung von Zahlungsflüssen[8] stößt ihrerseits auf rechtsstaatliche Bedenken[9] und wirkt eher hilflos.

So bietet sich für den Bürger im Jahr 2019 ein gemischtes Bild: Der gesicherte Friede innerhalb der EU wird als Selbstverständlichkeit empfunden und bietet keine hinreichende Legitimitätsgrundlage für eine „immer engere Union"; noch immer besteht ein Demokratiedefizit der Union selbst, und in den Mitgliedstaaten wird das Demokratieprinzip populistisch gegen das Rechtsstaatsprinzip in Stellung gebracht; beim Grundrechtsschutz schließlich fehlt ungeachtet des im Unionsrecht erreichten hohen Schutzniveaus die Bereitschaft des Europäischen Gerichtshofs zur Unterordnung unter gemeineuropäische Mindeststandards.

1.2 Die wirtschaftlichen Errungenschaften: Grundfreiheiten, Binnenmarkt, Wohlstand, soziale Gerechtigkeit

Unbestreitbar sind die großen wirtschaftlichen Errungenschaften durch die Errichtung eines Binnenmarktes mit derzeit noch 512 Millionen Einwohnern[10], in dem ungeachtet fortbestehender Unvollkommenheiten der freie Verkehr von Personen, Waren, Dienstleistungen und Kapital sichergestellt ist. In Verbindung mit dem Diskriminierungsverbot war die primärrechtliche Verankerung dieser vier Grundfreiheiten, nachdem der Europäische Gerichtshof ihnen als gerichtlich

[7] Rs. C-216/18 PPU *Minister for Justice and Equality v LM* (*Celmer*), Urteil v. 25.7.2018 ECLI:EU:C:2018:586, insbes. Rdnr. 68 (Vollstreckung in Polen erlassener Europäischer Haftbefehle bei Geltendmachung systemischer Mängel der Rechtsstaatlichkeit in Polen).

[8] Vorschlag für eine Verordnung des Europäischen Parlaments und des Rates über den Schutz des Haushalts der Union im Falle von generellen Mängeln in Bezug auf das Rechtsstaatsprinzip in den Mitgliedstaaten vom 2.5.2018, COM(2018) 324 final, 2018/0136 (COD).

[9] Rangel de Mesquita (2018), S. 287.

[10] Gesamtbevölkerung 2018 bei 512,6 Mio.; Bevölkerung des VK 66,2 Mio. (Quelle: Eurostat), daher wird die Binnenmarktbevölkerung bei Vollzug des Brexit am 29.3.2019 auf 446,4 Mio. sinken.

durchsetzbaren Individualrechten größtmögliche Durchschlagskraft verliehen hatte, der zentrale Faktor für die Öffnung nationaler Schutzräume und die Effektivierung des Binnenmarktes. Dies hat den Unionsbürgern wirtschaftliche Freiräume eröffnet, die zuvor allenfalls wenigen Privilegierten offenstanden.

Allerdings ist auch die Kehrseite dieser die mitgliedstaatlichen Grenzen und Beschränkungen aufbrechenden Marktöffnung nicht zu übersehen. Ein erstes Problem liegt im Ungleichgewicht zwischen „negativer" und „positiver" Integration, wie es treffend von Fritz Scharpf[11] beschrieben wurde: Einerseits schreiben die Verträge ein bestimmtes liberales Konzept der Marktöffnung primärrechtlich, also mit Verfassungsrang fest, das von Kommission und Gerichtshof durchgesetzt wird und den Spielraum der Mitgliedstaaten selbst auf Gebieten empfindlich einschränkt, die in unterschiedlicher Ausprägung von allen Staaten dem Wettbewerb entzogen waren (insbesondere im Bereich der Daseinsvorsorge). Auf der anderen Seite sind Begrenzungen der Marktfreiheiten zugunsten des Allgemeinwohls oder schwächerer Marktteilnehmer nach Maßgabe der Verträge zwar durchaus möglich (und auch erfolgt), setzen aber ein gleichgerichtetes Handeln der Organe ungeachtet aller Interessengegensätze insbesondere zwischen den Mitgliedstaaten voraus: Als sekundärrechtliche Maßnahmen hängen solche Regulierungen zunächst von einem allein der Kommission vorbehaltenen Rechtssetzungsvorschlag ab, müssen dann nicht nur vom Parlament, sondern auch vom Rat mit qualifizierter Mehrheit (im Bereich des Steuerrechts sogar einstimmig) verabschiedet werden und können nach ihrer Annahme auch nur in diesem Verfahren geändert werden.

Ein besonders schwerwiegender Aspekt dieser Asymmetrie sind die primärrechtlichen Festlegungen vieler Politikfelder auf ein bestimmtes Markt- und Politikkonzept, das auf nationaler Ebene immer zur Disposition des (einfachen) Gesetzgebers steht, während es auf EU-Ebene als solches dem Zugriff der Gesetzgebungsorgane entzogen und aufgrund der Schwerfälligkeit des Vertragsänderungsverfahrens auch auf Primärrechtsebene einer Änderung nicht wirklich zugänglich ist. Diese besonders von Grimm[12] kritisierte Über-Konstitutionalisierung entzieht Kernbereiche der Wirtschaftspolitik viel weitergehend als im Nationalstaat dem politischen Diskurs und verstärkt damit das demokratische Legitimitätsdefizit der EU. Wenn die Stimme des Bürgers aber zum einen nichts bewirken kann, weil bestimmte Politikfelder schon konstitutionell determiniert sind; wenn er darüber hinaus weder die Zusammensetzung der Exekutive noch wirklich den Kurs ihrer Politik bestimmen kann, schwächt dies die demokratische Legitimation europäischer Politik nachhaltig. Die eilige Aufnahme vermeintlich populärer Stimmungen ohne verfahrensrechtliche Grundlagen zur Berücksichtigung des Volkswillens wie der Vorschlag zur Abschaffung der Sommerzeit als Folge einer ungeregelten Internet-Konsultation[13] vermag diese Schwäche nicht wirklich auszugleichen.

[11] Scharpf (2008), S. 49-87, spricht von „Asymmetrie".

[12] Vgl. zuletzt Grimm (2016) besonders V. Die demokratischen Kosten der Konstitutionalisierung.

[13] Vorschlag der Kommission vom 12.9.2018 für eine RL „zur Abschaffung der jahreszeitlich bedingten Zeitumstellung", COM(2018) 639 final in der Folge einer zwischen dem 4. Juli und dem 16.

Während die Verwirklichung des Binnenmarktes in den Mitgliedstaaten unzweifelhaft zu Wohlstandsgewinnen führte, kann deren Verteilung zwischen den Mitgliedstaaten nicht als gleichmäßig bezeichnet werden, wie sich zum Beispiel an der Entwicklung der nationalen Bruttoinlandsprodukte oder der Arbeitslosenquoten ablesen lässt. So fiel die Jugendarbeitslosenquote in der EU-28 zwischen 2014 und 2016 von 22,2% auf 18,7% und im Euroraum von 23,8% auf 20,9%, während sie in Deutschland bei 7,7% bzw. 7,0% und in Griechenland bei 52,4% bzw. 47,3% lag.[14] Nimmt man den Wert des kumulierten Bruttoinlandsprodukts aller EU-Staaten pro Einwohner als Referenzgröße, dann lag 2016 der Luxemburger Pro-Kopf-Wert bei mehr als 250% und der bulgarische bei weniger als 50% des europäischen Durchschnittswerts; zwischen 2006 und 2016 erhöhte sich der Luxemburger Vergleichswert leicht von 260% auf 270%, während der griechische von 95% auf 70%, der spanische von über 100% auf 90% und der italienische von 110% auf 95% fielen.[15]

Auch wenn die EU mit den gut dotierten Programmen ihrer Struktur- und Investitionsfonds den wirtschaftlich rückständigen Mitgliedstaaten hilft, ihre Position im innergemeinschaftlichen Wettbewerb zu stärken, ist das Auseinanderdriften der wirtschaftlichen Entwicklung der Mitgliedstaaten ein systemadäquates Ergebnis einer primär auf Marktöffnung und die Beseitigung von Wettbewerbshindernissen ausgerichteten Integration. Der Effekt wird verstärkt unter den Bedingungen einer Währungsunion, deren Mitgliedern kein währungspolitischer Instrumentenkasten mehr zur Verfügung steht. Es ist leicht nachvollziehbar, dass unter solchen Bedingungen Zweifel am Nutzen des europäischen Integrationsprojekts laut werden, die integrationsfeindlichen Strömungen nutzen.

1.3 Integrationspolitik und öffentliche Wahrnehmung

Ein weiteres Legitimitätsproblem des europäischen Projekts in seiner konkreten Gestalt als EU liegt in der Divergenz zwischen Schein und Sein, zwischen öffentlicher Wahrnehmung und konkreter Ausgestaltung. Man hat oft den Eindruck, dass die Bürger (manchmal gilt das auch für nationale Parlamente und Regierungen) erst nach vollzogener Souveränitätsübertragung verstehen, was sie da aus der Hand

August 2018 durchgeführten öffentlichen Konsultation, bei der von 4,6 Mio. Antworten sich 84 % für eine Abschaffung der Zeitumstellung aussprachen; ein Quorum war weder auf EU- noch auf mitgliedstaatlicher Ebene vorgesehen; 3,1 Mio. Antworten (67 %) kamen aus Deutschland (COM staff working document SWD(2018) 406 final).

[14] Eurostat, Youth unemployment rate and ratio, 2014-2016 https://ec.europa.eu/eurostat/statistics-explained/index.php?title=File:Youth_unemployment_rate_and_ratio,_2014-2016_(%25)_YB17-de.png.

[15] Eurostat, GDP per capita at current market prices, 2006 and 2016 (EU-28 = 100; based on PPS per inhabitant) https://ec.europa.eu/eurostat/statistics-explained/index.php?title=File:GDP_per_capita_at_current_market_prices,_2006_and_2016_(EU-28_%3D_100;_based_on_PPS_per_inhabitant)_YB17-de.png.

gegeben haben. Besonders klar hat dies als Methode bereits 1999 Jean-Claude Juncker beschrieben: „Wir beschließen etwas, stellen das dann in den Raum und warten einige Zeit ab, was passiert. Wenn es dann kein großes Geschrei gibt und keine Aufstände, weil die meisten gar nicht begreifen, was da beschlossen wurde, dann machen wir weiter – Schritt für Schritt, bis es kein Zurück mehr gibt."[16] Es ist allerdings unvermeidlich, dass diese zuletzt auch von Präsident Macron in seiner Sorbonner Rede getadelte[17] Methode zu Frustrationen führt – bei den ihrer Kompetenzen verlustig gegangenen nationalen Entscheidungsträgern ebenso wie beim Bürger, dessen gewohnte Muster politischer Entscheidungs- und Verantwortungszurechnung ungültig geworden sind ohne dass er erkennen könnte, was an deren Stelle getreten ist. Wenn man auf nationaler Ebene „nichts mehr machen kann", weil für den Bürger überraschend die Zuständigkeit jetzt „in Europa" liegt, vermittelt diese Verlusterkenntnis der verlagerten Zuständigkeit eben noch keine Legitimation. Im Gegenteil wird die Zustimmung zur neuen europäischen Regelungszuständigkeit dann nur davon abhängen, dass „Europa" tatsächlich liefert – erst die vom Bürger wahrgenommene oder zumindest wahrnehmbare europäische Problemlösung vermag neue Legitimationsstränge zu schaffen.

Das unvermeidbare Legitimitätsdefizit des Elitenprojekts wird besonders deutlich, wenn die Integration starken demokratischen Signalen zum Trotz durchgesetzt wird – man denke nur an die Ablehnung des Verfassungsvertrages im Frühjahr 2005 in Frankreich und den Niederlanden bei hoher Stimmbeteiligung[18], der nach einigen kosmetischen Retuschen als Lissabonner Vertrag vier Jahre später doch in Kraft gesetzt wurde. Man denke an die negativen Referenden über die Verträge von Nizza und Lissabon in Irland, denen das irische Volk im jeweils zweiten Durchgang nach mehr oder weniger gehaltvollen Zusicherungen durch die europäischen Partner dann doch zustimmte, oder an die dänische Ablehnung des Maastrichter Vertrages 1992, die allerdings wesentliche, bis heute fortwirkende Änderungen des dänischen Rechtsstatus („Opt-outs")[19] in der dann angenommenen modifizierten Vertragsfassung zur Folge hatte. Es ist bezeichnend, dass spätere Versuche der Rücknahme dieser Opt-outs in Volksabstimmungen 2000 und 2015 wiederum scheiterten[20]. Das schwelende Misstrauen des demokratischen Souveräns gegenüber

---

[16] Der Spiegel (1999), Ausgabe 52, 27.12.1999, S. 136.

[17] Rede vom 26.9.2017 an der Sorbonne: „Il est tellement plus simple de ne jamais expliquer où on veut aller, où nous voulons conduire nos peuples et de rester avec des arguments cachés… Et je pense que nous n'avons pas eu raison de faire avancer l'Europe malgré les peuples. » *Discours du Président de la République – "Initiative pour l'Europe: Une Europe souveraine, unie, démocratique" (Paris, 26 septembre 2017), https://ue.delegfrance.org/souverainete-unite-et-democratie.*

[18] 69,5% der Stimmberechtigten in Frankreich und 63 % in den Niederlanden, vgl. Andreas Wehr, Zur Ablehnung des EU-Verfassungsvertrags in Volksabstimmungen in Frankreich und in den Niederlanden vor zehn Jahren, in: Junge Welt, 29.5.2015.

[19] Im wesentlichen Nichtteilnahme Dänemarks an der Währungsunion und der gemeinsamen Justiz- und Innenpolitik.

[20] Volksabstimmung über die Rücknahme des Opt-out zur Währungsunion vom 28.9.2000; Volksabstimmung über die Rücknahme des Opt-out zur Innen- und Justizpolitik vom 3.12.2015.

europäischen Initiativen tritt in Volksabstimmungen immer wieder deutlich hervor;[21] es zeigte sich in der Ablehnung des schwedischen Beitritts zum Euro[22], zu dem das Land primärrechtlich eigentlich verpflichtet ist, ebenso wie in der Ablehnung des Assoziierungsvertrages mit der Ukraine im niederländischen Referendum vom 6. April 2016[23] und besonders dramatisch im Brexit-Referendum vom 23. Juni 2016, welche Gründe auch immer im einzelnen zu den negativen Ausgängen der jeweiligen Abstimmungen geführt haben mögen.[24]

Dieser Widerspruch zwischen erklärtem Bürgerwillen und Stand oder Fortschritt der europäischen Integration bezeichnet nicht nur einen Legitimationsmangel des europäischen Projekts in seiner konkreten Ausprägung, sondern beschreibt darüber hinaus ein kaum auflösbares Dilemma: Wenn die Fortsetzung der Integrationspolitik ohne Bürgerbeteiligung das Legitimationsdefizit verstärkt, so verspricht eine stärkere Einbeziehung der Bürger doch solange keine größere Identifizierung mit einer Politik der „immer engeren Union", wie die Bürger konkreten Integrationsschritten skeptisch gegenüberstehen.

Eine beharrlich auch gegen den Bürgerwillen betriebene Vertiefung der Union aus vermeintlich nur der politischen Führung zugänglichen besseren Einsichten ist dagegen geeignet, den allgemeinen Politikverdruss zu stärken und radikalen EU-Gegnern Zulauf zu verschaffen, ein Phänomen, das inzwischen in fast allen Mitgliedstaaten zu beobachten ist. Der vor allem von der deutschen Politik vertretene paternalistische Grundsatz, Volksabstimmungen über komplexe europäische Fragen überforderten die Bürger, verkennt, dass die Übertragung zentraler staatlicher Kompetenzen auf die europäische Ebene durchaus auf einfache Grundfragen zurückgeführt werden kann, die der Bürger nicht weniger zu verstehen in der Lage ist als der durchschnittliche Abgeordnete.[25]

Im Hinblick auf die Legitimität des europäischen Projekts ist festzuhalten, dass eine gegen den erklärten Willen der Bürger forcierte Integration ihre Legitimation jedenfalls nicht demokratisch ableiten, sondern allenfalls auf die Kraft des (politisch oder moralisch) vermeintlich überlegenen Arguments stützen könnte. Dies ist

---

[21] Vgl. Pierre Moscovici am 14.11.16 in Harvard (nach EuZW 17, 128): „Let's be realistic. Each time a referendum on Europe is called, the answer is no."

[22] Volksabstimmung vom 14.9.2003.

[23] Klaus Hänsch bezeichnete diese Abstimmung in der FAZ vom 31.8.16 als „deutliches Warnzeichen" gegen eine immer weitergehende Erweiterung der EU, die inzwischen den Zusammenhalt der Union selbst bedrohe: „Je größer die Union wird, desto weiter entfernt sie sich von ihren Bürgern."

[24] Vgl. Hubert Védrine in der FAZ v. 13.6.16: „Es ist schon erstaunlich, dass die Anhänger des Rufs nach ‚mehr Europa' in ihrem unerschütterlichen Glauben (und ‚Glauben' ist hier das richtige Wort) diesen Rückzug der Bürger niemals analysieren und keinerlei Selbstkritik üben."

[25] Dies sieht offensichtlich auch das Bundesverfassungsgericht so, vgl. Lissabon-Urteil 2 BvE 2/08 vom 30.6.2009, http://www.bverfg.de/entscheidungen/es20090630_2bve000208.html, vgl. Rn. 113, 228, 270. Der Verfasser erinnert sich übrigens sehr gut, dass nach der Verabschiedung des gescheiterten Verfassungsvertrages durch den Deutschen Bundestag bezeichnenderweise die befragten Abgeordneten keineswegs korrekt anzugeben wussten, welche Kompetenzen durch den Vertrag auf die EU übertragen und welche in nationaler Herrschaft – i.e. ihrem eigenen Zugriff – verbleiben würden.

aber eine demokratietheoretisch höchst fragwürdige Denkfigur. Denn wenn in der auf Gleichheit der Bürger gegründeten Demokratie niemand für sich in Anspruch nehmen darf, mit besserem Recht als andere die Politik des Staats zu bestimmen, dann muss dies erst recht für die Frage gelten, ob der Staat seine Zuständigkeit über die Bestimmung eines Teils seiner Politik auf eine andere politische Einheit überträgt, denn anders als der Kurs der nationalen Politik lässt sich die Übertragung einer Kompetenz nicht durch die Entscheidung einer neuen Mehrheit revidieren; einmal übertragene Zuständigkeiten sind für immer verloren.

2 Die künftige Entwicklung der EU: „ever closer Union" oder „united in diversity"?

"If a politician, as we are always told, should never say 'never', should he [ever] say 'ever'?"

Geoffrey Howe, Formal inauguration of the Congress Centre of the Academy of European Law, Trier 1998

2.1 Vision und Wirklichkeit

Das zu Beginn dieses Beitrags zitierte Bild Victor Hugos von der „europäischen Nation" steht für eine Vielzahl von Visionen, die seit Jahrhunderten das Streben engagierter Vorkämpfer der europäischen Einigung beflügelt haben und für die das Wort von den „Vereinigten Staaten von Europa" ein weiteres Synonym ist. Mag auch die reale Europäische Union diesem Bild in vielen Aspekten erstaunlich nahe kommen[26], so kann doch derzeit bei ihr von einem europäischen Bundesstaat noch keine Rede sein, wie das Bundesverfassungsgericht in seinem Lissabon-Urteil zu Recht festgestellt hat. Zu diffus sind die Erwartungen der Mitgliedstaaten an die europäische Integration; zu divergent ihre Interessen; und zu eng sind die Bürger ihrem Nationalstaat verbunden, als dass sie ihre Loyalität auf einen europäischen Bundesstaat in Gestalt der Europäischen Union übertragen wollten. Die politischen, gesellschaftlichen und kulturellen Bedingungen für die Entstehung einer europäischen Föderation aus historisch gewachsenen Nationalstaaten mit einer Vielfalt lebendiger Sprachen unterscheiden sich eben grundlegend von denen für die Entwicklung der Vereinigten Staaten von Amerika aus einer Gruppe homogener englischer Kolonien mit einer einzigen Staatssprache.

Darüber hinaus veränderte die nach dem Fall der Mauer politisch unausweichliche Erweiterung der EU von zwölf Mitgliedstaaten 1994 auf 28 im Jahr 2013 den

[26] Im Vergleich zur Vision Victor Hugos weist die EU heute bereits „unité de monnaie, unité de mètre, unité de méridien, unité de code …" auf, doch fehlt es dauerhaft an der „unité de langue"; und von Paris als europäischer Hauptstadt kann keine Rede sein (auch der gemeinsame Nullmeridian ist anders als von Hugo unterstellt nicht der Pariser, sondern der von Greenwich…).

Charakter der Union nachhaltig. Ist die Bildung eines gemeinsamen politischen Willens in einem größeren Verbund schon per se schwieriger als im kleinen, so machte der Beitritt elf ehemals sozialistischer Staaten mit völlig anderen politischen, ökonomischen und gesellschaftlichen Erfahrungen die Union nochmals heterogener.

2.2 Staatenverbund oder „Europäische Republik“?

Im November 2018 machte vor allem in der deutschsprachigen Presse für kurze Zeit das Projekt der Ausrufung einer „Europäischen Republik“ von sich reden. Von „geschichtsträchtigen Balkonen in ganz Europa“ verlasen hundert Jahre nach Ende des Ersten Weltkriegs die Initiatoren Ulrike Guérot, Robert Menasse und andere ein Manifest zur „Entnationalisierung der europäischen Demokratie“[27], das „das Europa der Nationalstaaten“ (also die EU) für gescheitert und die [nicht näher definierte] „Idee des europäischen Einigungsprojekts“ für verraten erklärt. Daher müsse „die Macht in den europäischen Institutionen erobert werden, um den gemeinsamen Markt und die gemeinsame Währung in einer gemeinsamen europäischen Demokratie zu gestalten“. Der Europäische Rat sei „hiermit“ abgesetzt; an die Stelle der Souveränität der Staaten trete die Souveränität der Bürger; Träger der Europäischen Republik seien die „Städte und Regionen“.[28]

Es ist bezeichnend, dass die Aktion in der Öffentlichkeit eher als kulturelles Happening denn als politische Aktion wahrgenommen wurde und eine (zustimmende oder ablehnende) Reaktion der angesprochenen Bürger weder bei der Verlesung des Manifests noch später erkennbar wurde. Das von den Initiatoren zweifellos ernst gemeinte Projekt der Neugründung eines europäischen Staates wird politisch offensichtlich von niemandem ernst genommen, am wenigsten von den Bürgern, die sich weiterhin in erster Linie ihren Nationalstaaten verbunden fühlen. Nicht nur Günter Verheugen kennt in Europa „kein einziges Volk, das bereit [wäre], seine Eigenstaatlichkeit zugunsten eines europäischen Staates aufzugeben“.[29] Unter diesen Voraussetzungen der europäischen Wirklichkeit ist das Streben nach der Utopie einer Europäischen Republik nicht legitimer als ihre Ablehnung.

Auch die Frage, ob die Fortentwicklung der Europäischen Union in einen Bundesstaat überhaupt ein wünschenswertes Ziel sei, ist aus den gleichen Gründen ebenso legitim wie der Ruf nach ihrer Vertiefung.[30] Denn die Übertragung einer

[27] „The European Balcony Project“, vgl. https://wemakeit.com/projects/the-european-balcony-project?locale=de.

[28] Manifest zur „Proklamation einer Europäischen Republik“, die ausdrücklich als „Theatre event“ bezeichnet wird, https://europeanbalconyproject.eu/en/manifesto.

[29] In einem Tagesschau-Interview am 29.9.2017 sowie im Interview mit der NZZ vom 28.11.2018. Ähnlich Wolfgang Schäuble in der FAZ v. 25.1.16: „Die Bindekraft der Nation ist in den allermeisten Mitgliedstaaten viel stärker als die einer gesamteuropäischen Idee.“

[30] Vgl. Hans-Jürgen Papier, FAZ v. 17.10.16: „Die Behauptung, es gäbe nur noch die Alternative Ausbau der EU zum Bundesstaat oder den Verfall Europas, ist nicht mehr als ein … Märchen. Man

Kompetenz auf die höhere Ebene einer europäischen Föderation garantiert für sich noch keine bessere Sachentscheidung, entzieht aber der nationalstaatlichen Ebene die Möglichkeit eigener möglicherweise sachnäherer Entscheidungen und unterbindet in jedem Fall den Wettbewerb unterschiedlicher, für sich jeweils adäquater Lösungsmodelle. Um es zugespitzt zu sagen: Die Schaffung einer europäischen Armee unter zentralem europäischem Oberkommando gewährleistet per se noch nicht den Frieden und keine europäische Friedenspolitik; die Bereitstellung eines solchen Instruments auf europäischer Ebene bietet aber eine vorher nicht vorhandene Möglichkeit des militärischen Eingreifens mit allen Risiken und zu heute nicht bekannten Zwecken: Die Verlagerung möglicher „imperialistischer" Zielsetzungen auf eine höhere europäische Ebene würde diese nicht weniger verwerflich, sondern allenfalls gefährlicher machen.

Wenn die Verlagerung von Zuständigkeiten von den Mitgliedstaaten auf die europäische Ebene also nicht per se die bessere Lösung darstellt, bedarf jede Kompetenzübertragung einer besonderen Begründung, umso mehr, als das Subsidiaritätsprinzip des Artikel 5 Abs. 3 EUV schon für die Ausübung einer bereits übertragenen (geteilten) Zuständigkeit eine Begründung fordert. Dabei ist stets zu bedenken, dass die einmal übertragene Zuständigkeit für den Mitgliedstaat dauerhaft verloren sein wird und eben nicht durch Berufung auf das Subsidiaritätsprinzip wirksam beschränkt werden kann. Jedenfalls ergeben pauschale Forderungen nach „Mehr Europa" politisch solange keinen Sinn, wie die konkrete Ausgestaltung des „Mehr" nicht thematisiert und diskutiert wird.

2.3 Eine offene Debatte über die Entwicklung der Europäischen Union

Das europäische Projekt hat seit der Einheitlichen Europäischen Akte 1986 eine von den Unterzeichnern der Römischen Verträge kaum vorhersehbare quantitative und qualitative Entwicklung genommen. Viele Errungenschaften wie der Binnenmarkt, Freizügigkeit und Wegfall der Grenzkontrollen, natürlich die Friedenssicherung nach innen und vielleicht auch die grenzüberschreitende Zusammenarbeit der Justizbehörden werden von den Bürgern heute als selbstverständlich angesehen. Anderes funktioniert weniger gut oder ist unvollständig geregelt, wie Asyl- und Flüchtlingsrecht in einem Raum ohne Binnengrenzen oder die Währungsunion. Wieder andere Regelungen mögen als zu weitgehend, bevormundend oder überflüssig angesehen werden – wie Datenschutz, Verbraucherschutz oder die Liberalisierung bestimmter Wirtschaftsbereiche.[31]

muss vielmehr mehr denn je darauf achten, dass Europa nicht an einer Überdimensionierung seiner Staatlichkeit scheitert".

[31] Zu Recht wird häufig die Proliferation sehr detaillierter technischer Regelungen als solche negativ wahrgenommen, vgl. Präsident Macron in seiner Sorbonne-Rede vom 26.9.2017: „Si la vigueur du droit fait la force de l'Europe, la profusion des normes en précipite le rejet."

Die Auseinandersetzung über den richtigen Weg, über wichtige politische Ziele, über den effizientesten Lösungsansatz, ja selbst über strukturelle Reformen wie Vertiefung der Integration hier oder Rückgabe anderer Bereiche an die Mitgliedstaaten dort ist jedoch Teil des normalen politischen Willensbildungsprozesses in jeder politischen Einheit und sicher im politischen Mehrebenensystem. In dieser Auseinandersetzung sollte jede vertretene Auffassung a priori als legitim gelten. Die Debatte über europäische Fragen ist jedoch häufig ideologisch belastet, insbesondere wenn es um die Diskussion neuer Integrationsschritte geht: Hier werfen Integrationsbefürworter den Gegnern Europafeindlichkeit, Nationalismus oder Rechtspopulismus vor, während die Europakritiker ihren Gegnern umgekehrt Beschönigung oder Selbstbetrug vorhalten.[32] Anstatt sich mühsam mit Argumenten auseinanderzusetzen fordert oder verurteilt man Haltungen. Höhepunkt einer solchen jenseits der Fakten geführten Debatte war sicher der britische Abstimmungskampf über den Brexit.

Die Europäische Union mag in der Krise sein, doch ist sie anders als in den Zeiten der Eurosklerose nicht entscheidungsunfähig. Sie mag an vielen Stellen reformbedürftig sein, doch unterscheidet sie das nicht grundsätzlich von den sie konstituierenden Mitgliedstaaten. Wie jedes Menschenwerk ist sie unvollkommen und fehlerhaft. Die Europäische Union ist aber auch dann nicht am Ende, wenn die Vertiefung der Integration nicht als Selbstzweck betrachtet wird. Die Metapher vom Fahrrad, das stürzt wenn es nicht mehr getreten wird geht fehl. Die „immer engere Union" des Artikel 1 EUV ist kein rechtliches Gebot, sondern eine politische Zielsetzung;[33] die Vielfalt ihrer Völker und Mitgliedstaaten ist Reichtum nicht weniger als Herausforderung.

References

Grimm D (2016) ERuropa ja – aber welches?, Zur Verfassung der europäischen Demokratie. 2. Aufl. 2016

Kainer A, Persch J (2018) Das Prinzip der Einheit des Binnenmarkts: Keine Rosinen für Drittstaaten. EuZW 2018, Heft 22, S. 932, S. 935

Rangel de Mesquita MJR (2018) The commission's proposal to protect the EU budget against threats to the rule of law. ERA Forum 19(2):287

Scharpf FW (2008) Negative und positive Integration. In: M. Höpner und A. Schäfer (Hrsg.), Die politische Ökonomie der europäischen Integration, Frankfurt am Main, S. 49–87

[32] Statt vieler vgl. zum einen Udo Di Fabio, FAZ vom 23.5.2016: „Jeder politische Herrschaftsverband braucht Kritik. Es war dem gemeinsamen Projekt letztlich nicht zuträglich, dass die europäischen Funktionseliten jede Infragestellung des jeweils nächsten Integrationsschritts als mangelnde Loyalität zum europäischen Friedenswerk diskreditiert … haben."; zum anderen Thilo Sarrazin, FAZ vom 7.3.2016: „Die Mängel beider [der Währungsunion und des Schengen-Raums] haben zu tun mit einer europäischen Neigung zu Beschönigung und Selbstbetrug, die in eine symbolische, nicht zu Ende gedachte und zutiefst widersprüchliche Politik gemündet ist".

[33] Kainer and Persch (2018), S. 932, S. 935; die auch aus Art. 1 EUV eine rechtliche Verpflichtung der Union auf ein Fortschreiten der Integration ableiten wollen.

Europa muss noch enger zusammenwachsen

Katarina Barley

Das Kongressprogramm zur Feier des 25jährigen Bestehens der ERA sprach mit Blick auf Europa vom „Legitimitätsdefizit eines Elitenprojekts". Diesem Befund kann ich so nicht zustimmen. Ich sehe Europa keineswegs als Elitenprojekt: Zahllose Bürgerinnen und Bürger der Europäischen Union profitieren von offenen Grenzen, InterRail-Reisen, Erasmus-Austauschprogramm und dem Euro. Ich muss meinen Kindern heute bei einer Reise durch Europa erklären, wie das vor gar nicht allzu langer Zeit mit den Grenzkontrollen und den unterschiedlichen Währungen war.

Vom Sitz der Europäischen Rechtsakademie in Trier ist es keine halbe Stunde nach Luxemburg und gerade einmal eine Stunde nach Frankreich oder Belgien. Auch die Niederlande erreicht man schnell. Ohne die offenen Grenzen wäre Trier nicht in der Mitte Europas, sondern am Rande Deutschlands. Eine Stadt, die einstmals die größte Stadt nördlich der Alpen im römischen Weltreich war.

Von den Vorteilen offener Grenzen und einer gemeinsamen Währung profitieren nicht nur irgendwelche Eliten, sondern alle Bürgerinnen und Bürger Europas – auch wenn die Chancen und Möglichkeiten für uns alle inzwischen selbstverständlich, vielleicht allzu selbstverständlich geworden sind. Und so schienen denn auch nach dem überraschenden Brexit-Votum die Briten selbst nicht minder geschockt als das übrige Europa.

Wir haben es noch nicht geschafft, einen Weg zu finden, das Projekt Europa richtig zu erklären. Wir erreichen zumeist die bereits interessierten Bürgerinnen und

---

Katarina Barley, Bundesministerin der Justiz und für Verbraucherschutz; Mitglied des Stiftungsrats der Europäischen Rechtsakademie Trier (ERA). – Der Beitrag gibt im Wesentlichen die Stellungnahme der Verfasserin zur Podiumsdiskussion Die Zukunft des europäischen Projekts Krise des europäischen Projekts unterminiert die Autorität des Unionsrechts – Die EU auf der Suche nach Legitimität im Rahmen des Jubiläumskongresses der ERA vom 20. Oktober 2017 wieder.

K. Barley (✉)
Federal Ministry of Justice and Consumer Protection, Berlin, Germany
e-mail: fuerst-ma@bmjv.bund.de

W. Heusel, J.-P. Rageade (eds.), *The Authority of EU Law*,
https://doi.org/10.1007/978-3-662-58841-3_26

Bürger. Deswegen ist eine Veränderung an dieser Stelle vonnöten, wir müssen einen aufsuchenden Ansatz stärken und noch besser nah am Alltag den Bürgerinnen und Bürgern Europas die Vorteile der EU vermitteln. Leider lässt sich tatsächlich ein Legitimitätsdefizit der Europäischen Union an vielen Stellen beobachten, wie die Ergebnisse mehrerer Volksabstimmungen in verschiedenen Mitgliedstaaten zu den unterschiedlichsten europäischen Fragen gezeigt haben.

Dem europakritischen Trend zu nationaler Abschottung und fremdenfeindlichem Populismus in viel zu vielen Mitgliedstaaten der Europäischen Union kann nur durch ehrliche Aufklärung und überzeugende Argumente begegnet werden: Wir dürfen uns nicht der Illusion hingeben, das Zusammenwachsen Europas als Selbstläufer und alternativlosen Prozess zu betrachten.

Alle, die wir in Politik, Justiz, Verwaltung, Wissenschaft, Wirtschaft, Kultur und Medien Verantwortung tragen, müssen konkret und immer wieder aufs Neue die vielen Vorteile darlegen und begründen, die die Menschen in den Ländern Europas durch den voranschreitenden Einigungsprozess genießen. Zu einer ehrlichen Debatte gehört aber auch, politische Erfolge in Europa nicht immer wieder mit der eigenen nationalen Durchsetzungsstärke zu begründen und zugleich für politische Niederlagen irgendwelche Bürokraten in Brüssel verantwortlich zu machen.

Die Europäische Union und ihre Organe sollten verstärkt die großen Zukunftsaufgaben in den Blick nehmen, die wir nur mit gemeinsamer europäischer Kraft meistern können.

Die Europäische Rechtsakademie ist 1992 gegründet worden, um Experten des Unionsrechts aus ganz Europa zusammenzuführen, fortzubilden und in mehrsprachigen Veranstaltungen auch ein Stück weit eine gesamteuropäische Öffentlichkeit im Bereich der Rechtswissenschaft und Rechtspolitik zu schaffen. Inzwischen sind – mit einer einzigen Ausnahme – alle Mitgliedstaaten der Europäischen Union auch Stifter der Europäischen Rechtsakademie. Trier wurde damals zum Standort gewählt, weil der Europäische Gerichtshof in Luxemburg quasi gleich um die Ecke liegt. Die europäische Einigung machte eine Stadt am Rande Deutschlands zu einem Treffpunkt mitten in Europa.

Trier ist heute sehr stark mit unseren westlichen Nachbarländern verbunden. Dabei liegt die Stadt auf einem Gebiet, das in der Geschichte regelmäßig ein Schlachtfeld war. Allein der Gewinn, dass ein vereintes Europa keine Kriege mehr gegeneinander führt, ist für jeden Menschen, der noch den Zweiten Weltkrieg erleben musste, das erste und wichtigste Argument für das europäische Projekt – ein Friedensprojekt. Denn wie ein Leben ohne Grenzen ist auch ein Leben in Frieden mit Blick auf unsere Geschichte keineswegs selbstverständlich. Mit dieser historischen Errungenschaft dürfen wir nicht leichtfertig umgehen.

Zur Wahrheit über die Notwendigkeit der europäischen Einigung gehört aber auch, dass in der globalisierten Welt von heute kein einziges Land in Europa mehr in der Lage ist, seine eigenen Interessen allein gegen andere Weltmächte durchzusetzen. Dies gilt wirtschaftlich, vor allem aber auch politisch: Nur gemeinsam können wir Europäer auf der Weltbühne im Konzert mit den Vereinigten Staaten von Amerika, Russland, China und anderen aufstrebenden Mächten mitspielen. Insofern bedeutet mehr Europa keinen Verlust, sondern einen Gewinn an Souveränität. Nur wenn wir in Einigkeit handeln, können wir auch in unserem Sinne globale Standards setzen, bevor dies andere in einer Art und Weise tun, die nicht unseren rechtsstaatlichen und demokratischen Ansprüchen genügen.

In diesem Zusammenhang will ich auch betonen, dass es die Europäische Union nicht akzeptieren kann, wenn einzelne Mitgliedstaaten darangehen, die rechtsstaatlichen Prinzipien in ihren Ländern in Frage zu stellen, die Gewaltenteilung aufzuweichen und die Unabhängigkeit der Justiz einzuschränken.

Das Recht ist sicherlich nicht alles. Aber ohne eine funktionierende Rechtsstaatlichkeit ist alles andere nichts. Die EU kann nur dann als „Raum der Freiheit, der Sicherheit und des Rechts" ohne Binnengrenzen wirken, wenn alle nationalen Behörden und alle Unionsbürger auch Vertrauen in die Rechtsordnung der anderen Mitgliedstaaten haben können. Wer in einem Mitgliedstaat der EU an den rechtlichen Fundamenten unseres Zusammenlebens in Frieden, Freiheit und Gerechtigkeit rüttelt, muss darauf eine ebenso klare wie entschiedene Antwort aus Brüssel bekommen. Gleichzeitig ist die Argumentationsstärke und Leidenschaft von überzeugten Europäerinnen und Europäern gefragt, wenn es darum geht, den Bürgerinnen und Bürgern dieser Länder zu verdeutlichen, warum Autokratie und Populismus keine gangbaren Wege sind.

In unserer globalisierten und vielfach vernetzten Welt halte ich auch nichts von einem exklusiven Heimatbegriff, der darauf abzielt, andere Menschen als Fremde auszugrenzen. Vergangenheitssehnsucht und Abschottungstendenzen sind ebenso realitätsfern wie am Ende selbstzerstörerisch für einen Kontinent, der wirtschaftlich und kulturell von offenen Grenzen lebt.

Um unsere kulturelle, religiöse und soziale Vielfalt zu leben und zu gestalten, brauchen wir keine von oben verordnete Leitkultur – was auch immer das genau sein soll. Wir brauchen vielmehr einen gründlichen Prozess der gesellschaftlichen Selbstvergewisserung, der sich an unseren rechtsstaatlichen und demokratischen Werten sowie einem positiven Bekenntnis zu den Errungenschaften und Erfolgen einer freiheitlich-offenen Gesellschaft orientiert.

Im geeinten Europa tritt eine politische Vertrags- und Verantwortungsgemeinschaft an die Stelle nationaler und nationalistischer Mythen. In Europa ist gesellschaftliche Vielfalt eine Chance, die es anzuerkennen und politisch zu gestalten gilt.

Zu den grundlegenden Werten einer europäischen Verantwortungsgemeinschaft gehört die gelebte und wechselseitige Solidarität ihrer Mitglieder. Das bedeutet mit Blick auf die seit spätestens 2015 erkennbaren massiven Migrationsbewegungen, dass die Europäische Union ihre südlichen Nachbarn nicht mit der großen Zahl an Menschen allein lassen darf, die vor Krieg und Terror zu uns fliehen. Das heißt aber auch, dass sich kein EU-Land der humanitären Verantwortung entziehen darf, Geflüchtete bei sich aufzunehmen und gemäß internationalem und europäischem Recht zu behandeln.

Nur wenn es uns in der EU gelingt, klare Regeln für die Gemeinschaft zu formulieren und diese im Zweifelsfall auch wirksam durchzusetzen, werden die Bürgerinnen und Bürger in den Mitgliedsländern das notwendige Vertrauen in die europäischen Institutionen fassen.

Wir alle bleiben gefordert, die europäische Einigung zu einem dauerhaften Erfolg zum Wohle aller Bürgerinnen und Bürger zu machen. Und wir alle müssen dafür werben und arbeiten, dass Europa weiter zusammenwächst, wenn es nicht zerfallen und in Bedeutungslosigkeit versinken will. Denn Europa ist unsere Zukunft.

Quo vadis Europe? The future of Europe under pressure

Wiebe de Vries

1 Introduction

Peace has been the cornerstone of the European project. For centuries, countries have been battling over territory, power, religion or various political principles. Our troubled past inspired individuals to envision a peaceful and united Europe where the possibility of a war would become unthinkable. Visionaries such as Arturo Spinelli and Ernesto Rossi, imprisoned by a fascist regime during the Second World War, carved out a way towards a better future in the Ventotene manifesto *For a Free and United Europe*.[1] This future was Europe.

The European Union, as we know it today, built its foundations with the aim to secure lasting peace. It started in 1952 with the European Coal and Steel Community. Later, in 1957, the Treaty of Rome created the European Economic Community (or 'Common Market') to unite European countries economically and politically in a common market where people, goods, services and capital can move freely. The founders of the EU came to an important realisation: if nations stand united, there is a lower risk of conflicts and greater cooperation. Years later, in 2012, the EU was honoured with the Nobel Peace Prize *"for over six decades having contributed to the advancement of peace and reconciliation, democracy and human rights in Europe"*.[2] The Prize recognised the role of the EU in transforming most of Europe,

[1] Altiero Spinelli; Ernesto Rossi, The Ventotene Manifesto. Ventotene: The Altiero Spinelli Institute for Federalist Studies.

[2] "The Nobel Peace Prize 2012 to the European Union (EU) - Press Release". Nobelprize.org. Nobel Media AB 2014. Web. 3 Aug 2018. <http://www.nobelprize.org/nobel_prizes/peace/laureates/2012/press.html>.

W. de Vries (✉)
Immediate Past President, International Association of Young Lawyers (AIJA), Brussels, Belgium
e-mail: vriesw@bloom-tax.com

W. Heusel, J.-P. Rageade (eds.), *The Authority of EU Law*,
https://doi.org/10.1007/978-3-662-58841-3_27

from a continent of war to a continent of peace. Standing united, the European project achieved the longest period of peace in written history in Europe.

In October 2017, the International Association of Young Lawyers (AIJA) spoke at the Academy of European Law Jubilee Congress "The Authority of EU Law", in Trier, Germany. We had the pleasure to present the results of a survey conducted on the future of Europe. The survey was distributed among 1400 young lawyers—active AIJA members under 45 and based in Europe. When asked about the EU's main achievements to date, 52% of respondents confirmed that maintaining long-lasting peace across the Continent has been indeed the greatest achievement.

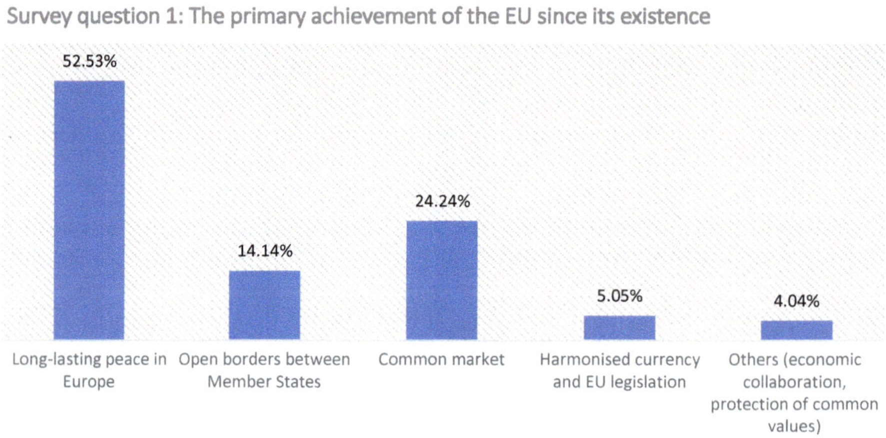

The same survey asked the young legal community about the biggest threat to the EU today. Close to 49% of respondents believe that the biggest threat is the lack of solidarity between Member States. This is followed by the lack of European leadership (19.39%), migration (13.27%) and others, such as populism or lack of transparency.

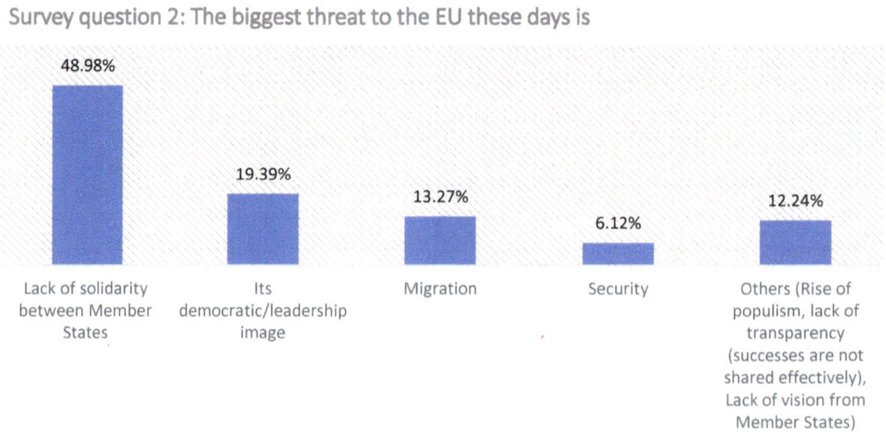

2 Europe's future in uncertain times

Uncertainty is looming over the future of Europe. Today, we witness a growing sentiment of mistrust towards the EU on the back of concerns about security and borders, the downfall of the economy, rise of populism and the challenges of a post-Brexit EU. The surge of the anti-EU sentiment sweeps the Continent as the 2019 elections for the European Parliament approach. Voters will be faced with a completely different political, social and economic environment from the previous round of elections. The future of Europe is at stake, but Europe cannot seem to decide on a compelling counter-narrative to deal with its multiple crises.

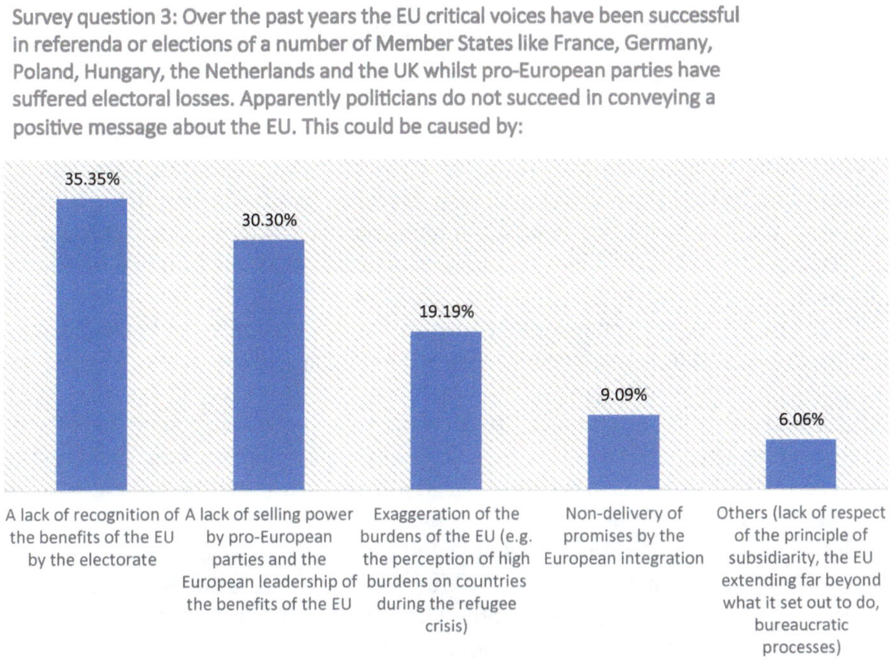

There is no doubt that populism will stay at the centre of Europe's debates in the next years. Over the past decades, populist parties have steadily increased their popularity across several Member States such as France, Germany, Poland, Hungary, the Netherlands or the UK while pro-European parties have suffered electoral losses. When survey respondents were asked about the causes of the rising populism, young lawyers (35%) claim that this is because the voters do not understand or recognise the benefits of EU membership. 30.30% of them believe that pro-European parties and the European leadership have failed to convey these benefits to their voters. This brings to light a more profound issue—there is no clear narrative on the benefits of EU membership. The truth is, voters often receive mixed messages and fall prey to the ambiguous agendas of populist leaders.

The Ventotene manifesto rightly called for unification and cooperation years ago. There is no better time to reflect on this. Europe needs to be reminded of the sacrifice of previous generations. In today's rapidly changing world, Europe needs to reclaim its founding principles and values and re-think the process of integration. Building on solidarity, dialogue and cooperation at grassroots levels can spark some hope among citizens and build a way forward for a common future.

3 The rule of law in Europe is challenged

While reclaiming its founding principles and values, the EU also needs to defend these more effectively. The EU is based on the rule of law. Respect for the rule of law, as outlined in Article 2 of the Treaty on European Union, is also one of the prerequisites for the accession of new Member States. Among the other values of Article 2, we find democracy, human rights, freedom and protection of minorities. The EU is not just a common market, but a community of shared values.

Over the last years, some Member States have been confronted with judicial deficiencies related to the independence of their national justice system. The EU has struggled to respond effectively to these violations. However, it has also taken unprecedent actions. For instance, the European Commission recommended triggering Article 7 against Poland for breaching European common values and rule of law. The institution has also recently raised concerns towards the current judicial reforms in Romania that may weaken the independence of justice.

During these troubled times, dialogue and trust in the judiciary will be vital to ensure an effective implementation of rule of law across the Member States. Euroscepticism is and will stay profoundly embedded across the civil society, national governments, new and traditional media. It will further erode democracy and the rule of law in Europe. In this context, we must show unity, vision and leadership to bring solutions to meet European citizens' expectations and defend our shared common values.

4 Scenarios for the future of Europe

Just under 40% of respondents believe that the EU will be broken into small groups of unions, with different levels of integration. 31% of respondents believe that the EU will remain as it is today. The form in which it will continue will depend very much on a variety of factors, such as the performance of the global economy and the economy of individual Member States. The impact of Brexit will also affect how the EU develops and how each Member State will re-evaluate its role and EU membership.

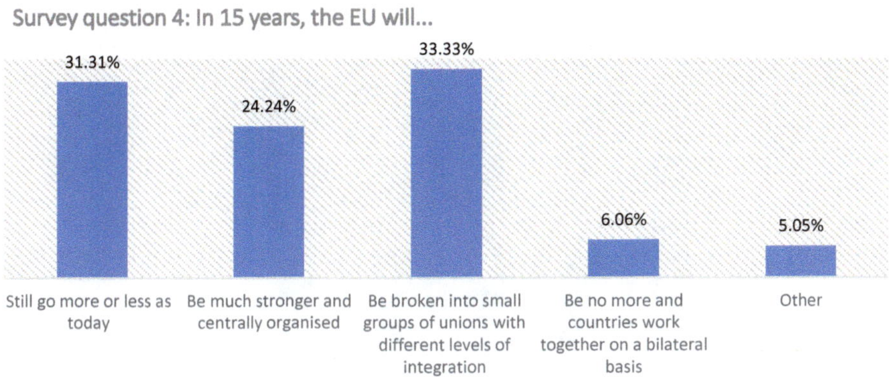

However, too often the debate about the future of Europe is limited to having to choose between more or less Europe. In 2017, the European Commission's White Paper on the Future of Europe listed five scenarios for the future of Europe by 2025. The starting point for each scenario is that the 27 Member States move forward together as a Union. The possibilities covered in the White Paper range from the status quo, to a change of scope and priorities, to a partial or collective leap forward.

AIJA and its members have decided to take a position regarding the possible ways forward based on the five scenarios presented in the White Paper. We consider that the way forward should focus on the elements of Scenario 3 "Those who want more do more". 40% of respondents were in favour of further cooperation and unity among Member States that want to do more. This also means that the rights of citizens would vary depending on whether they live in a country that has chosen to do more. Only 23% of respondents believe in Scenario 1 "Carrying on" and that the EU should stick to its course, while focusing on implementing and upgrading its current reform agenda.

Survey question 5: On 1 March 2017 a White Paper was released on "The future of Europe". The White Paper describes five scenarios. Which of the below do you believe to be the most likely scenario the European Union will develop towards?

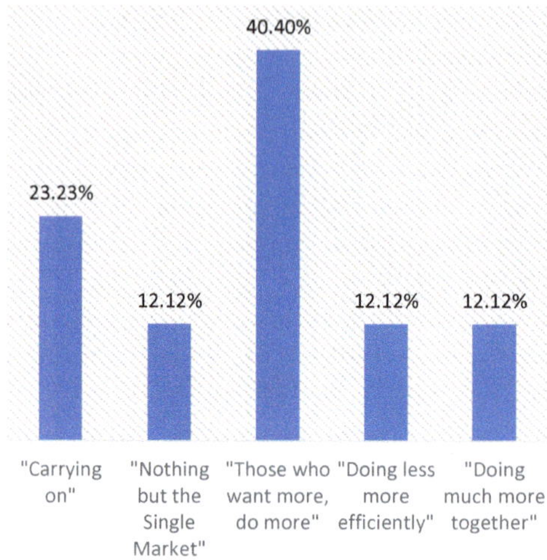

5 The future of the EU at the crossroads

Despite all the current challenges, it is important to recognise that the vision of a unified Europe has come a long way in the last decades. The European project has gone through multiple crises in its history and these have only made it stronger. With the rise of populism, the EU must find ways to contain this threat. More and more, we see that pro-European parties and the European leadership have reduced their efforts to advocate the benefits and achievements of the EU to its European citizens. In front of the most pressing challenges confronting the EU, the leadership has remained silent. If it continues to stay shy, this will only add momentum to the arguments of Eurosceptics.

The future of the EU is at the crossroads. In the current context, Europe may need to reconsider its own agenda: maintaining its course at full speed on a track of more integration, more members and more “power to Brussels”, or taking a slower pace where the concerns of the European citizens are understood and addressed.

Many European citizens don’t feel heard in the ambitions of the European Union. This could be an interpretation of the results of recent referenda, such as the Brexit referendum but also the Dutch referendum on the European Association Treaty with the Ukraine. The accomplishments of the European Union as they surface from the AIJA survey: long-lasting peace, a common market and open borders, appear by now a given rather than the achievements of the EU. In the perception of many, these historical successes fade away against the more recent and less beneficial consequences of the EU project such as the European migrant crisis and the financial crisis. Unsurprisingly, the most important threat to the EU in this respect, as seen by AIJA members, is the lack of solidarity between the EU Member States.

If we are at a crossroads, if we are facing the choice of going at full speed ahead while ignoring the current lack of electoral support from the EU citizens, or moving at a slower speed to address the concerns that have risen from recent electoral results: The choice should be obvious. As the saying goes: Rome was not built in one day. Neither is the project we call the EU. We could even question whether the European project could ever be considered finalised. If we have trusted the EU to be the best way to safeguard peace and prosperity in Europe for hundreds of years, there is clearly no hurry in making it perfect in the first minutes or hours after its birth. Listening to its citizens, more advocacy on the achievements of the EU and increased transparency on the EU governance may be items that deserve a higher attention in the priority list of the European leadership. The future will always belong to Europe.

The European Union's never-ending search for legitimacy

Pedro Silva Pereira

1 The EU's search for legitimacy: introductory remarks

Sixty years after the Treaty of Rome and 10 years after the Treaty of Lisbon, the European Union's (EU) search for legitimacy still continues. In a strange way it reminds us of Don Quixote's epical quest for "the impossible dream". I suppose we can all agree this is not a good sign.

Let me be completely clear about the real nature of the basic challenges we face. As I see it, the crisis of the European project is fundamentally a crisis of values and a crisis of purpose, but also a crisis of results—results for citizens, results for workers, results for families, results for businesses and results for Europe as a whole at a time when convergence seems to be a forgotten ambition. To some extent, those shortcomings are a direct consequence of increasing global competition and a dramatic legacy of the Great Recession, but—let's face it—they are also due to poor leadership, wrong economic policies and, last but not least, serious structural problems, in particular those related to the architecture of the Economic and Monetary Union (EMU) and to the general institutional framework for political and economic governance at the European level.

The much discussed "democratic deficit" surely is one of those major structural problems, but make no mistake: the calls to "take back control" and the rise of populism in Europe are much more an expression of discontent with the results delivered

Paper based on the author's intervention at the Jubilee Congress of the Academy of European Law (ERA), "The Authority of EU Law - Do we still believe in it?", Trier, 20 October 2017.

P. Silva Pereira (✉)
Member of the European Parliament, Vice-Chair of the Committee on Constitutional Affairs, Brussels, Belgium
e-mail: pedro.silvapereira@europarl.europa.eu

W. Heusel, J.-P. Rageade (eds.), *The Authority of EU Law*,
https://doi.org/10.1007/978-3-662-58841-3_28

by the European economic and migration policies than a sign of political disappointment with the lack of obscure institutional and democratic reforms in the EU.

The idea that we would get better results if we just turned back to our old borders, our old national sovereignty and our old national parliaments is nothing more than a mere illusion. In fact, every one of our major challenges today—from migration to globalisation, from economic growth to climate change, from terrorism to tax evasion—would be impossible to tackle if we were apart. However, it is also true that we can and must do better together, build on our common values, regain the notion of a common purpose and work in a more effective manner to deliver results that meet the expectations of the European citizens—that is what we must do.

Having put things into perspective, I will enter into the discussion of the EU's long-running search for legitimacy.

2 The "democratic deficit" in the EU: Reality and perception

While we have to recognise the existence of a "democratic deficit", it would be unfair to disregard the institutional advances for more democracy that have been introduced in Europe over the last 60 years, from Rome to the Lisbon Treaty.[1] Those democratic improvements are real and should not be undermined.

As in any other representative democracy, the European Union has now a Parliament elected by direct universal suffrage that represents all the European citizens. Besides, since the signing of the Lisbon Treaty, voters have been given additional democratic control over EU institutions through their elected representatives. The introduction of the so-called "Spitzenkandidaten" procedure gave voters the chance to know in advance—and therefore to take into consideration at the time of voting—the proposed candidates to the position of President of the European Commission. Electoral results do indeed matter: the EU Council is now legally obliged to take into account the results of the European elections when proposing a new President of the Commission to Parliament and the President and the entire College of Commissioners have to be voted on by the European Parliament.[2] Moreover, from the day it takes office the Commission is fully accountable before the Parliament through the usual parliamentary paraphernalia: questions, debates and inquiries of all sorts. Last but not least, the Commission can be dismissed by the Parliament at any time and for any reason, as in any other parliamentary regime.

Taken together with its equally important legislative competences, the political powers of the European Parliament give to the only European institution directly

[1] Besides introducing an entirely new chapter on the democratic principles of the European Union and the so-called "citizens' initiative", the Lisbon Treaty has also strengthened the political and legislative powers of the European Parliament in a substantive manner.

[2] The Parliament votes if the proposed Commission as a whole is "fit for purpose" but, in practical terms, it can also politically reject individual candidates and force their substitution.

elected by the European citizens a decisive role within the institutional functioning of the Union.

We must also not forget that the European Council is composed of representatives of national governments democratically legitimised by the citizens at the national level and acting under the control of national parliaments, in accordance with the constitutional rules of each Member State. This double source of legitimacy—a directly elected Parliament and a nationally legitimised Council—is one of the distinctive characteristics of the European institutions and the basic foundation of their democratic functioning.

If democracy means a democratic definition of political goals, a democratic selection of leaders and a democratic system to ensure proper accountability and control over the use of political power, it would be difficult to argue that the EU institutional setting does not fulfil all those basic requirements. Nevertheless, the key issue of the "democratic deficit" still remains. It is the question of its causes and potential solutions that we now need to address.

3 Three core reasons for the "democratic deficit" in the EU

Analysing the European model, Dan Rodrick[3] has told us about the famous triangular dilemma: if we take political and economic integration, national sovereignty and democracy, one can only have two out of three. Looking to the current institutional picture of the EU, an optimist would say that the choice has been made: we have accepted to lose—or at least to share—some of our sovereignty in exchange for more political and economic integration within a European framework where we have kept our democratic way of life. The only difference would be that for the purpose of exercising European competences we have replaced our democratic national institutions with European ones.

Unfortunately, this really is a very optimistic view. For many, at least, the shift from national political systems to the European institutional system is far from being understood as equivalent from the point of view of democracy. This can be explained by three fundamental reasons.

First, there is an undeniable lack of true European dimension in the European elections. In fact, European elections are widely "decentralised" and voters often select among national parties mostly on the basis of national political issues. To make things worse, many citizens believe that the European elections are not so important because they have little idea of what happens in the European Parliament which is rarely given suitable coverage by the media. As a consequence, many citizens simply abstain from voting in the European elections.

---

[3] Rodrick (2012).

Second, the link between the vote of citizens in the European elections and the concrete political decisions of European institutions, including the political decisions of the European Parliament itself, remains weak. To be fair, this is not a problem unique to the European project, but a well-known issue which plagues our national representative democracies as well, in part due to the enormous increase in the role and competences of the State in the last few decades. The tenuous link between the electoral choices made by citizens and the myriad of decisions taken by political and administrative bodies forced the introduction of several mechanisms—such as public consultations or public hearings—designed to establish an open procedure allowing citizen's participation in decision-making as a way to compensate for the perceived lack of democratic legitimacy of many of those decisions. Of course, the unavoidable geographical distance between European citizens and European public officials based in Brussels, together with the immense bureaucratic missions of the EU, could only exacerbate this sort of problems at the European level. In this context, it should come as no surprise that Europe is seen by many as a distant technocratic project, not a democratic one.

Third, there is also a particular and very serious problem regarding the lack of democracy in economic governance at EU level. In fact, democracy is about choices, beginning with the choice of fiscal policy—the number one mission of democratic parliaments. However, in the last few years, people have been told that there are no choices to be made simply because "There Is No Alternative" (TINA). Consequently, economic governance within the Eurozone was presented to the European citizens essentially as a strict rules-based framework where there was not much room left for true political choices.

Moreover, a maddening range of legal instruments—Growth and Stability Pact, Two Pack, Six Pack, Fiscal Compact, European Semester, preventive evaluation and veto of national draft budgets, Country Specific Recommendations, control of macro-economic imbalances, macro-conditionality and sanctions—were created to limit the political room for manoeuvre of Member States, either within the European institutions or through new informal bodies, as the Eurogroup, or even outside the community method in pure intergovernmental terms. While these tools were conceived to promote "economic coordination" and to ensure "fiscal discipline", they were in fact used to fight any substantive deviation from the only policy allowed. This madness reached the unthinkable when the EU politically endorsed pure technocratic governments in countries such as Italy and Greece.

The real democratic improvements introduced in the European institutions over the last few decades were severely overshadowed by this state of affairs regarding economic and fiscal policy. It is hard to overstate the impact of these EU-level "technocratic solutions", which turned out in fact to be quite ideological ones. To a large extent, this systemic and systematic exclusion of real political alternatives explains better than anything else the growing discontent with the lack of democratic legitimacy of the European project.

4 "Democratic deficit" in the EU: What can we do about it?

Having identified the main reasons for the "democratic deficit" in the EU, we can now point out the three fundamental issues we have to address if we really want to tackle this problem:

- First, to promote a true and meaningful European dimension in the European elections;
- Second, to strengthen the link between the vote of the citizens and the decisions of the European institutions;
- Third, to ensure enough room for real political alternatives and democratic choices at national level within the economic governance of the Eurozone.

5 For a true and meaningful European dimension of the European elections

The so-called "Spitzenkandidaten" procedure—where prior to the vote the most important political families announce their proposed candidates to the position of President of the European Commission—should be seen as a real improvement in increasing the European dimension of the elections. Introduced for the first time in the 2014 elections, this procedure should be continued,[4] even if it is understood to be a mere "political indication" in order to give to the Council and the European Parliament enough room for manoeuvre, if needed, to find a workable political solution taking into account the political composition of the newly elected Parliament.

However, while we should maintain the "Spitzenkandidaten" procedure, it would be a serious political mistake to institute the direct election of the President of the European Commission. Firstly, such a solution would be totally misleading to voters, suggesting an illusionary concentration of power in the President of the Commission, when the process of European integration, by its own nature, requires that there be a myriad of political compromises, including with national governments of Member States. Secondly, this would introduce a confusing presidential element in a regime which has been designed—and continuously reinforced—as being essentially parliamentarian. This would have the dramatic consequence of immediately stripping the European Parliament not only of its current right to vote for the President of the Commission, but also of the decisive political power to dismiss him and his entire Commission. On the contrary, we need to design a more coherent European political system as a true parliamentary regime, where the Executive—meaning the European Commission—is fully accountable to the

[4] Agreement between the European Parliament and the European Commission amending point 4 of the Framework Agreement on relations between the European Parliament and the European Commission (OJ L 45, 17.2.2018, pp. 46–46).

European Parliament, which is the only European institution that can directly and democratically represent European citizens.

Some suggest that another way to promote the European dimension of European elections would be to establish a "joint constituency" open to the so-called "transnational lists".[5] These lists would possibly be headed by each political family's candidate for the post of President of the Commission.[6] After instigating a huge political debate both in the Council and in the European Parliament,[7] this idea was finally rejected by a clear majority in Strasbourg in February 2018.[8] As far as it can be predicted, it looks like there is no future for "transnational lists" in the EU.

Perhaps more viable are a number of less far-reaching proposals made by the European Parliament in order to reform the European electoral law and to promote the European dimension of elections.[9] Two of those proposals deserve special attention: first, that the name and logos of the European political parties should also be placed on the ballot papers and on relevant campaign broadcasts and materials; second, that the deadline for the nomination of lead candidates for the office of President of the European Commission should be codified in the Electoral Act to enable political debates between the candidates to be organised and Union-wide electoral campaigns to be mounted. Unfortunately, after many months of political discussions, the Council failed to find an agreement on any of these issues.

Besides these and other measures that can be introduced to improve the perception about the European dimension of the European elections, it is of utmost importance that we overcome another serious obstacle: the systematic boycott waged by the media on almost everything that happens in the European Parliament. In fact, most news which focus on European issues pertain either to decisions and declarations of the European Commission or meetings of the European Council, and not about the political discussions and deliberations of the European Parliament. Of course, citizens can only understand the democratic functioning of the European Union and the utility of voting in the European elections if they get to know about what happens in the European Parliament and who is doing what about this and that issue. This change, however, cannot happen through laws and regulations, it can only come about through the collective will of responsible journalists.

[5] Report on a proposal for a modification of the Act concerning the election of the Members of the European Parliament by direct universal suffrage of 20 September 1976 (2009/2134(INI)).

[6] European Parliament Resolution of 11 November 2015 based on the legislative initiative report on the reform of the electoral law of the European Union 2015/2035(INL).

[7] In the context of the debate of Danuta Hübner and Pedro Silva Pereira report, which lead to the European Parliament Resolution of 7 February 2018 on the composition of the European Parliament (2017/2054(INL) – 2017/0900(NLE)).

[8] 368 against, 274 in favour.

[9] European Parliament Resolution of 11 November 2015 based on the legislative initiative report on the reform of the electoral law of the European Union 2015/2035(INL).

6 Strengthening the link between the vote of the citizens and the decisions of the European institutions

It should come as no surprise that the "standard remedy" for the "democratic deficit" in the EU is to strengthen the role of the only institution directly elected by European citizens: the European Parliament. Give more power and competences to the European Parliament,[10] increase the role of Parliament in decision-making and make the Commission more accountable before the Parliament—these are the sort of things that have to be done to strengthen the link between the vote of the citizens and the decisions taken by the European institutions.

It should be stressed that this is of particular importance in terms of economic governance. In fact, if we really want to address the widespread concern about the lack of legitimacy of European decisions, the top priority should be to reinforce the democratic legitimacy of economic and fiscal policy—, which obviously leads us to the need for reform of the Economic and Monetary Union.[11] As the Eurozone's instruments have been considerably extended over the years, it is only natural that their democratic legitimacy and accountability be upgraded.[12]

The European Parliament recently gave an important contribution to this debate through two own-initiative reports on the reform of the EU: the Bresso/Brok[13] and Verhofstadt[14] reports. The first is meant to improve the functioning of the EU "building on the potential of the Lisbon Treaty"—that is to say, without Treaty change. The second considers more far-reaching "adjustments to the current institutional set-up of the EU", proposing a comprehensive democratic reform of the Treaties.

At this stage, however, we should recognise that there is a lack of common vision about the future of Europe, which is the basic prerequisite for any successful political process seeking to revise the Treaties. This is why we should focus on what can be done to improve the democratic functioning of the European Union within the framework of the Lisbon Treaty. In fact, there is a lot we can do.

First of all, the role of the Parliament in the functioning of the Economic and Monetary Union should be substantially enlarged, ensuring proper legitimacy and full accountability. For that purpose, there is no need to create a new Parliament for the Eurozone: the European Parliament is the Parliament of the whole EU, therefore it is also the Eurozone's Parliament. What we need is a stronger parliamentary dimension throughout the entire European Semester process to ensure democratic

[10] Including a reinforced right of inquiry and the right of legislative initiative, under certain conditions.

[11] The 2012 report of Herman Van Rompuy on the reform of the Eurozone already pointed out the need for more democratic accountability, but progress has been rather slow.

[12] The Five President Report: Completing Europe's Economic and Monetary Union (2015) and The White Paper on the Future of Europe (2017).

[13] European Parliament resolution of 16 February 2017 improving the functioning of the European Union building on the potential of the Lisbon Treaty (2014/2249(INI)).

[14] European Parliament resolution of 16 February 2017 on possible evolutions of and adjustments to the current institutional set-up of the European Union (2014/2248(INI)).

legitimacy of economic and fiscal policy, regarding both coordination and implementation. In concrete terms, this implies instituting co-decision between the Council and the Parliament on the Annual Growth Survey and the Integrated Guidelines for economic and employment policies, but also Parliament's participation in and control over a number of the Commission's tasks: evaluation of national budgets, issuing of Country-Specific Recommendations, monitoring of macroeconomic imbalances and managing of excessive deficit procedures.

The same democratic control by the European Parliament should be ensured for the new policy instruments introduced in the framework of the EMU reform, including the reformed European Stability Mechanism[15] and the financial instruments to manage the future fiscal capacity of the Eurozone.

Another idea supported by many—and endorsed by President Jean-Claude Juncker himself[16] would be to merge the position of President of the Eurogroup with the position of Commissioner for Economic and Financial Affairs, generating a "double-hatted" EU Finance Minister that would also be Vice-President of the European Commission. This solution should be seen as an important step forward in terms of democratic accountability because the President of the Eurogroup—currently the leader of an important but informal and rather obscure body of the Eurozone's Finance Ministers—would become automatically accountable before the European Parliament, just like any other Commissioner.

The good news is that to implement these solutions no Treaty change is required. In fact, they can very easily be laid down in an inter-institutional agreement on democratic European economic governance. The only thing required is political will.

More demanding from a legal point of view, but equally important, would be to turn the intergovernmental instruments created during the financial crisis—like the European Stability Mechanism and the Single Resolution Fund—into instruments under EU law. Those intergovernmental instruments totally bypassed the Community or the Union method, diminishing transparency, avoiding accountability and escaping from any form of effective democratic control by the European Parliament.

Of course, other reforms can also be pursued to further develop European democracy, namely improving the workings of the "citizens' initiative" introduced by the Lisbon Treaty; promoting "e-democracy" in order to facilitate citizens' participation; organising public hearings and "citizens' conventions" (such as the ones recently proposed to discuss the future of Europe); and ensuring full transparency and access to information on rule-making and decision-making at EU level.

There is room, as well, for further engagement of national parliaments in the democratic functioning of the EU. However, it must be recalled that the role of national parliaments is essentially to mandate and scrutinise their respective governments in European affairs, while the European Parliament is elected by direct universal suffrage precisely to ensure democratic legitimacy of all European decisions

[15] Pedro Silva Pereira and Vladimir Manka report on the Establishment of the European Monetary Fund (A8-0087/2019).

[16] "The State of the Union Address" by Jean-Claude Juncker, 13 September of 2017.

and full accountability of the European Executive. As the sum of national democratic mandates does not produce a European democratic mandate, democratic legitimacy at EU-level depends fundamentally on the role of the European Parliament elected by the European citizens.

Nevertheless, the Lisbon Treaty went already as far as giving national Parliaments an active role in controlling the subsidiarity principle in European rule-making. A "green card" procedure has also been proposed by some to allow national parliaments to submit legislative proposals to the Council.

Additionally, cooperation between national parliaments and the European Parliament can and should be intensified, namely through the existing joint inter-parliamentary bodies, such as the Conference of Parliamentary Committees for Union Affairs of Parliaments of the European Union (COSAC), the Inter-parliamentary Conference on Common Foreign and Security Policy (CFSP-IPC) and the Inter-parliamentary Conference foreseen in Article 13 of the Treaty on Stability, Coordination and Governance in the Economic and Monetary Union (TSCG). However, inter-parliamentary bodies are illusory solutions to the democratic problems we face at EU level. In fact, it should be said that the existing joint bodies are more than enough and it would be a serious mistake to try to grant them any kind of decision-making powers which would only bring more confusion to the European institutional setting. On the contrary, these inter-parliamentary bodies should be taken as what they are: important *fora* for consultation, information-sharing and political dialogue.

7 Ensuring enough room for political alternatives and democratic choices at national level within the economic governance of the Eurozone

Reducing solutions to the "democratic deficit" to a dichotomy of "more Europe" or "less Europe" sounds simplistic, because it just so happens to be true. It is quite surprising that for so many "more Europe" is the only conceivable political response when "Brexiteers" and other populist and nationalist movements are pushing in the opposite direction and successfully turning vast parts of the public opinion against the European project under one single cry: "take back control".

The combination of this sudden federalist impulse with the prudent "no Treaty change" formula—obviously conceived to avoid unpleasant referendums—reveals how fragile this single note project is. On the contrary, a more balanced approach is needed: besides promoting a true and meaningful European dimension in the European elections and reinforcing the link between the vote of the citizens and the decisions of the European institutions, particularly through a stronger role of the European Parliament, it is paramount that we give back to national democracies and national parliaments some control over political choices on economic and fiscal policy.

Although very important, control of subsidiarity or even giving European legislative initiative to national parliaments will not be enough. The same also goes for any kind of institutional political dialogue between national parliaments and the European Parliament. From our point of view, the completion of the EMU—which is urgently needed—should go hand in hand with reinforcing national democracies by way of respecting national parliaments' competences to approve national budgets.

No doubt, the EMU needs common rules and regulations, as well as common targets and policy goals that must be fully respected by Member States in their national budgets. But it is important to realise that we have come to a point where nearly everything is under European surveillance: scenarios and forecasts, goals and concrete measures, economic policy and fiscal policy, structural reforms and social policies, estimates and results, all leading to constant warnings, opinions and Country-Specific Recommendations, if not the threat of sanctions or the veto of national budgets by the European Commission.

From the point of view of democracy, this high degree of European intervention in national budgets raises two serious problems. On the one hand, it must be said that the democratic legitimacy of many of these European interferences is more than questionable. For instance, how legitimate is it for a European bureaucrat to issue a "binding recommendation" against the increase of the minimum wage by a Member State? On the other hand, this level of European interference in the concrete choices of economic and fiscal policy—that were supposed to be made by national governments and parliaments—undermines the real meaning of national democracy. Taken together, these two problems are the most serious democratic challenges in today's European project.

More room for manoeuvre and for political alternatives in national democracies, clear distinction between European common targets and the national competence to choose fiscal policy measures, respect for the national Parliaments' competence regarding the approval of national budgets—these are all part of the solution to the problem of the "democratic deficit" in the EU.

8 Time for a "democratic offensive" in the European Union

Time has come for "a democratic offensive" in the EU to ensure full legitimacy of European decisions and full respect for the political will of European citizens. For that to happen, we do not have to wait for any reform of the Treaties. All we need is political will to explore all potential of the Lisbon Treaty to upgrade European democracy.

From all the suggestions made throughout the long debate on the EU's "democratic deficit", none is more important than deepening the democratic legitimacy of economic governance in the Eurozone. This primarily concerns the role of the European Parliament within the Economic and Monetary Union in terms of decision-making, control and accountability. But, at the same time, we need to respect the role of national parliaments in the budgetary process, allowing enough room for political alternatives and democratic choices at national level. This double-sided movement is of utmost importance to address in a balanced and successful manner the current democratic challenges we face in the European project.

A lot still has to be done, but neither is the European Republic a utopia, nor is democracy in the EU an "impossible dream". It is just an unfinished job. Our unfinished job.

References

Agreement between the European Parliament and the European Commission amending point 4 of the Framework Agreement on relations between the European Parliament and the European Commission (OJ L 45, 17.2.2018, p. 46)

European Commission (2015) The Five Presidents Report: Completing Europe's Economic and Monetary Union

European Commission (2017) The White Paper on the Future of Europe

European Parliament, Resolution of 11 November 2015 based on the legislative initiative report on the reform of the electoral law of the European Union, 2015/2035(INL)

European Parliament, Resolution of 7 February 2018 on the composition of the European Parliament (2017/2054(INL) – 2017/0900(NLE))

European Parliament, Resolution of 16 February 2017 on possible evolutions of and adjustments to the current institutional set-up of the European Union (2014/2248(INI))

European Parliament, Resolution of 16 February 2017 on improving the functioning of the European Union building on the potential of the Lisbon Treaty (2014/2249(INI))

Juncker J-C (2017) The State of the Union Address. 13th September 2017

Report on a proposal for a modification of the Act concerning the election of the Members of the European Parliament by direct universal suffrage of 20 September 1976 (2009/2134(INI))

Report on the Establishment of the European Monetary Fund (A8-0087/2019)

Rodrick D (2012) The globalization paradox: democracy and the future of the world economy. Paperback Editions, New York

Van Rompuy H (2012) Towards a Genuine Economic and Monetary Union

L'UE: quelle légitimité ? Quel avenir ?

Jean-Luc Sauron

1 Quelle légitimité ?

La question de la légitimité de l'UE (1.1) se déroule dans un contexte de crise démocratique sur le continent (1.2).

1.1 Un problème de légitimité descendante : L'UE est un syndic de copropriété sans capacité d'intervention chez les copropriétaires

L'UE n'a été rejointe, depuis 2004, que pour son dynamisme économique. Elle se limite à une structure subventionnaire incapable ou illégitime à parler d'autres choses que de répartition des enveloppes entre les États membres. Le règlement de copropriété se limite aux parties communes, sans pouvoir intervenir à l'intérieur des États membres. La crise migratoire a été la fin d'un cycle : non seulement il n'est pas possible d'imposer des mesures aux États sans adhésion de leur population (refus polonais, hongrois, tchèque) d'accepter un fardeau de populations étrangères, mais les mesures prises par ces derniers États membres pour rejeter les migrants font l'objet aujourd'hui de demandes de remboursement de frais, telles que les constructions de barrières barbelées.

Conseiller d'Etat, délégué au droit européen chez Conseil d'Etat ; professeur à Université Paris-Dauphine. Les opinions avancées ici n'engagent que leur auteur et non les institutions dans lesquelles il travaille.

J.-L. Sauron (✉)
Vice President, Council of State, Paris, France
e-mail: jean-luc.sauron@conseil-etat.fr

W. Heusel, J.-P. Rageade (eds.), *The Authority of EU Law*,
https://doi.org/10.1007/978-3-662-58841-3_29

Mais l'UE est-elle légitime à s'immiscer dans les questions intérieures des États ? Elle accepte de contrer l'indépendantisme catalan, mais a refusé de participer au débat du Brexit en Grande Bretagne. Actuellement, les Italiens se sont livrés à une gesticulation politique pour trouver un gouvernement au bout de plusieurs mois de campagne. L'UE n'aurait-elle été légitime à demander aux Italiens de sortir de leur nombril et de demander à la 3ème économie de la zone euro d'arrêter de jouer avec l'avenir économique du continent après avoir été soutenue par l'UE dans la partielle remise en selle de son système bancaire ?

1.2 Un problème de légitimité ascendante : le révélateur européen de la crise nationale de la démocratie

L'analyse est simple à faire. Nos concitoyens ont cru un moment que la crise décisionnelle et démocratique se situait à Bruxelles. L'actuelle Commission européenne a achevé de convaincre les eurosceptiques les plus endurcis que les institutions européennes fonctionnaient dans le vide.

Le résultat, c'est qu'il devient évident que la vraie crise démocratique est une crise démocratique de chacune des entités nationales européennes. L'AKP mobilise dans plusieurs États européens des partis « pro-turcs » par lesquels il essaie de peser sur les élections nationales. Les Russes et les Américains agitent leurs réseaux d'affidés politiques dans chacune de leurs zones d'influence en Europe. Nos concitoyens sont les cibles des « fake news » diffusées par les médias pour déstabiliser les votes – durant le Brexit ou la dernière campagne présidentielle en France.

L'Europe est gangrénée par la corruption. Malgré des affaires dramatiques à Malte et en Slovaquie, seules les opinions publiques ou les pools de journalistes se mobilisent. Aucune position d'importance ou décision d'action n'a été prise par le Conseil européen ou la Commission européenne. Dans ces conditions, comment reprocher aux agriculteurs honnêtes des problèmes de calculs des fonds ?

60 ans après 1957, l'Union européenne n'a pas commencé sa post-puberté.

2 Quel avenir ?

Pour pouvoir parler de l'avenir de l'Union européenne, il conviendrait de casser le cadre issu des années 50 (2.1) et de remobiliser l'opinion publique nationale sur les enjeux générationnels (2.2).

2.1 *Le cadre institutionnel issu des années 50 est obsolète et doit être bouleversé*

Ce cadre a été mis en place sous l'impulsion des Etats-Unis, dans un contexte de guerre froide et dans une configuration économique très loin de la mondialisation. Le monde actuel est instable, durablement multipolaire et définitivement ouvert.

Le schéma fédéraliste n'est pas le bon. La mondialisation a clairement sonné le retour pérenne des États. Ce retour est la condition de l'avenir démocratique de l'espace européen. Il faut fonctionner sur un modèle d'organisation très souple et au plus proche des acteurs nationaux, en favorisant systématiquement les convergences entre les économies européennes, à deux ou à trois, sur des initiatives venues des secteurs et acteurs nationaux.

Il faut, en revanche, européaniser tout ce qui concerne les relations avec l'extérieur : armée et commerce. Dans ces deux matières, il faut organiser un système collectif de négociation et d'action avec des compensations internes au bénéfice des régions touchées (commerce) ou plus actives (défense).

A l'époque du tout numérique, les transhumances du Conseil européen ou du Parlement européen soulignent un côté théâtral et presqu'uniquement lié aux questions de communication.

2.2 *Remobiliser l'opinion publique nationale sur les enjeux générationnels*

L'Europe se dirige tout droit vers un amoindrissement démographique qui se traduira par sa marginalisation économique, politique et civilisationnelle. Le propos paraît violent. Mais la plupart des pays ont amorcé un déclin de leur population (Allemagne, Italie, Russie, et la plupart des pays d'Europe centrale) ou s'y dirigent (France, Irlande, Espagne).

Le niveau européen est le bon niveau pour s'attaquer à cette problématique qui rend vaines toutes les manifestations sur le maintien du niveau de vie. Cela demandera de prendre des mesures de politique familiale, sans remettre en cause les avancées telles que le droit à l'avortement, en intégrant une politique migratoire rendue inévitable par une absence de prévisibilité sur ces questions, mais aussi de construire une Europe de la santé ambitieuse, un domaine où l'échelon étatique ne saurait être durablement pertinent.

Il serait très important de donner mission à l'UE de réfléchir sur le long terme. La force des démocratures ou des régimes autoritaires est de souligner combien ils raisonnent sur l'avenir de leur peuple. L'aspect « course du hamster » dans sa roue que renvoie la gestion au jour le jour des démocraties européennes s'en trouverait corrigé.

Modestes réflexions d'un Européen convaincu, qui demanderaient à être complétées par des propositions institutionnelles.

The role of government and trust in the market economy

Nadja König and Ludger Schuknecht

Paper presented at the ERA jubilee congress in Trier, 20 October 2017, updated in April 2018. The authors wish to thank Otmar Issing, Niklas Potrafke, Helmut Herres, Torsten Arnswald, Florian Meyerhöfer and Holger Zemanek for their valuable comments.

This paper studies the role of governments and its link to trust. We argue that the public's trust strongly depends on governments delivering on their core tasks in a market economy. In some economies, a neglect of core tasks can be observed and there seems to be some erosion, notably in terms of securing sound rules of the game in industrialised countries. We find very little correlation between government expenditure and trust but a strong correlation with delivering on core tasks. This leads us to conclude that it is not government spending per se that needs to increase to build trust, but rather better focused government activities.

1 Introduction

Growing populism, market scepticism and euroscepticism are, above all, a reflection of a lack of trust. Governments create expectations and build or destroy trust depending on whether they deliver. This has an important link to economics.

First, governments are tempted to promise too much to everybody. This is bound to create frustrations instead of building trust because people's desires are unlimited while financing is not. Moreover, the ability of governments is limited by the "laws"

Ludger Schuknecht: Since September 2018, he has been Deputy Secretary-General of the OECD in Paris.

N. König (✉) · L. Schuknecht
Chief Economist, Federal Ministry of Finance, Berlin, Germany
e-mail: Nadja.Koenig@bmf.bund.de; Ludger.Schuknecht@bmf.bund.de

W. Heusel, J.-P. Rageade (eds.), *The Authority of EU Law*,
https://doi.org/10.1007/978-3-662-58841-3_30

of the market against which adverse policy measures can only temporarily prevail.[1] Moreover, there is the risk of contradictions between extensive promises to different groups (high social welfare versus low taxes; security versus open borders). Governments may find it hard to resist this temptation which would require dealing with the scarcity of their means and prioritising their tasks.

This leads to the second argument: governments spend more and more money but less of it is spent on what people expect from governments as their core tasks. The first and foremost core task is public order and security, both in a non-economic and an economic sense: implementation and enforcement of the basic rules of the game (including absence of physical and economic crime), reasonable economic stability, education, infrastructure and basic social safety nets.[2] Doing well on their core tasks allows governments to promote equal opportunity, prosperity and social welfare. It allows people to see a better future even if they are not privileged from birth. People would then see their expectations met, which builds trust.

But governments are subject to political pressure, which potentially leads to over-commitment in the social sphere and to neglecting core tasks. This can contribute to disappointed expectations and poor trust.

A third political economy argument is relevant here. Trust in governments in delivering outcomes is closely linked to the process of decision making. People are more likely to develop trust when their own preferences have entered the decision making process. And they are more willing to cope with disappointment if they themselves participated in the decision. In Europe, many decisions are elevated to the EU level without first gaining the support of the population. If people feel they are not participating in the process leading to certain policy choices and if these policies then fail to deliver the desired outcome, people tend to blame the EU and their own governments rather than taking responsibility themselves.

In this paper we focus on the first two issues and argue that governments need to deliver on their core tasks to build trust. We find some indications that governments are at risk of neglecting their core tasks while over-committing in the social sphere in particular. Certainly, a much more thorough analysis of these claims is needed.

The following Sect. 2 provides a framework regarding what people expect from governments as their core tasks. Section 3 contains some stylised facts on how governments exercise their core tasks and how this has changed over time. Section 4 provides some policy recommendations and a conclusion.

2 Core tasks of government: Some conceptual issues

The link from the role of government to trust in government and the market economy is indirect (Fig. 1). If governments perform well on their core tasks, we are likely to witness more growth and prosperity, better opportunities and more

[1] Böhm-Bawerk (1914), and Issing (2009).

[2] Musgrave (1959), Buchanan (1975), and Friedman (1977).

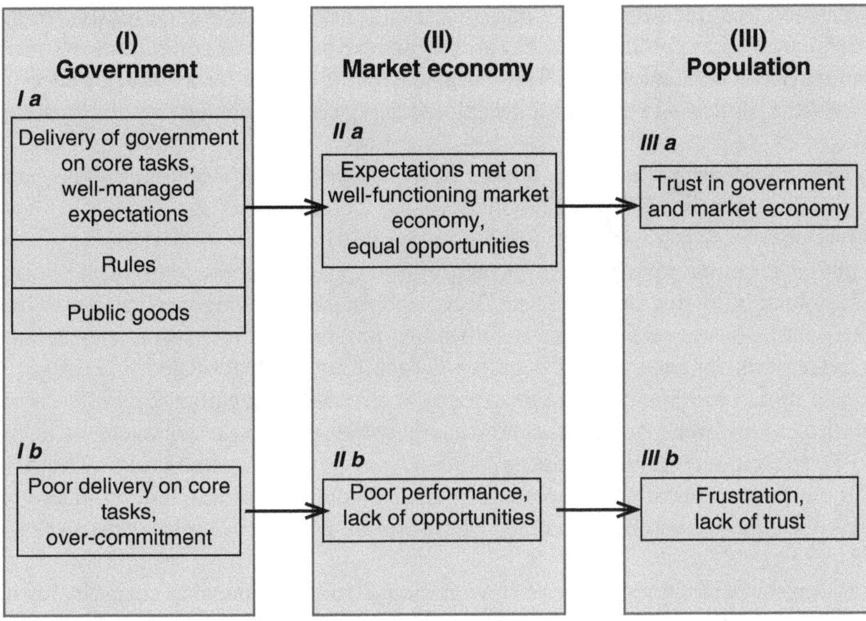

Fig. 1 The link from government performance to trust

satisfaction by people in the ability of governments to deliver on their expectations. This builds trust.

However, if this is not the case, we are also likely to see poor performance of the economy, parts of society without opportunities and a general sense of frustration with the economic and political system. Worse, the poor performance of the market economy may induce governments to blame the market instead of themselves. This risks discrediting the economic system and may create a spiral of new intervention, worsening performance and further undermining trust.

What are the core tasks of governments to boost prosperity and opportunity?

The economic literature since Adam Smith sees a key role of governments in setting the rules of the game for market economies. These rules need to define safe property rights and a framework for their exchange in functioning markets. Externalities are a reason to intervene in markets (Coase 1960; Pigou 1920, 1928; Musgrave 1959). Hence, there is a need for a well-functioning public administration with a good code of law and environmental regulation. Governments should also prevent an obstruction of markets and competition by providing a well-functioning antitrust system and open international trade rules.

In recent years, the potential for externalities in financial markets has received increasing attention. Information problems and the sheer size of externalities have resulted in a growing recognition that regulation needs to better align the incentives in the financial system to avoid the socialisation of losses.

Beyond this rule-setting role of government, there is also a good reason for the provision of other public goods. Security is an obvious case in point: (almost) every country needs a defence force. There is also a strong reason for a domestic security force—the police—to protect internal security, complemented by a system of justice.[3]

Beyond security, there are further public goods worth discussing. The best-known is public infrastructure, such as roads, water and sewage systems. Private provision of such infrastructure is often impossible or at least difficult because construction requires collective action and consumption is non-exclusive. Although today much infrastructure can be produced and financed privately because user fees such as tolls or network charges have become possible, there is still a considerable need for public engagement through regulation if not production and financing.

The most prominent public good today is probably education. Since the nineteenth century, free public education has become a common achievement in the world, starting with primary education but now also including secondary education. Without public education, people and societies would not invest enough in knowledge formation, thereby reducing the potential for society-wide progress and prosperity.

A further public good relates to governments' role in enhancing social inclusion and reducing income inequality. Government provision of basic social safety nets, including health, poverty alleviation and elderly care, is not only socially desirable but has a strong public goods component. Health services prevent diseases from becoming epidemics. Poverty reduction measures prevent people from becoming criminals out of desperation. Basic safety nets for the elderly reduce the need for costly self-insurance against longevity risks.

Finally, governments have the means to stabilise the economy in downturns (or finance wars if needed) by incurring debt which is then paid down in better times. On average, so the orthodoxy goes, governments should have balanced budgets which would leave room for dealing with new tasks and unforeseen developments without incurring critical or destabilising debt.

The benefits to society from such measures are twofold: first, sound rules of the game, security, education and social safety nets as well as public infrastructure provides everybody with opportunities to participate in economic and social life. In former times, being born to a poor family meant that you had no opportunity if you survived childhood at all. Today, everybody in a well-functioning industrialised market economy has the opportunity to access clean water and learn basic life skills at school. In the past, living in a poor quarter meant little access to the justice system and primitive, if any, roads. The provision of basic rules of the game, public goods and social safety nets has, hence, enormously increased people's opportunities. And

[3] These examples show in fact that the conceptual distinction between rules of the game and public goods that complement the rule-setting role of government is rather fluid. Good laws make no sense without police and justice. There can be no environmental protection without an agency to enforce it.

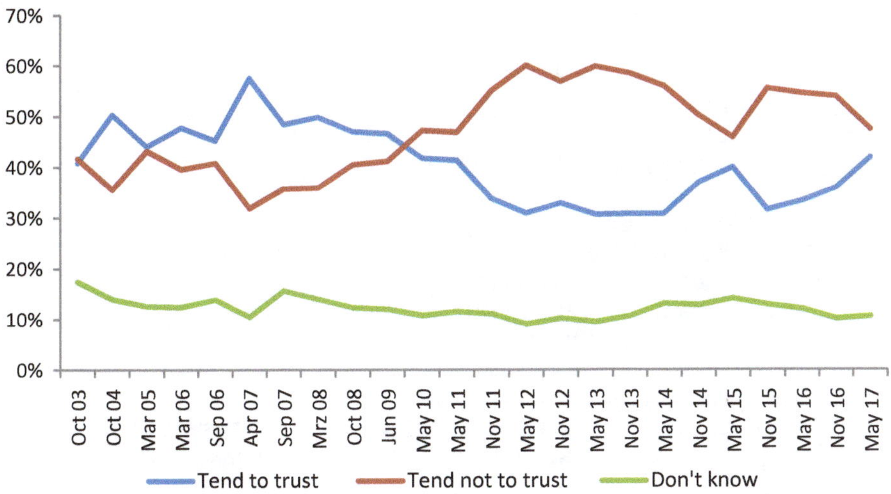

Fig. 2 Trust in the European Union. Source: Eurobarometer

it has made growth much more inclusive with much smaller wealth and income divergence than, say, 200 years ago. This is often forgotten in today's debate.

3 The role of government and trust in the market economy: Some stylised facts

In this section, we will look at fulfilment of the core tasks of government, that people expect to be met and at some indicators of trust in governments. This is not an easy task.

Regarding the second issue, do we really have a trust problem in Europe? That is a difficult question to answer, but there is some indication to the affirmative. The European Commission conducts an ongoing survey to get insights about citizens' opinions about EU institutions.[4] Since 2003, a question about citizens' "Trust in the European Union" has been added to the survey. Figure 2 tracks responses to this question over the past 15 years. On balance, trust was higher during the first decade of this millennium than thereafter, although trust has rebounded somewhat recently. But even during the first decade, the trusting group was only slightly larger than the non-trusting one.

[4]The Eurobarometer was established in 1974, but with only a very limited number of survey questions.

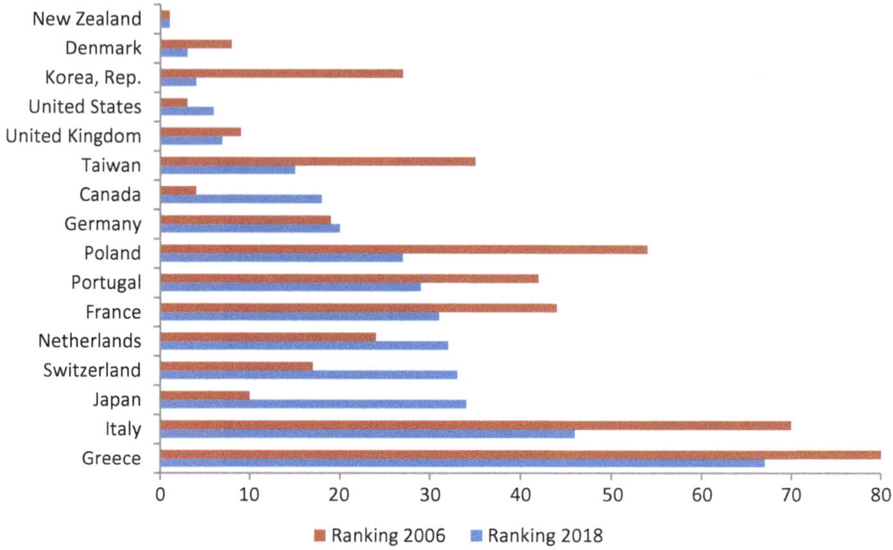

Fig. 3 Doing Business Indicators, rankings for 2006 and 2018. Source: The World Bank: Doing Business Indicators; http://www.doingbusiness.org/

3.1 *Rules of the game*

As outlined above, one of the most important tasks of the government in a market economy is to facilitate market exchanges, manage risk and encourage growth by providing a well-functioning legal framework. Suitable and efficient rules of the game are central to ensuring efficient economic processes and hence economic success. The latter, in turn, is an important element in establishing and maintaining the trust of businesses and citizens in both the government and the economic system.

Measuring rules of the game is not easy. And the link between rules of the game and trust is rather indirect. A popular indicator to evaluate an economy's regulative framework is the "Doing Business Indicator", which has been published annually by the World Bank since 2004. The "Doing Business" report compares locational conditions of 190 economies regarding their regulatory conditions. A high-quality regulatory framework should be a sign of "good" rules of the game for the market economy. It enhances the trust of businesses in governments and, through better economic performance, also affects positively the sentiment of the population more generally.

Figure 3 shows the World Bank's ranking on ease of doing business in 2006 and 2018.[5] We look at the rankings instead of the index as data for the latter is only

[5]The rankings for all economies are benchmarked to June 2017. For more information see: http://www.doingbusiness.org/reports/global-reports/doing-business-2018. The report looks at different categories that impede or support businesses. In total ten sub-categories are evaluated: "starting a business", "dealing with construction permits", "getting electricity", "registering property", "getting

available from 2010 onwards. Although, information on the absolute performance would be more interesting from the perspective of this paper's hypothesis, the rankings still provide a good indication for relative performance. New Zealand ranked first when the indicator was launched in 2004 and first in 2018. Many European economies, however, have important shortcomings. Even Germany, ranked 20th in 2018, performs only moderately well. Italy and Greece both rank low, at 46th and 67th, respectively.

While this figure illustrates the deficiencies of many industrialised countries when it comes to the basic rules of the game for business activity, the fact that the relative rank of many industrialised countries has declined since 2006 gives greater cause for concern. Figure 3 shows selected countries' rankings have changed since 2006. A strengthened legal-institutional framework (or better rules of the game) would be indicated by an increase in the respective countries' ranking. One can see that the overall picture is mixed for industrialised countries. By contrast, many emerging economies are catching up. Korea, for example, has improved its rank from 27th in 2005 to 4th in 2018. Indeed, relative to many emerging economies, industrialised economies have lost ranks.

The "rule of law" is probably the most important element of a well-functioning and well-governed market economy[6] where people trust the government. A neutral and fair legal system and secure property rights are essential to levelling the playing field for all agents in an economy. The Fraser Institute annually publishes the *Economic Freedom of the World Report* (Gwartney et al. 2017), which provides a suitable measure of the quality of the legal system and property rights.[7] Figure 4 displays the respective index in 2005 and 2015. Generally, the performance of governments on this core task has deteriorated over the past decade for the countries in our sample. The Nordic countries perform best; Southern European countries least well.

3.2 *Public goods*

We will now take a closer look at further public goods. As mentioned, the provision of high-quality infrastructure is central to creating an attractive environment for the private sector, thereby ensuring innovation, employment and productive

credit", "protecting minority investors", "paying taxes", "trading across borders", "enforcing contracts", "resolving insolvency". The average value of the sub-categories determines a country's rank. It is important to note that the methodology of "Doing Business" has changed since it was first published in 2004. Care should therefore be taken when interpreting the data.

[6] Hayek (1960).

[7] https://www.fraserinstitute.org/studies/economic-freedom. This is one of five sub-indicators of the Economic Freedom of the World (EWA) Index. The other indicators are: Size of Government, Sound Money, Freedom to Trade Internationally and Regulation. Afonso et al. (2005) studied public sector performance and distinguished between "opportunity indicators" and "Standard Musgravian indicators".

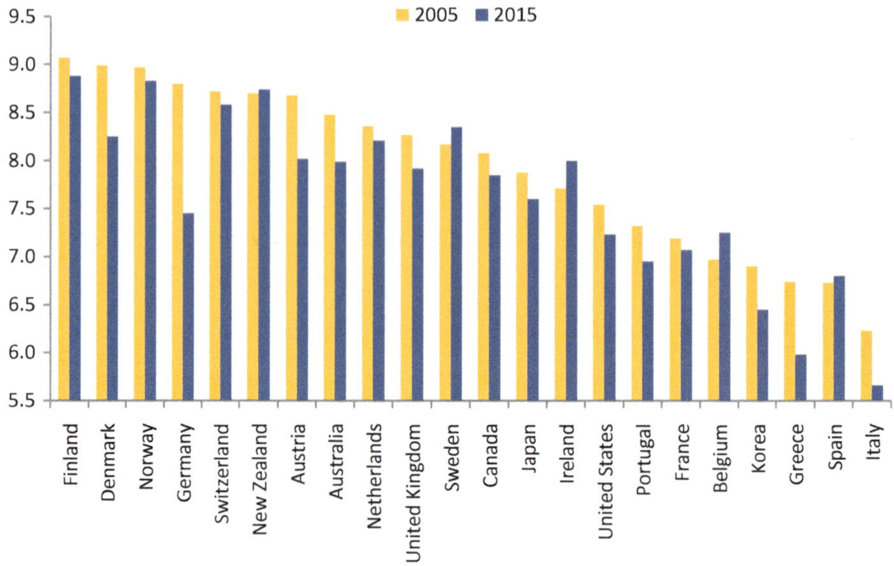

Fig. 4 Legal system and property rights sub-index. Source: Economic Freedom of the World: 2017 Annual Report

growth—and hence trust in the market economy. Providing good infrastructure for everyone is also important for economic inclusion, i.e. for ensuring equal standards of transport, communication, health, etc.

In this respect, public investment expenditure constitutes an important input factor in ensuring high-quality infrastructure. Table 1 displays how expenditure in public investment has changed since the 1980s. Across most economies, we observe a decline in public investment. The decline is largest in Japan, which had however extremely high rates of investment in the 1980s. The only two economies with positive changes in public investment in the past 35 years are Canada and Norway. Public investment in Germany is rather low, but significant parts of infrastructure investment (energy, communication, health) are classified as private investment. It is also interesting to note that the decline in public investment expenditure seems to be much smaller or there is even no decline at all in countries that have a relatively "lean" public sector. This includes for example Australia, Canada, Korea and Switzerland.

When it comes to the quality of infrastructure, there is a sparse amount of international data available. Some information can be gained from a sub-indicator on infrastructure of the Logistics Performance Index[8] (LPI), which is published by the World Bank. It reveals some surprising facts. Figure 5 illustrates the most recent results for 2016 and 2007. The most striking improvement exhibits Korea. Contrary

[8] The LPI is a weighted average of country scores on six dimensions: Customs, Infrastructure, International Shipments; Logistics Competence, Tracking & Tracing and Timeliness.

Table 1 Public investment expenditure, % of GDP

	1980	2000	2016[a]	Difference between 2016 and 1980 in percentage points
Australia	3.5	3.0	3.3	−0.2
Austria	5.3	2.7	3.0	−2.3
Belgium	5.2	2.4	2.3	−2.9
Canada	3.5	2.9	3.9	0.4
Denmark	4.2	2.8	3.7	−0.5
Finland	4.8	3.5	3.9	−0.9
France	4.1	3.9	3.4	−0.6
Germany	4.1	2.3	2.1	−2.0
Greece	3.2	5.1	3.1	−0.1
Ireland	5.6	3.5	1.8	−3.9
Italy	3.5	2.9	2.1	−1.4
Japan	9.4	6.8	3.7	−5.7
Korea	4.7	5.5	4.4	−0.3
Netherlands	4.5	3.8	3.5	−1.0
New Zealand		3.1	4.0	
Norway	4.9	3.4	5.4	0.5
Portugal	5.1	4.6	1.5	−3.6
Spain	2.4	3.7	1.9	−0.4
Sweden	6.4	3.9	4.4	−2.0
Switzerland		3.1	3.0	−0.1
United Kingdom	3.1	1.7	2.6	−0.4
United States	3.9	3.6	3.2	−0.7
Average	4.6	3.5	3.2	−1.1

Source: OECD government accounts, European Commission
[a]Or latest available

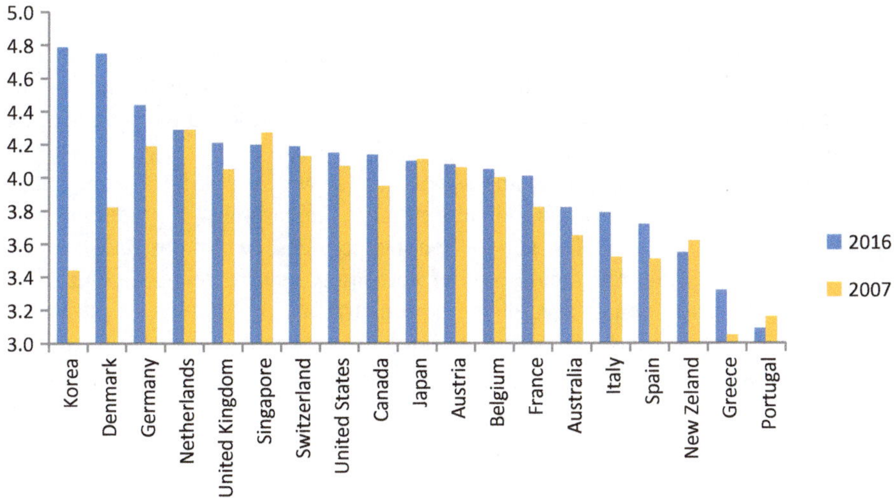

Fig. 5 Index for infrastructure (Sub-Index of the Logistics Performance Index). Source: The World Bank, Logistics Performance Index, https://lpi.worldbank.org/

Table 2 Core public administration expenditures, % of GDP

	1995	2005	2015	Difference between 2015[a] and 1995 in percentage points
Australia		10.1		
Austria	18.3	17.0	15.6	−2.6
Belgium	20.5	19.7	17.5	−3.0
Canada	19.5	13.3		−6.2
Denmark	17.3	12.6	13.8	−3.5
Finland	19.9	14.1	16.0	−3.9
France	16.3	14.8	14.9	−1.4
Germany	20.8	12.4	11.7	−9.1
Greece	23.2	16.7	21.6	−1.6
Ireland	14.0	9.2	8.9	−5.1
Italy	21.8	15.8	15.0	−6.7
Japan		9.9	9.5	−0.4
Netherlands	16.4	13.4	12.1	−4.3
Norway	15.0	11.0	12.4	−2.6
Portugal	16.4	14.7	16.0	−0.4
Spain	17.2	13.2	14.0	−3.2
Sweden	19.7	14.2	13.7	−6.0
Switzerland		11.0	10.5	−0.5
United Kingdom	10.3	10.3	10.2	−0.1
United States	13.1	11.5	10.8	−2.3
Average	17.6	13.2	13.6	−3.3

Source: OECD, Government expenditure by function database, own calculations
[a]Or latest available data

to some observers' claims, also Germany is performing well having improved the quality of infrastructure in the past 10 years. This can largely also be ascribed to the creation of a favourable framework for private-sector investment and the preceding privatisation of parts of the infrastructure (telecom, energy). On the whole, the picture is very mixed and there was little change for most advanced economies. Again Southern European infrastructure seems to be judged more negatively on average despite some improvement in the past decade.

Turning to other public goods and services, it is worth looking at core public administration expenditures as an indicator of government input for producing such goods. This category includes general public services (which include various administrative expenditures),[9] public order and safety, and recreation, culture and religion. We refer to them as core public administration expenditure, as they serve to provide key public goods, including the implementation of an economy's rules of the game. People therefore rightly expect these functions to be fulfilled by the government.

[9] Executive and legislative organs, financial, fiscal and external affairs; foreign economic aid; basic research; general public services; public debt transactions; transfers of a general character between different levels of the government.

Table 3 Expenditures on public order and safety, % of GDP

Year	1995	2005	2015	Difference between 1995 and 2015 in percentage points
Australia[a]		1.6		
Austria	1.5	1.4	1.4	−0.1
Belgium	1.4	1.7	1.8	0.3
Denmark	0.9	0.9	1.0	0.0
Canada				
Finland	1.4	1.3	1.2	−0.1
France	1.5	1.5	1.6	0.1
Germany	1.6	1.6	1.6	−0.1
Greece	0.9	1.5	2.1	1.2
Ireland	1.8	1.4	1.1	−0.8
Italy	1.9	2.0	1.9	−0.1
Japan		1.2	1.3	0.0
Netherlands	1.4	1.7	1.8	0.4
Norway	1.0	0.9	1.1	0.1
Portugal	1.6	1.9	2.1	0.5
Spain	2.0	1.8	2.0	0.1
Sweden	1.4	1.3	1.3	−0.1
Switzerland		1.6	1.7	0.1
United Kingdom	1.9	2.4	2.0	0.1
United States	1.9	2.1	2.0	0.1
Average	1.5	1.6	1.6	0.1

Source: OECD, Government expenditure by function database (Differences refer to latest available data)
[a]No or only limited data available

The data (Table 2) show how much governments spend on these key areas and how they set priorities in spending.[10] In almost all countries, spending on these categories has been declining over the past 20 years. Only the UK has seen virtually stable core public administration expenditures between 1995 and 2015. Germany's ratio was particularly high in 1995, at 20.8% as a share of GDP, mostly due to reunification expenditures, which somewhat overstates the drop thereafter.

Table 3 gives a more detailed view of the category of public order and safety. Due to different definitions of public order and safety and possible changes in the concepts over time, comparability of data is difficult and interpretation should be handled cautiously. One can see that expenditure trends for public order and safety as a share of GDP are quite different across economies. In Germany, for instance, expenditures on public order and safety have declined marginally over the past 20 years. Other countries also report small declines or increases. On the whole, these data do not point to a general erosion of internal security-related spending. However, it is hard to say whether expenditure trends were adequate relative to widespread public perceptions of rising crime. They are also difficult to evaluate in economic terms, in

[10] For more detailed information see OECD (2017), Government at a Glance 2017.

the absence of information about the demand for such services and the appropriate deflator. This, in conjunction with a frequent perception of decreased security, would need to be analysed in more depth.

In the area of education, there is probably less cause for concern as regards the overall level of public spending. Public expenditure has increased modestly in recent decades from about 5% of GDP in 1980 to 5.5% in 2015 for the average of industrial countries. Germany's expenditure ratio is slightly below average; the Nordic countries show the highest and Southern European countries the lowest spending ratios.[11] Furthermore, here again, it is hard to say whether spending has kept up with increasing demand, given that a much larger share of young people attend secondary and tertiary education today than was the case 20 or 40 years ago.

When it comes to education outcomes and opportunities, results are mixed. Overall, results from the OECD's PISA study point to higher PISA scores in advanced economies compared with the beginning of the millennium. In particular, most Nordic countries and Asian economies as well as Canada are performing very well and far above the international average. Germany's performance has improved in the past 15 years and was above average in 2015 in all three performance categories.[12]

The most concerning issue in education is probably the lack of quality education for the poor and disadvantaged. In this respect, PISA further aims to assess the provision of quality education regardless of students' socioeconomic background. Performance tends to be relatively independent of students' socioeconomic background in the Nordic and Asian economies, while there is a strong link in many Western and Central European economies. Whereas most countries do not exhibit any changes in the impact of students' social background for their performance since 2006, Germany and the U.S are exceptions, with slight improvements. In tertiary education, however, which is outside the scope of PISA, cost dynamics have been very strong in many countries, meaning that access concerns are mounting.

3.3 Social safety nets

Rules of the game and public goods are not enough. If the poor and needy do not benefit from public expenditures, they will be left too far behind in terms of welfare and opportunity and it is likely to exert negative influence on trust. Here, the record of social expenditure as a measure of government inputs seems to be exemplary at first sight: Social expenditure trends in Europe have been well above GDP growth in recent decades (Schuknecht and Zemanek 2018).

---

[11] However, as is also the case for infrastructure, cross-country comparisons on public spending on education are to be treated with caution as the share of public and private schools differs strongly across countries.

[12] PISA assesses three categories: Maths, Reading and Science.

Table 4 Social expenditure, aggregated data, % of GDP

	1980	2000	2016	Difference between 1980 and 2016[a] in percentage points
Australia	10.3	18.2	19.1	8.8
Belgium	23.1	23.5	29.0	5.9
Canada	13.3	15.8	17.2	3.9
Denmark	20.3	23.8	28.7	8.4
Finland	17.7	22.6	30.8	13.1
France	20.2	27.5	31.5	11.3
Germany	21.8	25.4	25.3	3.5
Greece	9.9	18.4	27.0	17.1
Ireland	15.7	12.6	16.1	0.4
Italy	17.4	22.6	28.9	11.5
Netherlands	23.3	18.4	22.0	−1.3
New Zealand	16.7	18.5	19.7	3
Norway	16.1	20.4	25.1	9
Portugal	9.5	18.5	24.1	14.6
Spain	15.0	19.5	24.6	9.6
Sweden	24.8	26.8	27.1	2.3
Switzerland	12.8	16.3	19.7	6.9
United Kingdom	15.6	17.7	21.5	5.9
United States	12.8	14.3	19.3	6.5
Average	16.6	20.0	24.0	7.4

Source: OECD, Social Expenditure Statistics
[a]Or latest available, 2015

Social expenditure in industrial countries has increased from about one sixth of GDP in 1980 to about one quarter of GDP in recent years (Table 4). This is a huge increase in just one generation. Social expenditure almost everywhere in Europe is comparatively high. In Germany, social expenditure was already very high in 1980, at over one fifth of GDP. It has increased further to one quarter of GDP which is slightly above average. Social expenditure has increased very strongly in the Mediterranean European countries and exceeds 30% of GDP in France. The Netherlands is the only country to have reduced social expenditure since the 1980s. Anglo-American countries and Switzerland spend less than average, at around 20% of GDP.

Increasing public social expenditure is indicative of another problem that we outlined earlier: governments promise to do too much and thereby risk to reduce rather than to increase trust. First, rising social expenditure has in many countries come at the expense of other core government functions (see Schuknecht and Zemanek 2018 for an empirical analysis).

Second, high social spending does not necessarily mean effective and efficient (i.e. well-targeted and well-prioritised) use of the money. In many economies, social protection has been extended to a broad range of people who do not necessarily require social support. When looking at the definition of social spending, the sheer number of sub-categories is striking. In Germany, a survey of family-related benefits shows a large number of different programmes which are hardly coordinated and, in some cases, even contradictory in their objectives (Bonin et al. 2013). Most of the programmes do not have much to do with the underlying objective of providing basic social safety nets.

The result is a spiral of growing benefits via a growing number of programmes while efficiency and consistency suffer. The process is likely to be reinforced in the coming decades by population ageing, which may bring more countries to the limits of solvency and occasion a need for significant further reform. This, in turn, may bring about a new round of frustration and loss of trust.

Third, growing benefits to some leave others disgruntled about not benefitting or not benefitting equally from such spending. Deaton (2015) rightly points out that people are doing better than ever in history: living standards, life expectancy and quality of life have been growing and may continue to do so in the future. Yet, poverty reduction has remained imperfect and poverty elimination elusive, as much in societies is measured against relative and not absolute standards.

The perception of social injustice, in particular towards the elderly, often stands in stark contrast to reality. It is worth taking a look at old-age poverty rates as an example. Table 5 shows the percentage of households with incomes below the 50% of median household disposable income. It is true that old-age poverty still exists. And it is, relatively speaking, larger in countries with lower social expenditure. That said, old-age poverty has declined significantly in recent decades and is often lower than poverty amongst children or other disadvantaged groups. The old have benefitted much more from income gains than other groups in the past decade (Chen et al. 2018). In some countries, retirees and pensioners tend to be richer on average than the rest of the population.

According to a study by the Institut für Wirtschaft (IW) Köln[13] on income inequality and the perception thereof, perceived inequality within a society and actual income inequality deviate substantially. Most people perceive inequality as relatively large, i.e. they assume that more people are at the bottom of income distribution than is actually the case. An exception is the U.S. where people tend to strongly underestimate the share of households at the bottom of income distribution.

The financial crisis is likely to have contributed to the distributional struggle within Western countries. How can it be that well-paid bankers are bailed out by tax-payers, violating the fundamental principle that capitalists are responsible for profits and losses while social benefits are frozen or cut as high debt needs to be brought down? This is linked to the earlier discussion of governments not delivering on their core mandate while benefitting the rich. And it is linked to the question about rules of the game: we have failed in setting the rules of the game in the financial sphere appropriately, which would have prevented the need for bail-outs in the first place.

[13] https://www.iwkoeln.de/__extendedmedia_resources/176927/index.html.

Table 5 Percentage with incomes below 50% of median household disposable income, 2012[a]

	People aged over 65	Whole population
Australia	33.5	14.0
Austria	11.4	9.6
Belgium	10.7	10.2
Canada	6.7	11.8
Denmark	4.6	5.4
Finland	7.8	7.1
France	3.8	8.1
Germany	9.4	8.4
Greece	6.9	15.1
Ireland	6.9	8.4
Italy	9.4	12.7
Japan	19.4	16.0
Korea	49.6	14.6
Netherlands	2.0	7.9
New Zealand	8.2	9.9
Norway	4.1	8.1
Poland	8.2	10.2
Portugal	8.1	13.0
Spain	6.7	14.0
Sweden	9.3	9.0
Switzerland	23.4	9.1
United Kingdom	13.4	10.5
United States	21.5	17.6

Source: OECD Income Distribution Database
[a]Or latest available (2013 for Finland, the Netherlands and the United States. Korea 2009, 2012 for all others)

3.4 *Economic stability*

A stable economic environment is essential, not only for businesses to flourish and develop, but also for social stability. A sound fiscal position is conducive to economic stability. It allows governments to undertake their tasks in a well-ordered and reasonably prioritised manner, with reserves and capacity to act during recessions or crisis. In countries with fiscal problems, governments have had to carry out emergency measures and cuts. And typically, such cuts do not affect the least productive spending but the least politically difficult, such as public investment. When unsound government finances coincide with inflation, this often erodes public salaries and with them morale and integrity. It is perhaps no surprise that low-deficit and low-debt countries such as Scandinavian economies or Switzerland seem to have more effective governments.

Table 6 Public debt, % of GDP

	1980	2000	2016	Difference between 1980 and 2016 in percentage points
Australia		19.5	41.1	21.5
Austria	37.2	65.9	83.9	46.7
Belgium	76.4	108.8	105.5	29.2
Canada	45.3	80.7	92.3	47.1
Denmark	33.2	52.4	39.9	6.7
Finland	10.9	42.5	63.6	52.7
France	20.8	58.6	96.6	75.9
Germany	33.1	58.9	67.6	34.6
Greece	22.5	104.9	181.3	158.8
Ireland	67.5	36.1	76.4	8.9
Italy	64.8	105.1	132.6	67.8
Japan	50.0	139.0	239.2	189.1
Korea		17.1	38.6	21.4[a]
Luxembourg	9.7	6.5	22.6	12.9
Netherlands	44.6	51.4	62.6	18.0
New Zealand		26.0	29.5	3.5[a]
Norway	46.7	28.1	33.2	−13.5
Portugal	37.7	47.9	130.3	92.6
Spain	16.6	58.0	99.3	82.7
Sweden	42.3	51.3	41.7	−0.7
Switzerland		54.6	45.4	−9.2[a]
United Kingdom	42.8	37.3	89.2	46.4
United States	45.7	59.0	107.4	61.7
Average	39.3	56.9	83.5	44.1

Source: IMF, World Economic Outlook
[a]Difference between 2016 and 2000

Sound public finances and low public debt can, from that perspective, also be considered public goods because they can help stabilise the economy during crisis.[14] But from this point of view, too, many industrialised countries are failing. Table 6 shows public debt as percentage of GDP. In 1980, only few industrialised countries had public debt in excess of 60% of GDP. Today, public debt averages about 120% of GDP in the G7 countries, several industrial countries report near or above 100%, and one country, Japan, even well above 200% of GDP. In addition, several European countries have experienced fiscal crises and required financial bail-outs that went hand in hand with stringent adjustment programmes.

[14]There is a large amount of literature on the potential damage of public debt. A negative link between high public debt and growth has been found by Pattillo et al. (2004) and Kumar and Woo (2010). Checherita-Westphal and Rother (2012) focus exclusively on the euro area and confirm that particularly high debt levels can have a detrimental impact on growth.

Table 7 Correlation coefficients between trust and input/outcome variables (2005–2015)

Input variables		Outcome variables		Pre-enlargement Europe Outcome variables	
Social spending	0.0858	Rule of law	0.6849	Rule of law	0.6878
Total spending	0.0277	Index on regulation	0.3337	Index on regulation	0.3751
Spending on education	0.4187	Index for infrastructure	0.4227	Index for infrastructure	0.4784
Investment spending	0.0618	PISA	0.3282	PISA	0.3156
		Income share of lowest 40%	0.3223	Income share of lowest 40%	0.5394
		Public debt	−0.4523	Public debt	−0.7331
		Globalisation Index, KOF	0.4392	Globalisation Index, KOF	0.3873

Source: OECD for all input variables and PISA; IMF WEO for debt; World Bank for the index for infrastructure, Fraser Institute for the indices on rule of law and regulation; WDI for income share of bottom 40%; KOF globalisation index

4 The link between trust and government activities

In this section we will look at the link between the core functions of government and trust as hypothesised in Sect. 2. At this stage, we limit ourselves to a simple correlation analysis between government expenditure (inputs) and government performance (outcomes) on the one hand and trust in governments on the other hand. Table 7 provides the correlation coefficients for 21 European[15] countries for the period 2005–2015.

There are a number of interesting findings. First, public expenditure (input variables) seem to matter only little for trust. Higher total and—perhaps more importantly—social expenditure are not correlated at all with more trust in government. The only expenditure component where the correlation coefficient is reasonably positive is education.

Second, outcome indicators as regards core roles of government are mostly well correlated with trust. The correlation coefficient is highest for good rules of the game ("rule of law" variable) and moderate for regulation. Also, high quality infrastructure shows a correlation of almost 0.5, which could be seen as relatively strong. The picture is more mixed as regards education. High PISA scores—as an indicator of high quality education—are not strongly correlated with trust. Only in pre-Eastern enlargement Europe the figure is higher, at almost 0.3.

As regards basic social safety nets, we chose the income share of the bottom 40% of households as indicator. While this is not a perfect measure of basic safety nets,

[15] Pre-eastern enlargement economies are Austria, Germany, Belgium, Denmark, France, Ireland, Italy, the Netherlands, Portugal, Sweden, Spain, Greece, Luxembourg and the United Kingdom. Eastern European economies include Czech Republic, Hungary, Poland, Slovenia and Slovak Republic, Estonia and Latvia.

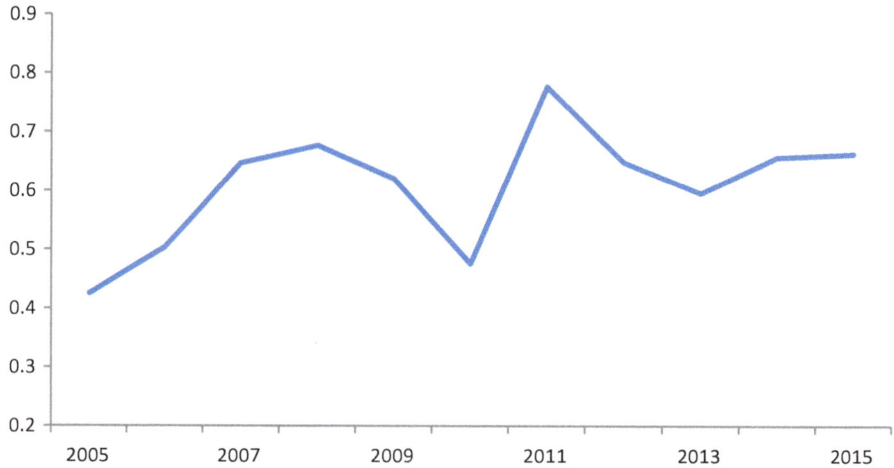

Fig. 6 Correlation coefficients 2005–2015 between trust and rule of law. Source: Fraser Institute, own calculations

it is relatively reliable. For this, the correlation coefficient is moderate at 0.32. Sound public finances, as reflected for example in low debt-to-GDP ratios are also correlated with trust: the coefficient is relatively high at almost 0.5. Overall, the correlation between trust and outcome variables tends to be considerably stronger in Pre-Eastern enlargement economies.

Finally, we also include an index for globalisation in the analysis. Globalisation is often blamed for a loss of trust or the rise of populism (Potrafke 2015). From the perspective of this paper, open markets and trade integration are a core function of government which boosts prosperity and high-quality jobs. Therefore, we would expect a positive correlation between the two. The correlation results confirm the latter claim: trust and globalisation (represented by the KOF globalisation index) are positively correlated where an index value of almost 0.44 can be considered as relatively strong.

Third, the correlation between outcomes and trust has been growing over time. Figure 6, for example, shows that the correlation coefficient for trust and the rule of law started out near 0.4 in 2005 before increasing significantly, ending near 0.65 in 2015 (with some bumpiness around the financial crisis as all countries were affected by a loss of trust in 2009/10 before trust recovered in the more stable high-trust countries in 2011).

Another angle from which to look at the relationship between trust and government performance is the experience with European adjustment programmes. Such programmes (which focussed in particular on reforms strengthening the rules of the market economy) have gone hand in hand with a resurgence of trust in governments, as Eurobarometer data shows (Fig. 7). Trust has recently increased most in Portugal and Ireland, and modestly in Cyprus and Spain. This confirms the role of sound

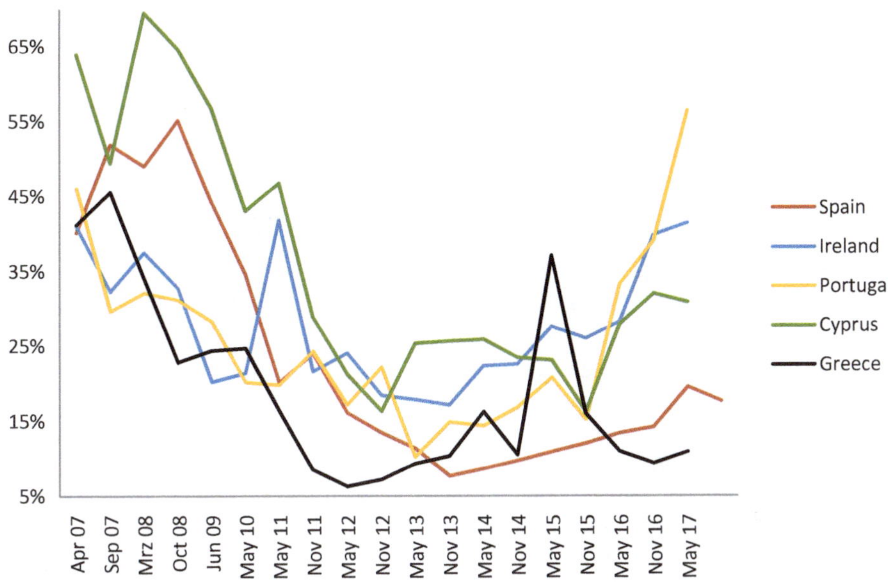

Fig. 7 Trust in own governments. Source: Eurobarometer

policies and the opportunity offered by reforms when it comes to re-building trust. This brings us to the conclusion of this study.

5 Conclusions

The results of this study provide some indications that the erosion of trust in governments and in the EU along with the rise of populism may have to do with governments' neglecting some of their core tasks, i.e. setting societies' rules of the game and providing core public goods. There is some indication of declining government performance, most notably as regards the "rules of the game". Moreover, there is little relation between trust and public expenditure (inputs) but more between "good" rules and strong basic public good provision (outcomes) and trust. This leads us to conclude that it is not government spending per se that needs to increase to build trust, but rather better focused government activities. Moreover, there is no relation between trust and growing social expenditure, but growing correlation between outcomes, most notably rule of law and trust over time. Yet, we have only scratched the surface in analysing this important question.

There is a risk that the neglect of core tasks and the decline of trust may continue in the future. Population ageing coupled with the political dominance of social spending may exacerbate over-commitment in the social sphere. This, in turn, could further undermine growth, prosperity and trust in the future. A vicious circle of higher social spending, non-delivery on core tasks and less trust may contribute to a continuing spiral of populism. It will potentially hit hardest those countries where welfare states (and expectations in the state) are already the largest.

What are the policy implications? We suggest that governments should refocus on their core activities. This has been argued by many economists for decades. Governments should give priority to setting people- and market-friendly rules of the game, and to providing core public goods such as security and education. Social safety nets and the spending involved should be much better targeted. The agenda should also include fiscal stability with low deficits and debt as this enhances governments' ability to fulfil their core tasks and react to new challenges. All this contributes to overall economic, financial and social stability, and to less disappointment with governments. The favourable experience and the re-emergence of trust in countries that have reformed governments in recent decades (including most recently in Europe) are a case in point.[16]

One important issue here is when to tackle reforms. In most cases, it is an acute crisis or the threat thereof that causes governments to act: the financial crises in the Nordic countries in the early 1990s, the post-unification bust in Germany after the turn of the millennium, and the crisis in Southern European countries in recent years. Good times with high growth, which economists argue should be the time for reforms, have typically been times of over-commitment and over-spending, laying the roots for later crises.

Another important point relates to the role of fiscal policy when it comes to achieving government core tasks. As outcomes matter, we need to change fiscal policy to prioritise key outcomes related to core tasks.

We close with a few more observations on the most difficult issue of participation and trust.[17] Two schools of thought seem to prevail. The first school emphasises participation, for example via referenda. This certainly reduces the risk of dissatisfaction and hence potential loss of trust. But it may be slow and cumbersome. This is broadly the Swiss model. Weiler (2012) calls this "process legitimacy" where decisions are taken via democratic process.

The second school emphasises paternalism. Important decisions including many decisions on centralisation in Europe are taken this way. Weiler (2012) calls this "political messianism" because the decision will take people to the "promised land", sometimes decidedly against their will. If centralisation is a success, it will gain "results legitimacy" ex post. Of course, if things then go wrong and the "promised land" remains elusive, people blame their governments, other governments and

---

[16] In light of this, it is also no surprise that relatively small and efficient governments in Switzerland, New Zealand and Canada fulfil their core functions reasonably well with moderately sized welfare states and public expenditure ratios around or below 40% of GDP (Tanzi and Schuknecht 2000). Some more inefficient European governments with big welfare states do less well, with public spending over 50% of GDP. Scandinavian countries are the exception, with big but effective public sectors, following significant reforms in recent decades.

[17] There is some literature examining the implications of centralisation, with very mixed results at best. The abolition and merging of local communities and the effect on citizen participation has yielded little in terms of administrative efficiency while reducing participation and identification (Lassen and Serritzlew (2011), Blesse and Rösel (2017) and many more).

Brussels. This is particularly relevant when one country's economic weakness results in another country's financial risks leaving all societies frustrated. There are perhaps important lessons from this, not least with regard to trust in the euro and the further integration of the euro zone.

References

Afonso A, Schuknecht L, Tanzi V (2005) Public sector efficiency: an international comparison. Public Choice 123(3–4):321–347

Blesse S, Rösel F (2017) Gebietsreformen: Hoffnungen, Risiken und Alternativen. Ifo Working Paper No. 234

Böhm-Bawerk E (1914) Macht oder ökonomisches Gesetz? In: Zeitschrift für Volkswirtschaft, Sozialpolitik und Verwaltung. Band 23

Bonin H, Fichtl A, Rainer H, Spieß CK, Stichnoth H, Wrohlich K (2013) Lehren für die Familienpolitik: Zentrale Resultate der Gesamtevaluation familienbezogener Leistungen. DIW Wochenbericht Nr 40.2013

Buchanan JM (1975) The limits of liberty – between Anarchy and Leviathan. The University of Chicago Press, Chicago

Checherita-Westphal C, Rother P (2012) The impact of high government debt on economic growth and its channels: an empirical investigation for the euro area. Eur Econ Rev, Elsevier 56(7):1392–1405

Chen T, Hallaert J, Pitt A, Qu J, Queyranne M, Rhee A, Shabunina A, Vandenbussche J, Yackovlev I (2018) Inequality and Poverty across Generations in the European Union. IMF Staff Discussion Note No. 18/01

Coase RH (1960) The problem of social cost. J Law Econ 3:1–44. The University of Chicago Press

Deaton A (2015) The great escape - health, wealth, and the origins of inequality. Princeton University Press

Friedman M (1977) Fair versus free. In: Selections from the collected works of Milton Friedman, pp 135–137

Gwartney J, Lawson R, Hall J (2017) Economic Freedom of the World 2017 Annual Report. Fraser Institute

Hayek FA (1960) The constitution of liberty. University of Chicago Press

Issing O (2009) Politischer Wille oder ökonomisches Gesetz? Einige Anmerkungen zu einem großen Thema, CFS working paper series; No. 2009, 24

Kumar MS, Woo J (2010) Public debt and growth, IMF Working Paper 10/174. International Monetary Fund, Washington, DC

Lassen DD, Serritzlew S (2011) Size and equal opportunity in the democratic process: the effect of the danish local government reform on inequality in internal political efficacy. World Polit Sci Rev 7:1–15

Musgrave RA (1959) The theory of public finance: a study of public economy. McGraw-Hill, New York

OECD (2017) Government at a glance 2017. OECD Publishing, Paris. https://doi.org/10.1787/gov_glance-2017-en

Pattillo C, Poirson H, Ricci L (2004) What are the channels through which external debt affects growth?, IMF Working Paper 04/15. International Monetary Fund, Washington, DC

Pigou AC (1920) The economics of welfare, 4th edn. MacMillan, London, 1932

Pigou AC (1928) A study in public finance. MacMillan & Co. Ltd, London

Potrafke N (2015) The evidence on globalisation. World Econ 38(3):509–552

Schuknecht L, Zemanek H (2018) Social Dominance, CESIfo Working Paper 6984

Tanzi V, Schuknecht L (2000) Public spending in the 20th century – a global perspective. Cambridge University Press
Weiler JHH (2012) Europe in crisis – on 'political messianism', 'legitimacy' and the 'rule of law'. Singapore J Legal Stud:248–268